STUDIES IN PHILOSOPHY

KRISHNACHANDRA BHATTACHARYYA

STUDIES IN PHILOSOPHY

Edited ny

GOPINATH BHATTACHARYYA

Vols. I & II Bound in One

MOTILAL BANARSIDASS PUBLISHERS
PRIVATE LIMITED • DELHI

Third Revised and Enlarged Edition: Delhi, 2008
First Edition: Calcutta, 1958
Second Revised Edition: Delhi, 1983

ISBN: 978-81-208-2972-5

MOTILAL BANARSIDASS
41 U.A. Bungalow Road, Jawahar Nagar, Delhi 110 007
8 Mahalaxmi Chamber, 22 Bhulabhai Desai Road, Mumbai 400 026
236, 9th Main III Block, Jayanagar, Bangalore 560 011
203 Royapettah High Road, Mylapore, Chennai 600 004
Sanas Plaza, 1302 Baji Rao Road, Pune 411 002
8 Camac Street, Kolkata 700 017
Ashok Rajpath, Patna 800 004
Chowk, Varanasi 221 001

Printed in India
BY JAINENDRA PRAKASH JAIN AT SHRI JAINENDRA PRESS,
A-45 NARAINA, PHASE-I, NEW DELHI 110 028
AND PUBLISHED BY NARENDRA PRAKASH JAIN FOR
MOTILAL BANARSIDASS PUBLISHERS PRIVATE LIMITED,
BUNGALOW ROAD, DELHI 110 007

PREFACE TO THE SECOND EDITION

I am extremely grateful to Messrs. Motilal Banarsidass of Delhi for their kind offer of Printing both volumes of Krishnachandra Bhattacharyya's Studies in Philosophy, particularly when all the copies of the first edition having been sold out the original publishers, for reasons of their own, expressed inability to print the two volumes.

Printing the two volumes could have been expedited if only I could collect a copy of each earlier. But that, precisely, was the most difficult task for me. My own copies had long back slipped out of my possession, and for months I went on enquiring at diffrent places. At long last I could get a copy of the first volume from Professor Pradip K. Sengupta of Visva-Bharati just a few days back and a copy of the second volume from one of my old students, Smt. Sabita Datta, some time earlier. They came forward with their copies when they learnt that I had for months been frantically seeking them. I do not know how properly I can express my indebtedness to them.

I again thank Messrs. Motilal Banarsidass of Delhi, particularly Shri N.P. Jain, who did not mind waiting all these months for my finding the copies.

Kalidas Bhattacharyya

EDITOR'S PREFACE
TO VOL. I

These 'Studies in Philosophy' represent all the published and only a few of the unpublished philosophical writings of Krishnachandra Bhattacharyya. There remains over an immense mass of manuscripts which will, perhaps, remain unpublished for all time to come.

The present volumes comprise the following tracts:—

Vol. I

1. Studies in Vedāntism (Published in 1907)
2. Śaṅkara's doctrine of Māyā („ 1925)
3. The Advaita and its spiritual significance („ 1936)
4. Studies in Sāṁkhya Philosophy (Unpublished)
5. Studies in Yoga Philosophy (")
6. The Jaina theory of Anekānta (Published in 1925)
7. The Concept of Rasa (Unpublished)

Vol. II

1. The Subject as Freedom (Published in 1930)
2. The Concept of Philosophy („ 1936)
3. The Concept of the Absolute and its alternative forms („ 1934)
4. Studies in Kant (Unpublished)
5. Some aspects of negation (Published in 1914)
6. The place of the indefinite in Logic („ 1916)
7. Definition of 'Relation' as a category of existence (Unpublished)
8. Fact and thought of fact (Published in 1931)
9. Knowledge and Truth („ 1928)
10. Correction of error as a logical process („ 1931)
11. The false and the subjective („ 1932)
12. The objective interpretation of percept and image („ 1936)
13. The Concept of Value („ 1934)
14. The reality of the future (Unpublished)

Each of the above tracts is preceded by an Analysis. The first one was made by the author himself and the others have been done by the editor. Of the foot notes, those marked in numerals are by the editor.

In presenting these studies the editor is happy to offer his most grateful thanks to the enterprising publisher, Sree Sushil Kumar Basu, the proprietor of Messrs. Progressive Publishers. It was he who very generously volunteered to undertake the publication of the book and see it through the press.

My warm thanks are also due to Professor G. R. Malkani, the Director of the Indian Institute of Philosophy, Amalner (Bombay) for his ready permission to reprint 'The Subject as Freedom' which was originally published by the Institute; to Dr. S. Radhakrishnan and Messrs. George Allen & Unwin Ltd. for their kind permission to reprint from their 'Contemporary Indian Philosophy' the essay 'The Concept of Philosophy'; and to the R. K. Mission for their permission to reprint 'The Advaita and its spiritual significance' which first appeared in their 'Cultural Heritage of India'. The editor is also obliged to a pupil of his and to his daughter for their assistance in preparing the copy for the press.

It is very much regretted that a number of typographical errors have crept in in spite of earnest endeavours to avoid them. In the 'Errata' at the end of the volume, only the major errors have been listed and corrected.

THE EDITOR

EDITOR'S PREFACE
TO VOL. II

The second volume of Studies in Philosophy is now presented after about twenty months since the issue of the first volume. For this inordinate delay the Editor alone is responsible. The Publisher tried his level best to expedite the publication, but owing to a number of circumstances which were beyond the control of the Editor, it was not found possible to bring it out at an earlier date.

This volume contains the fourteen tracts mentioned in the Preface to Vol. I, but in a slightly varied order. As in the case of the other volume, the order is not a chronological one.

In (1) *The Subject as Freedom,* the author works out his conception of Spiritual Psychology and the theory of the subject as freedom, and attempts to trace out the progressive stages of cognitional freedom. In (2) *The Concept of Philosophy* we have an analysis of the nature of philosophy and the conception of Philosophy as symbolic thinking not amounting to knowledge. (3) *The Concept of the Absolute and its Alternative Forms* elaborates the doctrine of the trinal absolute. (4) In *Knowledge and Truth,* we have an analysis of the distinctive level of consciousness occupied by theory of knowledge and of the theory of the mutual implication of knowledge and truth. (5) *Fact and Thought of Fact* attempts to give a definition of fact without assuming any fact and seeks to establish the position that fact does not admit of an impersonal definition. (6) In *Correction of Error as a Logical Process,* the author develops the Advaita theory of illusion and emphasises that correction is an epistemic function without any unitary logical content and that falsity has no reference to the time-position of a cognition. In (7) *The False and the Subjective,* the author elaborates the thesis that the false and the subjective imply one another. In (8) *Some Aspects of Negation,* the author presents a non-subjectivistic interpretation of the position that 'truth is manifold' and tries to establish that there are radically different types of logic based on incommensurable views of negation. (9) *Place of the Indefinite in Logic* lays down the thesis that the indefinite is not merely a subjective entity and that logic should find a place for the absolute indefinite. (10) In *Definition of Relation as a Category of Existence,* an attempt has been made to formulate a definition of 'relation' in purely objective terms as against the subjectivistic interpretation of Green and others. In (11) *Objective Interpretation of the Percept and Image*, an attempt has been made to translate the subjective terms 'perceived' and 'un-perceived' into objective terms. (12) In *Reality of the Future*, the author develops the thesis that the reality of the future expected on a known ground cannot be said to be an object of knowledge and that the future is real only to will and to faith. (13) *The Concept of Value* gives an analysis of the concept of value in its different forms, and establishes the position that value is absolute and that speakability of value as information is a necessary illusion. (14) The *Studies in Kant* gives us a speculative interpretation of a number of Kantian themes. As with the other constructive interpretations contained in Vol. I, we have here also quite a large number of improvisations.

In the Introduction to this voiume, the Editor has made an attempt to analyse the major philosophical doctrines of Krishnachandra Bhattacharyya. The analysis has been done, as far as possible, in the author's own words. This is for two reasons: first, the Editor was not sure that he had got at the exact logic of Krishnachandra's writings in a large number of places; secondly, and this is to some extent connected with the first, he felt that his own language was far less effective and elegant than that of the author, even when the latter's manner of presentation was quite thoroughly severe.

The Editor regrets that he has not been able to capture the inspiration or the insight that saturates almost all the writings of his father. It is because of this that he has all along felt that it was presumptuousness on his part to have undertaken this editorial work.

The Editor feels that he would be failing in gratitude if he did not emphasise that all the credit for this publication belongs to his friend, Sri Sushil Kumar Basu of Progressive Publishers. The undertaking would never have been completed but for his unfailing generosity, constant encouragement and spirit of dedication.

The Editor.

TABLE OF CONTENTS

VOL. I

TABLE OF CONTENTS

Vol. II.

ABBREVIATIONS

CAAF	—	The Concept of the Absolute and its Alternative Forms.
CP	—	The Concept of Philosophy.
CV	—	The Concept of Value.
CELP	—	Correction of Error as a Logical Process.
DRCE	—	The Definition of Relation as a Category of Existence.
FS	—	The False and the Subjective.
FTF	—	Fact and Thought of Fact.
KT	—	Knowledge and Truth.
OIPI	—	Objective Interpretation of Percept and Image.
PIL	—	Place of the Indefinite in Logic.
RF	—	Reality of the Future.
SAN	—	Some Aspects of Negation.
SK	—	Studies in Kant.
SF	—	The Subject as Freedom.
CPR	—	Critique of Pure Reason.
CPrR	—	Critique of Practical Reason.
CJ	—	Critique of Judgment.
BV	—	Bhoja-Vṛtti
SK	—	Sāṁkhya-Kārikā
SPB	—	Sāṁkhya-Pravacana-Bhāṣyam
SS	—	Sāṁkhya-Sūtram
STK	—	Sāṁkhya-Tattva-Kaumudī
TV	—	Tattva-Vaiśāradī
YB	—	Yoga-Bhāṣyam
YV	—	Yoga-Vārtikam

EDITOR'S INTRODUCTION TO VOL. I

Krishnachandra Bhattacharyya was born in a Brāhmaṇa family of Serampur (Bengal) on the 12th of May, 1875. The grandfather, Umākānta Tarkālaṅkāra was a Sanskrit scholar trained in the indigenous seminaries of learning. The father Kedarnath had not much of academic education and was employed in a mercantile house at Calcutta. He was a man of slender means with a numerous family to maintain and was hardly in a position to bear the educational expenses of his children. Krishnachandra was sent to the local school at the usual age and after passing the Entrance Examination of the Calcutta University in 1891, he entered the Presidency College at Calcutta. He graduated with triple Honours in 1896 and was awarded the P. R. S. of the University in 1901. The academic record during the school and college periods was uniformly brilliant.

Krishnachandra joined the Education Department of the Government of Bengal as a Lecturer in Philosophy in 1898, and after serving with great distinction as a teacher of Philosophy in almost all the Government Colleges in Bengal, he retired from service as the Officiating Principal of Hughly College in 1930. He joined the Indian Institute of Philosophy at Amalner (Bombay) as its Director and remained there from 1933 to 1935. He also acted as the George V Professor of Mental and Moral Philosophy at the Calcutta University from 1935 to 1937.

Krishnachandra Bhattacharyya was warm and generous in his temperament but was rather shy and was almost 'afraid' of publicity. He was nevertheless a man of very strong principles and also of strong likes and dislikes. He had great independence of spirit and he never submitted to official bullying. He was a genial personality and those who came in close contact with him were profoundly attracted towards him. He was an admirer of classical Indian music and study of good literature was one of his recreations for a long time. He spoke moderately but always impressively and had a keen sense of humour. His relations to his students were extremely cordial and many of them almost adore his memory. He was of a medium build, had a fairly strong constitution and was a man of active habits for the greater part of his life. In his later years, however, when he was afflicted with asthma, he developed complete sedentariness. He was generally abstemious in his habits. His private life was one of austere purity and he was a conspicuous example of the Hindu ideal of plain-living and high thinking. He died on the 11th of December, 1949.

Krishnachandra was deeply interested in current Indian affairs and though his office debarred him from taking an active part in politics, he was ever since the Swadeshi Movement an ardent champion of extreme nationalism. In socio-religious matters, he was a conservative Hindu, both in his habits and in his outlook. He had unmixed contempt for the exponents of 'liberal' Hinduism and he looked upon the so-called 'social reform' movements in Hindu society as unmitigated evils. He was a firm believer in the Hindu code of values and was a bitter opponent of all who maligned it.

Krishnachandra possessed a profoundly original mind. He had an acute analytic intellect combined with imagination and insight of a very high order. Though he was widely read in Indian and Western philosophies, classical German philosophy and Advaita Vedānta were the two forces that exercised a major influence on his intellectual development. He had great intellectual energy and almost upto the end of his life he used to revel in sustained philosophical discussions. He wrote extensively. But his writings present a striking contrast to his oral disquisitions. When he spoke, even his serious discourses were used to be interspersed with quips and sallies; they were remarkable for their lucidity and thoroughness and he would develop his points without any reserve. But when he wrote, he often became almost a different man. He seemed to lose his expansiveness, became reserved and instead of lucidity he tried almost to be aphoristic in his expression. Far from developing a point he was content just to set down a cryptic thesis leaving the bewildered reader to elucidate for himself as best as he could. Though he wrote vastly, he published little. And this was due to the fact that he would complete very few of his writings. The present editor has with him an immense mass of unpublished documents containing reflections, studies, fragments, notes etc. on a large variety of subjects and at different stages of completion.

The philosophical writings of Krishnachandra Bhattacharyya are mainly of two kinds: (a) constructive interpretation of other systems and (b) construction of a new system of his own. The two are not indeed unconnected; but in giving an account of his philosophical contributions, it seems desirable to keep the two apart. The author's philosophical position will be analysed in some detail in the Introduction to Vol. II which will contain all the basic writings in which his philosophy has been formulated. In the present Introduction, an attempt will be made to bring out the distinctive features of the interpretational writings which form the contents of the first volume.

In his 'Studies in Vedāntism' the author suggests that his method is one of constructive interpretation and disclaims that it is an 'exposition' in the ordinary sense of the term. A perusal of the contents of the present volume will go to show that this method is also the one which the author has employed par excellence in all his studies in Indian philosophy. The method has also been described as 'speculative'. But the author has not anywhere indicated its precise nature. From a consideration of his actual procedure it would appear that by 'constructive interpretation' the author means much more of construction than of interpretation, and the method in substance amounts to speculative re-construction based on a few pivotal tenets rather than an objective exposition based on a detailed study of the more important texts of the particular school of philosophy that is claimed to be interpreted. The method is apparently a risky one and may easily be taken to be a fanciful reading of one's own thought into others' thinking. The author was quite conscious of this risk, but then he was of the opinion that it could be eliminated if the construction were not repelled by the letter or spirit of the system to be interpreted; or, in other words, if it could be made to fit without any disharmony into the general frame-work of that system. And this is exactly what the author used to claim for his interpretational writings. It is to be noted, again, that the constructive effort is prominent more specially in connection with those doctrines which are prima facie the most removed from the common consciousness. The major task of this kind of interpretation was, in the author's view, to render esoteric doctrines intelligible in terms of the contents of common consciousness.

Much of what the author has here said of Vedānta, Sāmkhya and Yoga is not to be found in the extant original literature on these subjects. It is an extension or a development in new directions of some fundamental tenets of the several schools. It is development not in the sense of necessary amplification of what is potential therein: it is rather the discovery of new potentialities and is in that sense a genuine addition to the existing corpus of the philosophy of the relevant schools. The extension, again, is always the result of the application of certain principles which constitute the fundamentals of the author's own philosophy. It would be unfair to suggest that this is nothing but subjectivism in the sphere of interpretation. For, the so-called 'objective' interpretation is as much 'subjective' in this sense as 'constructive' interpretation. The mind that interprets is not a tabula rasa; neither is it just a calculating machine or an electronic brain. The interpreter is a thinking being and as such he will have to interpret with a mind having a system of beliefs and from a stand-point which he happens to occupy at the time of his interpretative activity. Subjectivism in this sense is inevitable in all human thinking. It is not any blemish either unless, indeed, the belief-system is proved to be unfounded or the perspective distorted, or, again, unless its application turns out to be wrong or illegitimate.

It is to be expected that in such an interpretation as the present one, there would be improvisations and deviations from the standard interpretations holding the field. In the first tract on Vedānta, viz., 'Studies in Vedāntism' some of the innovations are as follows:—(a) the conception of 'levels of consciousness'; (b) the conception of dream-experience as constituting a new 'dimension' of existence; (c) the exhibition, on the strength of conscious dream, self-conscious dream and dreamless sleep respectively, of 'the objective possibility of perception without sensation, of the self-conscious knowledge of all space as one object and of all time as one unfolded panorama, and of the self swooning into the realisation of noumena'; (d) the re-interpretation of the conceptions of adhyātma, adhibhūta etc.; (e) the re-interpretation of the concept of devatā as the absolute unity of subject and object; (f) the interpretation of the concept of loka as the absolute intuition-medium for this unity; (g) the re-interpretation of the concepts of parā-prakṛti, śakti and aparā-prakṛti; (h) the ethico-theological elucidation of the concept of jīvan-mukti; and (i) the interpretation of some cosmogonic myths.

In the second tract, viz., 'Śaṅkara's doctrine of māyā', the writer has tried to understand the doctrine of acosmism from the common phenomenon of illusion. The improvisations relate to the concept of māyā. The interpretation of the phrase 'sad-asat-vilakṣaṇa' is, no doubt, more in accordance with the detractors of the concept of māyā, but it is remarkable that the author has tried to make the concept of 'neither sat nor asat' intelligible from an analysis of the different aspects of the experience of illusion. The second innovation concerns the analysis of the three stages in the phenomenon of correction of perceptual error, correlating them to the three aspects of māyā as vāstavī, anirvācyā and tucchā and connecting them with the different aspects of creative and destructive activities of the Lord.

In the third tract, viz., 'The Advaita and its spiritual significance', an attempt has been made to elucidate the doctrine of the illusoriness of individuality from the ethical experience of repentance. It is to be remarked here that the author has not generally tried to establish the Vedāntic doctrines with the help of arguments. He has rather sought to understand them with the aid of the contents of common consciousness.

In the Sāṁkhya and Yoga studies, the innovations are as follows:—(a) the conception of 'reflection as a kind of introspective insight to unravel the nature of the Sāṁkhya tattvas and also as a freeing process from aviveka; (b) the distinction drawn between the causal and the non-causal manifestations of prakṛti and some of its evolutes; (c) the theory of the phenomenality of the world of experience in regard to its character and not being; (d) the re-interpretation of the concept of bhāva as the referential function of the mind; (e) the interpretation of the concepts of buddhi, ahaṁkāra and tanmātra as self-knowing, self-willing and self-feeling respectively; (f) the interpretation of the tanmātras as at once mind-stuff and the matrix of the bhūtas; (g) the characterisation of Sāṁkhya as a religion of 'spiritual naturalness'; (h) the distinction drawn between causality in the phenomenal world and causality in the world of tattvas; (i) the conception of qualitative combination in Sāṁkhya; (j) the theory of anticipatory response of buddhi and the lower tattvas; (k) the theory of the guṇas as the absolutes of the three modes of feeling which are to be understood in terms of freedom; (l) the conception of ākāśa as the functional form of prakṛti distinguished from ākāśa as bhūta; (m) the re-interpretation of the conceptions of time and causality in Sāṁkhya and Yoga; (n) the enumeration of as many as *thirty* major points of difference between the Sāṁkhya and the Yoga schools.

In the tract on 'Anekānta', the author tries to show that neither the category of 'identity' nor that of 'difference' can be regarded as fundamental in philosophy, that the alternation of identity and difference is a more satisfactory conception than either pure identity or pure difference, and that a new interpretation of the Jaina theory of anekānta is possible in the light of the concept of alternation.

In 'The concept of Rasa' an attempt has been made to assign the exact 'level of consciousness' on which aesthetic experience stands; and according to the author's analysis, artistic enjoyment stands on a par with 'duplicated sympathy' which is on a level higher than that of common sympathy which, in its turn, is higher in level than the ordinary experience of joy. The writer also seeks to give a new account of the genesis of bībhatsa-rasa.

The above will give an idea of the wide range of improvisations which the author has presented in these Studies. It is for the competent reader to judge whether they are legitimate or not. But to come to a right decision on the point, it is necessary to have a fair acquaintance with the writer's own philosophy which, however, is not reported in the present volume and which the editor hopes to analyse in some detail in his Introduction to Volume II.

EDITOR'S INTRODUCTION TO VOL. II.

The published writings of Krishnachandra Bhattacharyya date from the year 1908, but his characteristic philosophical position assumes definite shape in the writings during the years 1928-1936. The publications of this period outnumber and far outweigh those that fall during the previous twenty years. Of the twentyone tracts published in these two volumes, as many as fourteen belong to this later period, the other seven covering the previous years. The earlier writings are not indeed entirely unrelated to the subsequent ones. Some of the salient positions elaborated in the author's later and maturer thinking are to be found adumbrated therein.

For the purpose of this Introduction, it would be convenient to present the author's philosophical position under the following heads:

I. The nature of Philosophy.
II. Theory of knowledge.
III. The theory of the subject and grades of cognitional freedom.
IV. The theory of the trinal absolute.

I. THE NATURE OF PHILOSOPHY.

a. The Concept of Philosophy.

The nature of Philosophy is elaborated in 'The Concept of Philosophy', published in 1936. Philosophy is there taken to be an expression of theoretic consciousness which, at its minimum, is the understanding of a speakable. But since what is spoken must be in the first instance believed, theoretic consciousness always involves belief in something as known. Philosophy is theoretic thinking. It is not, however, literal thinking. Literal thinking can be expressed as genuine judgments, but philosophical thinking cannot be so expressed. A genuine judgment is that in which the predicate either amplifies or explicates the meaning of the subject that is already believed. In philosophy, however, we do not have judgment of this genuine brand. What we have is pseudo-judgments, that is to say, statements which are 'self-evident elaborations of the self-evident'. The content of philosophical thought is necessarily speakable; it is yet independent of the spoken belief of an individual mind. It is in the sense of possessing this kind of independence that a philosophical content has been described as 'self-evident'.[1] Again, the elaboration of this self-evident as we have it in philosophy is itself self-evident. To explain. A believed content that has necessary reference to the speaking of it is not spoken of as information or, in other words, as a judgment in the proper sense of the term. In a judgment proper, the subject never presupposes the predicate. But in the apparent judgments that constitute the body of philosophy, the subject is understood as presupposing the predicate. Philosophy is, in this sense, a kind of self-evident elaboration of the self-evident.

It has been said that the contents of philosophical thinking are speakable, but they are not literally thinkable. Now, if a content is literally thinkable in a judgment, the belief in it is actual knowledge. If it is only symbolically thinkable, it should not be said to be *known* but to be only believed as known. In philosophy, the content is spoken as at least partially symbolised. Philosophy cannot, therefore, be regarded as a body of knowledge. It is concerned only with contents that are not actually known but are believed as demanding to be known without being literally thought. Philosophy is thus systematic symbolism.

Philosophy is the elaboration of different kinds of spiritual experiences. The abstractions of high-grade metaphysics are based on spiritual experience and derive their whole value from the experiences which they symbolise. No metaphysical concept is entirely intelligible without reference to the spirit.

b. The organon of Philosophy.

According to the author, the organon of philosophy is 'reflection' which is a sort of subjective activity yielding immediate knowledge. This insight-yielding activity has been described as a sort of 'experimentation with the knowing activity'.[2] It is an introspective exercise that 'can be specifically regulated'. Logical reason is its accessory. Inference does not enable us to reach philosophical beliefs, though it has value as an instrument of exposition. Metaphysical reasoning is only the systematic exposition of symbolic concepts. The elaborate parade of deductive proof in metaphysics is just a 'make-believe.'[3]

c. The *scope of Philosophy.*

Philosophy is a form of theoretic consciousness involving the understanding of a speakable. Theoretic consciousness is of four

[1] C.P. 9.
[2] SK. Ch. III.
[3] C.P. 29.

grades : (a) *empirical* thought which involves reference to an object perceived or imagined to be perceived; (b) *pure objective* thought which has reference to an object but not necessarily to a perceived object; (c) *spiritual* thought which has no reference to an object and is subjective; and (d) *transcendental* thought which has reference neither to the subject nor to the object. Philosophy is based on the last three kinds of thinking.

It has been said that philosophy is the elaboration of the self-evident or that which is independent of the spoken belief of any mind. Now this self-evident may be spoken in the objective, in the subjective and in the transcendental attitudes. Pure objective thinking is concerned with the self-evident in the objective attitude and its content may be called the 'self-subsistent.' Subjective or spiritual thinking is concerned with the self-evident in the subjective attitude and its content is the 'real'. Transcendental thinking is concerned with the self-evident in the transcendental attitude and its content is the 'truth' or the absolute.

These self-evidents are all speakables. The objective self-evident is spoken as 'the relation of A and B is' where the 'Is' means an objective content that is self-subsistent or existing apart from relations. Here the objective attitude is retained in its fulness. The subjective self-evident is spoken as 'I am' where 'am' means reality or something that is subjectively 'enjoyed'. Here the objective attitude is explicitly dropped and the content is spoken as though it were objectively contemplated. The transcendental self-evident is spoken as 'the absolute self is'. Here the self-evident is not even literally spoken as in the above two cases. Still it is not meaningless and it symbolises 'truth' i.e., what is belived and is not literally speakable.

In the author's view, the self-subsistent object demands to be known in absorbed contemplation; the real 'I' demands to be known in the unobjective attitude of 'enjoyment'; the transcendental 'truth' demands to be reached in speechless realisation. It is to be noted here that the precise nature of this 'demand' is not explicated by the author.

d. The branches of Philosophy.

Corresponding to the three attitudes and the threefold nature of the philosophic content, there are fundamentally three grades of philosophy, viz., the philosophy of the object, the philosophy of the subject and the philosophy of truth. Under 'philosophy of the object' the author places metaphysics and logic. Empirical psychology and axiology, it may be presumed, will also come under the same rubric. The 'philosophy of the subject' or philosophy in the subjective attitude covers epistemology in the current sense and also in the author's special sense of the term. The 'philosophy of truth' is a distinctive discipline quite other than either metaphysics or epistemology. The author's Transcendental or Spiritual psychology appears to be a blanket term for the last two grades of philosophy.

e. Philosophy of the object.

In his CP the author takes 'fact' to be that in which the reference to the subject or the speaking function is not necessary. This fact is dealt with in science. The object that has necessary reference to the subject is called by him the 'self-subsistent' and is taken to be what is dealt with in philosophy. 'Objectivity' which is common to these two objects is itself no fact, being only the self-subsistent form that is elaborated in logic. The spoken fact and the spoken self-subsistent agree in having certain unavoidable speech-created forms. Logic presents a system of these unavoidable forms. The concept of the object is first reached by contrast with the subject as the self-evident content of spiritual consciousness. The object is thus understood as self-subsistent before fact is understood as object. Since the object is apprehended before the form, logic may be said to presuppose metaphysics. And since metaphysics presents alternative theories in connection with the object, there may conceivably be alternative systems of logic. Logic is thus no science but only a branch of objective philosophy. The pure object whose forms are discussed in logic is the metaphysical object. Logic and metaphysics are thus the two basal branches of the philosophy of the object. It is to be noted here that metaphysics involves the objective attitude and there is no metaphysics of the subject.[1]

f. Metaphysics and Science.

Metaphysics has been characterised as philosophy of the object and is taken to be based on the thought of the *pure* object. This raises two questions: (a) what is this *pure* object; and (b) is there any discipline which is concerned with the non-pure object. It appears that, according to the author, the 'pure object' is the self-subsistent object i.e. to say, the object as object considered apart from its usability. It is to be noted that there is a dualism in the author's conception of the 'self-subsistent'. The self-subsistent has two features—one extrinsic and the other intrinsic. Extrinsically, it is that

[1] SF. II; CP. 28.

which is believed to exist without being knowable or usable. Intrinsically, it is that which has necessary reference to the subject. Per contra, the non-pure object would be that which is believed to be necessarily knowable and usable and which has no reference to the subject. It is the task of the first grade of philosophy to view the object as self-subsistent i.e., not as necessarily knowable and usable. In science, however, the object is just what is known and though it may be unknown, there is no question of its being unknowable. Science has no interest in formulating the concept of the self-subsistent object and it implicitly believes in the necessary knowability or usability of the object. Philosophy questions this implicit belief and offers a speculative theory of the object. Science may be said to be 'predatory' in so far as it believes that the object exists only to be used or exploited and the concept of the self-subsistent object is taken by the author to be the first corrective that philosophy offers of the predatory outlook of the scientific intellect. The attitude of philosophy is thus contemplative or aesthetic while that of science is frankly utilitarian. As a sort of corollary, the author believes that many problems which are usually regarded as philosophical are wrongly taken to be so. He lists three such main problems in his CP :—(a) the problem of piecing together the results of the sciences into a world-view, (b) the problem that is connected with the so-called philosophy of Evolution, and (c) the problems concerning the formulation of the postulates or the structural concept of science.

g. Philosophy of truth.

The contrast of logic with metaphysics suggests the distinction between the self-subsistent and the real. The forms of thinking discussed in logic are a kind of entity that must be said to be believed in, but they are believed in as not real and yet as not nothing. The suggested distinction between self-subsistence and reality is verified in the 'enjoying' consciousness of a content. The content of this 'enjoying' understanding is understood neither as fact nor as the self-subsistent object. It is understood as what object is not, as the speaking subjectivity, as 'I'. The study of all contents enjoyed in explicit reference to the subject 'I' may be called 'philosophy of the spirit'.

h. Philosophy of truth.

There is, according to the author, a theoretic consciousness of 'I am nought'. But the denial of 'I' is possible because we already believe that the absolute is. The absolute is a positively believed entity that is only negatively understood as what the subject 'I' is not. It is an entity that cannot be understood as it is believed and is speakable only by way of symbolism. The positive character of the absolute is expressible only by the negation of 'I' and, as such, is not literally expressible at all. If then it is said that the absolute *is,* the 'is' means not reality but 'truth'. Reality is enjoyed but truth is not. The consciousness of truth as what is believed in but not understood either in the objective or subjective attitude and as a speakable in a non-literal or symbolic way is transcendental consciousness. Truth is belived as independent of speaking i.e., as self-revealing. 'Truth' then is absolute. But the absolute is not to be equated to truth. It may be 'truth' as in Advaita-Vedānta; it may be what truth is not or the absolute 'freedom' beyond being as in the so-called nihilistic Buddhism; it may again be 'value', or the indetermination oif truth or freedom as in Hegel. The study of this triple absolute belongs to the transcendental grade of philosophy.

II. Theory of Knowledge

a. The concept of 'knowledge'.

In presenting the author's theory of knowledge it is desirable to start with a clarification of what he means by the term 'knowledge'. It is well-known that the word has been used in a wide variety of senses. But, whatever the variety, it is generally not in dispute that knowledge is a kind of awareness. In one usage it is identified with awareness as such. But our author does not accept this usage and has often contrasted knowledge to mere awareness. Awareness is of two fundamentally opposed types—, awareness in the objective attitude and awareness in the subjective attitude. The former is primarily exemplified by the awareness of physical objects, where what one is aware of is distinguished from the subject that has the awareness. The latter is primarily illustrated by one's awareness of oneself and of one's 'knowing', where what one is aware of is not so distinguished. Following this difference in attitudes, we may have studies in the objective attitude and those in the subjective attitude. Theories of knowledge and metaphysics of the subject are usually regarded as coming under the former class. Our author, however, deviates from this prevailing view and holds that any study about knowing and the subject must be carried on in the subjective attitude .Not merely that:

he speaks of a 'cultivation'[1] of the subjective attitude and the interpretation of objects from the subjective attitude. He goes even further and appears to hold that awareness in the subjective attitude is far more authentic than the other kind of awareness. The subjective attitude, in his view, yields the self-evidencing truth.

Of the two types of awareness, it is the one in the objective attitude that the author primarily takes to be what is signified by the term 'knowledge'. Not that the other type of awareness is altogether denied that appellation. The awareness of the subject—which is an awareness in the subjective attitude—is taken to be a case of knowledge. The awareness of the knowing 'function' and other functions of freedom like feeling, willing etc. is definitely not knowledge. But though knowledge is chiefly awareness in the objective attitude, it is not co-extensive with objective awareness. It is only one species of the latter, there being other kinds, as for example, thought, feeling, imagination, memory etc. Objective knowledge is distinguished from these latter varieties in having intuition (in the Kantian sense) as one of its elements.[2] The author here appears to accept the Kantian convention that intuition and thought are the two necessary elements of what properly should be termed 'knowledge'. He further draws a distinction between knowledge and belief. Knowledge involves belief, to be sure; but as distinct from mere belief, it involves the distinctness of the believed object from the belief.[3] There is finally the distinction, presumably on the scope of validity, between knowledge on the one hand and illusion and imagination on the other. Thus it appears that the word 'knowledge' in the author's usage stands *primarily* (and not exclusively) for a valid and certain awareness in the objective attitude, having intuition for one of its factors and involving the distinction of the object known from the knowledge itself. Primarily, because the author is quite categorical that one's awareness of oneself is an instance of knowledge, even though it is neither objective awareness nor intuitional in character. One thing is not clear however, and that is whether the author would agree to describe what he calls 'knowledge' as a state or as a 'function'. That would perhaps depend on whether he would like to designate awareness itself as a 'state' or a 'function'. If knowledge were to be regarded as a 'state', it would have to be regarded as a sort of precipitate of the 'knowing'-function. If,

[1] SF. 16.
[2] SF. 49.
[3] SF. 33-34.

however, it were to be described as a 'function', it would be just the function of 'knowing' itself. There is not surely a knowledge-function over and above the knowing-function. Certain trends in the author's mode of thinking would seem to favour the assumption that, according to him, knowledge and knowing-function are one and the same thing. But the editor is not at all sure on the point.

About the nature of knowing or 'to know', the author is quite explicit. Know*ing* is a function and not a passive state of the subject, as many would have it. 'Function' appears to be a sort of activity. To know is to act or to do something. But it is activity neither in a physical nor in the volitional way. It appears to be sui generis and the author says that it is activity only in a symbolical sense.

Knowing activity is a 'free reference of the subject to the object'. It represents, according to the author, a positive mode of freedom of the subject to relate to object without *getting related* to it.[1] The freedom of the subject lies precisely in the fact that it is known by itself and that in relating to the object, it does not get related to the latter. That the subject has really such freedom is, as it appears, a matter of immediate certainty to the author. It might be suggested that the position is paradoxical, for if A relates to B (freely, it may be) it cannot but get related to B. It does not appear, however, that to the author this presents any paradox. To him it is not self-evident that the function of relating precipitates the state of relatedness, especially when it is free functioning. It is rather the case that the subject has an immediate feeling of relating itself to the object without having a feeling of getting related to it.

b. The object of knowledge. The theory of psychic fact.

Knowledge is primarily of a definite object and is to be distinguished from the awareness of the indefinite. The author is positive that the indefinite is as much an object as the definite and is exemplified by such entities as the aesthetic object, alternation, the image as being formed, the 'fringe' of a psychic fact etc.

Knowledge or cognition in the objective attitude is either of the physical fact or of the psychic fact. The author accepts the ordinary view of the physical fact, but as to the nature of the latter, he deviates widely from the usual view of the matter. In the ordinary and prevailing view, a psychic fact is a purely mental occurrence. It is just anything that happens in the mind, and, if immediately accessible, it

[1] SF. 13.

is accessible only to introspection. In the author's account, however, a psychical fact is never a pure mental event. It is not a 'pure' mental entity, because it is always an aspect of the non-mental object. Not that it is itself non-mental, as advocated by the Behaviourist. Neither is it any 'experience-unity of subject and object' as we have it in Ward.

It has been said that the psychic fact is an aspect of the non-mental object. This requires clarification. The object has certain 'modes of relatedness' to the subject, e.g., knownness, feltness etc. This relatedness viewed as a character of the object is, according to our author, the so-called psychic fact.[1] Knownness or relatedness is 'a floating adjective like beauty'.[2] A psychic fact constituted by this relatedness is a character of the physical object and exists, like the object. even apart from introspection.

Two negative criteria are laid down in this connection :— (i) what does not involve 'knowledge' of object is no psychic fact;[3] (ii) what introspection does not reveal is no psychic fact.[4] It follows from the above that the following kinds of awareness, among others, do not come within the author's definition of a psychic fact :—

(i) the awareness of the imaginary,
(ii) the awareness of the illusory,
(iii) the introspective state or process,
(iv) objectless feeling,
(v) belief in the past fear of some illusory object.

These are placed in a separate category and designated as 'non-psychic fringe of a psychic fact'. It is to be noted that though they are non-psychic, they are not for that reason physical entities. It is unfortunate, however, that the author has not given us any hints as to the precise status which hë ascribes to these fringe-entities.

c. *Presentation.*

Psychic fact is essentially 'presentation' as embodying belief. It is thus not imaginary or non-factual. It is not, however, completely accomplished as fact but only to be accomplished.[5] It is not completely accomplished as fact in the sense that it is not isolated or freed from the object.

It is necessary to explain what the author means by the term 'presentation'. Knowledge involves belief but, as distinguished from mere belief, it involves the awareness of the distinction of the object

[1] SF. 25.
[2] SF. 25.
[3] SF. 27.
[4] SF. 28.
[5] SF. 40.

believed from the belief.[1] This distinction is something more than the object itself and is what the author calls 'presentation' of the object.[2] Presentation as a psychic fact and object as a non-psychic entity are mixed up with each other in a peculiar way. The object is *given* as distinct from the presentation. The latter, however, is not *given* as distinct from the former: it is only abstracted or distinguished from the object in introspection. It is to be noted that it is in non-perceptual knowledge only that the object appears distinct from its presentation and not in perceptual knowledge. In perception, again, the presentation is not *known* as distinct from the object but it is believed and symbolised as what should be distinct.[3]

Presentation is not necessarily perceptual. In addition to external perception, we have presentation in the following modes: (i) feeling of the body from within; (ii) immediate apprehension of absence; (iii) memory of an object as past; (iv) imagination of the object as formed or becoming formed to be a perceptible object; (v) inference of the perceptible object as involving the unperceivable character of necessity etc.

Perceptual knowledge is, to the author, the actual standard of knowledge. The other modes of presentation imply it and involve a belief in something not yet known but which may be known in some ideal mode of realisation.[4] Perception not only lends cognitive character to the other modes of presentation: it prevents them from reaching their ideal completion.[5] Contrasted to perception, the other modes are knowledge of certain adjectival facts or floating adjectives. They are not known as substantive though they are wanted to be so known.

d. Belief, thought and feeling.

It has been said that the author does not take the word 'knowledge' to mean any and every awareness. Knowledge is only one kind and is contrasted to certain other kinds of which belief, thought and feeling are the most frequently mentioned. It is necessary to distinguish these different kinds. Belief is the awareness of a fact as fact. Thought is a presentation that does not exclude belief in the object. Its object is presented as unpicturable meaning. Thought is a completed product and is about a definite object. It is 'complete' in the sense of being dissociated from the forming or ideal timing that

[1] SF. 33.
[2] *Ibid.*
[3] SF. 56.
[4] SF. 38.
[5] SF. 39.

characterises the image. Thought is a form of theoretic consciousness which involves the understanding of a speakable. It is either literal or symbolic. Literal thought appears to be identified with 'empirical thought'. The latter is explained as consciousness of a content involving reference to an object that is perceived or imagined to be perceived.[1] Symbolic thought is other than this literal thought and is of three kinds, the nature and object of which have already been explained in connection with the author's conception of philosophy.

By 'feeling' the author appears primarily to mean the intuition of of the Intuitionists—i.e. an awareness that is non-sensuous, immediate and completely certain. But far from agreeing with the Intuitionist in taking this feeling to be a superior type of 'knowledge' he does not regard it as 'knowledge' at all. In knowledge, there is almost always reference to an object, while feeling is explicitly unobjective. It is a positive subjective fact without any reference to any objective fact[2] and is typically exemplified by the feeling of the body from within or of freedom. It is an awareness in which there is no conscious reference to the object even in the way of dissociation from it.[3] It is not denied that feeling has any content whatsoever. It has indeed one, but this content is unthought and unmeant and appears to introspection as only distinct in itself and not as distinct from feeling. A psychic fact like thought is distinguished in introspection from its object and is accordingly believed to exist also outside introspection. But as feeling is not thus distinguished from its content, it cannot be believed to exist outside introspection as a merely conscious fact.

In feeling there is the positive consciousness of detachment from meaning. 'Feeling is the knowledge of the purely unknown as such, the unknown that is not even meant'.[4] It is only symbolised as knowledge of the unknown. It is to be noted that as the unknown here is the unmeant, the preposition 'of' in the phrase 'knowledge of the unknown' has no meaning and is used as a mere exigency of language.

e. Theory of introspection.

It is necessary at this stage to advert to the author's theory of introspection. Introspection is usually taken to be internal perception or the non-inferential awareness of a mental fact, and so far as its character of immediacy is concerned, it is placed on a par with the sense-perception of the physical object. According to the author,

[1] CP. 8.
[2] SF. 101.
[3] *Ibid.*
[4] SF. 106.

however, introspection is a process of abstracting from the object of its character of 'relatedness to the subject'. The author agrees that a psychic fact is what is introspected. He does not agree, however, that the psychic is a purely mental fact. He holds that it is a character of the physical object, like knownness feltness etc., and that introspection consists in the distinguishing of knownness etc. as an abstraction from the object.[1] The author deviates from the ordinary view of introspection on another important point. In the ordinary view, perceptual states no less than the non-perceptual ones are accessible to introspection : in the author's view, there is no direct introspection into perceptual knowledge[2], and the knowledge that we have of perceptual presentations is obtained through our introspection into non-perceptual presentations.

This introspection is called 'psychological' introspection and is to be differentiated from 'spiritual' introspection which consists in distinguishing the functions of knowing etc. as other than the character of knownness etc.[3] A function like 'knowing' represents a mode of freedom from the psychic fact of knownness, and to the author, the consciousness of modes of freedom like knowing is as direct as that of a psychic fact like knownness.

In the above account which is found in SF, the author appears to recognise psychological introspection in the objective attitude as a variety of introspection. In CP, however, he withdraws this recognition and confines the term 'introspection' only to what he calls 'spiritual introspection' which is there identified with the 'enjoying understanding' of the subject or the 'I'. Here 'introspection' is awareness in the subjective attitude, and the author is quite definite that 'introspection proper is a form of theoretic consciousness that implies an abjuration of the objective attitude'.[4]

Spiritual introspection is speaking in the first person—either actually or ideally—and involves the explicit consciousness of *being* what is spoken. In KT, the author speaks of 'epistemological' introspection, i.e., a species of introspection which is at the basis of epistemology, especially of the Kantian type. The particular method by which Kant passed from the logical forms to the apriori functions is, according to the author, a self-evident process in self-consciousness and, as such, should be taken as a kind of introspection which is quite other than internal perception or psychological introspection in the usual sense of the term. Epistemological introspection is possible

[1] SF. 17.
[2] SF. 34; 36.
[3] SF. 17.
[4] CP. 32.

only in the subjective attitude and appears thus to be a variant of spiritual introspection. The so-called psychological introspection in the objective attitude is either not introspection proper or is only a degeneration of spiritual introspection.[1]

f. The concept of 'Truth'.

The author has used the term 'truth' in at least two quite distinct senses. In one usage the term means that which is self-justifying or self-revealing (viz. the absolute) and has 'real' for its antithetic term.[2] In the other usage, it stands for true or valid cognition and is contrasted to error.[3] The author holds that the doctrine of truth and error should belong to a discipline other than logic or epistemology.

In connection with 'truth', it is held that knowledge and truth have to be defined in terms of each other, the former as what alone is true and the latter as what alone is known.[4] Three consequences follow from this : There is, in the first place, no such thing as false knowledge. Since knowing is known only as the implicate of the awareness of truth, to know an object is to know it as implicitly true. Truth cannot be taken simply as additional confirmation of what already is known indifferently. The second consequence is that there is no knowledge of objects as merely distinct and not otherwise related to one another. The known content must be explicitly coherent and not merely co-existent with other known contents. The third consequence is that interpretations of knowing in terms of feeling or willing do not amount to knowledge.

g. Analysis of error.

The author has devoted more attention to the problem of error than to that of truth. The first analysis is found in his Vedāntic tracts where we have explicitly the Śaṁkarite analysis of perceptual error or illlusion. The second analysis—largely independent—is to be found in his CELP. The problem recurs also in SF and FS.

In analysing the phenomenon of illusion the author deals chiefly with the following problems :—(i) the stages constituting an illusion. and its correction; (ii) the nature and status of the content that is corrected and (iii) the precise nature of the corrective process. The analysis, it is to be noted, is fundamentally on the lines of the Advaita-Vedānta school, though the author has always something of his own to say on a number of important points.

[1] C.P. 32-33.
[2] C.P. 39.
[3] KT.
[4] Ibid. 8.

In the first analysis, the stock Vedāntic example of mistaking a rope for a snake is analysed in three stages :—(a) The snake is presented and believed to be real. (b) The belief is corrected by the perception of the rope as rope. The objective snake of the first stage now loses its objectivity and persists only as a possible object. The past percept as a subjective fact is, however, not yet questioned. (c) The snake is contemplated not only as non-existent now but as non-existent even when it appeared to be perceived. *That* snake is no possible object and there is a doubt even about the past perception of it is a subjective fact. *That snake* is thus shorn of its objective reality in the second stage and of its reality either as objective or as subjective in the third stage. It is still given to us as a positive unthinkable and in absolute mockery of all thinking.

In the second analysis, the author makes out the following points. (i) The correction is an epistemic function without any unitary logical content. It cannot be adequately expressed by any single sentence like 'this that I believed as this snake is not snake'. It has to be expressed in two sentences. There is no unitary logical form to express correction. (ii) Falsity has no reference to the time-position of a cognition at all and what is taken as false cannot be specified in purely objective terms. (iii) Taking the disbelief implied in correction to be adequately expressed in the form 'this snake is not', the *this* in it would not mean a perceived substrate or the snake-character. *This,* here, is not even a believed substrate but only an imagined specification of an imagined snake. *This* in 'this snake' stands for no fact at all. The disbelief is absolute and is not capable of being expressed as a negative judgment. It cannot, again, be said that 'what *this* was believed to be was not presented, nor that it was presented as *this*'. 'I cannot now describe in objective terms what I then believed, nor can I say that there was only the subjective fact of contentless belief. I believed in a content that was neither fact nor absolute nought'.

So much for the author's analysis of error. He has also something to say about the relation between the false and the subjective. According to him, the consciousness of the false and the consciousness of the subjective imply one another. The false is what is corrected and disbelieved. The content said to be disbelieved cannot be expressed except as 'what was believed'. Correction has thus to be taken as a form of reflective consciousness. Again, the consciousness of the subjective is consciousness of a belief. There is no consciousness of a subjectivity that is not consciousness of a content referred to fact. Now the consciousness of belief is the consciousness of having the belief *as past* for present rejection or re-affirmation and is never a mere non-committal consciousness of the content as merely subsistent.

III. Theory of the Subject and Grades of Cognitional Freedom.

a. *Theory of the Subject.*

The subject or the self is conceived after Advaita-Vedānta as consciousness and is interpreted as free-function or freedom. This, according to the author, is Kant's view also. But while to Kant this self is only thinkable and is never knowable, to Krishnachandra it is never literally thinkable though it is knowable. It is not, however, ordinarily known in itself, though the possibility of its knowledge will have to be admitted.

That the self is not literally thinkable follows from the author's definition of 'thought' which, in his view, must *mean* or refer to some object. Since the subject is other than the object and the object is just what is meant, the subject cannot be a meant something. That the subject cannot be anything meant follows also from the author's conception of 'meaning'. A word is taken to *mean* something when the speaker and the hearer could use the word to understand the self-same entity. But the word 'I' cannot be so used. As used it has a uniquely singular reference.

Though the subject is not the object, it is somehow found blended with the latter. The object is given in various stages and correspondingly there are various grades of subjectivity. Spiritual realisation is the realisation of these different grades as dissociated from the object.

The subject as consciousness is not, as has just been stated, realised in its purity in common consciousness. It is, however, recognised to be present throughout the different stages of objectivity. In his *The Subject as freedom,* the author makes an attempt to trace out in detail these different grades of subjectivity. What follows here is largely a summary, practically in the author's own words, of his general position as developed in this treatise.

b. *Grades of cognitional freedom.*

There are three broad stages of subjectivity :—(A) the bodily, (B) the psychical and (C) the spiritual.

(A) The subject is primarily intended by the word 'I' and as the body is identified with the 'I' it is permissible to speak of the 'bodily subject'. The bodily stage has three substages :—(i) the body as externally perceived, (ii) the body as internally felt and (iii) the absence of object known as a present fact. In the bodily or sub-psychic stage, the body as observed and felt is the subject in relation to the environment. (i) Though the body represents a stage of being of the subject, yet one's own body, even as a perceived object, has a unique singularity. The objectivity of other perceived objects is constituted by their space-position relatively to the percipient's body. It is not, however, so with the percipient's own body which is in this sense dissociated from the external world. A person's own body is uniquely different from other perceived objects and has no place in the objective world that he conceives to be presentable to him. Even if the subject is taken as nothing but one's own perceived body, it involves knowledge of something that cannot be understood in terms of the perceptible object in the merely objectivistic attitude. (ii) There is the awareness of the body from within in the 'feeling of the body'. The felt body cannot be distinguished from the perceived body though the latter is distinguished from the former. The felt body is, in this sense, potentially dissociated from the perceived body. It is, again, imperfectly dissociated from the perceived object and the latter is fully distinguished from the former. The feeling of detachment from the object is the feeling of freedom and the first hint of this freedom is reached in the feeling of the body. (iii) There is such a thing as a sense-conditioned cognition of an absent object, or of the absence of an object. It is not ordinary perception and is yet undissociated from it. It is a kind of imaginative perception conditioned by conscious non-perception of that which is cognised. The subject that imaginatively perceives the absence of an object is, like the felt body, not consciously dissociated from the perceived body; but the subject that knows absence through conscious non-perception is consciously dissociated from it. Conscious non-perception is thus a transitional stage between body-feeling and imagination with which the psychical stage begins.

(B) The psychical stage has four substages :—(i) image, (ii) idea-image, (iii) pictorial idea and (iv) non-pictorial idea. The image of the object whose absence is known in conscious non-perception marks the transition to the psychic stage. The image appears as a substantive something from which the object is distinct. The psychic stage begins when attention is shifted from the objective fact of absence to the image. As attended to, (i) the image appears as imaging or the forming of a form, the process and the product being presented at once. The consciousness of the form as evident in the forming process and as a product that does not yet come in time *after* it is (ii) the idea as undissociated from the image. A later stage is (iii) the idea as dissociated from the image; it is pictorial thought which wants to be imaged and is definite so far as it is imaged. (iv) Non-pictorial thought comes next. It is thought that is definite in itself and has properly no image, though an image may serve as its symbol. These grades of image and thought are the grades of presentation which is explicitly felt to be dissociated from the object. Such dissociated presentation is known in introspection to have no space-position and is at least not known to have time-position. The image still appears, however, as though it has spatial form and to be forming as though it were a temporal process. Some trace of this quasi-temporal process may persist in thought, but thought as a non-pictorial meaning is felt to be free from it and to be eternally complete. Still such meaning appears as though it were object. Its presentational character is explicitly indicated by the consciousness of the absence of accomplished meaning in the phenomenon of *trying to think*. This may be taken as pointing to the positive freedom from objective meaning such as characterises non-presentational or spiritual subjectivity.

(C) Spiritual subjectivity has three substages :—(i) feeling, (ii) introspection and (iii) beyond introspection.

(i) Feeling.—The introspective awareness of meaning as distinct from the image is awareness of the explicitly unobjective. Feeling is also explicitly unobjective. The consciousness of the merely unknown as distinct from what is known as object that is also unknown is 'feeling'. It is purely subjective in the sense that there is no conscious reference to object even in the way of dissociation from it. In introspection into feeling, the distinction of feeling from its presentative content is appreciated as definitely not known but only felt and symbolised. With this awareness of meaning as the symbol of feeling, the objective reference lapses altogether.

Feeling is the positive consciousness of detachment from meaning. It is the awareness of a content as *unmeant*. But as it is non-denial of a possible meaning, it is not without the persisting will to objectification. When a feeling has purged itself of this will, there is the awareness not merely of the unmeant but of the unmeanable as well. This is exemplified from the analysis of the experience of the illusory. The content there is the 'indescribable'. Two stages of feeling can thus be distinguished : the lower stage where there is freedom from actual thought and the higher stage where there is freedom from possible thought.

The feeling of not having a feeling is itself a feeling : it is the feeling of a feeling. We are aware of the un-meanable in two stages, as the meant unmeanable and as the mere function of meaning. The knowledge implied in the former is of a contradiction while that implied in the latter is not of anything : it is merely knowing. The feeling of feeling is the former kind of awareness, while the latter is just introspection which is the pure knowing *function* and is a complete detachment from felt being.

(ii) Introspection.—Introspection into feeling implies the possible detachment from the being of feeling. This possible detachment from all distinct being is introspective awareness. The self is taken by Kant as the thinking function and also as an accomplished meaning. But in the author's view, the self is identified with the function of introspection and detached from thinking and feeling. It is the first person 'I' which is neither meanable nor unmeanable. The word 'I' has a meaning-function but not a meaning. It is the expression of introspection or the I-function. The meaning function of the word 'I' is to the speaker his actual introspection, but the understanding of the word by the hearer is indicative of a form of consciousness subtler than introspection. It is the awareness of a possible introspection.

(iii) Beyond introspection.—Actual introspection is unrealised knowledge because it is actually only self-evidencing to another and not self-evident to itself. One's own self should be self-evident and should be intuited by oneself even as it is intuited by another. The self should be at once self-evidencing and self-evident, but as a matter of fact the self is self-evidencing and evident to another. The other self is to the self-evidencing self a possible introspector whose intuition of the latter is a possible intuition to the latter. The awareness of these possibles in oneself indicates the necessity of a spiritual discipline of realisation of the self already implied by introspection.

Introspection into the awareness of a possible subjective state is a possible or imaginary introspection. It is half-dissociated from the actually introspective self. Complete dissociation from this actual awareness is reached when the content of it is a subjective state that is illusory. There are actually illusions about the subjective just as there are illusions about the objective.

Ordinarily, introspection is the awareness of a subjective fact as owing its facthood to itself and is, in this sense, its appropriator. But there are experiences where one gets the hint of an introspection that is not appropriative. This kind of introspection would be self-intuition. The possibility of a silent self-enjoying 'I' is intelligible only because we are aware of certain subjective modes previously appropriated as utterly unappropriable and as appearing only as though they are distinct. The absolute intuitable self is only understood if the non-being of distinction is understood. This non-being is finally understood in the awareness of subjective illusion which is the explicit awareness creating a distinction that is no fact at all.

c. *The Subject as Freedom.*

It is in introspection that we are aware of the demand for the consummation of the freedom that is felt in every grade of subjectivity in respect of the object presented to it. The introspective subject is free from possible objectivity and is thus freedom itself. But it knows itself not as itself but as a distinct subject that is only possibly identical with itself. It is thus aware of a demand to know this subject as *actually* itself. This demand is for the intuition of the subject as absolute freedom. The subject is understood as freedom that is real. The idea of realising the subject arises only because we are identified with the body while we are introspectively aware of ourselves as not objective and yet as definitely positive. We do not *know* ourselves as dissociated from the object, yet we are aware of a possible dissociation or freedom. Actual freedom from the object is *known* in some measure in bodily subjectivity. In higher stages, there is only the *feeling* of it. The higher the stage of subjectivity, the less is the freedom felt to be achieved though the more assured is the faith in its achievability. In the introspective stage, the feeling of achieved freedom lapses altogether, but the faith in its achievability is completely assured.

IV. Theory of the Trinal Absolute.

Although the term 'absolute' in the sense of the unconditioned or the non-relative occurs frequently in the earlier writings of Krishnachandra, a distinctive theory of the absolute is to be found only in two of his later writings, viz., *'The Concept of the Absolute and its Alternative Forms' and 'The Concept of Philosophy'*. The present account is based chiefly on the former. In CAAF, the absolute is defined as 'what is free from the implicational dualism of content and consciousness'. The definition requires to be clarified. Consciousness is always the consciousness of a content and we are reflectively aware of the content as distinct from and in necessary reference to consciousness. This peculiar relation between content and consciousness is described as 'implicational dualism'. An entity that is free from such dualism would be an entity that is distinct but not in necessary reference to consciousness. Such an entity seems to be what the writer designates as the absolute. Now, as consciousness is of three kinds—knowing, feeling and willing—the implicatory distinction is also threefold. There are, again, three ways in which freedom from this distinction can be understood : (a) the content may be freed from its reference to consciousness and we have *truth*—the absolute for knowing; (b) consciousness may be freed from the content and we have *freedom* of the will—the absolute for willing; (c) the implicational relation of content and consciousness may be freed from their distinction as a unity and we have *value*—the absolute for feeling. In the case of knowing, the absolute would be a content that has to be understood as what need not be the content of any knowing, i.e., as utterly unrelated to knowing. In the case of willing, the reality of willing has to be understood as the negation of being or of an emergent distinct. In the case of feeling, the being of value has to be understood as a being from which known being is distinct; it is to entertain an indifference of being and non-being. All the three—unrelatedness, negation of the emergent and the indifference of being and non-being—are unmeaning modes of negation to reflection. But to admit the absolute in any form is to admit a negation that is unintelligible to the logic of the understanding.

The absolute has to be formulated in a triple way. It is meaningless to assert, however, that there are three absolutes or one absolute, for the absolute is not a *known* content and it is only about anything known that the question 'one or many' has any meaning. There is no sense, again, in speaking of the absolute as the unity of truth, freedom and value.

It will be seen that the absolute of Krishnachandra's conception is not the same as the overpersonal reality that is enjoyed in religion. It means what the subject 'I' is not. It is a positively believed entity that is only negatively understood. It is an entity that cannot be understood as it is believed and is speakable only by way of symbolism.

The absolute as transcending the enjoyed reality of religion is positive being (truth) or positive non-being (freedom) or their positive indetermination (value). In the author's opinion, the absolute is conceived as truth in Advaita-Vedānta, as freedom in Buddhist nihilism' and as value in Hegel.

The absolute, it has been said, has to be formulated in a triple way as truth, freedom and value. Each is absolute, but what are here understood as *three* are only their verbal symbols : they themselves are undersood together but not *as* together.

The author describes the mutual relation between truth, value and freedom as 'alternation', and employing the term, 'reality' to mean freedom, he offers the following explanation. "... it appears meaningless to speak of truth as value, of value as real or of reality as true; while we can significantly speak of value as not false, of reality as not valueless or of truth as not unreal, although we cannot positively assert value to be truth, reality to be value and truth to be reality. . . . In one direction their identity and difference are alike meaningless and in another direction their identity is intelligible though not assertable. Truth is unrelated to value, value to reality and reality to truth; while value may be truth, reality value and truth reality. The absolute may be regarded in this sense as an alternation of truth, value and reality". For further clarification of this relation, the reader is referred to sections 44 to 47 of CAAF.

It appears that 'alternation' in the present context is not merely epistemic, and truth, freedom and value are not just alternative descriptions of the absolute. 'Alternation' in the author's view appears to be constitutive of the absolute. But if, as the author holds, it is *meaningless* to assert that the absolute is one or many, it is difficult to see how the absolute can be asserted to be of the nature of an 'alternation' in the ordinary sense of either-or, or in any other extraordinary sense that can be conceived.

The above is a quite imperfect and inadequate report of the major aspects of the philosophy of Krishnachandra Bhattacharyya. It will be seen that though it is possible to recognise traces of Vedāntic or Kantian influence here and there, the philosophy as a whole is remarkably original. There are undeniably obscure points which the editor would have liked to clarify if he could. But despite this occasional obscurity, in going through these studies there is the ineradicable feeling that one is in the presence of an extra-ordinarily powerful and wonderfully inventive mind.

STUDIES IN VEDĀNTISM

INTRODUCTION

The following studies in Vedāntism are not so much expositions of the traditional Vedānta as problematic constructions on Vedāntic lines intended to bring out the relations of the system to modern philosophical systems. The work of construction has, however, been subordinated to the work of interpretation. A wide latitude of interpretation has been claimed throughout.

The studies follow the traditional authorities, the Upaniṣads, the Brahma-sūtras, and Bhagavad-gītā, and confine themselves to the monistic interpretations of Śaṅkara. They draw on treatises like Pañcadaśī, Vedānta-siddhānta-muktāvalī, etc., propounding what may be called the later Vedānta, for such definite views as may be regarded to be legitimate systematisations of the earlier but looser Vedānta. No attempt has been made here to trace the historical evolution of the Vedāntic school.

The historical study of a school of thought must have methods and aims different from those of a philosophical study, though the studies are mutually supplementary. The philosophical study should come first in the order of time; the historical study of an ancient system of philosophy, to be of any use at all, must be preceded by an earnest study of the philosophy, in the expositions traditionally accepted as authoritative. The correctness of these expositions—at any rate, the perspective—may be impugned afterwards by historic research. But the historian here cannot begin his work at all unless he can live in sympathy into the details of an apparently outworn creed and recognise the *truth* in the first imperfect adumbrations of it. The attitude of the mere narrator has, in the case of the historian of philosophy, to be exchanged as far as possible, for that of the sympathetic interpreter. There is the danger, no doubt, of too easily reading one's philosophic creed into the history, but the opposite danger is more serious still. It is the danger of taking the philosophic type studied as a historic curiosity rather than a recipe for the human soul, and of seeking to explain the curiosity by natural *causes* instead of seriously examining its merits as philosophy. This unfortunately is sometimes the defect of Western expositions of Eastern philosophy and religion,

It springs from a tacit conviction, which, to say the least, bespeaks a lack of historic sense, that the common-sense evolved at the present day is absolutely infallible; though if the history of philosophy were rightly studied, it would show that many of the modern speculative *discoveries* are but reaffirmations of old truths, and that the present-day common-sense itself is a complex structure in which are imbedded types of thought which are ordinarily taken to be completely outworn and superseded. We have heard of Indian pessimism and fatalism disposed of by a sapient reference to the climatic and political conditions of the country; and the very name of philosophy has sometimes been denied to Indian speculation on the ground, apparently established historically, that the Oriental intellect is not sufficient dry and has not masculine virility enough to rise to anything higher than grotesque imaginative cosmogonies. When history thus sits in judgment on philosophy, an Indian student of Vedānta may well be excused if to him a reproduction of the philosophy, such as may bring it into contact with modern problems, appears far more important than any mere historical dissertation.

A fair instance of how principles of historical research are sometimes allowed to prejudice a right appreciation of philosophy is afforded by Dr. Thibaut's otherwise valuable introduction to his translation of the Vedānta-sūtras, with Śaṅkara's commentary (Sacred Books of the East, vol. xxxiv). Referring to the attempts of Śaṅkara and other scholiasts to evolve a complete philosophic system from the Upaniṣads, he says: "On later generations, to which the whole body of texts came down as revealed truth, there devolved the inevitable task of establishing systems on which no exception could be taken to any of the texts; but that the task was, strictly speaking, an impossible one, i.e., one which it was impossible to accomplish fairly and honestly, there really is no reason to deny" (p. cvi). The texts "do not allow themselves to be systematised because they were never meant to form a system" (p. cxiv). "......But the task of systematising once given, we are quite ready to admit that Śaṅkara's system is the best that can be devised" (p. cxxii). The contention here apparently is that the task is *not* given, except to one who believes the texts to embody revealed truth.

Now, what precisely is the task to which Śaṅkara has addressed himself? It is not that of the critical historian, it is the task of piecing together the several texts into a philosophical system, of developing a hypothesis on a necessary basis which will cover all the texts. But it may be asked, why should it be assumed that all the texts should find place in a necessary system? May not some of them embody false speculations altogether? Here, then, we have to consider the special nature of the Upaniṣad texts. They may or may not have been revealed; but as they are, they are presented not as mere guesses from the outside to explain the facts of the Universe, nor even as leisurely philosophisings conducted on a necessary basis, but as embodying mystic intuitions, often the products of what has been called the mythologic imagination which *sees* philosophy in poetic symbols. There are sometimes attempts at reasoning, too, but then by themselves they are hardly logically convincing, having not unoften an almost infantine naiveté about them. Now, the question here is, what should be our attitude towards these texts which, apparently at any rate, embody intuitions? So long as no obvious mark of spuriousness is discovered, they are to be regarded as genuine, though even a genuine intuition may be false in its content. The falsity, however, is not to be judged apriori but only after a strenuous endeavour to reproduce, if possible, the intuitions through such means as may have been laid down, in the śāstras, or, what we understand better, after an attempt to systematise all the texts into a well-rounded philosophy. The latter is the task which Śaṅkara and other commentators have set themselves to accomplish. Hence admitting that the texts were never meant to be strung together into a system, it can still be held that the task of systematising is inevitably given to every student of the Upaniṣads.

Dr. Thibaut does not appear to have sufficiently distinguished the role of the philosophic systematiser from that of the critical or historical scholar when he lays down the caution that "we must refrain from using unhesitatingly and without careful consideration of the merits of each individual case, the teachings direct or inferred, of any passage to the end of determining the drift of the teaching of other passages". A commentator is certainly open to severe censure when he asserts that a text bears a certain *meaning* which it cannot bear in a particular context. But when he simply means that the truth embodied in a particular text is inadequately expressed and should be developed or rendered more explicit in the light of other texts, or when he interprets a mythologic metaphor differently in different passages under the conviction that it is a natural symbol of many correspondent truths of different potencies or grades, he is to be deemed as perfectly within his rights as a philosophic interpreter and systematiser. A philosophic commentator, especially on unsystematised texts embodying speculative truths, has a far wider latitude than a literary commentator. Exegetical interpretation here inevitably shades off into philosophic construction; and this need not involve any intellectual dishonesty. We may readily admit that "what he (the commentator) from his advanced standpoint looks upon as an inferior kind of cognition" was not "viewed in the same way by the authors of the Upaniṣads", but that may have been because the teacher of the inferior wisdom had not in view the antithesis between it and the superior wisdom. Śāṇḍilya, the teacher of the Śāṇḍilya-vidyā in the Chāndogya-Upaniṣad, may not have "looked upon it as anything else but a statement of the highest truth accessible to man". but that is no reason why Śaṅkara may not look upon it as the inferior wisdom. It would appear, too, as though the distinction between the higher and the lower wisdom was taken by Dr. Thibaut and some others to be wider than what Śaṅkara himself intended; to Śaṅkara, the Saguṇa (determinate)-Brahman and the Nirguṇa (indeterminate)-Brahman were not so much distinct gods as the contrasted aspects of the same reality.

A misconception of the latitude allowed to philosophic systematisation may be traced in Dr. Thibaut's remarks on Śaṅkara's doctrine of Māyā. He tries to demonstrate that Śaṅkara's doctrine of Māyā is nowhere to be found in the Upaniṣads except probably in an undeveloped form in a few doubtful passages, and contends that the doctrine should not, therefore, be read into other passages which are intelligible without it. Let it be granted for the present that the demonstration is satisfactory. Later on he admits that the doctrine of "the final absolute identification of the individual self with the universal self is indicated in terms of unmistakable plain-ness" (p. cxxii) in the Upaniṣads. Now if the point were discussed as one of philosophy rather than of historical scholarship, it would not be difficult to perceive that the doctrine of Māyā is a necessary corollary of this doctrine of the individual being Brahman in Mokṣa (absolute liberation): for it is only in this identification that he realises that individuality was an illusion and that the distinction of subject, object, etc., possible only through this individuality, was an illusion too.

In a reproduction of Vedāntism such as we have proposed, no attempt need be made to distinguish the points common to the Indian systems from those which are specifically Vedāntic. Special care, however, should be taken to develop from first principles such Vedāntic positions as being distinctively Indian present a marked contrast to European habits of thought. There are sundry deep-seated differences between Eastern and Western speculation. To European common-sense, certain forms of Indian speculation may appear absurd or puerile at the best; while now and then there are presented heights and depths of thought which take away and stifle one's breath, and which an all too comfortable rationalism designates hyper-subtle and mystical. An attempt should be made to show that in some cases at least the contradiction to European common-sense or scientific thought is only apparent, and that the Indian position, properly understood, whether true or false, is a development of thought in an unsuspected direction, though by no means incompatible with Western thought: while in certain other cases where there is real contradiction to European common sense, an analysis of this apparently absolute standard may, peradventure, yield dissolving views in which the Eastern thought is found to alternate with its Western counterpart with the naiveté of a summer dream. As to what is vaguely called the mysticism of Vedānta a clearing-up should be attempted in a more than ordinarily strenuous spirit of rationalism. Only it should content itself with a problematic indication of the direction in which the dark truths lie without pretending to furnish omniscient *explanations*.

The attitude to be borne towards the present subject should be neither that of the apologist nor that of the academic compiler but that of the interpreter which involves, to a certain extent, that of the constructor, too. It is too late in the day to *defend* a system like the Vedānta with a theologian's animus; it is hardly necessary, except probably to silence a class of persons whose ignorance of the system is matched only by their zeal in combating it. And it is, to say the least, unwise, even for one who has implicit faith in the system, for, to drag it into the theological arena is to effectually scare away all open-minded men from it and relegate it for good to the limbo of oblivion. The Vedāntic propagandist cannot do better than appeal through a literature wholly expository, without a word of dogmatic lecturing in it, which will invite readers—it may be, a select class of them—to contemplate with something of an aesthetic sympathy an ancient life-ideal animating an organised body of ancient thought, just to quicken, it may be for a moment, the consciousness, always very torpid, that the dominating ideal of the day is only one among many possibles; and then if Vedānta has any real vitality in it, it will set them thinking till it leads to a real division of the spirit. A true philosophic system is not to be looked upon as a soulless jointing of hypotheses; it is a living fabric which, with all its endeavour to be objective, must have a well-marked individuality. Hence it is not to be regarded as the special property of academic philosophy-mongers, to be hacked up by them into technical *views*, but is to be regarded as a form of life and is to be treated as a theme of literature of infinite interest to humanity.

ANALYSIS

CH. I. AN APPROACH THROUGH PSYCHOLOGY (SEC. 1-31)

Importance of the psychology of waking, dream and dreamless sleep (1). Empirical account of a dream; no sensation; consciousness of the body at a minimum (2-3). Does it demand a new dimension of psychical existence? Impression and idea qualitatively distinct. Dreams as pure ideas turned into percepts (4-5). Which is more real, dream or waking? Not sensation but idea gives truth, though idea in presence of sensation is felt to be less real. Dreams, though illusory, have wider possibilities than waking (6-9).

Possibilities of self-conscious dream and dreamless sleep (10-11). Timeless synthetic concepts behind concrete knowledge on the same level as dreamless sleep, where the self is immediately self-conscious (12-14). Vedāntic discussion of this state (15-16). Parallelism between different views about this state and those about self-consciousness in European philosophy. Kant, Hegel and Vedānta on self-consciousness (17-19). Difference between Kant's self and Vedāntic ātman (20). Spencer and Kant on indeterminate consciousness of the Unknowable (21-22). Vedāntic view of knowledge (23).

Samādhi (two forms), the concrete form of this indeterminate consciousness; actualised states of waking, dream and dreamless sleep (24-25). Difference between dreamless sleep and samādhi (26-27). Samādhi and discursive reason compared (28). Relation between savikalpa and nirvikalpa samādhi (29).

Waking, dream, dreamless sleep and ecstasy constitute the gradation of existence; gradation between subject and object, truth and untruth (30). Projections of dream, etc., on waking plane; parallelism with empircal and apriori psychology (31).

CH. II. VEDĀNTIC METAPHYSICS (SEC. 32-83)

The theory of adhyātma, adhibhūta, etc., dimly traceable in the Upaniṣads, brought out (32-38). Devatā the absolute unity of subject and object (33). Loka, the absolute intuition-medium for this unity (34). Necessity of loka defended against possible objections. Relation of the theory to Absolute Idealism (35-38).

Are the devatās *universalia ante rem?* Is Vedānta realistic (39)? Yes; the sun the unity of the particular eyes and the visible things (40). But is not this aspect-realism rather than class-realism? Yes, but these sense-aspects are substantial realities or primal matters. Reconciliation of empiricism and rationalism (41). Grades of matter; formless matter one pole and full-blown reality the other. The full-blown reality minus the formless matter is māyā, the matrix of eternal 'names and forms' or *principia individuationis* (42). Realistic class is also admitted. Vedānta versus Nyāya on Jāti. Jāti not co-ordinate with vyakti (43-44). Three (five) systems of eternal entities in Vedānta (45).

Vedānta versus Hegel on the identity of contradictories. Vedāntic discussions bearing on the law of contradiction (46-47). Does Vedāntic Realism furnish a principle of change (48)? Śaṅkara's discussion of causality (49-51). Pañcadaśī on Śakti or power (52-53).

Brahman and māyā, by mutual reflection, become Īśvara with parā-prakṛti, śakti, aparā-prakṛti, (54). These the archetypal concretes of sattva, rajas, tamas (55). Parā-prakṛti is the active buddhi of the Lord (56). Discussion of buddhi, ahaṁkāra, manas, citta (57). Buddhi both the object and the (determinate but undifferentiated) body of Īśvara. Parallelism of sattva and tamas with Aristotle's actuality and potentiality. Difference between Vedānta and Aristotle (58).

Two forms of Īśvara: triguṇātīta and śūddha-sattva-upādhi. Their relation to Brahman (59-60). Distinction between the higher god and the lower god misleading (61-62). Why Brahman becomes determinate, an illegitimate question (63-64). Difficulties in the conception of Īśvara as creator (65). A preliminary discussion of the relation between moral discipline and absolute consciousness (66) necessary to understand Īśvara (in His two aspects) as the Absolute of both, the unity of the individual spirits (67). A further discussion of the progressive realisation of individual spirits necessary (68-69) to understand Īśvara as the Good, the Just, as exercising śakti or power. as in grace maturing the Karma of individual spirits (70). Sthāvaratva, the extreme punishment (70). Fate of sthāvara bound up with jīvan-mukta souls (72), through whom as deputies, Īśvara creates. Creation and dissolution. Trinity of Brahmā, Viṣṇu, Maheśvara (73-74).

Onward course of creation (75). Discussion of the five Koṣas and the three bodies of the individual, to introduce the universal emanations Hiraṇya-garbha, etc. (76-77). Vedānta on the five primal matters; their relation to the elements of chemistry; 'quintupling' of these matters (78-81).

Interpretation of two cosmogonic myths to illustrate the above (82-83).

CH. III. VEDĀNTIC LOGIC (SEC. 84-126).

Vedāntic truths said to be revealed; do they admit of proof? Necessity of revelation (84). Position of manana in Vedānta (85). Six pramāṇas (86). Two kinds of knowledge (87).

Pratyakṣa:—Perception is Brahman; knowledge timeless, its empirical mode in time (88). Conditions of perception explained (89-95). Perceptual judgment (96). Perception of object as object (97). Perception of the self (98). Discussion of illusory perception (99-101).

Anumāna:—Nyāya account of svārtha inference (102-103). Four Vedāntic objections connected with European Logic (104-106). Major premise reached through positive instances (107). Number of the instances inessential (108). Nyāya versus Vedānta on parārtha inference; deduction of Vedānta's position from its position on svārtha inference (109). The absolute syllogism after Hegel (110).

Upamāna (111).

Āgama:—How vākya is a pramāṇa explained by the identity of thought and language (words, sentences, mantras) (112-115). Objection of Nyāya to this identity (116). Vedānta on eternity of the Word (117). Śakti (meaning) of the Word like the śakti (power) of Īśvara (118). Two kinds of meaning (119-120). Conditions of valid vākya (121). A sentence by itself induces belief (122).

Arthāpatti connected with hypothesis in Inductive Logic (123).

Anupalabdhi:—**Abhāva** a percept but not the result of a perceptive process directed towards it (124). What is implicit perception from the point of view of the self? **Anupalabdhi** a positive function of the mind (125). Discussion of the illusion of **abhāva** (126).

CHAPTER I

AN APPROACH THROUGH PSYCHOLOGY

1. The psychology of waking, dream, and dreamless sleep constitutes the pivot of the Vedāntic system and of certain other systems like the Yoga, which may be regarded as ancillary to it. It is to be regarded as a clear addition to ordinary psychology, the importance of which is not a whit exaggerated if it is claimed that it recognises a new dimension of existence altogether. Its importance will be appreciated by connecting it with kindred Western speculations on the one hand, and with Vedāntic speculations in Metaphysics on the other.

2. What would be the empirical account of a dream? Physiological speculation on the point has hardly anything to offer except certain platitudes which do not touch the speciality of the phenomenon; and so the psychological exlpanation alone is worth referring to here. When a man goes to sleep, images are roused in his mind, sometimes by sensory presentations, but most often with apparent spontaneity, although even in such cases the absence of an ideal suggestion, *continuous with a sensory presentation*, cannot be absolutely proved. In waking perceptions, illusions, and hallucinations, the ideational elements are generally copies of previous percepts (sometimes involving new construction also); but these do not appear at random, being attracted into definite grooves of suggestion by the presentative elements and by attention as determined by practical interests. In dreams, too, we have copies of waking percepts, but imaginative construction is here far freer, there being normally no restrictive and directive action of sensation on the one hand, and of connective attention on the other. Many events and combinations of events which would be at once deemed to be impossible waking life would not be questioned at all in a dream. In waking life, many associations or constructions are ruled out, prevented from even appearing in consciousness, by certain beliefs determined by our practical necessities. Even sensations and percepts are occasionally so ruled out. At the same time, in waking life, there are different degrees of seriousness or concentration of attention on what directly subserves life; there are stages of listlessness, play, aesthetic and philo-

sophic consciousness. So long, however, as the consciousness of a body is there we cannot 'become a living soul'; the body always demands a measure of attention, while outer stimuli are continually stirring it up and starting ever-renewed trains of associations. In dreams, the distractions of this 'heavy' body are reduced to a minimum, sometimes disappearing altogether; the necessity of practical life is not so tyrannic, and hence there is unrestrained credulity. But why should there be a belief at all? Objectification carries a naive belief with it, unless it is definitely contradicted by some other belief. The idea of the object is not known to be a *mere* idea, unless contradicted by some perception or by a more vivid or coherent idea.

3. We may conceive a stage of dream proper—there being transitional stages between waking and dreaming—where there are no sensations and the consciousness of the body is at a minimum. Here the object-consciousness must be purer than in the waking stage, i.e., freer from reference to body; the self, too, is not mere idea of body but is the seer of ideas cf. Dṛṣṭer draṣṭā or seer of seeing). So in a dream, things appear to come in and go out without startling or surprising us: they are recognised as matters of course. Space and time tend to lose their reference to the body, and so violations of continuity occasion no surprise at all. There is no tyrannic continuous memory, no rigid demand for uniformity, no compunction for not being in a line with truth—a glorious life of thoughtless thoughtfulness.

4. Does this account of a dream justify us in taking it to belong to a *new dimension* of psychical existence? The continuous gradations from waking consciousness to dream proper need not preclude us from admitting such a new dimension. Dreams may be described as perceptions without sensation. Is there any difference in kind between perception with sensation and perception without sensation? The question would roughly resolve itself into the old question about the existence of a qualitative difference between impression and idea. The differentiae of impression and idea that are ordinarily proposed are not really satisfactory. As to the criterion of vividness, it is altogether adventitious to knowledge as knowledge; besides, ideas appear less vivid than sensations only when they coexist, and that, too, not in all cases. The criterion of being affected by movement is unsatisfactory, for in dreams where we have admittedly nothing but ideas, objects

are affected by our dream-movements; here, too, the test is useful only when impression and idea coexist. As to the other criterion, inner coherence, it may be pointed out that the incoherence of a dream is not felt as such within the dream; besides, sensations as sensations have no coherence, and we may have incoherent perceptions riding roughshod over all our expectations. There is nothing left but the felt abruptness or *given*-ness (independence of self would be going too far, as self-consciousness may not have been developed) of the impression, as distinct from the freedom, the play-like easy, unquestioning movement of attention in ideas and dreams. In framing to ourselves a difficult combination of ideas, in introspection, in the effort to recollect, a resistance no doubt is offered by percepts or habits of thought generated by sense-experience; but as the self prevails against it, the ideal functioning is felt to be free, the easiest to the self.

5. This shows that sensation and idea are not co-ordinate in reality[1], and to overlook this is a fundamental vice of Empirical Psychology. The idea may unconsciously animate the sensation (perception is a 'presentative-representative' cognition); but this unconscious working is absolutely different from its conscious existence. The conscious idea, while recognising itself to have been operative in the percept, absolutely disown its unconscious sensuous character; e.g., when an illusion is corrected by careful observation, the idea simulating a percept is known to be a *mere* idea, but the illusory percept vanishes altogether without caring to court a comparison with the true percept. Thus we have three distinct mental states throwing light on one another; (1) perception in which idea unconsciously works, (2) such perception coexisting with a conscious idea, where the idea is regarded as inferior in reality to the percept, and (3) the pure idea, hardly ever realised in waking consciousness (except probably in the fluid transparency of the poet's intuition, in spontaneous clairvoyance, or in the settled vision of the Yogin), to which the waking world would appear unsubstantial. The last state is one to which all have not access, and would be disbelieved altogether, were it not for the fact that we have a daily illustration of its *possibility* in our dreams. In dreams, the ideas do not consciously remember the corresponding waking percepts; they are at once percepts.

1 Because the one is free while the other is constrained or given.

6. Not that dream is truer than waking percept. Each is true within itself; but while 'the former is daily sublated, the latter is sublated only under exceptional circumstances' (Śaṅkara). The truth of this or that waking percept may sometimes be denied in a dream as it may be denied in waking life itself; but dreams do not deny the truth of waking life as a whole, for they never doubt their own waking character. Waking, however, always denies the truth of dreams.

7. We have already, however, found reason to believe that the dream-world is wider in *possibility* than the waking world. The dependence of waking perception on sensation shows its limitation. Sensation, far from being the final standard of truth, is by itself the farthest from the truth [2]; belief is easiest in self-consciousness. Internal perception is prior to external, logically if not chronologically. The sensation is felt to give us reality, only because the idea unconsciously animates it. The element of representation in perception is the element of interpretation or knowledge. But then it must be borne in mind that this unconscious working of the idea is known only when we have come to be reflective or self-conscious. Even then the sense-conditioned consciousness informed with the idea is felt to be higher in point of truth than the mere idea set over against it. But that is because practical attention or the self is not yet dissociated from the body; anything not directly ministering to the life of the body is taken to be unreal. With the development of the mind, the self and its interests come to be more and more dissociated from the body—we come to infer and deliberate and have abstract interests; still, except in very rare cases, the imperious call of the body is not silenced, and the body-dissociated mental processes are still felt to be rational only when ministering to the bodily life, though it may be indirectly. A solemn, but often ineffective, protest is recorded by our moral, aesthetic, religious, and speculative aspirations, though they, too, sometimes appear to accept bribes of the emissaries of this body.

8. Will is essentially a denial of the existing sense-order; knowledge, too, by its very nature, is an emergence from the body, i.e., from sense-homogeneity. Yet both are ordinarily *for* the life of the body. But the moral will, on the one hand, and

2 This seems to be written under Hegel's influence. It is to be noted that the author completely outgrew this influence in his later years.

aesthetic intuition on the other (not to speak of other forms of absolute consciousness [3]) disown this slavery and affirm the independence of the idea. The body, however, does its best to ignore their protest. They are felt to be only aspirations for pure knowledge, not knowledge; they tell us only that the body *ought not* to be the truth, though it unhappily seems to be the truth. The ineffectiveness of their protest is explained from our present point of view by the contrast felt between the sense-percept and the idea when they coexist, it being erroneously supposed that our ideas always coexist with some sense-percept, with the presentation of the body at least, if no other presentation is forthcoming. That with mere idea, we may have what may be called a 'feeling of knowledge', the consciousness of knowing as distinct from thinking or imagining, is brought out, however, in dreams. This explains the importance that is attached in Indian Philosophy to this unique psychological phenomenon. There is no other phenomenon in our ordinary psychic life like it; even in hallucination, as has been recently pointed out, there is some real sense-objective and some real peripheral excitation from within.

9. Dreams are, however, illusory. An idea is felt to be true so long as it is not contradicted by sense-perception. For though sensations do not produce knowledge, they signalise the occasions, cosmically determined, when breaches are effected in the leaden walls of insensibility, when the idea, in fact, unconsciously follows the law of truth [4]. The ideal of knowledge is, however, attained when the idea freely or consciously follows law, without being drawn down to interpret a sensation. Dreams, no doubt, are illusory; but then if only we possessed ourselves in dreams, if only we could exercise the control of attention over the riotous dance of the images which there comport themselves as percepts without sensations, if only, having cut away from the moorings of this oppressively constant presentation of this body, we could find secure anchorage in a freer, purer, more comprehensive self, we could assure ourselves of a far more complete vision of the truth than we could conceive ourselves to attain in this waking life. We could then transcend this space and time which

3 i.e., consciousness unreferred to the body.

4 Cp. Hegel.

have the body and the present moment as their points of reference, this space and time which coop us up and cabin us in; we could, then, not only intuitively perceive the distant, the past, and the future, take in at a glance what we have now to explore piecemeal—dimly, slowly, laboriously—, we could aspire to know noumenon, life, self.

10. All this may be entertained as a hypothesis, if not as a demonstrated fact. That, however, it may not be deemed inadmissible even as hypothesis, its 'objective possibility' has to be exhibited by tracing its *vera causa*. There are three suppositions: (1) perception without sensation; (2) the self-conscious knowledge of all space as one object, and of all time as one unfolded panorama; (3) the swooning into the realisation of noumenon, life, self. The *verae causae* respectively are (1) conscious dream, (2) self-conscious dream, and (3) dreamless sleep. That the conscious dream explains the possibility of perception without sensation has already been explained. The other two require elucidation.

11. Most of our dreams are self-conscious. Here the self's relation with the object is peculiarly different from its relation in waking life. In waking life, as has already been indicated, the object reports itself by a sensational shock; here, however, the object comes in and goes out unquestioned without startling us. Besides, here the self is, or seems at least to be, free from the body; sometimes it even sees the body lying asleep; it is not located anywhere and yet it books at space. Violations of continuity do not surprise it at all (section 3), though the objects are still in space. This could be understood in the merely conscious dream, where each isolated image, as it floats up, turns into a percept; but how can there be *self-conscious knowledge* of such *spatial* objects violating the laws of space-conntinuity, unless we suppose that the self sees here *with the whole of space as one* function? Similarly with time. Besides, here seeing is apparently creating (for here is no *given* abrupt sensation); the self seems to freely create its world, its space and time, its joys and sorrows. No doubt it only *seems*; really these creations are the images of waking percepts now freely accepted and so apparently created.

12. But why should there be this or that specific combination of images rather than any other? That implies the functioning of certain synthetic[5] concepts from behind. i.e. concepts on

5 i.e., synthesising.

the same level as the self[6]. We have here to admit, therefore, a new level or 'plane' of consciousness. These synthetic concepts might have been generated by individual experience or inherited as the capitalised value of ancestral experience—anyway they are now timeless[7] psychic forces ordering the distribution of the images.

13. A similar question may be asked with regard to sense-experience also. The sensations have been described as the cosmically determined occasions on which knowledge is permitted to manifest itself from within. But why should the right interpreting idea materialise itself on the occasion of a sensation? There must be some correspondence between the life within that supplies the right idea and the life without that supplies the sensation. It reminds one of the objection sometimes taken to Kant's doctrine of the forms that it does not explain why the manifold of intuition does not get into wrong forms. Dualism of subject and object has to be admitted, at least so long as we conceive ourselves to be individuals; only this correspondence between them is mysterious. It will not do to say that the object not only gives the sensation but also begets the association-traces which bring the right idea to the interpretation of the sensation. For so long as we admit that to know anything is to assimilate it, the *primum cognitum* cannot be explained by the causality of the object. We must admit an idea behind all presentation: a *regressus in infinitum* has to be accepted. So why a person should have certain sense-experiences rather than any other can only be understood in the light of the principle that every man freely accepts, if not makes, his circumstances. Every man is born with the seed of all his future psycho-physical existence, with instincts for action and original dispositions for certain forms of cognition. How these themselves have been generated is an enquiry which will lead us away from our present topic. It will suffice here to indicate that the knowledge-seeds and the action-seeds are not absolutely distinct, and that it is a community of these *Karma*-seeds, as they might be called, of different persons, that gets manifested into this common phenomenal world.

14. Can we rise in knowledge above these functioning concepts or *Karma*-seeds? In self-conscious dream, there is time,

6 Because they are timeless.
7 i.e., not having any specific time-location.

though it is apparently created at every moment. But the hidden springs of these creations cannot themselves be in time. They are in timeless unity with the self. How, then, can knowledge transcend them? This. however, is shown to be possible by dreamless sleep or suṣupti as it is called. In this stage, the self, dissociated not only from the body but also from the mind[8], rests in itself. It is then *immediately* conscious of itself, not conscious of itself as returning to itself, in reflection. It is then identical with what Kant calls 'transcendental unity of apperception'; only it is then not the mere 'fringe' of determinate empirical consciousness but is in complete isolation. It is not a mere thought, an unreal abstraction, but a concrete reality.

15. Here we meet with an objection from ordinary psychology. Admitting the existence of the self as an entity behind the mental states, one may hold that in dreamless sleep, the self is unconscious, not self-conscious. Let us dwell on the stock Vedāntic argument on the point. When a man rises from dreamless sleep, he becomes aware that he had a blissful sleep during which he was conscious of nothing. This he knows directly from memory. Now memory is only of a presentation. Therefore the bliss and the consciousness of nothing must have been *presented* during the sleep. If it be objected that only the *absence* during sleep of disquiet and knowledge is *inferred* from a memory of the state before the sleep and the perception of the state after the sleep, it is asked in reply: can we *infer* anything. the like of which was never presented? If reasoning is only a manipulation of rarefied images, the images can have been derived only from percepts. But it may be urged that the negative concept, at any rate, could not have had any percept corresponding to it, and therefore one may justifiably hold the *absence* of knowledge and disquiet during sleep to have been inferred. To this it is replied that absence cannot be inferred, unless it be conceivable. The absence of knowledge cannot be referred to, unless the absence be the object of a direct consciousness of it *during the absence.* Like knowledge, the absence of knowledge cannot be known by external perception or any form of inference founded on it, but by internal perception or self-feeling. No *inference* can ever warrant us in attributing absence

8 'mind'= empirical consciousness.

of consciousness to any object. If the paradox were allowed, a psychic thing or absence of a psychic thing, if conceived, is actual: its *esse* is its *concipi*—a peculiarity of hypothesis in Psychology which deserves to be noticed. Not that the absence of determinate knowledge need be known explicitly during the absence; one who is born blind is not conscious of not seeing. But if such a man comes to see, like Cheselden's patient, he will have an explicit perception of the previous absence of seeing which will at the same time be a *re*cognition of the absence as that implicitly cognised during the absence.

16. If, then, the direct consciousness during the absence be granted, then the consciousness of the absence immediately after the absence, i. e., immediately on waking, would be called memory rather than inference. Now what is the direct consciousness of the absence of knowledge and disquiet during deep sleep? It can only be the 'undifferenced knowledge and bliss' set over against negation. The mind or empirical consciousness lapses here altogether; we have pure consciousness against a 'dark ground', pure consciousness of a blank objectivity[9] or 'object in general' (Kant). All sensation and all concrete image then lapse into a blank homogeneity. Through a right understanding of this suṣupti state, we reach the conceptions of caitanya or the pure self, and of avidyā or the primal blank which is rendered definite by the self; so that to say that the pure self is immediately conscious of itself in deep sleep is only to state a verbal proposition.

17. The nature of the self, as pure consciousness, is often disputed, and the dispute turns on the way in which this suṣupti is understood. It has been variously held against the foregoing view that in this state, the self is (1) non-existent, or (2) unconscious, or (3) both conscious and unconscious. All these views find their parallel in the views which have been held about self-consciousness. To know is to *re*cognise: when the self first comes to know itself, it recognises itself. But recognition means a previous moment of self-forgetfulness. Now when the self forgot itself, was it non-existent or only non-intelligent? (1) If the *esse* of the self is its *percipi*, the unknown self would be the non-

9 i.e., of *some* object though not of any object in particular.

existent self. (2) But if the present self-consciousness be taken as a proof of the eternal existence of the self, then the self should be taken as sometimes unconscious, sometimes conscious—unconscious when dissociated from the empirical mind, conscious when associated with it. (3) Or if self-consciousness means consciousness of the self as having been *operative*, not merely existent, in the consciousness preceding it (and giving the whole truth to it), then when the self forgot itself, it was both conscious and unconscious. Finally, if the self, as it comes back to itself, feels that its self-alienated stage was utterly illusory, then it is not only eternally existent and consciously operative, but eternally *self*-conscious, too.

18. The empiricist, of whom the dogmatic nihilist and the absolute sceptic are the logical descendants, holds the self before self-consciousness to be immediate negation. The abstract conceptualist holds it to be immediate position, and that essentially, even during self-consciousness, as to him 'being cognised' is adventitious to the being of an object. The Kantian takes the self before self-consciousness to have been immanently operative in consciousness; yet when the self comes back to itself in empirical self-consciousness, in recognising itself it still feels that it does not know its essential nature, for the same thing cannot be at once subject and object. The self, as it comes back, just gives a flash of recognition, but anon it shoots forward, by its inertia, as it were, in a spiral rather than in a circular orbit. The self constantly aspires to catch itself and as constantly slips from itself. As long as self-consciousness is a process—and no determinate knowledge that is not a process is conceivable—it is thus a spiral motion, apparently beginningless and endless. The rapidly intermittent flashes of recognition appear to give a continuous line of light or a knowledge of the self, which is, however, only a 'paralogism of the pure reason'. The Hegelian takes the motion to be an eternal *circular* or perfect motion, consciousness before self-consciousness being only an arc of the circle setting up for itself, each minute arc itself a straight line; but when the circle is completed (i.e., when self-consciousness arises), the self recognises that these straight lines are only *for* the circle, that the circle is the truth that contains in itself the ideality of the straight lines. Here the Vedāntist will, however, hold that the self at each point only illusorily *fancies* itself to be moving in a straight line; and

as long as it moves, it can never take in the entire circle at once; and so even when it recognises itself, the illusion does not completely disappear. The blind impulse forward is real by reason of its very imperiousness; the flashes of self-recognition appearing now occasionally, now frequently, and at last continuously, the self feels at once in triumph and in humility that it is moving in a spiral inwards towards the centre of light (the true self), though the centre is still infinitely remote, content only to have more and more light; and ever as it presses forward with accelerated speed, it takes the past dimness as due only to his limitation of ignorance, till behold, it has reached the centre of light itself where it quiescently spins a circular motion. Who could have imagined that the spiral had the centre within a finite distance? This quiescent circular motion was all along the ideal of the process of knowledge; this was the contentless aspiration towards the thing-in-itself, this the formless indefinable sense of the Beyond in all determinate knowledge. Nor was the circle of light, constituted by the flashes of self-recognition, ever becoming more and more refulgent. altogether a 'paralogism'; for though the spread-out character of the process was false, the light was the reflection of this central self-manifesting light. Thus Vedānta reconciles Kant and Hegel by admitting the impossibility of the self being caught in a process of self-consciousness; and yet holding the process to be a self-manifestation of the self.

19. Does not, however, Hegel too admit that the self's movement in a circle is illusorily self-alienated in consciousness and that it is self-contained in self-consciousness? Does not Vedānta admit that even at the centre, the self, though quiescent, is spinning a circular process? The difference, as will be more fully explained afterwards, is that whereas Vedānta takes even this central motion to be the reflection of the self on the negation which falls beyond it, i.e., to be absolutely free self-creation, Hegel takes this reflection on the negation to be the ultimate reality. Not that even Hegel takes it to be *necessity* or God's *given nature*. No one is a more strenuous advocate of freedom; but then freedom has two sides, the quiescence of self beyond will and its quiescence in pure will. The former is Vedāntic Brahman, the latter is Vedāntic Īśvara, a point to be cleared up later on. The latter is also Hegel's Absolute Idea, to which will and intellect are the same.

20. This difference between Hegel and Vedānta is connected with a fundamental difference regarding the conception of self between Kant's synthetic unity of apperception and the Vedāntic ātman or caitanya. They are generally regarded as the same, and in fact there is a good deal of similarity between them. Kant's self, though transcending empirical consciousness, is individualised in a sense, for it is this which becomes practical as will, emerging as a postulate directly implied by morality. Even if we do not allow the conclusions of the practical reason to prejudice those of pure reason, even if we take the self to be the formless prefix of all cognition, transcending even the categories and forms through which it works in knowledge, we have yet to admit that in Kant, this self is *for* knowledge of the thing-in-itself, is relative to a constant something, has the thing-in-itself constantly before it; its very nature is aspiring to know the thing-in-itself, the 'object-in-general' being the obverse of this aspiration, the blank canvas on which it wants to have the thing-in-itself pictured (what, however, is never accomplished). So whether individualised or not, it is still *agent,* the form of *knowing* rather than of knowledge. In Vedānta, however, the self is the breath of this knowledge, the light of consciousness, something eternally accomplished rather than being accomplished. The accomplish*ing* self cannot be said to have finally triumphed over empiricism or absolute scepticism. This seems to be the trend of Spencer's views also. He would not admit the current argument against absolute scepticism, that it is proving the falsity of reason by reason; that, he would say, at best shows that within the sphere of determinate cognition, the self (or rather the dominating cohesion of the ideas of subject and object) is the highest truth; but then this cognition itself tells us that it is a cohesion generated by experience, and that, therefore, we cannot pronounce it to be absolutely necessary. Who knows that even this cohesion may not break down with further experience? That it cannot be conceived is no argument, for the moment something is said to be inconceivable, it is pronounced to be conceivable by implication. The subject of the proposition, 'this cannot be conceived' is in fact a *conceived* inconceivability. This is only a negative conceivability, however. It is only an 'indefinable sense of the Beyond', mere *matter* of knowledge without positive *form.* In the very humility of accepting absolute scepticism as a possible

view, there is the transcendence of it, in which, however, there is no differenced self to enjoy the triumph.

21. Hegel does not admit the possibility of an absolute scepticism impugning the reality of the self or reason, and therefore does not recognise an undifferenced consciousness. Kant's pronouncements are rather uncertain on the point; but then his 'Refutation of Idealism' may be taken as founded essentially on the recognition of a form of cognition other than the determinate. Much has been made, ever since Schopenhauer's unfortunate pronouncement on the point, of the so-called inconsequence in Kant of taking causality to be a category of the self and yet riding out on this category beyond the self to the thing-in-itself as the cause of our sensations. Kant, it should be remembered, expressly points out a fundamental difference in applicability between the dynamical and the mathematical categories. The difference comes out again in the different solutions he has given of the first two cosmological antinomies on the one hand and the last two on the other. The mathematical categories have no reference except to phenomena in space and time, but the dynamical categories while referring to phenomena refer essentially beyond them to the free and the self-existent, although this reference cannot be concreted by intuition. The thing-in-itself in Kant is not, however, to be confounded with his noumena or Ideas of the Reason, which are only the reason-pictures of the essentially unknowable. The self, as causality imbedded in all determinate cognition, asks for the cause of itself. Experience demands its own cause; the causal aspiration is like a flame informing the fuel of experience and yet freely existing by itself. This demand of the self is not satisfied by the idea of the reason, for that is only the way in which the cause of the self, i.e., of causality, i.e., of experience, would be known, if it could be known at all. This difficulty with regard to causality applies more or less to the whole of the understanding, i.e., the self as knowing objects; for even when the self recognises itself, it is puzzled to find itself *unconsciously* informing objects. It asks 'Why did I know object at all?', just as it might ask in another connexion, 'Why did I sin at all?'. It feels the ground insecure beneath its feet. So Spencer finds that the cohesion within our knowledge of subject and object demands itself an object beyond knowledge, the Unknowable, from both the points, object-cons-

ciousness and subject-consciousness. Now this demand, alike in Kant and in Spencer, is indeterminate but none the less real.

22. Neither Kant nor Spencer has brought out in full the implications of this indeterminate consciousness. They have not made it clear whether it is a subjective process only or the absolute reality. As indeterminate, can it be said to be different from the thing-in-itself or the Unknowable? It seems to have equal relations with the self and the Unknowable. The self itself becomes real in it. It is the undifferenced consciousness that plays on all determinate cognition. Beyond the will, there is the self-affirmation of the intellect; but beyond this self-affirming pulsation, there is the pure undifferenced self or Caitanya. The thing-in-itself cannot be said to be different from this undifferenced Caitanya, cannot be said to be its reference. Yet it is significant that neither Kant nor Spencer calls this undifferenced self-doubting consciousness the self or the subject. This vacillation on their part is explained by the fact that when this consciousness and the determinate consciousness (which is always accompanied by the former) coexist, the former, though felt to give all the reality that the latter has, still appears to be a formless shadow in comparison with the latter which is informed by it. It is in fact the old difficulty about the percept and idea reappearing on a higher plane. Schelling and Hegel disregarded the contrast and imagined they found, in the aesthetic and religious consciousness especially, the consciousness negating individuality to be much more real than determinate experience. Kant, however, would have argued against them that these coloured conciousnesses, the aesthetic and the religious, can never warrant us in taking the de-individualised consciousness as more than a mere aspiration, i.e., as knowledge, as the absolute self, as an eternally accomplished cognition. If Hegel argues that his Absolute Idea is not accomplish*ed* only—for then there would be no difference between him and Schelling--but that it is eternally accomplish*ing* itself also, that it eternally mediates itself through that absolute consciousness which denies individuality, it is replied that this, too, is only *thought*, only the shadowy fringe of determinate consciousness.

23. It may, accordingly, be asked : does not this argument of a Kantian against Schelling and Hegel press against Vedānta too? Knowledge, according to Vedānta, is not only different

from the knowing activity, it cannot even be described as the (contingent) result of the activity. Its essential character is its eternity, its self-manifestation (s v a y a m - p r a k ā ś a t v a). The mental mode, however, in which knowledge manifests itself is contingent, being the result of mental activity. So, too, in the case of such knowledge as leads to m o k ṣ a or 'liberation', there is first a hearing of the Scriptural texts, a reflecting on them, a refutation of doubts, and a final fixing of the mind on the texts—all this repeated times without number, till the transparency of the mind is secured, and then knowledge shines through and is recognised to have been eternally complete. So, too, the M o k ṣ a that is reached is taken to be B r a h m a n itself, 'unchangingly eternal' (K ū t a s t h a n i t y a); it is not only quiescence itself : as just passing into it, one feels all the past strife[10] after it to have been utterly illusory, and, what would sound paradoxical, the feeling of illusion itself lapses, there being nothing left but the self shining by itself. Of knowledge, not of B r a h m a n only, but of any object, the object is not the cause in any sense. The knowledge, as it shines forth, is felt to shine as it were in free grace. So neither the activity of the self nor the activity of the object can be said to be a *means* to it; as Ś a ṅ k a r a characteristically declares there is no *claim* to knowledge. All this is expressed in another way by saying that perception[11] as an (apparently) processless *accomplished* cognition is B r a h m a n or the self itself—of course in the murky atmosphere of sensation which, however, is only *our* limitation. Yet so long as we seek to know this self, this breath of knowledge, as a determinate object, it necessarily eludes our grasp. It is only to be characterised as n e t i n e t i, 'not that,' 'not that'.

24. Yet is not this suicidal, one might ask, to call this breath of knowledge the absolute self and yet to deny its positive conceivability? One feels as if the triumph gained over absolute scepticism was more imaginary than real, only a fond hope, not an accomplished reality. But here V e d ā n t a points out that as the objective possibility of 'perception without sensation' and of knowledge of noumenon was demonstrated by dream and dreamless sleep, so the objective possibility (which is here indistinguishable

10 i.e. striving.
11 See Sec. 88.

4

from actuality) of this undifferenced consciousness of the absolute lies in a concrete psychological state called the turīya or samādhi state where this consciousness is isolated and is not a mere fringe of determinate consciousness.

25. The discussion of suṣupti or dreamless sleep has thus brought us over to the consideration of this samādhi or ecstatic consciousness. Waking, dream, and dreamless sleep are intelligible facts easily performing the role of *veræ causæ*, but this samādhi seems to explain *obscurum per obscurius*. It accordingly requires an elucidation. In the suṣupti state, the mind is dissociated wholly from the self which is then in the immediately conscious attitude. It is conscious, but conscious of a blank only. It has then the direct cognition of the absence of specific cognition, the consciousness of a positive nothing, and hence it flashes back on itself. It is the light flashing in circumambient gloom, revealing nothing but the gloom. The suṣupti state. however, gives the possibility only but not the actuality of the knowledge of noumena; the self does not here swoon into the knowledge of noumena. Like the dream-state, it is a state in which the self has no control over itself. not a state to which the self rises by a continuous effort. So if we could control ourselves in this state, we could promise ourselves the attainment of a far more potent and comprehensive species of knowledge than we could attain even in the actualised dream-state. The progress of knowledge in the waking state might be conceived to be in a line stretching away from us to infinity. and the end is the knowledge of all finite phenomena in their relations to one another. The progress of knowledge in the *actualised* dream-state as distinct from the passive uncontrolled state, is *in* infinity, though the knowledge is still phenomenal; the end here is the knowledge of the infinite of phenomenon getting determined into finites. The progress of knowledge in the *actualised* suṣupti-state is from infinite to infinite and not phenomenal. The phenomenal infinite is turned by noumenal screws which are fixed like the axle of a revolving wheel. We may distinguish three stages here (1) the objective possibility of the self being isolated in suṣupti, (2) the actualised but determinate self-isolation in what has been called savikalpa-samādhi or determinate ecstasy, (3) the actualised indeterminate self-isolation in nirvikalpa-samādhi or indeterminate ecstasy. These stages are often not

distinguished, especially in earlier Vedāntic literature. They are all absolute stages where the sense of duality is non-existent.

26. Now what is the difference between suṣupti and savikalpa-samādhi? The difference, as ordinarily given, is that in the former the (empirical) mind with all its modes lapses altogether, whereas in the latter it does not lapse but only gets concentrated into one absolute irrelative mode which thus becomes actualised in the highest degree. The one represents the greatest *dispersion*[12] of attention, the other its utmost *concentration.* In both, the consciousness of duality lapses; in both, the self enjoys undifferenced bliss; in both, the timeless seeds of knowledge and action (vidyā-karma) persist, accounting for the recognition of the past on awaking from them. But whereas on awaking from suṣupti, the self remembers that it was in the attitude of knowing object though the object was there a blank, on rising from samādhi it ought to remember it *was* the object in that state and not in the object-knowing attitude at all. In the former, the self as always limited was simply isolated: in the latter, it burst its bonds, destroyed the barrier between subject and object, and became the absolute.

27. The ecstasy, far from being unconsciousness or bare consciousness, is supra-consciousness. If Hegel's 'speculative con sciousness' or 'notion' be the truth of discursive understanding, this intellectual or ecstatic intuition of Vedānta is the truth of the speculative consciousness. If Hegel's thought is concrete and creative, it is not so as thought but as reality or being, i.e., as ecstatic identity of thought and being.

28. The method of attaining this ecstasy is not the method of scientific investigation. A phenomenon has not only a relational aspect but also an intrinsic *aesthetic* aspect merging into a mystic aspect. The former aspect is caught by our discursive reason, the latter by imagination which is in fact intuitive reason. Here, too, as in the case of the moral intuition, it has been objected that the notions reached through this imagination are "heuristic rather than determinative" (Kant). But the consideration of the dream-state has already demonstrated the possibility of these notions being isolated and so turned into eternal percepts. This

12 Because there is no determinate object to which the attention may be directed.

imaginative isolation is effected by prolonged attention. Discursive thought about the relations of an object may no doubt help in this imaginative isolation, for it means a detaining of the aspects of the object in the mind, an oscillation of the mind round it, though it may not always be followed by a definite settling of the mind on it. Generally the mind buzzes round an object, and then moves on to another and then returns to it; and thus if making progress at all, it moves in wider and more complicated figures, but still never effectually settles on any object. While science or philosophy is thus ever and anon *moving* in its figures, with or without a consciousness of the whole, one quite loses sight of the other discipline, viz., that of contemplating an individual object, of getting glued down to it, of sinking into the heart of it, by suppressing within us the urgency of distracting desires and the subtle caprices of thought, and by tranquilising the surface of the mind while holding before it a symbol of the object we are seeking to know, instead of struggling to catch the object with a self-stultifying eagerness.

29. There are different grades of noumena (devatā) which the self may realise in ecstasy. From the ecstatic intuition of all other determinate objects, there is waking; but there is no waking from the ecstatic intuition of God, for the simple reason that so long as there is limitation or the slightest trace of individuality, there can be no intuition of this Infinite Determination, no becoming infinite. This is the highest stage of savikalpa-samādhi. The mind-capsule of the self, persisting in all such samādhi, and ever expanding, reaches here its utmost tension and utmost tenuity. This perfectly transparent envelope still constitutes the determinateness of God as Īśvara. He is the actualised 'Ideal of Pure Reason' of Kant, the 'Absolute Idea' of Hegel, self-realised not in thought but in ecstasy. Although, said Kant, this is the most adequate reason-picture of the thing-in-itself, the thing-in-itself is the real, negating even this picture; of the thing-in-itself, as Spencer would have put it, there is only an indeterminate consciousness, an 'indefinable sense'. Vedānta's addition to this is the suggestion that both the reason-picture and the indeterminate consciousness are capable of being isolated and actualised in the concrete states, savikalpa-samādhi (intuition of determinate noumena), and nirvikalpa-samādhi (intuition of the reality transcending

all determinateness). The latter is undifferenced not only in the sense that the consciousness of duality is absent, as it is even in susupti, not only in the sense that the unconscious ring of the Unknown constituting the limitation of all noumena lower than God is removed, as it may be in savikalpa-samādhi, but also in the sense that even the consciousness of this removal is absent. This is the highest stage, this is the truth, this is Brahman.

30. Waking, dream, dreamless sleep, and ecstasy with the intermediate stages constitute, then, a *new dimension* of the mind. This is not only *a* dimension of the mind but *the* one dimension of existence in which even the deepest of all distinctions, viz., that between the subject and object, has place. The ordinarily conceived duality between them gives place in Vedānta to the conception of a gradation of existences, one pole of which is the lowest waking stage in which the self completely forgets itself, the stage of the mere object, and the other pole, the ecstatic stage in which the self not only denies the existence of everything else but denies the denial itself, the stage of the pure subject. The gradation is not eternally spread out; the samādhi state is not only a stage among stages, it is the truth of the other stages. So, too, in the series, each stage is the truth of the preceding stage. The gradation between subject and object is also the gradation between truth and untruth, between good and evil. The self, as identified with any stage, feels the stage below it to be illusory; thus there is a reconciliation between the absolute distinction of truth and untruth on the one hand, and the continuous gradations of truth on the other. The final duality of Brahman and Avidyā (illusion) which at the same time is no duality of positives, is the exemplar of the relation between truth and untruth.

31. It remains to recognise the fact that each stage is not only present in its isolation but also unconsciously informs the lower stage. In fact on the waking plane we can trace the projections of all the other planes. Psychology recognises the stages, perception, imagination (reproductive and productive), thought (understanding) with the explicit consciousness of subject and object, and the indefinable consciousness of the beyond (Spencer). Now the last three, as we have pointed out, might be regarded as the projections of dream, dreamless sleep, and ecstasy on the

waking plane. Of these, the earlier stages adumbrate the later, and the later react on the earlier. This is the empirical counterpart of Kant's apriori psychology. In the perception of object, there is the given matter of the sensations, fitted, partly as reproduced ideas, into the forms of space and time (generated, it may be, out of ideas; this time again shooting forth the rays of productive imagination, the schemata, to touch the categories which are the eyes of the self or the synthetic unity of apperception: this self all the while feels the pressure of the thing-in-itself and so thinks the object under the form of infinity, i.e., in relation to the infinite world, to the subject, and the *ens realissimum,* still failing, however, to catch the thing-in-itself and having only a contentless aspiration towards it. Vedāntism finds the concretes of these apriori elements which all operate in waking perception, in the distinguishable internal characters of the several stages, waking, dreaming, etc. The general correspondence between the Vedāntic stages and the Kantian elements has been sufficiently made out; a more detailed correspondence can be exhibited only after a modified presentation of Kantianism. This, however, space will not permit.

CHAPTER II

Vedāntic Metaphysics

32. The position of the pure subject and the material object in the Vedāntic system has been indicated. The primary duality of self and negation, which is no duality of positives, has been found to transfigure every stage of existence. As a consequence of this unconscious transfiguration, each stage in the series, waking, dream, etc., in its unconscious form, becomes *co-ordinate* with the lower stage. This is particularly apparent in the waking stage where the distinctions among the several aspects of existence, adhyātma, adhibhūta, adhideva, adhiloka, etc., come out explicitly as co-ordinate with each other. These distinctions are intelligible only in the light of a metaphysical view which is dimly traceable in the Upaniṣads and which can hardly be said to have been completely brought out even by the commentators. The exposition of it, to be attempted presently, would therefore require to be justified by an elaborate discussion of all passages in the Upaniṣads which lend colour to it. For the present it is set forth only as a hypothesis.

33. In the waking stage, the sentient body is the adhyātma or subjective aspect, and the objects of sense-experience constitute the adhibūta or objective aspect. They are so distinct here that language is strained in calling them *aspects* of the same thing. But they are related to one another. The self as identified with the body takes the object to be 'useful', to be subservient to its pleasure and pain. The experience of the object rouses desire, desire again begets experience—a restless whirl of relation. In the aesthetic consciousness, however, such as is roused in rapt contemplation or upāsanā, one rises to a universal standpoint from which is witnessed the *identity* of the different sentient elements, of the body with the different aspects of the object. The restless relations, the attractions and repulsions between the body and the object, are then felt to be illusory differentiations of quiescent unities. The eye and the visible aspect of things, for example, constitute a unity. The Upanisads bristle with aesthetic intuitions of such unities, ranging from the most profound to the most superficial, viewed as devatās or objects for upāsanā.

This upāsanā consists in a *continuous* direction of the attention to an aesthetic symbol revealed by the śāstras, i.e., by some seer. The attitude in it is quite the reverse of the attitude of that cheap rationalism which makes a parade of its independence of authority; the existence of the devatā or the aspect of the object worshipped may not have been proved by reason or may not have at once appealed to one's leaden aesthetic sensibility, but through the will to believe or śraddhā, through prolonged contemplation, the devatā may be seen to be gradually shining out.

34. The adhideva aspect is to be understood in relation to the adhiloka aspect, which requires an elucidation. Every devatā demands a loka. Psychologically put, an absolute unity, to be real, must be not only thought but realised in some sort of intuition. In aesthetic (visual) intuition, for example, we realise a devatā, like the sun, the unity of seeing and the visible world. Now as here the realised object ceases to be an object and gets manifested as the absolute identity that it eternally was, though unrecognised because of the individual's limitations, so the intuition, too, is divested of its merely subjective aspect and appears as an eternal shining world (div) with which the limited subject is raised to identity. The distinction between the subject and object in ordinary knowledge appears in the absolute sphere as a distinction between loka and devatā. Only in ordinary knowledge, the subject takes the lead, whereas here the devatā which corresponds to the object, is the higher reality. What is from the lower standpoint *my* intuition of an object is from the higher standpoint, a devatā shining, revealing himself in a loka.

35. It may be urged, however, that the distinction between subject and object is altogether annulled in the absolute sphere and therefore a devatā must be conceived to shine by itself. The demand for a locus for such intelligible entities springs from a feebleness of the mind which will have sensuous symbols where it ought to entertain pure concepts of the reason; it springs in fact from that hypostasising tendency with which Plato has been charged with regard to his Ideas.

36. To this it is replied that an existence that is nowhere is unintelligible and that the demand for a locus even in the sensuous sphere springs from a necessity of the reason. The locus of an extended object involves the conception of the *attribute* of

extension (which is nothing but the whole of space) being in space. The sensuous conception of an object in space would thus be utterly unintelligible *unless a relation be conceived to be dual—a being and a process*—the being transcending the process and yet resting on the process.

37. This necessity of the reason applies not only to such a sensuous relation, it applies to the highest relation, the relation of subject and object. To Absolute Idealism, the Self is the absolute identity of subject and object. It is self-relation, the being and the relation being here identical; and so far it is self-existent, it might be deemed absurd to demand any *locus* or external relation. To this, Vedānta will reply that such an absolute or irrelative reality *is*, or is realisable only in, an ecstatic consciousness (which Hegel does not admit) and that to us who have not reached it, who only *think* of it, this has to be thought of as resting on the relation to an individual. To ecstatic consciousness, such relation is not; but mere thought has to postulate a dual absolute—the absolute for the absolute consciousness as resting on the absolute for the individual, the unknowable absolute on the knowable absolute. The self that excludes the object as absolute negation is at once the same as and higher than the self that has the negation within it as a moment. If the self be but relation,[13] as Hegel takes it, it must be taken to depend on the *nature* or the limitation of the terms of the relation; even in the self-relation of the self, the selves that are related to each other are bounded by negation[14] and hence their relation cannot be wholly free. If it be said that the relation is prior in reality, that it is the universal which freely particularises itself, it is replied that such a particularising is inexplicable in the last resort and therefore the universal that is in and through particulars is a *fact* to be accepted, not a free function of the reason. The last principle of philosophy *for us* must be a *necessity* of the reason founded on a *given fact*, though the aspiration of philosophy must ever be to reach a principle that is wholly rational. Brahman, the self-existent, must therefore be conceived by us to rest on His own glory (sve mahimni tiṣṭhati). So lower down, every devatā is to be conceived to be in a loka.

13 Of *identity* of subject and object. See above.

14 Because 'nature'=limitation=negation.

38. The necessity of the several aspects, adhyātma, etc., has been vindicated at what might appear to be a disproportionate length, were it not for the fact that these are just the conceptions which require to be raised above the mythologic region in which they are supposed to be. Given a loka or intuition-ground, we have against it a devatā or an absolute unity of subject and object. A concrete intuition-medium, a Platonic heaven is necessary to ensure to these devatās or Ideas reality. It will not do to say that they exist in thought or reason: that appears from the waking standpoint to be too thin to support reality.

39. The doctrine of adhyātma, etc., is thus capable of being affiliated on Absolute Idealism, as modified by Vedāntic transcendentalism. The devatās have the character of absolute identities but do they resemble the Platonic Ideas in being *universalia ante rem*? Is the Vedāntic view one of (conceptual) realism? The fact that Schopenhauer's view finds room for the eternal ideas, the grades of the objectification of the will, encourages us to look forward to something like them in Vedānta.

40. A devatā is differentiated transversely[15] into adhyātma and adhibhūta, but is it also longitudinally[16] differentiated into particular individuals? It would appear to be so, for a devatā like the sun is said to be the unity of the senses of sight supposed to be severally possessed by different persons and of the visible aspects of things. There is an instructive difference in this respect between Vedānta and Sāṅkhya; according to the latter, each sense, as sense, i.e , as aḍhyātma, is one, and different souls partake (by reflection) of this one sense; but according to the former, a sense as sense is many, being different in different individuals, but then these many are only the illusory differentiations of one devatā which corresponds to the particular sense. (The difference is explained by the Sāṅkhya view that the individual soul is real and that there is no such thing as *one* cosmic illusion but only individual illusions of separate eyes, separate minds, etc., there being one real prakṛti which eternally and really evolves into mahat, etc, including the archetypal senses. The Vedāntic view is that this prakṛti is but Māyā or cosmic illusion, and that therefore not only the indivi-

15 i.e. element-wise or aspect-wise.

16 i.e. as recurrent.

dual illusions but also the *archetypal* senses and the correlated primal matters are but its differentiations). In any case, the many particular senses of sight and the many visible aspects of things are said to find their unity in the Sun-deïty.

41. But still this would be *aspect*-realism rather than true class-realism. The aspects, visibility, audibility, etc., have their Ideas, concrete basal d e v a t ā s as they might be called; but are not these only superficial aspects of things? What of the natural kinds like man, gold, etc.? Have not they, too, their Ideas? V e d ā n t a, while admitting that not only the class but every individual has got its eternal 'name and form' (n ā m a - r ū p a) will demur at first to an implication of the objection. These sense-aspects in V e d ā n t a are the *primal matters*, the absolutes of the senses, hearing, touch, sight, taste, and smell. They constitute no superficial aspect but the central substance, and 'names and forms' are but the illusory differentiations of this substance. When, by means like u p ā s a n ā, we have risen to the absolute consciousness in the waking state, these external sensuous aspects are viewed as the basal d e v a t ā s (they themselves are the illusory differentiations of still higher, more substantial realities, as we shall see presently): they are viewed as the substance (relatively speaking) of the object of which the form (taken in its widest sense) is only the manifestation or illusory differentiation. Within the form, there are again relations of matter and form, for each stage of the form is matter in relation to a further differentiation of it. Now each of the stages is capable of being actualised into d e v a t ā s by ecstatic contemplation. Now when a rationalist takes the sensation to be lapsed thought or thought become unconscious, and when an empiricist holds that our thoughts are only the complex manufactures out of sense-material, by themselves, only illusory refinements and useful only in reference to sense-reality, their antagonism is transcended by the V e d ā n t i s t who reinstates both by pointing out that without an absolute intuition-continuum, the thought cannot be real and that the d e v a t ā is therefore the sense reality, divested of its limitation of unconsciousness.

42. These d e v a t ā s again have an order among them—an order really of emanation but capable also of being viewed as of evolution from the human standpoint—the absolutely formless indeterminate matter being one pole, and the full-blown waking reality the other pole. We may notice two orders of differences,

the one comprising the several grades of matter, the other comprising the forms as manifested in each grade. Yet the grades themselves are formed or determinate matter. The same (formless) matter *persists* through all the grades in all the forms; so, too, each formed matter persists in its differentiations in the grades below it, the grades corresponding to dreamless sleep, dream, etc., the successive materialisations of the same reality. This then is the difference between ordinary realism and Vedāntic realism; the Ideas are not only concrete universals but *substantial matters* of different grades from the pure subject to the grossest material object. The pure subject is the formless matter, the sole reality, the truth of the grades of materialisation, and of all the determinate objects therein. The full-blown reality minus this formless matter is absolute negation, the very principle of illusion. Yet what are the multitudinous 'names and forms' of this full-blown reality? These empty husks of reality are not reality: but they get filled in with the formless matter. Why does the reality enter these unreal forms? It shows that these forms are neither real nor unreal. Such a contradictory thing can only be the principle of illusion; it is darkness only that can be at once revealed and destroyed by light. This is the famous principle of Māyā, which is one yet manifold, the matrix of all 'names and forms.' These, too, must be eternal, coeternal with the pure subject. Yet this does not necessarily argue a despair of explanation. Of the forms which constitute individuality, no explanation is possible except that illusion is at its root. No universal can exhaust the infinite variety of the individual. If even we could trace a consecutive differentiation from the highest universal downwards, each step of the differentiation would be unintelligible. It is the very essence of differentiation to escape the universal. To recognise the necessity of this unknowability is to recognise the principle of māyā.

43. Not that universals among these shadowy names and forms, concatenating them, are unknown in Vedānta. The realistic jāti or universal is admitted both in Nyāya and Vedānta, though the latter emphatically disclaims the eternal jāti of the former. According to Nyāya, this jāti is an eternal reality inhering in the vyakti or individual things and is eternally connected with it. Vedānta denies both its eternal reality and its being co-ordinate with individual things. As has

been already indicated, to Vedānta nothing is an eternal reality except the pure self. As to the other point, if an individual and its jāti be taken to be distinct (and co-ordinate in reality), they cannot be unified in any way. The inherence, according to Vedānta, is a fiction. (This recalls the famous criticism of the Platonic doctrine of Ideas by Aristotle in his Nicomachæan Ethics). In 'A is B', if B the concept is distinct from A, their copular relation is a fiction; for it is asked, what connects A or B with the relation? If another relation, what connects that with its members? And so there is a regress to infinity. Once you set up two utterly distinct things, you cannot bridge over the gulf; only you may pronounce the effort to combine to be itself illusory. Without an admission of identity-in-difference, not only this inherence, but also any kind of connexion even space connexion, would be inconceivable. What view, then, does Vedānta itself hold? It understands the jāti not as the denotational real but as the connotational real, not as co-ordinate with and distinct from the vyakti or individual, but *identical* with it on the one hand and of a different grade of reality on the other. The identity between attribute and substance dharma-dharmin is characteristic of the hylozoistic speculations of Vedānta and Saṅkhya (regardnig māyā which is one yet many, or regarding prakṛti which really evolves), following logically on the denial of inherence as a distinctive principle. This dharma or attribute is again the essence. the persisting matter in relation to the dharmin or thing, infinite in every individual, having the whole of the phenomenality behind it.

44. Vedānta might very well admit the co-ordinateness of jāti and vyakti in the sphere of the pure 'names and forms', that realm of shadows. The relation between jāti and vyakti, which has already been discussed, is in the region of formed matter where the more differentiated is less in reality. The realm of shadows or māyā may be compared to space, the principle of separation or 'spread-out-ness', the nearest determinate symbol of the principle of difference, in which a mode may be said to be different from another in which it is included.

45. We have thus to recognise three systems of eternal entities in Vedānta: (1) in regard to matter, formless matter and its several emanatory grades corresponding to the stages, samādhi, suṣupti, etc., including the intermediaries; (2) in re-

gard to formed matter, the basal devatās, corresponding to the primal matters, and also the essences like 'cow-ness', 'horse-ness' (gotva, aśvatva) incarnated in the above grades; (3) in regard to the 'names and forms', the abstract differences, which are neither real nor unreal. We have still to recognise two other orders, (4) the Karma-unities or will-unities in the several grades, and (5) the universal unities of these with their cosmic reactions, the universal emanations of Brahman, including the lesser gods, the inquiry into which is for the present postponed.

46. Lest the identity-in-difference implied in Vedāntic realism be taken to be an unwarranted importation of Hegelianism, it is necessary to refer to discussions bearing on the law of contradiction in Vedāntic philosophy. It may be noted at the outset that in this Vedāntic conception of identity-in-difference, as distinct from a simliar conception in Hegel, the identity is the truth and the difference is illusory and even the negation of the difference through which the identity is affirmed is illusory. In connexion with the discussion of illusory perception, as of the nacre taken for silver, the point is raised: when the appearance of the silver is corrected and the nacre in its real nature known, can it not be held that the thing is *sometimes* silver and *sometimes* nacre? The reply given is that it is the very nature of the later or correcting perception to deny the truth of the former perception once for all. When the illusion of silver ceases, one is not conscious of the real silver being absent but only of the illusory silver having disappeared. But a further difficulty may be raised: when the silver is known to be illusory, is not the knowledge itself self-contradictory, as expressible in the form 'the (existent) silver is non-existent'? The reply is: the knowledge is rather expressible in the form, 'the illusory silver is absent'. The very perception of the illusory character of a thing is the perception of the illusory thing being absent: to light up the darkness is to destroy it. The question really is: if illusion is known through contradiction, is not contradiction itself conceivable? The Vedāntic reply appears to be that the contradicting perception completely destroys the phenomenal reality of the contradicted percept. The contradiction is therefore not real[17]. We have really two cognitions here, (a) *this* phenomenally real silver, (b)

17 Because one of the terms is non-est.

that illusory silver is absent. The cognition of this phenomenally real silver, *plus* the contradicting percept of the nacre amounts to the cognition of the illusory silver being absent. In identity of contradictories, the identity is known through recognition: the relation of identity is nothing but the identical thing. The union of contradictories is uncritically accepted at first, only to be rejected when it is known to be a union of contradictories. This view of illusory perception is only the reappearance in a lower plane of the dualism of Brahman and māyā which yet is no dualism of positives.

47. In this connexion, we may refer to a discussion of Śaṅkara in his commentary on Bṛhadāraṇyaka Upaniṣad V—i, where he combats Bhartṛ-prapañca's views of Brahman being at once one and dual (dvaita-advaita, the causal Brahman different from the effect Brahman, though identical at the retraction of the world). Śaṅkara argues that although rules of action may admit of exceptions or alternatives, a truth does not; truth does not depend on any one's choice. Two contradictory attributes, dvaita and advaita, dual and single, cannot both be true of the same thing. The Vedāntic doctrine of adhikāri-bheda (accommodation), that the truth to be taught must be relative to the students' capacities or qualifications, is not only a practical principle of pedagogy, secular and religious,—it is founded on an epistemological truth. The duality of Brahman and the world is true to one steeped in desires, and encased in individuality; their unity is true to one who has come to *know,* to transcend individuality. Truth is relative to the knower. This, however, is no Protagorean subjectivism. So long as the individual is an individual, there is duality between teacher and taught, the teaching appearing to be something foreign, imposed from without; but when there is a flashing from below, there is one homogeneous flame of advaita-jñāna or monistic knowledge, when, however, the individual does not remain an individual to recognise the contradiction between it and the previous dvaita-jñāna or dualistic knowledge. To us, from the outside, dvaita and advaita are both true, as possible stages of knowledge, but dvaita is inferior in reality to advaita; they are not co-ordinate. In every act of knowledge, the duality between subject and object presents itself only to give way to their identification.

48. It may be urged against the foregoing account of Vedāntic realism that it does not provide for a principle of *change,* as distinct from one of mere difference, whether change is regarded as emanation (vivarta) or as evolution (pariṇāma). The three orders of eternal entities which we have recognised are all static; where is the dynamic principle?

49. One would imagine such a principle is likely to be met with in a discussion of causality. Referring, however, to an elaborate and acute discussion of the subject in Śaṅkara's commentary on Bṛhadāraṇyaka Upaniṣad I, ii, we find only a clearer enunciation of the static view of the world which we have already presented, but the dynamic principle appears to be nowhere. It would not be, however, quite out of place here to present, in a slightly modern garb, the salient features of Śaṅkara's argument, both as a specimen of his reasoning and as a further explication of the foregoing views.

50. Before the world began, no difference was manifest; everything was shrouded by death. Not that there was a mere void, for then causes and effects were in their seminal unmanifested condition. (To justify this, he proves first that the cause, meaning by it only material cause, and next that the effect, meaning by it the effect-form, are eternally existent.) (1) *Eternity of cause.* That effects are possible only when the causes are present is a matter of experience. It might be objected that when a pot is fashioned out of a lump of clay, the lump is first destroyed and then the pot comes into being and so the cause is not immediately antecedent to the effect. But it is replied that not the lump-form but the clay is the cause. All causes in their causation destroy their previous manifestation in introducing their present manifestation, for the same cause cannot exist in two different forms at the same time. But the cessation of the previous manifestation does not mean the cessation of the cause itself. Yet why not take the lump-form also to be a cause, seeing that the clay cannot exist except in some form? Because the form is variable but the matter is persistent. But still must it not have some form? No: in the production of the pot, the clay for a moment has left the lump-form and is passing over to the pot-form. (That is the *mystery* of production. Change means the conflict of manifestation and the consequent momentary *nakedness* of the substance.) But is this naked substance perceived? May it not be

that the lump of clay only *resembles* the pot that is made out of it without the clay persisting identically in the change? No; the identity is *perceived* but the similarity is only *inferred*. Inference is based on perception, and if perception were to be questioned by inference here, there would be an illicit regress to infinity. The denial of identity would mean the rapid succession of momentary acts, which means the denial of knowledge *of* any object. For where is the evidence for the object? If in another act of knowledge, where is the evidence for this again? And so on. Similarly if you do not trust in your immediate perception of identity and ask 'what is the evidence for it' and reply 'because there is the felt similarity', you must ask for the evidence for that again, and so on. which means that you cannot *affirm* anything. Besides, the consciousness 'this is like that' is possible if the same self or knower is present to both the momentary cognitions, 'this' and 'that', which, however, cannot be admitted by one who denies identity. Is it replied that whether there be a self or not, the likeness is a feeling (itself an event of the mind)? But it is no blind feeling; 'this' and 'that' refer to each other; it is an objective assertion. If it were only a subjective feeling, 'this' and 'that' also, being individually known by assimilation with their likes, would be merely subjective, false: and then the knowledge of this subjectivity or falsity would itself be merely subjective or false. (Such a sceptical suicide then is the only alternative to the view that the cause is perceived to be persisting self-identically in the effect.) (2) *Eternity of effect.* The effect-form, too, does not accidentally emerge into existence but is eternally existent. (i) As an object hidden under darkness or behind an opaque wall manifests itself when a lamp is lighted or when the wall is removed, so is the form of the pot hidden under the previous form of the clay, the lump-form, and is manifested when the previous form is removed by appropriate means. *Objections*:—(a) In order to prove that all that is manifested was previously existent, it is necessary to know that what was previously non-existent is not manifested, but the absence of manifestation cannot be perceived. Hence it can only be said that a thing is existent when manifested. *Reply*:—It cannot be held either that it is existent *only* when manifested, for that amounts to saying that all existents are manifested, which, however, is not true. (b) The previous form, lump-form, as agent producing manifestation, is different in nature from the darkness or the opaque wall; for the wall occupies a space-position distinct from that of the object hidden by it, but the lump-form does not do so. *Reply*:—This difference is not important; in milk, the milk-form prevents the manifestation of the water-form and yet occupies the same position as the latter. (c) But there is another difference: to *see* the pot hidden under darkness, one has to make an exertion (light a lamp, etc.), but to *see* the pot emerging from the lump of clay, no such exertion is required (though it is required in the production of it). *Reply*:—In both cases, to see does not require any exertion: the exertion put forth is for production only—in the former case for investing the pot with the attribute of lightedness, in the latter case, for destroying the lump-form, etc.

(ii) The past being of the future being of an object may be peculiarly distinct from the present being, but it is still being. Knowledge of the future is knowledge of some *existent* object, for otherwise how is the future *willed?* Willing (as distinct from merely desiring) means directly an objectification of the future. The Yogin in his clairvoyance is said to *see* the past and the future as we see the present. Besides, God's foreknowledge would be meaningless, if the future object were not eternally existent (cf. Anselm's reconciliation between divine foreknowledge and man's free will). (Existence or reality immediately means 'transcending time.') Again, what does non-existence of the future object, 'pot' mean? Only that some other object is now present. Non-existence of pot itself is not existent positively: it is not defined by being distinguished from other non-existences, as that of the cloth. And what is non-existence *of* pot? Is non-existence an attribute of pot? Then it means non-existence of non-existent pot, not of the positive pot. Finally, if we say, 'A is produced or comes into being', A, the subject, must be already existent in order to have the predicate, 'comes into being'.

51. This elaborate discussion of causality leads to the recognition of Brahman as the material cause of the universe and of the primal hiding principle, co-eternal with Brahman, viz., māyā which by itself is nothing, like the blue tint which seems to pervade objects viewed through blue glasses. Still therefore the dynamic principle remains undiscovered.

52. What is śakti or power? It is sometimes identified

with the principle of illusion or māyā. In Pañcadaśī, for example (Chapter II, slokas 47 seq.), we have pronouncements to the following effect:—māyā, or the power of the Lord, is no reality (in the presence of Brahman), is inferrible from its effects, and only from these. The power of the Existent is not the Existent, even as the power of the fire is not the fire. What, then, is it apart from the Existent? It cannot be called the void, as that is taken to be the effect of māyā; it is something then which is neither the void nor the existent. Yet it exists only as through the Existent, for substance and attribute are not separate entities. It may, no doubt, be manifested in effects, but before creation, such manifested power did not exist, and so power cannot be a principle separate from Brahman. (Yet to show that Brahman transcends it, it is added) this power does not pervade all Brahman but only a portion or aspect of Him (it). This Universe is only a quarter of Him; full three quarters are self luminous. So in Bhagavad-gītā Kṛṣṇa says, 'by a portion of myself, do I pervade the Universe'. So too śruti, 'having pervaded the universe, He extends a space beyond' (atyatiṣṭhad daśāṅgulam); and there is the Vedānta-sūtra, 'Also there is a form of the Lord not abiding in effected things' (Thibaut's translation). (It is admitted, however, that this attribution of parts to the Indiscerptible is only provisional). 'That power, as residing in the Existent, produces effects'. The power that creates ākāśa (space or ether, its first effect) creates also its identity with the Existent and thus (in the inverse order) makes the existent an attribute of ākāśa as substance. It is really the Existent that becomes ākāśa; to take the existence as *of* ākāśa is what might be expected of māyā or the principle of illusion.

53. We have to note four points in the above passage:—(1) that this *power*, by itself, is only māyā: (2) that it exists and functions only as residing in Brahman, i.e., only as Brahman informing māyā; (3) that though thus informed, it is transcended by Brahman; and (4) that Brahman existing in the power becomes the effect: the effect is thus not non-existent. The passage presents both sides of the Vedāntic doctrine of māyā—the world being unreal apart from Brahman and real in the reality of Brahman. The latter side is frequently overlooked.

54. Power then as existent is the Existent assuming forms, i.e., making the unreal real. The One Existent Blissful Intelligence, entering māyā becomes self-dirempted into Īśvara and aparā-prakṛti, i.e., the Determinate God (and the 'object in general', the primordial matter in which God) is to energise. Brahman against the 'dark ground' of māyā is Īśvara, māyā against the light of the self is aparā-prakṛti. Yet Īśvara is said to be *free*, to be related to the dark ground, yet floating on it, to have conquered it once for all, employing it 'only as a servant'. This attribute of freely relating Himself to the dark ground, being itself absolute (for in Him attributes and aspects are concrete realities), is to be viewed as an entity by itself, viz., as parā-prakṛti, and the nisus of this again towards aparā-prakṛti is to be taken as a third entity śakti, or power of the Lord.

55. This parā-prakṛti is the intelligence of Īśvara, appearing in its determinate form only as reflected from the aparā. As Brahman, the undifferenced intelligence, shines on this māyā; it turns it into an object and forthwith becomes the Determinate Subject of this object, functioning towards the object. This triply stratified māyā with the reflection of the Lord, viz., as comprising parā-prakṛti, śakti of the Lord, and aparā-prakṛti, may be considered to be the concrete archetype of the abstractions, sattva, rajas, and tamas (light, intelligence, or goodness; activity; darkness, insentiency, heaviness, evil), those universal aspects of existence to understand which is to understand the differential genius of Hinduism itself. Conformably to the general trend of Vedāntism, one would expect a projection of parā-prakṛti and śakti on aparā-prakṛti: thus aparā-prakṛti is of the three guṇas (attributes, elements), sattva, rajas, and tamas, all compact. The Sāṅkhya principle pradhāna, is this aparā-prakṛti, a stage more determinate than mere māyā, differing from it much as Aristotle's matter as potentiality differs from Plato's *me on*, the negation-soil in which he plants his Ideas. Sāṅkhya, however, takes it to be an ultimate reality incapable of being derived from higher principles.

56. The parā-prakṛti has been taken to be the determinate intelligence (buddhi) of the Lord, but it should be noticed that this buddhi is also taken to be an evolute of

the aparā-prakṛti, in fact its first and most perfect evolute. So we have to understand the parā as the buddhi in its subject-aspect, i.e., as informed with Brahman; the other buddhi is its passive aspect, its object aspect, for active buddhi knows passive buddhi, as the eye sees light. But what is this buddhi, active and passive, as distinct from Brahman? Here an understanding of the psychology of the faculties recognised in Vedānta, viz., buddhi, manas, ahaṅkāra, and citta is necessary.

57. All knowledge is self-affirmation. The Vedāntic self is as we have seen already, beyond this self-affirmation, something transcending determination the indeterminate, the unknown and unknowable, that which being presupposed in all knowledge is incapable of being caught in any determinate mode of knowledge. This determinate self-affirmation, too, as (eternally) *completed* or *accomplished*, is beyond the self-affirming activity. This activity implies the consciousness of a limited, unrealised agent proceeding or functioning towards an object. The consciousness of such a limited agent or subject as (illusorily) identified with the self (which is really *absolute*, not only in the sense of being above duality but above all determination also) is what Kant calls empirical self-consciousness. This activity itself is to be conceived as manifested in two grades, the intellectual and sensory, the synthesis of concepts and the synthesis of apprehension. The self is manifested in self-affirmation or knowledge; knowledge is manifested by the self-affirming activity of the self-conscious individualised self; the activity is that of the interpretation of the sense-manifold, *given* as *one* apprehension. The relation of the senses to the objects will be discussed later on. The senses are only blind receivers and incapable of being themselves perceived (atīndriya). The essential character of the four faculties of antaḥkaraṇa here discussed—manas, citta, etc, (manas in its widest sense comprising all the four) is that they have both spontaneity and receptivity and are capable of being self-perceived. Manas in the narrower sense is the faculty of simple *apprehension* (not a mere *sense*). It has for its specific function, saṁśaya (doubt), saṁkalpa and vikalpa (assertion and negation, intellectual or conative). These functions, so widely different, are capable of being connected with one another. As an organ of simple apprehension, manas just raises the ques-

tion, 'what is it' (sensation), but answers it not, just gives a start to attention; so its function on the intellectual side is to doubt. Saṁkalpa is mental impulse (mānasa karma), conation as it appears in desire or motor impulse, in attention, even in objectification. This blind spontaneity is essentially that element in an assertion which goes out beyond the mere judgment, the element of free will in intellection to which Descartes attributed error. Vikalpa is just the negation of this saṁkalpa, a mental impasse, attention as homeless, not as fixing itself on an object but as moving away from it or in its transition from one object to another, will in the air appearing as aversion, hesitation, doubt or as consciousness of difference, the stress of the will in and beyond the negative judgment. Citta is the faculty of intellectual synthesis as distinct from mere apprehension, intellectual, in a wide sense including smaraṇa (remembering), anusandhāna (inquiring, seeking to know *what*), etc. Citta thus is intellectual pravṛtti or self-affirming activity directed outwards, i.e., towards the object; the consciousness which is directed inwards, i.e., the consciousness of self as agent or subject being ahaṁkāra. Buddhi is the faculty of knowledge (as distinct from knowing), intellectual synthesis (niścaya or adhyavasāya) not as activity but as an eternally accomplished (pariniṣṭhita) affair, the unquestioning, quiescent self-affirmation in the copula of a judgment, in belief, in the feelings of pleasure and pain. The relation of knowing to knowledge is peculiar; the latter is manifested, eternally accomplished, not effected as a contingent product or result. In knowledge, however, two elements may be distinguished, the vṛtti or mental mode (section 88), and the light of cit or self playing on it and investing it with its timeless or eternal character. The former can be described as the result of the knowing activity, of the ripening of the seeds of vidyā-karma or the saṁskāras; and so buddhi or mahat in this aspect—the completed organism of knowledge—has been sometimes described as the adhibhūta aspect of citta, the knowing activity, which is thus the corresponding adhyātma or limited subjective aspect. Buddhi then as the faculty of determinate knowledge is the immediate home of the self, which is the light of *knowledge* transcending all determination and yet transfiguring all determinate mental modes.

58. This buddhi is either the immediate reflector of the self or the immediate envelope or body of the self. As reflector or object, it is the finest evolute of aparā-prakṛti. As the body with which the self is identified, it is parā-prakṛti. The two prakṛtis, therefore, interpenetrate one another; they have been described as the primal male and female principles, a division which appears at different stages in Hindu cosmogony but does not, therefore, necessarily involve confusion of thought. The light of the self not only gets reflected from the surface of māyā, turning it into aparā-prakṛti, it transfigures māyā in all its strata, everywhere differentiating it into sattva and tamas, itself getting next identified with the sattva and then functioning (rajas) towards the tamas. Thus it is that the sattva aspect of aparā-prakṛti is at the same time the adhyātma or subjective aspect, tamas being the adhibhūta or objective aspect. One is tempted to identify this distinction between sāttvika and tāmasika in Vedānta with the distinction between actual and potential in the Aristotelian system; there is a good deal of agreement, too, between the systems in respect of the connected doctrines, viz., that matter is unredeemed potentiality, that the soul is the entelechy of the body, and that God is *noesis noeseus,* the purest actuality (cf. Īśvara having the transparent garment, śuddha-sattva-upādhi of buddhi). But it must be remembered that whereas all the differentiation is taken to be ultimately real by Aristotle, Vedānta takes it to be real only within the sphere of māyā or illusion. In fact, as has already been pointed out, Aristotle's matter is aparā-prakṛti but not māyā; and although he recognises that there are different grades of reality, that actuality is the truth of potentiality, and that God though pure actuality still contains in Himself ideally all potentiality, yet he does not rise to the conception of Brahman to whom 'being the truth or actuality of anything' is itself an upādhi or envelope, who is absolute in being devoid not only of all external relation but also of all internal relation, who is said to be ekamevādvitīyam, one without a second, transcending svagata-bheda (having parts), sajātīya-bheda (having something similar), and vijātīya bheda, (having something different from it). He rises as far as the Vedāntic Īśvara, the first emanation of Brahman, Brahman in the attitude of creation. This Īśvara, though the

determinate God as distinct from the indeterminate Brahman, is still undifferentiated within Himself. This follows from the very nature of buddhi, which is pure self-affirmation, which is distinct alike from pure caitanya on the one hand, and from citta and ahaṁkāra on the other. This buddhi, has been identified with the state of the self as in suṣupti, or better still, as in savikalpa-samādhi which is its actualised state. Yet buddhi is not an abstract state but rather the concrete faculty or body in which the self is inclosed. The undifferenced character of buddhi appears still more explicitly when we consider that it is the faculty of *feeling* pleasure and pain, which is most intimately related to the self though different from it.

59. Īśvara, then is the self as shining on and in māyā which has the three guṇas (attributes or elements) of sattva, rajas, and tamas, and is accordingly both triguṇātīta (transcending these guṇas), and śuddha-sattva-upādhi (invested with a transparent body of sattva). Of Him as triguṇātīta, parā-prakṛti or the determinate actualised intelligence is the immediate prakṛti or nature; or rather as intelligence itself is an evolute of aparā, taking on two aspects (male and female) in the light of Brahman, He as triguṇātīta is the unity of parā (intelligence as facing the self) and aparā (the same intelligence in its objective or passive aspect, the sattva aspect of aparā facing its tamas aspect) and yet prior to it. This unity next gets identified with and thus contracted into the parā or the transparent garment of sattva which thus has before it the aparā, with tamas as the predominant, though not the sole element. Hence comes the peculiarity that the parā-prakṛti is both different from Brahman and an aspect of Brahman. Hence, too, the possibility of sattva being here absolutely pure, though everywhere else the three guṇas imply one another. It is the lighted surface of māyā, as reflected from which Brahman is Īśvara; to this lighted surface, all the interior is darkness, negation. On the outer confines of māyā, the 'sacred influence of light' appears, and as 'chaos retires', 'dim night' too retires, rendered dimmer by contrast. The alchemy of light turns that which it shines on into light. What was dark, negative, utterly false, becomes light, existent, parā-prakṛti which again shoots inward, stratifying aparā-prakrti which is the equipoise of the

guṇas into its sattva and tamas aspects, and getting at every stage identified with the sattva-aspect. while the tamas-aspect is for ever retiring.

"But now at last the sacred influence
Of light appears, and from the walls of Heaven
Shoots far into the bosom of dim Night
A glimmering dawn. Here Nature first begins
Her farthest verge and Chaos to retire."

60. From the standpoint of Brahman, all this transfigured māyā is false. From the standpoint of Īśvara, as invested with the transparent body of sattva. sattva alone is real, tamas is unreal—they are not co-ordinate. The 'glimmering dawn' shot inwards is only the promise of the conquest of the entire realm of chaos, promise of the ultimate perishableness of tamas.

61. Brahman and Īśvara have sometimes been called the higher god and the lower god. The distinction is, to say the least, misleading, and probably the over-definite language of some of the systematising scholiasts is responsible for it. No doubt there is a distinction between the conceptions. Yet Īśvara is not in reality different from Brahman. As has been already indicated, Īśvara is the absolute of savikalpa-samādhi, whereas Brahman is of nirvikalpa-samādhi, these states being continuous yet different. As a conception, however, Īśvara as triguṇātīta is different from Brahman.

62. An image will make it clear—a light-sphere in circumambient darkness. From the centre of it, the fulness of light radiates all around, without a thought of the darkness: it is the indeterminate infinite Brahman. At the circumference, however. it reaches its limit (not a resistance) and retires into itself, the limiting darkness falling outside of it; the sphere, as viewed from the circumference inwards, is the determinate Infinite or the closed-in Absolute, Īśvara. The limit, however, determines its quality, not as darkness but as darkness lighted up, which again defines the darkness (thus the darkness gets stratified). Let us view all this from the standpoint of the individual. In the dim light of reason, in that 'glimmering dawn' in the bosom of night, the individual is lulled by the bright dreams of the morn, not unaccompanied by frightful nightmares; this is the soul-clearing work of morality (sattva-śuddhi), with its lapses and its

despairs, with its toilsome march and its intervals of serenity. At length he wakes up to the glory of a sunrise, is lifted up to absolute consciousness when all the dreams which constituted life and the world he feels to be illusory, for he has now reached his *true* self which he always was but knew not. Still the dreams are there remembered, though now known to be dreams. He exclaims, 'Lo! the Sun (Īśvara) is there: He has revealed Himself unto me in grace and I am absolute in the Absolute. All that past individuality of mine was but a dream'. Forthwith the duality vanishes in the rapt feeling, 'I am the Sun', which still means 'I am nothing and the Sun is all. I am no longer the limit outside the object; the limit is but the determination of the object the object which is conscious of the limit'. Both these stages are the aspects of Īśvara, the former being the śuddha-sattva-upādhi aspect, the latter the triguṇātīta aspect. 'In the former, He reveals Himself in me, in my absolute consciousness, puts on my absolute consciousness as a garment; in the latter, I become His very self—He not only shines in me but passes out unimpeded and I am dissolved in Him'. In the former, the light of that sphere passing outwards impinges on darkness, lighting it up; in the latter, the light retires backwards to the centre. But in either case, the light is determinate; in both, there is an awareness of the darkness; the light at first makes it an object and then unites ecstatically with it. Īśvara as triguṇātita still remembers His feat of transcending māyā; the self is conscious of its difference from Īśvara being illusory. It is just the *passing* into the indifference of Brahman, not the indifference itself. It is the indifference rendered conceivable; yet such is the nature of the conception that its content spurns the form, proclaims its own inconceivability. This conceived inconceivability is the ultimate formula; as conceived, it is the triguṇātīta Īśvara the inconceivability that is conceived being triguṇātīta Brahman. They constitute one unit, one scintillating star; that noble verse in the Chāndogya Upaniṣad, śyāmāt śavalaṁ prapadye śavalāt śyāmamprapadye, 'May I pass from the dark blank to the figured determinate and from thence to the blank again' points to this mystic scintillation of the One reality. No wonder, therefore, that the highest epithets should be applied to Īśvara, as for example, in the Śāṇḍilya-vidyā in the Chāndogya, such as one would expect to be applied to Brahman from the characterisations, lower Brahman and higher Brahman, the misleadingness of which must be now apparent.

63. Yet after all it may be asked, why this limitation of a darkness at all? Why the illusion of an individuality at all? As we have seen already, the question itself is illegitimate, for while the individuality is there, it necessarily sees no beginning or end of itself, for all that it knows, it knows under the form of individuality; and when the individuality is transcended, not only is *it* felt to be an illusion; even its having been illusorily present in the past is felt to be so; so nowhere does it appear as a *contingent reality* of which only we can demand an explanation.

64. But then how should the inconceivable be thought of, referred to at all? It must be because it *reveals* itself in a form which it at the same time condemns. But are not those to whom it reveals illusory also? Why then this illusory revelation in an illusory form to illusory subjects? Once again, this 'why' is an illegitimate demand, an atipraśna, as it has sometimes been called. As the individual is just passing into Brahman, it feels all this to be illusory and then the illusion vanishes. The highest consciousness then for the individual as individual is this consciousness of the illusoriness of his own individuality. This has to be simply accepted: there is no 'why' for this or for Brahman.

65. Before the moment of passing into Brahman, the individual is raised to absolute consciousness (parā-prakṛti, as invested with which Īśvara is śuddha-sattva-upādhi), when Īśvara is known to be knowing the world as His reflex, i.e. as created by His will. Not that the world is created out of nothing: for Īśvara assuming śuddha-sattva-upādhi, i.e., knowing attitude, means at once having aparā-prakṛti before Him as object and material for His will to mould. But certain old difficulties at once start up. How does this will meet the matter? How does it actualise particular groupings of 'names and forms' potentially contained in this matter, and this in time, according to law? Why does He will at all, seeing that he, as perfectly actualised, cannot have anything to attain or avoid? The will meets the matter as identical with it, just as the energising body can act on the object, the body being, as we saw, but sentient space continuing itself in its move-

ment through space. As to the other questions, a preliminary discussion is required to introduce the Vedāntic solutions.

66. The absolute consciousness in which Iśvara is revealed is reached only when there is a perfect chastening of the spirit, when it is made the still mirror of truth, not simply by a discipline of the intellect but by an ethical discipline of the will, when all the desires of the individual self have been completely eliminated and the spirit is broadened out so as to comprehend the truest interests of all beings. Ignorance is but the intellectual reflex of evil willing, the shadow of which again deepens the evil, and thus it goes on ad *infinitum.* We have already introduced the notion of every man being born with the seed of all his spiritual life, intellective and conative. Each such seed of vidyā-karma (knowledge and action) has a measure of ignorance or evil in it, and the self as embodied in this seed sees no beginning of itself, for it can explain its evil or sin only as due to an ignorance which is not a temporary cloud but is ingrained in the character which constitutes its body, and further it can explain this ignorance only as due to self-imposition, i.e., free sinning, for the self cannot have anything imposed upon it from without. The absolute consciousness is reached only when this substantial ignorance has been dispelled by good willing. So when Fichte said that every man could, if he would, i.e., if he had not a sinning will, rise to intellectual perception and when Schelling thought the very reverse, that 'the capacity for it, like the poetic talent, is possessed by a select few', that the true philosopher, like the true poet, is born, not made, they held views which are reconciled in the Vedāntic doctrine which has already been presented. The ignorance that is ingrained in the seed of vidyā-karma with which a man is born shuts out certain forms or planes of thought *ab initio* from his mental horizon, which no effort of mere thinking can make accessible, just as an instinctive tendency or an ingrained habit cannot be annulled by a single fiat of the will. At the same time there are rational elements or good tendencies in that seed or 'noumenal character' which the will primarily, and the intellect secondarily (with the help of the will), can help to develop, gradually working out the ignorance and the evil. Accordingly when Hegel holds, as against both Fichte and Schelling, that the 'wonderful power of the understanding' alone can be trusted to lead us to every level of thought by a necessary

dialectic development, that therefore a bad man can rise step by step up the thought-ladder alone to the highest conceptions of philosophy, Vedānta will press against him the old objection that thought is not knowledge, that even the large range of thought to which the bad man has access is due to the fact that he is not all bad, and that though the thought is continuous with absolute knowledge or intellectual perception, yet at every step this thought, necessary as it is, has the alternative of absolute scepticism beyond it. The smoky flickering flame of mere thought clears up only when the moisture of evil and ignorance in the 'noumenal character' (Schopenhauer) is completely burnt off in the fire of morality.

67. This Vedāntic view may now be made the individualistic platform from which we may view the question already suggested, 'Why does Īśvara will at all'. Īśvara is the crown of the moral consciousness, the unity of all the 'noumenal characters' or the unities of vidyā-karma (including not only human spirits but spirits above and below, as is apparent from the Vedāntic doctrines of the continuity of spiritual gradations and of metempsychosis). He is again the organism, not only of the spirits—for ignorance, the mother of Karma, cannot have place in Him—but of nature, too, furnishing the experiences appropriate to their Karma (the *malum poena* to their *malum culpa*). He is the joint organism of moral law and natural law, the latter being only the obverse of the former, the two being the differentiations, mainly sāttvika and tāmasika, of aparā-prakṛti as interpenetrated by parā-prakṛti. [Were it not for the ignorance begetting karma and *begotten* of karma, every one would *see* the unity of moral law and natural law, see that he is the architect of his own fortune, though now 'virtue and happiness seem to be synthetically connected' (Kant) with each other]. Īśvara, however, is not the immanent unity but the transcendent, the latter being his true nature. There are grades of transcendence, too. As primarily transcendent or triguṇātīta, He is in dreamless sleep, with the homogeneous unity of parā and aparā-prakṛti as the objective blank before Him, the primal glory in which He rests (sve mahimni tiṣṭhati). This unity is the avyākṛta ākāśa, the unmanifested archetype of space and matter, the absolute buddhi (though sometimes taken as only objective, as

the first objectivity of buddhi), the Vedāntic substitute for the pradhāna of Sāṅkhya. It is the home of all 'names and forms', 'unevolved but about to be evolved' (avyākṛta-vyācikīrṣita) because of its being in immediate unity with the individual wills or noumenal characters, which last in the reflection of Īśvara are the jīvas or individual souls, called prājñas in this connexion, who rest, unconscious of their individualities in this dreamless sleep of the Universal Spirit (Parameśvarāśrayā māyāmayī mahasuṣuptih yasyām svarūpa-pratibodha-rahitāh śerate saṁsāriṇojīvāḥ.—Saṅkara's commentary to Brahma-sūtras). Next Īśvara becomes invested with parā-prakrti, and as such transcends the *processes* of this unity of parā and aparā. The individual will-selves have here as much a dual nature as Īśvara himself. In dreamless sleep, their mind dissolves into māyā and they attain their eternally free (mukta) state, their identity with the triguṇātīta; the same souls, in relation to their life-processes and reincarnations, are viewed as invested with the first individualising sheath, the 'noumenal character' (the Kāraṇa-śarīra or the will-self). But a difference emerges here; for whereas the envelope of Īśvara in this aspect is śuddha-sattva or transparent, that of the jīva is malina-sattva or impure, partly opaque, dimming the light that shines through it. The impurity is the limitation that constitutes the individuality. But just as the aparā-prakṛti has buddhi as its evolute, so too these malina-sattva individual souls gradually move towards the śuddha-sattva type, the jīvan-mukta souls (i.e., those who have burst their bonds of individuality and ignorance in this life) being just a stage removed from the śuddha-sattva Īśvara.

68. A further understanding, somewhat after Schopenhauer of the progressive realisation of these individual spirits is necessary for a clearer explication of the nature of Īśvara. The individual wills, asserts himself against the world, nature and society; and as his will spends itself, the world recoils on him. As his willing necessarily means a limitation of vision, the recoil seems to be foreign to him; hence all the misery and apparent injustice of the world. He sets it down to blind nature (or unjust selfish society). This rough tussle with nature and society, however, de-

velops in some spirits a generalised and moralised reason, whereas in others it deepens unreason, leading them through impoten strife gradually, through a diminution of life, to the level of stocks and stones. Those in whom reason is developed come to perceive that the recoil is their own work, that a punishment as well as a reward is something that is their due, something to which they have a claim. But the Universe is not quite so simple, and it puzzles the reason to lead it peradventure to serener heights or to hurl it down again. For are not the rewards and punishments, notoriously the latter, very often disproportionate to one's Karma in this life? What is stranger still, why should evil Karma be acquired at all? Why should reason every now and then lapse into irrationality which is the essence of sin? Why again should there be the sudden conversions, the lightning flashes of good inclinations, now and again bursting forth from the leaden cloud of habits? It is only the 'noumenal character' that can explain all this, the character which may not get completely manifested in any one stage of the phenomenal life, not even in one's whole life. The self as identified with it moves freely in the (knowing and), willing process; at every stage, the self recognises the character then manifested to have been pre-existent, unconsciously constituting his individuality. This noumenal seed is not explained by heredity and accidental variations which explain only the outward, naturalistic side of it. The individual self sees no beginning of itself and looks out beyond its life-processes to an uninterrupted existence before birth. The existence of a life before this is intelligible in the light of the relation between the (naturalistic) evolutionary view and the apriori view on the one hand and the Vedāntic view on the other. The concrete self or the noumenal character is known apriori, at any rate recognised in empirical consciousness to have been beginninglessly operative. The empirical account of the origin of this concrete self does not prejudice the validity of the notion of its eternal pre-existence. If its pre-existence is admitted, is it (1) timelessly transcendent, or (2) timelessly immanent in experience or rather in the most concrete experience-system, the whole species regarded as one? Vedānta will hold that it is both. A doctrine somewhat like traducianism is traceable in a passage in Bṛhadāraṇyaka-Upaniṣad (I, V. 17-8) on the relation between father and son: other passages may also be referred to. At the same time just as every object and every combination of objects were found to presuppose eternal 'names and forms', so every individual soul has its individuating principle in a distinctive Kāraṇa-śarīra. This śarīra is timeless by itself, though its concrete nature, viz., its being the matrix of specific instincts and unconscious cognition-traces points to the experiences of this distinctive body before the present life. Every such will-self, itself only a name apart from Brahman—the name being what alone is said to persist after death, after the body has relapsed into the elements, gross and subtile—is a centre of many names and forms, the shadows of the objects of its experience in all time, with which, however, it is at this height in immediate unity. Such a will-self then, ranging as it does over many lives of the same individual, furnishes us with a solution that considerably lightens the heavy unintelligibility of the Karma-system.

69. From the stage, therefore in which the individual feels himself freely claiming his rewards and punishments, he passes again to the stage in which the recoil is felt to be foreign to him till that mist, too, clears up in the recognition in a far wider sense than before of himself being the *eternal* architect of his own fortune. Here, however the difficulty comes back in an accentuated form. He does not indeed ask himself, 'why was I cursed with such a noumenal character'—that would be the voice of the 'devil that is an ass'—for to ask this, one should first be dissociated from the noumenal character which, however, in this dissociation would be illusory. But in the light of the moralised reason that has been developed in him, he will cry out in Augustinian despair, 'Am I then never to escape from this self-imposed self, this radical evil in me? Is final liberation or Mokṣa impossible for me?'. In this stage of deep vairāgya (denial of the will, repentance), he learns, emotionally and intellectually, of a higher soul (a guru) from the revealed Scriptures, or sometimes by spontaneous intuition (sources which are identical in the last resort), that Īśvara is the Truth and that his individuality is a lie, that it is only through His light, in His grace (Karuṇā) that he has been hungering and thirsting for mokṣa (liberation) so long, that he, the unregenerate self, has not learnt the blissful truth by an effort establishing claim to it, but that his knowledge is but God knowing in him.

70. We are now prepared to understand why Īśvara is said to will, i.e., to actualise in grace the Karma of individual souls

in order that they may reach m o k ṣ a or identity with Himself. By Himself, He is t r i g u n ā t ī t a ; but as the individual necessarily takes himself to have been beginninglessly existent, Ī ś v a r a is to him the *good person*, willing this evolving world into existence out of compassion for him, in order that he, by himself, may work out the evil in him. In this stage of duality, he at first takes his experiences of pleasure and pain as the reward and punishment meted out to him by a *Just* God; but as he comes to recognise that they are the necessary reflections of his own nature, he realises that justice is but mercy as viewed through the ignorance which separates him from God, the good principle that has led to this realisation being felt to be the inshining of God Himself. This mercy, then, does not conflict with justice; neither v a i s a m y a (injustice) nor n a i r g h ṛ ṇ y a (heartlessness) can be predicated of Ī ś v a r a. In mercy, He becomes the good principle in individual spirits, He actualises them, He neutralises the evil in them by inflicting on them punishments (or, as Christians put it, by inflicting on Himself their punishments). Yet his mercy is not indiscriminate; it descends on them according to the measure of their K a r m a. In reality, however, *He* does not work at all, *He* does not suffer at all, except in their persons: K a r m a and pain are to Him alike illusory. His willing to actualise them is but the evolution of their s a t t v a, through the dynamic of their K a r m a. He is but the breath of the K a r m a system, the organism of justice which is at the same time the organism of grace. His ś a k t i or power is but the K a r m a of individual spirits pressing outwards towards fruition. His i c c h ā or will to create is no bondage to Him. To Him, it is a glorious divine disport or l ī l ā; to us, individual spirits, the influx of grace or K a r u ṇ ā.

71. Ī ś v a r a, as Justice, has His dread aspect, too. Through Him, those in whom s a t t v a is dominant rise higher and higher, but those in whom t a m a s is dominant sink deeper and deeper. *Facilis descensus Averni.* Yet if He is universal reality, why is He specially identified with goodness, with all that is 'glorious and beautiful and potent'? It is the old problem of evil—is evil positive in V e d ā n t a ? As in Schelling, it is ultimately but the 'dark ground' of goodness. As indicated already, s a t t v a is but t a m a s actualised. To most men, however, in whom s a t t v a is but imperfectly developed, the evil is co-ordinate with the good, and therefore positive. But as the evil deepens, spiritual vision

also gets dimmed; and the misery that follows drags the sinner lower and lower; instead of chastening his soul there is an increasing helplessness till the struggle between s a t t v a and t a m a s ceases, s a t t v a getting completely involved in one dull cloud of unconsciousness (s t h ā v a r a t v a). But, apparently, this does not serve the ends of Divine Justice, far less of Divine mercy. For to whom is the unconsciousness a punishment at all? It may be replied that to the individual left with the last spark of freedom, the passage to this s t h ā v a r a t v a will appear like a sinking into 'eternal perdition'. But how is Divine mercy vindicated? The last fury of the Divine wrath is followed by unconsciousness. The last embrace of Divine love means, too, a lapse of differenced consciousness. Extremes tend to meet.

72. Let us now consider the state of the j ī v a n m u k t a which is just the antipodes of the state of s t h ā v a r a t v a. The j ī v a n m u k t a is one who after repeated births, repeated terms of probation passed successfully, at last kills off all ignorance, all K a r m a, all evil, and reaches absolute knowledge. How does he still remain j ī v a t, living, embodied, the body being only a materealisation of K a r m a ('objectification of the will'—Schopenhauer)? K a r m a is divided by Indian philosophers into three sections, s a ñ c i t a, ā r a b d h a, and k r i y a m ā ṇ a. Not all the K a r m a acquired in previous lives receives fruition in this life. The noumenal character does not become fully phenomenalised in *one* life. The part that is manifested, that has started on its course of fruition in this life, is called ā r a b d h a (that which has begun), the part that is unmanifested is called s a ñ c i t a (hoarded) and the new K a r m a which is being generated in this life is the K r i y a m ā ṇ a. Now the J ī v a n m u k t a, having killed off his ignorance, no longer feels the solicitations of desire, and hence acquires no new K a r m a. The s a ñ c i t a K a r m a is burnt off in the fire of knowledge, destroyed in its embryonic stage. The ā r a b d h a, being a unity, must run out its course and cannot be stopped half-way. As in the case of an arrow shot through the air or of the revolving wheel of the potter, the momentum must spend itself out. But then it may be asked: while the momentum is there in life, how can there be abosolute knowledge or m o k ṣ a? If, too, s a ñ c i t a be destroyed by this knowledge which shows forth all K a r m a to be illusory, how can the momentum of ā r a b d h a be there still? It is replied that to the j ī v a n-

m u k t a himself, the momentum of his bodily life is nothing in reality: it is positively existent only to others with dim vision. The world, including the bodies of individuals, is but the community of the self-energising K a r m a - unities (energising in the grace of God, which is the deepest sense of self-energising). Natural law is but the obverse face of the moral law. If the body of the j ī v a n - m u k t a were annihilated for others also, there would be violation of this law, which is absurd. To the j ī v a n - m u k t a himself, however, the emergence of this knowledge of the illusoriness of his body must appear to be abrupt. He seems to be raised to divine grace without any merit of his own. But to Ī ś v a r a, justice does not admit of being baulked. K a r m a can be killed out only by K a r m a; the will can be denied only by the will (Schopenhauer). Yet the will, which has thus completely denied itself would stand out in spiritual pride, were it not for the fact that it gets at this stage (and even earlier) transfigured by reverence (the obverse of grace). In this reverence, in this assurance of free forgiveness, these individual souls elect to continue the divine system of justice and grace by remaining in the body, by freely continuing in the illusory form in relation to other souls. So the j ī v a n - m u k t a souls assist as the high priests at the cosmic y a j ñ a or sacrifice, the incense from which is for ever and for ever mounting to the Highest in heaven. They move about like the impersonations of the Divine grace that is dimly stirring in the bosom of the age, the beacon lights of the universe, the realised hopes of the army of the good—never self-assertive, sometimes even despondent—fighting out the great battle with the army of the evil. The good triumphs: evil is vanquished and reduced to s t h ā v a r a t v a (unconsciousness). Peace reigns once again; Ī ś v a r a passes into a deep sleep. This is p r a l a y a, Universal Death to the last of the army of the evil just swooning into s t h ā v a r a t v a, the ecstasy of life to the resplendent heroes of the army of the good. When, at any stage of the world, all the j ī v a s come to be ranged under two classes, j ī v a n - m u k t a and s t h ā v a r a, there comes on this p r a l a y a or dissolution; i. e., the system of K a r m a - forces that started on the course of fruition, the cosmic ā r a b d h a, as it might be called, becomes completely dissipated; the m u k t a or liberated need not work, the s t h ā v a r a cannot work. The cycle closes; there comes the turn for the cosmic s a ñ c i t a (it may be, only a part of it) to mature itself; this includes not only the sañcita of those who have been reduced to sthāvaratva in this cycle, but also of those so reduced in other cycles. Īśvara, the soul of the Karma-organism, awakes; there is begun sṛṣṭi or creation over again.

73. And how does he create? He matures this sañcita. He proceeds according to law, according to the Vedas. The uniformity of the course of Karma-fruition is but the reflection of the Impersonal Reason, which is an emanation of Brahman co-eternal with the creative Īśvara. Īśvara, having recognised it, has breathed it out in the form of Revelation (vāk or veda). The mukta (free) souls, who have had their sañcita all burnt off by knowledge (or, it may be conceived, only those of them whose sañcita was acquired in reciprocity with the cosmic sañcita, going to be actualised in this creation), now freely, joyously get incarnated as deputy-creators of Īśvara, as the strands of His creative buddhi or grace, as His mānasa-putras (sons begotten of buddhi), as the Vedic seers (Ṛṣīs who see the mantras constituting Impersonal Reason), to quicken the sthāvaras once again into life, who now look out with young eyes of wonder on the renovated world.

74. Thus sṛṣṭi (creation) succeeds pralaya (dissolution) and pralaya succeeds sṛṣṭi. Sṛṣṭi, as through Buddhi (the will and the intellect being the same to Him), is the function of Īśvara in rajas-envelope, i.e., of Brahmā. Pralaya, its obverse, is the function of Īśvara in tamas-envelope (envelope of unconsciousness), i.e., of Maheśvara; while sthiti (or subsistence of the world) with its upward and downward trends is of Īśvara in the envelope of sattva as Providence or Viṣṇu. The alternation of the Trinity is eternal; it is only the nothingness of Karma artistically exhibited on the stage of time, the empirical picture of Īśvara being triguṇātīta an *emanation*, from His being. It may also be viewed as *evolution* from the point of view of individual souls who, in their moralised reason as evolved with the procession of cycles, recognise an increasing moral purpose in the procession, assured of their progress towards mokṣa along this "eddying yet advancing stream" of Ka ma.

75. The nature of Brahman and Īśvara has been explicated at some length. It will suffice now only to indicate the main

stages in the onward course of creation, along the three lines (1) Īśvara (as invested with parā-prakṛti). (2) individual souls as embedded in this parā and constituting the forces or the weapons of Īśvara's activity, and (3) aparā-prakṛti as gradually differentiated in response to this activity.

76. (1) and (2). In nirvikalpa-samādhi, the individual is no longer an individual, he is undifferenced Brahman. In suṣupti, he is like Īśvara, dual; Īśvara in one aspect is triguṇātīta and in another aspect invested with śuddha-sattva-upādhi or transparent envelope of sattva (section 70), and so the individual is merged in Brahman on the one hand (cf. svamapiti, attains his self) and is invested with an envelope of undifferenced buddhi on the other. On waking from deep sleep, the individual recognises that he has slept blissfully. This constitutes evidence for the envelope of buddhi and explains why it is called ānandamaya-koṣa or envelope of bliss. This ānandamaya is called the puccha or tail of Brahman who is ānanda or bliss itself without an envelope. As having limitation in the individual, it is said to be malina-sattva or partly opaque, as opposed to the śuddha-sattva or transparent envelope of Īśvara. This opacity or limitation is due to the saṁskāras or the timeless traces of the vidyā-karma (knowledge and action) of a past life which constitute the dormant individuality in suṣupti, making up what is called the Kāraṇa-śarīra (will-self) which is viewed as merged in ānandamaya. These traces again in their kinetic aspect, i.e., *viewed as operative functions*, constitute the vijñāna-maya koṣa, the envelope constituted by the original springs of thought and volition, the tendencies which may be indifferently regarded as inherited habits or as 'reminiscences of a life before this' Thus these saṁskāras or vijñānas, too, are double-faced like Janus, and lie as it were in the borderland between suṣupti and dream, 'Manomaya' is the name applied to the body constituted by manas, the receiver or unity of presentations, images and desires (as distinct from the instinctive springs which belong to vijñānamaya). Prāṇamaya is the unity of the five sense-organs (not the bodily sites but the supersensuous principles of seeing, hearing, etc..), the five organs of action (not the limbs supplied with muscles, but rather the radical 'kinaesthetic' presentations—articulation, locomotion, prehension, etc., and

lastly the five prāṇas (not 'airs' as they are often translated, but rather the five strands or currents of vital functions in the body). (Without attempting a detailed explanation of prāṇa, apāna, etc., we may point out that these are explicitly distinguished from air, e.g., in the Brahma-sūtra 'na vāyu-kriye pṛthag-upadeśāt, where Śaṅkara describes these as the adhyātma counterparts of air. In fact it would appear from other contexts that air is taken to be life instead of life being taken to be air). Liṅga-śarīra or the subtile body is the name given to the complex of the three envelopes, vijñānamaya, manomaya and prāṇamaya, which thus comprises seventeen elements (buddhi, manas, five sense-organs, five organs of action, and five vital functions). Another name is sūkṣma-śarīra, called also śiśu and madhyama-prāṇa in the Upaniṣads, where it is not often distinguished from the Kāraṇa-śarīra. The next body or envelope is the annamaya or sthūla-śarīra, the material body which the soul enters in waking life but abandons in dream etc., and after death.

77. The individual soul, as identified with the material body is the jīva or dehin; the unity of all these jīvas, the collective or cosmic self in the waking state is Virāj or Vaiśvānara. As identified with the subtile body, the individual is the liṅgin or taijasa, and the unity of all taijasas is Hiraṇyagarbha or Sūtrātman. Lastly, as identified with the Kāraṇa-śarīra, the individual is prājña, and the unity of all prājñas is Īśvara. From Īśvara to Virāj, from prājña to dehin, is the order of sṛṣṭi or progressive materialisation, the reverse being that of pralaya or progressive idealisation or deindividualisation. As the progress is continuous each stage is double-faced, and so what is predicated of Īśvara is sometimes predicated of Hiraṇyagarbha, and so on.

78. (3). We have already traced the stages of (a) māyā as co-ordinate with Brahman, (b) the unity of parā and aparā-prakṛti as co-ordinate with the triguṇātīta Īśvara, and (c) aparā with tamas predominant as co-ordinate with śuddha-sattva Īśvara. Ākāśa in the strictly adhibhūta aspect is the last, for the second, though called avyākṛta ākāśa (Section 67), is the indifference of adhyātma and adhibhūta. This ākāśa, then, is the obverse face of buddhi, the first evolute of aparā the blank of objectivity, the

prius of space and matter. Next comes vāyu, more determinate in character than ākāśa, the primordial force or motion filling this ākāśa and poising the heavenly bodies each in its proper sphere, force conceived not in its mechanical aspect but as the cosmic life-force, that which constitutes the śakti or power of the prājñas, binding the saṁskāras, individual and cosmic, to the buddhi-units and which, lower down in the course of materialisation, is the nerve-force and the objective face of undifferentiated sensitivity (touch). The attribute of ākāśa is said to be not only emptiness or blank objectivity, but also sound. This sensuous sound, though generated by air-wave, *is* not air-wave; the sense of hearing (not the bodily apparatus) apprehends the sensuous sound (as distinct from the air-wave); the locus of this sound is ākāśa. Sound again is the necessary sensuous basis for even the most abstract thoughts; so Īśvara has been said to apprehend the Impersonal Reason co-eternal with Him and to breathe it out in the shape of that potent sound-system, the Vedas. Vāyu or air has not only these attributes of ākāśa—blankness and sound—but also touch. It is thus more determinate than ākāśa, although both are said to be amūrta (without form), amṛta (imperishable), yat (going in every direction, i.e., infinite) and tya (invisible or parokṣa), in contradistinction from the three other primal matters, tejas, ap, and pṛthivī (fire, water, earth), which are said to be finite and perishable (Bṛhadāraṇyaka Upaniṣad, II, iii). Here, then, is a nodal point in the gradual procession or emanation of the five primal matters, the Vedāntic analogues of the Sāṅkhya tanmātras (though with a difference), the probable explanation why very often the Upaniṣads speak of *three* (the last three) primal matters instead of *five*. Of the three, tejas has rūpa or colour in addition to the attributes of vāyu; ap has rasa or taste (which goes with liquidity in all its variations) in addition to those of tejas; and pṛthivī has smell in addition to those of ap.

79. It may be pointed out that the theory of these five primal matters does not, in any way, conflict with the theory of the *elements* in Chemistry. The principle of classification is altogether different. The five matters are the concretes or objectives corresponding to the five kinds of sensation, the sensations[18] being taken

18. i.e. the sensa.

as the attributes of objects (and attributes in Vedānta are identical with substance). Whether such a classification is fruitful of results or not is a different enquiry; at any rate it fits in with the peculiar idealism of Vedānta. One is tempted to connect it with Mill's dictum that the number of primary laws of nature cannot be less numerous than the distinguishable feelings of the human mind; only what is regarded as a mere abstract concept or law by the empiricist is taken in Vedānta to be substantial matter (Section 42).

80. Besides, it is to be noticed that if ākāśa is conceived to stand on the level of suṣupti, and vāyu on the borderland between suṣupti and dream, the three other elements stand on the level of dream, while the elements of Chemistry are all on the level of waking or the level of gross matter. On this waking level, Vedānta would introduce these primal matters, not in their simplicity but as compounded or pañcīkṛta (quintupled). Pañcīkaraṇa is the name given to the process of the combination of the matters according to a formula like $\frac{1}{2}$a, $\frac{1}{8}$b, $\frac{1}{8}$c, $\frac{1}{8}$d, $\frac{1}{8}$e where a, b, c, d, e, stand for the matters. Sometimes when the last three matters are alone taken, the process is called trivṛtkaraṇa or tripling ($\frac{1}{2}$a, $\frac{1}{4}$b, $\frac{1}{4}$c). The ākāśa, vayu etc., which are perceived by our senses, are only the modes of this compounded matter, the primal matters being supersensuous.

81. The shadowy 'names and forms' imbedded in the primal māyā get actualised as material objects in this pañcīkṛta matter. The noumenal will-self here gets materialised into a dehin; here then is the sphere of Karma-fruition and also of moral probation.

82. We may conclude the present study with a paraphrase (with interpretations) of two cosmogonic accounts from the Upaniṣads, in illustration of the Vedāntic views already discussed. The first is from Chāndogya Upaniṣad.

VI, ii,—This (empirical world), differentiated into names and forms) was barely existent in the beginning (was the bare 'that' as distinct from the 'what'), one without a second (homogeneous with it or heterogeneous). It saw (aikṣata, thought and willed, which mean the same thing to it). 'I shall be many: I shall generate', and accordingly created tejas (fire). Then tejas thought, 'I shall be many, I shall generate', and accordingly created water.

Water next thought, 'I shall be many, I shall generate', and created earth (annam).

[This one Existent (sat) is then intelligence and not the unintelligent pradhāna of Sāṅkhya. This creation according to Saṅkara, is emanation (vivarta), for nothing can be distinct from Sat. Fire, water, etc.. also thought, i.e., as embodied in these, Sat thought and instituted the successive steps of creation. Each link in the chain of causation is not only a medium but a true cause in the reflection of the First Cause. This amounts to saying that God creates reasonably, according to Law.]

VI, iii.—All living beings, whether oviparous, viviparous, or vegetable, generate their respective seeds (These are the Jīvas or the beginningless units of individuality.)

The One God (Sat) willed, "I shall introduce myself into these three gods (fire, water, earth, the basal devatās) through this Jīva (these beginningless *principia individuationis*, i.e., as Saṅkara takes them, the saṁskāras, in the buddhi of the Sat, of the forms of a past creation) and make names and forms' manifest. I shall render each of these (basal) devatās three-fold (trivṛt) which does not deny pañcīkṛta or quintupled, explained already'. So it did.

83. The next passage is from Bṛhad-āraṇyaka-Upaniṣad. I, ii. It exhibits the characteristic mystic imagination of the Upaniṣads. Here a large latitude of conjectural interpretation must be allowed. Śaṅkara's interpretations have been accepted wherever available.

There was nothing here in the beginning. Everything was shrouded by Death or Hunger. This Hunger is Death. He created manas, in order that He might feel Himself (invested) with a mind

(This Death is here identified by Śaṅkara with Hiraṇyagarbha. He is, in fact, Hiraṇyagarbha as passing into Īśvara. He is the Universal Hunger which has retracted into itself the entire evolved world. Again, as Hunger is at once the destructive and creative stress of the prāṇamaya, so the self of dissolution or death is the self of creation or life. Thus Death wanting to be Life, i.e., wanting to create, created to Himself a mind to anticipate the creation. The will-self is imbedded in intelligence. We have already explained the alternation of pralaya and sṛṣṭi.)

He worshipped and was satisfied. As He worshipped (fire and) water came into being, as the 'embodied parts of his devotion' (pūjāṅga-bhūtāḥ).

[Death has now passed into the living mind, which now reduplicates itself, becomes self-conscious. Creation here is self-consciousness, self-worship. Worshipping a god is becoming that god. Nature is sometimes spoken of as the '*processio* of the Holy Spirit' or as 'a sacramental system'. Of the 'embodied parts of the worship', fire (with special reference to the sacrificial fire of the aśvamedha sacrifice) is the direct embodiment, and water is the indirect embodiment; for, fire is said to be situated both within and outside water. The series from ākāśa to pṛthivī is one of growing determinateness, and after vāyu, of descending magnitude, too.]

(Fire thus situated) thickened the froth of the waters and turned it into Earth. As He thus created Earth, He became fatigued and forth exuded from within his fiery perspiration.

[The self-worship of Hiraṇyagarbha means the encasement of Himself in the primal matters evolved out of tamas (i.e., out of the imperfections or Karma of the individual selves) and then the irradiation of this envelope with the fire of the self within, which makes the whole a living, developing 'mundane egg'. 'Self-worship' means 'being at once the worshipped and the grosser worshipping self'.]

Now this fire or life (prāṇa) within this mundane egg divided itself into three parts, āditya (the sun, being the eye and soul of ākāśa), air and fire, without losing its identity. (Thus all the five matters are mentioned.) This last (fire) rests on water.

He (Death) wanting a second body (other than manas) effected a junction between His mind and vāk (the World). The generative seed (entering the waters) developed into the year (sam-vatsara).

[This second body is the pañcīkṛta body of Virāj. Vāk is objective or Impersonal Reason, that which is coined into words in the Vedas. He united thought with vāk, i.e., reflected on the order of creation as laid down in the Vedas, on the eternal Logos or the Law. The generative seed is the cosmic system of vidyā-karma acquired in a previous life of Hiraṇyagarbha, the collective self of all individual units of vidyā-karma. No creation out of nothing; the matter (fire, etc.) is but aparā-prakṛti, the ignorance constituting individuality, as encasing the self; the forms are the primordial *principia individuationis*, the Karma-units; the law is eternal and is only recognised by this mind-endowed (samanaska) Hiraṇyagarbha. He makes Karma fructify, in grace (its obverse being self-worship), according to law, by reflecting on it (for His knowing is willing). The Logos, quickened by reflection becomes the generative seed (parā-prakṛti) planted in the waters (in the primal matters generally, in aparā-prakṛti) and develops into the year. The year is the eternal Idea of the concrete year; the yearly procession of events as a whole, ever repeating itself in the kaleidoscope of sensuous apprehension, represents a single pulsation (differentiation) of His life. It is the prototype of the infinite of waking time, not yet born.]

It took a year for the egg to be hatched. Thus came the year into being; there was no year before this. When the babe Virāj was born, Death opened His jaws to devour it, and virāj screamed out in terror. Thus speech came into being.

[The babe is the waking world just beginning to see light. It is the first waking actuality, the potentiality of all the future. The phenomenal world, however, from the moment it comes into being, is in the jaws of death (cp. Chāndogya, mṛtyunā grastameva); it is an illusory differentiation. Virāj screamed as the babe just born would scream, as its blank consciousness emerges from the dark unconsciousness which still hangs over it. Sound is, in more senses than one, the bridge between the visible world and the invisible.]

Death paused and thought. 'Why devour the babe? (Let it have its spell of sensuous development.)' So it developed according to vāk (Impersonal Reason) into the articulate Vedas, Vedic metres, sacrifices, men, animals etc.

[Vāk has three forms: (1) Objective Reason. (2) this as actualised in thought or reflection. (3) this as sensuously developed into the Vedas........ The Vedas are again prior in reality to the phenomenal world. The position of sound (ākāśa) between phenomenon and noumenon is to be noticed.]

All this sensuous creation He seized to devour. Death desired to celebrate a second Aśvamedha (horse-sacrifice, the first being that performed in a previous life by virtue of which

He came to exist at the beginning of the cycle). He became weary and began to practise susterities (t a p a s). Forth departed from His body (the V i r ā j - body) sentiency and power, leaving it 'turgid and defiled'. But his mind never lost sight of it.

(The V i r ā j - body has to die, to be sacrificed in order to live. He was weary, impressed with the nothingness of the sensuous body as such, which is always in the jaws of death. But this sensuous life has to be lived through. Let it be a life of self-sacrifice then. Let the body be purified. So His heart was all along set on this purification.)

He thought, 'Let this body be m e d h y a first, i.e.. worthy of being sacrificed, and then I shall get embodied in it'. Meanwhile the body had become 'turgescent' (a ś v a t), and so as He entered it once again, He became an a ś v a or horse (a sensuous body which the higher self fills, but with which it does not get confused. May we not trace here something like the stages of modern Ethics : (i) naive sensuousness, (ii) a division in spirit and asceticism, the sensuous body to be thoroughly mortified, (iii) reinstatement of the sensuous self as conscious of its nothingness by itself yet justifying its existence as an organ of duty?)

He let the horse loose for a year (as they do at the A ś v a - m e d h a ceremony) and then tied it up and offered it as a sacrifice, offered up each animal as a sacrifice to its proper god (offered up Himself as a sacrifice to Himself) and thus attained the state of P r a j ā p a t i. Thus He conquered the second death (became the archetypal Life, and is not born again to be devoured by death).

[The year here stands for the cycle of s a ṁ s ā r a, the wheel of K a r m a from which j ī v a s fly at a tangent into m o k ṣ a (liberation), into a Death which has conquered itself, into Eternal Life. 'Letting Loose' represents the fact that God lets the individual eliminate his K a r m a by K a r m a, till in knowledge the individuality lapses altogether.]

CHAPTER III

VEDĀNTIC LOGIC

(Mainly based on Vedānta-paribhāṣa)

84. The central truth of the Vedāntic system, the pure self or Brahman as undifferenced 'being, consciousness, and bliss', together with other ancillary truths about supersensuous things, is taken by Vedānta to be essentially revealed, not ascertained by any human evidence like that of perception or inference. The self that is immediately perceived, for example, is not known to be existent, far less to be existent after death. (Śaṅkara says this in his introductory note to Bṛhadāraṇyaka-Upaniṣad, and it is pretty much the same as what Kant says about the 'paralogisms of the Pure Reason'.) True, even in Vedānta, arguments are advanced in proof of the existence and immortality of the soul, but these are *only suggestions of the Beyond by* phenomenal signs, not proofs positive, as they have been taken by Naiyāyikas. If the ecstatic intuition in which alone the supersensuous is knowable is not forthcoming at once, and if the phenomenal world only *suggests* the noumenon as a thought, though it may be necessary thought, how is the enquiry into it to begin at all? Some provisional belief (śraddhā) is required to start the enquiry. A mere thought, even though necessary, can never induce belief, can never be mistaken for knowledge; for in knowledge there is an unmistakable intuitive or 'given' character. This provisional belief can only be induced by authoritative statement (śabda or āgama) which may, for aught we know, be disproved afterwards. But the statement gains in reliability if on acting on it or after contemplation of it we attain a progressive *satisfaction or realisation*. That is the only justification which we may expect to have of the truth of what is claimed to be revelation, from below, i.e., before we have finally realised its truth. Whether metaphysical enquiry necessarily presupposes a revelation is an issue which need not be confused with the other issue whether the Veda itself is revealed or not. If it be granted that spirit can only teach spirit and that truth can only be *recognised* and not created by mental activity, it must also be granted that revelation is necessary, and that the Word is God, and that

accordingly there should be an eternal succession of omniscient teachers.

85. At the same time Vedānta allows that for the attainment of the knowledge of Brahman, there is required not only śravaṇa (hearing of revealed texts and trying to understand them) but also manana and nididhyāsana. The exact relation of these processes has been disputed, but the processes themselves are recognised in all Vedāntic schools. Manana is defined as 'the mental act which generates knowledge by means of arguments defending the truth embodied in the texts against objections preferred by other evidences' (pramāṇa). Inference, and the other natural sources of knowledge, cannot yield the sacred truths but only point to them. So the proofs of the existence of God in European philosophy have sometimes been pronounced to be no proofs, for the conclusion there necessarily transcends the premises: Inference, etc., however, show the direction along which one may proceed to the truths. They refute heretical objections; and by detaining the thoughts about the truths, they enable the mind to get a tight grip of them and thus prepare the way for realising them in ecstatic intuition.

86. Hence the position of logic in Vedānta. It considers all the pramāṇas or sources of knowledge. They are six in number: pratyakṣa, anumāna, upamāna, āgama, arthāpatti, anupalabdhi. It is advisable to keep up the Sanskrit names, instead of giving the ordinary translations, some of which are, to say the least, misleading. Other schools of Indian Philosophy give shorter lists, but Vedānta vindicates the necessity of each of these pramāṇas. It will be noticed that logic here is conceived to have a more extended scope than is ordinarily allowed to it, including as it does a consideration not only of mediate but also of immediate knowledge. It necessarily comprises a good deal of epistemological matter.

87. Knowledge is of two kinds: anubhava, reached through evidence, which may be both true (when it is pramā) and false, but which is always something *new*, previously unattained: and smṛti or memory-knowledge which, however, is not something new. In the persisting cognition of the same object, there is a single unchanging presentation illuminated by, i.e., subsumed under the form of the self. Such a persisting

determinate cognition (as distinct from the presentation) ceases, however, when it is contradicted by another cognition standing on stronger evidence. The theory of the persistence of the presentation fits in with the peculiar realism of Vedānta which demands an intuition-continuum for every grade of abstract thought (Section 34). The necessary thought of the identity between a presentation and an idea must have its basis in the continuity of the presentation in some real medium. Besides, as knowledge is viewed in Vedānta from the standpoint of the self as spontaneity and not from the empirical standpoint, the logical activity of the self (and not the presentation) is taken to determine *how long* a mode of cognition can be said to endure as one and the same; it is said to cease only when contradicted.

PRATYAKṢA

(EXTERNAL AND INTERNAL PERCEPTION)

88. Perception, as has already been explained (Section 23) is Brahman itself, the immediate identity of knower and known. In fact the attitude of nirvikalpa-samādhi is retained in the perception of phenomenal objects. There is a difference, no doubt, between the timeless knowledge of Brahman and the abrupt emergence of the perceptual knowledge; but even in the latter the knowledge by itself is timeless and quiescent, its manifestation only being in time. The image of dust-motes getting into a quiescent sunbeam will furnish an apt illustration. Presentations are in time; they manifest the self and limit it at the same time. All determinate knowledge is a self-abnegation, involving as it does a stratification of the pure consciousness or caitanya into three forms: Pramātṛ-caitanya or determinate self-consciousness, vṛtti-caitanya or modes of consciousness, and viṣaya-caitanya or empirical object.

89. In perception the manas (streaming out of the sense-orifices of the body in visual and auditory perception and keeping at its bodily seat in the other forms of sense-perception) is said to take the form of the object, i.e., get determined into a mode or vṛtti like the object, occupying the same position in space and time as the object, both being pervaded by an identical (determinate) consciousness or caitanya, provided, of course, the object is capable (yogya) of being cognised by the senses. An explanation is necessary.

90. That an influence from the object produces sensation in us need not be denied by Vedānta. The point here is the explanation of that extra-organic localisation which specially marks visual and auditory perception. Now in perception, there is a tendency to slur over the sensation-sign and pass at once to its significate, constituted by motor and other ideas. What is this *signifying*? Rapid association, mental chemistry may be granted, but what is it from the point of view of the self? From the standpoint then of the self, as invested with manas, as knowing the not-self *in space* viewed through the glasses of the manas, may it not be held that the Vedāntic account of the mind going out to meet the object is truer than the confused physiological account that the object or influence from the object comes to meet the mind as located in the body? Even in the grossest form of consciousness, when the body is taken to be the point of reference, not being distinguished from the self, Vedānta recognises in this going out the priority of the knower to the object and so still keeps the meaning of knowledge intact. If it be argued that growing reflection will shift the point of reference from the body to something more spiritual, it is replied that unless one rises to levels of consciousness higher than the waking, the self cannot be thought of except as located in the body. The objection that the streaming out of manas involves a materialistic conception is easily disposed of if we remember that Vedānta recognises no absolute distinction (Section 42) between the self and material object but admits grades of emanatory existences between them, each being material in relation to the grade before it, what we mean by matter coming last in the series. Ultimately no doubt Vedānta will hold that the body is phenomenal, this space also is phenomenal, and that this 'going out' of the mind is only illusory.

91. 'The mind takes the form of the object'. It is the idea of the conformity of the mental order with a *given* order. No idealisation can completely do without this *given* element. Below ecstatic intuition where this 'given'-ness completely disappears, dualism is inevitable.

92. The mind and the object occupy the same space-position. This distinguishes perception from inference. In inference, the mind only *thinks* of the inferred object but does not go out to meet it. The distinction is practically that drawn in modern psycho-

logy, only viewed from the point of view of the self's spontaneity, that in perception the given element and its interpretation are welded together in a unity, while in inference they are kept distinct. In perception the self as invested with the mental mode (the interpretative concept which, relatively to the sensation, is the beginningless v ā s a n ā or s a ṁ s k ā r a, analogous to the eternal names and forms actualised in creation) becomes further materialised into the particular function of the sense-organ excited by the particular stimulus (and this might be regarded as a maturation of its K a r m a). In inference the self just expects to be realised: it descends from its plane to a lower plane, but not to the lowest. (Sometimes the tension is so great that it discharges itself in the waking plane, in other words, inference lapses into a percept, as in 'I see my brother'. Does not this show that all perception is illusory, as it is always *seeming* to see, the mind forgetting itself and becoming the body)?

93. The perceptive act and the object occupy the same time-position. The object of memory precedes the act of memory. But it may be e k a d e s a with it, i.e., occupy the same position as it, in the same sense in which, in internal perception, a pleasure is said to be e k a d e ś a with the perception of the pleasure. What then is this d e ś a? It should be remembered that in V e d ā n t a, ā k ā ś a appears in all the stages, waking, dream, etc., and there is the theory of the intermediate existences between self and matter.

94. One c a i t a n y a pervades both v i ṣ a y a (empirical object) and v ṛ t t i (apprehending mental mode). This is readily understood in the light of Kant's theory of the self working unconsciously in the object-consciousness: all consciousness is *implicitly* self-consciousness. This 'implicitness', this indistinguishable blending of the subject and object, is precisely what is brought out in this identity of c a i t a n y a (self) covering v i ṣ a y a (object) and v ṛ t t i (mental mode).

95. Y o g y a t v a or 'the object being capable of being perceived' distinguishes perception from ś a b d a (knowledge through authoritative statement) which last can take cognisance of supersensuous objects as spiritual merit and demerit (d h a r m ā d h a r m a).

96. In the case of a judgment in which the subject is perceived but the predicate is inferred, or in which the terms are per-

ceived through different senses, if the judgment be *one* substantive mental state, the foregoing account of the perceptual process is not tenable; for how can manas at once go out of the body and be in it, or go out of two different sense-orifices at the same time? But then, according to Vedānta, the judgment is not *one* state but rather a process from the subject-thought to the predicate thought. It would appear, from its criticism of Nyāya, that a judgment, according to it, does not involve a conceptualistic universal, co-substantial with the terms and eternally connected with them (Section 43). Vedānta might hold that this transition from the subject to the predicate is a necessary thought of the union of the terms, but then this does not mean their concrete identity-in-difference. If the thought be concretely *realised* (in the Vedāntic sense, i.e., through the judging self being de-individualised), the relation will cease to be relation; one would *see* their undifferenced identity. When the copula is concretely realised, the terms are lower in reality; when the copula is only abstract, the terms are of higher reality.

97. The perception of object so long discussed may not amount to the knowledge of object as object, i.e., as distinct from the subject and yet related to it. Mere perception of object requires only the coincidence of vṛtti-caitanya with viṣaya-caitanya (Section 88), but the perception of object as object requires also their coincidence with pramātṛ-caitanya. It requires that the self should not be a mere logical pre-supposition: it should come out as determinate self-consciousness as distinct from object-consciousness. The vṛtti or mental mode in relation to which the object exists—for the object is only empirical object—is a determination of pramātṛ or the determinate self. The vṛtti then points two ways, towards the self and towards the object. At each moment, the whole of manas gets modified into vṛtti (this being vivarta or emanation, not pariṇāma or real modification), by the ripening of some saṁskāra or Karma-seed, under the stress of the cosmic Karma-organism appearing as stimulus. So on the one hand the saṁskāra gets materialised into a percept and the percept into a bodily (cerebral) impression; on the other the cosmic stress takes the form of the phenomenal object (and that gives the sense-stimulus). (This account has to be expanded a little to explain the extra-organic localisation in visual and auditory perception.) Thus the

pramātṛ-caitanya rests on the viṣaya-caitanya in the perception of the object as object.

98. In the internal perception of the self, the pramātṛ-caitanya does not rest on viṣaya-caitanya, but rests simply on vṛtti. Not that it is then the *pure self* seeing the vṛtti as object; it sees, only as *invested with* vṛtti, only as determined, i.e., as it sees in a dream. So Śaṅkara, in his commentary on Bṛh. Upaniṣad IV. iii, points out that in the stage of dream the self-luminous (svayaṁ-jyoti) self sees the dream-forms as object and therefore is itself revealed; but in the stage of suṣupti, where vṛtti or mental mode lapses altogether, the self-luminosity is *not* revealed, being present in its purity. To be visible, an object must not be perfectly transparent.

99. So it is held on the one hand that ahaṁkāra (section 57) requires a vṛtti or empirical mode and on the other that even in illusory object-consciousness, there is a real materialisation of the self. The last point requires explanation. When the nacre is mistaken for silver, the nacre, a mode of māyā (as every phenomenal object is) modifies the mental mode coincident with it by the idea of silver which it revives by similarity. The self looking through it sees the objective illusory mode, silver. This theory of an objective illusory mode or anirvacanīya existence is characteristic of Vedānta.

100. *Objections met*:—(1) If the illusory object, silver, is created in the absence of silver, we could see anything of which we have an idea, i.e., there could be no difference between image and percept. So it is held by the anyathā-khyāti-vādin that in such a case, the self freely, perversely applies to the nacre a predicate, silver, which does not belong to it but to something else. No illusory object, silver, is here created. We only *think*, pass *intellectually* to, the object silver which, however, exists somewhere. The reply is that to take the interpretative element in perception (true or false) to be merely intellectual or merely associational (representative) would be alike wrong: it is really a concept based on an associated image. This concept is the necessary *objective* element, the image is the *subjective* element. Yet though the subjective element is there, Vedānta would argue against the ātma-khyāti-vādin that the silver in this case is not *consciously* remembered. Such a subjectivity, unconscious of its subjectivity, is nothing but the anirvācya or

'inexplicable', prātibhāsika or illusory objectivity. The objectivity, however, which is contrasted with a conscious subjectivity, would be the phenomenal or vyāvahārika reality. In the presence of the thing-in-itself or pāramārthika reality, these two realities are just the same, both illusory; but this thing-in-itself is knowable precisely because in the reflection of its light, māyā itselt is differentiated into the (phenomenally) real and the illusory.

101. (2) How to know that this nacre is silver? Through the coincidence in position (ekadeśatva) of the two objective modes of māyā, the corresponding subjective modes, and pramātṛ-caitanya. (3) Why is not the illusory silver apparent to all? An object-determination is a determination of the particular subject who has the illusion. That most things, however, appear much the same to all is explained by a community of the Karma of different selves. (4) If in all judgments, there is a transition from one cognition to another (Section 96), how can there be a false perceptual judgment at all? It is replied that in the perceptual judgment 'this nacre is silver', there is a coincidence of the determinations of caitanya corresponding to 'this' and 'silver'; as a single cognition, therefore, it admits of truth and falsehood. (5) Why not say, 'this is sometimes silver, sometimes nacre'?—Because when the (apparent) percept of silver ceases, one is not conscious of the real silver being absent but only of the illusory siver having vanished (Section 46). When a percept is contradicted by another percept, there is indeed no final guarantee that the contradicting percept is not illusory instead of the contradicted percept—for there can be such a thing as illusion of illusion; still there is the psychological fact that while in the contradicting perception, one has to believe that it is true and that the contradicted perception is false. It is the abrupt disappearance of the silver when looked at carefully with the naive belief (coupled in many cases with a reflective inferential belief) that what is looked at carefully is real, that accounts for our disbelief in the persistence of silver.

ANUMĀNA (INFERENCE)

102. The Vedāntic theory of the nature of inference is best studied in relation to the Nyāya theory of inference in its two aspects, inference as the process of discovering truth for

oneself (svārtha), and as the form of proving or exhibiting the truth to others (parārtha). The main contention between Vedānta and Nyāya is in regard to the former.

103. Three stages in the inferential process are recognised in Nyāya. In the example, 'the mountain has fire, because it has smoke', there must have been established, first, a constant concomitance (vyāpti) between fire and smoke, from their occurring together in kitchens, etc.; then this smoke must have been perceived in the mountain (pakṣa-dharmatā); and finally this last relation is combined with the memory of the vyāpti (tṛtīya-liṅga-parāmarśa) in order to get the conclusion. 'the mountain has fire'. In other words, the middle term is first (inductively) related to the major, then to the minor, and then the two relations are related to one another. The three processes may be symbolised thus:—(i) Am connected with Ap, Bm—Bp, Cm—Cp......therefore m-p; (ii) Xm has m (is like Am, Bm, which have p); (iii) Xm has m, m-p; (reappearing in memory); the two together leading to 'therefore, Xm has p'.

104. To this account Vedānta has the following objections: (a) The first two stages precede the inference and are no part of it; (b) 'm-p' in the third stage is more a function (saṃskāra or vyāpāra) than a substantive mental state, though it is a conscious function. being quickened with the consciousness of the middle term; (c) 'm-p', the function, though retained in memory, is not operative as a conscious *remembrance*. (A conscious remembrance of it may sometimes accompany the inference though forming no part of it). (d) The whole proposition, 'Xm has p' is not inferred : p only is inferred, Xm being perceived.

105. The second objection, in a sense, comprehends all the others. It is connected with the Vedāntic position on jāti already explicated (Section 43). When Mill holds that the conclusion in a syllogism is drawn, not *from* the premises but *according* to them only, that not rules but facts constitute the evidence, he agrees with Vedānta (and Hegel) in disbelieving in the abstract universal being co-substantial with things and eternally connected with them. How can an eternal thing be eternally connected with non-eternal things? The so-called axiom of the syllogism cannot possibly subsume particulars under it, for the simple reason that no premise is absolutely true. From the purely conceptualistic

point of view (that of Nyāya), the unity of the inferential act is never really attained; the relation of relations, as in tṛtīya-liṅga-parāmarśa, is unintelligible. So long as the universal is regarded as a substantive state of the mind and not a spontaneity (a 'transitive' state, as James would call it), the judgment must be regarded as pieced out of terms and reasoning as pieced out of the separate judgments, instead of reasoning being regarded as the unity prior to them all. Not that Vedānta accepts the Hegelian solution of the identity of contradictories. To it, the entire inferential process is summed up in the single word 'function', which does not constitute a substantive unity with the given minor term and the major term. Hence, too, the conclusion is taken to be, not the whole proposition 'Xm has p' but only p. This accords with the Vedāntic view of the judgment, already presented under perception (Section 96). This is also intelligible in the light of the general Vedāntic position that a grade of reality (to which, for example, the jāti as the connotational universal belongs) (Section 42) is unconsciously immanent in the next grade (to which the corresponding vyaktis or individuals belong) which it transcends but where, if consciously emergent at all, it is taken as an abstract thought lower in point of reality. Buddhi which is the self-affirmation in the copula, transcends manas which is yet informed by it. The axiom of the syllogism, like axioms in general, stands on the level of buddhi and is a timeless saṁskāra.

106. It must not be supposed, however, that Vedānta takes this process or function to be merely blind expectation, the working of an anudbuddha or unawakened saṁskāra. The awaking of it helps on the function (tadudbodhasyāpi sahakāritvāt). It is in fact a conscious function, an intellectual synthesis and not an imaginative or associational synthesis. The major premise, according to Mill, is only a concurrent or subsequent justification of the conclusion. But is not the justification essential to inference as distinct from association? So Spencer holds in his Psychology (Special Analysis, Reasoning), where he says that though the major premise comes after the conclusion, it is recognised to have been operative before the conclusion, the recognition being the completion of the reasoning, without which in fact the reasoning would not be reasoning. In 'the mountain has fire because it has smoke', the perception of the

smoke rouses into conscious activity the saṁskāra of the relation between smoke and fire. This saṁskāra, though conscious, is not present as a conscious memory (smṛti). The logical ground of inference is objective; it is not subjective memory. In illusory perception and in dreams, the anirvacanīya object (Section 99) is a memory-image, unconscious of its memory-character.

107. As to the major premise itself or vyāpti, it is not an inference by itself, being only the saṁskāra generated by the observation of the concomitance (anvaya) between the major term and the middle term (and non-observation of non-concomitance), but not by the observation of the concomitance of the absences of the terms (vyatireka). As against Nyāya, it is argued that the positive evidence alone generates belief. The negative evidence only assures the reason, constitutes a collateral justification. It is clear that this criticism of Nyāya is directly connected with the Vedāntic position that the major premise is only a *function*, a consciously *operative* universal, and not an abstract reason only. All inference is then anvayirūpa, i.e., founded on positive concomitance. It is not, however, to be called Kevalānvayi, as arguments like 'this pot is knowable because nameable' are called, where according to Nyāya, vyatireka-vyāpti, i.e., concomitance between not-nameable and not-knowable is not ascertainable, because the terms do not stand for anything existent. According to Vedānta, there is no Kevalānvayi inference; as Brahman is the constant *ground* of all differenced reality, the negation of all things is existent. According to nominalistic existential logic, the negative concept 'not-A' which has no positive existent equivalent, is altogether inadmissible in logic; and therefore a positive concept like A, of which the negation is non-existent, is also inadmissible. According to conceptualistic logic (including Nyāya), there is a place for all that is conceivable, and therefore there is a place for a concept like A, though not-A be non-existent. In realistic Vedānta (realistic like Kantianism), even the self-contradictory, not to speak of a mere conceivable, is positive; and what would sound paradoxical, the self-contradictory is the only positive both in the sense that the phenomenon in which contradiction is immanent is the only thing determinately knowable, Brahman being indeterminate, and in the sense that, apart from Brah-

man to which all contradictory predicates aspire, the phenomenal system is a house of cards or mere negation.

108. Vedānta further holds that the *number* of the instances observed is inessential to the induction or vyāpti. How to reconcile this with the view of empirical logic that it is *the one* essential point in induction? Spencer, in his discussion of the Universal Postulate, holds, as against Mill, that though the belief in an axiom is generated by the instances, they are not separately registered in the mind but rather operate as a consolidated function, the inconceivability of the opposite being its negative justification. So the positively operative universal is not the separate instances but the knowledge of the objective relation between the middle term and the major term. How this knowledge or belief is itself generated, how the number of instances affects its *strength*, is a question for psychology rather than for logic. The so-called syllogism of inclusion or exclusion is no inference at all or is inference only because the number leads us to expect some necessary connotational connexion. Logic is concerned primarily with truth and only secondarily, if at all, with the intensity of the belief and degree of certainty.

109. So much for the process of inference (svārtha). To exhibit its cogency to others (parārtha), we require an ideal form like the syllogism which is no inference but only the form of inference. Here, too, a difference emerges between Nyāya and Vedānta. Where Nyāya states five members of the syllogism—(i) The mountain has fire; (ii) Because of the smoke; (iii) Whatever has smoke has fire, as the kitchen; (iv) This mountain has it; (v) Therefore it has fire.—, Vedānta states only three, either the first three, (analytical) or the last three (synthetical). The third member represents the major premise with the statement of an instance ('the kitchen'), other than the minor term, falling under the middle term, which is necessary to obviate the appearance of a petitio principii in the syllogism. The second or the fourth member represents the minor premise and the first or the fifth the conclusion. The two premises, appearing only as functions in svārtha inference, have to be exhibited as substantive propositions in parārtha inference. The considering of them together to secure the unity of the inference, which is taken by Nyāya to be a distinct step in svārtha inference, is exhibited by it in the parārtha inference by presenting the

minor premise twice, first as the second member which is the bare cognition of the middle term, and then as the fourth member which is this cognition spread out as a proposition, and sandwiching the vyāpti-function, here spread out as the major premise between them, the conclusion, too, is put both at the beginning and at the end. All this, apparently, according to Vedānta, is artificial; for in parārtha inference, we should trust the hearer to *function* for himself and content ourselves with sketching the outlines of the language-picture which might start the necessary functioning in his mind.

110. Hegel has taught us to look beyond logical forms, to the absolute realities of which they are shadows. Now the absolute of pratyakṣa or perception is Brahman (Section 88); it reveals Brahman even in a phenomenal object. To admit empirical reality is at the same time to admit the concept of reality. So inference reveals to us the unreality of the phenomenal universe, the members of the absolute inference being, 'This universe is unreal, because different from Brahman; all that is different from Brahman is unreal, like the silver in the nacre'. It has already been explained that when one is just passing into an intuition of Brahman, one feels that everything different from Brahman is unreal. Had it not been for the well-known difference between illusion and phenomenon (prātibhāsika and vyāvahārika) which gives us the concept of unreality, the unreality of phenomenon would have been inconceivable as being absolutely without analogy; mokṣa would have been an abrupt irrational affair. On the other hand, had it not been for the implicit consciousness of Brahman or Reality, there would have been no difference between truth and untruth within phenomena. Thus the absolute of inference is Brahman informing all knowledge against illusion within the phenomenal region and availing Himself of this self-created antithesis to negate the whole phenomenal existence, to work out Karma by Karma, and thus to return to His undifferenced self. This process of Brahman is Īśvara or Hegel's Absolute Idea.

UPAMĀNA

111. Upamāna is the source of the knowledge of similarity. It is an independent pramāṇa. Whatever gives us new and certain knowledge is pramāṇa. Now the knowledge of similarity

is certainly *new* knowledge, not mere memory. It is direct knowledge, not inferential, for it is felt to be so; besides, what possible proof can there be of similarity? Can it be called 'perception' of similarity? No; two like things may not be both presented at the same time. Yet, it may be urged that the idea of the one and presentation of the other are synchronous; and is not perception itself a presentative-representative process? The reply is, this will explain only the perception of the common elements, not the consciousness of the *relation* of similarity. If, however, the relation be taken *only as a feeling*, as it is taken by all thorough-going empiricists, e.g., by the Buddhists (cf. Śaṅkara's reply to this, Section 49), by Mill (in his Logic), and by Spencer (in his Psychology), it may no doubt be said to be perceived. But knowledge is always viewed in Vedānta, not from the empirical standpoint, but from the standpoint of the self as spontaneity. It may be objected that from this standpoint, the consciousness of similarity is the same as the recognition of identity (knowledge which is mere memory, no new knowledge or anubhava at all). But they can hardly be taken to be the same. It will not do to say with some psychologists that similar things have an identical element and that suggestion of a similar is only assimilation followed by contiguous association. The artificiality of such a view is manifest. Identity is no doubt the truth of the similarity, but the psychological difference between the two is absolute to us, so long as we are confined to empirical consciousness. In the ecstatic intuition of Brahman, one is not conscious of a similarity with (or difference from) other experiences. The consciousness of similarity lies midway between the blind feeling of familiarity and the ecstatic intuition of identity. In this consciousness, there is a process, a swinging of the self backward and forward, bespeaking a limitation of its freedom. Hence it is a new kind of pramāṇa. First B is felt to be like A and then, as a result of it, A is felt to be like B. B at first suggests its similar A through the *function* of similarity (cf. Bradley on Association in his Principles of Logic), though here, too, as in the case of the *function* of vyāpti in inference, it is consciously operative (Section 104); and then the self swings back from A to B (i.e., the functional activity of similarity is transformed into the substantive consciousness of similarity).

ĀGAMA

112. V ā k y a, a sentence or series of sentences in which there is a principal one to which the others are subordinate, is said to be a p r a m ā ṇ a or independent source of knowledge. The right appreciation of this p r a m ā ṇ a will depend on the understanding of a certain theory of language with which it is bound up. When we say 'a word *means* a thing', we do not mean that the word reminds us of the idea of a thing. We may no doubt consciously pause to remember or visualise the ideas. but this remembering is not understanding the meaning of the word, any more than any irrelevant idea, of which we are reminded by a word, is a part of the meaning. The word *directly* refers to the thing, expresses the thing, *touches* it (B ṛ h. U p a n i ṣ a d I, V, 3) in a sense. Psychologists speak of the primitive tendency to *reify* names, but have we got beyond this reification even now? With the same naiveté with which we objectify our ideas in perception, we *objectify the word*. The free concept not only requires the name for its support but is identical with it, though transcending it. Just as the presentative and representative elements of perception are not only associated but identified, being covered by the same determination of the self and objectified by it, so too in conception, the same determination of the self gives the name and the concept an identical object-reference. This unity of the name and the concept works unconsciously even in perception.

113. The sentence at once refers to an objective relation. The moment it is employed (provided of course it is a complete sentence, satisfying certain conditions, to be explained presently) a belief is generated in something objective. So Mill argued against the conceptualistic theory of judgment that 'the sun is hot' does not mean that the idea of the sun is the idea of hot. The copula of a judgment is the self[19] pointing necessarily to an object and the unity of the sentence is but this self clothed in language. The primordial objective reference of a judgment is a provisional belief, a belief, it may be, with a certain general cautiousness induced by experience: if it is only *thought*, it is at any rate *continuous* with knowledge. The mere absence of conflict with other evidence is sufficient to turn it into knowledge: we do not require a positive confirmation by other evidence.

19 The author, perhaps, means to say that the copula represents the assertive function of the self.

114. The understanding or the self in judgments transcends judgments and points to the Ideas of the Reason or noumena. They are to be realised only in ecstatic intuition, but till that is forthcoming, the necessary thought of them must have some intuition-basis, viz., a name. Yet just as an Idea of the Reason intrinsically spurns all sense-intuition as being completely inadequate, so too ordinary names constitute only the means by which such an Idea is pointed to, not its support or *expression*. Each noumenon demands its true expression, and as Schopenhauer remarked, a potent musical sound constitutes its direct objectification whereas other aesthetic symbols are mere imitations of its grosser objectifications. Such potent sound-symbols are supplied by the mantras, by such mystic syllables as the Om, the power of which is not to be judged by any apriori reasoning but only through the persistent attempt to realise them by devout intonation. A conventional word comes to *mean* a thing, to be provisionally *identified* with a thing, only through this necessary demand of the thing for its true sound-symbol.

115. The same result is reached in another way. Though every vākya, as having a direct objective intention, has the appearance of impersonality, yet as it may be ambiguous or false and may have reference to phenomenal truth, a subjective personal element has also to be taken into account. It is only in true statements about the supersensuous that this personal element is wholly eliminated. The supersensuous, as has been already explained (Section 84), to be thought at all, must have been revealed. The Vedas claim to be the repository of all such true statements about the supersensuous; and whether the claim is allowed or not, the true revelation, wherever it is found, must have also the true form, and therefore the perfection or the sacredness of it must transfigure every sound (or letter) composing it.

116. To this theory of the identity between thought and language, Nyāya takes an objection which easily connects itself with the conceptualistic theory of the judgment. The subject and predicate of a judgment are, according to it, subsumed under the same abstract universal. In modern language, the proposition states the 'congruence or confliction of concepts'. The sentence, then, has not an immediate, objective reference; the objective reference is mediate, i.e., gained through inference like the following: Sentences (satisfying certain conditions) in the past gave rise

to thoughts which were found to accord with objective relations; here is a sentence (satisfying these conditions), therefore it is expected to accord with objective relations. In the last resort, then, a word is taken to be eternally connected with its meaning by mere convention (saṅketa) or by the will of God (Īśvarecchā). In the case of the Vedas, they are taken to be a system of sounds *created* by the personal author, Īśvara (pauruṣeya).

117. Vedānta, however, holds that the system of sounds is not created but only manifested. When a letter is articulated it is not created but only manifested in sensuous form (dhvani). Whenever a sound is produced, we recognise it as 'that sound'. If we are to believe in this recognition, every distinctive sound-form must be taken to have a persistence, not as air-vibration, but as sound-form (in its immediacy, as sensuous objectivity). The manifestation alone is in time but the sound-form is eternal. Thus the eternity of 'names' (nāma-rūpa) and the impersonal reality of the Word are intelligible. The question of the *primum cognitum* naturally leads to the theory of the eternal pre-existence of all differences that come to be manifested (section 42). The Word which is thus manifested to us is to be regarded as the Word existent in all previous cycles, now freely *remembered* and manifested by Īśvara. So Virāj at birth remembered he has Brahman ('ahamBrahmāsmi'-Bṛh. Upaniṣad). To Īśvara, who is eternally free in intelligence and volition, all these remembrances before each creation (sṛṣṭi) are one, and all these sṛṣṭis are but the timeless actualisation of the same Vedas or objective Reason. To the individual, however, the manifestation in a particular cycle is *new*.

118. The Word is co-eternal with Īśvara, both being Infinite determinations of Brahman, and it is noticeable that the same word śakti or power is used to indicate both the relation of Īśvara to created (manifested) things and the relation of the Word (and therefore any word) to its objective meaning. In both cases, this śakti, though but māyā investing Brahman (Section 52), is turned into an impersonal reality by the irradiation of Brahman.

119. The meaning of a word is two-fold, direct (śakya) and implied (lakṣya). The object which is directly meant is that towards which the word functions through its śakti. A word refers to a thing through its jāti or class. The reference

to the individual is not independent of the reference to the universal (substance and attribute being taken to be identical in Vedānta), except in cases where the name directly points to the thing. The śakti is there said to be svarūpa-satī, i.e., functioning in itself but not jñātā-hetu, i.e., not functioning as known. No doubt the direct reference of a word to (or its identity with) the universal also is unaccountable, but it is still jñātā-hetu, i.e., self-conscious reference and not a mere pointing out with the finger. Although essence and an existent partaking of the essence (viśeṣaṇa and viśeṣya) are not different in reality, they are absolutely distinct aspects to the judging or discursive reason. The self of the understanding is, as Kant said, for the objective judgment, is unconsciously immanent in the empirical object, and at the same time it is an idea of the Reason, a noumenon transcending the empirical object.

120. The reference to the individual through the universal is to be taken as only an implied reference or lakṣaṇā. This lakṣaṇā is not the function of a single word but of the whole sentence. The sentence reacts on each word that it contains. How is that possible? How do śakya and lakṣya blend? Just as in perception, the concept unconsciously synthesises the intuition, so in a judgment the copular unity modifies each of the terms. 'A is B' is really equivalent to 'AB is AB'. The sentence is an organic unity and each word in it partakes of the common life. The judgment has a tendency to lapse into a concept. This is noticeable in eulogistic or abusive sentences which are not meant to be literally taken but express simply praise or abuse. Ultimately the sentence-unity is only for the knowledge of particular objects, and the members of this unity, the concepts, also refer to them.

121. Not every combination of words, however, constitutes a true sentence, but only such as has the conditions of ākāṁkṣā, yogyatā, āsatti, and tātparya. These might be roughly translated as 'syntactical connexion' (the mutual demand of the essential parts of a sentence for one another, as the demand of a verb for its subject of a transitive verb for its object, etc.), 'compatibility of meaning' (of parts of the sentence), 'proximity of the parts', and the 'objective intention'. The abstract assertive form of a sentence is determined byākāṁkṣāas the self thinks of object through the categories, though sometimes the assertive form appears

almost in its purity as in the appositional construction (abhedānvaya) 'this pot is a blue pot', where there is no ākāṁkṣā ('syntactical connexion' therefore is too wide a rendering). This assertive form, determinate or otherwise, may be perfect, though there may not be compatibility of meaning, as in 'this square is round'. This compatibility of meaning is what is ordinarily called consistency, though it has a material aspect, too, for in one sense even a self-contradictory sentence is conceivable through the propositional form. Āsatti or the proximity of the parts has reference to the articulatory or written form of a sentence rather than to the thought-unity, though this form is but the expression of the unity. It is that which makes us understand omitted words in elliptical constructions and unites the direct meaning of the words of a sentence with their implied meaning. Tātparya is the capacity of a sentence to produce objective knowledge. It is not the subjective intention of the person uttering the sentence, though in cases of ambiguity the subjective intention has to be taken into account. It is the objective intention which, in cases of ambiguity or the like, is not contradicted by the subjective intention. So a true sentence, even when uttered by one not understanding or misunderstanding it, has an intrinsic tātparya. If yogyatā be the formal compatibility of meaning, tātparya is compatibility in a material reference, the unity of the sentence and the corresponding objective relation. There might be higher unities, too, but these go beyond the sentence form.

122. The first thought roused by a sentence may be one of doubt or misunderstanding. Should it then be said that the objective knowledge produced by a sentence is dependent on a prior belief induced by other evidences? No, says Vedānta; a sentence by itself has the objective reference. The knowledge of the objective relations through other pramāṇas may no doubt remove doubts and misunderstanding, but is not necessarily demanded by the sentence. The sentence shines by its own light. The ascertainment of the meaning of a sentence, however, may be aided by the knowledge of the topic through other evidences, as in the case of sentences having secular reference. In the case of revealed texts, however, the meaning is evolved through mīmāṁsā of the texts themselves, i.e., through their mutual criticism and not through any extraneous pramāṇa; for no other pramāṇa can speak of the super-sensible.

ARTHĀPATTI

123. Arthāpatti is the supposition (or conception) of the premises, reason, or cause from the conclusion, consequence, or effect. Here is one getting stout though he does not take food during the day; the reason supposed is that he takes food at night. It includes all inference through vyātireki-liṅga, i.e., negative mark or middle term which, according to Vedānta, is not inference at all. In reference to the stock example given in Nyāya of Kevala-vyātireki inference, 'earth differs from other primal matters, for it has smell', Vedānta would point out that here earth, as a new primal matter, is conceived only, not inferred. It is like the framing of a hypothesis from given facts. So, too, where Nyāya holds that the major premise is reached both through positive and negative evidences, Vedānta holds that inference from it appeals to the positive instances or facts only; the negative instances simply define the positive instances, enable us to *conceive* the major premise clearly. The so-called inductive methods are therefore mixtures of anumāna and arthāpatti, deduction and hypothesis. In all inductive method there is an element of hypothesis, i.e., an assuring of ourselves, before the deductive verification, whether by tact or by conscious method, that in the absence of a certain antecedent, a consequent will also be absent. In the conscious framing of a hypothesis, our aim (though not always accomplished) is to find out something explaining facts that no alternative supposition will explain. In fact all hitting at the cause, all solving of riddles, all colligation by concepts involve a conscious or sub-conscious employment of negative instances, suggested by the positive data—and this is arthāpatti. This appears clearly in understanding omitted words in a sentence. So, too, a negation presupposes an affirmation, the presupposing being arthāpatti.

ANUPALABDHI

124. Abhāva is negation, including non-existence relative whether to all time, to particular times, or to particular natures. How is it known? It can no doubt be inferred but can it be perceived? It may be a percept, but the percept is then not the effect of a process of perception directed towards it. The self sometimes may not perceive a thing, even though it exerts the perceptive activity, yet the percept of the locus, *minus* that thing, is therefore the percept of the minus-ness or abhāva. But we cannot say

that the percept of this a b h ā v a is the result of the process of perception directed towards it; the perceptive process is directed only to the locus of the a b h ā v a, not to the a b h ā v a or to the thing that is non-existent. The non-existence of the thing, therefore, is an accidental percept *implicated* in the percept of its locus and not the intended objective of the actual process.

125. What is meant by saying that a percept is at once differentiated from everything else? Does it involve an explicit perception of the difference? No. In the stage of thought, the relation itself is definitely attended to, but in the stage of perception, it is only sub-consciously, implicitly present. The substantive presentation or percept is alone explicitly perceived. But then what is this *implicitness* of its relations from the point of view of the self's spontaneity? Need we admit a new process, a new p r a - m ā ṇ a for this implicit percept of difference? Why not call it implicit perceptive process only? From the point of view of the self knowing or functioning, this 'implicitness' is meaningless, being only a metaphor borrowed from the unintelligent object. So the language of implicit and explicit is not employed in V e d ā n t a at all. So in inference, where one might have said that the t ṛ t ī y a - l i ṅ g a - p a r ā m a r ś a of N y ā y a (Section 103) gives at any rate the *implicit* articulations of the inferential act, V e d ā n t a prefers to say that there is a single mediating function, and no substantive mental state somewhere out of the ken of consciousness, as the word 'implicit' would imply. It marks an essential difference between apriorism on the one hand, and intuitionism and empiricism on the other Should we not admit a passive or presentative side to this functioning? We may, but the self, while functioning in a particular way, cannot at the same time apprehend the functioning in its passive aspect as object, for the self is identified with the envelope of that passivity (or ignorance). It may view it, while shaking it off, as an outworn slough. When we speak of p r a m ā ṇ a or logical evidence, we view the mental process from the point of view of function and not of passivity. Hence it will not do to say that implicit perception is the process of which the result is the percept of a b h ā v a. For implicit perception, we have to substitute a distinctive positive function of the mind, a n u p a l a b d h i. When the a b h ā v a of a thing capable of being perceived is cognised where no other p r a m ā ṇ a can take cognisance of it, it is cognised through this a n u p a l a b d h i. It

has for its object not the absent thing but the absence itself. It is the bare awareness of the absence, though what is absent may not be known. Again, the thing that is absent must be. unlike spiritual merit or demerit (Section 95), capable of being perceived, i.e., it must be of the same order of reality as its locus which is perceived; otherwise the percept of its absence cannot be implicated in the percept of its locus. The negation must not be absolute indeterminate negation: it must be the negation of something intuitable.

126. An objection: If a b h ā v a be a percept, though not the result of a perceptive process directed towards it, is it a percept even in the illusion of a b h ā v a? In the case of the nacre taken for silver, the objectivity of the silver is constituted by its implicit subjective existence (Section 99) or a n i r v a c a n ī y a t v a. Has the illusory a b h ā v a also this 'inexplicable' existence? No, it may be replied: here we have a n y a t h ā k h y ā t i (Section 100). Objectivity is through implicit subjectivity in those illusions only in which the mind and the senses are in contact with the object mistaken. But here the object mistaken being a b h ā v a, they are not in contact with it, i.e., although the objective appearance is there, it has no subjective counterpart. If there is anything at all, it must be the implicit subjectivity of the absence of sensation, i.e., the implicit consciousness of the absence. This is only *partially* similar to the implicit subjectivity of the silver in the case of the nacre. The consciousness of absence is half-way between positive and negative, and because knowing comprehends and also transcends the known, it is, relatively speaking, phenomenally negative and really positive. Not that the illusory objective appearance of a b h ā v a is B r a h m a n, for though B r a h m a n is the substrate or a d h i s ṭ h ā n a of m ā y ā and so of all phenomenal and illusory existence, it is not their u p ā d ā n a or modifiable material. (B r a h m a n is still sometimes spoken of as the material cause of the universe. As against the non-intelligent p r a d h ā n a of S ā ṅ k h y a, V e d ā n t a proposes a spiritual material, B r a h m a n; but then it is not naked B r a h m a n but rather B r a h m a n as informing m ā y ā.) So the implicit consciousness of the absence of sensation is not the same as the implicit consciousness of the pure self but rather that of m a n a s (or its objective obverse) which is the material capable of being differentiated into the sensation-modes though now without them.

ŚAṄKARA'S DOCTRINE OF MĀYĀ

ANALYSIS

(1-3) The doctrine of M ā y ā is the logical pendant to the doctrine of B r a h m a n. It is the conceptual formulation of the feeling of vanity of life just as the other doctrine is of the demand for absolute certitude. Both m ā y ā and B r a h m a n are accepted in faith and only interpreted in thought. The 'vanity' of life means the lapse of its 'value' and does not apparently mean the lapse of its 'reality'. But in Ś a ṅ k a r a 's acosmism we have not merely the denial of value but also of all *given* 'reality'. This denial of the given would be unintelligible but for the fact that the illusory itself is *given* in our ordinary experience. (4-6) The stock V e d ā n t i c example of illusion—mistaking a rope for a snake—may be analysed in three stages:—(a) The snake is presented and believed to be real. (b) The belief is corrected by the perception of the rope as rope. After correction the snake continues to be a presentation to the mind though it comes to be invested with the quality of unreality. The first percept of the snake is *degraded into an illusion* when we have the affirmation of the rope. In this stage the snake persists as a possible object and the past perception of it as a subjective fact is not yet questioned. (c) The snake is contemplated not only as non-existent now but as non-existent even when it appeared to be perceived. There is the doubt even about the past perception of it as a subjective fact. *That* snake is no possible object. Existence is denied of it absolutely and the objectivity of the illusory content is called in question. The objectivity of the unreal snake, as persisting in the second stage, is now reduced to what is determinate neither as objective nor as subjective, to bare given-ness. (7-8) *That snake* then, shorn of its objective reality in the second stage and now of its reality either as objective or as subjective is still given to us as a positive unthinkable: it cannot yet be rejected as absolute nought. The indescribable *should* be nought but is still given in absolute mockery of thought. (9-12) The snake in the three *stages* of illusion is given respectively as implicitly real object, as unreal object and as the indescribable. The last stage leads to the realisation of absolute nought which is not given at all.

Corresponding to the stages there are the three *processes* in illusion as presented to uncritical thought, to critical thought and to faith respectively. Again, corresponding to the three processes, we have the stages of māyā as the predicate of the illusory object: (a) Vāstavī. (b) anirvacanīyā. and (c) tucchā. (a) renders intelligible the theory of māyā as cosmic magic turning up the unanticipable; (b) furnishes the clue to the conception of māyā as the absolute freedom. the unthinkable free power of the Lord to put forth and retract objective appearance; (c) makes intelligible the theory that the cosmic appearance is not merely retractable but that the retractation itself is unreal. (13-14) What is neither sat nor asat is nonsense and yet we have such unthinkable nonsense actually presented in the illusion—'the unreal. unobjective snake there'. The illusion has no longer to be logically corrected, that correction being finished; there is demand only for the correction of the hidden subjective defect through which it is still given. The nonsensical here is presented not through any caprice of a verbal combination but through a deeper subjective distemper. To say that the snake is nought though not felt as such is to express a faith in and a demand for its realisation by a cure of this distemper. (15) Though the snake is not an apparent object. it is not known for certain to have been perceived. To faith there was no perception of it; to reason the past perception is unproved; while to immediate belief it is a fact. There is belief now in the past perception as a subjective fact without a belief through memory in the snake having been perceived. The snake as a given unthinkable is but a percept *presented as an unreal subjective fact* to an eternal consciousness. (16-17) In an illusion in respect of a subjective fact, the subject knows the object through the wrong act of identifying with the Vṛtti. Now it is only as a subjective illusion is corrected that the distinction of pure consciousness from the Vṛtti and the unreality of the Vṛtti are suspected. This suspicion is in some sense a self-freeing act of the subject. though it is only incomplete self-freeing. Such freedom implies a faith in the spiritual possibility of progressively annulling the act of identification and thus attaining complete freedom. (18-20) That a given object should be a *given* unthinkable is a standing scandal to human reason. The faith that the given-ness is only apparent does not effectively remove the felt fact. The consciousness of the practicability of annulling the given-ness of a particular illusion is what alone yields the conception of truth as not given, as transparent, as self-certified or svayamprabha. That the unthinkable is still given though it should not be given brings up the thought and faith that the Vyāvahārika world is also just given and is not necessary, that its ultimate ground is dark and inexplicable i.e., māyā and that the system of relations is not self-justifying truth.

ŚANKARA'S DOCTRINE OF MĀYĀ

1. Śaṅkara's doctrine of Māyā is the logical pendant to his doctrine of Brahman as the undifferenced self-shinning truth. Both Māyā and Brahman are taken to be incapable of being established by reason, by any natural pramāṇa. They are believed to be scripturally revealed, though they are claimed as intelligible contents of pure consciousness. They are in fact to be accepted in faith and only interpreted by thought. For purposes of philosophy, we may generally substitute in place of faith in scriptures, spiritual experience and, in this connexion, the feeling of the vanity of life and the demand for absolute certitude. The doctrine of māyā and Brahman may be regarded as the conceptual formulation of this feeling and demand. The value or validity of the experience, feeling or faith is not to be questioned within philosophy which should start with it and seek only to interpret it. The present paper confines itself to the enquiry how far the interpreting concepts are intelligible and at what precise point, if at all, logical thought can make room for the faith in the illusoriness of things other than Brahman.

2. Is the theory of the illusoriness of the world the necessary formulation of the feeling of the vanity of life? The feeling implies the evanescence of value from the objects that interest us. Does the lapse of value mean lapse of reality? If the value of an object lapses to our consciousness, the given form of the object, it may be said, need not disappear or change into some other form. Even if the given form changes, the formless given-ness of the object may be said to persist, for the new form is not felt to be separately given. It may be supposed that the given form is turned with the lapse of value into a mere subjective idea but then the reality of the idea has to be admitted as given. Or it may be that the form is realised to be not a given idea but only the subjective activity of forming or constructing it; but even this free activity is given as the presented process of the becoming or defining out of the idea. The lapse of value does not mean the lapse of all given-ness; some given reality has apparently to be admitted, whether objective or subjective, determinate or indeter-

minate. The acosmism of Śaṅkara goes beyond both realism and idealism by reducing the world to absolute illusion, by interpreting the vanity of life as implying the denial of all given reality. Is such absolute denial of given-ness, with the correlated notion of truth as utterly ungiven, i.e., as self-luminous (svayamprabha) intelligible?

3. The denial or the illusoriness of the given would be inconceivable but for the fact that the illusory itself is given or experienced as such. Were it not for the experience of prātibhāsika or illusory being, the possible unreality of the vyāvahārika or empirically real world—the elimination of its given-ness—would be utterly unintelligible. The presentation of an object as illusory is, as will appear presently, fundamentally different from the presentation of a fact, objective or subjective. The difference between the given-ness of the illusory as illusory and that of fact, objective or subjective, can only be expressed as a difference in the felt quality of reality, the former being less real than the latter. The quality of reality is explicitly felt only when it is experienced as dissipated in an illusion. The experience of illusion thus marks an actual step towards the elimination of given-ness and is as such a unique datum for epistemology.

4. The metaphysical doctrine of māyā is best approached through the epistemology of illusion. We may analyse the stock Vedāntic example of illusion—mistaking a rope for a snake—in three stages. The snake is first presented, it is next corrected, and then it is contemplated as corrected. It is in the first place presented and believed as real, though it is not affirmed or judged as real, its reality being only not denied. The belief is next corrected by the perception of the rope as rope. The correction has to be accepted as an ultimate fact of consciousness. It is not yet a negative judgment. The rope is indeed affirmed or judged to be real but the snake remains a presentation[1] though invested with a new immediate quality of unreality. The affirmation of the rope and the peculiar presentation of the snake presuppose each other. The affirmative judgment need not presuppose a negative judgment: it presupposes only the presentation of immediate unreality. Illusion or the corrected and degraded percept is at least one form, if not the sole form, of the presentation of unreality.

1 i.e. something presented to the *mind*.

In the present example, the rope is affirmed as real in explicit contrast with the illusory snake; and the first percept of the snake is degraded into an illusion in reference to the affirmation of the rope. The affirmative judgment and the illusion[2] emerge together—as fact and not by any thinking necessity—as mutually implicated. Mutual implication is but a name for confusion which, however, in this stage is not realised as such. The attitude is still objective and the cognition does not appear as confusedly dual because the objective content that is known—viz., 'rope not snake'—is a related unity. The relation, it may be noted, is unique: the unreal implies the real[3] but real does not imply nor is it in any way affected by the unreal. The rope is a complete content which does not require to reject the content 'snake' and is neither the better nor the worse for having rejected. The snake, however, in the context is there *as* rejected or corrected by the other content, as illusory in its presence. The real has the unreal here as its free implication.

5. In the second stage we are directly concerned only with this objective content. The rope is affirmed as real and the snake though presented as unreal is still regarded as objective. Though corrected, the snake is neither forgotten nor presented as a mere subjective fact: it persists as an objectively presented no-fact. It is still a possible object and the past perception of it as a subjective fact is not yet questioned. The unreal object, however, here is a subordinate or implied element in the known content, the real object being the principal element. In the third stage, the unreal is made the principal element, the direct object of contemplation. The snake is known not only as non-existent now but as non-existent even when it appeared to be perceived. It is not now felt to be remembered and that means a doubt even about the past perception of it as a subjective fact. As now felt to be neither perceived nor remembered, is it a possible object at all? Snake, no doubt, is a possible object but *that* snake appearing at the previous moment to the particular observer is no possible object, as it never existed, does not exist and will not exist: existence is denied of it absolutely. The judgment in fact—'it does not exist' is inadmissible: its subject *it* lacks existential

2 i.e. the sense of illusion.

3 i.e the sense of the unreal implies the sense of the real.

import, standing as it does now for what was only apparently existent. The absolute denial of existence annuls the starting subject altogether and no judgment about the snake appears to be left over. The unreal snake which was still an object in the second stage now turns out to be no possible object at all. Not that, however, it is known now as a mere subjective image; it is known as what appeared to be perceived. The qualitative difference between what is perceived and what is imagined does not disappear even when the former is known to be perceived wrongly.

6. But is it still believed that the wrong perception of the previous moment was a real subjective fact? If it was a fact it must be vouched for by memory which however only tells us here that the snake was *felt to* be perceived, not that it *was* perceived. The past perception is known as a fact, only if its object is now felt to be remembered. The snake is not so felt and so the facthood of the past perception is at least not known. The facthood is not denied when the snake is taken to be an unreal *object* in the second stage. But now that its objectivity itself is called in question, the facthood of its perception becomes open to doubt. That is why memory testifies apologetically that it was only felt to be perceived. It means on the one hand that it is not felt to have been merely imagined and on the other that the facthood of the perception cannot be affirmed with certainty. Thus the objectivity of the unreal snake, as persisting in the second stage, is now reduced to what is determinate neither as objective nor as subjective, to bare given-ness.

7. In the third stage then the implied unreal object of the second stage turns out to be no possible object at all, to be incapable of being presented as the subject of a judgment of which existence can be denied. While existence is denied of the starting subject absolutely,[4] non-existence is not now predicable of it, for no possible object remains. The snake now is referred to not by a negative judgment but by a self-contradictory judgment which is no judgment. The judgment 'that snake is unreal'—the implication of the cognition 'rope, not snake'—is now realised to be a contradiction. The contradiction, however, is still felt to be given, unlike a contradiction like square circle which is but a verbal or thinking sport. All contradiction is, in a sense, given: the failure to

4 i.e. both as objective and as subjective.

think is not thought but only felt. The illusion—*that* unreal snake—which is a contradiction in the sense of being indescribable either as existent or as non-existent (s a d - a s a d - v i l a k ṣ a ṇ a)[5] is given in a deeper sense. Square circle is sought to be only imagined, not known, and the feeling of the failure tells us that it is absolute nought (t u c c h a). But '*that* unreal snake' is sought to be known, being felt to be perceived in the first instance. The problem of thinking is itself given or forced upon us and it is given as insoluble in the feeling of the failure to think. *That snake* then, shorn of its reality[6] in the second stage and now of its bare objectivity[7] also, is still given to us as a positive (b h ā v a - r ū p a) unthinkable (a n i r v ā c y a): it cannot yet be rejected as absolute nought.

8. There is a difference between the contradiction between existent and non-existent and that between 'not existent' and 'not non-existent'. The unreal object of the second stage might be taken as at once existent and non-existent but the 'indescribable' of the third stage is what is neither existent nor non-existent. Strictly speaking, the latter is no contradiction at all: the concepts 'not existent' and 'not non-existent' do not get related at all to contradict one another, being predicable of no assignable subject. At the same time they have been brought together not arbitrarily or accidentally, but under the constraint of a given presentation. They are not indeed thinkingly related but are *given* as related in the way of contradiction. As given, the relation may be regarded as a symbolism for thought-contradiction, as a problem or demand to realise the given-ness as false. The 'indescribable' should be nought but is still given in absolute mockery of thought. It marks, in a sense, the frontier between thought and faith, being the given limit of thought on the one hand and the promise of the annulment of given-ness on the other.

9. The snake in the three stages of illusion is given respectively as implicitly real object, as unreal object and as the indescribable. The last stage may be regarded as leading to the realisation of absolute nought which is not given at all; and each of the first two stages may be viewed as leading to the next stage.

5 Here the concept of 's a d a s a d - v i l a k ṣ a ṇ a' appears to be interpreted in a novel way.

6 i.e. reality as objective.

7 i.e. reality either as objective or as subjective.

We may thus speak of three processes in illusion[8] as presented to uncritical thought, critical thought and faith respectively. They would roughly correspond to the three views of māyā—viz., as concrete (vāstavī), as unthinkable (anirvacanīyā) and as nought (tucchā).

10. The first process in illusion is the reduction of an implicitly real object to appearance. The reduction cannot be regarded as merely subjective process, If the magic transformation of the present snake into an appearance to a particular mind could be taken as an objective process, it would mean the opening up of a new dimension of becoming in which objects come to acquire or lose reality. The hard reality of a world once and for all given would give place to a perpetual swing between dream and waking manifestation. The world would be intelligible as a system of appearances materialising and dematerialising to individual spirits, as a play of cosmic imagination or līlā. The emergence of the new in causality would be understood as the emanation or vivarta of an appearance from the timeless cause, the law of causality would be a law of appearances—the effect-appearance being as real as the causal appearance and so a pariṇāma of it, and causal power would be a name for cosmic magic. Thus the first process in illusion renders intelligible the pictorial conception of vāstavī māyā, the inexplicable world-process creatively turning up the unanticipable (aghaṭana-ghaṭana-paṭīyasī)—an analogue of the Bergsonian real time.

11. The second process in illusion, viz., the reduction of objective appearance to the given unthinkable, furnishes the clue to the conception of māyā as unthinkable free power, the freedom to put forth and retract objective appearance. It is because we thinkingly reduce objective appearance to the given un-objective or unthinkable that we can conceive or intellectually apprehend freedom—freedom of willing, for example, which is a process from the un-objective to the objective—as real. Māyā as the anirvacanīya power of the Lord means His absolute freedom, freedom to create or put forth as also to destroy or retract objectivity. It is the freedom of retractation that we first understand through the analogy of the dissipation of objectivity in an illusion. Creative freedom is intelligible as the reversed process of the re-

8 i.e. processes in the correction of an illusion.

tractive freedom. The common conception of creative freedom without destroying freedom[9], of the Lord being able to put forth will but not to retract it is not the conception of absolute freedom.

12. The third process in illuson is the reduction in faith of the given unthinkable to absolute nought, the elimination of the indescribable given-ness. The corresponding cosmic conception would be that of Tucchā māyā which the Vedāntist would accept as revealed or presented in faith. The conception of māyā as absolute nought is necessary for the vigorous monism of the Śāṅkarite school. The monism implies not merely that the world is an appearance and that this appearance is retractable but also that the retraction itself is unreal, is not even real as the free nature of Brahman. Brahman is not like Īśvara detached from or free in respect of a māyā that is present to him but has not māyā before him at all. He not only need not exercise free power: power is not real to him. Brahman is the truth and is not merely real. Neither the real nor the true as content requires to deny the opposite to be itself; but while the *knowledge* of the real as such depends on the correction of the unreal, the knowledge of the true as such is not dependent on the correction of the false. The knowledge of the falsity of the world is no necessary element of the knowledge of Brahman. The knowledge of Brahman is no mediate affirmation but an intuition which is not a result that is reached but is felt when it comes to have been eternally there. That means that the ignorance of Brahman was itself unreal, to the last vestige of which the correction of the world as false and its cosmic obverse, the retraction of free power, appeared real. The conception of eternal truth implies the falsity or tucchatva of given cosmic unreality, the mithyātva of given mithyātva, not only rejection of the world as unreal but absence of any reference to it by way of rejection. Such a conception is possible only through a consideration of what we have taken as the third process in illusion.

13. We have shown so far how the consciousness of illusion renders the conception of māyā intelligible. Our experience of illusion—as about the snake—supplies in its different stages not only *an* analogy but the only analogy for the conception of cosmic māyā as magic, as freedom and as nought. It remains however

9 i.e. freedom to destroy.

to show definitely where the transition is effected from a particular illusion to cosmic m ā y ā and how the faith in the latter fits in with logical thought. For this, a farther analysis is required of the consciousness of illusion in the stage where the given unthinkable appears to faith as absolute nought.

14. What is neither s a t nor a s a t should be a chimera but persists as given in the illusion. It is instructive to ask what this persistence implies and whether and how it can be got rid of. It was pointed out that when the objective appearance of the snake is known to be not objective at all, to be beyond affirmation and denial, the subjective facthood of the past perception of it itself becomes doubtful. The snake is not felt to be remembered, i.e., to have been perceived. At the same time it is not felt to be merely imagined but as given, though not to present perception or memory. It is given as an unreal but not as being subjectively constructed nor as what had but has lost reality. Though not objective, it is referred to a real point in the objective world as where it is *not*. It is not only contradictory but nonsensical to say that the square circle is or is not there; and yet we have such unthinkable nonsense actually presented in the illusion—'the unreal un-objective snake there'. The illusion has no longer to be logically or objectively corrected, that correction being finished; there is demand only for the correction of the hidden subjective defect through which it is still given. The nonsensical here is presented not through the mere caprice of a verbal combination as in the case of square-circle but through a deeper subjective distemper. To say that the snake is nought though not felt as such is to express a faith in and a demand for its realisation by a cure of this distemper.

15. If the snake is not even an apparent object, it should be known as what was not perceived. It is not actually so known; we cannot get rid of the belief that it was perceived, though as it is not felt to be remembered, it is not known[10] to have been perceived. To faith there was no perception of it[11], to reason the past perception is unproved[12] while to immediate belief it is a fact. There is belief now in the past perception as a subjective fact without the object of it being felt to be remembered.

10 i.e. known for certain, see sec, 6.

11 Because the indescribable is incapable of being perceived.

i.e., without a belief through memory in the snake having been perceived. It means then that the past appears to be now directly perceived; that the snake, as past percept[13] and not as a past objective fact, is presented to consciousness without an empirical psychosis or vṛtti. To say, however, that the snake is now presented as a past percept is not to admit that it is consciously presented as a real subjective fact. A percept is never like an image distinguished actually as subjective from the object perceived, being so distinguished only in name. In the case of an illusion indeed, it is actually distinguished but not as an assured subjective fact. The pastness of the percept does not mean that it was present, i.e., was a fact having a position in the objective time-order. Pastness here is but a *quality* of the percept, a name for the presented unreality of the subjective fact, which as timeless is presented to a timeless consciousness, is śākṣi-bhāṣya, 'lighted up by pure consciousness.'

16. We may say then that the snake as a given unthinkable is but a percept presented as an unreal subjective fact to an eternal consciousness. A subjective fact is but the subject with an empirical vṛtti, not the vṛtti with the form of the subject. It is the subjective act of identifying with the vṛtti, not the presentation of the subject as objectified in it. A subjective illusion[14] is an ethically (or spiritually) wrong act rather than a logically false cognition: it is the subject wrongly working through the vṛtti, not knowing the vṛtti, but knowing the object through the wrong act of identifying with the vṛtti. The identifying is a pure act of the self, the heart of will and is implied in all knowing short of the ecstatic intuition of the self. Now it is only as a subjective illusion is corrected that it is known as such, that the identifying act is known, that the distinction of pure consciousness from the empirical vṛtti and the unreality of this vṛtti are suspected. That suspicion of the distinction is already a distinguishing or self-freeing act of the subject; it is only by *being* free that the subject *knows* its freedom, detachment or distinction.

17. To suspect, however, the distinction of the subject from the vṛtti is not to get rid of it altogether. It is to be free

12 Because the snake now is only *felt* to be perceived.

13 i.e. as the 'content' of a perception.

14 i.e. illusion in respect of a subjective fact.

in a measure and yet to be identified. A contradiction like this is real to the spiritual will but not to thought, being intelligible only as a subjective act of incomplete self-freeing or realisation. Such freedom, however, as is already realised in the suspicion of distinction implies a faith in continued realisation, in the spiritual possibility of progressively retracting the act of identification. Now the snake as a given unthinkable corresponds to the suspicion of the self being free from the perception of it, a suspicion that does not yet exclude a belief in or identification with the perception as past or unreal. The given unthinkable again is in faith absolute nought. The faith corresponds on the subjective side to the faith in the practicability of progressively realising the subject's freedom from the past perception and of annulling the identification that the belief in it implies. But for the faith in subjective or spiritual practicability, that the given unreal should be nought would be no living faith but only a dreamy suggestion of it; and absolute certitude would be deemed unattainable.

18. That a given object, stripped first of its reality and then of its objectivity, should still be a *given* unthinkable is a standing scandal to human reason. The faith that the given-ness is only apparent does not effectively remove the felt fact. So long as it is not removed, absolute truth is only conceived but not known. It is possible however to go at least one stage beyond this Kantian impasse. The annulment of the objectivity of a given illusory object implies a doubt about the subjective reality of its perception—the starting experience of getting freed from empirical subjectivity. The unthinkable no-object is accordingly felt to be only non-empirically given to the pure self, the givenness is felt to be removed one step from a merely blind imposition and the persisting though enfeebled identification of the self with empiricality already presented as illusory is believed to be progressively retractable. That is how absolute truth, though unknown, is believed to be not unknowable but as demanding to be known. The faith emerges not only in truth but also in the knowability of truth.

19. Here then we have the transition from a particular illusion to the thought of and faith in absolute illusion or māyā. The consciousness of the practicability of annulling the given-ness of a particular illusion is what alone yields the conception of truth as not given, as transparent, as self-certified or svayampra-

bha. Such conception of truth is at once a faith in the knowability of truth. If in one case—viz., the case of a particular illusion, truth is believed to be attainable by the practicable spiritual process of freeing oneself from empiricality, absolute truth—absolute freedom of the self with the reduction of all empiricality to illusion—is conceived to be attainable. For what does the act of freeing in the particular case imply? If a given object turns into illusion, it is by fact and not by any necessity of thought. If the perception of it is suspected to be only a subjective illusion, it means that the self or pure consciousness has so far freed itself, that the conception of and faith in the self as truth has emerged. That implies the consciousness not only that the self is not identified with this perception, this particular empiricality, but that being unconsciously identified cannot be predicated of the self at all. The accomplished act of freeing from any empiricality is the consciousness of the act itself as free, i.e., of the self as not affected by the act, as *ever* free, transparent or svayamprabha and not merely *making* itself free or repenting of a previous helpless lapse.

20. A single act of freeing from an empirical subjectivity implies thus a faith that all such subjectivity and identification with it are illusory. The same faith is reached in another way. When the snake appears as an illusory object, the rope is taken to be real as against it. When the snake appears as a given unthinkable, the rope in contrast with it is believed not only to be real but as justifiable by reason or pramāṇa, as in a world of vyāvahārika, i e., thinkable and practical reality, as conformable to Veda or Objective Reason or—what amounts to the same thing—as in a world of laws or system of relations. That the unthinkable is still given though it should not be given brings up the thought and faith that the vyāvahārika world—with Veda itself as objective reason—is also given and is not necessary, that it is a free revelation, that its ultimate ground is dark or inexplicable, i.e., is māyā, that the system of relations is not self-justifying truth. What is given and justified by something else, i.e., logically thought is still only *real*, not *true*[15]. The

15 Here, 'real' is that which is justified by something else; and 'true' is that which is self-justifying.

Absolute must be the self-evidencing truth, not given to any *pramāṇa* but enjoyingly intuited.

21. How this enjoying intuition is to be reached, how the freedom of the self from empiricality is to be progressively achieved, how, in other words, the given-ness of illusion is to be finally eliminated are questions of metapsychological *sādhana* or discipline which bring out the spiritual aspect of *māyā*. This aspect is not discussed in the present paper.

THE ADVAITA AND ITS SPIRITUAL SIGNIFICANCE

ANALYSIS.

(1-4) *A d h y ā s a and spiritual detachment*—The illusoriness of the individual self is the central notion of A d v a i t a V e d ā n t a. Individuality which involves an identification of self with the body is never, however, *felt* to be illusory in our secular life. It is at best *thought* and accepted in faith. But this notion would not occur to a person who has no experience of himself as a spirit and of the object as distinct from the subject. That experience is furnished by a deepening of the moral consciousness in which we not only repent of our past actions but find it hard to imagine how we could perform them. In such a state one is aware of the self that is castigated as not merely 'me' but also as 'I'. In a further deepening of this stage, the past 'I' is not only sought to be disowned but is cognitively viewed as a sort of 'You' that is yet 'I'. One is aware here of the individual self as somehow at once true and false, true as the unobjective subject and false in so far as it appears as 'you'. The individual self means the self feeling itself embodied and the illusoriness of the embodiment is the illusoriness of the bodily self and not merely of the self's identity with it. (5-6) *Two illusions*—There are apparently two illusions—(i) of the 'I' appearing as 'you' (objective subject) and therefore also as 'me' (object), and (ii) of the 'you' appearing as 'I'. Under the first illusion one is aware of the 'me' or the body as only felt, as one's embodiment; and the correction is the realisation that such a body was only his individual illusion. In the other illusion that continues, the body appears to be distinct from him and yet as somehow 'he'. With the correction of the first illusion, he sees that this appearance should also be illusory, but still he does not actually disbelieve it. To be conscious of oneself as individual or 'me' is to be conscious of the 'me' as illusory and of the subject or 'I' as the truth. It is the illusion of the individuality that suggests the theory of objective illusion called a n i r v a c a n ī y a - k h y ā t i - v ā d a.

(7) *The Concept of M ā y ā*—This brings in the concept of M ā y ā which is neither real nor unreal. M ā y ā is the beginningless nescience that conditions the individuality of a finite self as also his subjective ignorance. Since there are many individuals, m ā y ā may be taken as the corpus of the many beginning-

less individualities and may be characterised as the manifold of nāma-rūpā. (8-11) *Brahman* and *Iśvara*—This last conception of Māyā is intelligible only as the cosmic principle of illusory individuality. As cosmic, Māyā is to be understood as what is not Brahman. Brahman, however, can but need not be understood as what is not Māyā. He is Īśvara, the Lord of individual selves and the creator of the world. Creation is understood as manifestation in the soil of Māyā. Brahman, in a sense, *becomes* the world without losing His transcendence. Brahman does not, however, *become* the Jīva: the Jīva is Brahman but wrongly views himself as other than Brahman. Īśvara is conceived as an absolute emanation of Brahman and not as merely relative to the individual's thinking. The creativity of Īśvara is like that of the magician. His śakti is neither absolutely real nor absolutely unreal. As absolutely free with his Māyā-śakti, Īśvara is not only not a false idea of the Jīva, He is not also an absolute appearance like the world. Īśvara has a dual form, as wielding māyā-śakti and thus immanent in the world (vikāra-vartin), and as dissociated from it, transcendent (triguṇātīta). As transcendent, Īśvāra is conceived as what is not Māyā: while Brahman is understood without reference to Māyā and the world. Īśvara and Brahman are characterised by the same epithets--nitya-śuddha-buddha-mukta.

(12-14) *Mokṣa and its means*—Mokṣa is not anything to be reached or effected but is the self itself or the svarūpa of Brahman. The individual, however, thinks that he is not free and wants to be free. For him, accordingly, there is the necessity of a sādnana. This sādhana must be such as will lead him to realise that his bondage is an illusion and that he is eternally free. To know the truth about himself can, therefore, be the only discipline for him. The sādhana, therefore, is primarily that of knowing (jñāna) and secondarily that of willing and feeling (karma and bhakti). The latter makes for clarity of spiritual being and is thus implicitly or explicitly the clarity of knowledge. Without rejecting any other sādhana, the religion of Advaita Vedānta regards knowledge of the self as its distinctive sādhana and regards it as self-sufficing and requiring no supplementation (samuccaya).

(15) *Universal outlook*—Advaitism as religion and philoso-

phy in one is at once individualistic and universalistic in its outlook. As religion, Advaitism insists on the conservation of one's spiritual individuality (svadharma), while as philosophy, it recognises the svadharma of everyone else as absolutely sacred. (16-17) *Practical Idealism*--Advaitism stands for a strong spirituality and for efficient practice of idealism. While it prescribes nivṛtti or renunciation of the world in spirit, it demands that it should be achieved through such discipline as is suited to the adhikāra or the spiritual status of each individual. The absolute freedom from law which Advaitism aims at is to be achieved by the willing of the law, by niṣkāma-karma or by merging one's individuality in institutional spiritual life which represents a sacrificial concert of gods and men. (18) *Toleration*—Toleration is to Advaita Vedānta a religion in itself. The Advaitin feels that the religion of others is not only sacred to them but to himself also. There is no prescription, however, of universal brotherhood and the duty to relieve distress is to be performed as duty rather than as a matter of altruistic enjoyment. The brotherhood that is practically recognised is the brotherhood of spirits realising their svadharma. (19-21) *Respect for individual differences*—The difference of spiritual status is not necessarily a gradation, and in so far as it is, it does not suggest any relation of higher or lower that implies contempt or envy. The notion of adhikāra means just an acceptance of realism in the spiritual sphere and the highest adhikārin should feel it a privilege to join in the worship of the humblest. The Advaitic scheme of life would view with positive disfavour iconoclasm in any sphere or form. There is no room in Advaitic religion for the duty of profaning one god for the glorification of another. The idea of hustling people out of their reverence in their own spiritual interest would be scouted in this religion as self-stultifying profanity.

(22-25) *An integral part of Hinduism*—Much of what is here attributed to Advaitavāda is the implied creed of Hinduism and Hindu society. Advaitism is sometimes characterised as rationalistic religion. But the abstract cult of self-knowledge derives its whole meaning from the concrete religion of ceremonial and worship. It represents a protest against concrete religion only in so far as the latter resists 'inwardisation'. Advaitism, far from encouraging premature quietism, positively prescribes Karma, though rigorously as a duty and not for gain. The religion of jñāna, however, is in no sense a protest against the religion of bhakti. The Advaita knowledge is understood as an intuition that amounts to ecstasy and does not in any sense mean a supersession of bhakti. Although bhakti implies individuality, it represents the individual's joy in surrendering his individuality.

THE ADVAITA AND ITS SPIRITUAL SIGNIFICANCE

1. The illusoriness of the individual self is apparently the central notion of Advaita Vedānta. Every vital tenet of the philosophy—Brahman as the sole reality, the object as false, Māyā as neither real nor unreal, Īśvara as Brahman in reference to Māyā, mokṣa (liberation) through knowledge of Brahman and as identity with Brahman—may be regarded as an elaboration of this single notion.

2. An illusion, unlike a thinking error, excites wonder as it is corrected. One's apprehension of something as illusory involves a peculiar feeling of the scales falling from the eyes. To be aware of our individuality as illusory would be then to wonder how we could feel as an individual at all. As we are, it is indeed only in faith, if at all, that we accept the illusoriness of our individuality. But even to understand the position, we have to refer to some spiritual experience in which we feel an abrupt break with our past and wonder how we could be what we were. A person behaves as though he believed he were his body, and although he never explicitly says that he is his body, he never also ordinarily feels detached enough from the body to wonder how he cannot yet get rid of the belief. The notion of adhyāsa or the false identification of the self and the body would never occur to a person who has no experience of himself as a spirit and of the object as distinct from the subject, as another person is from oneself. It is only one who felt such a distinction of the self and the body that would wonder at his own implicit belief in their identity. He can take the identity to be illusory, only if he feels it to be impossible and cannot yet deny its appearance. Vedānta starts with the notion of adhyāsa and presupposes such an experience of spiritual detachment from the body, including the empirical mind.

3. We can conceive this spiritual condition as a deepening of the form of moral consciousness in which we not only repent of our past actions, but find it hard to imagine how we could perform them. In this consciousness, our past being is felt not only to be strangely alien to us, but as an intellectual absurdity, as apparently at once subjective and objective, at once I and me. One at best

thinks of one's body as me and not as I; but in repentance, unless it is a senseless whipping of a dead horse. one is aware of the self that is castigated as not merely me but also as I; not only as a thing of the past, alienated or objectified, but as still tingling with subjectivity. In the further stage, in which the past appears unintelligible, this past I is not only sought to be disowned, but is cognitively viewed as a sort of you (y u ṣ m a d) that is yet I (a s m a d). a contradiction that yet appears. This alienated I which is not mere me is the individual self, and it is on this spiritual plane. and not lower, that one is cognitively aware of one's individuality. One is aware. however, here of the individual self as a contradiction, or as somehow at once true and false, true as the unobjective subject and false in so far as it appears as another I (you), as at once me and I. The notions of the individual self, of the individuality or me as false, and of the eternal self as the I that is never me, are born in one and the same spiritual consciousness.

4. The individuality is understood as me, i.e., as the illusory objectivity of the subject and not merely illusory identity with the object taken as real. The identity of the self and the not-self has the form of the self, being in fact the embodied self and not the conscious body. The individual self means the self feeling itself embodied, the embodiment being only a restrictive adjective of the self; and the illusoriness of the embodiment is the illusoriness of the body itself and not merely of the self's identity with it. The idea of the object. in fact, as distinct from the subject is derived from the idea of the embodiment, which itself is born in the consciousness of the individual self as false in respect of its individuality.

5. There is, however, a complexity. The me is taken as illusory not primarily because it is objective, but because the individual self already appears to itself false in so far as it takes itself to be an objective subject, to be a sort of you which is at once me and I. As the individual self is felt to be false, it is realised that the I cannot be me; but this does not prevent the me or the body from appearing as I. There are apparently two illusions—of the I appearing as you (objective subject) and therefore also as me (object) and of the you appearing as I. In the spiritual consciousness in which a person wonders how he could be what he cannot be, he corrects the former illusion, but not the latter, for

unless the past self were still present, there could be no sense of intellectual absurdity. His past self (you) is still somehow he, though he sees he cannot be that self. Under the first illusion he is aware of the me or the body as only felt, as his embodiment or limiting character; and the correction is his realisation that such a body was only his individual illusion. In the other illusion that continues, the body appears to be a substantive fact, distinct from him and yet as somehow he. With the correction of the first illusion, he sees that this appearance also should be illusory, but he still does not actually disbelieve it. Hence it is that he wants this illusion to be dissipated and meantime realizes that it is not his individual illusion, but a cosmic illusion, the dissipation of which would mean for him realization of the body and the entire world, of which it is the point of reference, as illusory.

6. To be conscious of oneself as individual or me is to be conscious of the me as illusory and of the subject or I as the truth. The me is the prototype of objectivity, and to feel it to be illusory is to be aware of the possibility of objectivity itself being illusory. We take a particular object to be illusory only as we believe in the objective world, but we could never conceive the illusoriness of the world itself unless we started with the illusoriness of the me. Were it not also for this starting illusion, an illusory object would not be conceived, as it is conceived in Advaita philosophy, namely, as anirvācya as an unassertable that is yet undeniable. The illusion of a snake being corrected rouses wonder. Wonder should mean that this (rope) being a snake is a contradiction that yet was presented, but there is apparently no actual consciousness here of a contradiction presented as such, viz., of this being at once snake and rope. The spiritual consciousness of one's illusory individuality is, however, explicit consciousness of the contradiction of the self having been believed as not-self. It is the illusion of the individuality therefore that suggests the theory of objective illusion called Anirvācya-khyātivāda.

7. This brings in the concept of Māyā or the principle of illusion as what cannot be characterized either as real or as unreal. It is primarily the illusion through which the self believes (in willing and feeling) that it is an individual. As this belief persists even when the individual sees that the self cannot be individual, the individuality appears neither as real nor as unreal, for if the belief were removed, there would be no individual self to see

the unreality of individuality. The principle of individuality, then, is prior to the individual's actual consciousness of himself as individual and of this world as his experience (b h o g a); and as yet this individuality is what cannot be real, it has to be taken as the cosmic principle of illusion. M ā y ā is the principle of individuality, the beginningless nescience that the individual self has to conceive as positively conditioning his individual being as also his subjective ignorance. To the individual there are many individuals, and so M ā y ā may be taken as the corpus of the many beginningless individualities. Again, as the world is understood as the system of experiences of the individual self, which apart from the self are but empty distinctions and forms, n ā m a-r ū p a as they are called, M ā y ā may be characterized as the manifold of n ā m a - r ū p a—the name and form—which has no self-identity and yet is undeniable.

8. This last conception of M ā y ā, however, is intelligible only through the conception of M ā y ā as the cosmic principle of illusory individuality. As cosmic, it has to be understood in reference to the unindividual self or B r a h m a n, though only as what is not B r a h m a n. B r a h m a n has, however, no necessary reference to M ā y ā: He can be, but need not be, understood as what is not M ā y ā. Understood as what is not M ā y ā, or as it is figuratively put, as shining against M ā y ā without being identified with it, or as a master using this principle as his servant, He is Ī ś v a r a, the Lord of the individual selves and the Creator of the world. The world is understood as the system of the experiences of the selves, and as they believe themselves to be individuals so far as they will, the experiences are to be taken as their b h o g a accordant with their k a r m a. Ī ś v a r a then is conceived as actualizing their k a r m a into their b h o g a or experience, and thus manifesting the manifold of n ā m a - r ū p a, which as experienced is just this world or j a g a t.

9. Ī ś v a r a has different relations to the individual selves and to the world. He is the Creator of the world, but not of the selves, the notion of creation of souls being foreign to all Indian philosophy and not to A d v a i t a v ā d a only. Creation is understood as manifestation in the soil of M ā y ā. B r a h m a n in a sense becomes the world without losing His transcendence. The world is an absolute appearance, at once real and unreal, real as B r a h m a n, the cause that continues in the effect, and un-

real as alienated from Him. It cannot, however, be said similarly that Brahman becomes the Jīva: the Jīva is Brahman and only views himself as other than Brahman, the otherness being no absolute appearance, but only the content of his wrong belief. As explained, however, the principle of illusion itself has to be taken by the Jīva as cosmic, and hence, though his individuality is not an absolute appearance, Brahman in relation to him appears absolutely as Īśvara.

10. Īśvara in Advaita Vedānta is conceived as an absolute emanation from Brahman, though He has been sometimes erroneously supposed to be Brahman as merely viewed by the Jīva in reference to himself and the world. This reference to himself and the world is not his thinking only; that creative thought (īkṣā)—'Let me be many', etc.—belongs to Brahman and is not simply referred to Him allegorically by the Jīva. At the same time this manifold that is manifested by him is manifested as (partially) unreal, as already 'in the jaws of death', as in fact as much retracted as created. Hence His creativity is like that of the magician; as the creativity of absolute appearance, His freedom or śakti is neither absolutely real nor unreal, and this is just how the cosmic Māyā is characterized.

11. As absolutely free in respect of creation as Brahman Himself, with this absolute freedom or Māyā-śakti—a determination that means no restriction of His being—Īśvara is not only not a false idea of the Jīva, a mere symbol adopted for his upāsanā (worship), He is not also an absolute appearance like the world. Īśvara is as much unconstituted by Māyā as Brahman, and both are characterized by the same epithets—nitya-buddha-śuddha-mukta (eternal, omniscient, pure, free). Īśvara has a dual form, as wielding Māyā-śakti and thus immanent in the world (vikāravartin), and as dissociated from it, transcendent (triguṇātīta) and merging back into Brahman. As transcendent, Īśvara is conceived as what is not Māyā, as determined not by Māyā but by freedom from Māyā, as other than the world that is put forth by Him as an appearance, while Brahman is understood without reference to Māyā and the world. The current conception of Brahman and Īśvara as the higher God and the lower God appears to be a fallacious exaggeration of this simple distinction.

12. Brahman is the eternal self that has not only no positive determination, but has not even the negative determination of consciously rejecting positive determination. He is indeed characterized as Sat (existence), Cit (knowledge) and Ānanda (bliss), but these are not determinations, being each of them the unspeakable Absolute viewed by us as beyond the determinate absolutes Sat, Cit, and Ānanda formulated by our consciousness. The individual self has not only to correct for himself his subjective illusion of individuality, not only to wait for the cosmic illusion of individuality to be corrected, but also to contemplate all correction to be itself illusory. He has to contemplate mokṣa not as something to be reached or effected or remanifested, not even as an eternal predicament of the self, but as the self itself or the svarūpa of Brahman. The self or the absolute is not a thing having freedom but is freedom itself.

13. The individual illusorily thinks he is not free and wants to be free. To his consciousness, accordingly, there is the necessity of a sādhana or discipline to attain freedom. This discipline to him must be such as will lead him to realize that his bondage is an illusion and that he is eternally free. To know the truth about himself can be the only way of attaining freedom, and the discipline, therefore, is primarily that of knowing (jñāna). and secondarily that of willing and feeling (karma and bhakti). The latter is in the first instance helpful as a preparation for knowledge, as securing the spiritual attitude in which the inquiry into spiritual truth can start. In reality it is more than mere preparation, since with the progressive transparency of the mind effected through any discipline, the truth begins to shine in, though it may not be in the intellectual way. Knowledge that is demanded for freedom is spiritual being rather than the detached consciousness of a spectator, being knowledge of the self not as distinct from but as one with the knowledge. The spiritual being that is secured by karma and bhakti cannot, therefore, be very different from jñāna. The clarity of spiritual being is implicitly or explicitly the clarity of knowledge.

14. Vedānta is primarily a religion, and it is a philosophy only as the formulation of this religion. All religion makes for the realization of the self as sacred, but the religion of Advaita is the specific cult of such realization understood explicitly as self-knowledge, as sacred knowledge, and as nothing but know-

ledge. Without rejecting any other sādhana, it prescribes knowledge as its distinctive sādhana and regards it as self-sufficing and requiring no supplementation (samuccaya). The self is to be known—accepted in the first instance in faith, which, as confirmed, clarified, and formulated by reason would be 'inwardized' into a vision. This work of reason is philosophy, which is thus not only an auxiliary discipline, but an integral part of the religion and its characteristic self-expression.

15. Advaitism as religion and philosophy in one is at once individualistic and universalistic in its spiritual outlook. Religion is nothing if not individualistic; it is an 'inwardizing' of one's subjective being, a deepening of one's spiritual individuality, this being the unspoken inner function even of a religion with the salvation of all as its professed objective. Philosophy, on the other hand, is essentially universalistic in its attitude, presenting a truth that is for all, and is not merely a mystic experience of the individual philosopher. As an explicit religion, Advaitism insists on the conservation of one's spiritual individuality or svadharma, while implicitly as philosophy, it recognizes the svadharma of everyone else as absolutely sacred, being in this sense the most catholic and tolerant among religions. Again, as an explicit philosophy, it takes every individual self as the one self or reality; and at the same time as an implicit religion, it denies the world that is common to all and retires into the solitude of subjectivity. In either aspect it appears to combine the boldest affirmation with the most uncompromising denial.

16. Advaitism stands for a strong spirituality, for efficient practice of idealism, for unworldiness that is neither sentimental nor fanatical. It not only asserts the detachment or freedom of the self from the world, it boldly denies the world, though it does not take even the illusory object to be merely imaginary (tuccha). So too, while it prescribes nivṛtti or renunciation of the world in spirit, it demands that it should be practically and methodically achieved through such discipline as is suited to the adhikāra or actual spiritual status of each individual, and may not involve even in the case or the highest adhikāin a literal adoption of the hermit's life. While the spirit is taken as the only reality, the object is understood not as absolute naught, but as absolute appearance, as a necessary symbolism of the spirit. Logic, law, and the revealed word itself are all in this sense.

symbolism—unreal in themselves and yet showing the reality beyond. The object has thus to be accepted in order to be effectively denied. One has to be a realist to outgrow realism. It is for the strong in spirit to attain the self, and strength consists not in ignoring but in accepting facts—accepting the conditions of the spiritual game in order to get beyond them.

17. Advaitism aims at the absolute freedom of the self, freedom from all relativity, including the relativity of good and evil. Freedom from law is, however, to be achieved by the willing of the law, by the performance of one's moral and spiritual duty without desire—desire not only for pleasure but even for spiritual merit, and by merging one's individuality in objective or institutional spiritual life which represents a yajña or the sacrificial concert of gods and men. It would imply the strenuous cultivation of a dispassionate serenity of soul and the strength that it implies to keep out illusions and stand unruffled in one's subjective being.

18. Toleration is to Advaita Vedānta a religion in itself; no one who realizes what any religion is to its votary can himself be indifferent to it. The claim of a religion on its votary is nothing outside the religion and is itself as sacred to others as the religion is sacred to him. While then an individual owes special allegiance to his own religion or svadharma, which chooses him rather than is chosen by him, he feels that the religion of others is not only sacred to them but to himself also. This, in fact, is the practical aspect of the Advaitic view of all individual selves being the one self. The oneness is not contemplated in the empirical region, and there is no prescription of universal brotherhood in the sense that the happiness of others is to be promoted as though it were one's own happiness. There is indeed the duty to relieve distress, but such work is to be performed as duty rather than as a matter of altruistic enjoyment, the dry detached attitude of duty being consonant with the spirit of the religion of jñāna. The brotherhood that is practically recognized in this religion is the brotherhood of spirits realizing their svadharma, the dharma of each being sacred to all. If then, in this view it is irreligious to change one's faith, it is only natural to revere faiths other than one's own. To tolerate them merely in a non-committal or patronizing spirit would be an impiety, and to revile them would be diabolical. The form in which

the truth is intuited by an individual is cosmically determined and not constructed by him, and the relativity of truth to the spiritual status of the knower is itself absolute. Even the illusory object in this view is a mystical creation (prātibhāsika-sṛṣṭi), the three grades of reality that are recognized—the illusory, the relational, and the transcendental—being in fact grades of this absolute relativity.

19. The doctrine of adhikāri-bheda is an application of this epistemological notion of absolute relativity to the specifically religious sphere. The difference of adhikāra or spiritual status is not necessarily a gradation; and so far as it is a gradation it does not suggest any relation of higher and lower that implies contempt or envy. The notion of adhikāra in fact means in the first instance just an acceptance of fact or realism in the spiritual sphere. It is a question of duty rather than of rights in this sphere; and a person should be anxious to discover his actual status in order that he may set before himself just such duties as he can efficiently perform in spirit. It is a far greater misfortune here to over-estimate one's status than to under-estimate it. A higher status does not mean greater opportunity for spiritual work, since work here means not outward achievement, but an 'inwardizing' or deepening of the spirit. Again, from the standpoint of toleration, one not only respects the inner achievement of a person admitting an inferior status, but can whole-heartedly identify oneself with it; the highest adhikārin should feel it a privilege to join in the worship of the humblest. There is aristocracy in the spiritual polity; spiritual value is achieved by the strong and is much too sacred a thing to be pooled. At the same time every individual has his sacred svadharma and has equal opportunity with everyone else to realize or 'inwardize' it.

20. The merit of Advaitavāda lies in having explicitly recognized that spiritual work is this 'inwardizing', the deepening of faith into subjective realization, the striving after self-knowledge. This work can start from any given point, any spiritual status or situation that happens to be presented. Men are intrinsically higher and lower only in respect of this inner achievement. The problem of altering traditional society, of equalizing rights in order to create opportunities for self-realization, has accordingly a subordinate place in the Advaitic scheme of life, being recognized mainly negatively as the duty of abstaining from

acts of conscious injustice. This scheme of life would view with positive disfavour iconoclasm in any shape or form, any violent tampering with an institution that is traditionally held to be sacred; but it would not also apparently require one to vitalize artificially such an institution if one believes—not by hearsay, but after loyally trying to work it—that it is moribund or dead. Spiritual realism would demand both reverence for and dissociation from what was sacred. One sacred custom can only be superseded by another sacred custom, the former being either reverently allowed to die a natural death or incorporated in an ideal or symbolic form in the latter. There is no room in Advaita religion for the duty of profaning one god for the glorification of another.

21. The idea of hustling people out of their reverence in their own spiritual interest would be scouted in this religion as a self-stultifying profanity. Social life and tradition are viewed as sacred, as a yajña being performed through the ages, the sacredness being the shine of the one Self, the shadow of Eternity. It is the life of the gods, and we can help it best by merging into it, by realizing it as our subjective life. This subjective realization may sometimes come spontaneously, but so far as it can be effected by sādhana, it can be effected by each individual for himself. He can indeed help others in the work by education, but he can educate only in the measure he has himself realized this life. He can wish and pray that other's self-realization might be expedited; but for an *ordinary* person to suppose that he can and ought to emergize and vitalize other spirits is, to the religion of Advaita, a delusion and a curious mixture of arrogance and sentimentality.

22. Much of what is attributed here to Advaitavāda is the implied creed of Hinduism and Hindu society. This philosophy is the most satisfying formulation of the distinctive spirit of Hinduism, and in this sense it may claim to be a synthesis of other systems of Indian philosophy, which all seek to formulate this spirit; and it has also explicitly influenced the historical evolution of Hinduism. As it is not only a formulation of the religion, but is itself the religion in the simplified and unified form of the realization of subjectivity or self-knowledge, it is sometimes characterized as a rationalistic religion; and there is a tendency to isolate it in the abstract and to interpret it as disowning all Vedic and post-Vedic worship and ceremonial. But the abstract cult of self-

knowledge derives its whole meaning from the concrete religion of worship and ceremonial, and is recognizable as a religion only as its concentrated essence. It represents a protest against the concrete religion only so far as the latter resists 'inwardization'; but it implies no rejection but only an interpretation of the concrete religion. The *Advaitin* would whole-heartedly join in the traditional worship and would be false to himself if he professed contempt for it, though he would recognize that the contemplation of the abstract significance is itself a part of the worship and at a certain stage may be the whole spiritual activity.

23. The contemplation that is demanded is more than mere philosophic thought, being a specific enjoyment of the thought as sacred and representing a new stage of spiritual consciousness. The truth has to be felt as a self-revelation, as a light that shows itself. Light is a sacred symbol, not a mere metaphor, from the contemplation of which the *Vedāntic* conception of the self itself may be taken to have emanated.

24. The *Advaita* discipline of *jñāna* is primarily a protest against the discipline of *karma*, of moral (and ceremonial) activity which is apt in all ages to be taken as a self-sufficing religion. The discipline of *karma* is important as a preparatory chastening of the soul, but taken as a religion by itself, it is understood to work against the attainment of *mokṣa*. To will is to energize in *ahaṅkāra* (egoism), even though it be willing without desire, the specific willing to deny will, to sacrifice one's individuality. At the same time, such willing without desire tends unconsciously to dissolve the *ahaṅkāra*, though the tendency requires to be confirmed by *bhakti*, by the dedication of the spiritual merit of the willing to the Lord, or by the feeling of merging oneself in the cosmic *yajña*, the symbol of the life divine. All good willing means self-purification, and although it requires to be superseded so far as it involves *ahaṅkāra*, the supersession is itself effected through willing in an attitude of detachment, in the implicit consciousness of the self being beyond *ahaṅkāra*. Hence *Advaitism*, far from encouraging a premature quietism or renunciation of *karma*, positively prescribes *karma*, though rigorously as a duty and not for gain, and conceives it possible even for one who has risen above morality to perform *karma* in *lokānugraha*, for the education of others and for the conservation of the social order.

25. The religion of jñāna, however, is in no sense a protest against the religion of bhakti. To it the higher stages of bhakti at any rate not only mean soul-clearing, but also involve the enjoyment of the truth in one's being. It is indeed demanded that the felt truth may be self-revealed as known truth, but this knowledge is itself understood as an intuition which amounts to ecstasy and does not in any sense mean a supersession of bhakti. Although bhakti implies individuality, it represents the individual's joy in surrendering his individuality. The bhakta may feel his individuality restored through the Lord, but that is a mystery of divine life with which the Advaitin would not dally. The individual's own achievement terminates with the surrender of individuality.

STUDIES IN SĀṀKHYA PHILOSOPHY

PREFACE

Much of Sāṁkhya literature appears to have been lost, and there seems to be no continuity of tradition from ancient times upto the age of the commentators. In such systematic works as we have, one seems to have a hazy view of a grand system of speculative metaphysics There is so much that is clothed in a poetic or mystic garb on which commentators do not help us much but which are suggestive enough to tempt us to construct the system anew. The interpretation of all ancient systems requires a constructive effort; but while in the case of some systems where we have a large volume of literature and a continuity of tradition, the construction is mainly of the nature of translation of ideas into modern concepts, here in Sāṁkhya the construction at many places involves supplying of missing links from one's imagination. It is risky work, but unless one does it one cannot be said to understand Sāṁkhya as a philosophy. It is a task that one is obliged to undertake. It is a fascinating task because Sāṁkhya is a bold constructive philosophy. Sāṁkhya is not the avowed formulation of religious experience which Vedānta is primarily, nor analytical and critical like Nyāya but is based on speculative insight and demands imaginative—introspective effort at every stage on the part of the interpreter.

ANALYSIS

CH. I. PAIN AS EVIL (SEC. 1-15).

(1-2) M u k t i or freedom from pain is believed to be attainable. The wish for freedom from pain is necessary; for what is not wished to be terminated is not felt pain. The wish thus has to be regarded as conditioning the facthood of pain and is thus itself an evil. Reflection on pain thus develops into reflection on itself as evil, freedom from which too is necessarily wished. Of the two wishes the one for freedom fiom pain is *secular*, while the wish for freedom even from this secular wish itself is *spiritual*. (3-6) To the spiritual wish the feeling of pain is not a fact in the sense in which it is to the secular wish. To the latter, pain is an undoubted fact and yet a puzzle because the self *as subject* appropriates something that is known as an object and is thus opposed to itself. To the spiritual wish, however, pain is no absolute fact though it is not eliminated from consciousness. The feeling of pain is regarded both in N y ā y a and S ā ṁ k h y a as real; to V e d ā n t a it is only phenomenal fact and not real. (7-8) All the views admit that the feeling of pain involves an illusion. Pain appears to developed reflection as the self opposing itself. The self knows itself as object as it opposes itself and it opposes itself as it objectifies itself. The objectification is intellectual illusion and the self-infliction is conative evil, the two as inseparable making up spiritual illusion or a v i d y ā. (9-10) Error about the self and wrong will condition each other in the reflective self, but views differ as to which of them is immediately presupposed by spiritual freedom. In V e d ā n t a and S ā ṁ k h y a the last evil that is sought to be got rid of is error, so that freedom is ultimately through knowledge alone. Pain, in all the views, involves spiritual illusion. Pain, felt pain and the feeling of pain are the same to the V e d ā n t i s t and the B u d d h i s t but are taken by them to be synthetically or analytically identical with spiritual illusion. They are distinguishable in S ā ṁ k h y a, felt pain being real evil, unfelt pain real but not evil and the consciousness of pain being evil but illusory. (11-15) Freedom from actual pain is an affective experience of the mind to S ā ṁ k h y a, freedom from the mind itself being absolute freedom or a p a v a r g a. The first freedom for its completion demands the second freedom and is continuous with it. But there is in S ā ṁ k h y a no discipline for freedom over and above reflective detachment which, again, is the beginning of freedom.

CH. II. REFLECTION AS SPIRITUAL FUNCTION (SEC. 16-32)

(16-17) Reflection is primarily reflection on pain and is at all stages a freeing process. It is spiritual in the sense that it is as much conative as intellectual. It may indifferently be called the will to deny will or the knowing function. In Sāṁkhya, there is really no will to deny will as in Yoga. The reversion of the will is nothing but the knowing process. and its consummation is viveka in which the mind detaches itself from the body and gets lost in unmanifest prakṛti. (18-19) Two processes of mind—the progressive one which is natural life and the regressive one which is reflection or the spiritual function of freeing from natural life. Sāṁkhya admits a continuity between life and reflection, while Yoga does not. To the former, life starts reflection and viveka comes as a stage in the process that is conditioned by aviveka. But to the latter the upward movement of the mind is utterly distinct from its downward course. (20-23) This difference between Sāṁkhya and Yoga is connected with their difference regarding the relation between viveka or self-knowledge and absolute freedom. According to Sāṁkhya, viveka is the residual mind which *spontaneously* drops off; but according to Yoga, a further effort of the mind, namely, asamprajñāta is necessary to terminate itself. Sāṁkhya, like Vedānta, recognises no positive prescription to achieve mukti, but it differs from Vedānta which holds that the reflective process towards mukti starts miraculously and is no part of natural life. Reflection to Sāṁkhya is no ascetic effort and is itself an experience. (24-25) To one who has begun to reflect, the only prescription of Sāṁkhya is not to will at all but to let reflection naturally deepen or fulfil itself. The process of yoga is taken as a natural self-deepening of reflection; it is a process of active freeing, though it is not any voluntary doing. Reflection as a spiritual process is above ahaṁkāra, but the voluntary striving for yoga would still imply ahaṁkāra. (26) Sāṁkhya thus presents a religion of spiritual naturalness or reflective spontaneity. Its metaphysics springs from this religion and reflection which is the spiritual freeing process is also the organ of metaphysical knowledge of tattvas or *noumena* of

S ā ṁ k h y a philosophy. (27-32). The t a t t v a s are known by inference, faith and y o g a, but these are all understood as implied in different ways in the one natural-spiritual process of reflection. A metaphysical condition is immediately known in reflection to be constitutive of a fact. Such reflection involves inference which is reduced to a view of the conditioned getting distinct from itself as its condition, of a self-distinguishing process in the content *as still given*. Reflection involving such internal perception is *transcendental reflection*. Transcendental reflection in S ā ṁ k h y a involves inference that implies a faith in its continuous passage into intuition. The self-concretion of reflective perception is y o g a and faith in such y o g i c intuition about metaphysical entities is faith in scriptures. Assertorial certitude about metaphysical reality cannot in the S ā ṁ k h y a or V e d ā n t a view be yielded by inference apart from scriptural testimony.

CH. III. THE BODY OF THE SELF (SEC. 33-47)

(33-37) S ā ṁ k h y a admits a dualism of subject and object, but the object has a necessary reference to the self. This reference is characterised as unconscious teleology which is a metaphorical description of the objective process being real only as an identifying of the object with or its distinguishing from the self. (38-41) The body is understood as a complex of elements having its unity in their non-distinction from the self and the distinction of two bodies is not understood as existing in the pure object. Object not constituting any body would be unmanifest p r a k ṛ t i: manifest object must be the body of a self. There are two broad grades of the manifest object viz.. mind and matter constituting the mental and the material bodies of the self. Each is a body in the sense of being a complex of objective t a t t v a s undistinguished from the self. (42-47) The two bodies are known in two grades of reflection which are identical with the two kinds of reflection—secular and spiritual—mentioned in Ch. 1. To reflection on the mind, the mental body and the material body are presented as two distinct bodies..the vanishing and the standing. The material body has the mental body immanent in it; but though the mental body stands or lapses as a whole, the material body is taken as capable of lapsing before the lapse of the mental body.

CH. IV. CAUSAL AND NON-CAUSAL MANIFESTATION (SEC. 48-61)

(48-49) Concepts of liṅga and bhāva interpreted anew. Bhāva as the subjective function of referring to the bhogya. Two kinds of manifestation of buddhi: the causal and the non-causal. The world as the non-causal manifestation of the body. (50-52) The world related to the perceiving body as the content of a thought is related to the thought. The world as bhogya is the projection or necessary construction of the feeling body. (53) The world as construction out of unmanifest guṇas. (54) The manifestation of prakṛti into buddhi as at once a causal and a non-causal process, causal in regard to the existence of buddhi and non-causal in regard to the content of buddhi. (55) The eight bhāvas of buddhi and the two grades of bhāvas. (56) The bodily self as a bhoktṛ. (57) The caused and uncaused manifestations meet in the material body which is constituted by all the manifest tattvas. (58) The analysis of the feeling body into liṅga and bhāva gives the clue to the Sāṁkhya theory of Evolution. (59) The views of Nyāya, Sāṁkhya and Yoga on the referential relation of the world to the experiencing self elaborated. (60-61) The Sāṁkhya and the Yoga views on the constitution of the phenomenal world compared.

CH. V. TIME, SPACE AND CAUSALITY (SEC. 62-75)

(62-64) Causality in the phenomenal world versus causality in the world of tattvas. Pariṇāma as self-distinction and its two varieties, the unmanifest and the manifest. The causal process as an unfolding or self-distinction and the effect as the cause unfolded. (65-66) The implication of causality as *unfolding* brought out. Unfolding as immediately known in reflection on the mental object which is known as necessarily dual. (67-69) Causation as a process of the object towards bhoga conditioned by immanent aviveka. The views of Sāṁkhya and Yoga on the function of nimitta in causation and on the distinction between immanent change and transitive change. (70-71) The concept of kāraṇa-ākāśa or space as a function of prakṛti distinguished from ākāśa as bhūta. (72-73) The Sāṁkhya versus the Yoga theory about the ontical status of time-order (krama). Their difference on this point connected with the difference in their views re prakṛti-vikṛti. (74) The concept of qualitative combination or Involution in Sāṁkhya. (75) The concepts of sūkṣma and sthūla in the context of causality.

CH. VI. THE OBJECTIVE TATTVAS (SEC. 76-92)

(76-77) The significance of the different groupings of the objective tattvas. The constituents of the mental body and the material body. (78) The mind as functional versus the mind as *standing*. The standing character of the mind explained. (79-88) The concepts of tanmātra, bhūta and indriya explained. The concepts of aviśeṣa and viśeṣa analysed. (89-92) Relation between ahaṁkāra, tanmātras and indriyas explained.

CH. VII. THE OBJECTIVE TATTVAS (CONTD.) (SEC. 93-110)

(93-96) Ahaṁkāra and buddhi as functional tattvas. Buddhi, ahaṁkāra and tanmātra as the counterparts of self-knowing, self-willing and self-feeling. Abhimāna as the function of ahaṁkāra. Ahaṁkāra as willing towards bhoga analysed. Willing towards freedom—What? (97-98) Buddhi is mind as knowing and has for its essence certitude (niścaya). The inward meaning of the evolution of ahaṁkāra from buddhi or its dissolution into buddhi brought out. (99-101) The concept of buddhi as certitude analysed in detail. (102-104) Bhāvas interpreted as functions of certitude. (105-106) Bhāvas and vṛtti as mode and function at once. Relation between bhāva and vṛtti. (107-108) The concepts of ālocana and saṁkalpa connected with the indriyas and manas explained. (109-110) The anticipatory functions of the senses and of the mind.

CH. VIII. THE SELF OR PURUṢA (SEC. 111-126)

(111) Anticipative response as at once construction and apprehension. The dual function of mind, as bhāva projecting the object and as vṛtti reflecting the object, illusorily referred to the self. (112) A new theory of 'mutual reflection' put forward as against the one advocated by Bhikṣu. (113) The self by itself not known as object. (114) Two grades of reflection implying a distinguishing from the self, the first one yielding the concepts of bhūta and tanmātra and indriya, the second yielding those of ahaṁkāra and buddhi. (115) Avidyā distinguished from asmitā. (116) The concept of viveka ana-

lysed. The self as mukta conceived as contentless consciousness. (117-118) The grounds for inferring the existence of self as in Sk. explained. The self inferred primarily for the explanation of the unity of the body. (119) The inferred self as knower. The self in its essential nature as *knowledge*. (120) Sāṁkhya pluralism interpreted. (121-125) The self known as infinite i.e., as involving all selves. The self known in buddhi as having within it a community of selves. (126) Sāṁkhya versus Vedānta on individuality.

CH. IX. PRAKRTI (SEC. 128-140)

(128-130) Prakṛti as potential being with the actual function of appearing. Dualism inside prakṛti of *substantial being* as potential and aviveka as actual but without standing being. The difference between Sāṁkhya and Yoga on this point explained and connected with their views of sadṛśa-pariṇāma and sāmyāvasthā. (131) The last two concepts further elucidated in relation to Sāṁkhya and Yoga. (132) The concepts of sadṛśa-pariṇāma and self-causation in its two aspects differently interpreted in Sāṁkhya and Yoga. (133) The reality of guṇa as in the two systems. Bhikṣu's interpretation questioned. (134) The quantitative inequality of the guṇas as qualitative distinction between dominant and recessive. (135) Sāṁkhya and Yoga on immanent change. Dharma-lakṣaṇāvasthā-pariṇāma. (136) The concept of guṇa analysed. (137-138) Private and 'public' affective characters of the phenomenal object. (139) The guṇas as absolutes i.e.. as at once the potentialities of feelings and felt contents. (140) The guṇas as affective absolutes constitute the object.

CH. X. RELATION OF THE GUṆAS (SEC. 141-148)

(141) The three guṇas as the 'absolutes' of the three modes of feeling which are to be understood in terms of freedom. (142) In Sāṁkhya. the guṇas understood primarily in terms of feelings and secondarily as qualities of the object. (143) In Yoga. the guṇas understood as the triplicity of mental functions. (144) Existent object as a complex of guṇas. (145) The three grades of *felt-ness* in relation to the object. (146-148) The co-existence and mutual relation of the guṇas. The Sāṁkhya and Yoga views on the point.

CHAPTER I

PAIN AS EVIL

1. Indian philosophy starts with the belief in the attainability of mukti. Mukti, whatever else it implies, is understood as absolute freedom from pain. Is there any ground for the belief that such freedom is attainable?

2. To reflect on the feeling of pain is necessarily to wish to be free from it. To wish anything is to think that it may be attained. To necessarily wish something is to believe that it not only may but can be attained, that it cannot be unattainable. The necessary wish for freedom from pain is then the unquestioned belief that it can be attained. The necessity of the wish further implies that it is constitutive of the feeling of pain which yet is distinct from it. The wish presupposes the belief in the facthood of pain and yet if the wish were absent, there would be no feeling of pain, for what is not wished to be terminated is not felt pain. The wish for freedom is the reflective self or reason itself which thus has to be regarded as conditioning the facthood of pain and as, therefore, acting suicidally. Reflection on pain, though implying the possibility of freedom from it, is in this sense an evil, the potentiality of pain. Reflection thus develops into reflection on itself as evil, freedom from which too is necessarily wished. The wish for freedom from the reflective wish to be free from pain is spiritual wish, the latter wish being secular. It is the necessary wish for absolute freedom, freedom not only from pain, but from the potentiality of pain, and implies the belief not only that it can be attained but also that it has already begun to be attained. The belief in mukti is belief not only in its possibility but also in its actuality and in the indefinite realisability of the actuality.

3. To the wish for freedom from the secular wish to be free from pain which is the potentiality of pain, the feeling of pain is not a fact in the sense it is fact to the secular wish. To the secular wish and the reflection implied by it, pain is an undoubted fact and yet a puzzle. It is known to be given to the reflective self but not in the sense an object is given to it in sensation. In reflection on the object as perceived, the object

is known as only given, the given-ness being the sensation which the reflecting self is not aware of as its function, there being no introspective consciousness of sensing. The given-ness of pain to reflection is the feeling itself in the form 'I feel': I am directly aware of *myself* feeling, but not of *myself* sensing. In introspective consciousness then, pain is known to be as much myself as given to or foreign to myself. The facthood of pain is not questioned though somehow it appears as both distinct and non-distinct from the introspective self. That the reflective self itself conditions the pain and thus functions suicidally is not known in secular reflection. What appears here is the contradiction that the self appropriates what it knows to be opposed to itself, the puzzle that it is not detached from pain as it must or should be. Pain is still a fact though its relation to the self is unintelligible.

4. To the spiritual wish for freedom from the secular wish, or in other words, to reflection as reflection on itself, pain is no absolute fact though it is not eliminated from consciousness. To some, as for example, to the Buddhist, its given-ness disappears, being reduced to the contradiction in the reflective self, the suicidal function that reflection is. By others its foreignness is still admitted but not as absolutely real. It is taken either to be real but *essentially* terminable or to belong to a lower grade of reality. Nyāya, which does not admit grades of reality, takes pain to be real even to the final reflection though the necessary wish for its absolute cessation implies its necessary terminability. To the Vedāntist as to the Buddhist, the wish for freedom from the reflection which conditions pain is wish not only for the non-persistence of pain but also for the present pain to be realised as a contradiction. To the Buddhist, this wish is already such a realisation though it may require to be deepened. The Vedāntist, however, would take the consciousness of the contradiction as faith in its realisability rather than its realisation. The faith is still the beginning of the absolute detachment from pain, but the demand for its further deepening implies that this initial detachment is not yet a realisation of the contradictory nature of pain. Pain, therefore, still appears given though as what cannot or ought not to be given, appears as impossible and yet as fact, unintelligible yet undeniable.

5. The Sāṁkhya view on this point is the Vedāntic view with a difference. There is the faith not only in the terminability but in the contradictory character of the feeling of pain. At the same time the contradiction is not regarded as absolute. That the self should be one with the feeling that is intrinsically opposed to it is no doubt a contradiction, but that the feeling should be non-distinct from the self is no contradiction but a terminable fact. Distinction in Sāṁkhya is not a given fact: distinction is but distinguishing which, however, is a function not of the subject but of the object, being the real objective process of the object defining itself. The object either defines itself from the self, thereby itself tending to lose its manifest character or does not define itself, in which case it tends indefinitely to put forth further manifestation. Both are real processes in the object, the second process being known in the first as what was and has been terminated. Thus the non-distinction of the feeling of pain from the self is a real fact known in reflection on it which involves its distinction from the self. In secular reflection, the distinction is only possible but in spiritual reflection, the distinction is an actuality that has begun. Pain as actually distinct from the self is thus distinct from the feeling of pain, unfelt pain being an unmanifest reality which is equated in Sāṁkhya with rajas, one of the three guṇas that make up prakṛti, an unanalysable factor of eternal objective reality.

6. In other views, pain means the felt pain, unfelt or unmanifest pain being a contradiction in terms. To Sāṁkhya, unfelt pain as distinct from the felt pain is not only real but eternally real, being known as such in spiritual reflection, while the feeling of pain is real but essentially terminable, involving as it does along with a contradictory notion of the self a real non-distinction from the self, the termination of which has already begun. To Nyāya also, the feeling of pain is non-eternally real as involving an illusion about the self, though it involves the illusion only as its cause and does not embody it, as it is taken to do in the other views. To spiritual reflection, the feeling of pain is regarded both in Sāṁkhya and Nyāya as still real; while apparently the Vedāntist takes it to be only undeniable but not positively possible and therefore not assertible, to be only phenomenal fact and not real, and the Buddhist denies its reality altogether, understanding it to be

no longer a given feeling but an illusion that somehow persists.

7. All the views spring from spiritual reflection and all admit that the feeling of pain involves an illusion. The nature of the illusion requires elucidation. The feeling appears to ordinary reflection to be at once myself and opposed to myself, to be appropriated and rejected at the same time. The reflection implies the belief that I am free and also wonder that I am still affected in the way of pain: I do not thus wonder at being affected by the object in the way of sensation. The wonder leads to the further reflection that I am affected not from without but by myself, that I let myself be affected[a], that if I would. I could refuse to be affected—what I do not think about sensation as an affection. Sensation I do not resent but I resent the feeling of pain though the sensation is apparently more foreign than the feeling. Sensation is in the first instance at least foreign, not opposed to the self while pain is opposed precisely because it is of the self. Pain thus appears to this new reflection to be the self opposing itself.

8. The illusion that is involved in the feeling of pain is thus at once intellectual and conative. The self opposes itself and is thus object or not-self to itself. This self-opposing or self-objectifying self is the reflective self. It knows itself as object as it opposes itself and it opposes itself as it objectifies itself. The objectification is intellectual illusion and the self-infliction is conative evil, the two as inseparable making up spiritual illusion or avidyā. They are inseparable in the sense that each conditions the other so that avidyā has to be conceived as a beginningless series of wrong knowledge and wrong will that is necessarily terminable, because illusion is known as such only when correction has begun. The feeling of pain as belonging to the reflective self involves this beginningless self-caused avidyā which is indifferently spiritual illusion or spiritual evil.

9. Error about the self and wrong will condition or imply each other in the reflective self, but views differ as to which of them is immediately pre-supposed by spiritual freedom. In some views (e.g.. Vedānta and Sāṁkhya) the last evil that

[a] Cf. Kant—'the outer object is given to the inner sense by the self itself.'

is sought to be got rid of is error, so that freedom is ultimately through knowledge alone. In others (e.g., Yoga and Nyāya) the self is unfree even in knowledge, has still the conative tendency to be passive to itself and can be free only through a specific freeing activity, unconscious or conscious. There are again views (e g., the Buddhist view) to which error and wrong will are not synthetically but analytically connected, not causing but implying one another, so that neither lapses while the other remains, freedom being through their simultaneous lapse. To Sāṁkhya as to Vedānta, error survives wrong will and freedom is in the last resort through correction of error.

10. Pain in all these views involves spiritual illusion. To the Buddhist, it is but the illusion; the Naiyāyika takes it to be only caused by the illusion, while in Vedānta and Sāṁkhya, it is at once the effect and the embodiment of the illusion. To all but the Buddhist, pain has a natural being. Nyāya regards it as wholly natural though it is conditioned by spiritual evil, Vedānta and Sāṁkhya take it to be both natural and spiritual, its natural being being constituted by its spiritual being and yet distinct from it. To Vedānta, its natural being is accordingly only phenomenal, being nought apart from its spirituality. To Sāṁkhya, however, the natural being is self-subsistent though undistinguished from the spiritual evil, pain being on the one hand a mental fact and on the other an illusory affection of the self. By pain is meant here felt pain; and if unfelt pain be a fact as it is to Sāṁkhya, it is not understood to be an evil at all, evil being only to the feeling consciousness. Felt pain is an evil which, however, is still distinct from the feeling consciousness, being a mental fact that is the unfelt pain itself with the induced character of feltness or manifestness due to its non-distinction from the self. Pain, felt pain, and the feeling of pain are the same to the Vedāntist and the Buddhist but are taken by them to be synthetically or analytically identical with spiritual illusion. They are distinguishable in Sāṁkhya, felt pain being real evil, unfelt pain real but not evil and the subjective consciousness of pain being evil but illusory. Felt pain, however, is taken as in Vedānta and Nyāya to be synthetically connected with spiritual illusion, not merely caused by it as in Nyāya but embodying it as in Vedānta, though not therefore merely pheno-

menal. The illusion is to all an evil in itself, not as transcending or superseding the natural evil of pain but as wholly immanent in it.

11. Felt pain is thus to Sāṁkhya a real evil at once natural and spiritual and as such both terminable and corrigible Hence it is that, as in Nyāya, the striving for secular freedom from pain is regarded as continuous with the striving for spiritual freedom from the secular strife itself. Mukti is regarded as desired, not as it is to the Vedāntist as something eternal, the achievement of which is itself illusory. The unfree state of the self (bandha) is real to Nyāya, beginninglessly real though terminable. To Sāṁkhya, it is unreal as a state of the self, the self being essentially incapable of modification, but it is real as a state of the mind as object, as the beginningless but terminable non-distinction of the mind from the self. The mind is in time and its termination (which is its potentialisation into prakṛti) is as much an event in time as the termination of any particular pain. The only difference between secular and spiritual desire for freedom is the difference between freedom from actual pain and freedom from the mind that is the potentiality of all pain.

12. Freedom from actual pain is still a bhoga or affective experience of the mind to Sāṁkhya, freedom from the mind itself being apavarga or absolute freedom. The first freedom for its own completion demands the second freedom. The process towards the first is continuous with the process towards the second in Sāṁkhya, while in Yoga it is otherwise, the mind being likened to a river with two entirely opposite currents at once, one towards bhoga and the other towards apavarga. So too in Vedānta, there is the irreconcilable dualism of śreyah and preyah, of mokṣa and svarga, of spiritual will (śāstrīya karma) and natural will (svābhāvika karma), the former in each dualism implying an absolute rejection of the latter, although the latter might be phenomenally continuous with the former—what would not be admitted by the Buddhist. Nyāya like Sāṁkhya admits a continuity of secular freedom with spiritual freedom, though it does not admit with Sāṁkhya that the latter as a freeing process is not egoistic willing but only a distinguishing of the mind from the self.

13. There is apparently in Sāṁkhya no sādhana or

discipline for freedom. Even the secular process of freeing from pain is a reflective detachment rather than a willing to achieve one's good or pleasure, though the reflection happens to go with such willing. The spiritual process of freeing from the mind or the general potentiality of pain is nothing but reflection and is already above the egoistic attitude (ahaṁkāra) that conditions willing. Reflection or knowledge is at no stage to Sāṁkhya a sādhana or means to freedom but is the beginning of freedom[a]. Evil is throughout taken as correlative to freedom and not to the good, reflection being the freeing process started by the feeling of evil itself and not supervening from without. The current of the mind as non-distinct from the self towards bhoga turns of itself and continuously backward as reflection: viveka or the self-defining of the object (including the mind) from the self emerges in the natural process started by aviveka or the beginningless non-distinction from the self.

14. What is the Sāṁkhya conception of the good? As pain is the only evil, pleasure is the only good, both being at once natural and spiritual. Pain is not opposed to pleasure, nor is it a limitation of pleasure, nor the positive of which pleasure is but the cessation, but is only different from pleasure, both being positive. As in Nyāya, pleasure is not in itself an evil, being evil only as it is mixed with and shot over with pain. Not that unmixed pleasure is not attainable, as held by Nyāya, though such pleasure is still of the mind as identified with the self and not the self itself as it is to Vedānta, and is not in itself the potentiality of pain as it is to Yoga. It is indeed terminable but only as it terminates of itself into absolute freedom, being in fact the beginning of freedom. Pain leads to reflective detachment while pleasure as pleasure is the initial stage of such detachment.

15. The good, therefore, in Sāṁkhya is pleasure which by itself does not entail pain and tends of itself to be detached

[a] Vide Māṭhara in his gloss on Sk. 37—Na hi bhagavatah kapilasya mate kimapi kartavyamanuṣṭheyatayā, kintu sāmkhyānām pañcaviṃśati-tattva-jñānameva sādharmyeṇa vaidharmena ca niḥśreyasahetuḥ. Uktam ca—Ilaśa piva lala moda nityam viṣayānupabhuñja kuru ca mā śaṃkām; yadı viditam te kapila-matam tat prāpsyase mokṣa-saukhyam ca.

from the self. It is indeed in the first instance a b h o g a or given experience, but it is already in the process of vanishing as experience into the free function of knowledge. Hence even if the secular freedom from pain be a pleasure or good, it tends to abolish itself into freedom that is no given experience at all. Pain as evil, therefore, is correlative to absolute freedom which implies freedom from pleasure also as good. It is because evil is correlated in the last resort with freedom and not with the good that freedom from pain is understood as the spiritual goal.

CHAPTER II

REFLECTION AS SPIRITUAL FUNCTION

16. Reflection starts as reflection on the feeling of pain. To wish to be free from pain is the primary reflection on the bodily self, the self that appears to feel in the body, pain unlike pleasure being always explicitly felt in the body. Pleasure may not be explicitly felt in the body, and even when it is so felt, it is felt as being dissociated from the body. The feeling of pleasure is already a feeling of freedom, the initial actuality of the reflective consciousness. Pain appears distinct from the reflective wish to be free from it, although the wish is consciously constitutive of the pain. Hence the feeling of pain, unlike that of pleasure, is only implicitly reflective and appears to be followed by but not continued in the reflection. No bodily feeling is *necessarily* followed by reflection: pleasure and pain alike may be followed by m o h a or the feeling of indolent passivity. But when they are followed by reflection, pleasure alone and not pain appears to be continued in it. To be felt in the body is to be felt in m o h a : pain is felt as struggle with m o h a and pleasure as conquest over it, which as positive is felt in the mind as detached from the body. Were it not, however, for the reflective consciousness of struggle in pain, the conquest in pleasure could not be reflectively apprehended as such. The body-detached character of pleasure or its essentially reflective being is known as such in further reflection, only because the body-bound character of pain is first known in the reflective wish to get rid of it. Reflection, accordingly, is primarily reflection on pain.

17. Reflection is at all stages a freeing process, the mind freeing itself from the body or from itself as a subtle body of the self. The process is spiritual in the sense that it is as much conative as intellectual a detaching activity which may be indifferently called the will to deny will (will to n i v ṛ t t i) or the knowing function. It is in reflection that the self-assertive will (will to p r a v ṛ t t i) is known to have been one with the body that is sought to be freed from; and it is in reflection that the given object is negatively willed to be detachedly known. In S ā ṁ k h y a there is really no will to deny will as in Y o g a :

it is just the knowing process, knowledge as mental being a process. In Sāṁkhya the consummation of this reversion of the will, which is the knowing process, is conceived as viveka which is not eternal quiescent knowledge which would be the self but the mind distinguishing, defining or detaching itself from the self and thereby losing itself in unknown or unmanifest Prakṛti, the self consequently standing in its eternally manifest solitariness.

18. It is in the regressive movement of reflection towards mukti that the progressive movement of the self towards bhoga is known to have been a fact. The forward process is life, reflection as the backward process being the spiritual function of freeing from natural life and of knowing it as being arrested. The further question arises if reflection is continuous with natural life, whether the movement towards bhoga arrests itself and turns back of itself as the process of freeing from bhoga. Does reflection tell us that it has emerged from life or that it has inexplicably supervened on it? That unlike life which is perpetually self-caused, reflection absolutely begins is generally admitted, but there is difference as to whether it is started by life itself. If even pain be admitted to start the reflective wish to get rid of it, is the further reflection on this wish, the consciousness of the wish being itself foreign to the self, also started by the wish which is the primary reflection? This further reflection would be the same as reflection on pleasure, the consciousness of pleasure being foreign to the self, but is reflection on pleasure started by pleasure itself? Is spiritual reflection continuous with the wish to be free from pain which is natural reflection?

19. The Sāṁkhya view admits this continuity. To Yoga as to some other views, there is discontinuity between life and reflection and between the so-called natural reflection and spiritual reflection. There is no natural reflection to Yoga, the natural urge towards freedom from pain being to it no conscious or reflective wish as it is to Sāṁkhya. The conscious wish for freedom is not natural but spiritual, and it supervenes on the blind movement of life as inexplicably as the further reflection supervenes on this reflection. To Sāṁkhya, the urge towards freedom from pain is conscious wish and as such at once natural and spiritual; and this wish again is implicitly reflective on itself

which of itself becomes explicit. The freeing process of reflection is at once a part of life and a detachment from life. Life starts reflection and viveka comes as a stage in the process that is conditioned by aviveka. Yoga agrees with Sāṁkhya in regarding both aviveka and viveka as predicaments of the mind and not of the self but does not admit that viveka comes in the natural course of the maturation of aviveka, holding as it does that the upward movement of the mind towards freedom is utterly distinct from its downward course towards bhoga.

20. This difference between Sāṁkhya and Yoga is connected with their difference on the question of the relation between self-knowledge and absolute freedom. Self-knowledge is to both viveka. the spiritual discrimination of the mind from the self, which is a mental fact, the terminal stage of the self-attenuating process of the mind called spiritual reflection. Viveka to Sāṁkhya is the residual mind which spontaneously drops off or distinguishes itself from the self. To Yoga, a further effort of the mind—called asamprajñata— is necessary for the mind to terminate itself. The mind has to make an effort to lose itself in prakṛti, this effort being itself conscious, a conscious transition into unconsciousness. The freeing movement of reflection, accordingly, is in all stages a strain or effort to Yoga, while to Sāṁkhya it is absolute spontaneity continuous with the flow of life.

21. Pain, it has been said, is in Sāṁkhya only implicitly reflective, appearing as it does distinct from the reflective wish to get rid of it, although reflection on the wish tells us that the wish is constitutive of the pain. Before this latter reflection emerges, the reflective freeing from pain appears as an effort from without, which however is realised in the latter reflection as due to and embodying an illusion, as what was an effort only so far as the wish for freedom was blind or natural and was not reflection. Even the first reflection was as reflection a spontaneity of the mind and was not an effort but only accompanied by it. The reflective detachment of the mind from the body or pain involves an accidental strain, but the reflection that detaches the mind from the self does not involve it, being, as we said, freedom or detachment that has already begun to be actual.

22. Such effortless reflection consciously emerges in the first

instance as reflection on pleasure. Pleasure is felt as the already started process of the mind freeing from the body, as the immediate actuality of reflection so that reflection on pleasure is pleasure itself freeing from its apparent given-ness in the body, pleasure spontaneously withdrawing from itself as objective. Sāṁkhya Kārikās 59 and 60 may be interpreted as asserting this spontaneity of the detachment of pleasure as bhoga from the feeling self, of pleasure starting reflection on itself. With this accords also the passage from Māṭhara's gloss on Kārikā 37, quoted in section 13, which seems to suggest that the feeling self cures itself, spontaneously reflects on feeling, and frees itself in reflection without any effort of the will.

23. Sāṁkhya like Vedānta recognises no positive prescription to achieve mukti. But while Vedānta holds that the reflective process towards mukti starts miraculously and is no part of natural life, Sāṁkhya takes it to spring from life and to be continuous with the life-process. Reflection is not only no ascetic effort but is nothing foreign to experience, being itself an experience (of the vanishing of experience). To reflect is not only to abstain consciously from willing, to feel the lapse of willing but to feel the lapse of feeling also. Reflective feeling is not a self-abolishing feeling to Vedānta as it is to Sāṁkhya but only a feeling of the blindness or given-ness of feeling (bhoga) being abolished through the lapse of willing. Sāṁkhya conceives it not as standing joy as it is to Vedānta but a joy in the process of lapsing, joy that is as much objective experience as pain, though not itself a pain as it is to some other views. To neither is there such a thing as reflective pain or reflective effort: what appears such is blind feeling or willing as going along with and inspite of reflection. To both, reflection and the freedom from pain that it implies is a positive joy, but while to Vedānta the joy is consciousness itself under a limitation, Sāṁkhya takes it to be the manifest character of the mind as passing away.

24. To one who has begun to reflect and to realise that the reflection has come naturally, the only prescription of Sāṁkhya, if it is a prescription at all, is not to will, or if willing is already there, to make an object of it, to view it as itself a pain that should not be. In more explicit spiritual reference, the prescription is to avoid ascetic effort or antagonism to nature or life. It is not to push on reflection nor to wonder at it as miraculously

there but to let it, as what has naturally come, naturally fulfil itself. To one to whom reflection has not come, the prescription to rouse reflection is meaningless. One to whom it has come but not in full measure can do nothing to deepen it but can only let it complete itself, avoid misdirecting it or scaring it away by attempting to force it. One can indeed will to attend (bhāvanā) to the content of reflection, but such attention cannot of itself deepen the reflection, though reflection by its spontaneous deepening may lead to the fixation or unfolding of its content.

25. Apparently to Sāṁkhya the process of yoga is a natural self-deepening of reflection that has naturally emerged. In Yoga philosophy itself, the yoga process is voluntary attention passing of right into concentrated reflection or intuition. Not that Sāṁkhya takes yoga to be a passive process, for reflection that gets deepened into yoga is a process of active freeing though it is not a voluntary doing. There is accordingly no prescription of yoga in Sāṁkhya though it is admitted as a stage in the spontaneous consummation of reflection. The spiritual process of reflection is from the beginning above ahaṁkāra or the egoistic will. The voluntary striving for yoga would still imply ahaṁkāra. In Yoga philosophy, the will to yoga is not egoistic but spiritual, being ultimately the activity of asamprajñāta.

26. Sāṁkhya may thus be said to present a religion of reflective spontaneity or spiritual naturalness. Its metaphysics springs from this religion, reflection which is the spiritual freeing process being the organ of metaphysical knowledge. Reflection is started by experience or bhoga, unless it is prevented by moha; and it is a freeing from bhoga unless the same moha misdirects it towards bhoga again. Thinking which is not thus misdirected to the service of sense is real only as the spiritual process of freeing from sense, and it is this spiritual thinking that yields metaphysical knowledge. The freeing from sense is a knowing of the self as what the body, with which is bound up the experienced or bhogya world, is progressively detached from. The mind too is a body of the self in some sense and the detachment means a gradual distinguishing of the material body and of the mental body from the self with which they were identified. To distinguish the body from the self, to make the body an object of reflection is on the one hand to know the self better and on

the other to see the possibility of its dissolution into impersonal or objective but unexperienceable realities, experience being possible only through the body. The self, which is known only as distinguished from, and these objective non-empirical realities are the metaphysical t a t t v a s or noumena of S ā ṁ k h y a philosophy. Reflection is at once a freeing of the self from the body and the knowing of these metaphysical entities. The freeing and the knowing, the religion and the philosophy, are not means to one another: each of itself passes into the other. There is no freeing except in the knowing of the object as metaphysical, as absolutely distinct from the self, or—what is the same thing—as what was illusorily confused with the self as its body; and there is no knowledge of the metaphysical object except as what was its body and now disowned.

27. The nature of reflection as the organ of metaphysics requires further elaboration. Are the S ā ṁ k h y a t a t t v a s known by inference or accepted in faith or reached only through y o g a? Inference, faith and y o g a are none of them denied in S ā ṁ - k h y a as leading to metaphysical knowledge, but they are all understood as implied in different ways in the one natural-spiritual process of reflection. Inference in metaphysics is necessarily of the regressive type from the conditioned to the condition and ultimately to the unconditioned condition. Within phenomenal reality, condition and conditioned are in reciprocity, but what is conditioned by a metaphysical condition never conditions it again. Besides, metaphysical condition unlike phenomenal condition is always constitutive of and embodied in the conditioned which yet is distinct from it. Inference of the metaphysical condition is, therefore, always regressive; and the inferred condition is known to be embodied in the conditioned in some immediate way and not by inference again. The constitutive condition[a] is knowable as such as the immediate self of the conditioned, from which the conditioned is still distinguished. Inference may at best indicate its necessity but cannot yield assertorial certitude about it. How then is such certitude attained?

28. A metaphysical condition is immediately known to be constitutive of a metaphysical or phenomenal fact in reflection. Such

[a]A is said to constitute B when B without A is nothing that is known, though as embodying A, B is distinct from A.

immediate knowledge would be intellectual intuition if it involved no inference or superseded inference. But in the first instance, at any rate, it involves inference which is not superseded but reflectively reduced to a view of the conditioned getting distinct from itself as its condition, of a self-distinguishing process in the content *as still given*, the view therefore amounting to an internal perception though not yet to intellectual intuition. Yoga or samādhi would be this intuition in which the self-distinguishing process is conceived to be completed, so that the dualism in reflection of internal and external perception lapses, the internal perception being but the perception of the lack of completion in the process, which is just lack of perception of the given. That a content should be but is not perceived *in the given object* is what is known in the internal perception of the content. Reflection that involves such internal perception is transcendental reflection. Inference of a phenomenal condition is knowing something about the conditioned, not knowing it better or knowing its very self. But inference of a metaphysical condition is a better knowing of the conditioned, a *reflectively* synthetic cognition of it or an insight into it. Kant's transcendental reflection is the same process : only what is founded on it is epistemology, not metaphysics.

29. Transcendental reflection as in Sāṁkhya involves inference that implies a faith in its continuous passage into intuition. The inferred content is meant, in the reflection, to be intuited in the given content and believed to be intuitable. This intuition is not complete perception of the given, for the immanence of the inferred in the given cannot itself be given; and as yet a fulfilment of reflection, it must be more concrete than the internal perception that the reflection implies. This self-concretion of reflective perception is yoga, and the faith in such yogic intuition as involved in reflection which is assertorial certitude about the metaphysical entities is what is really meant by faith in the scriptures. Thus inference, faith and yoga are all implied in the transcendental reflection that is the organ of Sāṁkhya metaphysics.

30. What is reflectively believed and understood as unprovable by secular pramāṇa is not merely thought apriori but *presented* to thought independently of it, vouched for by an authority other than the thinking self. To believe in such presentation is to believe in a revelation; and to believe in any testimony as scriptural or absolutely authoritative is to believe that its con-

tent is given to our thought by something other than thought and other than sense. What testimony should be taken as revealed is a different question, legitimate or illegitimate. The primary point is whether we have reflective belief in a content as real and as yet unknowable by perception or inference. If we have, we have faith in revelation, for no content is believed unless it is presented. and what is presented but not by sense is 'revealed'.

31. Assertorial certitude about metaphysical reality cannot in the Sāṁkhya or Vedānta view be yielded by inference or necessary thought. To Sāṁkhya as to Kant, the certitude emanates from outside theoretical thought which, however, yields the concept of metaphysical reality. The concept does not depend on faith nor does it of itself carry belief. To Vedānta, metaphysical thought is itself an emanation of faith, being spiritual thought that is utterly distinct from secular thought which is only competent to refute secular doubts about the validity of spiritual thought. To Nyāya as to Sāṁkhya, metaphysical thought is nothing other than secular thought. Unlike Sāṁkhya, however, Nyāya holds that metaphysical thought is validated in precisely the same way as secular thought, although certitude from outside thought viz., from revealed scriptures is also admitted on the basis of thought as having concurrent jurisdiction with secular certitude about the metaphysical.

32. Vijñāna-bhikṣu discusses the question if the tattvas are known by inference independently of scriptural testimony and opines that they are inferred though the inference is in interpretation of scriptural testimony[a]. Vācaspati in his gloss on Sāṁkhya-Kārikā 6 indicates two kinds of contents that have to be known through scriptural testimony and not by inference only, viz., the order of emergence of the tattvas, mahat etc., on the one hand and things like heaven, karma devatā etc., on the other. Of these the former apparently are at once inferred and admitted in faith, the kind of content that we have taken as necessarily conceivable by thought but deriving its assertorial certitude from the scriptures. The latter would appear to be further removed from thought, though here too the contents cannot be inconceivable. There must be a way of understanding the meaning of devatā, for example, in terms of the contents of our ordinary consciousness. Faith-content of this type is not, like the cosmic evolution of the tattvas, purely intellectual and has to be understood apparently as a postulate of some kind of non-cognitive consciousness, of feeling or willing on the nonsensuous or spiritual level.

[a]SPB.—65.

CHAPTER III

THE BODY OF THE SELF

33. Sāṁkhya admits a metaphysical dualism of subject and object, the existence of each being conceived as independent of the existence of the other. At the same time, the nature of the object is understood in necessary reference to the self, while the self is taken to be intelligible by itself. The nature of the object is ultimately its character of manifestness to the self, for every other character of the object involves this character. The character is objective and is not the mere circumstance of the self knowing it or of being aware of knowing it. But it implies a reference to the self : the object is known as manifest to the self, though what constitutes this character is not the self but distinction from the self. The nature of the object presupposes the distinction in point of existence between the object and the subject. The reference of the object to the self is, in this sense, a necessary synthetic character and not a defining character of the object. The object may be conceived to exist without being the content of consciousness, but a character of the object can only be conceived as the content of consciousness, which is yet objectively real.

34. The essential character of the object—viz., its manifestness is understood to be at once a being and a process. The object, in fact, is known as getting manifested. To get manifested is for the object to be defined out of its own unmanifest condition, to be in this sense distinct from itself ; and to get unmanifested is for this outward distinction to lapse or become retracted into itself. Either process is explicitly for the self and is intelligible only in reference to the self. To reflection on the object as known, the object appears as what was being manifested and now arrested in manifestation and as, therefore, beginning to be unmanifested. With the arrest of its further manifestation, its present manifestation gets an evanescent character, for nothing merely stands as manifest before reflection. The conscious evanescence of the manifestness of the object means a perception of its reality being independent of or distinct from the self and of the manifestness, therefore, having been conditioned by the non-distinction of the object from the self. Thus the manifesting process of the object, which is its

defining from itself, implies its non-distinction from the self and the lapsing of this definition implies a distinguishing of the object from the self. The object defines itself when it does not distinguish itself from the self and it gets undefined in character when it distinguishes itself as an existent from the self.

35. The non-distinction of the object from the self is the fact corresponding to the illusory identification of the self with the object. The self is identified with the object in the consciousness of being embodied. The body is itself a real but terminable organisation of the object, the unity of which consists entirely in its not distinguishing itself from the self. Distinguishing, as has been indicated, is a contingent but real function of the object itself, implying the termination of the equally real predicament of not distinguishing. The body as not-distinct from the self is the conscious body (and not embodied self), with consciousness not as a quality but as an associated thing. The oneness with the self from the side of the object means only undistinguishedness, but from the side of the self it means the embodiment of the self in the object. The body is thus an objective fact known as such when it has begun to be distinguished from the self (and thus dissolved) in reflection, or, in other words, when the embodiment of the self has begun to be realised as an unreal modification of the self.

36. The intrinsic process in the object of its manifestation or unmanifestation is thus reducible to the process of the object forming or unforming the body of the self. By 'object' is meant here metaphysical object (or objective t a t t v a), not the object of sense-experience and feeling (b h o g a), the status of which will be discussed later. The object in which one is illusorily conscious of being embodied, the object that can appear one with the self is not the spatial object which is experienced as out there and never as oneself. The object that is taken to manifest or unmanifest itself is the object appearing as conscious body or ceasing to appear such, the object that is as real as the self and can appear as the self, or, in other words, the object that is metaphysically real. This object is known to have a character that necessarily refers to the self.

37. The necessary reference of the object to the self beyond is characterised as unconscious teleology. The object is not conscious though it may be sometimes undistinguished from consciousness: and if it necessarily manifests or unmanifests itself *for*

consciousness or self from which it is distinct, if its entire process consists in the formation and the dissolution of the body of the self, it may be said to be spontaneously moving towards or unconsciously willing the ends of the self. Not that the self has really any end or purpose, though it illusorily appears to have it, nor also that the purpose is of the unconscious object. Unconscious teleology is thus apparently a metaphorical description of the objective process being real only as an identifying of the object with the self, or its distinguishing from the self, or—what is the same thing—as the formation or the dissolution of the body of the self, formation for the bhoga or experience of the self and dissolution for its freedom from bhoga. These are ends of the embodied self which, on the correction of the illusion of the embodied self, turn out to be no ends at all. The objective process is, however, real and has to be understood as having spiritual significance before it can end for the self.

38. The body is understood as a complex of elements having its unity in their non-distinction from the self. A metaphysical complex is intelligible only as for the self, as really undistinguished from the self and as having the self illusorily immanent or embodied in it. The unity of the body is necessarily understood to be a spiritual function. To reflection, it appears as what the self has become and also as what the self is getting freed from, being really a plurality of objects associated with the self forming a unity or a unity dissociated from the self dissolving into the plurality. The unity and the plurality of metaphysical objects are thus known alike as processes, processes of synthesis and analysis making up the being of the body. The body represents in itself the entire process of nature for the self.

39. The body undistinguished from the self and the impersonal objects that are its constituents are known together. One knows one's body as a complex of such objects which, again, are known only as forming or having formed the body. There is to Sāṁkhya no metaphysical object or objective tattva that is manifest except in a body that is forming or dissolving. Not that in reflection, we know our body as actually forming or dissolving. We actually think it only but with the faith that it is actually happening. We have faith in mukti and in the body getting detached from the self in reflection and thereby becoming resolved into impersonal object to the freeing self. The implication is that

as the self becomes completely free, the object ceases to be manifest to it. Must it then continue to be manifest to other embodied selves? As a matter of fact, indeed, when one self is reflective, other selves blindly press on towards bhoga: the freedom of one does not mean freedom of all. But is there any necessity that the object should be manifest in some body and that the *same* object that constituted my body should constitute some other body? It depends on whether my body in appearing as object to my reflection appears distinct from the object that another body appears to be to my reflection. Taking 'body' here to mean the material body, the matter of it as forming the body is conceived as undistinguished from myself, as constituting me or myself as object and is, therefore, not taken as a part of the external or experienced world—which never appears to reflection as one with me. This matter is then noumenal matter and is not like the experienced object taken to be in space; and as I believe at the same time in another's body, I take the matter of it also as out of space. There is thus no intelligible distinction between the two bodies other than that they are identified with distinct selves. So, too, my mind and another's mind are understood to be distinct only in reference to the distinction between ourselves.

40. The distinction of two bodies is not understood as existing in the object and hence the same object that constitutes my body can be said to constitute another's body. But why must the object be conceived to constitute some body? Noumenal object is known only as constituting a body; and although reflection on the body yields the knowledge of the object as a reality distinct from the self, it is only as still identified with the self that it is manifest as object. Object not constituting any body would not be denied but it would be only unmanifest prakṛti: manifest object must be the body of a self. But when this body dissolves to a mukta self, must the stuff of it constitute at the same time the body of an unfree self? The object as manifest has a necessary reference not to this self or that self but to self in general i.e., to *any* self *as self*, as subject embodied in the *same* object. 'Self in general' means self-hood which is constructively one as implying identification of each self with the one object[a]

[a]As will be shown later, to be aware of oneself is to be aware of other selves, all as embodied in the same object, the object as thus embodying the self in general being known as devatā.

The object that is manifest to a freeing self as unmanifesting itself is manifest to it as manifesting to other selves[a]. The potentialisation of the knownness of an object to one self means to the self its actualisation to another.

41. The metaphysical object is one in the sense of being indivisible, but it admits of many distinct grades, the many objective tattvas being such grades. There are two broad grades of the manifest object--viz., mind and matter, known as constituting the mental body and the material body—what are called the subtle and the gross bodies of the self. These bodies are known in the first instance, the grades of object being known as these detached from the self in reflection. Each is a body in the sense of being a complex of objective tattvas undistinguished from the self. The material body is the complex of the five matters (bhūta), and the mental body is the complex of the mental karṇas or organs—including buddhi, ahaṁkāra and the eleven indriyas—on the one hand, and of the mental stuff including the five tanmātras on the other. These constituents of the body are the objective tattvas to be explained later.

42. The two bodies are known in two grades of reflection, one in which the material body is distinguished from the mental body which here appears as the self, and the other in which the mental body is distinguished from the pure self. The first reflection is identical with the reflection that has been taken to be implied in the wish to be free from pain which is explicitly felt in the body. The second reflection is what was called spiritual reflection, reflection on the first reflection. Reflection is the consciousness of oneself as objective, of the *me* as what appeared as *I*. In the first reflection, the *me* is the material body which no longer appears as *I*. In the second reflection, it is the mental body which still appears as I. The *me* as distinct from the *I* is the body which is material if it cannot be reflectively called *I* and mental if it can be. The mental body as at once *me* and *I* is thus explicitly self-distinguishing. More accurately, it is what is manifest as the *me* or the body forming or dissolving, as the lapsing of I into *me* or the turning of *me* into mere object, object that is explicitly not myself.

[a]To know an object as ceasing to be manifest is still to know it as manifest

43. The material body is also like the mental in the process of making or unmaking. but the process is not explicit in the first reflection and only comes to be suspected in the second reflection when the mental body is known to involve the process. The material body appears to have a finished being like that of the experienced object, but unlike it a being that is self-sustained and independent of the mind or self. That it only appears to be and is not a standing independent being is realised as possible in the second reflection. Even then it does not cease to appear as such, while the mental body is manifest to reflection as in the process of cessation. Hence to reflection on the mind, the mental body and the material body are presented as two distinct bodies, the vanishing and the standing. The reflection implies the thought but not the actual knowledge of the mental body as isolable from the material body, though it is actual knowledge of the latter body being constituted by and distinct from the former.

44. The unity of the body is understood to consist in the non-distinction of its elements from the self, in its being the *me* as distinct from the *I*. The non-distinction is real as objective identity with the self. not as the subjective function of identifying with the object. The identity of the matters (bhūta) with the self is, however, mediate, being their identity with the mind as immediately one with the self The material body has the mental body immanent in it. The mental karaṇas or functioning organs are taken to be the life-functions that hold the material body together[a], and the mental stuff (tanmātra) is conceived to causally become the stuff of the material body. The mental elements including the life-functions, however, hold together as the mental body through the transcendental function of the mind which is the original aviveka manifested as the bhāvas of buddhi.

45. There are apparently only these two bodies to Sāṁkhya. Does Sāṁkhya like Vedānta admit a kāraṇa-śarīra over and above the mental body (sūkṣma-śarīra) and regard the latter as a complex of bodies (koṣas)? There is mention, no doubt, of a body of the unfree self existing even at the time of pralaya, but apparently it is conceived at this stage either to be no body at all, being aviveka itself or karma by itself or to be the mental body of a previous cycle as surviving

[a]SK. 30, 32

it[a]. The mental body, again, is conceived as a complex of tattvas but not as a complex of bodies (koṣas), there being no suggestion of the sense-body lapsing while ahaṁkāra and buddhi stand as body, or of the will-body (ahaṁkāra) lapsing with buddhi alone standing as the body. Apparently the three karaṇas—buddhi, ahaṁkāra and manas stand or lapse together. In the regressive process of dissolution (pratisañcara) manas indeed lapses into ahaṁkāra and this into buddhi, but so long as buddhi does not tend to lapse (in its pure bhāvas), the mental body stands represented in buddhi with its impure bhāvas—which may be regarded as the ideality or *manifest* potentiality of the lower tattvas making up the body.

46. But if the mental body stands or lapses as a whole, why should the material body be taken as capable of lapsing before the lapse of the mental body? As already explained, the material body is only mediately identified with the self. The lower factors of the mental body, however, cannot be said to be identified with the self mediately through the identification of the higher factors with the self. To reflection, the material body does not appear conscious as the mental body appears, though the consciousness is not its attribute but its undistinguished associate. There is thus a felt discontinuity of the mental with the material body. There is no such discontinuity among the factors of the mental body. Each appears conscious and none appears as an unconscious object to any other in the way the material body appears to the mental body. The knowing mind is aware of the willing mind not as an object but as subjective or conscious like itself, and so, too, is the willing mind aware of the sentient mind. Mind as a whole is object to viveka, but below the stage of viveka, every factor of the mind appears endowed with the I-form and never as mere object relatively to any other factor.

47. Viveka itself is a *mental* function appearing conscious and does not imply an immediate lapse in being of the mental body into pure objectivity (unmanifest prakṛti) though it is knowledge of this lapse as already begun. This explains the state of jīvanmukti which is detachment of the body from the self in knowledge but not yet in being. The self that has reached viveka no longer subjectively confuses itself with its body though the body still inexplicably remains non-distinct from the self.

[a]SS. VI. 67-69.

CHAPTER IV

CAUSAL AND NON-CAUSAL MANIFESTATION

48. Na vinā bhāvaiḥ liṅgam
Na vinā liṅgena bhāva-nirvṛttih.
Liṅgākhyaḥ bhāvākhyaḥ tasmāt
Dvividhaḥ pravartate sargaḥ.

(SK. 52)

Liṅga here means the manifest objective tattvas from buddhi downwards. Bhāva is apparently subjective function of the body, mental or material, function implying the *I*-form, function of the object as non-distinct from the subject and as illusorily taken to be function of the self. We have said that the metaphysical object as known is known only as constituting the body, the body being taken as one with the self through beginningless aviveka. The bhāvas would be the different aspects of this oneness as manifest in the manifest metaphysical object—meaning specially the grade of the mind called buddhi. Aviveka runs beyond manifestation, being taken to be the function of prakṛti even at the time of pralaya. The bhāvas, therefore, may be taken as the specifications of this primordial function, manifested in the first manifest object—viz., buddhi and, therefore, also in its evolutes. The above kārikā then denies that the metaphysical object can be manifest without appearing to function as a subject and also that the subject really or apparently functions without being identified with a body; and it asserts two kinds of manifestation of buddhi viz., into the outward grades of objective *substance* on the one hand and of objective *function* appearing as subjective function on the other. As will appear presently, these two kinds of manifestation of buddhi may be characterised as causal and non-causal manifestation of the metaphysical object.

49. We may start with the presented dualism of the (material) body and the external world. The external world is external to the body which yet appears to be comprised within it. This implies a confusion which is cleared up by reflection showing that the body to which the world is external is not in space, being felt as distinct in itself and known as distinct from I (the mental self)

but not from the world i.e., from space. Felt as undistinguished from or one with space, it is not *in* space: and every external object is known as in space which is itself distinguished from or external to the body as felt from within. Perceived object necessarily refers to the body and implies distinction from it but the body does not imply distinction from the object but implies only distinction from I. In this sense, the external world depends on the body but not vice versa. Not that the body causes the world in the sense that it becomes the world, nor that it makes anything else (e.g. unformed matter) become the world. It is neither the immanent cause nor the external cause of the world: not immanent cause because the effect would then be distinct *in* it, not *from* it as the world is actually, and not external cause because then its material would be other than the material of the world. The world, as will appear presently, has for its material not indeed the manifest matters (bhūtas) that compose the body but their primordial potentialities, the guṇas that make up prakṛti. The world, therefore, is a non-causal manifestation of the body.

50. A non-causal manifestation of a real is just what is called its 'phenomenon'. The real in fact at any stage is understood as what phenomenon implies to reflection. The external world to reflection immediately implies reference to the body as real, the metaphysical appearing in the first instance as one's body. The world is a manifestation of the body in the sense that, in point of existence, it is not other than the body, though in respect of its manifest character it is distinct from and dependent on the body. A causal manifestation of a real is a distinct real, existing distinctly *in* the cause and not as distinct *from* it. The perceived world has no manifest reality apart from the percipient's felt body though it is manifested as distinct from or external to it, externality of the world to it being a function of the body.

51. The externality of objects in the world to one another is implied in the externality of the world to the bodily or percipient self. The world is space as cut up into objects and the externality of this variegated space to the conscious or perceiving body means only that this space is the content of the bodily consciousness, distinct from it as any content is distinct from the consciousness of it, being at the same time nothing manifest apart from the consciousness. By 'bodily consciousness' we mean perceptual cons-

ciousness, consciousness or self as illusorily identified with the material body, the corresponding fact being the conscious or perceiving body, the material body as undistinguished from the self as an associated thing. The external world is related to the perceiving body as the content of a thought is related to the thought—viz., as constituted by and distinct from (not distinct *in* the perceiving body).

52. The external world is nothing manifest apart from the perceiving body or bodily consciousness, being manifest through it as distinct from it. The perceiving body is the body as feeling the object and the object as presupposing it may be regarded as its feeling projection or necessary construction, the necessity being the necessity of the manifestation of aviveka as bhoga. This projection as bhogya (phenomenon) through the necessity of bhoga (experience) of the self as identified with the bhogāyatana (body) is the external world. The entire manifest aspect of this world, spatial and qualitative, is an appearance projected by the feeling body. It is the appearance of the real matters constituting the body, appearance as distinct *from* the body and, therefore, not as their immanent determination. The space (-time) of the world is no mode of the metaphysical substance ākāśa, and the qualities of the world—colour etc., which presuppose this space cannot also be regarded as the other substances appearing under a limitation. The world is not a construction by the percipient *out of* the noumenal bhūtas, being a construction in respect of its material as well so far as it is manifest.

53. The world as external to the body is distinct from the matters that directly constitute the body and from the other manifest tattvas that indirectly condition its manifestation. Yet we are aware of it in our experience (bhoga) as *given* and have accordingly to conceive it as a construction (in the interest of bhoga) out of *unmanifest* real matter (which is the three guṇas of prakṛti) out of which the body and its constituents have emerged by real causal combination and not by imaginative construction. Thus prakṛti gets manifested in two ways—in the causal way as the manifest tattvas that constitute the body (including the mental) and in the non-causal way as the external world[a]. As the world is manifest primarily through buddhi (and *only* through it to the jīvanmukta), the dual manifestation

[a]Cf. SK. 15 'avibhāgāt vaiśvarūpasya'

may be said to be the bifurcation of buddhi (dvividha-sarga)

54. Apparently, then, the manifestation of prakṛti into buddhi has to be understood as at once a causal and a non-causal process. Both the existence of buddhi and its content—viz., the external world are the manifestation of prakṛti. The former is what prakṛti becomes and the latter what it appears, neither being intelligible apart from the other. Manifestation as buddhi is thus as much a causal becoming as a non-causal appearing, for the distinction between them emerges only through buddhi—as distinction within buddhi between its existence and content (or function of reference to content). Buddhi begins to get un-manifested and its reference to the object begins to be withdrawn in one and the same act—viz., in the reflection that distinguishes buddhi from the self, and thus we have to conceive the manifestation of prakṛti into buddhi as the in-difference of a dual process. The two manifestations of buddhi are also inseparable but distinguishable as the evolution of lower objective tattvas on the one hand and as the emergence of its bhāvas or the subjective functions referring to the bhogya or experienceable world on the other. The world is a given appearance or phenomenon of prakṛti, being as much given to a bhāva as constructed by it, as much a perceived object as a percept.

55. The world as a percept is a construction of the 'subjective function' that is primarily resident in buddhi and, therefore, resident in the lower tattvas (that are distinct *in* and not *from* buddhi) as well, being in fact the function of the material body with the mental body immanent in it. Sāṁkhya-Kārikā speaks of eight bhāvas of buddhi and also of two grades of bhāva—karaṇāśrita and kāryāśrita, meaning respectively bhāva as resident in the mental body comprising the karaṇas or psychic organs and bhāva as resident in the material body. The unity of the body, as has been indicated, consists in its non-distinction from the self, in what appears as its self-form or subjective function. Thus the unity of the material body is kāryāśrita-bhāva presupposing indeed the karaṇāśrita-bhāva (comprising the eight bhāvas of buddhi) but distinct from it as the subjective function of feeling non-distinct from the external world, feeling of being an actual experient un-

detached from the world or one with space. The psychic bhāva involves the feeling of being a detached possible experient, of being one who might experience or is going to experience or experienced in the past.

56. The conscious material body or the bodily self is the actual experient (bhoktṛ) undistinguished from the experienced (bhogya) world. The experience is primarily a feeling, being knowledge of and conation towards a content as felt. The world to reflection is the content of bodily feeling or projection of the feeling body which is yet felt to be given to the self as distinct in existence from it but not from the body while being distinct from both in its manifest character. It is never mistaken like the body for the self, being thus manifested as distinct from it, though it is nothing manifest apart from the bodily self or feeling body. It is a phenomenon in the sense that it is manifest only through the bodily self but as yet given to it.

57. The caused and the un-caused manifestations of the unmanifest reality are respectively noumenal and phenomenal; and they meet in the material body which is constituted and conditioned by all the manifest tattvas from the bhūtas up to buddhi and is undistinguished from the external world, appearing immediately as a part of it but to reflection as one with the whole of it. Not that this reflective awareness is complete and amounts to the positive accomplished knowledge of one-ness with the world, there being a persisting feeling of a part of the world as *mine* (abhiniveśā). Some other parts of the world (viz., my property etc.) are also felt as *mine*, but they are known definitely to be not *me* or my felt body, unlike my observed body which is not known as not *me* though not also known as *me*, being only felt as me, felt in fact as at once *me* and *mine*. The material body, felt as the bodily self feels a part of the world as undistinguished from itself and knows it at the same time as an appropriated object. Why this should be so is as much inexplicable as why there should be an external world, the uncaused manifestation of objective reality being just, as a matter of fact, given as thus related to the body. The further significance of this ultimate fact will appear later in our discussion of solipsism.

58. The given-ness of the world or the non-causal appearance of reality as thus related to the body (felt as the self) is what suggests the central Sāṁkhya enquiry into the causal evolu-

tion of the manifest objective tattvas. The guiding clue in the enquiry is the analysis of the body into liṅga and bhāva, into its constitutive elements and its apparently subjective functions unifying them. Bhāva is a function of the body appearing as conscious, the function of referring to the external world. The causal and the non-causal processes of manifestation are the strands of the single cosmic process of prakṛti towards the bhoga of puruṣa.

59. The external world is generally viewed in Indian philosophy as having necessary reference to the experiencing self. In some systems, it is taken as entirely constituted by the subjective demand for bhoga or the necessity of aviveka to lead to bhoga; while in others, it is taken to be constructed by it out of some given material. In Sāṁkhya, no manifest or actual material is admitted as given as in Nyāya and yet the world is taken to be given, the implication being that the given is here the unmanifest reality. Yoga philosophy appears to present a view intermediate between those of Sāṁkhya and Nyāya. With Sāṁkhya, it holds, though not in the same sense, that the world is an imaginative or phenomenal construction out of given material and not a real combination of it in the sense it is conceived to be in Nyāya. But it differs from Sāṁkhya and agrees with Nyāya in holding that the material is the five actual matters that constitute the body. Sāṁkhya has been so far taken to present the view that not only are the finite spatio-temporal aspects of the experienced object a construction of buddhi in the interest of bhoga but even its qualities like colour etc., are projected into this cut-up space by buddhi, its given material being thus utterly unqualified or unmanifest. Is there any justification for such an interpretation of the Sāṁkhya view?

60. Can Sāṁkhya admit with Yoga any real or causal combination of elements in the phenomenal object? The phenomenal object, indeed. appears as having a plurality of qualities. but is the mode of their combination more than spatio-temporal appearance? The body is conceived as a unity of elements that is illusory from the side of the subject but real from the side of the object, being the real but terminable non-distinction of the elements from the self. It is only as the elements can be really non-distinct from or one with the self that their combination into the

body can be real and cause a real unity. But the external object cannot in any aspect be really or even appear as one with the self and cannot therefore present a real or causal combination. Even that part of the phenomenal world that is my body as observed appears only as *mine*, not as *me*, not as undistinguished from the self.

61. Yoga admits a real combination of the bhūtas within the phenomenal object apparently because its view of the unity of the body differs. The metaphysical elements that constitute the body are taken to be as much appropriated by the self as the body as external, and even the extra-organic objects are appropriated. Primordial avidyā, in fact, is conceived in Yoga as conative appropriation, identification of the self with the body as object in sva-svāmi-sambandha, while in Sāṁkhya the identification with the body is intellectual from the side of the subject, a mistaken *knowing* of the self as the object (which is real non-distinction from the side of the object), consciousness of the body not as *mine* but as *me*, while the external object is not *me* and can be *mine* only. There is appropriation of or sva-svāmi-sambandha with the external object only and not the object constituting the body. In Sāṁkhya, there is real combination only of the objects that are not appropriated, enjoyed, or experienced, objects that are regarded as *me* and not as *mine*. Since then there is no real combination in the phenomenal object, the object cannot have real elements too as the manifest substratum of its phenomenal (spatio-temporal) unity. The phenomenon is a manifestation that is not distinct *in* the body (like its manifest constituents) but distinct *from* it as its projection or transeunt appearance. The external world does not emerge at the end of the causal evolution of the tattvas. Sāṁkhya and Yoga agree that it is not a new or transeunt tattva caused by the bhūtas (tattvāntara-pariṇāma); but Yoga asserts, what Sāṁkhya would deny, that the material substratum of the world is an immanent modification (dharma-lakṣaṇāvasthā-pariṇāma) of the bhūtas. In fact the distinction of phenomenon and noumenon emerges in Sāṁkhya with the emergence of buddhi as a liṅga with bhāva (which is reference to or anticipation of phenomenon as its content). The course of causal evolution of prakṛti is from the beginning co-ordinate with and has explicit reference to its non-causal manifestation, the bhogya world or phenomenon. Although there is bhoga or experience only when the causal evolution is completed, there is the necessary anticipation of the bhogya in the emergence of the very first stage of the evolution—viz., of buddhi.

CHAPTER V

TIME, SPACE AND CAUSALITY

62. The external world being an uncaused manifestation or phenomenon of prakṛti has no place in it for causal change through real combination. Causality is understood in Sāṁkhya only in connection with the evolution of the tattvas from buddhi downwards. There is indeed an appearance of causation or change through combination in the external world, which implies space and time as mutual determinants. But the causation being only an appearance, space as the form of combination and time as the form of change in the world are also mere appearances. The phenomenal implies the real (though not as its manifest substratum) and we have accordingly to admit causation with space and time as its moments in the real world and within unmanifest prakṛti itself. Prakṛti has to be conceived as the potentiality of change through combination, as an unmanifest plurality of elements which is manifest only as it becomes a unity by being together. Its reference to the manifest unity and to its coming to be through combination is intrinsic, the unmanifest being understood only as the presupposition of the manifesting process. The manifest unity is buddhi, the form of the manifest in general; and its becoming through combination is the form of the causal process as the unity of time and space, is ākāśa as causal, as the manifesting process of the unmanifest as distinct from ākāśa as effect or evolute, the first bhūta which is space-time as a manifest being. Buddhi is in this sense in the making i.e., as ākāśa within prakṛti*.

63. To Sāṁkhya there is real object, distinct from the self, which is eternal-in-change (pariṇāmi-nitya) unlike the self which is unchangingly eternal (kūṭastha-nitya). Pariṇāma as manifest is change but since an unmanifest pariṇāma within prakṛti is admitted, pariṇāma in general means either the process or the product of self-distinction. Distinction, as already pointed out, is to Sāṁkhya the distinguishing process which is a function of the (real) object referred by a necessary illusion to the subject. Self distinction would be the process of

*Cf. Vijñāna-bhikṣu SS. II. 12; V. 25

being distinguished from itself, the emergence from a real of another real which is yet the same. Within prakṛti, a guṇa is only as it reproduces itself, becomes *merely numerically* distinct from itself as effect; and within the sphere of manifest reality, the real that emerges from a real is, as it emerges, distinct in *nature* also from the cause, though in all cases the effect is distinguished *in* the cause as resident in it, is evident as the cause itself unfolding a distinction. The effect as the unfolded cause and the unfolding process also are called pariṇāma of the cause.

64. Self-distinction of the object means its unfolding, the causal process being an unfolding. Where the effect is manifest, it is manifest as having been unfolded: the product appears immediately to reflection as the terminus of the unfolding process. The effect is not only the cause unfolded but is manifest as such, as with the cause within itself unmanifest and manifesting. The cause is evident in the effect as its dark ground or implicit being. To paraphrase Sāṁkhya-kārikā 9, the effect is immediately known as what was implicit in the cause, as what has now the cause for its matter or material, as the only determination of the cause, as what the cause alone can become and as partaking of the nature of the cause. The cause in fact is manifest in the effect as its very self, the effect immediately showing it. The effect reveals the cause as having become it, as still becoming it and, so far as it is itself manifest, as including the manifest effect within it.

65. Such are the implications of causality as self-distinction or unfolding. Mental being is immediately evident to introspection as self-distinct; and apparently the mind or, more specifically, buddhi is taken in Sāṁkhya as the pattern of all metaphysical or body-forming object. Unfolding in fact is knowable only in internal perception about the mental object or in what is on the same level, viz., aesthetic perception of the material object. The matter constituting the material body does not immediately reveal its cause to reflection on the bodily self. But to reflection on the mental self, the elements constituting the mental body more or less reveal their cause, and hence comes the suggestion of gross matter also as having a subtle counterpart, viz., mental stuff (tanmātra) as its cause. Elements of the mental body lower than buddhi are only imperfectly manifest as self-distinct, but buddhi is manifest to reflection as self-distinct only, as the process of distinguishing from itself—distinguishing from itself as

manifest and as ultimately unmanifest—, and as being in the making and no standing being at all.

66. Psychologists speak of the content of introspection being modified by the introspection. What is not ordinarily noted is that the modification *as such* is known in the *same* introspective act. The implication of this circumstance is that to be reflectively aware of the mental is to be aware of a dual content—viz., of the modification and also of that of which it is a modification. The latter is again presented to the same reflection as modification of a further content and so on, the endless series pointing to the unmanifest beyond of which the mental in general is a modification. Now what is known of the mental is known in introspection. Hence the mental as known is necessarily dual, explicitly distinct from or manifestation of itself. The mental may also be known in introspection as independent of it in being, and so far as it is so known, it is not known as self manifested. Such independence is not, however, known as itself a content independent of the introspection and hence the lower grades of the mind are and are not at once known as self-manifested, or, in other words appear partially as being self-manifested and partially also as standing. The mental as buddhi, however, is not known as distinct from the reflection on it, being, as will appear later, the absolute mind which lapses of itself into prakṛti and not through any further reflection on the reflection.

67. Such we imagine is the metaphysical basis of the Sāṁkhya theory of causality as self-distinction, the further implications of which have now to be elaborated. Causation is understood as a process of the object towards bhoga, the self-manifestation of the object conditioned by its beginningless non-distinction from the self. The cause is the substance of the effect, substance that is only as it of itself becomes the effect (or retracts its becoming) and aviveka as the condition of the becoming is not a circumstance outside the substance but a beginningless (and terminable) predicament of it. The immanent cause (samavāyi) and the external cause (nimitta) of the Vaiśeṣika school are here undistinguished: the cause not only persists in the effect but becomes it of its own motion. It can also retract the becoming and there is no necessity that the cause should become, for there is no necessity of the primitive illusion (or non-distinction) continuing. Illusion is known only as it is corrected, being

only undeniable but not assertible as a fact. *When* the illusion comes to be known as such, *when* in fact reflection sets in is utterly indeterminate, though as the corrective or retractive reflection comes it is known as continuous with the becoming. So it may be said that the cause freely—i.e., not only spontaneously but without necessity—becomes the effect. In Yoga philosophy, the cause necessarily becomes, though only when an external nimitta—God's absolutely free will in the last resort—removes the starting arrest; and the becoming is arrested and retracted through the equally free operation of nimitta. Sāṁkhya and Yoga agree in taking the cause as an inherently active substance that becomes without being acted on; but Yoga still demands a nimitta to remove the circumstance that prevents the becoming and thus to *let the cause cause*. Sāṁkhya does not demand such nimitta.

68. Pariṇāma is self-distinction where the effect, if manifest (as in all visadṛśa-pariṇāma) is distinct in nature from the cause, (not merely numerically distinct as in sadṛśa-pariṇāma). Buddhi, for example, becomes ahaṁkāra where a new character emerges. Within buddhi, too, one state (vṛtti) of it appears to become another: and it may be asked if this is also pariṇāma. Yoga philosophy distinguishes it as immanent change (dharma-lakṣaṇā-vasthā-pariṇāma) from transitive change (tattvāntara-pariṇāma) like that of buddhi into ahaṁkāra. Can Sāṁkhya admit real immanent change? The question is about the relation of the modes of a tattva to one another and to the tattva. Sāṁkhya would not apparently admit any unmodalised tattva. Buddhi, for example, is never without vṛtti: there is nothing in this system like the saṁskāra-śeṣa-buddhi conceived in Yoga to be buddhi that has not yet lapsed into prakṛti though its vṛttis have lapsed. In Sāṁkhya apparently, the lapse of all vṛtti means the lapse of the tattva that has vṛtti, the substance apart from its modes being nothing but the substance that is its cause. An effected substance is manifest only in its modes and so the relation of a mode with its naked substance is but relation of the effect-substance with the causal substance. As to the relation of the modes to one another, one mode is only distinct from another and is not what the latter becomes, or, in other words, is not distinct *in* the latter. Each mode is indeed noumenal,

is the tattva, but it succeeds another mode only phenomenally, being noumenally merely distinct from it. Each mode in fact is distinct as anticipatively referring through its resident bhāva to some external bhogya object: vṛtti and bhāva as will be shown later, are indeed distinct but involve one another.[a] Now the apparent succession of the modes of a tattva is but their bhāva-reference to succession within the phenomenal world. The real relation of the modes is distinction which is indeed a one-directional process like succession, the process of self-distinction, but does not amount to change, being like the process of self-reproduction (sadṛśa-pariṇāma) of a guṇa the self-reproduction of the tattva. The tattva is in fact *any* mode as involving all others so that the distinction of one mode from another is the simple self-reproduction or merely numerical self-distinction of the tattva.

69. Sāṁkhya then admits real change only in the sense of change of one tattva into another, this alone implying real manifest time. The so-called immanent change of Yoga is real as simple self-distinction and not change, being in time only reflexively in reference to the time of the phenomenal world. Sāṁkhya may admit it as pariṇāma in the wide sense that includes sadṛśa-pariṇāma, as immanent pariṇāma that is not change, being conceivable as the manifest form of sadṛśa-pariṇāma. This interpretation accords with the Sāṁkhya-sūtra II. 12.—Dikkālāv ākāśādibhyaḥ, where Vijñānabhikṣu explains dik-kāla as nitya karaṇa-ākāśa, a character or function of prakṛti. As already pointed out, this ākāśa, is the causal prototype of ākāśa as bhūta, both being real ākāśa, as distinct from the constructed space-time of the phenomenal world.

70. This kāraṇa-ākāśa has already been interpreted as the form of changes implied in every metaphysical object and, therefore, in prakṛti itself. Change is through combination and combination is for change. What changes is a complex and elements combine for the production of a new unity. Change is real time and combination is real space. Each implies the other, their unity being called ākāśa, ākāśa as the general form of change that is inherent in the real object. Such ākāśa is implied

[a] In Yoga, there may be bhāva without vṛtti, as in asamprajñāta.

in prakṛti as the potentiality of change. The form or function of change is not potential, for the distinction of actual and potential is intelligible only of what changes and the function does not change. Prakṛti is conceived as avyakta in being only, but the function which is the primal aviveka itself is still taken to be vyakta within it. Kāraṇa-ākāśa is this manifest function of unmanifest being.

71. Time as a moment of this ākāśa is understood as real becoming (pariṇāma) which is change only when it is becoming of a different and not simply of a numerically distinct, or, in other words, becoming of a manifest effect. Within prakṛti, it is becoming as mere self-reproduction of a guṇa. Nothing is real if it is not becoming either in the sense of self-reproducing or in the sense of changing and when it is not yet changing, it is still self-reproducing which is active persisting. As change is to this active persistence, so is combination to bare plurality. So ākāśa as the function of prakṛti is the active persistence of each of an unrelated plurality (triplicity) of guṇas, persistence being the time-function and unrelated plurality the space-function of prakṛti.

72. The procession of the manifest tattvas from prakṛti is conceived in Sāṁkhya as in or rather as one manifest real time. The evolution of prakṛti from buddhi downwards is a single process of which each tattva is a nodal point, a real continuity of discontinuities. In Yoga philosophy, each change (whether of tattva or of phenomenal object) is a real instant (kṣaṇa) but the succession (krama) of the instants is not real as time. The krama of kṣaṇas is still real as eternal law to the creative buddhi of Īśvara. In other words, though the change of A to B and that of B to C are each real time, we cannot speak of the series A—B—C as real time, which only appears to be a continuity through the constructivity of our intelligence (vikalpa or buddhi-nirmāṇa). In Sāṁkhya, change of tattva alone (and not of phenomenon) is real time, antecedent and consequent being understood as abstractions from causal process so that in the causal series A—B—C, A, B, C, are three kinds of real object, cause only (A), at once cause and effect (B), and effect only (C) respectively. To Yoga apparently, prakṛti-vikṛti does not indicate any new kind or grade of reality; it is not as in Sāṁkhya effect with an immediate causal

character, something at once emergent and becoming, a transitive being—but is only alternately cause and effect having only the speciality of being l i ṅ g a or immediate expression of a l i ṅ g a or unmanifest p r a k ṛ t i—the v i k ā r a s being without this character of manifesting their causal self.[a] There is nothing special in their causal character, the speciality being in their expressive character. Hence k ṣ a ṇ a - k r a m a is real not as a causal process or becoming but as an absolute thought-content (logos). The S ā ṁ k h y a view of A—B—C (which is a scheme of the entire process of evolution) as a real temporal continuity is bound up with its recognition of p r a k ṛ t i - v i k ṛ t i as a qualitatively new grade of reality and a new category within becoming.

73. Change of the object in the interest of b h o g a is a free process in S ā ṁ k h y a, not a necessary process with God as the n i m i t t a letting it start as in Y o g a. Change is of a permanent that is in three stages—as what can change but has not begun to change (p r a k ṛ t i), as what has begun to change and can yet change (p r a k ṛ t i - v i k ṛ t i), and as what it has changed to and no longer changes (v i k ā r a). The causal process is one—the potential becoming actual, where the becoming is a distinguishable real—distinct from the potential which does not necessarily actualise (as in Y o g a) and having the finished actual distinct from it, there being no necessity for the process to terminate (cp. sleep, beginning to wake, persistent wakefulness—freely and not necessarily continuous at each change). It is accordingly a continuity of discontinuities, a line of nodal points (Hegel). Now each of these three is substantial being, whatever is distinguishable as real being substantial in S ā ṁ k h y a. Thus the object is causality and causality is a triplicity of substances of which the intermediate (p r a k ṛ t i - v i k ṛ t i) is the concrete continuity of the extremes, (manifest) time being this continuity in the abstract. Concrete continuity is cause and effect in one and hence implies the notion of its reversibility (p r a t i s a ñ c a r a). For a process to be substantial is to have its sense or direction cancelled by admitting the backward direction as continuous with the forward direction. Thus time is to S ā ṁ k h y a cyclic.

74. Space is intelligible as the manifest form of noumenal combination which is represented in the unmanifest as unrelated

[a] Cf. YB. II. 19.

plurality. The character of real combination is bound up with the character of real change, combination and change being understood as not *in* space and time but space and time themselves. Combination in Sāṁkhya is throughout understood as qualitative, as having one element explicit—i.e., dominant in manifestation—involving the others as implicit in different senses. The elements are together not as phenomenal objects are together, each outside the others but as one with the others internal to it, i.e., modifying its quality, forming with it a qualitative unity and not a quantitative whole (extensive or intensive). (Cp. combination of feelings or of musical notes.) Involution and not spread (or degree) is the character of qualitative combination and the form of involution is intelligible space. All visadṛśa-pariṇāma implies combination in such space of the unmanifest guṇas ultimately; and mediately it may be of the manifest reals also. The body, for example, is a combination of manifest reals not indeed as making up a cause (for the body does not become anything) but as making up an effect (for the body has come to be); the unity of the body thus implies intelligible space.

75. The causal elements are said to be subtle (sūkṣma) relatively to the effect which is said to be gross (sthūla) in the sense of being both actual and complex as contrasted with the cause or causes which are potential and simple. There are grades of the real object viz., the vikāras, which are only effects, not causes. These are not only relatively but absolutely sthūla or gross in nature, being wholly actual either as mental receptivity (indriya) or as inert matter (bhūta). They do not change into any further tattva and the so-called immanent change of Yoga, which in the case of the other tattvas implies a qualitative interpenetration of vṛttis, would here imply a mutual outsideness of their vṛttis. This outsideness is still qualitative, a spatial continuity of distinct determinations which yet are not in space, a combination that does not become any new qualitative unity but is only non-causally manifested in the external world. The space that is implied is not distinct from perceivable space which, however, is distinct from it. The vikāras are then sthūla in another sense—viz., they are undistinguished from the perceivable world, appear to be one with the perceived.

CHAPTER VI

THE OBJECTIVE TATTVAS

(Bhūta. Tanmātra and Indriya)

76. Sāṁkhya philosophy is mainly the philosophy of the twenty-four objective tattvas in reference to the self taken as the twenty-fifth tattva. There is considerable difficulty in the interpretation of the objective tattvas and some light is thrown on it by the different modes of grouping of the twenty-three manifest tattvas. One grouping is into the seven prakṛti-vikṛtis and the sixteen vikāras. Another is the demarcation of the eighteen tattvas that constitute the mental body on one side from those five that make up the material body on the other. There is again the division into the thirteen karaṇas or organs (internal and external) and the stuff or material of the mind and the body—viz., the tanmātras and the bhūtas. A further point to be noted is that the senses on the one hand and the tanmātras on the other are taken to be co-ordinate (evolutes of ahaṁkāra) while the rest of the evolution is in a single line.

77. The grouping in reference to the two bodies presents the main clue to the interpretation of the tattvas. The constituents of the mental-body are taken to be buddhi, ahaṁkāra, and the eleven indriyas on the one side as the karaṇas and the five tanmātras on the other. The karaṇas or organs are the mind as through its Bhāva functioning towards the external world and the tanmātras appear in contrast to be the mind as standing or existent. Both are substances but they embody the self or are endowed with the self-form in different senses. Mind as karaṇa appears as subject—i.e., as the self experiencing—prehending (āharaṇa) and revealing (prakāśa) the external object (and also as holding the material body together), while mind as tanmātras (or their original bhūtādi) appears as the objectively persisting or standing self. The former aspect is sāttvika and rājasika while the latter is tāmasika.

78. To explain this standing character of the mind. The mind consciously stands so far as it feels or enjoys itself. The self or consciousness is beyond time, beyond persistence and change. The persistence of the self is therefore the persistence of the mental

body as non-distinct from the self which is illusorily taken as the mental self. Now to be conscious of the persistent self is to be conscious of the persistent *me* and not *I*, the consciousness of the mind as knowing or willing being that of the objective or embodied *I*. The consciousness of *me* is feeling, being unreflective when the *me* is the material body and reflective when the *me* is the mental body. The mental body, unlike the other body, is at once *me* and *I*, is the felt (me) as feeling (I). The persistent self then is the mind feeling itself as felt, and the mind as (narcissistically) felt by itself, as manifest objectivity of feeling is the standing stuff of the mental body called bhūtādi, the parent of tanmātra. The mind functions as the karaṇas and stands as the tanmātras.

79. The material body as distinct from the mental stands only as a complex of matters with no functions of its own other than the functions of the mind that animates it. If mental stuff is mind as felt by itself, the stuff of the material body is what is sensed by the mind. The relation of tanmātra and bhūta thus appears to be that between felt and sensed objectivity. If the pure sensed content can be shown to be a causal manifestation of the pure felt content, tanmātra would be intelligible as the subtle or causal form of bhūta. Again if sensing and sensed content are knowable only as immediately constituting bhoga or perceptual experience with its differentiation into pleasurable, painful etc., we can understand why the indriyas and bhūtas should be called viśeṣa-tattvas. What immediately constitutes bhoga *appears* i.e., is non-causally manifested in the bhogya or phenomenon: it does not become or change. That would explain why the indriyas and bhūtas are called mere vikāra or effects that are not causal again.

80. We may now consider the tanmātras, the indriyas and the bhūtas together, the two former being co-ordinate constituents of the mental body and the two latter co-ordinate as viśeṣas or vikāras. Tanmātra and indriya are directly manifest as with the self-form, the former as the (objectively) persisting self and the latter as the functioning self, and hence they are taken as belonging to the mind. Bhūta is manifest as with self-form only through them, only as they are immanent or undistinguished in the material body. Indriya and bhūta are alike distinguished as viśeṣa and vikāra

from tanmātra; which thus is undifferentiated and causal stuff and is just subtle or psychic matter.

81. To explain the undifferentiated or aviśeṣa character of tanmātra. To experience is to subjectively function in the material body towards the external world directly. The functioning is apparently of the self but really of the body undistinguished from the mind which again is undistinguished from the self. It is other than functioning in the mind or mental body which is consciously detached functioning towards external world, what may be called 'thinking feeling' or imaginative feeling. Experiencing is feeling the external world in an undetached or sensuous way. Experience as specific function of the material body is feeling and it is knowing only as the function of the mental body as immanent in the material body. Now the only function of the mind that is consciously immanent in the experiencing body is sensing. Bodily feeling is at once the standing being of the body and its experiencing function; and conscious sensing is one with the experiencing function which yet may be without it. The content of all subjective function is the external world which is distinguished from the function in all cases except when the function is sensuous experiencing. Experiencing and empirical world as feeling and the felt are indistinguishable and may be both designated sense-experience or bhoga.

82. Bhoga is, however, distinguished alike from the mere feeling and the mere sensing. The mere feeling is the standing being of the body and is in fact its constituent matters, the bhūtas. The mere sensing is the mind functioning in its lowest or outermost grade, being the indriyas. Each is one with bhoga which however is distinct from each; they necessarily imply one another in this sense. Each is understood as the non-causal presupposition of bhoga and not as causally becoming bhoga. Bhoga or bhogya is not their effect but the phenomenalisation of prakṛti as revealed by and reflected in them. As undistinguished from the bhogya, they are conceived as having the originals of its characters. Its characters are not only presentative but also affective. The sense-qualities of the phenomenal world are represented in the real world by the bhūtas on the one hand and by the indriyas on the other. But each quality has its distinguishable affective aspects—its pleasurable, painful and 'indolent' feel, these being the manifest

forms of the three guṇas of prakṛti of which the phenomenal is the non-causal expression. These distinguishable aspects are then conceived to be manifest also in the bhūtas and the indriyas which accordingly are called viśeṣas or the affectively differentiated tattvas.

83. The viśeṣas are also the non-causal vikāra-tattvas, being viśeṣas through their one-ness with non-causal manifestation. Affective differentiation and non-causal character are thus connected: what is affectively differentiated does not become and what becomes is not so differentiated. Becoming in fact is *for* bhoga or phenomenal manifestation and is distinct from it while what is undistinguished from bhoga no longer becomes. Thus what becomes is aviśeṣa-tattva which would include all the other tattvas. The term aviśeṣa, however, is actually used in the Kārika (38) to mean the tanmātras and in Yoga-bhāṣya (II.19) to include ahaṁkāra also.

84. So tanmātra is a causal tattva that is the content of feeling manifest to feeling but not manifested or reflected in the external object. It is not experienced in the body but is necessarily conceived as experienced in the mind. though our actual experience is always in our body. It is accordingly conceived as experienced by a devatā or a Yogin. As felt-content, it is, as already explained, stuff or matter and not function; as causal, it is the subtle counterpart of bhūta which is non-causal; and as affectively undifferentiated, it is taken to be pure joy in the objective and is accordingly designated devatā along with ahaṁkāra and buddhi. These prakṛti-vikṛtis are unlike the vikāras absolute entities in a sense. The derivation of tanmātra from ahaṁkāra will have to be understood in connection with their absolute character.

85. To discuss details about bhūta. indriya and tanmātra. There are the five bhūtas corresponding to the five presentative senses or jñānendriyas and the five tanmātras. There is some sort of development within each pentad but the five-fold character is suggested by experience of the external object and not apriori. The second bhūta—vāyu, for example, presupposes the first—ākāśa--but is not its evolute in the sense in which bhūta is evolute of tanmātra. The tattvas within each pentad present progressive concreteness, but apparently a pentad as a whole is taken to be evolved from its

cause. Now the five experienced or perceived aspects—viz., sense-qualities—of the external object have for their noumenal prototypes the five bhūtas which are by a sort of aesthetic abstraction or transcendental reflection known to be the reals symbolized by the phenomenal aspects. They may in fact be identified with the sensa with the metaphysical significance—not ordinarily assigned to the sensa—that they are like Platonic Ideas in the sensuous sphere of which the phenomenal or perceived qualities are the ectypes.

86. The space-aspect of the phenomenal object is pre-supposed by the other aspects which are ordinarily called sense-qualities. Admitting what is common to most Indian systems—viz., that space as the so-called bare form of the object is really the space of sound, the five sense-qualities appearing in space (of the phenomenal object) answer in the noumenon to five qualitied spaces—viz., ākāśa with the sound-quality, vāyu which is that ākāśa as restricted by the emergent touch-quality, tejas which is that vāyu as restricted by the further quality of colour and so on—sound-space and its four emergent but immanent determinations. These noumenal qualitied spaces—each infinite unlike the cut-up or finite space of the phenomenon—are the bhūtas. The qualitied spaces may as well be called spatial qualities, qualities by themselves real (not qualities of object *in* space which would be phenomenal).

87. These noumenal spaces or qualities make up the felt material body. Ākāśa as the eternal form of becoming is the causal space-time already explained. Bhūta as ākāśa is effect—ākāśa that no longer becomes. Indriya also is effect that no longer becomes, being, however, effect as function while bhūta is effect as matter. The non-causal function of sense is to *reveal* the external object while bhūta is matter that *appears* as external object. Sense is said to reveal object by coming in contact with it without leaving its place in the body (S. Sūtras V. 104-7). That appears to imply that the sense-function has to be symbolised in the phenomenal as a sort of standing motion. The vṛtti of sense as of the mind in any grade is constituted by its bhāva or subjective function of referring to the (phenomenal) object, vṛtti being the standing state or mode and bhāva the function of reaching the object and constituting the vṛtti at the same time—what is symbolised as standing motion. Thus the

sense-function like bhūta may be understood as non-causal ākāśa with the difference that it is time with space implicit in it, while bhūta would be space with time implicit in it. Bhūta is spatial quality that is referred or projected on to the object, while indriya is the time-function of instantaneously reaching the object. It is non-causal ākāśa in both cases with varying stresses on the space-aspect and time-aspect.

88. If bhūta means spatial sense-quality by itself, tanmātra would stand for non-spatial sense-quality. Spatiality as a character of sense-quality as distinct from a perceived object is extensity rather than extension, is spread that is no whole but a simple unity of (infinite) repetitions (units) of the same quality which yet persist in the unity in their distinctness and is thus neither extensive nor intensive quantity. Bhūta is thus conceived to be qualitatively spatial, with only two qualitative magnitudes—aṇu (here, simple unit-character) and mahat (here, bigness), the simple sensible unit being itself a complex of supersensible plurality, which explains also the 'degrees' of sensible bigness[a]. The supersensible constituents of the simple sensible unit are called tanmātra. Each tanmātra is one, and the five tanmātras are only intellectually distinct from one another unlike the bhūtas which present an intuitable continuous series of qualitative spreads[b].

89. Ahaṁkāra is conceived as predominantly rājasika or active, being—as will appear presently—the principle of egoistic conation. This conation matures into egoistic cognition and egoistic feeling which are respectively the sāttika and tāmasika developments within the conation. As one wills, one imagines the object willed and feels it in anticipation. To imagine is to anticipate sensing and to anticipate a feeling is to begin to be immobilised into a standing being The anticipatory sensing is the conation itself maturing as knowing, and the anticipatory feeling is the same getting accomplished into a restful or indolent being. Conation or ahaṁkāra in the former aspect is technically called vaikṛta, the original of indriya and in the latter aspect is bhūtādi, the original of the tanmātras. Neither vaikṛta nor bhūtādi is a tattva other than ahaṁ-

[a] SS. V. 87-88, 90
[b] STK. on SK. 38

kāra, but these now evolve the new tattvas viz., the indriyas and the tanmātras.

90. Sense or sensing has two aspects—as revealing (prakāśa) and as reaching or pervading (āharaṇa) the object—and is accordingly divided into the cognitive (jñānendriya) and the active (karmendriya) senses. Āharaṇa apparently would be the mental (āhaṁkārika) counter-part of the bodily use of the object that is revealed by the cognitive senses. Such use is as much a condition of sense-knowledge as it is conditioned by it—their correlation being through manas. To speak is for the mind (ahaṁkāra) to be the spoken sound, to pervade it, to cover it actively. To hear is for the mind to reveal (not to receive or be passive to) the sound, to anticipatively though undetachedly take its form. So in the case of the other senses, though what jñānendriya and karmendriya correspond to one another is obscure except in the case of śrotra and vāk. The mind *uses* the object in the sense of being or pervading it. Both kinds of indriya function by reaching the object (prāpti), though it is reaching without leaving its position.

91. As combining the two functions, manas is conceived as a further sense—the internal sense as distinct from the others called external, which is the lowest of the internal karaṇas or organs of the mind, having as their common function the holding of the material body together (dhāraṇā). Manas as internal sense not only co-ordinates the vṛttis of the external cognitive senses but also those of the external active senses, and these two sets of vṛttis with one another, having for its distinctive vṛtti—saṁkalpa (and vikalpa) which would be defining or characterising the sensed content.

92. It remains to explain how tanmātra as the felt or tāmasika transformation of ahaṁkāra is also the non-spatial sense-quality that becomes spatialised as bhūta. As felt, it is, as has been explained, the standing being or stuff of the mind. But why should pure or simple sense-quality be taken as the same as mental stuff? What is felt but not in the (gross) body is the mind as felt by itself. The mind here means the individualised mental body of the self, as embodied in which the individual self is a finitised ego excluding other egos, wills in other words to maintain its finitude. What finitises the individual self which is in-

finite is a h a ṁ k ā r a as resting in b u d d h i, the will anticipating its fulfilment. The finitising ego-hood is in fact the will in its objectivity which as transformed into felt fulfilment or standing being is the stuff of the mental body. This standing being is the *me* that was *I* or the ego but is not it any longer, having its place still within the mind only through its *conscious* absence of ego-hood. B h ū t a as making up the material body is also *me* but what was never reflectively taken as the *I*. The distinction of the material *me* from the mental *me* is the spatiality of the former. Spatial sense-quality as denuded of its spatiality by aesthetic abstraction is manifest as a pure aesthetic content. Aesthetic feeling and aesthetic content are one, the former being necessarily expressed in the latter which is immediately expressive of the former. Aesthetic feeling is self-enjoying and aesthetic content is self-enjoyed. The aesthetic (t a n m ā t r a) in fact is an absolute mentality like willing (a h a ṁ k ā r a) and certitude (b u d d h i).

CHAPTER VII

THE OBJECTIVE TATTVAS (Contd.)

(Ahaṁkāra and Buddhi)

93. Ahaṁkāra and buddhi are taken along with manas as the three internal organs (karaṇa); and along with the tanmātras as prakṛti-vikṛtis and as other than the viśeṣas. They are functional tattvas that are internal (mental) causal and aviśeṣa. Aviśeṣa, as has been shown, is manifest necessarily as mental and causal, and so it will suffice to characterise them as manifest functional aviśeṣas. The affective differentiations—pleasurable, painful etc.—are manifest only in the tattvas that do not become but are immediately reflected in the bhogya world that is distinct *from* them and not distinct in them. The affectively undifferentiated tattvas are also manifest as absolute in the sense of being *causa sui*, cause (prakṛti) and effect (vikṛti) at once and not alternately, or self-caused. The self-caused is understood in three forms—self-known, self-willed or self-felt; knowing, willing and feeling amount to self-becoming in the region of the absolute. Buddhi, ahaṁkāra and tanmātra are the absolute mind as corresponding respectively to the illusions of the self objectifying itself—knowing itself, willing itself, and feeling itself—objectifying in each form being really the self-distinguishing causality of the mind. These forms of the absolute mind are really three stages: buddhi as self-knowing becomes ahaṁkāra as self-willing which in its turn becomes tanmātra as self-feeling.

94. Buddhi, ahaṁkāra and tanmātra may be regarded as self-consciousness in the objective, as the real mental counterparts of the illusion of self-objectification. Tanmātra as the counterpart of self-feeling has been explained. Ahaṁkāra is taken as corresponding to self-willing. Sāṁkhya-Sūtra VI-54 says that the agent is ahaṁkāra, not the self. The finite ego-hood of the self (which is in essence an infinite individual) is manifested in willing. The knowing self may be finite but the finiteness is not manifest in the knowing. The feeling self is finite but is manifest as *me* and not as *I* or ego. Ahaṁkāra

is the finite ego-hood of the mind as willing. Now willing as in the (gross) body and directed towards the external object presupposes willing in the mind towards itself, the mind as active *I* becoming the standing *me*. This is the self-willing of the mind which answers to ahaṁkāra.

95. The specific function of the mind as ahaṁkāra is said to be abhimāna—what appears in the gross form as pride or vanity or complacency and is in essence the conscious identification of the self with a finite being—expressible as 'I am this being (and therefore not other being)'. This finitising function is, as intellectual, a bhāva of buddhi, the 'subjective' function of asmitā which is one of the viparyayas, not a causal manifestation of the objective mind. The function, however, is the transcendental or anticipatory form of conation as the causal function of becoming finite. Transcendental asmitā manifested as causal or conative is abhimāna: the consciousness (illusory) 'I am this being' matures into 'I am going to become this being'. This is the pure conative or rājasika manifestation which as partly fulfilled will is self-feeling (tāmasa) abhimāna, the self-immobilising activity of the mind, taking form as pride or complacency. Bhūtādi is this tāmasa abhimāna as self-felt and not self-feeling. It still implies conative activity (resting on asmitā), though as a recessive fringe only. With the complete fulfilment of this immobilising activity, abhimāna as self-felt mind is turned into tanmātra.

96. Ahaṁkāra is the mind as willing. Willing is understood as willing towards bhoga. Bhoga is in one's (material) body which is manifestly exclusive of other bodies. Willing towards bhoga too implies exclusiveness, being in fact the mental prototype of the bodily exclusiveness, and it is accordingly the nucleus of what has been called the mental or subtle body. Willing towards freedom has also been conceived, willing to get rid of the finitising body, of the will towards bhoga which though free in the sense of self-causing—the sense in which all the prakṛti-vikṛtis are free—is really self-contracting, being the mind acquiring *impotentia* (aśakti or anīsvaratva). The so-called willing towards freedom is properly free activity, activity that does not wait for the result, being intrinsically unimpeded, though there may be lapses from it. This unimpeded activity of the mind—activity and fruition in one or spiritual efficiency—is called

aiśvarya and is a function of buddhi. It is not willing at all because willing must have for its object what was not and is to emerge. Activity that is necessarily efficient is not willing because it has no object *to be* accomplished. The activity towards freedom is but the exercise of freedom.

97. As ahaṁkāra is primarily the mind as willing, though it may develop knowing and feeling aspects (as vaikṛta and bhūtādi), so buddhi is primarily the mind as knowing which may take the appearance of willing and feeling. The essence of willing is abhimāna while the essence of knowing is niścaya. Niścaya means certitude, the formula of which in subjective terms is 'I am I' as distinct from 'I am this being', the formula of abhimāna. The formulation of abhimāna is factitious, for it does not appear as a certitude though it involves certitude which, were it to be expressed as a judgment, would be expressed as 'I am this being'. Niścaya or certitude by itself is nothing if not explicit as a judgment. Both the formulas therefore express certitude, certitude with or without reference to willing, or—what is the same thing—certitude about object and certitude about the subject, the expression of which is synthetic judgment (identity of differents) and analytic judgment (self-identity). Identity, in fact, is the objectivity of what subjectively appears as certitude. Buddhi as object distinct from the self is mind as undifferenced manifestation[a], undifferenced either in the sense of not referring to difference at all or in the sense of superseding or anticipating difference. Even in the latter sense, the difference is not in buddhi, the anticipatory reference to which is an uparāga or reflection of tamas in buddhi[b]. So even the so-called synthetic identity is analytic, the difference of its terms being presupposed by but not constitutive of the identity.

98. Niścaya (certitude) or adhyavasāya (judgment) is primarily understood as synthetic in reference to willing. Knowledge may not lead to willing but willing presupposes knowing in the form 'this should be done' which in the last resort implies 'I as this ideal being have to be actual', or 'I am this being in possibility'. The asmitā ('I am') that starts willing is a synthetic identity of the differents—'myself as possible' and 'myself as actual'. This

[a]liṅgā-mātra or vyaktatāmātra—YB. & YV II. 19
[b]SS. II. 15

may be taken to be the original of a synthetic objective judgment like 'A is B': identity-in-difference is intelligible in reference to willing. The reference is anticipative or retrospective. Synthetic knowledge is to be or was necessarily embodied in willing (or feeling). This seems to be the inward meaning of the evolution of ahaṁkāra from buddhi or its dissolution into buddhi through reflection.

99. Certitude though primarily isolated in reflection on willing as a self-function which is objectively identity-in-difference is not what is primary in being. Synthetic identity presupposes (and lapses into) analytic identity, the subjective form of which is 'I am I', the pure sāttvika asmitā. Analytic identity as objective is nothing but the function of manifestation (liṅga-mātra) or manifest being in general (vyaktatā-mātra). 'I am I' really means that the self is not really the content of judgment; the content of judgment is objective, and the analytic identity is but the objective representation or symbolism for the self from which it is distinct. Mind is essentially buddhi or manifestation in general, manifest being and manifesting function. As function, it manifests not only all object constructed and caused, but also the primordial distinction of object from the self; and as being, it is the manifest form of the object as distinct from the self and as such unmanifest (prakṛti). As being, it is manifested by itself as function which as thus prior to manifest being has to be understood as actual and not lapsed in prakṛti[a], actual as aviveka, the vāsanās or memory-traces of a past life.

100. The primal certitude 'I am I' is thus equivalent to 'mind (buddhi) is not I'. The implication is that even analytic identity is not subjectively an intuition but thought or distinguishing reflection, a negative judgment. To Vedānta, it would be nirvikalpa perception (with the negation of the apparent relation of identity), and to Yoga, it would be asmitānugata samādhi, the highest grade of samprajñāta. To Sāṁkhya, knowing is distinguishing, even this final knowing called viveka. Niścaya as analytic identity appears indeed relatively to synthetic identity as intuition, but the intuition is only a higher grade of distinguishing, distinguishing itself from the being of the self on the one hand and from the un-manifest pra-

[a] Cf. SPB. II. 15; V. 25; VI. 12

kṛti on the other. Viveka is buddhi distinguishing itself as function (thinking) from puruṣa and as being (intuition) from prakṛti.

101. Certitude, identity or manifestness constitutes the substantial reality of the mind. Like ahaṁkāra, it is mind as self-objectifying or self-causing: self-knowing is also a becoming or causal self-distinguishing of the mind. The difference is that here the becoming is not a self-finitising, the mind as effect being as infinite as the causal mind. As already explained, even identity-in-difference is self-repetition: certitude of the form 'I am this being' confers the infinity of the *I* on 'this being' or *me*. Buddhi then may be said to present within itself the *manifest* form of sadṛśa-pariṇāma and hence the vṛttis of buddhi may be taken to be self-repetitions.

102. Certitude is explicit as knowing but it may appear also implicitly as the proto-type of willing and feeling. Mind as self-identity—whether analytic or synthetic—has four bhāvas or modes of referring to a content. These are jñāna, aiśvarya, vairāgya and dharma belonging to the mind as analytically self-identical or pure buddhi, and their opposites ajñāna, anaiśvarya, rāga and adharma—belonging to the mind as synthetically self-identical or buddhi with the uparāga of tamas. Now the first three bhāvas in each set correspond respectively to knowing, willing and feeling. The bhāvas in the second set have negative names though they are also positive as subserving bhoga unlike the bhāvas in the first set, which represent withdrawal from bhoga.

103. Ajñāna would mean such certitude as is implied in the knowledge of the object to be enjoyed or experienced, implied in what may be called empirical judgment. It is called ajñāna, as experience or bhoga implies wrong knowledge, the false identification of the self with the not-self. Anaiśvarya would mean conscious inefficiency, certitude about the will being impeded or having restricted efficiency. All willing is impeded willing, unimpeded willing or aiśvarya, as we have seen, being not willing at all. Willing would be ahaṁkāra, but the reflective certitude about its limitation is a bhāva of buddhi. Rāga or avairāgya (to distinguish it from rāga as a stage of ajñāna or viparyaya) is conscious attachment or reflective consciousness of being attracted or immobilised by the felt object.

Vairāgya is feeling of detachment or freedom from the bhogya object, disinterested feeling. Like aiśvarya, however, which is free activity that only appears as willing, vairāgya which is free being has only the appearance of feeling, disinterested feeling being only symbolised as feeling. Jñāna, however, is mental freedom and is understood literally as the mind knowing itself as distinct from the self and as a symbol of the self.

104. The pure bhāvas of buddhi are the spiritual functions, modes of freedom referred to the self but really belonging to the mind. The impure bhāvas are modes of being unfree which, however, are realised as such and, therefore, also imply spiritual mentality. Both are functions of the mind as infinite, as completely self-manifesting or self-identical, as with the form not only of the self but of the self *as self-conscious*. The two remaining bhāvas however—viz., dharma and adharma—do not have the conscious form of the self. They mean spiritual merit and demerit and not conscious spiritual activity, moral and ceremonial, as they have been taken to mean by some commentators. Merit and demerit are actual (manifest) but unconscious tendencies of buddhi, being included among bhāvas as due to self-conscious activity of the self (mind).

105. Bhāva and vṛtti of buddhi (as also of lower tattvas) have to be distinguished. Vijñāna-bhikṣu interprets vṛtti as dravyarūpā or substantial (mode of substance) like a flame, though he points out that it sometimes means self-maintaining function (sva-sthiti-hetu-vyāpāra[a]). Even in the latter sense, vṛtti is dravya-rūpā in the sense that it is the being of a tattva as self-maintaining. The former meaning is taken to be indicated by sūtra V.107 where vṛtti is said to be other than part (bhāga) and quality (guṇa), being at once in the tattva and outside of it, implying a sort of 'standing motion'.[b] Apparently then vṛtti is mode and function at once, one or other aspect being stressed in the two meanings (as dynamic state or standing motion). Bhāva is mere function —the function of referring to or appearing conscious of the objects

[a] Cf. SS. V. 105-8

[b] Cf. also Aniruddha-Vṛtti on the sūtra where vrtti is characterised as prasarat-rūpa.

is not dravya-rūpa or substantial. Bhāva and vṛtti are indeed dependent on each other: there is no bhāva without vṛtti (such as seems to be implied in the asamprajñāta of Yoga philosophy) and no vṛtti without bhāva (no merely mental state without conscious reference to the object). No tattva is without either: it has a standing form through its reference to the object (buddhi e.g., anticipatively, and really, takes the form of the object) and its reference is possible through its standing form, the two together making up its real pratibimbana or mirroring of the object.

106. With this is connected the Sāṁkhya theory of knowledge. Knowledge is a bhāva or subjective function through which a content or object is non-causally manifested. This manifestation is at once knowledge of the content as given and projection or construction of the content. The function is primarily of buddhi but secondarily of all the karaṇas. The karaṇas are the four—buddhi, ahaṁkāra, manas on the one hand as internal organs and the external senses on the other. The knowing function as through these karaṇas is called adhyavasāya, abhimāna, saṁkalpa and ālocana respectively. Each of these in reference to the particular object known is connected with a particular mode (vṛtti) of the karaṇa as substance. Jñāna as bhāva is a function of a vṛtti of a karaṇa. So adhyavasāya etc., are each a knowing function in one aspect and an existent mode in another of a substantial karaṇa-tattva.

107. The external (cognitive) senses yield knowledge of the object as barely given and not yet endowed with a distinguishable character, nor related to the willing and feeling ego, nor manifested as true or self-identical i.e., as the content of certitude. This bare acquaintance with the given is called ālocana. Some take it as knowledge of the object as vastu-sāmānya i.e., as without particularity (viśeṣa) which to them is distinguishing and distinguishable character known only in the way of saṁkalpa by manas. Others like Vyāsa[a] and Vijñānabhikṣu[b] take ālocana as of two grades—acquaintance with the vastu-sāmānya called nirvikalpa, and acquain-

[a] YB. III. 47
[b] SPB. II. 32

tance with it as this and not another, as particularized (viśiṣṭa) or savikalpa. Apparently to them this particularity is a distinguishing but not distinguishable character (the knowledge of which is saṁkalpa): the sense-datum may be sāmānya-viśeṣātmā, though the viśeṣa here does not appear as viśeṣaṇa distinct from viśeṣya.

108. Manas is called an indriya though it is also an antaḥkaraṇa. Its specific function saṁkalpa consists in distinguishing the viśeṣaṇa or determinant in the viśeṣya or determinate object of the external senses. As it only explicates what was already known implicitly in the determinate sense-cognition, manas is itself a sense, the internal sense; and in the words of Kant, every representation of the external sense is also a representation of the internal sense. Saṁkalpa is not judgment (adhyavasāya); or if the word 'judgment' is used in a wide sense, it is only a 'judgment of perception' (Kant) or an 'analytic judgment of sense' (Bradley). Manas shares with ahaṁkāra and buddhi the character of being concerned with all time, unlike the external senses which are concerned with the present only.[a] Memory, immediate expectation and immediate relating of sense-data would be among its functions.

109. Ahaṁkāra is specifically manifest as willing but it is also 'knowing' in its vaikṛta aspect, knowing of the sensed or sensable object as related to willing (—feeling) ego, as *mine* or to *be mine*, as object of *my* bhoga. It is not knowledge of a content as true, as fact independent of *my* experience or 'public' object which would be knowledge proper, adhyavasāya or niścaya. Certitude is explicit at least in the first instance in negative reference to one's private experience: to be aware of something as certain is to be aware of it as not merely a fact to me. A higher grade of certitude would be the positive knowledge of the pure self as a self-evident or analytic self-identity. Certitude as negatively referring to egoistic experience is only the implicit form of this certitude.

110. Now all these karaṇas are taken to refer to the object spontaneously. There is no idea of the external object affecting or causing an impression on them nor of any one organ affecting any other. The function of each is an anticipatory response:

[a] SK. 33, 35

each acts freely for the self.[a] The internal k a r a ṇ a s are said to have the common character of life, of holding the body together; and their knowing function is apparently an aspect of this life-function. Each anticipatively take on a v ṛ t t i reflecting the form of the object, the v ṛ t t i of each higher k a r a ṇ a being accordingly undistinguished from the corresponding v ṛ t t i of a lower k a r a ṇ a. The k a r a ṇ a s thus function in concert, as though each knew the mind of the others.[b] They function either simultaneously or in succession[c] so that although a higher function implies a lower, a lower does not imply and may psychologically precede a higher. All the lower k a r a ṇ a s yield their contents ultimately to b u d d h i. Object is reflected in a v ṛ t t i of external sense, that again in a v ṛ t t i of m a n a s and so on; b u d d h i - v ṛ t t i further is said to be reflected in the self but in a new sense to be discussed in the sequel.

[a] SK. 31
[b] p a r a s p a r ā k ū t a - h e t u k a - v ṛ t t i—SK. 31
[c] SK. 30

CHAPTER VIII

THE SELF OR PURUṢA

111. In the Sāṁkhya theory of knowledge, the mind in its many grades is understood to anticipatively take the form of the external object, to restrict itself to a vṛtti reflecting the object. This reflecting or mirroring is apparently also the projecting or constructing function of the mind. As pointed out, it is the mind getting modalised into a substantial vṛtti similar to the object and also non-causally functioning as bhāva apart from which the object has no manifest or known aspect. The mind thus as much casts its reflection, making a phenomenal object out of the given (prakṛti) as gets the reflection of the object constructed. Reflection means different things in the two cases: the idea is constitutive of the object and the idea is like the object. Anticipative response is at once construction and apprehension of the bhogya object. The object is ultimately projected by and reflected in buddhi as bhāva and vṛtti. Now mental function, whether substantial or otherwise is non-distinct from the self and appears to embody it. Vṛtti of buddhi accordingly appears as the self reflecting the object and bhāva as the self projecting the object. The dual function of the mind is illusorily referred to the self. The self appears to take the reflection (pratibimba) of buddhi-vṛtti which reflects the object and to be itself reflected in buddhi-bhāva which projects the object.

112. This is how the theory of mutual reflection of the self and buddhi may be interpreted. Vijñāna-bhikṣu who presents this double pratibimba theory, however, understands the reflection of the self in buddhi to mean the vṛtti for self-knowledge taking the form of the self (like the vṛtti for object-knowledge taking the form of the object), the presentation of the self as *me* and not as it has been here taken as bhāva of the form 'I know'. He assumes this presented *me* to explain self-knowledge: if the self is known, it is known in a vṛtti of the form of the self, a vṛtti reflecting the self. Such vṛtti, again, is reflected in the self in order that the reflected self may be

known, just as vṛtti reflecting the object is reflected in the self in order that the reflected object may be known. The reflection of the self in vṛtti is then real mode of buddhi, not the illusory embodiment of the self in bhāva as we have taken it to be. But the self-form as a real mode of buddhi would be the *me* and not the *I*, and the knowledge yielded by the further reflection of this mode in the self would be but the knowledge of the *me*. The real Sāṁkhya view, therefore, appears to be that the self is known as what buddhi (object) is not, known in viveka (the pure bhāva, jñāna) which indeed implies a vṛtti but vṛtti of the form 'I am I' or, less adequately, 'I am *me*' but not of mere *me*. This vṛtti is what has been called vyaktatā-mātra, the native form of buddhi, buddhi in the bare form of self-identity. The reflection of the self in buddhi or more generally in the mind is the embodied *I*, (the I as constitutive of the body or me), not the presented *me* or the body which is the object with the self-form.

113. The self then as what the mind is not is objectively manifest as constituting the mental body and as the non-causal subjective function or bhāva of this body. It is manifest both in the pure and the impure bhāvas but adequately in the pure bhāvas which have for their specific content the distinction of the mind from the self. The content of the impure bhāvas of buddhi is the mind (reflecting the object) as distinct from the self, buddhi being self-conscious in both. We know the self not as object but in knowing the distinction of the object from it or in knowing the object as distinct from it. The self is never known by itself: there is properly no intuition of the self.

114. All knowledge is reflective i.e., implies a distinguishing from the self. We start by distinguishing the external object from the self as embodied in the material body. Then we distinguish the material body from the self as embodied in the mental body, thus knowing the former no longer as *me* but as the impersonal cosmic bhūta. Next we progressively distinguish the mental body from the self as willing, thus obtaining the concept of the cosmic tanmātra on the one hand and the cosmic indriya on the other; and then from the self as knowing (or more generally, as self-certitude) and thereby coming to conceive the cosmic tattva, ahaṁkāra; and lastly from the pure self with the thinking of buddhi as the cosmic

tattva. This second reflection or distinguishing is progressive but the mental body holds together till buddhi itself is known as object. The knowledge of buddhi in its pure bhāvas as distinct from the pure self would be viveka, the goal and original of all reflection. The reflection that makes an object of the mental body is a single process in many stages, for that body does not lose its self-form till pure buddhi loses it.

115. The self is known as actual in all reflection but as embodied. The second reflection in its final stage is indeed a distinguishing of buddhi from the pure self, but the pure self is here known as what buddhi is distinguished from and yet embodies. In other words, the identity of the self with viveka as bhāva is known to persist in the consciousness of viveka as vṛtti. Viveka is the knowing function conscious of buddhi as a knowing state or mode. The identity of the self with the function persisting along with the distinction of the state from the self is just what is called avidyā[a] as distinct from asmitā.

116. Viveka as implying both identity and distinction of buddhi with and from the self is necessarily of a vanishing character. In fact as one in viveka knows viveka itself to be object. its manifest character as substantial buddhi tends to lapse. The knowing function also being of the same buddhi and not of the pure self tends to cease absolutely, the lapse of substantial buddhi being only a potentialisation into prakṛti. Hence. too. in the evolution of buddhi from prakṛti, the object-knowing function which conditions the evolution is understood as actual within prakṛti: buddhi as ajñāna-bhāva is actual within prakṛti. Thus the destiny of the knowing function of viveka is to end absolutely as function which means the termination of the illusion of embodiment on the one hand and of the content of knowledge on the other. The self as mukta or in its essential nature is accordingly conceived to be contentless consciousness.

117. The self is pure consciousness, not embodied consciousness nor consciousness of a content having the form of the object. It is known immediately in reflection and is not really inferred. Inference may indeed help in rising to and clarifying the reflection—which has been shown to be transcendental reflection in

[a] YV° II.6

Sāṁkhya. The self is taken in Kārikā 17 to be inferred on various grounds of which two—viz., saṁghāta-parārthatvāt and adhiṣṭhānāt—appear to be inferential grounds proper, the others being only aspects of the self immediately revealed by reflection. There is immediate introspective consciousness of the object being other than the self (triguṇādi-viparyayāt), of the self as feeling or experiencing (bhoktṛ-bhāvāt) and as striving for freedom (kaivalyārtha-pravṛtteḥ). 'Saṁghāta' means a combinational unity, all combination being understood as qualitative. All object, whether noumenal or phenomenal, is a saṁghāta of the three guṇas interpenetrating one another. In this connection, although this general sense is not excluded, what is immediately meant by saṁghāta appears to be the unity of the body. The body is obviously purposive, being for the bhoga and apavarga of the self; and hence the clue to the general proposition that the emergence of simple functional unity in a qualitative (interpenetrating) combination is necessarily teleological. It would be the Sāṁkhya version of organic unity. With this accords also the explanation of the other ground for the inference of the self—viz., adhiṣṭhānāt. The body has the self not only as final cause but also as immanent cause.

118. So the self is inferred primarily as the explanation of the unity of the body. The body and, in fact, any complex that functions as a simple unity can so function because of a simple unity from which it is undistinguished and which appears to function for its own good. If a simple real could act, as it cannot, it would achieve only value and be no new existent. If a complex acts as a simple, it must appear to achieve the good of an external simple unity which is reflected in it. The nature of this simple real thus inferred has to be recognised to be the self that immediately appears to reflection as what all object is distinct from, as enjoyer of object or as freeing itself from the object. The further understanding of the object being distinct from it brings out its character as the subject (sākṣin)—viz., as an absolute distinct (kevala, alone or unrelated), as affectively detached (madhyastha), as knower (draṣṭṛ) and as no agent (akartṛ).

119. The self that is thus inferred and immediately known in reflection as subject is called knower (draṣṭṛ) in reference

obviously to asmitā. But in the last resort, the self is conceived as knowledge or consciousness, though still, as will appear presently, as pure individual. The mukta self is no longer sākṣin, for to it there is no object to be conscious of. Viveka leads at once to its lapse into prakṛti and to mukti of the self, so that the self is essentially contentless jñāna and not jñātṛ. This essential nature of the self as beyond avidyā cannot be inferred: it is evident to the terminal reflection viveka.

120. Sāṁkhya admits a plurality of pure selves or puruṣas. The plurality is also taken to be inferred from the circumstance of the birth, death, organ, willing and feeling differing in different embodied selves[a]. A prior enquiry, however, is how a body other than mine is known to be of another self, for such knowledge is obviously assumed in the above inference. The kārikā starts with the common sense belief in other embodied selves, but the inference of many pure selves would be invalid if the datum can be shown to be due to illusion, as it is sought to be shown by the Vedāntist. The Sāṁkhya view then can be defended if buddhi in its pure asmitā-function is taken to yield knowledge of *I* as in a community of *I's* or in reference to the object, if my certitude about an object be taken to involve others' certitude about it. This would be holding that the common-sense belief in many selves *cannot be* due to illusion corrigible as in the Vedānta view within buddhi-knowledge.

121. Mere sense-knowledge (ālocana and saṁkalpa) is unreflective, not consciously referred to any self, though to reflection it belongs to oneself and not to others. The knowledge of the object as *mine*—or *to be mine*, such as willing involves (abhimāna)—is consciously referred to oneself to the exclusion of other selves. Of the knowledge involving conscious certitude about the object (adhyavasāya), one is aware that it is impersonal and does not belong *exclusively* to oneself or, in other words, that the content known is not affected by relativity to the knower. Such awareness is equivalent to—though only implicitly—to the awareness of its being knowable by all selves.

[a] SK. 18.

122. The self is known in buddhi in its pure bhāva not only as not finite, (i.e., as above ahaṁkāra) but as not me (i.e., as object to itself). Now the self as infinite *I*[a] can only mean *I* as involving all *I's*. Infinity in Sāṁkhya is infinity as in the finite. It is in reference to the finite phenomenal object the universal[b] and in reference to a constituent of one's exclusive body the corresponding cosmic substance, but what is it in reference to the subject '*I*'? There is the concept of puruṣa-sāmānya[c] which does not mean one self but the abstraction 'self-hood'. It cannot be taken as a universal in the sense gotva is a universal of individual cows, nor as a single substance like an objective tattva with an apparent differentiation within it corresponding to different bodies. It is an abstraction in the sense that it cannot be represented like a universal or a substance as really or apparently *comprising* individuals (or modes) under it, being intelligible only as the svarūpa (or character of being itself) of the individual. It is not abstraction in the sense of being a secondary character of a primary attribute (like intensity, brightness, universality). The subject is manifest as what has no character (nirdharmaka), but this characterlessness is itself taken as its character of self-manifestness[d]. Thus the subject is manifest simply as individual thing, as being itself. The pure individual is necessarily intelligible as individual among individuals. The subject that is consciously manifest as simply individual is manifest to itself as a self among selves.

123. Each self then in the pure buddhi-function of asmitā involves all selves. The self is essentially individual. *any* individual implying others. The term 'I' is to the person who uses it singular though he is necessarily aware that others can use it of themselves. Puruṣa-sāmānya or self-hood is this necessary universality of a singular, being universal only if uniqueness or the unique-in-general is universal. Unique-in-general means *any* unique, not *all* uniques. 'All A is B' indeed means 'any A is B' but 'any A is B' need not mean 'all A is B', for even the distributive *all* has an implied collective character. As

[a] Cf. sarve eva puruṣā īśvarā iti in SPB. II. 15.
[b] SS. V. 91. etc.
[c] SPB. I. 154; V. 116; VI. 66.
[d] prakāśa—SPB. I. 145-146.

applied to the object, *any* and *all* may be regarded as equivalents but not as applied to the subject. Subjects cannot be understood as together in *being*: they can be together only in *function*. In point of being, each subject is absolute, but they can be conceived to function in harmony. In this sense we may say that the self is known in buddhi as having with it a community of selves. The self is known in the form 'I am I' which is an analytic self-identity, the enunciation of which is significant only in its being the form of many such self-identities. I say 'I am I' only as I am aware of others saying of themselves 'I am I'. I am a spirit only in the recognition of other spirits and hence, too, my certitude about an object implies others' (possible) certitude about it.

124. So far as I know through buddhi, I know the object as not to me alone but to any knowing. This applies both to the phenomenal object and to the objective tattva. The bhogya is indeed relative to me as exclusive bhoktṛ but it is none the less taken by me as given, as having an existence that is for any bhoktṛ. So when the body, mental and material, is viewed through buddhi as object not only to me but to all, the constituents of the body become manifest as cosmic tattvas.

125. The self is thus known in pure asmitā as an individual involving a community of individuals, each being an infinite or Īśvara. There is no suggestion in Sāṁkhya of a self really or illusorily differentiated into many selves, nor of a single Īśvara as in Yoga distinct from the selves and mystically working within them. Each self is essentially an Īśvara and pure buddhi as revealing and embodying the many infinite selves is called mahat or the great which gets restricted by rajas and tamas conditioning the movements towards bhoga. Of the self as mukta which to one's final reflection is absolute (kevala), we cannot say if it is an individual aware of itself involving a community of individuals. There is no reason to regard it as not individual in being, but all we can assert of it is that it is contentless consciousness, not consciousness of itself or of object.

126. The distinguishability of puruṣa-sāmānya in the puruṣa known in asmitā lapses when the asmitā lapses, and hence the mukta self is at least not consciously individual. To Vedānta, unconscious being or individuality of the pure self or consciousness is meaningless. To Sāṁkhya the being of

consciousness can be manifest only to buddhi. When buddhi lapses, the self would not be aware of its being. Vedānta would take it to be then ecstatically self-conscious. Apparently to Sāṁkhya, the being of the mukta self or absolute consciousness is then unmanifest or unconscious. Whether it is then individual or not can never be asserted. The conflict between Vedānta and Sāṁkhya on this point may, therefore, yet disappear. Only Sāṁkhya would insist that through buddhi, you cannot know the individuality of the self as illusory. Apparently, Vedānta will rely on some spiritual feeling or Śāstra for its denial of individuality and seek not to disprove individuality by reason (buddhi) but only to disprove objections to the faith in its illusory character.

CHAPTER IX

PRAKṚTI

127. Prakṛti, the primal objective tattva, is best considered after puruṣa, for buddhi lapses only by revealing and distinguishing itself from puruṣa. Viveka is primarily the distinguishing of buddhi from puruṣa, through which the conception of prakṛti and of its unmanifest distinction from puruṣa emerges. In the order of being, the distinction of buddhi from puruṣa is derived from that of prakṛti from puruṣa; but in the order of knowing, the latter is conditioned by the former. The order of the tattvas may, therefore, be thus represented.

Puruṣa

Prakṛti—Buddhi—Ahaṁkāra etc.

The direct relation of puruṣa is with buddhi alone among the objective tattvas.

128. The reflection that distinguishes the mind from the self is also the consciousness of the mind as having been manifest through non-distinction from the self; and as the mind (as buddhi) is object with the sole character of manifestness (vyaktatā), the distinguishing of it from the self means its lapsing into the unmanifest (avyakta or prakṛti). To be aware of manifestness thus lapsing is to be aware of its having emerged, of the unmanifest having manifested manifestness, such manifesting being as much becoming as appearing. The unmanifest prakṛti is thus purely causal or potential being with the actual function of appearing which is but the beginningless aviveka or non-distinction from the self, the objective aspect of what is subjectively called the experiencing function (bhoga). 'I enjoy' is but illusion, the corresponding objective fact being that unmanifest reality (thing-in-itself) *appears* as the external world (phenomenon, bhogya). As it so appears, it *becomes* buddhi and the other tattvas (liṅga) constituting the enjoying or experiencing body (bhogāyatana).

This appearing function is beginninglessly actual and never potential, though it can end absolutely. Hence if the unmanifest becomes manifest, it does not require any external cause (like God's will in Yoga) to wake it up: it is already awake in its appearing function which in good time will actualise its being.

129. Prakṛti then presents, both potential being and actual function. As in the region of the manifest (which practically means 'within buddhi'), liṅga and bhāva are distinct but interdependent, so within unmanifest prakṛti, there is the dualism of 'substantial being' potential as the guṇas and of 'aviveka'—comprising the traces (vāsanās) of previous births—which is actual but without standing being. This aviveka is mere function that is somehow at once sat and asat, real and unreal, being the identity of subject and object (mind), which is real as objective non-distinction and unreal as subjective identification.[a] In Yoga, this dualism does not appear to be put within pradhāna or a-liṅga: the guṇas are conceived to be not determinate potential being as in Sāṁkhya but as an indetermination of being and non-being (niḥsattā-sattvam etc.)[b]; in other words, the indeterminateness that appears in the Sāṁkhya conception of the function of aviveka is transferred to the conception of potential being. In Yoga, sattā or being means vyaktatā or manifestness, so that the unmanifest guṇas are neither determinate being nor determinate non-being.[c] In Sāṁkhya, potential or unmanifest being as of the guṇas is still determinate being which has an indeterminate function.

130. This difference between Sāṁkhya and Yoga is reflected in their views of sadṛśa-pariṇāma and sāmyāvasthā. Prakṛti is taken as an indefinite plurality of elements which are not combined into a unity. The manifest object (tattva) is an effect and effect is a unity of elements in qualitative combination, having a manifest quality of its own. The elements by themselves are the causes which by qualitative interpenetration become a unity with a manifest simple quality. This becoming is called visadṛśa-pariṇāma. Cause then is a

[a] SS. V. 56.
[b] YB. II. 19.
[c] YV. II. 19.

plurality of elements which before the emergence of the effect is ununified and has no simple quality. The simple quality of the effect is the quality of one of the elements, the qualities of the other elements being either unmanifest or manifest in a way that does not affect the simplicity of the effect. The quality of one element is in this sense dominant and not in the sense of being more intense than the qualities of the other elements. This difference between dominant and recessive is not manifest in the cause where the elements are accordingly said to be in sāmyāvasthā, same in the *nature* of manifestation and not in manifest *degree*, the above difference being difference in nature of manifestation. The persistent interpretation of sāmyāvasthā as equality of degree of the elements appears to make no sense.

131. Sāṁyāvasthā of the elements called guṇas implies their utter unrelatedness and the consequent non-dominance of any one of them. Prakrti is these elements and is not their unity or substratum: it is each of them or their alternation and is not even their togetherness. Is sāmyāvasthā the defining character of prakṛti? Vyāsa[a] calls it a-liṅga-pariṇāma to distinguish it from the other tattvas, though he points out that the good of the self (puruṣārtha) which is the nimitta of the other pariṇāmas is not the nimitta of this pariṇāma which is pralaya nor of its termination in sṛṣti, God's absolute will being apparently the sole nimitta here. Sāṁkhya-sūtra[b] appears to take it as the definition of prakṛti, though Vijñāna-bhikṣu interprets it in the manner of Yoga-bhāṣya as a contingent character (upalakṣaṇa). Prakṛti is taken as nitya, persisting partially even along with the other tattvas; and this does not justify one in taking sāmyāvasthā as a contingent character. Sāmyāvasthā of prakṛti is retained even along with the visadṛśa-pariṇāmas emerging as distinct in prakṛti. But as these *come* to lapse again into prakṛti, is not sāmyāvasthā a contingent character as well? This lapse or retraction—whether for the mukta self or in cosmic pralaya—is properly no effect in Sāṁkhya and is even in Yoga an effect outside the causal process in the object. Causal process in the object is the

[a]YB. II. 19.
[b]SS I. 61.

downward process towards bhoga, the opposite process being utterly discontinuous with it to Yoga, and no causal process at all to Sāṁkhya though continuous with the causal process. Puruṣārtha or the good of the self is not the nimitta of this reverse process to Yoga and to Sāṁkhya; it is not nimitta even of the forward process, there being no nimitta-cause outside the immanent cause in this system; and unconscious teleology is just the nature or spontaneity of the (noumenal) object and no causal circumstance at all. The reverse process then to Sāmkhya is purely spontaneous, and so to its sāmyāvasthā which is its terminus is just the eternal existence of prakṛti as distinct from its manifestness, existence that is no character, either necessary or contingent but the existent itself.

132. Now sāmyāvasthā or prakṛti itself, being the cause or potentiality of all that is manifest, must be taken to have within it something corresponding to the manifest causal *process*. This appears to be the sadṛśa-pariṇāma of each guṇa as unrelated to the other guṇas. Sadṛśa-pariṇāma means mere self-reproduction of a guṇa, its self-repetition without the emergence of qualitative difference. A manifest tattva is understood as self-caused or self-causing, and buddhi—the highest of the manifest tattvas—is *manifest* as such. Substance, then, even as unmanifest guṇa must imply self-causation: there is no conception of a merely static substance in Sāṁkhya or Yoga. The reality of an object consists in its becoming. Manifest reality is necessarily what becomes different from itself and manifestness as reality is what has become different from itself as the utterly unmanifest and is becoming further specificated. As to be manifest is to be different from itself in nature, the self-caused-ness of the unmanifest can only mean bare numerical distinction from itself. Now a self-caused tattva may also be taken as self-causing but there is difficulty in Sāṁkhya about a vikāra-tattva which to it no longer causes, while to Yoga, it still causes though only immanent pariṇāmas of itself. There is difficulty also about prakṛti or guṇa in Yoga, for it can hardly be called effect of itself, if by effect is meant what has determinate being, guṇa being understood in this system as indeterminate. Thus Sāṁkhya would generally characterise objective reality as self-caused and Yoga as self-causing.

133. Consequently, in Sāṁkhya, the reality of guṇa

consists in its being self-caused, while in Yoga it consists in self-causing. It implies the cessation of self-distinction to Sāṁkhya and the emergence of self-distinction to Yoga: it is a being comprising self-distinction to the former and breaking up into self-distinction to the latter. To Sāṁkhya a guṇa is one, the material identity of many self-repetitions, presupposing but superseding their difference; while to Yoga it is a nominal universal, the many particular guṇas being the reality, though even here they are not co-existent as conceived by Vijñānabhikṣu. He reads this view of a guṇa being a mere name for many co-existent particular guṇas not only in Yoga but also in Sāṁkhya and takes it not only to be implied in certain texts,[a] but as the only explanation of quantitative variation of a guṇa and of immanent pariṇāma within a tattva. Sāṁkhya will, however, hardly admit such quantitative variation and immanent pariṇāma within the real, and even if it does, it will not necessarily explain them by the conception of particular guṇas.

134. There is properly no increase or decrease of the tattvas in Sāṁkhya. The so-called quantitative inequality of the guṇas in a visadṛśa-pariṇāma appears to mean only the qualitative distinction between dominant and recessive. Two tattvas or modes of a tattva may appear to have more of a certain guṇa, say sattva, in one than in the other; but this can be explained by saying that the guṇa is in one less manifest, less obscured by the other guṇa than in the other, the degrees of manifestness of a guṇa being really its qualitative relations to the other guṇas—called abhibhava, janana, mithuna and āśraya to be explained presently (sec. 147).

135. Immanent pariṇāma—what is called in Yoga dharma-lakṣaṇāvasthā-pariṇāma as distinct from tattvāntara-pariṇāma— as already explained is properly no change in Sāṁkhya. For one thing, it does not admit a tattva without vṛtti which changes into vṛttis: a tattva is always in a vṛtti. Buddhi, for example, as referring in its bhāva to a particular object is a particular buddhi-vṛtti. The vṛtti being the tattva itself is a causal fact unlike the bhāva, and so the pratibimba of

[a] SPB. I. 127-28; YV. II. 18.

viṣaya in the tattva is taken as a real pratibimba, though there is no such thing as the tattva without any pratibimba. The passing of one vṛtti into another, however, is not a causal process, being apparently only the non-causal passing of one bhāva into another. As still each vṛtti is the tattva, each in its bhāva referring to the others, the vṛttis only present mutual difference and not change and may therefore, relatively to the change of the tattva to the next tattva, be said to be in a sort of space arrangement. The so-called immanent change then need not be explained by a quantitative re-arrangement of particular guṇas. That there are different vṛttis does indeed imply that the guṇas have no static being[a], but that need not mean that each guṇa is perpetually changing in respect of attribute, temporal quality and state (dharma-lakṣaṇāvasthā). It may mean only that each is in sadṛśa-pariṇāma where bare numerical distinction and no distinction in nature emerges. So the conception of particular guṇas (guṇa-vyakti) seems to have no place in Sāṁkhya.

136. The object, whether phenomenal or noumenal is taken to be constituted by the three guṇas—sattva, rajas and tamas. Guṇa does not mean attribute; it is substantial reality, called guṇa as being for another (parārtha or paropakāraka)[b], for the bhoga of puruṣa, that being the character of object. The guṇas are three, corresponding to the three modes of bhoga—sukha, duḥkha and moha (prīti, aprīti, viṣāda). The object is for the self in these three modes, and the three guṇas being accordingly defined as having these feeling-modes as their ātmā, svabhāva or lakṣaṇa. An object is pleasurable not in the sense of being an external cause of pleasure in one's mind but as being, so far as it is pleasurable, the pleasure itself, as being manifested as the pleasure and manifested or shown by the pleasure as its implicit being or causal self. No object is all pleasurable and hence the pleasurable object is in its other affective aspects the other bhogas—duḥkha or moha—also. What is (dominantly) pleasurable to one person may indeed be painful to another, but this inconstancy in the mutual relation of the guṇas in the same object appears only in non-causal

[a] calam ca guṇavṛttam—YB. II. 15; III. 13.
[b] STK. 12.

or phenomenal manifestation. That an external object is the same to different persons though it affects them differently does not imply that it is really other than its affective character but only that its common or public character is also its affective character that is distinguished in some way in buddhi from the affective characters presented to some one individual only.

137. All characters of the external objects are affective, being non-causal manifestation of the guṇas. Even the 'private' characters are (phenomenally) real: prakṛti is conceivable as phenomenalised to each self as the public world with some aspects that are for that self only. There may indeed be doubts about which aspects are public: what are taken as such may turn out to be only private. But that does not invalidate the general distinction between public and private. The illusory is only what having appeared public now appears private, the previous appearance being still believed as having been given or put forth by prakṛti though as a corrigible manifestation. Thus the conception of the illusory as at once real and unreal (sadasat)[a] applies both to transcendental illusion (aviveka) and to objective illusion. Non-causal manifestation then may be not only public and private but also illusory in this sense.

138. The inconstancy of the mutual relation of the guṇas in the external object may thus be explained as constituting no bar to the conception of the object being nothing but affective experience. There is no dualism of experience (bhoga) and the experienced (bhogya), and even experience as knowledge (of the object as public) is affective bhoga. The apparent dualism of bhoga and bhogya is really the dualism between the body (bhogāyatana) and the object (bhoga or bhogya) which has emerged out of the same objective reality (prakṛti). Experience appears to be of the embodied self and the body is constituted by the manifest tattvas each of which is the causal manifestation of prakṛti—i.e., of the guṇas, the reals that are non-causally manifested as the three modes of experience or bhoga. The causal and non-causal manifestations bifurcate at buddhi: buddhi is aware of itself as having emanated both as being and function, liṅga and bhāva from prakṛti and as at once becoming the lower tattvas or orga-

[a] SS. V. 36.

nising the gross experiencing body on the one hand and constructing or projecting the world on the other. The same tattvas that make my body make also other bodies, the difference between the bodies being not in material but in the distinctive modes of aviveka with which the many selves are beginninglessly invested. Thus what appears as 'private' characters of the external object correspond to the distinctive modes of aviveka constituting the bodies.

139. The manifest object then, whether phenomenal or noumenal, is but the guṇas, the reals that are causally and non-causally manifested into the experiencing body and experience (or the experienced). The guṇas become the body and appear as experience. It is from the side of experience or the modes of bhoga that the guṇas are understood in the first instance; and it is as bhoga of itself leads to reflection, that the body, with the tattvas as matter and aviveka as form, is gradually traced back to the guṇas. Hence the guṇas are defined as what are manifest as the bhogas, as the potentialities of the three modes of feeling, as the feel*ables* that may not be actually felt. As further they are known in reflection to be constituents of the tattvas which make up the body undistinguished from the self that appears to feel, they may be regarded as the potentialities of the three feelings as well. Thus the guṇas are at once the potentialities of feelings and felt contents, being absolute in this sense. The external world also is both experience and the experienced, feeling and the felt, but the dualism does not appear here at all. The prakṛti-vikrtis, where the dualism of the feeling and the felt appears in the form of causal self-distinction, are absolute in another sense. In prakṛti, the dualism is unmanifest but has to be still inferred as subsisting between the potential being of the guṇas and the actual though unconscious aviveka which constitutes their function of sadṛśa-pariṇāma which may be called their self-feeling, both the being and the function being absolute as self-felt and self-feeling respectively. The vikāras alone are not absolute in any sense: the senses only feel and the bhūtas are only felt.

140. That guṇa or the absolute of feeling and felt-content is object itself that is utterly distinct from the self requires to be explained. Pain, which is bhoga par excellence, appears to be the only entity that is immediately intelligible as utterly distinct

from the self. The realistic view of the object as what can exist unknown or unrelated to the self would be unintelligible unless knowledge itself testified to the necessary existence of the object as unknown. The idealist's case is that reflectively the object is only known to be now unknown in some particular way (e.g. perception), being still known to be known in some other way: the object as utterly unknown is a self-contradictory notion. There is no perception and therefore no memory of an object existing unknown. We may indeed be aware in knowing an object that it *was* unknown but this is not to *remember* its past unknownness and hence we cannot expect or conceive that it may exist unknown, for we expect or conceive on the basis of memory. We can conceive a content to continue out of consciousness only if our present consciousness necessarily refers to such continuation. This can be said only about the consciousness of pain, for to be reflectively aware of pain is to wish to be free from it: the necessary wish is the necessary idea of the pain being foreign to and therefore ceasing to consciousness. There is the consciousness of the pain as given and, therefore, the idea of its ceasing to consciousness is not the idea of its ceasing to be real. It is then only here that we have the idea of a content of consciousness possibly existing out of consciousness. The exemplar of objective reality then is pain, and, as will be shown, the other bhogas are intelligible only in reference to pain. Hence objective reality is essentially feeling or felt content. Object as known is but such felt content to detached reflection. The guṇas as affective absolutes constitute the object.

CHAPTER X

RELATION OF THE GUṆAS

141. The three guṇas are the absolutes of the three modes of feeling—sukha, duḥkha and moha. Pleasure and pain are known as the two primary modes or tones of feeling, but what is moha? For one thing, it is a conscious feeling, feeling of not being able to feel, feeling of affective insensibility and not insensibility itself. It is the feeling of absence of affective freedom, pleasure and pain being feelings of restful freedom and restless freeing activity. It is a feeling of indolence, stupidity or fascination. Moha is thus intelligible as a primary mode of feeling co-ordinate with pleasure and pain, the three being understood in terms of freedom. The immediate manifestation of the guṇas in buddhi in its reference to the external object is feeling or bhoga. Of the modes of bhoga, pleasure even in the grossest form is as pleasure a conscious detachment or freedom from the object, implying a beginning of reflection. Pain implies the active wish to be free from pain which is, however, unfulfilled so long as it is pain. The feeling of pain is thus a freeing activity, ideal or actual willing. Moha is the feeling not only of the want of freedom (which pain also is) but also of not actively wishing or willing freedom. It is still a positive feeling, feeling of indolence in mind and body, feeling of being stupefied before the object or being fascinated by the object. The three feelings are all positive, different from one another but necessarily opposed, being capable of being combined into a unitary feeling.

142. The feeling of freedom is described as the feeling of lightness in the body or mind, lightness of mind being felt in the spiritual qualities of sincerity, mildness, truthfulness, purity, kindness, intelligence, forgiveness etc. So the restless and distracting activity of the mind in pain is reflected in the qualities of antipathy, hatred, anxiety, deceptiveness etc., and the feeling of moha in the qualities of indolence, ignorance, pride, fear, lack of faith etc. Necessarily the feelings are described in objective metaphors; and in Sāṁkhya at least the guṇas are understood primarily in terms of the feelings and secondarily as qualities of the object. Sukha, duḥkha and moha are primarily

the felt mental qualities of lightness (freedom. laghutva), restlessness (calatva) and heaviness (gurutva), and their analogues in the object are expression (prakāśa), action (kriyā) and standing being or persistence (sthiti). The necessity and sufficiency of the triple characterisation of the object are justified by the introspective testimony about the necessity and sufficiency of the elementary feelings.

143. Yoga philosophy starts with the triple characterisation of the object,[a] and then apparently, as the mind is also object, reads it into the triplicity of feelings or into the triplicity of mental functions—knowing, willing and feeling (prakhyā-pravṛtti-sthiti),[b] relying more on imagination than on introspection. Prakāśa as a quality of the object is its manifestness, definiteness or expression which is known-ness as an objective character. Knowability as a character of the object is its aesthetic character of expression or expressiveness. Beauty is the perfect form of presented intelligibility, the unobscured self-revelation of the object which may be called its freedom, corresponding to the feeling of freedom which is pleasure. Thus is prakāśa connected with knowing (prakhyā) and with pleasure; kriyā or activity in the object may be easily connected with willing (pravṛtti or self-assertion of buddhi) and with the restless character of the feeling of pain; and sthiti or persistence of the object is the obvious and aesthetic correlate of the feeling of moha. Whether sthiti as a character of buddhi should be taken as a feeling is not so obvious; and some take it to mean unconscious mental persistence as saṁskāra. But as prakhyā and pravṛtti are understood as conscious mental functions, conscious mental persistence appears here to be primarily meant by sthiti; and this can be nothing but feeling which in contrast with knowing and willing is consciously being unfree or undetached from the object.

144. That the elementary feelings are three will be taken by Saṁkhya as evident to introspection, and the triplicity of the conscious buddhi as also of the object that is its content would be derived from this introspective testimony. The three feelings constitute the immanent nature of the three guṇas, which is

[a] YB. II. 18.
[b] YB. I. 2.

characterised by the terms laghu (light, free or pliant), cala (restless or changing) and guru (heavy or stiff). Their transitive functional aspects are prakāśa (manifestation of itself or of others), upaṣṭambha (acting on or compelling others) and varaṇa (obscuring of prakāśa,—more generally, niyama or retarding or arresting of both prakāśa and kriyā). The substantial being of the elementary feelings is the guṇas. Existent object is a complex of the guṇas, their unity being conceived after the manner in which the feelings are introspectively found to be combined.

145. The object is the felt content. What is known or willed is still a felt content. The object even to the jīvanmukta is feelable content which he does not feel and is aware of in a disinterested way, such awareness being not bhoga but a seeing (sākṣātkāra) of the felt or the feeling. The known aspect of the object is its expression which, to the ordinary knower, is the embodiment of aesthetic feeling in the context of other feelings which pervert and obscure the expression; and it is presumably to the pure knower (jīvanmukta) the perfect embodiment. The willed aspect of the object is its going to be felt or going to be the expression of its felt non-being and its initial blind felt-ness or given-ness. The object is felt in three grades—detachedly felt as expressing itself, half-detachedly felt as going to be, and undetachedly felt as existent or persistent. The second grade of felt-ness is the most obvious form of objectivity, in reference to which the other two grades are appreciated. Without reference to it, expression would be regarded as only imagined and persistence would not be manifest to consciousness at all. Expression is regarded as *known* objective fact only so far as it is felt to be the continuous fulfilment of going to be; and one is conscious of the object as persisting only as it is felt to be prevented from being another. Pleasure appears objective to the self in so far as it is felt as relief from pain or different from pain co-existent with it; and moha appears to consciousness when one feels unable to wish or will away pain. We are reflectively aware of pain along with pleasure and moha and of the object in change as having its past integrated in its expression and as persisting in and through the change.

146. Pain, as pointed out, is what is immediately manifest as the not-self or object. An object is known as object only as

we are conscious of it as what may exist out of consciousness; and such consciousness is primarily of pain. We are aware of an object as such so far as it is painful and we know it as fact so far as it is at the same time pleasurable or expressive and blindly given or helplessly accepted in moha. Thus the experienced object is of pleasure, pain and moha, all compact, and it is in reference to the experienced object that the tattvas or noumenal objects are known. Object, whether phenomenal or noumenal, is manifest as pain (hostile to the self), and so far as it is manifest as pleasure or moha, it is manifest as with the heart of pain. The necessity of the co-existence of the three guṇas is derivable from the very conception of the manifest object.

147. How are the guṇas related to one another in the manifest object? They are related as the elementary feelings are found related in a complex feeling. Four kinds of relation are mentioned in S. Kārikā 12, which are differently interpreted by the commentators. Abhibhava means the arresting of manifestation, and janana appears to mean the excitation of manifestation. Each guṇa may arrest the manifestation of the others and each may also excite the manifestation of the others. Āśraya probably means being the object of another's function: each guṇa may function towards the others as object. Mithuna means being present along with and subordinate to another: each guṇa may be manifest as subordinate to another. Apparently one guṇa only can be dominant in an object, the others—one or the other or both— being recessive, either unmanifest or manifest. In the former case, the dominant may rouse an unmanifest guṇa into manifestation, and in the latter case, the dominant may have the others either as the object of its function or as adjectival to its substantive being. For example, in buddhi, sattva prevents rajas and tamas from being manifest (abhibhava); it may reveal (prakāśa) rajas and tamas as object or content (āśraya); it may lead to willing (ahaṁkāra) and consequent feeling (tanmātra)—i.e., excite the manifestation of rajas and tamas (janana); and it may be adjectival (mithuna) to rajas (to indriya as proceeding from sāttvika-ahaṁkāra) and to tamas (tanmātra as pure aviśeṣa pleasure). There may be consciously unmixed joy; one may aesthetically delight in the contemplation of pain or

moha; pleasure may lead to pain or moha; pain may have a pleasurable aspect or there may be pleasure in being 'fascinated'.

148. Yoga-bhāṣya II, 18 refers to the relation of the guṇas: ete guṇāḥ parasparoparakta-pravibhāgāḥ pariṇāminaḥ saṁyoga-vibhāga-dharmāṇah itaretaropāśrayeṇa upārjita-mūrtayaḥ parasparāṅgāṅgitve api asambhinnaśaktipravibhāgāḥ. Each guṇa as substantive or dominant with the others reflected in it tends to change; each may be associated with or dissociated from the others and as associated, becomes a manifest object; and each, while organically connected with the others, retains its distinction. The last part 'parasparāṅgāṅgitve api' definitely means something like organic unity.

STUDIES IN YOGA PHILOSOPHY

ANALYSIS

CH. I. SĀṄKHYA AND YOGA. (Sec. 1-15)

(The place of Buddhi, Ahaṁkāra and Asamitā)

(1-5) The nature of will and its place in spiritual life according to Sāṁkhya and to Yoga. The relation of will to ahaṁkāra and to buddhi. The concept of asmitā analysed. The nature of nivṛtti and pravṛtti to Sāṁkhya and to Yoga. The status of viveka and its relation to asamprajñāta. (6-7) The practice of yoga and its relation to mokṣa according to Sāṁkhya and to Yoga. Two kinds of yoga, samprajñāta and asamprajñāta, the former terminating in pure knowledge and the latter in the super-conscious free being of the spirit. Yoga as free willing for free being. (8) The nature of nirodha to Sāṁkhya and to Yoga. (9-11) The concept of Īśvara-praṇidhāna. The status of Īśvara as a tattva. The concepts of illusion and causality in the two systems. (12-15) Two aspects of bhoga: appropriation and objectification. Appropriation as a kind of conation to Yoga and as a kind of feeling to Sāṁkhya. Appropriation as primary and explicit to Yoga. the reverse being the view of Sāṁkhya. Bhoga as a function of buddhi-endowed self is real to Yoga and unreal to Sāṁkhya. Illusion as anyathākhyāti to Yoga and as sadasatkhyāti to Sāṁkhya.

CH. II. SĀṄKHYA AND YOGA (contd. Sec. 16-31)

(Causality, Becoming and Time)

(16) Bhoga as the final cause of the causal becoming of prakṛti. To Sāṁkhya the causal process is terminated by reflection and to Yoga by free negative willing.

(17-19) The nature of 'becoming' as the unity of succession and persistence. The difference between Sāṁkhya and Yoga on the nature of causal becoming. (20-21) The nature and function of 'nimitta' in Yoga. The concept of pratibandha. (22-24) The concept of 'time' in Sāṁkhya and Yoga. Time and ākāśa. Time to Sāṁkhya is prakṛti in its eternal function of manifestation. Two aspects of time—

kṣaṇa and krama—distinguished by Yoga: their ontical status analysed. (25-28) Three modes of real immanent change—viz., of dharma, lakṣaṇa and avasthā recognised in the Yoga school. These not accepted as real in Sāṁkhya. Implications of this difference between Sāṁkhya and Yoga brought out. (29-30) The Sāṁkhya theory about the relation between one mode of a tattva and another mode conditioned by it. (31) The nature of real time to Sāṁkhya and Yoga.

CH. III. SĀṄKHYA AND YOGA (contd. Sec. 32-48)

(The Empirical world: its status and constitution)

(32-37) The metaphysical status of the body and the external world according to Yoga, Sāṁkhya and Vedānta—fact, non-causal appearance and Illusion. (38) The tattvas according to Sāṁkhya and to Yoga. Different views on ahaṁkāra. (39-44) Bhūta and its atomic nature according to Yoga. The Sāṁkhya view on the point imagined. (45-47) Yoga atomism vs. Vaiśeṣika atomism. (48) Bhikṣu's ascription of Yoga atomism to Sāṁkhya gratuitous.

CH. IV. BUDDHI-VṚTTI (Sec. 49-65)

(Nidrā and Smṛti)

(49) Willing as becoming is to Yoga a prospective function, while to Sāṁkhya it is a retrospective one. (50) Twofold pariṇāma—sadṛśa and visadṛśa—explained. (51) Difference between Sāṁkhya and Yoga on the conception of self-identity or vyaktatā and sadṛśa-pariṇāma. (52-53) The Sāṁkhya concept of aviveka compared to the Yoga concept of avidyā. (54) Two kinds of dharma-pariṇāma—a-paridṛṣta and paridṛṣta—mentioned in Yoga-Bhāṣya.

(55-56) The Sāṁkhya conception of vṛtti versus the Yoga conception analysed. (57) The five vṛttis in the Yoga-sūtras as five types of presentation. (58-60) The nature of smṛti as a vṛtti analysed. Two kinds of smṛti distinguished by Vyāsa: Vācaspati and Bhikṣu differ in their analysis of these two kinds. (61-63) Vṛtti analysed in reference to samādhi. (64-65) The nature of nidrā as vṛtti analysed in detail.

CH. V. BUDDHI-VṚTTI (contd. Sec. 66-82)

(Vikalpa, Viparyaya and Pramāṇa)

(66-68) The concept of vikalpa as a vṛtti analysed. Vikalpa versus viparyaya. (69) The status of vikalpa in Vedānta. (70) Vikalpa and savikalpa-samādhi. Function of vikalpa in savitarka and savicāra-samādhi. (71) Vikalpa as āhārya cognition in Vaiśeṣika. (72) The nature of error to Yoga and to Vaiśesika, to Sāṁkhya and to Vedānta. (74) Analysis of empirical error according to Yoga and to Vedānta. (75-76) The concept and types of kleśa analysed. (77) Analysis of avidyā. (78) Analysis of asmitā. (79) Analysis of rāga, dveṣa and abhiniveśa. (80) Avidyā and pramāṇa. (81-82) Types of pramāṇa analysed.

CH. VI. THE FIVE LEVELS OF BUDDHI (Sec. 83-98)

(83) Analysis of certitude as the function of buddhi in reference to the self. (84) The five levels of buddhi : kṣipta, mūḍha and vikṣipta characterised by implicit asmitā, ekāgra by explicit asmitā and niruddha by lapse of asmitā. (85) Prakhyā, pravṛtti and sthiti variously operative in the different levels. (86) Self-identity inferred in buddhi, introspected in vṛtti and inexplicit in the other tattvas. (87-88) The second level, vikṣipta analysed. (89) The first and third levels analysed. (90) Progressive increase of freedom of knowing or 'knowing-duration' in the different levels. (91) The mind in the first three levels working within spiritual error. (92-95) Analytic elaboration of the first three levels. (96-98) The concept of vikṣepa and its implications.

CH. VII. THE NATURE OF YOGA (sec. 99-112)

(99) The nature of yoga as spiritual activity which is activity for achieving absolute freedom. (100-101) Spiritual activity is free activity for nivṛtti or arrest of the will to bhoga. (102) This free realising of freedom conceived as a knowing process in Sāṁkhya and in Vedānta, as a feeling process in the

Bhakti systems and as a willing process in Yoga and Kant. (103) Yoga is not necessarily the type of spiritual activity in systems other than the Yoga. (104-106) The apparently mystical concept of spiritual activity reduced to an intelligible practical psychology in Yoga Philosophy. (107) The religion of yoga is not a mere system of psychical gymnastics. Is there any place for the consciousness of the sacred in this religion? (108) The procedure for attaining super-religious freedom is either religious (i.e.. through grace) or super-religious (i.e.. through one's might). (109) Yoga is willing of miracle or magic. (110-112) Skepticism about yoga and bibhūti considered.

CH. VIII. THE KINDS OF YOGA (Sec. 113-131)

(113) Two grades of Yoga, samprajñāta and asamprajñāta, and the different sub-grades enumerated. (114) The concept of ābhoga in connection with the samprajñāta. The concept of vitarka. (115) The concept of vicāra. (116) Transition from savicāra to sānanda-samādhi. Vācaspati versus Bhikṣu on 'ānanda' in this context. (117-118) Triple aspect of the content in the four stages of the samprajñāta clarified. (119-121) The conceptions of videha, prakṛti-laya and vivekin clarified. They represent respectively the affective, conative and cognitive types of spirituality. (122) Bhoja on asmitā-samādhi. (123-124) The varieties of vitarka and vicāra-samādhi explained. (125-126) The object of vicāra-samādhi. (127-128) The concept of samāpatti analysed. (129-130) The nature of the prajñā or spiritual wisdom that results from this samādhi. (131) Transition to the asamprajñāta stage.

CH. IX. THE PROCEDURE OF YOGA (Sec. 132-146)

(132) Yoga as absolute will is 'beyond good and evil' and in that sense is super-religious; yet it is to be distinguished from Nietzsche's concept of absolute will. (133) The steps to samādhi two-fold—preparatory and constitutive. They are again either consecutive or alternative. (134) The concepts of abhyāsa and vairāgya analysed. Different aspects of prayatna conditioning yoga. (135) The different stages of discipline for the uttamādhikārin analysed. Auxiliary practices to counteract vikṣepa. (136) The discipline for the madhyamā-

dhikārin analysed. The eight-fold discipline prescribed for the common aspirant. (137-144) The nature of the eight aṅgas of yoga analysed. (145-146) The siddhis and the attitude of the yogin to them explained.

CH. X. THE NOTION OF ĪŚVARA (Sec. 147-159)

(147) The dual meaning of Īśvara-praṇidhāna in Yoga-sūtras. (148) Bhikṣu's interpretation of Sāṁkhya atheism. The place of meditation on God in the Yoga system. (149-151) The precise nature of the proof of God in Vyāsa's commentary brought out. (152-153) The relation between faith and God elaborated. (154-155) The eternal freedom of God and his buddhi. (156-158) God, grace and bhakti. (159) No reference in the Yoga-sūtras to God's creative powers.

CHAPTER I

SĀṄKHYA AND YOGA

1. The essential difference between Sāṁkhya and Yoga appears to lie in their conception of the will and of its place in spiritual life. To Sāṁkhya, willing is the function of ahaṁkāra and not of buddhi, being the activity of the finite agent to maintain its finiteness. The principle of self-maintaining finiteness or exclusiveness (not individuality which belongs to the self) is ahaṁkāra, while buddhi is infinite (mahat or vibhu) both in its existence and in its content. Willing indeed proceeds from self-conscious certitude which is the function of buddhi, certitude in the form 'this is what I am going to be' or as it might be put—'I (the infinite) am this prospective (finite) *me*'—which is just the certitude of asmitā, though willing is not asmitā. To Yoga, however, willing is asmitā: it not only proceeds from self-consciousness, but is self-conscious subjectivity, being never the mere object of asmitā-consciousness. The willing or active *me* is a continuation of the *I* that knows it: to be conscious of willing is to be conscious, explicitly of *I* willing, conscious not merely of *me* but of *I becoming me*. Since asmitā is not dropped when willing emerges as a finite mental object, ahaṁkāra is called in Yoga asmitā and is as a function taken to belong to buddhi and not to a separate tattva, as it is taken in Sāṁkhya.

2. Asmitā in both Yoga and Sāṁkhya is understood as a function of buddhi. Willing is not taken as a function of buddhi in Sāṁkhya where, therefore, asmitā is a judgment (adhyavasāya) or certitude (niścaya) of the form 'I am me' prior to willing, whence willing is supposed to spring. Asmitā in this form means indeed the consciousness of I willing, but willing is here distinguished as object (me) from the consciousness and the I is not so distinguished, so that the I-form is taken as only supervening on willing and not as intrinsic to it. Asmitā again is to both Yoga and Sāṁkhya not only of the form 'I am me' but also of the form 'I am I'. This would be in Sāṁkhya pure judgment unlike judgment in the other form which has reference to or has the shadow of willing. In Yoga,

not only the lower asmitā but also the higher is taken as willing, knowing being never divorced from willing, though willing as in asamprajñāta-yoga runs beyond knowing. Willing to both Yoga and Sāṁkhya is mental activity proceeding from knowledge. Mental activity has two directions positive and negative, called pravṛtti and nivṛtti. To Yoga both these forms are willing, while to Sāṁkhya the negative one is not willing but only reflection, a knowing process implying abstention from willing. In Sāṁkhya again, pravṛtti, which is to it the only willing, is essentially the finitising of the mind: it implies the lapse of the infinity or impersonal knowing certitude of buddhi and is as such the function of a lower tattva viz., ahaṁkāra. In Yoga, the finitising pravṛtti retains the infinity or freedom of buddhi; and there may even be a pravṛtti that is not finitising such as is said to be exerted by the yogin at a certain stage. Nivṛtti too is willing, willing explicitly to cancel finitising pravṛtti, willing in reflective knowledge where the knowledge is an aspect of the willing and is to be ultimately superseded by it. Both pravṛtti and nivṛtti emerge in knowledge, but while positive willing never outruns knowledge (as it is taken in Sāṁkhya to do necessarily), negative willing outruns knowledge in the last resort in asamprajñāta.

3. Buddhi to both Sāṁkhya and Yoga is the mind with the manifest form of *I am* or asmitā. Judgment or certitude that is said to be its distinctive function is or involves the consciousness of I *am*. What is called ahaṁkāra in Sāṁkhya has to it the form of *me* and not of *I* and is taken as having evolved from asmitā in the form 'I am the prospective me' which is a function of buddhi. In Yoga, ahaṁkāra is the same as this asmitā. Willing to Sāṁkhya is the function of ahaṁkāra having simply the form of *me* and not of I, while to Yoga it is a function always involving the I-form, even in the stage where it has the me-form and may not have the *me*-form at all. All willing then including what Sāṁkhya would call willing is to Yoga a function of buddhi, the ahaṁkāra of Sāṁkhya being to it the lower asmitā. Willing in fact is to it the essential function of buddhi which is implied in the certitude (with the I-form) that is admitted by both as its distinctive function and which may even supersede

the certitude. The perfect mode of this certitude is taken by both to be viveka—the knowledge of buddhi as distinct from the pure self, of the *I* that is the known content of consciousness as distinct from the content-less consciousness which is the pure self. To Yoga but not to Sāṁkhya even viveka involves willing, the knowledge of the distinction of buddhi as viveka from the self being an incipient willing to detach the self from viveka itself—what is actualised in asaṁprajñāta where even self-consciousness or the knowledge of *I* as content is said to lapse. Thus willing which always starts in certitude and can supersede it is understood in Yoga as a function of buddhi that is even more essential than certitude.

4. The Sāṁkhya term 'ahaṁkāra' occurs nowhere in the Yoga-sūtras. It occurs in Yoga-bhāṣya I.45. The term 'asmitā' occurs in many sūtras and is apparently used in different senses, which are not, however, altogether unconnected and means everywhere a function of buddhi. What is meant by ahaṁkāra is referred to in Yoga-bhāṣya on II.19, where asmitā-mātra is taken as included in the six aviśeṣas which are distinguished from buddhi as liṅga-mātra. Not that it is, therefore, regarded as not belonging to buddhi: 'liṅga-mātra' in the sūtra is the essential being of buddhi as distinct from its function as an antaḥ-karaṇa, the being of one stage of its function being taken to be asmitā-mātra as an aviśeṣa. Asmitā-function in this stage is still a buddhi-function, the substantive being of which is the sixth aviśeṣa which just corresponds to the ahaṁkāra of Sāṁkhya. In Yoga-bhāṣya I. 45, where the word 'ahaṁkāra' occurs, it is said—'asya (ahaṁkārasya) api liṅga-mātraṁ sūkṣmoviṣayaḥ. It need not mean that ahaṁkāra is separate as a tattva from buddhi. Buddhi as liṅga-mātra is subtler than buddhi as antaḥkaraṇa of which asmitā-mātra or ahaṁkāra is a mode. Every effect is not a new tattva. The immanent pariṇāmas of a tattva are sthūla relatively to the tattva and may admit of degrees of subtleness among themselves.

5. Thus willing which in Sāṁkhya is the self-manifestation of the being of ahaṁkāra as potential in buddhi is

taken by Yoga to be the function of buddhi that is constitutive of the being of ahaṁkāra. Yukti-dīpikā (p. 32), an old commentary on Sāṁkhya-kārikā, credits one Patañjali with the view that ahaṁkāra is but the asmitā-function of buddhi. This may be the view of the author of Yoga-sūtras, the apparent discrepancy as suggested by the inclusion of asmitā-mātra or ahaṁkāra within aviśeṣa being explained if the view is taken to imply that while the being of ahaṁkāra (as aviśeṣa) evolves out of the being of buddhi(as liṅga-mātra).the function of ahaṁkāra is but the asmitā-function of buddhi. To Sāṁkhya, ahaṁkāra both as being and function is a tattva separate from buddhi.

6. Willing then to Yoga is a function of buddhi and is in fact its essential function. It has the two directions—the positive and the negative, the former being towards bhoga and the latter towards mukti. Both would be forms of asmitā of which the former with the downward trend would correspond to the ahaṁkāra of Sāṁkhya. The higher asmitā with its upward trend is spiritual willing which culminates in the mode of samādhi called asmitānugata which involves viveka and leads to a further form of negative willing called asamprajñāta where viveka itself is dropped and dissolved. Spiritual willing or nivṛtti is willing to abstain from egoistic willing, willing implicitly or explicity to secure the freely quiescent being of buddhi called samādhi. This being or standing is itself an activity, a grade of spiritual willing consisting in the self-reproduction without change of buddhi or a buddhi-vṛtti in its changeless active flow (praśānta-vāhitā). Negative willing includes both the activity for samādhi and the samādhi itself, the latter being not merely the result of the former but its continuation in a higher potency. To Sāṁkhya, nivṛtti-activity is reflection, a cognitive and not a conative process. The quiescent being of buddhi called samādhi is its passive state and not an activity and is only the result or spontaneous (unwilled) concentration of reflection. No specific activity of reflection to secure this concentration is prescribed in Sāṁkhya. To it there is properly no spiritual willing, all willing being the function of ahaṁkāra or the finitised mind, though it need not be explicity to maintain its finitude.

7. To Yoga, the explicit activity to secure samādhi or the practice of yoga is spiritual willing and is an absolutely necessary stage in the discipline or sādhana for absolute freedom. To it as to other systems, freedom is reached through the correction of avidyā or spiritual illusion. To Sāṁkhya, such illusion is finally corrected or eliminated through knowledge while to Yoga, the final elimination is possible only through the practice of yoga, a form of willing that is conditioned by knowledge. Yoga to actualise knowledge that is already reached is the immediate antecedent of the attainment of freedom and is unconditionally prescribed for all, even if yoga be only an alternative way to reach knowledge. Yoga to actualise knowledge that is already reached—jñāna-janya-yoga as Vijñāna-bhikṣu calls it—is the specific subject-matter of Yoga philosophy. Two broad forms of it are mentioned—samprajñāta and asamprajñāta—of which the former terminates in knowledge again, the ultimate form of which is viveka, and the latter that is started by viveka is consummated not in any further knowledge but in a super-conscious free being of the spirit. The latter apparently is the pure or essential form of all yoga, yoga being generally spiritual willing for the free being or active quiescence of the spirit, of which quiescent knowledge is only a contingent aspect.

8. Yoga as discussed in Yoga philosophy is a form of jñāna-janya willing which means free willing, willing that not only springs from knowledge but continues and actualises it. Spiritual willing is free willing in this sense and yoga would be this free willing explicitly to secure free being of the spirit. Willing in Yoga philosophy is essentially free activity for free being, the activity called 'yoga' being only the explicit form of it which again in its absolute purity is asamprajñāta-yoga. As already stated, 'yoga' means both the activity towards samādhi and samādhi itself which is also an activity, the activity of changeless self-reproduction. The activity implicitly or explicitly towards samādhi may be called free willing and samādhi itself is free being. Yoga being thus free willing explicitly for free being is the conscious activity of the mind to arrest its helpless change or differentiation into states or vṛttis. In samprajñāta-yoga the mind stands in a vṛtti and resists its change into other states, while in asam-

prajñāta it is taken to withdraw itself from all vṛttis. The will to prevent the emergence of vṛtti is called 'nirodha' which is understood as the heart of yoga, free willing being in essence the activity of nirodha. The result of the willing which means its continuation as free being is samādhi which is conceived to be a return of the mind to its native being. It is the character that buddhi has in all the levels of its being in some measure or other, its sārvabhauma-dharma as it is called in Yoga-bhāṣya.

9. Samādhi is the result of nirodha or the vṛtti-arresting will. The result is a return of the mind to its native being and may accordingly be taken to be as much reached of right by the will as coming spontaneously to fulfil it. In Sāṁkhya, nirodha is no activity at all, being the same as samādhi which is only a passive quiescence that comes spontaneously as the concentration of the cognitive activity of reflection. In Yoga, nirodha and samādhi are both activities and samādhi as a free or active quiescence is not only a new grade of freedom but is also continuous with the freedom of the nirodha-will. These two aspects of samādhi are distinct in samprajñāta: as a mode of being, it is reached of right by the nirodha-will, but as a mode of self-manifesting knowledge (prajñāloka), it comes spontaneously as the fulfilment of the will. In asamprajñāta, however, where there is no self-manifesting knowledge, the effected aspect and the spontaneous aspect appear as one free being with alternative stresses. Hence the nirodha-will that leads to it is taken as itself coming spontaneously, as the content of a cognitive reflection other than, though emerging in, viveka. This cognitive reflection is what is meant by Īśvara-praṇidhāna in Yoga-sūtra I. 23.

10. Asamprajñāta-samādhi may according to Yoga come with absolute spontaneity in the case of certain devatās but it has to be reached by us through spiritual activity. The activity may be nirodha involving śraddhā (faith), vīrya (strength of will) etc.,[a] in the super-intense form or it may be a unique mode of reflection on God (Īśvara-praṇidhāna). The conjunction 'or' (vā) in Yoga-sūtra I.23. has to be

[a] YS. I. 20-21

interpreted as meaning that the praṇidhāna is a sādhana alternative to nirodha-will, and is itself a surrender of willing. Nirodha is negative willing, willing to arrest positive willing. The praṇidhāna may be called willing but it is the willing to arrest negative willing and therefore all willing, to reverse in fact the entire attitude of willing, to secure the attitude of knowing though there is no knowledge beyond viveka. This will to be in the knowing attitude for freedom from knowledge (asaṁprajñāta) as the end is the will to contemplate a mystery, the mystery of its own spontaneous emergence, of the absolute freedom through which free will itself emerges, the freedom to create freedom, which is just the mystery of God as conceived in Yoga. The will to secure asamprajñāta-samādhi then is at once the culminating phase of willing and a contemplative surrender of the willing attitude. It is the necessary alternation of willing and not-willing where the willing is negative, being withdrawal not only from vṛtti of buddhi but from buddhi itself as manifest, and the not-willing or surrender of willing is positive contemplation of the mystery of absolute freedom or God.

11. Īśvara-praṇidhāna in Yoga-sūtra I.23 is surrender of the whole willing-attitude and not simply of ahaṁkāra or of the fruits of willing, which praṇidhāna in Yoga-sūtra II.1 (also II.32) is taken to mean in the Bhāṣya. The latter praṇidhāna is taken as a kriyā-yoga, a mode of willing while the former is no kriyā or doing at all and is understood as contemplation,[a] as a bhakti-viśeṣa —a kind of 'intellectual love of God' (other than the love that consists in the committing of the fruits of action to God),[b] where God appears to be only a postulate of the contemplative attitude and not the content of knowledge reached prior to the contemplation. God is regarded as a tattva admitted by Yoga over and above the twenty-five tattvas of Sāṁkhya. Apparently, however, Yoga would not—any more than Sāṁkhya—admit knowledge of a tattva that is not implied in viveka, knowledge reached of right by the metaphysical method of distinguishing the object from the self. The knowledge of God is not thus reached: in fact, God as self-revealing is an object of faith that

[a] tajjapah tadartha-bhāvanam—YS.I.28
[b] parama-gurau arpaṇam—YS.II.1

emerges only in the characteristic attitude of contemplation (praṇidhāna) which comes after viveka along with the will to drop viveka itself which is, in fact, the will not to know. Some proof of God is attempted indeed in the Bhāṣya, the value of which, however, would be shown later to depend on this contemplation. God, therefore, does not appear to be a tattva co-ordinate with the Sāṁkhya tattvas that are implied in viveka.

12. Are the other tattvas conceived in the same way in Sāṁkhya and Yoga? They are all implied in viveka, being, in fact, reached in the process of reaching viveka, and the answer to the question depends on the conception of the nature of the process in Sāṁkhya and in Yoga. The process is conceived by both as opposite in direction to the process towards bhoga or affective experience, being, in fact, the reflective retracing of the causal process by which such experience is rendered possible and which is conditioned by an illusory identification of the self and the object. Are illusion and causality understood in the same way in the two systems?

13. Bhoga involves the illusion of identity of the self and the not-self in both the systems, this illusion being the parent of all illusion. The identification is understood both as regarding the not-self—ultimately a buddhi-vṛtti—as the self and as viewing the self which is no content of consciousness as though it were an objective content, a mode of the not-self or buddhi-vṛtti. The former is the appropriation of the object implying what is called sva-svāmi-sambandha or relation of the possessed and the possessor. The latter may be called objectification of the self in contrast with which appropriation would be the subjectification of the object. Appropriation is apparently to Yoga a function of willing and to Sāṁkhya a function of feeling. Objectification is also understood differently in the two systems—as the affective apprehension of the self as with the form of the object or of buddhi-vṛtti in Sāṁkhya and the cognitive apprehension of the form of the self in buddhi-vṛtti in Yoga. The reflection of the vṛtti in the self is indeed admitted by Yoga, but it seems to be taken not as constituting bhoga—the jīvan-mukta who is above bhoga being conceived also to have it—but as only the cognition of possible bhoga.

14. Of the two aspects of bhoga, appropriation is apparently taken by Yoga as the primary and explicit aspect and objectification as secondary and implicit, the Sāṁkhya conception of bhoga being just the reverse. To Yoga, the illusion in bhoga is the conative appropriation in which empirical knowledge of the object is taken to be rooted, while Sāṁkhya takes the illusion to consist in the affective objectification, a feeling of the self as wearing the form of the buddhi-vṛtti or object. Yoga would admit objectification as implicit in appropriation and understand it as the consciousness of the reflection or pratibimba of the self in a vṛtti, the reflection being as objective as the vṛtti. It is from this objectified form of the self that the self proper is known[a] just as the form of the empirical object in vṛtti is taken as the medium of knowledge of the object. The difference is that the object is *given* to the vṛtti wearing its form while the self is not given to the corresponding vṛtti. The form of vṛtti is an anticipatory construction of buddhi in either case, but while the form of the experienced object is as much given as constructed, the form of the self is only constructed and is a mere vikalpa, the self being no object of experience. The reflection of the self in vṛtti—which is the so-called objectified self—is not the self at all, while the reflection of the felt object in vṛtti is not other than the object, the presentation of the object being the object though the object is distinct from the presentation. Similarly Sāṁkhya would admit appropriation as implicit in objectification and take it as the felt non-distinction of the object from the self which, unlike the felt identity of the self with the object or the affective objectification, is not illusory but a factual predicament of the object or buddhi.

15. Bhoga is no function of the pure self either to Yoga or to Sāṁkhya; but as a function of buddhi-endowed self, it is real to Yoga and unreal to Sāṁkhya. It is real conative appropriation to Yoga, real perpetration of an illusion or contradiction, real willing of the contradiction of the object being the self. This willed contradiction is the real significance of the theory of anyathā-khyāti, the theory of illusion accepted by Yoga and Nyāya. The root of conative

[a] YS. II. 20

appropriation is called in Yoga 'a v i d y ā' which is defined[a] as the viewing of the not-self as the self etc., the false viewing being explained in the B h ā ṣ y a as not the mere failure to distinguish the not-self from the self but a positive knowing (of their identity-in-difference) other than true knowing,[b] which must be understood as an *act*, for there can be no differenced *presentation* of the not-self and the self as one. Illusion is a cognitive act, act of identifying what are indefinitely known as distinct and not a mere confusing or failing to distinguish; and a v i d y ā, the primordial illusion, is just the transcendental act of appropriation, the beginningless act of relating in s v a - s v ā m i - s a m b a n d h a.

16. To S ā ṁ k h y a, b h o g a is the feeling of the self being the not-self, wearing the form of the v ṛ t t i, getting objectified or modified into the form of the affective object in the last resort. It is an affective identification of what are here also indefinitely known as distinct, identification of the self with the not-self which is known at the time as given to the self and as distinct from the self only in this sense and otherwise non-distinct in fact. The root of the affective illusion—as distinct from the willed contradiction in Y o g a—is a v i v e k a which, too, like a v i d y ā, is not merely privative, being the positive feeling (not presentation) of the self being impossibly affected or modified like the object. The object is actually non-distinct i.e., not yet distinct from the self while the self is felt as though it were the object (v ṛ t t i). The non-distinction of the object from the self is an actual objective situation, factual or s a t though terminable, but the positively felt identity of the self from the object is unreal or a s a t. Hence illusion is taken in S ā ṁ k h y a as s a d a s a t - k h y ā t i. The illusory identification of the self and the not-self then which is at the root of b h o g a is understood differently in Y o g a and in S ā ṁ - k h y a. Hence the theory of the causal process, too, which is the movement towards b h o g a as distinct from the reflective, spiritual or free process towards m u k t i is different in the two systems.

[a] YS. II. 5

[b] v i d y ā - v i p a r ī t a m j ñ ā n ā n t a r a m

CHAPTER II

SĀÑKHYA AND YOGA (Contd.)

(Causality, Becoming and Time)

17. Bhoga is understood in both the systems as the final cause of the evolutionary process of the object, the downward process of the causal becoming of prakṛti. The process of dissolution (pratisañcara) is taken by neither as a causal process, being to Sāṁkhya connected with the spontaneous cognitive act of reflection and to Yoga with free negative willing. The causal process is taken by the former to stop of itself with emergence of reflection and by the latter to be arrested by free negative willing which is to it willing not to exercise causality, *not* willing to exercise an opposite causality. To both, the causal process is the function of ahaṁkāra or the will to bhoga, the will to be finite and to progress in finitude. Causal becoming (pariṇāma) is the process of a tattva becoming finite, 'becoming' being understood as the continuing of the cause into the effect in a finitised form.

18. The concept of becoming requires to be further analysed. Becoming is understood as a unitary process presented objectively to consciousness. There are systems like Nyāya which would not even admit the presentation of becoming, its so-called unity being only the content of a wrong *thinking*, thinking of distinct contents as one. Others like the Vedāntist and the Buddhist would admit it as presented though as appearance only and not as fact. To Sāṁkhya and Yoga, becoming is presented as fact. Becoming implies both succession and persistence, both of which are presented, their unity, too, being admitted by all except Nyāya as presented and not merely thought. To them the object that conditions experience is nothing but becoming, being constituted by the causal process which is immediately presented as a becoming. Causality is presented as the cause becoming the effect, the cause as a whole at once altering and continuing into the effect, not merely altering in one respect and continuing in another. This presentation may be regarded as ultimately a false appearance, being false either as succession or as persistence. It is regarded as objectively real by Sāṁkhya

and Yoga, but they appear to differ in their conceptions of the unity of succession and persistence.

19. The difference is deducible from their conceptions of the will. Causation is to both willing to be finite, willing being a function of the object, of buddhi or ahaṁkāra which is object and does not belong to the self. To Yoga, all willing including the will to be finite is a function of buddhi, being, in fact, the self-actualisation of knowledge. Causality as the will to be finite is the self-conscious thought (or thought with the I-form) of the finite (*me*) achieving its being: cause becomes effect as the *I* willing becomes the me. To Sāṁkhya, willing which means willing to be finite is the content of knowledge and not the self-actualisation of knowledge into being. It is the object as *me* getting further manifest as *me*, and getting known as having been self-manifested. Causation is the self-manifestation of a pre-existent objective being: being is not achieved but is known to have been only manifested, to have had only known-ness induced in it by itself. The being of the effect with its limitation is already in the cause in an unmanifest form i.e., without its known-ness, the cause as distinct from the effect existing only as manifesting, expressing or unfolding the effect. The manifest-ness or known-ness of the effect and not its existence is constituted by this manifesting function of the cause which exists as the effect itself getting self-manifested. Yoga does not appear to take the effect with its limitation as pre-existent in the cause. The effect is indeed the cause with a limitation but the limitation was not in the cause, having been turned up and not merely manifested by the cause. The being of the effect implies limitation and is, therefore, taken to be constituted by the causality of the cause, not as manifested by it. The causality of the cause again does not, as in Sāṁkhya, constitute the being of the cause. The cause, so far as it is distinct from the effect and is not itself the effect of another cause, is no being at all but a function. In Sāṁkhya the cause has the being of the effect and its distinction from the effect consists in its manifesting the being.

20. The cause to both Yoga and Sāṁkhya manifests itself as the real limited being of the effect which is recognised either as the fulfilment or as the definition of the cause. Fulfilment and definition are respectively the conative and cognitive formulations of the identity-in-difference of cause and effect. Causation is will-

ing in both the cases and the result of willing is identical with the willing of it. Willing involves knowing, being to Yoga knowing itself as achieving its existence and to Sāṁkhya an existent content of its own knowing. The existence of knowing which is the result of the willing is identical with the willing in the sense of being its fulfilment, while the known or manifest existence of the willing which is the result of itself as unknown or unmanifest is identical with it as its definition. The identity of cause and effect in the case both of fulfilment and definition is not mutual but is only in one direction. In Yoga, the cause constitutes the effect which, however, as *being* is distinct from it. In Sāṁkhya, the effect is pre-existent in the cause which, however, as being defining itself is distinct from the defined being of the effect. To Hegel apparently the identity is mutual: fulfilment is definition and definition is fulfilment—what would be denied by Yoga and Sāṁkhya respectively. Becoming as at once fulfilment and definition is affective specification where the cause as the (relatively) unspecified content is realised and explicated in the effect as the specified content. Cause becomes effect which is recognised as cause. In Yoga, cause becomes effect as the *I* becomes *me;* in Sāṁkhya as the *me* becomes a more definite *me;* in Hegel as the *I* becomes *me* and the *me* becomes *I*. To Yoga, for the *me* to be recognised as the *I* is retraction of becoming, not becoming; to Sāṁkhya, the *I* as distinct from the *me* does not come in at all—there being retraction of *me* into *me* which is reflection; to Hegel becoming or causation includes retraction.

21. Becoming to both Yoga and Sāṁkhya is the self-determination of the cause. The cause freely determines itself either in the way of self-fulfilment or in the way of self-manifestation: prakṛti is svatantra. In Nyāya, the samavāyī or material cause does not determine itself, being determined by another cause, an external circumstance called nimitta, in the production of the effect. To Yoga and Sāṁkhya the material cause is the only cause: the samavāyī of the effect turns up or manifests the difference in itself called the effect. Sāṁkhya admits no nimitta at all, the so-called conjunction of the object with the self, which is sometimes called the nimitta of becoming, being nothing other than the object. Yoga admits a nimitta which is, however, taken as no cause[a] and is

[a] aprayojaka—YS.IV.3

conceived to be what simply removes a counter-acting circumstance or pratibandha. The latter is not an opposed cause: it may be an inoperative circumstance in the presence of which the cause does not operate, being as it were hypnotised by the mere presence. When the cause becomes the effect, the effect is known to be nothing but the cause fulfilled or manifested. But the cause is sometimes found not to act and even when it acts, it takes time to produce the effect. The implication is that there is some inoperative counter-acting circumstance which prevents or delays causation. Its absence is a negative condition of causation and the positive circumstance that causes the absence is nimitta, the ultimate nimitta being the absolutely free will of God.

22. The question of pratibandha or nimitta arises only when the cause is known prior to the effect. If, as Yoga takes it, willing is the self-actualisation of knowledge that is already there, the cause is known prior to the emergence of the effect. If the cause does not operate in any case, a counter-active has to be admitted and hence when the cause operates, the absence of the counter-active and the nimitta causing the absence have to be inferred. Where however, as in Sāṁkhya, the cause is known only through the effect as the prior datum, the cause is known as having already operated so that the admission of the absence of counter-active as a negative condition is superfluous, being like the admission of the absence of the absence of A after the admission of A. Hence in Sāṁkhya the question of the nimitta does not rise at all and it is unnecessary to admit a divine will as a co-operant condition of becoming along with the self-determining function of prakṛti.

23. The difference between Sāṁkhya and Yoga about the nature of causality is reflected in their views on the nature of time. Neither system admits time as a separate tattva: time is to both concrete becoming or pariṇāma which is not conceived as an event in time. Pariṇāma may be understood as the cause turning up its own limitation or as the limited effect having got manifested. In the former conception, the real objective fact is the act of the cause, its act of turning up or the production, the succession of cause and effect being only a retrospective construction as in the Bergsonian view. In the latter conception, the real fact is the antecedence of the cause to the effect, the prior becoming of the effect, but the causal act as the initial

moment of this becoming is but an abstraction. Hence to Yoga which presents the former conception, time is real as the causal act, the initiation or the initial moment of becoming (kṣana) —what may be called the living present—and the so-called time-relation of sequence of cause and effect is not real, for the past or future moment with which the real present appears to be related is not real at all. To the latter or Sāṁkhya conception of becoming, the effect being pre-existent in the cause is never turned up so that the time-relation of sequence alone—the prior process of manifestation constitutive of the manifestness of the effect—is real time.

24. The views of time require further elucidation. Time is taken by some commentators on Sāṁkhya-kārikā as nothing but ākāśa as bhūta viewed in reference to experienced motion—say, of the sun in the sky. This conception, however, would hardly apply to the procession of tattvas and would at best interpret becoming in the world of experience. Yukti-dīpikā,[a] the commentary on Kārikā already referred to, suggests that time may be the causal process (kāraṇa-parispanda) itself, the general process of becoming. This accords with Vijñāna-bhikṣu's commentary on Sāṁkhya-sūtra[b] where the ākāśa of which space and time are taken to be differentiations is taken not as a bhūta but as an aspect of prakṛti itself. Time as an aspect of prakṛti is nitya-kāla or eternal time which appears to be nothing but the eternal becoming of prakṛti, the eternal procession of the tattvas. This ākāśa is understood along with buddhi to be manifest within prakṛti as function though not as being and may well be taken as the same as this buddhi. Time then to Sāṁkhya appears to be prakṛti itself in its eternal function of manifestation through which the tattvas from buddhi downwards have their manifest character.

25. The Sāṁkhya view of time has to be mainly guessed at but the Yoga view of time is pronounced both in the Yoga-sūtras and in the Bhāṣya.[c] The two aspects of time—kṣaṇa (instant) and krama (continuous sequence of instants)—are dis-

[a] p. 89, II. 8-9
[a] II. 12. dik-kālāvākāśadivyaḥ
[c] YS. III. 13-15, 52; IV. 12. 32

cussed in YB. III. 52 and IV. 32. The instant is explained in the first instance as infinitesimal duration, the time taken by an atom of infinitesimal magnitude to move out of its position or to reach the next position. Apparently this applies to an action in the empirical world only, but kṣaṇa and krama are understood in the metaphysical world also[a] and hence kṣaṇa would generally mean the time taken by a thing to give up its present mode or to take up a new mode. Ultimately it would be the changing act of guṇa which is as much substantial as the guṇa,[b] not the time taken by the act but the act itself as substantial.

26. Three modes of immanent change of a tattva (as distinct from its change into a new tattva) are mentioned in YS. III. 13—viz., change of dharma (character or capacity), change of lakṣaṇa (stage of actuality) and change of avasthā (state), each later of which is consequent on the former. The lakṣaṇas are taken to be three-fold—viz., future, present, and past, these being understood not as temporal modes but as stages of actuality—what in the process of causation (willing) respectively is to be actual, is actual and was actual, the three being the eternal stages of the same thing, of which the present is vyakta (manifest to all) and the other two sūksma (manifest to yogin).[c] The instant is primarily understood in reference to lakṣaṇa-pariṇāma, being the passing from the future stage to the present stage or from this to the past stage, there being no passing from the past.[d] The stages are not temporal but eternal, but the passing from one stage to another or the changing act is time which as necessarily simple or indivisible is called kṣaṇa or instant. An effected thing has all the three stages or lakṣaṇa-pariṇāmas and time as instant is also a pariṇāma, the transition of a thing from one lakṣaṇa to its 'causal next' (samanantara), being pariṇāma in the sense of act of change as distinct from pariṇāma as mode of being.

27. Kṣaṇa as the causal act is the living present—emerging or evanescing—as distinct from the present as a lakṣaṇa or stage of actuality. We may speak of the present stage of a thing,

[a] YB. IV. 32
[b] YV. III. 52
[c] YS. IV. 12-13
[d] YB. III. 14

as eternally together with its past and future, but the living present of a thing is unique and cannot be literally spoken of as being together with a past or future kṣaṇa. The passing of the future into the present and the passing of the present into the past are not together in the sense the future, present and past are together. Yet we speak figuratively of a past or a future instant and hence have the apparent concept of krama or sequence of kṣaṇas. This sequence is not an objective fact but is only a thinking (speaking) construction (vikalpa), a thought-content constructed 'at the moment of the termination of a change'[a] i.e., retrospectively. It is, in fact, a figurative representation of the order of the lakṣaṇas or the stages of actuality, which as an intelligible or non-temporal order is an objective fact. What then is ordinarily called time—viz., a duration differentiated into a succession—is to Yoga nothing real, being but a symbolism for the intelligible order within a change which is real time only as the durationless transition from one stage of the change to the stage that is causally next to it, the transition being the self-changing act of the thing, or its immanent causal function, the thing itself as kṣaṇa.

28. Apparently time, whether as real instant or the fictitious order of instants, is understood by Yoga only in reference to the immanent change of a tattva; the change of a tattva to another tattva and hence the entire procession of the tattvas presenting only an intelligible order is not time at all. To Sāṁkhya this intelligible order among the tattvas is the only real time, the eternal function of prakṛti. There is, as will appear presently, no real immanent change in Sāṁkhya, and the *entire* order alone is time, the passing from one tattva to the next being not a real part of it but an abstraction. Time as the function of prakṛti is one and not many and accordingly it is called (kāraṇa or functional) akāśa. The instant or, for the matter of that, any finite determination of time is an unreal abstraction.

29. Sāṁkhya would certainly admit many characters (dharma), stages of actuality (lakṣaṇa) and states (avasthā) of a tattva and an order among them but cannot take this order to be causal. In fact, dharma, lakṣaṇa and

[a] YS. IV. 32

avasthā are to it abstractions, not changes of the tattva and causality is a relation to change as effect. The emergence of a difference in a substance by its own activity or the substance as with this difference is called pariṇāma of the substance as without this difference emergent in it. In tattvāntara-pariṇāma, the effect has all the characters of the cause with an additional distinctive character of its own. A so-called immanent change lacks some characters of the previous change and has some characters that it lacks. So the latter cannot be said to be the effect of the former. Are both to be taken as effects of the one substance? Unless the substance be admitted to exist without any accidental character, there appears to be no sense in speaking of it as the cause of any accidental character emerging in it. Immanent (causal) change then can only be admitted if the substance can exist without any differentiation in it, without any feature other than its defining features. Yoga appears to admit such existence of the substance—e.g., buddhi as in the asamprajñāta stage is admitted to be without any vṛtti or actual state (avasthā). Sāṁkhya cannot admit an undifferentiated substance: a substance exists only in its modes. A tattva may be admitted to exist before the emergence of the tattva that is its effect. But a tattva cannot by itself exist before the emergence of any mode and cannot, therefore, be the cause of this mode: there can be no immanent causality to Sāṁkhya.

30. What then, according to Sāṁkhya, is the relation between one mode of a tattva and another mode conditioned by it, between two buddhi-vṛttis, for example? Vijñānabhikṣu's conception of buddhi-vṛttis as like flames of the same fire or waves of the same sea does not apparently interpret Sāṁkhya view. A vṛtti to Yoga is what buddhi causally contracts itself into.[a] In Sāṁkhya, vṛtti is buddhi as referring in its bhāva-function (not causal function) to its content[b] as having the form of the content not as its real contraction but as an aupādhika or reflectional construction. The form of the content as reflected in buddhi is real only in the sense the image of a red object in

[a] YB. IV. 10
[b] SS V. 106

the mirror is really presented as red, not real as a modification of buddhi nor unreal in the sense the reflection of a vṛtti in the self is unreal, which again is like the image in the mirror in so far as it is presented but not as *really in* the mirror. The form of the object is *really presented* in buddhi as the form of the vṛtti which, however, is presented as only *unreally* or *magically* in the self.

31. Vṛtti then to Sāṁkhya is buddhi really in the form of object, which form, however, is not its causal modification, as it is to Yoga, (though the causality admitted by Yoga is that of buddhi itself and not of the object). It is, therefore, a non-causal but real manifestation of buddhi, belonging to its bhāva-sarga as distinct from its liṅga-sarga.[a] The relation of a vṛtti to another conditioned by it is like the relation of their contents non-causal. In the sphere of non-causal manifestation of buddhi, whether in its subjective or objective aspect, there can only be an appearance of causation and no real causation. The so-called immanent change of a tattva then (dharma-lakṣaṇa-avasthā-pariṇāma) is to Sāṁkhya an appearance of change or causal manifestation, which is neither real change nor, therefore, illusory, being in fact a phenomenally real manifestation of prakṛti.

33. To Sāṁkhya then real time is the eternal procession but not illusory differentiations and their succession would be, like the succession of their contents, not time but an appearance of time. To Yoga which regards the vṛttis as real changes of a tattva through its immanent causality, their succession would indeed be a non-causal construction or vikalpa, but the emergence of a vṛtti would be a real kṣana.

33. To Sāṁkhya then real time is the eternal procession of the objective tattvas, the order of phenomenal objects as also of the tattva-vṛttis corresponding to them being only apparently temporal, though not illusory. To Yoga real time is the act of a tattva of causing an immanent change, the succession of such immanent changes is only constructed time, a construction or vikalpa of buddhi and the order of the tattvas is non-temporal.

[a] SK. 52

CHAPTER III

SĀṄKHYA AND YOGA (contd.)

(The empirical world: its status & constitution.)

34. Sāṁkhya would not apparently admit the Yoga contention of the immanent causal change of a tattva. Such change, as for example of buddhi into the vṛttis, would be to it only an appearance though not illusory, a non-causal or reflectional construction which is yet really in the tattva. A vṛtti is taken both in Yoga and Sāṁkhya as implying a bhāva (rūpa in Yoga) or non-causal reference of buddhi beyond itself to the facts of experience, though it is itself regarded by Yoga against Sāṁkhya as causally manifested. What is the metaphysical status of the facts of experience according to these systems?

35. Both would deny that the empirical world is a tattva other than the vikāra-tattvas (bhūta and indriya) with which the evolution of the tattvas is taken to end. Yoga takes it, however, to be an immanent pariṇāma of the vikāra-tattvas.[a] This cannot be the Sāṁkhya view, to which the notion of immanent change is, as pointed out, generally inadmissible. In the Vedāntic view the empirical world is false, but then it is of the same status as the objective tattvas so that to vyāvahārika knowledge it is as real as the body—subtle and gross—through which the self experiences the world. The bhogya (experienced) and the bhogāyatana (experiencing body) would be, as in Yoga, immanent changes of the same stuff.

36. If Sāṁkhya denies immanent change, what would be its view of the body and the external world? The body is undoubtedly real, as real as the tattvas constituting it. The unitary form of the body is the form of the self from which its elements are undistinguished, this non-distinction being the principle of beginningless aviveka. Aviveka has here, however, a manifest form, being manifest in buddhi as its bhāva or its function of bhoga which is its non-causal reference to the

[a] YB. II. 19; III. 13; IV. 14. etc.

objects of experience or the external world. The body then is one through the buddhi-bhāva immanent in it, i.e., through its response to the external world, being itself called a kāryā-śrayi-bhāva. The body as one is real as bhogāyatana or the substratum of the bhoga-function. What, however, then is the bhogya object which cannot be said to be such substratum?

37. The object of experience is not only not an immanent pariṇāma of the tattvas that are manifest in the experiencing body : it has not even like the body the real unity of a non-causal function. As experienced, however, it cannot be unreal unless experience as the function of buddhi be taken as in Vedānta to be unreal. To Sāṁkhya, experience or bhoga is indeed illusory content. but the illusory is to it not utterly unreal but real in one aspect while in Vedānta it is what cannot be asserted to be real or unreal. If the sense-experience is real, its content or the object of experience is real. Experiencing is real not indeed as a causal activity (state) of buddhi as in Yoga but as a non-causal subjective function of (the) buddhi (-self), of buddhi endowed with the form of *I*. The function is reference to the object and cannot be real without its content, the object being also real. The object of bhoga is felt to be given and this feeling does not cease even when the object is realised as nothing apart from the bhoga, as constituted by the illusory identity of the self with the not-self. It is thus unlike a manifest tattva which is known as other than the self i.e., through the correction of illusory identity. At the same time it is not an illusory appearance. because it is not. like the snake that a rope appears to be. known in reflection as what was not given as such to bhoga. To know that experience is an illusion is not to know that the experienced object is an illusion: even the jīvan-mukta is supposed to perceive the empirical object as fact though he has no experience of it. The empirical object is manifest as fact though it is not a manifest tattva: as fact it is the unmanifest tattva—prakṛti—and as manifest, it is only an appearance non-causally manifested—constructed and known—by buddhi as the content of its bhāva-sarga. It cannot be an immanent change in bhūta as vikāra-tattva, as it is taken to be in Yoga because there is no real immanent change and because it is not manifest like bhūta etc., by the correction of the identity of the self and the not-self.

38. Yoga admits immanent change and specifically takes empirical objects as the pariṇama of atomic bhūta (bhūta-sūkṣma) which again is the pariṇāma of the tanmātra.[a] At the same time the spatio-temporal distinctions within the empirical world are apparently taken by Yoga along with Sāṁkhya as non-causal constructions of buddhi—i.e., as vikalpas. Vikalpa as buddhi-vṛtti is as much an immanent change of buddhi as the other vṛttis, but the content of vikalpa is a non-causal construct or buddhi-nirmāṇa which is no fact (vastu) though not illusory or is, in other words, a given appearance such as the entire empirical world is taken to be in Sāṁkhya. In Yoga, while the empirical object is otherwise a real change of vikāra-tattva, its distinguishing space-time limitations are only given appearances. The guṇas constituting a tattva are perpetually entering into new combinations[b] and hence the multiplicity of immanent changes. Of these pariṇāmas each is in essence every other[c] though one only gets manifest at a time (emergent, present or udita), the others not emerging because of some counteractive circumstance—which the particular space-time characters of the emergent change are taken to be.[d] A particular immanent change emerges only with its proper time, place, shape and occasional cause, these being no changes themselves but only the context for a change. Its time means its position in time-series or krama which is definitely taken[e] as a construction of buddhi; and presumably the same status would be assigned to the other circumstances—place, shape etc.—constituting the context for a pariṇāma.

39. An empirical object is then to Yoga an immanent change of bhūta in a buddhi-constructed context. To Sāṁkhya it appears to be wholly a buddhi-construction (so far as it is manifest), having place in the bhāva-sarga as distinct from the liṅga-sarga of buddhi; or, more accurately, it is the content of a buddhi-bhāva as immanent in the gross or bhautika body i.e., as kāryāśrita-bhāva, content that is constructed so far as it is manifest but not so far

[a] YB. IV. 14; III. 44

[b] calam ca guṇa-vṛttam—YB. III. 13, etc.

[c] sarvam sarvātmakam—YB. III. 14

[d] YB. III. 14

[e] YB. III. 52

as it is given. It is thus a non-causal manifestation of *prakṛti* referred to or experienced by the bodily self as constituted by the experiencing function but not by the matter of the body. The body is itself *bhūta* though not its immanent *pariṇāma*, *bhūta* with *buddhi-bhāva* really resident in it though not as a modification. *Yoga* appears to take the empirical object to be of the same status as the body experiencing it.

40. The consideration of *Yoga* and *Sāṁkhya* views on the nature of illusion, causality, time and the empirical world prepares the way for an answer to the question asked before as to whether the objective *tattvas* are conceived in the same way in the two systems. The *Sāṁkhya* (objective) *tattvas* are referred to in the *Yoga-sūtras* in the enumeration of the four *guṇa-parvas*.[a] The *guṇas* are taken to exist in four stages—*viśeṣa* comprising the *bhūtas* and *indriyas*, *aviśeṣa* including the five *tānmātras* and also *ahaṁkāra* called *asmitā-mātra*, *liṅga-mātra* which is *buddhi*, and *a-liṅga* which is *prakṛti* or *pradhāna*. The difference in respect of *ahaṁkāra* in the two systems has been already brought out, their conceptions of *aviśeṣa* being otherwise the same. As to the *viśeṣas*, the main difference is about the atomic nature of the *bhūtas* which is admitted by *Yoga* and would be apparently denied by *Sāṁkhya*. Important differences, however, appear in their conceptions of *buddhi* and *prakṛti*.

41. As already pointed out, *Yoga* holds that *bhūta* emerges out of *tanmātra* in the form of perceivable *sthūla* atoms in the first instance, out of which again *sthūla* complex objects emerge as immanent *pariṇāmas*. A *bhūta* in its essential form as a new evolute of *tanmātra* is atomic, being called *bhūta-sūkṣma* or *sthūla-sūkṣma*—having much the same status as the *trasareṇus* of *Vaiśeṣika* philosophy. The *bhūta-sūkṣma* is a simple perceivable, though it is still a complex of the unperceivable *tanmātras* which are elementary manifest matter.[b] The manifest object is in the last resort composed of the *guṇas* which are absolutely simple and not only unperceivable but unmanifest (without the objective

[a] YS. II. 19
[b] YB. IV. 14

character of known-ness). Apparently then to Yoga there are three grades of sūkṣma matter—the guṇas, the tanmātras and the bhūta-sūkṣmas. Of these, bhūta-sūkṣma is definitely called paramāṇu[a] and mahābhūta or viśvarūpa, in the form of composite bhautika objects which are taken as its pariṇāma, is presumably composed of or immanently caused by many such paramāṇus. Each paramāṇu is composed of tanmātras, an earth-paramāṇu by all the five tanmātras, a water-paramāṇu by four (excluding smell) and so forth. The question is if Yoga admits many tanmātras or many guṇas of the same species like many paramāṇus of the same species which are very likely admitted. Are there, for example, many individual sound-tanmātras or many individual sattva-guṇas?

42. If a mahābhūta is taken by Yoga as composed of many paramāṇus (trasas), these are understood not as exact similars but as 'having different qualitative viśeṣas.[b] The mahābhūta as avayavin is taken to be an immanent pariṇāma[c] of each paramāṇu as avayava. A paramāṇu, again, is avayavi-pariṇāma of many tanmātras of the same kind (with tanmātras of other kinds combined with them but not making an avayavin with them). A tanmātra unlike a bhūta does not admit of qualitative variations and hence its immanent (avasthā-) pariṇāmas can only be quantitatively different as degrees. Tanmātras of the same kind as the avayavas of a paramāṇu are then together as the units of an intensive, as distinct from an extensive, quantum are together and may be symbolically described as mutually interpenetrating (cf. the Vaiśeṣika conception of two paramāṇus making up a dvyaṇuka with the same magnitude as that of a paramāṇu), their togetherness being here felt and not perceived. A unit-tanmātra is further conceived like any other tattva as a unity of the three guṇas that is predominantly tāmasika. Does this predominance, which is apparently a quantity, imply the co-existence of many individual tamoguṇas?

[a] YB. III. 44; IV. 14
[b] YB. III. 44
[c] YS. IV. 14

43. The dominant character of a g u ṇ a in a manifest object may not be merely relative to the other g u ṇ a s constituting it : it may be relatively to the same g u ṇ a in other objects where also it is dominant. In the latter aspect, the g u ṇ a as constituting an object may appear to be a quantum requiring to be conceived as a synthesis of units. Hence on certain other considerations V i j ñ a n a - b h i k ṣ u admits an infinite number of units of the same g u ṇ a. Is the conception tenable? As a g u ṇ a is conceived in Y o g a and S ā ṃ k h y a, it can hardly be intelligibly spoken of as having a given finite quantity. One object may indeed appear to have more of a particular g u ṇ a than another, but the quantity here is understood metaphorically rather than literally. It is like taking the knowledge of a greater as itself greater than the knowledge of the less.

44. The g u ṇ a s are understood in terms of the b u d d h i - function of b h o g a in its three forms—s u k h a, d u ḥ k h a and m o h a—as their unmanifest potentialities. The three b h o g a s are regarded not only as subjective experiences but as experienced characters of the object. Subjectively they stand for three apparent predicaments of the self, being the feelings of being free, being at once free and unfree, and being unfree respectively. Objectively they are presented as the three fundamental aesthetic characters—p r a k ā ś a, k r i y ā and s t h i t i; and these understood as unmanifest or independent of the subject are the three g u ṇ a s. Apparently even an aesthetic character has a degree but the degree here is like the degree of the freedom of the self. If subjective freedom be taken as freedom of the will—as it would be taken in Y o g a, 'greater freedom' would be felt in making an effort—what is described as willing to reinforce a previous willing—which is not really adding to the previous willing but is on a higher level of self-consciousness. It is willing the willing itself, which is not a greater degree of the first willing but is creative of a greater degree. Degree of freedom and, therefore, degree of s a t t v a or p r a k ā ś a as an objective character would then be understood in Y o g a as not an accomplished or existent quantum but a quantum in the making. So generally the degree of a g u ṇ a as in a manifest object would have to be regarded as a factitious quantity.

45. Now a quantum in the making cannot be said to be composed of co-existent units. More or less of a g u ṇ a in

an object then is only a coming into being of the object, the becoming being thinkable as *any* number of becomings. The object even as tanmātra which admits of no distinguishable qualitative variations and only of distinguishable degrees admits still of qualitative peculiarities which are un-isolable in thought. These are really aesthetic characters and can be present as more or less. When an object is said to have more or less of any such character, we say loosely that it has more or less of a guṇa. Here: the fact is that it has the guṇa with more or less of the aesthetic character as its upādhi, the guṇa itself being a causing function which may be thought as any number of functions and is thought as a particular number because of the upādhi.

46. Apparently then Yoga admits many paramāṇus (having nameable qualitative viśeṣas) of the same bhūta in the corresponding mahābhūta and many *degrees* (each with an un-nameable qualitative viśeṣa) of the same tanmātra in the corresponding paramāṇus explaining these viśeṣas but not many vyaktis of the same guṇa as explaining such un-nameable viśeṣas. Not that an un-nameable viśeṣa is eternal like a Vaiśeṣika viśeṣa, for the tanmātra of which it is viśeṣa is an effect. As an effected viśeṣa, it too admits of magnitude. But such magnitude cannot be a synthesis of units as the viśeṣa of a mahabhūta is a synthesis of those of the paramāṇus and not even as the viśeṣa of a paramāṇu is a synthesis of those of the tanmātras. The synthesis of paramāṇus is extensive and that of tanmātras is intensive; and if a tanmātra, again, has an effected magnitude, it cannot be the result of an extensive or intensive synthesis. As a manifest character, this magnitude must be simple, unanalysable into manifest units. But as the tanmātra of which it is a character is effected, this manifest simple must be effected. Its effectuation, however, can be only an unmanifest process. Manifest synthesis is of co-existent units which retain or lose their manifest distinction as units in the compound, though their co-existence is still manifest in the latter case, the case of intensive synthesis, where the units are felt as flowing into each other. In the un-manifest effectuation of the viśeṣa of a tanmātra, if it be called a synthesis at all, there is not even this felt flowing existence and, therefore, no

vyaktis or self-identical units at all. A guṇa constituting the tanmātra is here a pure flow, not the flow of one self-identical unit into another, not the emergence of a self-identity followed by its cessation but a flow in which self-identity does not emerge at all. Yet self-identity as emergent in a manifest tattva is an effect, the cause of which, viz., a guṇa must be understood as the *causing* of self-identity. This causing process in which the guṇa consists is just what is called its sadṛśa-pariṇāma.

47. Yoga thus presents some kind of atomic theory which, however, differs from the atomic theory of the Vaiśeṣika. Paramāṇu, tanmātra and guṇa of Yoga correspond roughly to trasa, dvyaṇuka and paramāṇu of the Vaiśeṣika, these being inferred for the explanation of the magnitude-variations of a sense-perceived bhautika object. The cardinal difference between the two atomic theories is in respect of the conception of the ultimate simple constituent of objective reality—the guṇa of Yoga or the Vaiśeṣika paramaṇu. Yoga would not admit the Vaiśeṣika notion of the eternal co-existence of many simple constituents of the same kind which are absolute repetitions of one another. Objection has been taken to this notion by others on the ground that there can be no such thing as two exact similars, that what are numerically different must be also different in some character. The Vaiśeṣika reply to the objection would be that a given thing with a finite magnitude is necessarily inferred to be a synthesis of things of smaller magnitude that are exactly similar and that, therefore, ultimately exact similars of infinitesimal magnitude must exist, each with an eternal un-analysable viśeṣa. There must be co-existent exact similars because there is finite magnitude, though how they retain their distinction may not be conceivable. Yoga would admit that the notion of finite magnitude implies the notion of exact similars but not of their co-existence, that their co-existence cannot be inferred from the existence of the finite magnitude but is otherwise known where it is a fact, that exact similars cause a thing of finite magnitude without necessarily being the parts of it. Even where the parts of a thing with finite magnitude have finite magnitudes (e.g., trasas), *each* part causes or causally becomes the whole, the other parts being relatively to it only nimitta which to Yoga, as has been

pointed out, is no cause but only what removes the pratibandha of the effect. The co-existence of the parts, therefore, is no causal circumstance in reference to the effect, though it is a fact. In what is called saṁkhyā-ja-parimāṇa (magnitude due to mere number) in Vaiśeṣika where the magnitude of the effect viz., trasa is admitted to be not due to the co-existence of the dvyaṇukas, they are still regarded as vyaktis under a jāti. This would correspond in Yoga to the magnitude of a trasa (called paramāṇu) as caused by the tanmātra-magnitudes which are apparently synthesised like the units of a degree. A tanmātra then may be conceivably regarded as vyaktis under a jāti. Like a Vaiśeṣika dvyaṇūka a tanmātra-unit is an effect of something subtler viz., guṇa. If a guṇa appears as more or less in such a unit this magnitude cannot be said to be saṁkhyā-ja-parimāṇā. In Vaiśeṣika, a trasa has dvyaṇūkas in it, each of which is composed of paramāṇus. the magnitude of both trasa and dvyaṇuka being saṁkhyā-ja. Apparently here, however, we have not two grades of saṁkhyā-ja magnitude. The cause of the trasa-magnitude is as much the number of the dvyaṇukas as the number of the paramāṇus. there being no dvyaṇuka except as constituting a trasa. The magnitude of a dvyaṇuka does not differ from that of a paramāṇu, both being 'aṇu' and therefore not admitting of more or less. Yoga would take a tanmātra-unit as admittedly of more or less of a guṇa, though it cannot understand it as due to the number of guṇa-units.

48. The relation of the three grades of sūkṣma matter in Yoga—viz., guṇa, tanmātra and paramāṇu has to be more closely compared with the relation of the three Vaiśeṣika grades of matter of minimal magnitude—paramāṇu, dvyaṇuka and trasa. A guṇa (along with other guṇas) causes a tanmātra (and in fact any manifest object) but is not present as many units constituting the parts of the tanmātra. To the Vaiśeṣika, paramāṇu as causing a dvyaṇuka is two units, though it is doubtful if these units should be called parts of the dvyaṇuka. The paramāṇus causing a trasa are units that are parts of the trasa. The causal constituents of a whole that is greater in magnitude than any constituent are called its parts If the paramāṇus are causal constituents of a

dvyaṇuka that has the same magnitude as each paramāṇu, they cannot be called its parts. Even if this objection be waived, we have to take the paramāṇus not as spatially next to one another but as only temporal 'nexts'. Everywhere else a temporal next has a space-position other than that of the persisting antecedent that forms a unity with it, but here a temporal next is not a spatial next. Whether we call the paramāṇus-parts of the dvyaṇuka or not, they are not spatially co-existent units as they are even in the trasa. So if they are two units, they are *together* in their product in quite a unique sense. To Yoga, a guṇa constitutive of a tanmātra as its effect is not many units at all. Number is a character of what are each already self-identical, but a guṇa is creative of self-identity that appears only in the manifest and is manifestness itself. The cause of self-identity is not a self-identity but a self-becoming or self-reproducing function (sadṛśa-pariṇāma).

49. Again, to the Vaiśeṣika, the paramāṇus cause the trasa, causing the dvyaṇuka as implied in the trasa. The emergence of the trasa and that of the dvyaṇuka is aparently a single process, the dvyaṇuka in fact being the trasa in one aspect. Although the paramāṇus are said to cause a dvyaṇuka and the dvyaṇukas a trasa, a dvyaṇuka cannot be inferred to exist *apart* from a trasa nor a paramāṇu *apart* from a dvyaṇuka, though their existence in trasa is inferred from the change (due to heat) of one trasa into another. The emergence that requires to be explained may be indifferently expressed as that of trasa as embodying dvyaṇuka or of dvyaṇuka as necessarily embodied in trasa, and hence the causation of the dvyaṇuka and that of the trasa are coincident processes. To Yoga a tanmātra is not necessarily formative of a paramāṇu (-trasa): a higher tattva can exist by itself without causing or being embodied in a lower, causing as it does the lower only when there is a nimitta to remove pratibandha. If the Vaiśeṣika admits that a trasa breaks up into free dvyaṇukas and these into free paramāṇus at the time of pralaya though not within sṛṣṭi, admits in other words the possible destruction of saṁkhyā-ja-parimāṇa, it can be, according to him, only through the will and in the knowledge of God (Iśvara-buddhi), through and in which creation also is

possible. To our buddhi, a trasa breaks up into dvyaṇuka etc., only in passing into a different trasa: its breaking up into free parts would mean its passing out of perceptibility, which is never perceived and cannot be inferred. The tattvas in Yoga and Sāṁkhya are not properly inferred but are known through some kind of 'transcendental' reflection through which their *free* being is also known. Tanmātra, for example, as the cause of bhūta is not inferred in the sense dvyaṇuka is inferred as the cause of trasa in Vaiśeṣika philosophy. While then the causation of the dvyaṇuka and that of the trasa are taken in this philosophy to be temporally distinct only to the knowledge of God, Yoga would take the two causations —of the tanmātra and of the bhūta (-paramāṇu)—as distinct to our (transcendental) buddhi also.

50. Sāṁkhya does not admit the atomic theory either of Yoga or of Vaiśeṣika. The atomic conception in fact is alien to the spirit of Sāṁkhya, although Vijñāna-bhikṣu attributes to Sāṁkhya the atomistic notions of Yoga philosophy. To Yoga, units of the same tanmātra or of the same bhūta (as paramāṇus) would be the immanent pariṇāmas of the tanmātra or bhūta. Sāṁkhya, as has been pointed out, cannot admit immanent change at all. The so-called immanent change would be to it only aupādhika, being not real modifications but real reflections in each tattva of the objects of experience. As to Vijñāna-bhikṣu's hypothesis of guṇa-units (attributed by him both to Yoga and Sāṁkhya) to explain *more or less* of a guṇa, the conception of sadṛśa-pariṇāma has been shown to be sufficient for the explanation. That conception is entertained both by Yoga and Sāṁkhya though with a difference. The difference will come out in the discussion of buddhi.

CHAPTER IV

BUDDHI-VṚTTI

(NIDRĀ AND SMṚTI)

51. The object is to both Yoga and Sāṁkhya pariṇāmi-nitya: its reality unlike that of the self involves becoming or dynamic, as distinct from static, self-identity. Becoming is real in the sense willing is real, willing in abstraction from consciousness being real becoming. Willing (towards the object) is understood in Yoga as consciously becoming finite and in Sāṁkhya as having consciously become finite, as a prospective function in the former and a retrospective function in the latter. As not yet abstracted from the self, we are aware of it as 'I going to exist as *me*' or '*me* having come to exist'. If 'me' be taken as the type of the objective existent, objective reality would be to Yoga going to exist and to Sāṁkhya coming (or having come) to exist. It is only in the conative consciousness—consciousness of willing or having willed—that going or coming to exist is appreciated as real fact. To the mere cognitive consciousness, going to exist would be but an imagined content, a construction (vikalpa), according to Yoga; and coming to exist a mere abstraction from the emergent or manifest existent, according to Sāṁkhya. The real object is then to Yoga what is going to exist or becoming and to Sāṁkhya what has come to exist or has become.

52. Two kinds of becoming or pariṇāma are admitted in Yoga and Sāṁkhya—sadṛśa and visadṛśa. Visadṛśa-pariṇāma is causal becoming where the two terms of becoming which are identical in difference are different in character, not mere self-repetitions. Sadṛśa-pariṇāma is becoming, the terms of which are only numerically different, not different in character. Mere numerical difference may be denied as a fact, as for example, by Leibnitz; or it may be admitted as an eternal or timeless fact, as by the Vaiśeṣika, about paramāṇū or manas, or by Sāṁkhya and Yoga also about the self. *Objects* as merely numerically distinct are admitted in Yoga and Sāṁkhya not as timelessly together as in Vaiśeṣika but as terms of becoming. The second term of becoming

is not necessarily an effect distinct in character from the first : the ultimate cause, viz., guṇa, is also real as becoming, as what becomes or has become itself over again, there being no eternally real (kūṭastha-nitya) object. Distinction to both Yoga and Sāṁkhya as objective is not eternal being but the process of becoming distinct. This applies even to merely numerical distinction which in its manifest form is presented as self-identity. A manifest objective tattva is explicitly known as known object, unlike the unmanifest guṇa on the one hand which is known as unknown and unlike the experienced object on the other which is known but not as known or unknown. The self also is known as known but it is not known as object; and although it is an explicit self-identity, it cannot be conceived as becoming itself. Objective tattva is manifest in the sense of being a self-identity involving the process of becoming itself. Of the manifest tattvas, buddhi has the sole character of manifestness which is just this self-identity, the lower tattvas having other characters emergent in them more or less obscuring the pure self-identity. The pure self-identity of buddhi is itself an effect and its cause, the guṇa, has to be understood as having the potentiality of self-identity or—what is the same thing—as in sadṛśa-pariṇāma.

53. In Yoga the self-identity or manifestness (vyaktatā) of the object is taken to constitute its existence[a] or presence. In Sāṁkhya it is a character caused by the already existent guṇa in itself, manifestness being known-ness rather than existence. The cause or potentiality of self-identity is accordingly conceived differently in the two systems. In Yoga a guṇa is real but not yet existent, being what is going (or has ceased) to exist, is neither existent nor non-existent and lacks self-identity.[b] In Sāṁkhya, 'real' and 'existent' would mean the same thing : guṇa is existent without self-identity or manifestness, what is known as not self-identical, *not* like the object of experience that is not known as self-identical. The existence of buddhi is self-conserving, as contrasted with which the existence of guṇa is simply emerging, just as ahaṁkāra is self-conserving finitude and buddhi (as the lower asmitā) is only the emerging of finitude. Determinate tattva contains

[a] YB. II. 19; YV. II. 19.
[b] *Ibid*.

the prior process of emergence or becoming determinate ideally within it. It is never known without the emergence being known : the determinate is never merely given as determinate. The emergence, too, which is fact and no mere abstraction is known only in the determinate. Yoga would, however, admit that becoming may be known prior to the emergence of determinate being in the form of going to exist though not in the form of coming to exist or emerging. Sāṁkhya would deny it but admit that emerging is known in the knowing of the determinate—as constitutive of its determination. Whether in the form of going to exist or coming to be determined, becoming as prior to determinate being i.e., as an indeterminate being has to be conceived as the transition between two determinate beings in abstraction from them as its terms, the abstraction being possible through the conception of the terms being exactly similar. The identity of two terms implies one term *becoming* the other term as merely numerically distinct from it, the becoming being understood either prospectively as in Yoga, or retrospectively as in Sāṁkhya. Sadṛśa-pariṇāma is this becoming as implied in identity. the function of a being going to be itself or coming to be itself. its projection of itself in the future or its retraction of itself as past. its willed self-propagation or its felt self-integration.

54. This difference between Yoga and Sāṁkhya on sadṛśa-pariṇāma indicates their difference on the nature of prakṛti and buddhi. Existence to Yoga means manifest existence; buddhi is indifferently sattā-mātra or liṅga-mātra, prakṛti being accordingly niḥsatta or a-liṅga (avyakta). To sāṁkhya, manifestness is a contingent character of the existent, existence being no character and, therefore, not contingent: guṇa is the bare existent and buddhi is guṇa with the sole character of manifestness. The guṇas to both are the three unique modes of freedom, but freedom is understood conatively in Yoga and cognitively in Sāṁkhya, so that to the former guṇa is self-becoming before existence and to the latter self-becoming of the existent or the existent having become itself, self-becoming being perpetual in either way. The difference in the conception of freedom is connected with the difference in the conception of ahaṁkāra in the two systems already brought out.

55. Sadṛśa-pariṇama, the function of prakṛti, is understood prospectively in Yoga and retrospectively in Sāṁkhya. It may be equated with the function called avidyā or aviveka understood as the function of anāgata or atīta-buddhi—as distinct from present or manifest buddhi—incipiently operative or unmanifestly persistent within prakṛti. As in Yoga, guṇa has no existence yet in prakṛti but is only the real function of going to exist, it may be conceived to be avidyā itself as in Vedānta, though it is taken to be objectively real as the function of sadṛśa-pariṇāma, not what is neither real nor unreal but the real that is neither existent nor non-existent. In Sāṁkhya, aviveka or the function of sadṛśa-pariṇāma is real as the retrospective function of the existent guṇa.

56. In Yoga the first manifest or existent form of prospective self-repetition is apparently the immanent change of buddhi. Buddhi is liṅga-mātra or sattā-mātra which is the existent freely getting differentiated into many real modes, each of which being the undivided buddhi is every other (sarvam sarvātmakam). Immanent pariṇāma is the self-repetition of a tattva, where each repetition has a distinct identity or existence, is a vyakti, unlike a repetition of a guṇa which has no identity at all. An immanent pariṇāma of buddhi may be dharma, lakṣaṇa or avasthā. Buddhi has two kinds of dharma-pariṇāma—unconscious and conscious (a-paridṛṣṭa and paridṛṣṭa).[a] Yoga-bhāṣya mentions seven a-paridṛṣṭa dharmas—of which nirodha, dharma and saṁskāra may be specially noted. Nirodha or negative attention, the essential function of yoga, is an unconscious willing to arrest the helpless change of buddhi, unconscious at all levels of buddhi and is inferred from the saṁskāras left by such willing which, again, are inferred from the facilitation of subsequent nirodha. Negative willing, unlike positive willing, is not known by introspection (though its fulfilment as such may be conscious in samprajñāta-samādhi) but is inferred (even in the case of asamprajñāta) from the progressive spontaneity of the practice of concentration (as remembered in vyutthāna).

[a] YB. III. 15.

Dharma and adharma (merit and demerit) are the saṁskāras left by previous willing leading to bhoga or mukti, while what is specially called saṁskāra' in the enumeration of the seven a-paridṛṣṭas is saṁskāra of previous bhoga (experience), otherwise designated vāsanā, which leads to memory (smṛti). As opposed to the a-paridṛṣṭas, there are the conscious pariṇāmas of buddhi including the five vṛttis to be mentioned presently and also the conscious activities and feelings.

57. All these are the dharma-pariṇāmas of buddhi and the vṛttis among them are its specific dharma-pariṇāmas or avasthās. Apparently there may be unconscious functions but not unconscious states or vṛttis of the mind. Vṛttis are conscious modes of buddhi which are concrete things comparable to the flames shot forth from fire, presentations and not mere functions (dharma) or degrees of actuality (lakṣaṇa). Conscious activities and feelings are also sometimes called 'vṛtti' but they appear to be both function and presentation, function bound up with vṛtti in the narrow sense of presentation. The functions—conscious and unconscious—would roughly correspond to the bhāvas of Sāṁkhya (which, however, has no place for nirodha). Vṛtti is understood in Sāṁkhya not as presentation, not as a real mode of buddhi but as a constructive mode, as the being of buddhi understood as characterised by a specific function.

58. Vṛttis are understood in Yoga as cognitive presentations which alone are real modes of buddhi. Five classes of presentation are mentioned—viz., pramāṇa, viparyaya, vikalpa, nidrā and smṛti—which are respectively presentation of object as real, as unreal, as constructive, as absence of presentation and as presentation. The classification of vṛttis is at once psychological and epistemological, psychological so far as presentation is itself a differentiated mental object and epistemological so far as presentation is *of* an experienceable object. The function of referring to an object is itself constitutive of a real mode (and not merely of a constructive mode as in Sāṁkhya which is still existent) of buddhi, though it may be real without constituting it as in asamprajñāta where buddhi is saṁskāra-seṣa having a-paridṛṣṭa dharma only. Presentation is at once mental object (grāhya)

and anticipatory reflection (image) of object (grahaṇa which is not subjective function or bhāva but objective function or rather subjective function in abstraction from the subject or grahītā), the kind of mental object being determined by the kind of anticipation of object or anticipated object.

59. The epistemological modes of anticipation of object or anticipated object are interesting as indicating a unique system of objective categories. Real, unreal, constructive, unpresented and presented are the ultimate predicates of the object in the sense of presented content, content of a self-identical mental state. What we assert of a presented content is either about its reality or about its presentedness. We assert about its reality in three forms—it is real or it is not real or it is as though it were real; and we assert about its presentedness in two forms—viz., that presentation or its absence is presented. Presentation of a content that is known as real is pramāṇa, of a content that is known as unreal is viparyaya and of a content that appears real even when it is known as unreal is vikalpa; while presentation of a content *as* presented—i.e., presentation of presentation is smṛti and presentation of the absence of presentation is nidrā. The distinction between reality and presentedness is the epistemological distinction between object of presentation and presentation of object, both presentation and its object being object in the wider sense of dṛśya or what is distinct from dṛk or self.

60. Each vṛtti has to be understood in reference to the corresponding subjective certitude i.e., to the self as apparently functioning through the vṛtti. No vṛtti is admitted in Nyāya, buddhi being but an attribute of the self, not a thing seemingly or really distinct from the self, as it is in Vedānta, or in Sāṁkhya or Yoga. To Vedānta, buddhi is but a manifest mode of ajñāna: ajñāna is intelligible only as a positive limitation of jñāna, self or consciousness and not as a thing by itself. Vṛtti is accordingly conceived in the system from the subjective side only, as the apparent mode of the self functioning and not as a real independent thing undistinguished from the self. In Sāṁkhya and Yoga, it is an independent thing (or state of a thing) which is indeed only as associated with the self, being dissolved in dissociation with it; but the association is a real character of the thing and an apparent character of the self. Vṛtti which is thus really objective also appears subjec-

tive and it is in reference to the apparently subjective vṛtti that the objective vṛtti has to be understood. Pramāṇa, for example, as an objective mental state has to be understood as an implication of the subjective function of true knowing.

61. To begin with smṛti or memory. It is defined as the re-presentation of an object as presented. It is not merely a second presentation of the object but an implied presentation of the first presentation. The first presentation may have been any of the five vṛttis, not merely pramāṇa or merely perception. The first presentation may be of any object, real or unreal etc.; a presentation is always itself an object to the self[a] and can never exist unknown. The object of memory is at once the object of the primary presentation and the presentation itself.[b] The explicit consciousness of the presentation or of the knowing (vyavasāya) involving the presentation is called anuvyavasāya. It is a 'subjective' function, an apparent function of the self; but if the self knows a content, it knows through a vṛtti i.e., as identified with a presentation. This is true even when the content is itself a presentation and hence a vṛtti which must be known by a self[c] is not merely sākṣi-bhāṣya but is known in a second vṛtti with which the self is identified.[d] The second vṛtti in its subjective aspect is anu-vyavasāya and, as a mental state, is memory. Memory is in this sense presentation of presentation, although it is presentation explicitly of the object of the primary presentation and only implicitly of the presentation itself, as distinct from anuvyavasāya which is presentation explicitly of the presentation and only implicitly of the object of presentation. The presentation of the object and the presentation of the presentation have both the form of the object, the latter having the form of the object with the additional character of being distinct from the primary presentation.

62. Memory (like nidrā to be considered presently) is a secondary or derivative vṛtti. Yoga-bhāṣya brings in the interesting conception of memory being either bhāvita-smartavyā as in the dream-state or abhāvita-smartavyā as in the waking state. Vācaspati interprets the two as

[a] YS. IV. 18.
[b] YB. I. 11.
[c] YS. IV. 21.
[d] YB. IV. 22.

productive and reproductive imagination ('bhāvita' meaning kalpita or constructed), although the former, being admittedly what deviates from the primary presentation of the object, does not fall under the given definition of smṛti and is only loosely described as such. Vijñāna-bhikṣu understands 'bhāvita' in the sense of bhāvyartha-sūcaka or prognosticative of the future object (or more accurately of object of future knowledge). Memory as revival of past presentation of object need not involve the memory-judgment (*'that* object which *was* presented) or a certitude about the past as such: it may be prognosticative of the future. Dream involves revival of past presentations and also a construction out of them which is no revival of the past but a free anticipation of the future, of some object to be presented, all dreams being thus apparently taken on the authority of śāstra as veridical.

63. A vṛtti has to be understood not only in reference to the corresponding subjective certitude (vyavasāya) but also in reference to samādhi which may be regarded as the pure isolated form of this certitude. Unlike an ordinary vyavasāya which is implicitly or explicitly in transition to another vyavasāya, samādhi such as is reached through yoga is a consciously standing certitude, the standing being pure self-reproduction or becoming of itself over again. What aspect of samādhi does smṛti as a certitude represent? Memory-knowledge is knowledge by the self as identified with a vṛtti of an object as presented to another vṛtti. Since a vṛtti is as it is presented to the self which knows it only as identified with a second vṛtti with the form of the object of the first vṛtti, there is apparently an infinite regress of vṛttis. But a vṛtti presented to the self is not necessarily known explicitly by the self, being known only when some doubt arises about the object of the vṛtti (of the form 'is the object presented as A or as B?). Memory of a perceived object, for example, which need not be explicit knowledge of the perception is such knowledge when the object which presents some indeterminateness about its perceived character is sought to be known more determinately. So, too, there is no explicit knowledge of memory as vṛtti unless some indeterminateness appears about the remembered character of the object. A remembered character is indeed a perceived character but it is not simply its repetition but its further unfolding. The changing

of an object is perceived but when it is remembered, certain doubts about the specific character of the changing (e.g., how much of it was perceived in one act of perception) emerge which would not emerge in the perceptual consciousness. Thus a fresh and more fundamental indeterminateness about the object emerges at the memory-stage, which leads to the explicit knowledge of memory as vṛtti, which knowledge again involves a new vṛtti, —a memory of memory. How far this regress will go will depend on the number of grades of indeterminateness about the object that can be actually conceived.

64. The presented object is sought to be known better by being remembered over and over again. Here, although the memories refer to the same presented stratum of the object, each later memory may refer also to the memory just before it, so that the latest memory would present an involution-series of memories of the primary presentation. If a later memory refers immediately to the object presented, the series is interminable; but if it refers to it through the previous memory, a qualitative difference would emerge between the first, second and third memories. The second memory would be thinking (cintā) and the third would be contemplation (dhyāna) in which it is conscious of itself as a series. A memory later than the third would have the same character and thus as a qualitative grade, the third memory is the terminus. Samādhi would be the grade beyond it which is no longer memory but intuition of the object presented as completely unfolded. Samādhi itself, however, would be of different grades which also has a terminus in the sense already explained.

65. A presented object is known *better* by having what is implicit in the presentation explicated or unfolded through presentation of the presentation, i.e., through memory in its three grades including thought and contemplation. There is again presentation not merely of presentation but also of the absence of presentation. An object that is unpresented in one way may be presented in another: an object, for example, that is not perceived may be remembered. Memory involves the consciousness of the object being presented though not perceptually presented. To be thought is also to be presented, the presentation being explicit in dhyāna or contemplation: that thought and contemplation are but grades of memory is known in contemplation. But there may be

a consciousness of presentation being altogether absent, though this consciousness is itself bound up with a presentation. This presentation of no presentation is nidrā or sleep. What was implied in a previous presentation and is now explicit in memory is remembered as having been only implicit. If the implicitness is remembered, it must have been then presented. The presentation of implicitness is sleep in general and hence in this case we may say, there was sleep along with waking. Generally it may be said that all waking short of the highest samprajñāta is overlaid with sleep (or pure feeling?).

66. Sleep as a vṛtti is taken in Yoga to be directly remembered on waking in the form 'I know no object' or 'nothing was presented to me'. It is remembered because of the saṁskāra left by sleep which because it left a saṁskāra must have been an actual vṛtti presented to the self, because no vṛtti can exist without being thus presented. Vedānta would not admit that sleep is a vṛtti of buddhi: the absence of presentation during sleep is indeed known on waking but it is known without the medium of a vṛtti (being sākṣi-bhāṣya) and is not really remembered. Some Vedāntists admit nidrā-vṛtti and its saṁskāra, not as belonging to buddhi but as belonging to raw ajñāna in which buddhi is taken to be dissolved in sleep. The difficulty however is, as pointed out by Vijñāna-bhikṣu, that then such ajñāna-vṛttis might be present in dream and waking also, so that there would be no necessity to admit a buddhi at all. So if sleep is remembered it must have been a vṛtti known then to the self presumably without any further vṛtti, there being in any case nothing in the nidrā-vṛtti to raise the question at all.

67. Sleep as a vṛtti may be of many kinds—blissful, restless or heavy and may include states like swoon which are not remembered but only inferred on waking, inferred as presented to the self without being explicitly known by it. Normally sleep is remembered as a vṛtti known to the self during sleep, the self itself being then known in the knowing of the vṛtti. Vedānta emphasises this self-knowledge during sleep and does not admit that it is knowledge of vṛtti also, the pure ajñāna-vṛtti which is sometimes admitted being not known during sleep, and not remembered on waking but only inferred. Suṣupti according to Vedānta is, so far as it is conscious.

pure undifferenced self-knowledge and has the same form as nirvikalpa-samādhi. The difference between this samādhi and suṣupti would presumably lie in the character of the unconscious saṁskāra in the two states. In the former, over and above the unsterilised saṁskāras of experience which make for re-awaking or vyutthāna, there is also the saṁskāra of the conscious contemplative or abstracting activity (dhyāna etc.); and besides, unlike the latter, it leaves a saṁskāra of itself facilitating the re-attainment of the ecstatic condition. The waking consciousness of the samādhi or suṣupti just ended accordingly differs. The self that was in these states is known as having been without ahaṁkāra in samādhi and with ahaṁkāra in suṣupti. In the latter case, however, ahaṁkāra is known to have been only implicitly present: and implicit presence is apparently to Vedānta an ajñāna-vṛtti that is not only not explicitly known but is not even presented to the self. In Yoga, suṣupti is remembered as having been a buddhi-vṛtti known to the self. Samādhi is not remembered but is known on waking (as suṣupti too is known according to Vedānta) without a vṛtti. It is known as having been no vṛtti identified with the self but as the self identified with a function or a-paridṛṣṭa-dharma of buddhi, the function of nirodha. In the case of samprajñāta-samādhi, a vṛtti is indeed remembered but not as what the self was identified with. Again, the saṁskāra left by samādhi is not a vāsanā conditioning the memory of an experience or empirical vṛtti but a karma-saṁskāra that facilitates later activity and feeling attainment in the same direction.

CHAPTER V

BUDDHI-VṚTTI (contd.)

(Vikalpa, Viparyaya and Pramāṇa)

68. The vṛtti called 'vikalpa' is implied in the consciousness of a content that is not real and is still verbally meant. The verbal expression of the content generates the vṛtti but even a vṛtti referring to an unreal content that is otherwise generated but is verbally expressible would appear to come under vikalpa. The content which is known at once as unreal and as verbally expressible is presumably what characterises the vṛtti. Viparyaya or error as a vṛtti also refers to an unreal content and may be generated by a form of words but the content is not verbally expressible (except as a contradiction) when it is known to be unreal. The content was meant by the generative verbal expression as a real object, and not as a possible object plus its reality, so that now that the reality is negated, it is not reduced to possible object only. The content that vikalpa refers to is a possible object but the content of viparyaya is not the unreality of a possible or thinkable object. The possible or the imaginary as such which is the content of vikalpa is never reached by the mere correction of error Where then a verbal expression generates an error, the content of the error is not rendered by the expression after correction; and in fact after correction, the content of an error, however generated, is not verbally expressible at all except as a contradiction. Vikalpa as generated by a verbal expression is, however, significantly expressed by it though known to be unreal. We may be imaginatively aware of a content as unreal when there is no question of error at all; and it is not necessary that such content should be generated by the understanding of a verbal expression, though it always admits of a significant verbal expression.

69. Patañjali defines vikalpa as —'Śabdajñānānupātī vastu-śunyo vikalpaḥ.[a] The first adjective may mean 'generated by śabda-jñāna' or 'expressible as implied in śabda-jñāna'. The latter is the interpre-

[a] YS. I. 9

tation of Vijñāna-bhikṣu who explains the compound as 'what has śabda-jñāna as its anupatī', not as what others explain it viz., 'anupātī of sabda-jñāna'. The statement in the Bhāṣya—'vastu-śunyatve api śabda-jñāna-māhātmya-nibandhano vyavahāro dṛśyate' may refer to the vyavahāra either before or after the vikalpa. The examples given in the Bhāṣya are indeed all of meanings generated by language, but one is not precluded from admitting under vikalpa imaginary contents of which one is aware otherwise than through the understanding of language. There is no other heading of vṛtti under which they could come and the text does not rule out the extension. Even the perception of the mere appearance as such e.g., the image in the mirror—may come under vikalpa, since it stands, though it is (inferentially) known to be no fact. Whatever being known as unreal is actually presented is the content of vikalpa, for whatever can be asserted to be now presented is verbally expressible. Of the erroneous content as such we can say that it appeared to be presented but never that it is presented. Error may still be called a presentation because we cannot deny that some content was presented though we cannot specify what was presented.

70. The content of vikalpa is presented as an unreal but possible object, as the imaginary as such which stands before the mind through the meaning function of language, if not through anything else. The image in the mirror may also be called an imaginary object standing indeed through the perceiving function but not as excluding the meaning-function, because to stand before the mind is to appear self-identical which is possible only through thought or the meaning-function. As distinct from it the content of error known as such is the unreal without self-identity, of which we can say that it appeared to stand but never that it stands—what we can say about the imaginary object. The self-identity of the unreal is presented not as real nor as unreal but *as though* it were real. Vikalpa is the presentation of an unreal not as real (which would be viparyaya) nor as unreal (which would be pramāṇa) but as though it were real i.e., *as* appearing as real. The appearance of a content is itself a content and the vṛtti referring to this secondary content is vikalpa. It is not like memory the presentation of a content as presentation but is the presentation of a content as apparently

presented or apparently objective. The verbal expression of such a content is only figurative and the content as figuratively expressed has a presented character due to the expression. Vikalpa is the presentation of the factitious character of a content. We speak of the head *of* Rāhu (who is all head), of *in*activity or *un*causedness as a character of an object or of appear*ing* as an activity of an object. All these are figurative expressions which are understood by being actually imagined while being taken as unreal. Ordinary language is largely figurative though not always suspected as such and the understanding of it involves vikalpa almost at every turn.

71. The importance of vikalpa will be realised when it is remembered that time itself as krama and, therefore, all space-time position of the objects of experience are taken in Yoga philosophy to be only presented to vikalpa, not to pramāṇa as it is taken by common-sense or to viparyaya as it is taken by Vedānta. What is called savikalpa perception, however, is not vikalpa (as it is taken by the Buddhist) but pramāṇa, its content being not unreal though the space-time position of the content is unreal. In Sāṁkhya, too, where not only the space-time position but even the presented quality of the object of experience is a mere appearance, savikalpa perception is not mere vikalpa, since the object is unaccountably *given* and is a non-causal but real manifestation of prakṛti. In Yoga the object of experience is an immanent causal pariṇāma of vikāra-tattva, though its space-time position is constructed. What is given as a manifest or unmanifest tattva but with a superinduced vikalpa (though not bhrama or error) is not a vikalpa but a pramāṇa.

72. In savikalpa (or samprajñāta) samādhi, the vṛtti that is concentrated on may or may not be a vikalpa in the Yoga sense. Its content may be imaginary or a real object of experience or a real metaphysical object; and where it is a real object, it may or may not be overlaid with vikalpa (or the memory of vikalpa), though even when it is overlaid, it does not cease to be the object of pramāṇa. In savitarka and savicāra-samādhi, the content, if real is riddled with vikalpa,[a] is an object of experience (sthūla) with a space-

[a] YS. I. 42.

time limitation, or a tattva (sūkṣma) as constituting such an object. Vikalpa is the appearance of a unity of word, thought and thing (śabda, pratyaya, artha) which are really distinct. This appearance is the primary object of the contemplation leading to samādhi that develops through stages in which it is gradually dissolved. In passing from savitarka to nirvitarka, vikalpa (or its smṛti) in the sthūla object is dropped but continues in the sūkṣma object in savicāra which is dropped in passing to nirvicāra. Later stages of samprajñāta are free from vikalpa and there is no vṛtti at all in asamprajñāta.

73. The difference between vikalpa and viparyaya has already been discussed. The Vaiśeṣika takes vikalpa as a form of āhārya or fictitious knowledge. thus including it within viparyaya.[a] Vedānta apparently would bring viparyaya under vikalpa: all error is construction, object as distinct from the self being false as a construction of avidyā. Since the object is the self (or reality) itself under the limitation of avidyā, it is mithyā (though till it is *actually* sublated like the appearance of the rope as snake, it is empirically real) and not tuccha but apart from the self, it is tuccha, being but a vikalpa. The object is to the eye of reason miṭhyā or anirvācya but to the eye of faith it is tuccha. or as it may be put. it is tuccha or mere vikalpa to the jīvan-mukta. Error in the last resort would be mere vikalpa: all difference in the object is but a verbal construction (vācārambhaṇa). though the vāk or speech here is cosmic and impersonal. To Yoga. however. error and vikalpa are utterly distinct as vṛttis. The world of experience, so far as it is a construction. is not false but phenomenally real. It is not reality with false limitation and therefore false in the last resort as it is conceived to be in Vedānta but reality with constructed limitation and therefore still real. for the construct though unreal does not falsify but only limits the manifestation of reality.

74. Viparyaya or error is to Yoga a vṛtti that has not the form of the object that it purports to refer to.[b] It is

[a] YV.I.9
[b] a-tadrūpa-pratiṣṭhām—YS.I.8.

then possible to refer to an object without a presentation having its form. To Vaiśeṣika, cognition—true or false—refers to its object without presentation and, therefore, there is no special difficulty about false cognition. To Yoga cognition is through presentation and the difficulty about false cognition is how the presentation implied by it refers to the object without taking its form. Has the vṛtti called viparyaya a form at all? The form of object only but not that of vṛtti can be an apparent form: it cannot be said that the presented form of the vṛtti is cancelled. by correction or bādha. The form of the object that is cancelled then never even appeared in the vṛtti. That is why the content of error known as such (through correction) cannot be intelligibly stated; it can be verbally expressed only as a contradiction (like 'this rope as snake'). There is no vṛtti for the consciousness of a contradiction. The vṛtti for a cognition is known in reflection on it, the reflection being an anuvyavasāya in other cases and in the case of false cognition the correction or bādha itself. The vṛtti for a false cognition as indirectly revealed by the corrective reflection is known as not having had the form of the content that is now cancelled. It cannot be said—as it would be presumably said by the Vedāntist—that the vṛtti is known neither as having nor as not having the form of the cancelled content, or, in other words, that the content was neither presented nor unpresented, for some content was certainly presented which is also definitely known in the bādha as not the content cancelled. This definite knowledge of the vṛtti as without the form of the object that it yet referred to is knowledge of a contradiction that implies no vṛtti. The knowing or mistaking of the rope as snake is a fact but there is no knowledge or consciousness reflected in a standing vṛtti of the rope being a snake: a contradiction is committed but is not known, being a content that is unpresentable or unknowable as known.

75. That a contradiction is committed but not presented is just what is implied by the theory of anyathā-khyāti—advocated both by Yoga and Vaiśeṣika. The latter does not admit vṛtti or presentation in any knowing and hence the taking of the rope as a snake (previously known in some other time-space position)—or the commission of a contradiction—without its presentation implies no special difficulty, though the

contradiction is no object at all. Yoga, however, admits presentation though in this case it is not presentation of the form of snake or of the contradictory 'rope as snake' but some indefinite unnameable presentation and understands the committed contradiction to be the taking as this (rope) not an actual snake known elsewhere (as in Vaiśeṣika) but the unreal content of the present vṛtti or what is presented as unpresented.[a] In Vedānta, the contradiction is itself presented as a content that neither is nor is not (prātibhāsika-sṛṣṭi, anirvācya) while in Sāṁkhya it is presented as a content that *both* is and is not.[b] The presentation here to Vedānta would apparently be a vṛtti not of buddhi but of raw avidyā—such as suṣupti is sometimes taken in this system—while to Sāṁkhya it would be a buddhi-vṛtti. In Yoga, there is presentation not of the contradiction but of *some* content as unpresented, the contradiction itself being utterly unpresented and only committed. The contradiction is the *function* of avidyā, while to Vedānta it is a presentation of avidyā and to Sāṁkhya an indeterminate presentation of buddhi.

76. To understand empirical error, both Yoga and Vedānta have to refer to raw avidyā, to avidyā beyond asmitā (as it would be expressed in Yoga) or the transcendental principle of error, which is conceived in Yoga as a function and in Vedānta as a presentation conformably to the different views on the nature of knowing in the two systems. There is no knowing function or activity in Vedānta: what appears as such is the quiescent being of knowledge with the willing function of buddhi as its upādhi. In Yoga, buddhi is as much a knowing function as a willing function, the latter being the actualisation of the former (and amounting to its supersession in asamprajñāta). The self is indeed knowledge (consciousness) itself as in Vedānta and Sāṁkhya but it knows the object only as identified with the knowing buddhi or buddhi-vṛtti and not the willing buddhi which is no vṛtti, that being why it knows no content at all in asamprajñāta. Error is a knowing function intermediate between the bare willing function in asamprajñāta and the

[a] YV.I.8.

[b] sadasat-khyātir bādhābhāvat SS.V.56.

knowing—willing function involving the vṛttis other than viparyaya which differs from them in being formless. Error cannot be merely an exercise of free will, nor is it a mere presentation with conflicting determinations but an utterly indeterminate presentation explicitly embodying an exercise of free will. This free will is just avidyā which is constructive of vṛtti—the viparyaya-vṛtti—in the first instance and destructive of vṛtti—of the viveka-vṛtti ultimately—in asamprajñāta.

77. Empirical error unlike other vṛttis referring to the object explicitly embodies avidyā, the transcendental principle of error. Yoga mentions five transcendental errors—avidyā, asmitā, rāga, dveṣa and abhiniveśa of which avidyā is taken as at once starting and pervading the others.[a] Each is the nimitta of the next and is loosely regarded as its source. Avidyā leads to and does not become asmitā, though it continues with asmitā. Asmitā too leads to avidyā, and may co-exist with it though it need not. Asmitā and rāga, rāga and dveṣa, dveṣa and abhiniveṣa are apparently related similarly. Each lower may also cease in the presence of the higher, the cessation being gradual. The continuously manifest stage (udāra) as embodied (labdha-vrttika) in a presentation may pass to the intermittent (vicchinna) stage, that again to the tenuous, half-manifest or sub-conscious (tanu) stage and then again to the un-manifest or unconscious (supta) stage. From each later stage, a kleśa may hark back to the former stage, but there is a fifth stage, viz., dagdha-vīja-bhāva whence there is no return. When avidyā, the primordial kleśa which may co-exist with the other kleśas and also function in their absence (as in asamprajñāta), reaches dagdha-bījatā and ceases altogether, buddhi itself ceases or lapses into prakṛti.[b]

78. These principles are 'transcendental' in the sense of being 'subjective' functions, functions indeed of the mind but necessarily referred to the self, being unconscious as mental and conscious only as subjective and empirically conscious as embodied in objective presentations. They may as well be regarded as grades of spiritual error or kleśas as they are called, understood more as willing function than as knowing function. Yet

[a] YS. II. 4.
[b] YB. II. 10.

they are errors and not merely wrong willing—errors, because the primordial and pervading kleśa viz., avidyā is the conative actualisation of false knowing. Willing is a more essential function of buddhi than knowing, but it is necessarily understood through knowing as its actualisation.

79. Avidyā is explained in YS.II.5 as the taking of the non-eternal as eternal, of the unclean as clean, of the painful as pleasurable, of the not-self as the self. Essentially it is the wrong viewing of the object as the self and derivatively in cognitive, moral and hedonistic reference to the object of experience, the viewing of it as though it were as real, as clean or sacred, as dear or enjoyable as one's own self. The nature of avidyā is best understood by contrast with empirical illusion on the one hand and with asmitā on the other. The content of all error is known in the correction of it as a contradiction or an unintelligibility, and it is in this sense that it has been said to be verbally inexpressible. In the case of an empirical illusion, however,—e.g., in the taking of a rope as a snake, one is aware in the correction that the unintelligible appeared as intelligible, that the contradictory 'this (rope-) snake' was explicitly known as 'this snake'. In the correction of the illusion of taking my body as myself—a form of avidyā, I am not similarly aware of my body having been *explicitly known* as myself. I am aware only of having acted or felt in a way that has to be interpreted as *implying* the cognition of my body as my self. The cognition is here implicit not in the sense that its content is undistinguished in an explicitly known content but in the sense that it is not and does not involve explicit cognition at all, that it is only inferred (or imagined) to be a cognition from the manner of willing or feeling and not from any explicit cognition as the datum. Such implicit cognition of the self is not cognition of a presented content and is in this sense a transcendental function. If it is still taken as viparyaya-vṛtti, it is because the false knowing is remembered, showing that there *must* have been some unspecifiable presentation though it can not be asserted that there *was*.

80. Asmitā is also a transcendental error and is explained in YS.1.6. as the consciousness of the apparent identity of the self and buddhi. It is the consciousness of the identity either as the self only or as buddhi only, not as their relation.

Avidyā would be consciousness of their identity as a relation or rather the function of relating them in the way of identity. Viveka which is knowledge of their distinction still implies the self knowing as identified with buddhi, the identification here being the avidyā-function of relating explicit distincts as identical. In asmitā, there is no consciousness of their distinction: it is consciousness of the product of the avidyā-function, viz., the undifferenced appearance of their unity either as the self or as buddhi,[a] as for example when one says 'I enjoy' or 'my enjoyment' ('I knowing' or 'knowing me'). Avidyā is the implicit identifying of explicit distincts, while asmitā is the explicit consciousness of the unity of implicit distincts. The explicit unity is the result of the implicit identifying, the terms of the unity losing their distinction in the result.

81. Avidyā and asmitā are conceived as functions of false *knowing*, but the other three kleśas or transcendental errors are conceived as affective functions only implying or presupposing false *knowing*. They, too, are primarily functions and become consciousness only when embodied in presentation. Rāga is the craving for pleasure or object of pleasure implying memory of pleasure or of the object of pleasure. It is an error in the sense that the memory or perception (or the anticipation that it implies) is not detached knowledge such as the jīvanmukta may be conceived to have but a craving for one's exclusive self, thus involving asmitā; and it is yet distinct from asmitā in so far as the consciousness here is explicitly of pleasure as object and only implicitly of the enjoying self (*me*). Similar considerations apply to dveṣa or antipathy for pain and object of pain. As an affective function, however, it necessarily presupposes rāga and is accordingly less self-conscious, implying asmitā more remotely than rāga. Both rāga and dveṣa admit of different grades and specifications in reference to different classes of objects. The last viparyaya, viz., abhiniveśa is positively a clinging to life and negatively the fear of death. The positive moment is less (self-) conscious than the negative moment which thus directly involves dveṣa. Abhiniveśa is conscious even in its positive aspect and is called ātmāśīḥ—an instinctive desire about

[a] YV.II.6.

oneself of the form 'let me not cease to be' 'let me be' (mā na bhuvam, bhūyāsam). It is not due to the saṁskāra of any experience in this life but is due to the vāsanā of the experience of death in a previous life and is the most obvious datum for the inference of a previous birth.[a] As a conscious desire, it is reckoned as a vṛtti.

82. Error as avidyā which is implied in every other error is implied even in pramāṇa or true knowing. Viveka which is the highest form of true knowing still involves avidyā which demands to be corrected through asamprajñāta or the activity of getting rid of all knowledge. Knowledge means knowledge of content which is possible only through the erroneous identification of the self with buddhi. If the self is taken to be jñāna, it is not jñāna of any content, being contentless consciousness understood merely as a being and not as a knowing function. The erroneous identification or avidyā and, therefore, also its retraction or purely conative correction which is the function of the same avidyā thus run out beyond pramāṇa, viparyaya being in this sense a more fundamental vṛtti of buddhi than pramāṇa. Within explicit knowledge, error indeed presupposes true knowledge, but knowledge itself presupposes conative error which is implicitly cognitive also. While pramāṇa may be said to be nearer than error to pure consciousness, error as avidyā is closer to prakṛti, being as vṛtti the immediate evolute of prakṛti and as function continuous with it. In the retractive movement towards mokṣa, the self regains its character of functionless consciousness immediately in knowledge (viveka) but through pure willing.

83. Pramāṇa or true knowledge is of three kinds—pratyakṣa, anumāna and āgama. Of these, pratyakṣa is understood to be a vṛtti having the form of a real object and referring more to its particularity than to its sāmānya or universal, as distinct from anumāna which refers more to its sāmānya than to its viśeṣa, the object being taken in both as having both sāmānya and viśeṣa. Āgama in referring to an object beyond pratyakṣa refers through its sāmānya but yields knowledge of its viśeṣa. An object is known as individual i.e., with its viśeṣa either through pratyakṣa or through āgama, not through anumāna. The viśeṣa

[a] YB. II. 9; IV. 10.

of an object as thus known is, however, known as apparently one with or co-implicated (saṁkīrṇa) with the remembered meanings of words that express it—i.e., with verbal universals which are, in fact, vikalpas. It is known in its purity in samādhi or samāpatti of a type to be considered later, which amounts to perfect perception (param pratyakṣam). Absolutely true knowledge through āgama and anumāna can only be reached through such pure perception of viśeṣa. One must have such perception for oneself as the basis of the knowledge of the supersensible through anumāna and āgama.[a]

84. Pramāṇa is a direct or indirect knowing of the real individual as having a real or verbal universal, an absence and even an unreality undistinguished in it. The pure individual is sought to be intuited, known in the way of para-pratyakṣa or sākṣātkāra by the elimination of the undistinguished excrescences through the practice of yoga. Pramāṇa is in itself a demand for its purification and actualisation in samādhi. As knowledge of the real individual, it is not direct except in perception, and even as perception it is mixed up with the other pramāṇas and, therefore, is indirect knowledge in some aspect also. It is further mixed up with vṛttis other than pramāṇa and thus refers to contents other than the real along with the real. Normally then what is taken as truly known is known neither with absolute directness nor in isolation. Not that, therefore, it is not known : it is known but with an indefinite background which partly obscures its definiteness and threatens its certitude without, however, actually challenging its known-ness. Reflection on such knowledge shows its unrealised character without negating it as an actual presentation and without falsifying its content. The unrealisedness is, in fact, a transcendental or spiritual character but is not, therfore, without any bearing on the psychology and logic of the knowledge in question. The known content is felt to require further definition. Logical definition may be sought to be reached inductively but that is only a preparation for a new insight into the nature of the content to be defined. To have the insight is to have the presentation of the content or the vṛtti steadied and clarified. The islolating fixation of the knowing vṛtti for the definition of the known content is just the yoga process of realisation.

[a] YB. I. 42

CHAPTER VI

THE FIVE LEVELS OF BUDDHI

85. The distinctive function of buddhi is niścaya or certitude which is (or is implied in) the consciousness of a content as to the self, as making a difference to or (illusorily) modifying the self. The nature of certitude cannot be understood except in such reference to the self. Consciousness or the self is indeed associated with the mind not simply as buddhi but also in its lower stages, but the mind does not refer to the self as content or to a content *as to* the self except in the stage of buddhi. Certitude as such implies asmitā or the consciousness of 'I am'. The consciousness may be implicit or explicit but in any case certitude without this consciousness is unintelligible. Certitude may be directly about the self or about the object, in which latter case it is indirectly about the self and may be either implicit or explicit. Direct and explicit certainly about the self may again lead to a stage of buddhi where the consciousness of 'I am' lapses into the mere being of *I*, where the distinction between *I* as content and the consciousness of it ceases to be conscious.

86. Yoga-Bhāṣya[a] mentions five citta-bhūmis or levels of buddhi—viz., kṣipta, mūḍha, vikṣipta, ekāgra and niruddha. Of these the first three levels appear to be characterised by indirect and implicit asmitā and the fourth by explicit asmitā which is indirect in its earlier stages and direct in the latest stage. The fifth represents the stage where direct and explicit consciousness of *I* lapses into the mere being of *I*. The sub-stages of the fourth stage together with the fifth stage are sometimes specifically called citta-bhūmis, being the levels of buddhi as concentrated in yoga or samādhi. Samādhi is ordinarily understood to mean the concentrated state of buddhi but sometimes it is used in a wider sense to mean its general character of standing, of being self-identical or flowing as self-identical which is its character at all levels (sārvabhaūma-dharma), being just

[a] I. 1-2

what is meant by its manifestness. Buddhi is the manifest as such, manifesting or reflecting the eternal changeless self directly or indirectly, explicitly or implicitly. Buddhi is nothing without samādhi in the wide sense and the five levels of buddhi are distinguished by different measures and qualities of this samādhi.

87. Buddhi like every other objective tattva is a unity of the three guṇas. The sattva-element is dominant while rajas and tamas are more or less recessive and may be altogether suppressed or reduced to mere saṁskāra; and sometimes in the fifth or niruddha level the sattva element also may be reduced to saṁskāra and buddhi stands manifest as bare being with all differences suppressed in it. The guṇas in reference to conscious buddhi have the characters of prakhyā, pravṛtti and sthiti. Prakhyā would be the expressive character (prakāśa) in reference to the content of buddhi which is the self either directly or indirectly, being thus the function of revealing the self or self-conscious knowing. Pravṛtti would be activity (calatva) in reference to the self, the apparent activity of the self to become finite or self-conscious willing; and sthiti or persistence in reference to the self would be apparently self-conscious feeling. When pravṛtti and sthiti of buddhi are actual or emergent functions, they modify the dominant character prakhyā; and where they are abhibhūta or reduced to mere saṁskāra, they do not modify. In the kṣipta stage, both pravṛtti and sthiti are actual, the former being more explicit than the latter. In the mūḍha stage, pravṛtti is suppressed and sthiti is explicit while in the vikṣipta stage, sthiti is suppressed and pravṛtti is actual. In the ekāgra stage, both are suppressed and prakhyā alone is actual, and lastly in the niruddha stage prakhyā also is suppressed or rather retracted.

88. All these stages are stages of buddhi as manifesting the self. Buddhi manifests the self not necessarily in the sense of conditioning the consciousness of the self—there being no consciousness of the self in asamprajñāta—but in the sense of taking the changeless form of the self, while changing. Buddhi is indeed the same even in a flow of vṛttis, but the sameness here is inferred and is not evident to introspection.

Each vṛtti, however, is a flow in which there is a sameness that is introspectively evident. Buddhi without vṛtti—as in asamprajñāta—is also a flow with the form of self-identity, as is evident to the memory of it in vyutthāna. Flow with the explicit form of self-identity is samādhi and is evident to introspection or memory about at least some section of the flow that constitutes the being of buddhi. A tattva lower than buddhi is a flow in which the form of self-identity is not explicit at all.

89. The first three levels—kṣipta, mūḍha and vikṣipta—are, as has been pointed out, characterised by indirect and implicit asmitā. The mind is here directly occupied with objects *as to* the self. The indirect reference to the self is further implicit in the sense that it here appears as a value of the object felt or willed and not as a knowing presentation *detached* from the object presented, as it appears in the ekāgra stage. We may begin with the vikṣipta stage and work backwards and forwards to the other stages. Here the tamas element of buddhi is suppressed or reduced to mere saṁskāra so that it does not affect its prakhyā or self-consciousness. As this self-consciousness is indirect i.e., is primarily object-consciousness, its non-limitation by tamas means that buddhi here reveals the objective universe. Yet the revelation is of the possibility rather than of the actuality of the universe: there is consciousness in this stage of an indefinitely extendable series of objects beyond the attained definite object. This objective beyond is not actually experienced because it is the content of cognition as conatively qualified, prakhyā being here still restricted by pravṛtti or rajas, though not by tamas. The sthiti of buddhi or its self-conscious persistence (feeling) affects its prakhyā by limiting its field of vision, by making it stick to the object actually attained and shutting out the beyond from its view. The pravṛtti of buddhi or its self-conscious activity (willing) affects its prakhyā by making the beyond appear indefinitely as what is to be or can be experienced. The objective beyond is thus presented to consciousness as a possibility. In the kṣipta and mūḍha stages this consciousness of possibility is absent; and in the ekāgra stage, there is consciousness of the beyond as an actuality.

90. In the vikṣipta state, the mind is said to reveal all

objects[a] and in the ekāgra state, to reveal the true nature of its object or reveal its object as luminous or self-evident.[b] The former refers to the indefinite extent of knowledge and the latter to the depth of knowledge or insight into the essence. As vikṣipta precedes yoga, it cannot be said to yield knowledge of the actual infinite and hence it can only be understood to reveal the possible infinite. The objects that *can* be known in a stage of knowledge are only thought as an *all* in that stage and can be *known* as an actual or accomplished universe in the form of a more essential object in a deeper grade of knowledge. The possible universe is only thought in connection with actual objects that are known and thus knowledge in the vikṣipta state may be said to be of actual objects in a possible universe. The thought of the universe is the knowledge of relation within the objects of actual knowledge as continued in the thought of relation between them and the possible objects beyond them. Thus knowledge in the vikṣipta state may be taken as our ordinary thinking or discursive knowledge.

91. Knowledge in the mūḍha or kṣipta stage is to be conceived as lacking this consciousness of the universe, the thought of internal and external relation of the known object. In the mūḍha stage, the mind is fixed on a particular object and is aware that it cannot move on to other objects. In the ekāgra stage also, the mind is fixed on a particular object but is aware that it freely does not move out of it. The mūḍha state presupposes the kṣipta state, since to be aware that it cannot move, it must have had experience of moving (without the consciousness of relating as in the vikṣipta state). To be aware of passing from one object to another without relating them is to know on the kṣipta level. The mind here is aware of moving out from the object on which it was fixed, and getting fixed on another, moving out of it again and so on. There is an alternation of moving and standing, pravṛtti and sthiti within knowing while in the mūḍha state, there is no pravṛtti, but only sthiti, there being only a helplessly

[a] sarvataḥ pradyotamānam.

[b] sad-bhūtamarthampradyotayati—where 'sad-bhūtam' is explained as paramārtha-bhūtam or as śobhanam nitāntāvirbhūtam sattvam.

fixed or standing cognition. In the *vikṣipta* state the mind moves only and does not stand though in moving it relates, relating being a free standing or consciously keeping self-identical inspite of movement. In the *ekāgra* stage, the mind does not move from object to object but freely stands or fixes itself on an object and enjoys its self-identity in the activity of standing.

92. What is this freedom of knowing? The mind as *prakhyā* or self-conscious knowing is free, is aware of keeping self-identical, of actively maintaining itself in *samādhi*. It is aware of itself not as the persisting object that it is but as the persisting subject, as the self willing to stand (not eternally standing), or, in other words, as consciously achieving its duration. The *sthiti* of the mind that is due to *tamas* is an objective or helplessly given duration, which is not consciously realised as its self-identity. Knowing in the different levels of *buddhi* differs not in respect of this *sthiti* but in respect of *sthiti* as *samādhi* or *praśānta-vāhitā*[b] or self-achieved subjective duration. There is progressive increase of such knowing duration as one passes from *kṣipta* to *ekāgra*, not of the duration of the *vṛtti* involved in knowing. The subjective duration, however, is undistinguished from the objective duration in the stages before *ekāgra* and hence the duration of a cognitive *vṛtti* appears to increase gradually in passing from *kṣipta* to *vikṣipta*. It is greatest in *vikṣipta* not in respect of the knowledge of the substantive object but in respect of the knowledge of the relations within the object, while in *ekāgra*, duration is felt mystically to lapse into eternity.

93. The difference among the first four levels of *buddhi* has been considered so far in reference to knowing. But it is really a spiritual difference of which the cognitive aspect is only one aspect which is specially stressed because it is through it that the other aspects can be precisely characterised. In contrast with *vikṣipta*, *ekāgra* is said not only to be a new quality of knowing which reveals its object as luminous or self-evident but also to attenuate the *kleśas* or spiritual errors, to loosen the bonds of *karma* and to make for freedom from the knowing or objective attitude altogether. *Vikṣipta* does

[a] YB. I. 13

not thus work—at least directly—against spiritual error, does not seek to reverse the downward current of karma and positively maintains the objective attitude. The vikṣipta mind is said to work for dharma, jñāna, vairāgya and aiśvarya, and the mūḍha mind to work for their opposites—adharma, ajñāna etc.—both attaining 'subjective' good or evil—while the kṣipta mind directly wills and enjoys viṣaya or object. These spiritual characters of the mind—good and evil—are rooted in the kleṣas or spiritual errors. The mind in the first three levels works within spiritual error in which saṁsāra or natural life is rooted. The spiritual problem of cutting the root of natural life and of turning the will backwards towards the attainment of mukti as strong un-ruffled self-possession does not arise in these mental levels. The mind here has only natural characters which receive their spiritual complexion from the memory of its spirituality in the higher levels—ekāgra and niruddha, memory of samādhi in the restricted sense of the term.

94. As immediately antecedent to explicit spritual mentality. vikṣipta mentality is implicitly spiritual, seeking to attain but not consciously enjoying the attainment of dharma, jñāna, vairāgya and aiśvarya as the forms of 'subjective' good. Explicit spirituality is more than the enjoying attainment of 'subjective' good which as such is good for the striving self, self that is identified with buddhi as with the moral pravṛtti for the good. But it is only as this moral pravṛtti is satisfied that the good is enjoyed as good in itself or spiritually good: striving for the subjectively good is consummated in the enjoyment of the spiritually good. Spirituality is more than even this spiritual enjoyment: it is implicitly a detachment or withdrawal from the enjoyment which is actualised in a transcendental or superconscious state of buddhi called asamprajñāta. This detachment from spiritual enjoyment in the enjoyment itself comes spontaneously according to other systems, but in Yoga philosophy it is taken to be effected through a specific withdrawing activity of the mind—viz., the practice of yoga. Vikṣipta is thus the pre-spiritual mentality, conscious as pre-spiritual, as a striving mentality that makes for but is not the enjoying attainment of spirituality and much less the detachment from the enjoyment.

95. The mūḍha mentality as just preceding the vikṣipta, is the opposite of the moral striving towards the subjective good in which vikṣipta consists, being thus what makes for the subjective evil in the form of adharma, ajñāna etc. As there is no pravṛtti in the mūḍha state, the making for evil is not a striving but is still self-conscious. In mūḍha and vikṣipta, the evil or the good is felt as of the finite self, as subjective, but in kṣipta, it is not so felt. There is no consciousness of evil in kṣipta where the attitude is non-moral striving towards and enjoyment of the object or viṣaya felt as good but not known as such, as good for the self. That, however, the object is still felt as good shows that the mentality is implicitly self-conscious and belongs to buddhi. The consciousness of evil comes first in the mūḍha state as the result of the baffled striving for natural good in the kṣipta state. It is indeed the consciousness of natural evil but as baffled striving rouses the consciousness of the self also, the natural evil is felt as an evil for the self. Such subjective evil is implicitly a moral evil which is recognised as such in the vikṣipta state. What is felt as a natural good is implicitly a subjective evil: and what is felt explicitly as a subjective evil is implicitly a moral evil. What is explicitly felt as morally good is an implicit spiritual evil recognised as such in the explicit spiritual consciousness; explicit spirituality recognises itself as an absolute evil to be superseded.

96. The mūḍha state represents the tendency towards subjective evil and it comes midway between the kṣipta and the vikṣipta representing the tendencies towards natural good and moral good respectively. There is no helpless movement of the mind or distraction in the mūḍha stage. Its immobility is felt in the state as a subjective disability but not as a moral evil: it is, in fact, implicitly enjoyed, being suicidally sought to be continued by blind resistance to distraction (implicit pravṛtti). It is moral indolence which is recognised in vikṣipta as the fundamental moral evil, as the parent of adharma, ajñāna etc. The vikṣepas are the causes that keep the mind in the vikṣipta or morally striving state and prevent it from passing into the spiritual activity of yoga. Nine such vikṣepas are mentioned and five derivatives from them (vikṣepa-sahabhuvaḥ), the former being apparently what directly prevent

yoga and the latter what are only incompatible with yoga.[a] The nine vikṣepas are disease, mental dullness, doubt, unconscious omission or lapse of will, bodily dullness, greed, error, hesitancy in rising to a higher spiritual level and unsteadiness on the present level. Of these, mental dullness and greed appear to be the persistence of the mūḍha state itself within the vikṣipta and are opposed not to yoga-practice (spirituality) only, but to moral striving also, being thus specifically moral evils. Disease, unconscious lapse and bodily dullness are felt as evil even in the pre-moral or mūḍha stage. Doubt, error and the last two vikṣepas are specifically spiritual evils.

97. The mind passes from object to object in the kṣipta state not freely but because it is at the mercy of the objects which attract it successively. The operation of tamas is here implicit and the operation of rajas as expressed in the passing or transition is explicit, though the former really determines the latter. The former becomes explicit in the mūḍha state where rajas ceases to operate though, as sattva or prakhyā is the ground of all this variation, there is a consciousness of the absence of movement or transition. In the vikṣipta state tamas lapses and the movement from object to object is free in a sense and not conditioned by the attraction of the object as in the kṣipta state. The movement, however, is judged from the standpoint of yoga or the spiritual consciousness as an inability to stand, as unfree, as due to an internal necessity—the intrinsic instability of a vṛtti—though not to an external necessity, viz., the attraction of the object. The kṣipta mind is at best aware of moving towards an object but not of moving out of an object. The vikṣipta mind is aware of moving out of an object freely and does not realise that this freedom is only apparent and that it really cannot stand due to its inherent instability. It is only in spiritual consciousness, the yoga-level of mentality that the inherent cause of its movement is understood as a vikṣepa opposed to freedom. Freedom is conceived as the conscious power of the mind not to move from vṛtti to vṛtti, such power being lacking in the mūḍha state where the mind only helplessly stands and is unable to move. The yoga-level of the mind implies the conscious ability to move and the actual

[a] YS. I 30-31.

exercise of this ability not in moving from object to object (vṛtti to vṛtti) but in the mind or a mental vṛtti flowing as self-identical—which is in fact the conscious arrest of mental change or ruling out of vikṣepa.

98. Vikṣepa is thus distraction not merely of attention but of the free flowing being of buddhi. Buddhi as prakhyā is not merely knowing but the will to realise knowing, which is more than the will to attend. The will to attend may be variously motived and when the motive is explicitly to secure the free being of the mind, freedom from the inner tendency to change, from its own instability or unfreedom, the will to attend is the will to realise the mind. It is in the first instance a realising of freedom in a vṛtti that has itself come through change but ultimately it means a realising of freedom from vṛtti altogether. Vikṣepa is understood in this will to realise freedom as a mode of unfreedom of the self-conscious mind, as a tendency of the spirit to be in a vṛtti and as a necessary consequence to pass on to a new vṛtti. There is no vṛtti with vikṣepa[a] actual or potential. In the vikṣipta state, the vikṣepa is actual, while in the yoga state (short of the final asamprajñāta) it is potential, waiting to be actual as vyutthāna. Vikṣepa is not itself a vṛtti but the conscious passing to a vṛtti or the mental cause of the passing, which may be conscious or unconscious.

99. The fact that vṛtti necessarily implies vikṣepa is taken in Yoga-Bhāṣya I.33. to disprove the Buddhist view of the mind being but a series of momentary cognitions (pratyaya). If each pratyaya or vṛtti stood by itself in the series that mind is taken to be, each would be an ekāgra mentality and there would be no vikṣipta mentality at all—which is not the fact. Since then the difference between vikṣipta and ekāgra is an undeniable fact, the mind must be one with many vṛttis, either similar or dissimilar.

100. The continuity of one vṛtti with the next is conscious in both the levels: to be aware of a vṛtti is to be aware of passing beyond it. In the vikṣipta mind, the conscious passing to a dissimilar vṛtti is specifically called vikṣepa. In the ekāgra mind, the passing is conscious self-reproduction of a

[a] YB. I. 30

vṛtti, its conscious achievement of duration and is itself vṛtti though not another vṛtti, while in vikṣipta the passing is conscious function of the starting vṛtti and not itself vṛtti. As the self-reproduction of an ekāgra-vṛtti is itself the vṛtti, vikṣepa is here not all potential as in asamprajñāta but both potential and actual, potential in respect of the subsequent vyutthāna-vṛtti and actual in respect of the insight into the essence of the object of the starting vrtti. The insight here implies not a subsequent (anāgata) vṛtti but a present vṛtti involved in the starting vṛtti. The relation of the ekāgra-vṛtti to the involved vṛtti of insight is not a passing or vikṣepa in the sense of a conscious self-losing of the initial vṛtti but in the sense of its conscious self-realising. It is still the conscious passing of a vṛtti and is as such a subtle vikṣepa which is, however, absent in the fifth or niruddha level. Vṛtti as necessarily implying vikṣepa is an evil and the consciousness of this evil is what impels the mind to pass from vikṣipta to ekāgra and from ekāgra to niruddha.

CHAPTER VII

THE NATURE OF YOGA

101. In Yoga philosophy, 'yoga' is understood as spiritual activity or the result achieved by spiritual activity. Activity is conceived in this system as willing, knowing and even feeling as a process being taken as implicit willing. The process or activity of knowing or feeling is not necessarily understood in other systems as willing; and willing itself may be regarded as a mode of knowing or feeling. Spiritual activity, however, if admitted at all, is taken in all systems as a specific conscious function, the function of achieving freedom from evil as such. Non-spiritual activity may be a freeing from evil but it need not be freeing from evil explicitly understood as evil. Again, spiritual activity is activity explicitly for achieving freedom. Activity in the merely moral stage is a freeing from evil as such but is not explicitly *for* freedom being either for some good form of being (objective or subjective) or in pure obedience to the law, while spiritual activity is for freedom as the good but not as a good form of being. By 'good form of being' is meant here what is desired; and in desire the agent necessarily conceives his desiring being to continue unaltered at the time of fulfilment. Freedom which is the end of spiritual activity is not desired in this sense, being conceived in the activity not as what will satisfy the self retaining its present mentality at the time of satisfaction but as freedom from this mentality itself. Spiritual activity, in other words, is for the good in itself conceived indeed by the agent but not as good for the agent with his present mentality, conceived by him as an impersonal satisfaction, whether or not he remains a person at the time of satisfaction. Lastly, unlike other conscious activities, spiritual activity not only makes for the end and is anticipatively conscious of it but is explicitly aware of being the activity of the end. It is not only avowedly for freedom but is itself self-consciously free from evil, being in this sense the self-deepening of a satisfaction already attained. The activity of the impersonal end is more readily intelligible—though only figuratively—in spiritual knowing and feeling than in willing. Yoga philosophy may claim the merit of making it literally intelligible

in the conception of y o g a as the essential or spiritual form of willing.

102. Freedom and evil are connected notions: evil is intelligible only as implying a limitation or privation of freedom while freedom is known in the first instance as freedom from evil though it may not mean it. One is conscious of being unfree in the consciousness of freedom: un-freedom is realised as such in consciously not knowing, feeling or willing what ought to be known, felt or willed. The concept of 'ought' is understood literally in reference to willing and has only a figurative meaning in reference to knowing and feeling. What ought to be known or felt is what is good to know or feel, something that is already known or felt but necessarily wished to be realised, known better by introspective clarification of the presentation of it and felt more intimately by imaginative inwardisation of its significance for the self. Realisation here is no willing except to Y o g a and although it is a process or activity terminating in a result, the result is felt to come of itself and not to be achieved by right. There may be a preparatory willing to remove the obstacle to its spontaneous emergence but the emerging process itself and not merely its result is felt to be a miraculous fulfilment of a wish involving the conscious dropping of the willing attitude. Yet it appears as though the fulfilment was achieved by willing; and there are figurative imperatives like 'know the self' or 'love your neighbour' (representing as it were, the will of an Oversoul). To systems other than Y o g a, not willing but the symbolism of willing is necessary to the spiritual realisation of knowing and feeling; and even the realisation of willing may not be literal willing but only a symbolic willing, a wishing that the realised will may come. To Y o g a all realisation is willing though it is not willing outward but inward and is will to n i v ṛ t t i and not to p r a v ṛ t t i. The will to n i v ṛ t t i, will not to will, will to retract willing is the one spiritual activity. The self-retracting will may rest in the first instance in realised knowledge or feeling but ultimately it shoots beyond them. Spirituality is essentially the will to retract the forward will, and though it may yield the capacity of energising the forward will also, the exercise of this capacity except in the retractive interest would mean a fall from spirituality.

103. Spiritual activity is essentially for n i v ṛ t t i or arrest of the will towards b h o g a. It may be an overt striving towards

an object but the motive of the striving is a good other than bhoga. Starting from the conative tendency towards bhoga as natural, spirituality may be taken to consist in viewing it, so far as it is self-conscious as evil, as the un-freedom of the self. The natural tendency may not in itself be an evil, but to be explicitly aware of it as an activity of the self is to be aware of it as evil. One is thus aware of it when pleasure is viewed as to be appropriated or enjoyed as a possession and not as an expansion of the self, as the self being better. Pleasure may not be viewed as for the self, and even when so viewed may be taken—as on the merely moral level—as a presented mental fact that does not affect the being of the self. It is viewed on the spiritual level as affecting the being of the self, as either expanding it—yielding the sense of freedom, or contracting it—yielding the sense of possession and as evil in the latter case. It is only when the self seeks pleasure to appropriate it that the will to bhoga is taken as evil willing. Spiritual activity is the activity to arrest evil willing, to be freed from willing viewed explicitly as evil. activity for the avowed end of freedom from unfree willing. Such freedom may or may not be a desirable form of the being of the self, but in any case it is not sought to be realised *as such*. The activity is spiritual as a realising of freedom only from unfree willing; and it is spiritual in the further sense that it is itself free which it would not be if freedom were sought to be realised as a good *being* of the self.

104. The free realising of freedom is regarded in Sāṃkhya and Vedānta as a knowing process and in bhakti-systems as a feeling process. In Yoga it is taken as literal willing, willing not necessarily to the exclusion of knowing or feeling, nor merely along with them but willing as their essential implication and as capable of outgrowing them. In Kant also it is taken as willing. willing to be freed however not from the evil will to bhoga as in Yoga, but from natural inclination (and also it may be from the evil being or the intelligible character of the self); and it is willing to realise freedom not as the good nor as potentially outgrowing knowing and feeling as in Yoga but as the practically known and respected law of holiness. Spiritual activity is in Yoga willing to free oneself from the will to bhoga regarded as evil. All willing is in this system self-conscious, the function of buddhi called asmitā. Spiritual

willing is willing behind willing, willing in reference to objective willing, higher asmitā controlling lower asmitā essentially in the negative or inhibitive way but capable of positively starting or energising it also either in the interest of freedom or as an expression of an unconscious evil in one's being deeper than the will to bhoga. Willing to control willing in the negative or the positive way is just what is meant by yoga in the system. All spiritual activity is yoga.

105. In other systems spiritual activity is not necessarily yoga in the sense of spiritual willing and yoga may be a spiritual condition other than activity. Although yoga either as an activity or as a passive condition is admitted as a fact in most Indian systems, it is only in Yoga philosophy that yoga is identified with spiritual willing and understood to be the essential form of spirituality. Spiritual willing is complete at every stage, neither complacent nor impatient but strong in its detachment and masterful in its activity. At every stage it is dual, willing not to be finite as against willing to be finite, ever succeeding beyond success, ever retaining and achieving its free infinitude. As free willing not to will, it is at the same time a possible willing to will, the possibility being here unlike the possibility on the moral level which is real to willing but not to knowing, an actuality that is known to be really annulled within the annulling willing. It is not preventing a desire from passing into willing but making it pass into willing to be killed by or subordinated to the spiritual willing. A jīvanmukta is said to create a body (nirmāṇā-kāya) to work off his karma, this being the terminal factual form of a willing annulling other actual willing within itself.

106. Willing as explicitly free both in the act and in the end, these being identical, is yoga. It is the merit of Yoga philosophy to have reduced the apparently mystical consciousness of spiritual activity to an intelligible practical psychology of willing. Psychology is ordinarily conceived to be a science based on reflection of the grade to which the mental states are only presented facts without any bearing on the consciousness of freedom and evil. Even the psychology that is based on moral reflection, if it refers to freedom at all, refers to it as extra-psychological or transcendental which mental states presuppose but do not determine or specificate. Hence it is that in the spiritual consciousness one feels an instinctive antagonism to the

reduction of it to psychology. Such reduction, in fact, is generally a denial of the unique value, obligatoriness or sacredness of distinctively spiritual activity; and where it is not a denial, it stands confessed as inadequate psychology presenting the husk and not the kernel of spirituality; for the value here constitutes the fact. Spiritual value or freedom, however, is not other than mental fact though the latter is distinguishable from the former. Freedom is mental fact as constituting, not as constituted by, mental state while mental state is fact as constituted by freedom. Freedom or value is not the pure self, for it has a necessary reference to mental being, nor is it the mental being which presupposes it. Freedom is a mental fact constituting mental state or being which is distinct from it. There may thus be a psychology dealing with freedom as the mental function of making and unmaking mental being; and the reduction of spirituality to this mental function neither denies its value nor presents an inadequate analysis.

107. Freedom as constituting mental state is psychologically intelligible only as freedom of the will. The purely logical or formal relation of 'constitutiveness' has indeed no necessary reference to willing: A is said to constitute B when B is distinct from A, but apart from A is nothing knowable. If B stands for knowable being in general, either there is no A to constitute it or A stands for a knowable real non-being which is just what is meant by freedom. Now mental state may be taken as representing knowable being in general, for if there be knowable non-mental being, freedom cannot be said to constitute it without constituting a mental state---viz.. knowledge of the being. If freedom, as shown, is still a mental fact, it can be said to constitute mental state or knowable being in general if it can be real as non-being even without constituting being. This can only be understood about freedom of the will. Free knowing or feeling, unless taken as an aspect of free willing, is fact only to the mystical consciousness. Free willing as a psychologically intelligible spiritual fact is y o g a.

108. Spirituality is reduced to a procedure of practical psychology in Y o g a philosophy, to a methodical willing to unmake or withdraw from mental state or knowable being in the first instance and then to make or freely put forth mental state, if and when necessary. The religion of y o g a has accordingly

been called a psychological religion. In one sense any religion that emphasises the inner or subjective spiritual attitude in contrast with objective spiritual life, social and ceremonial, is a psychological religion. The religion of Yoga is called psychological in a specially disparaging sense on the assumption that it is merely a system of psychic gymnastics and does not imply like the subjectivistic religions of jñāna and bhakti the realisation of sacred truths and values. The assumption is wrong. yoga being—as has been shown—exercise of explicitly spiritual and not of merely psychic willing. Such willing is also realisation of truths and values though it seeks to go beyond them. But it may be contended that as seeking to achieve freedom by right or might, yoga leaves no room for the consciousness of the sacred which is essential to religion. The charge requires to be examined.

109. Knowledge or feeling of the sacred content as such is as realisation of it itself sacred. The realisation is not a production or causation of the sacred and may accordingly be understood as the activity of the content itself. It is difficult to understand the conative realisation or *my* willing as the activity of the content or end willed without dropping the conative attitude altogether. The primary willing of freedom as end may be knowingly or feelingly realised as the activity of the end: but is it realised in the conative way? if the realising will were a surrender to a categorical imperative, to freedom as the sacred law (as in Kant) and not as an end, its sacredness might be intelligible as the activity or motivation of the law. But in the Yoga system, yoga as the realising will has freedom as the end or good though it does not exclude a surrender to freedom as the law, to Īśvara as holy will. As the end or good is supposed to be achieved by right and not to come to the agent through its free grace, how can the achieving be sacred? It has to be admitted then that so far as yoga is the will to realise freedom of the will as an end and not as an imperative, it is the will to transcend the sacred and to supersede religion. At the same time the activity of realising it is at the start a sacred or religious willing that is known or felt to come. Even the will to overcome this religious willing (in asamprajñāta) may come (though it need not) through the religious will to surrender to God as the eternally realised law, the will to

Īśvara-praṇidhāna (as understood in YS.I.23 and not in YS.II.1,32). The freedom that comes through such religious willing, however, is conceived as super-religious, as the freedom of asamprajñāta. The striving after it and the praying for it (as Īśvara-praṇidhāna may be called) are alternative activities which both bring in super-religious freedom. The discipline of Yoga may then be taken as alternatively religious and super-religious activity for super-religious freedom as the end.

110. The procedure for attaining super-religious freedom (as in asamprajñāta) is either religious or super-religious. The religious procedure in the last resort would be Īśvara-praṇidhāna in response to which Īśvara in his grace is said to help the passage into asamprajñāta. The super-religious procedure would be the spiritual effort of yoga, the intensification of śraddhā, vīryya etc.[a] This effort is not religious willing: there is no religious willing, for to reach an end through one's might and not through grace is not an activity that is felt as sacred. Nor is it the ordinary egoistic will, for it is the effort to get rid of the ego or the finitising ahaṁkāra. It is a willing negatively to avoid willing on any interest including the religious interest and positively to will itself or the freedom of self-possession or active self-identity. As willing, it is activity for an end or good, but the good here is conceived as itself and nothing else. If to act for a good is to act in an interest, the interest here is in the freedom from all interest. Yoga is an absolutely dis-interested willing (not the surrender of willing like certain forms of religion including Īśvara-praṇidhāna), being even in the asamprajñāta stage a super-religious spiritual activity. In other systems also there is the conception of super-religious spiritual activity, though the activity may not be conceived as willing. All activity for mokṣa (as distinct from svarga)—activity as opposed to self-surrender—where the good is conceived as absolute and not as co-ordinate with evil, not, in other words, as satisfying an interest is super-religious. Self-knowledge, for example, is a super-religious good in Vedānta; so is bhakti in Vaiṣṇava systems.

[a] YS.I.20-21

111. Yoga as spiritual willing is not for jñāna but is started by jñāna. In the case of samprajñāta it leads to jñāna also, though not as an intended result. Again yoga, unlike jñāna, is said to make for the cessation of prārabdha bhoga or experiences in this life due to the karma of a previous life.[a] Jñāna leads to vairāgya and this to the attenuation of karma, but such attenuation does not at least normally work against prārabdha and tends only to destroy or 'burn the seed' of sañcita-karma. The jīvanmukta waits for the prārabdha to work itself out and is not supposed to be competent to arrest its operation. In Yoga philosophy, jñāna is supposed (through vairāgya) to start the specific kind of willing called yoga which works against all karma and tends to arrest the operation of even prārabdha. Yoga is not only like the other spiritual functions generally reversive of the current of life, the downward course of causality towards bhoga, but is specifically directed against the causal course within the present life, being thus the will not to will, the self-conscious will to nirodha. Nirodha is not merely the anticipative prevention of a possible causality but the present conquest of a causality that has actually begun to function. Yoga in this sense is interference with natural causality, nature being understood as a system of experiences (bhoga) that has already started into being and includes a determinate future. It is thus tantamount to the willing of miracle or magic.

112. There is general scepticism at the present day not only about any mental activity actually yielding the capacity of producing magical effects in nature but even about the possibility of willing in the mistaken faith in such magic, scepticism not only about the yoga-vibhūtis but about the psychological possibility of yoga itself. Even if such scepticism be waived there is the dispute already noticed as to whether yoga is a necessary stage of spiritual discipline; and there is besides the doubt whether magic has any place in spiritual life at all. Whoever admits free willing, however, in any sense admits magic in some form or other. Even if free willing is admitted in the sense simply of willing as determined by the knowledge of the end to be achieved, the causality of the knowledge, though not implying

[a] YV.I.1

that *I* could have caused a natural effect other than what I actually cause, implies that nature *could* be and not merely *might* be otherwise, could suspend its causal operation or, in other words, that nature is free. If freedom of willing is admitted in the further sense of the real possibility of willing what I do not will, it would mean an indetermination not only in external nature but even in mental nature, the external indetermination being conditioned by the internal. If further there is freedom of willing not to will, the willing that is said to be abstained from, has to be understood not merely as a real possibility but as an actuality that is annulled or 'reduced to ideality' in the abstaining will. There is not only indetermination in the mind, but the indetermination is a determinate moment in the spiritual willing, or, in other words, magic not only *can* be willed but *is* willed—at once put forth and retracted—in the freedom of yoga. If freedom is admitted at all, it is admitted as the causality or self-energising of knowledge (of the end willed). Freedom is not a hypothesis unless willing as causality is a hypothesis. The only causality that we are directly aware of is willing whence we derive the conception of causality in nature on the one hand and of spiritual causality on the other as the starting and retraction of willing itself as the effect. If knowledge has causality, the knowledge of knowledge also has its causality which would be just the magic efficiency of yoga. Free will in the different senses is, in fact, the same activity in different stages of realisation and implies the possibility of magic at every stage. To doubt yoga-vibhūti is to doubt yoga itself and to doubt yoga is to doubt the freedom of the will.

113. The fundamental doubt is about willing as the causality of knowing. Knowledge that starts willing is knowledge of a content to be brought into experienceable existence or to be prevented from emerging in it. Is the experience of attaining or avoiding literally *caused* by such knowledge? Is such known-ness of the content the cause of its emergence or non-emergence into existence? Is it of itself materialised into positively or negatively experienceable actuality? To deny the causality of knowledge in respect of the actuality of its content is to hold that knowledge is but a by-product of nature, that object that exists of itself causes its own known-ness. This would be materialism in which one inexplicability is only substituted for another. If the causa-

lity of knowledge be magic, the emergence of knowledge or known-ness as effect is also magic. Knowledge whether as cause or as effect of the experienceable actuality of its content implies an inexplicability. We start with the belief in our willing as a real causation. The belief may be held to and inwardised into the theory of yoga as a system of magic willing. Or it may be sought to be rejected, but the rejection also requires a specific discipline to realise it—realise the emergence of known-ness as a continuous change of the object—which would be yoga again though of another type. Materialism to be asserted as a theory demands to be realised. Realisation is yoga and one can only choose between different types of yoga. There is no escape from magic.

114. So much as to the general possibility of yoga and yoga-vibhūti. The possibility of specific vibhūtis will be discussed later.

CHAPTER VIII

THE KINDS OF YOGA

115. Two grades of yoga are mentioned by Patañjali—viz., samprajñāta and asamprajñāta. Samprajñāta is said to present four sub-grades as having for its object the content of vitarka, vicāra, ānanda and asmitā. The first two are each sub-divided into two stages, the first into savitarka and nirvitarka and the second into savicāra and nirvicāra. Again, three kinds of yoga are distinguished according as its object—the content concentrated on—is grāhya, grahaṇa or grahītṛ. These stages and kinds of yoga require to be explained.

116. Samprajñāta implies concentration on a vṛtti corresponding to an object. The object is in the first instance sthūla or perceptual which has sūkṣma aspects apprehensible by the mind without the mediation of the senses. Concentration on the presented sthūla aspect leads to its clarification, to the explication of all its implicit sthūla particularity, to the mind being 'completely filled' by it (ābhoga) or intuiting it in its fulness. The presentation of an object prior to the concentration implies the consciousness of a gap between the mind and the object : the mind does not completely reflect the object and the object is not completely unfolded, these being different sides of the same fact. The given-ness of the object in ordinary perception is not an ultimate inexplicability as it is to Kant but implies the consciousness that I have to know it better and the object has to reveal itself more frankly. It is an implicitly conscious gap—an absolute entity at once subjective and objective—between the mind and the object, the explicit fulfilment of which is yoga as concentration, this too being an absolute entity. Ābhoga or the mind being 'filled' by the object or intuition is the general character of the samādhi reached through concentration. When the intuition is of the sthūla object as sthūla, it is called vitarka.[a]

117. The concentrative intuition called vitarka explicates only the sthūla particularity of the sthūla object. The comple-

[a] YB.I.17

tion of the process furnishes the occasion for the next stage of concentration called vicāra which yields intuition of the sūkṣma aspect of the sthūla object. 'Sūkṣma' means both what is imperceptible to sense and what is the constitutive cause of the sthula object and is understood here as the metaphysical reality immanent in the sensible object that is concentrated on. Vitarka leads to the intuition of the implied sensible aspects of the sensible object of concentration. The supersensible essence of the sensible object is not implied in it in the sense its sensible particularity is implied : the implicitness or immanence of the constitutive essence in the sensible object is of another grade. To intuit the object in its full sensible particularity is to be aware of the problem of intuiting its metaphysical essence. The sensible object is a construct of the vikāra-tattvas or viśeṣas—bhūta and indriya, these being accordingly themselves taken as sthūla, although neither is by itself perceptible to sense.[a] The sūkṣma essence of the sensible object is a gradation of objective essences from tanmātra upwards to prakṛti. Vicāra is concentration on these essences, on the eight prakṛtis mentioned in sāṁkhya.

118. The completion of vicāra in respect of any of these essences raises the problem of ānandānugata yoga. The meaning of 'ānanda' here is disputed. Vācaspati takes it to mean the pleasure that consists in the mind being 'filled' by indriya, sense-pleasure self-consciously understood as the intuition of the senses themselves as object, as the mind freely one with indriya. Vijñāna-bhikṣu holds that 'ānanda' has here no reference to sense, sense-pleasure as self-conscious being to him only a form of vitarka: ānanda is the pure joy that emerges after the realisation of the essence or heart of the object. To Vācaspati as to some others, while vitarka and vicāra are concentrated on the grāhya or apprehended object, ānanda is concentration on grahaṇa or the act of apprehension—which would be denied by Bhikṣu. The point will be discussed presently but Bhikṣu appears to be right at least so far as he implies that ānandānugata represents a higher grade of yoga than vicārānugata. Asmi-

[a] Bhūta is sthūla-sūkṣma and indriya is also such, the former representing the substantive being and the latter the sense-perceptibility or manifestness of the bhautika object.

tānugata is a still higher grade: ānanda, whatever else it implies, is not presentation of an object like vitarka and vicāra but is a mental state that is itself presented as an implicitly 'subjective' content while asmitā is presented as the subject itself, explicit either as the mind with the form of the self or as the self with the form of the mind. Concentration on implicit subjectivity (ānanda) prepares the way for concentration on the explicit subject (asmitā).

119. In YS.I.41 which will come up for later discussion, there is reference to the content of samprajñāta-samādhi or samāpatti as either grāhya (apprehended object), grahaṇa (apprehending act) or grahītṛ (apprehending subject). There is dispute as to whether the content of each of the four stages of yoga has these aspects or whether yoga as vitarka and vicāra has grāhya only as content, while ānanda and asmitā have grahaṇa and grahītṛ respectively. The first view is apparently held by Vijñāna-bhikṣu and the second by Vācaspati and others. It may be suggested, however, that although the content of vitarka and vicāra has the triple aspect, the grāhya aspect is alone explicit, the grahaṇa and the grahītṛ aspect being explicit in ānanda and asmitā respectively. In each of the four stages, the content has a triple aspect, for yoga is concentration not of cognitive attention only but of the whole being of the mind. In the first two stages the attitude is mainly cognitive or cognitively objecttive, while in the last two it is mainly subjective, being the feeling attitude in the third stage which is subjective but not opposed to the objective attitude and in the fourth stage either the pure conative attitude which is subjective and opposed to the objective or the attitude of knowing the self and not the object as in vitarka and vicāra.

120. The important point appears to be that the subjective attitude of mind presupposes the objective attitude and that it is only when the object of experience is known as constituted by objective metaphysical essences that the feeling and willing aspects of the object are explicitly detached from the object as free subjective function and subject. The correction of the objective attitude of the mind is effected through the pure or metaphysical knowledge of the object. With all this accords the interpretation of the different stages of samprajñāta given in Bhoja-vṛtti I, 17.

The content of samādhi is the grāhya in vitarka and vicāra. The content of ānanda-samādhi is buddhi itself with the self implicit in it, buddhi as subjective function, not pure buddhi but with a touch of rajas and tamas in it and hence not freed altogether from the objective attitude, such content being ānanda or joy, the self-conscious 'absolute' being of subjective function or grahaṇa. The objective attitude of the first two samādhis implies the conceit of a body—gross and subtle—in which the mind is finitised. In ānanda-samādhi, this conceit of a body drops, such samādhi being said to be enjoyed without self-knowledge by the videha-devatās. Next comes asmitā-samādhi of which the content is pure buddhi freed from the objective attitude altogether and itself object in the sense of the bare existent or manifest self-identity, identified with the pure self and reflecting no viṣaya at all. This samādhi has two forms according as the identity of the self and buddhi is taken as buddhi only or as the self only. The former would be the samādhi said to be enjoyed by the devatās called 'prakṛti-layas and the latter would be viveka-khyāti as the consummation of samprajñāta.

121. The conception of videha and prakṛti-laya requires to be interpreted. Both are understood to be free from ahaṁkāra or the conceit of the body. Freedom from ahaṁkāra does not by itself mean knowledge or realisation of the self (or Īśvara). It is in the first instance a merging or forgetting of the self in a tattva higher than ahaṁkara, a free identification of the self with infinite buddhi—either in the form of feeling or in the form of willing. Free identification means identification in the explicit subjective attitude as distinct from unconscious or erroneous identification which implies the objective attitude and the conceit of the body. It means consciousness of infinite buddhi as one self, such consciousness being feeling the self as content, or willing as the self. The self is not the content of consciousness nor does the self will and hence the self as apparently content or apparently active is really buddhi undistinguished from the self or the self undistinguished from buddhi. The identity of buddhi with the self—as the content of consciousness—is the subjective object, feeling itself being the object felt; and the identity of the self with buddhi—the activity of consciousness—is the subject as willing towards

buddhi. Videha apparently represents the former and prakṛti-laya the latter. The videha may be taken as actively feeling out towards feeling as absolute object or tanmātra and as in this activity feeling infinite buddhi as the self. The prakṛti-laya in willing towards infinite buddhi feels infinite prakṛti as the self. Both are devatās, for to feel an infinite tattva as the self without being unrestricted to a body is to be a devatā or an absolute feeling. One feels an infinite object as the self, in being active towards something lower which is the finite absolute or tanmātra (lower than buddhi) in the case of videha and the infinite absolute or buddhi (lower than prakṛti) in the case of prakṛti-laya, 'absolute' meaning here manifest identity of subject and object. The former is in sānanda-samādhi and the latter is sāsmitā-samādhi, neither knowing the self (or God) as a tattva beyond the object, neither achieving freedom from the object. As unfree, though without the conceit of body, they are reborn but reborn as in samādhi which has not got to be achieved, the former apparently in the highest samprajñāta, or viveka-khyāti and the latter in samprajñāta; each being re-born in a samādhi higher than its present samādhi.

122. The videha, the prakṛti-laya and the vivekin appear to represent the affective, conative and cognitive types of spirituality or realised consciousness of the self. In terms of samādhi, the first stands for sānanda and the last two for two stages of sāsmitā, sānanda and sāsmitā having grahaṇa and grahītṛ or subjective function and subject as their respective contents. Realised feeling as of the videha is the objective absolute, the identity of subject and object appearing as impersonal. Realised willing as of the prakṛti-laya is the subjective absolute or the identity appearing as personal. Realised knowing or viveka would be detached from these two absolutes and as such would be the over-personal self as correcting or dissolving the self-conscious or free identity of subject and object. This correcting is still a buddhi-function with which the self is identified and is not accordingly explicitly aware of being over-personal. The subjective absolute or absolute will like the objective absolute or absolute feeling is identified with the substantive buddhi and not merely buddhi-function, but

unlike it is identified with the implicit or unmanifest form of buddhi which is just prakṛti.

123. The videha and the prakṛti-laya are conceived to be freely merged into or identified with the object and not knowing the self (or God) as beyond the object. The freely feeling self is aware of the self but not as distinct from buddhi and the freely willing self is aware of the self as distinct but not as known. The prakṛti-laya as absolute will may be further taken in Yoga as implicitly aware of God working in him (or in prakṛti with which he is identified)—that is why he is supposed to be reborn as janyeśvara—but not therefore as known. The vivekin is conceived in Yoga as knowing not only the self but also, it may be, God.

124. Is asmitā-samādhi necessarily dual as absolute knowing and absolute willing, viveka and prakṛti-līnatva as apparently conceived in Bhoja-vṛtti? It does not appear that one in the sānanda stage has to pass through the prakṛti-līna form of asmitā in order to attain the viveka stage. It was pointed out before that intensive effort and the contemplation of Īśvara are only alternative ways of reaching asamprajñāta. May not the two forms of asmitā be similarly alternative processes? Viveka or absolute self-knowledge need not be reached through the realisation of absolute will: sānanda or absolute feeling seems to pass directly either into absolute willing or into absolute knowing. Two courses appear to be open at every stage of the free willing of freedom. Freedom is understood both in the act and in the end of willing: the end remaining the same, a higher freedom or grade of efficiency in the act may be developed or the form of the act may be the same while a higher quality of freedom as the end may be achieved. Apparently the end of the videha and of the prakṛti-laya is the same—viz., to freely merge into the object; but the act of the latter is freer as willing towards buddhi itself than the act of the former which would be actively feeling out towards tanmātra. Again, the act or subjective function of the vivekin and the videha is the knowing of the mind, not willing towards it which is the act of the prakṛti-laya; but while the latter seeks to merge in it, the former seeks to be detached from it. Similarly the passage beyond vicāra also is in two directions—towards the knowledge of

ānanda and towards ānanda itself. But ānanda as free samādhi is at once both, unlike asmitā which is alternatively knowing and willing. The knowing of ānanda as subjective function and the feeling of it are indistinguishable.

125. So far as to the samādhis in the subjective attitude (i.e., with grahaṇa and grahītṛ as content)--viz., ānanda and asmitā. As to the objective samādhis—vicāra and vitarka (with grāhya as content), each presents two forms which are distinct and co-ordinate (not alternative). The two forms of vitarka are savitarka and nirvitarka, 'vitarka' in these terms meaning wrong vitarka.[a] Similarly about the two forms of vicāra—savicāra and nirvicāra. In both savitarka and savicāra, the content is presented with an adventitious distinction which drops out in nirvitarka and nirvicāra. In savitarka this distinction is a vikalpa generated by verbal knowledge,[b] while in savicāra, it is the specific spatio-temporal or causal position[c] of the content concentrated on, this being also avikalpa in the wider sense. This adventitious distinction in the content is a buddhi-construct which is sought to be eliminated in the next higher samādhis—nirvitarka and nirvicāra.

126. In vitarka the object concentrated on is a perceptible whole of perceptible parts. In savitarka, it appears with the fictitious unity of the name, meaning and thought[d] called vikalpa. Not that the object as thus known is false, for the adventitious character is a mental construct and not the content of error. But it is known inadequately, known as indefinitely confused with presentation owing to the mind-created limitation. To be known adequately within perceptual limits—in parapratyakṣa[e] is to be known in nirvitarka. Here the factitious character of the vṛtti drops off, the elimination being called smṛti-pariśuddhi[f] or the removal of the memory or thought of the verbal meaning. The object in savitarka

[a] YV.I.17.
[b] YS.I.42.
[c] YB.I.44.
[d] YS.I.42; III.17.
[e] YB.I.42.
[f] YS.I.43.

appears within the vṛtti and yet as distinct from it because of the verbal reference. In nirvitarka, as the verbal reference lapses, this distinction of vṛtti and its object also lapses so that the vṛtti appears to lose itself (svarūpa-sūnyeva) and shines as the object only (arthamātra-nirbhāsā). This object is still a whole of parts, an avayavin the unity of which is real and not a vikalpa.

127. The object of vicāra is sūkṣma in the sense of being the imperceptible cause or cause of cause etc. of the sthūla or perceptible object. Savicāra is the intuition of the sūkṣma object as present with the limitations of deśa, kāla and nimitta.[a] The intuition is of the sūkṣma as manifest in the sthūla and having the objective time-position of the sthūla, which is position in the causal series of spatio-temporal phenomena. (Such sūkṣma corresponds to what Kant calls substance or cause in *phenomenon*). This objective time-position is presumably a vikalpa, as implying krama which is taken in Yoga-bhāṣya[b] to be a vikalpa,[c] though apparently not in the sense of a verbally generated construct. As this time-position necessarily involves deśa and nimitta, they too are vikalpas; and the incidental implication is that there is no real causality in the succession of phenomena. In nirvicāra this time-position of the sūkṣma object is eliminated, the noumenon being known as integral and unrestricted to any specific immanent pariṇāma.[d] As in nirvitarka, the vṛtti appears to lose itself and shines as the artha only.

128. Nirvicāra yields intuition of the supersensible causes of the sensible world, beginning with the tanmātras and ending with prakṛti, a gradation of objective essences as standing by themselves without being manifest in this world. An object of normal perception under savitarka-concentration is isolated from all its external relations but is still known as an avayavin[e] unfolding its internal perceptible characters such as were implicit in the presentation of it. Under vicāra-concentration, this isolated object reveals a gradation of imperceptible constitutive

[a] YB. I. 44.
[b] II. 52.
[c] Vastu-sūnyo buddhi-nirmāṇaḥ śabdajñānānupātī
[d] YB. I. 44.
[e] YB. I. 43.

causes terminating in the a-liṅga, object that is unmanifest and manifests nothing, object as unrelated to the self in this sense. The viewing of the sensible object as thus resolved into prakṛti, as unrelated to the self, as unknowable leads to the lapse of the objective attitude altogether and to the emergence of the subjective attitude. The objective attitude implies attention to the grāhya (apprehended or known object) which ultimately reduces it to a known unknowable (a-liṅga), grāhya-a-grāhya as it may be called. The subjective attitude emerges when the object thus turns out to be a puzzle, if not a contradiction. The consciousness of the subjective not only presupposes the consciousness of the objective but the reduction of objectivity itself to an apparent or real contradiction. Attention is thus turned from the grāhya or apprehended object to grahaṇa or apprehending act or subjectivity whence again, as has been explained, it is turned to the grahītṛ or apprehending agent or the subject.

129. All these are stages of asamprajñāta-yoga. The general character of samprajñāta is best understood in reference to its result which is technically called samāpatti. Samāpatti is the fixation of the mind on a content (the mind being tatstha 'in it') and its assumption of the form of the content (it being tadañjana—'taking its smear or complexion'). In all knowledge, the mind may be said to be fixed on the content and to take its form, but this has to be understood in a special sense about the super-normal intuition that samāpatti is taken to be. The mind here self-consciously fixes itself on the content and self-consciously identifies itself with it. Self-conscious fixation is not only the awareness of the mind as fixed on the content but also the awareness of willing to withdraw the mind from other contents, not provisionally—as in ordinary reflective knowing—in order to know more about the object fixed on but to know it better, willing to conquer vikṣepa as a spiritual evil, evil conceived to be a limitation of freedom (of self-possessed contemplation). As the result of such disinterested fixation, the mind overcomes the gap between knowing and its object or their dualism, gets 'filled' by the object and thus rises above the subjectivism that ordinary reflection involves. The mind takes the form of the object, is tadañjana in the sense that the dualism of knowing and known lapses. The lapse may take two forms :

either the mind or the mental vṛtti that is fixated finds the object within itself, the object being still distinct within, though not from, the mind as mirror, or the mind may freely merge itself into the contemplated object, give up its self as it were, (svarūpa-śūnyeva) so that the object alone shines out (artha-mātra-nirbhāsā). Even in the latter case, the object that shines is the mind or vṛtti appearing as the object by freely retracting its subjectivity. These two forms are distinguishably continuous in vitarka and vicāra where there is samāpatti in respect of the grāhya object. In ānanda and asmitā—where the samāpatti is in respect of grahaṇa and grahītṛ as content, the two forms either coincide or are exclusive alternatives.

130. Samāpatti is attained by the mind that is kṣīṇa-vṛtti, abstracted from all vṛttis other than that concentrated on and with the functions of rajas and tamas that make for vikṣepa attenuated by abhyāsa and vairāgya or disinterested spiritual practice. The abstraction or the arrest of vikṣepa—the retractive spiritual will—is the essential activity of yoga which in samprajñāta terminates or rests in a particular vṛtti. In attention in the vikṣipta stage, concentration appears to be the activity, abstraction being only its passive concomitant and result. In yoga, abstraction is the explicit activity of which concentration is the result which, too, is not passive but a restful activity, the activity of keeping self-identical in a vṛtti. Abstraction is negative or retractive willing which is real only through the spiritual interest, interest in the freedom from interest. The willing, however, rests in the vṛtti from which as ālambana it starts. There is no vṛtti, however, that does not imply an actual or potential vikṣepa,[a] and even in ekāgra, there is potential vikṣepa in the form of a persisting reference to the objects of bhoga or experience, reference that is, however, only a saṁskāra. Hence samādhi in samprajñāta is said to be savīja—with the seed or potentiality of suffering in it. At the same time this seed or saṁskāra is gradually devitalised by the saṁskāra left by the samādhi itself—prajñā-kṛta-saṁskāra as it is called—which as the saṁskāra or as conditioned by the saṁskāra

[a] YB. I. 30.

of the retracting activity tends to arrest the tendency to relapse into the vikṣipta level.

131. Prajñā that shines out in samādhi is spiritual wisdom implying not only intuition of the viśeṣa or particularity of metaphysical objects, which āgama and anumāna only postulate and do not establish, but also a purity or transparency (vaiśāradya) of the buddhi-self in which one views suffering souls as from a height.[a] It need not mean the wisdom that is reached in nirvicāra-samādhi alone (in which prajñā is first mentioned in YB.): it includes viveka (param prasaṁkhyānam—YB.I.2.) which also is called prajñā in YS.II.27. Prajñā in this wide sense leaves its saṁskāra which militates against the saṁskāra of vikṣipta mind that persists in ekāgra. The saṁskāra of vikṣipta does not persist in asamprajñāta which is accordingly called nirvīja-samādhi. This samādhi arrests vṛtti altogether, arrests even the terminal vṛtti, the prajñā called viveka and militates against the saṁskāra left by the prajñā. Nirvīja-samādhi or niruddha also leaves its saṁskāra, as may be inferred from the facilitation and increased duration of later niruddha. This saṁskāra works against the saṁskāra of savīja-samādhi.

132. The prajñā that emerges in the final samprajñāta —viveka as it is called—is the perception of itself as buddhi-vṛtti distinct from the self and as accordingly savīja, tending through its implied avidyā towards bhoga or potentially evil. The perception is spiritual as implying para-vairāgya or final detachment of the self from the object, detachment not only from the object of the mind but also from the mind itself as object, from the mind even in its final actual state viz., viveka. Vairāgya is not mere desirelessness but a free conquest (vaśīkāra) of desire—whether for natural (dṛṣṭa) or for spiritual (ānuśravika) good through the perception of the evil implied in desire. Vairāgya is the condition of all yoga, the one motive of the will to nivṛtti. The perception of the evil even in viveka-samādhi in so far as it is a vṛtti leads to para-vairāgya which is no longer the conquest of desire —for viveka already means a cessation of desire—but the free

[a] Bhūmisthāniva śailasthāḥ—YB.I.47.

annulment of unfreedom that viveka itself as vṛtti is perceived in viveka to imply. Freedom is the positive end—the freedom of the mind to stand like the self. Negatively it is freedom from desire—and therefore is not said to be desired—and even from knowledge which as viveka knows itself to be but vṛtti, as dependent on the object and as, therefore, the initial form of unfreedom. There is no knowledge except through vṛtti and freedom though achieved through knowledge is freedom from knowledge itself, freedom as the super-conscious activity of the mind to stand like the self, to be and not to know.

133. This super-conscious activity or freedom beyond knowledge is asamprajñāta-samādhi. It is still the activity of buddhi, not of the self which is pure consciousness and no activity. In all lower stages the activity of buddhi is bound up with a vṛtti though even there as the will to nivṛtti, it also transcends the vṛtti. Here it is the will to withdraw from all vṛtti and is, therefore, no function of vṛtti, being the function of buddhi without vṛtti, i.e., with vṛtti reduced to saṁskāra within it. It does not mean a lapse of buddhi into prakṛti, as the retraction of all vṛtti would imply in Sāṁkhya. This saṁskāra-śeṣa-buddhi lapses into prakṛti only in the final asamprajñāta which of itself passes into mukti or kaivalya. Otherwise there is relapse from asamprajñāta to samprajñāta—waking or vyutthāna means this relapse here—to viveka-prajñā whence through the saṁskāra left by asamprajñāta there is easier elevation to the super-conscious stage. The alternation goes on till viveka reaches its full maturation in the four-fold knowledge of evil (heya), cause of evil (heya-hetu), freedom from evil (hāna) and means to freedom (hānopāya; and then comes the final asamprajñāta with its three stages—para-vairāgya, citta-laya (in prakṛti) and kaivalya (cessation of the possibility of re-emergence of citta) spontaneously succeeding one another without the necessity of fresh sādhana. The four stages prior to final asamprajñāta make up what is called kārya-vimukti (interpreted by Bhikṣu as kartavya-samāpatti or cessation of duty) and the last three citta-vimukti which is freedom from the mind.[a]

[a] YB. II. 27.

CHAPTER IX

THE PROCEDURE OF YOGA

134. Yoga or the free willing of freedom is a super-religious spiritual activity. It may presuppose a moral and religious discipline, and religious activity in the form of Īśvara-praṇidhāna may be an alternative procedure co-ordinate with the yoga procedure for the attainment of yoga or the freedom of samādhi as the end, but freedom whether in the yoga act or as its end is conceived to be super-religious. The absolute will that yoga implies is as much 'beyond good and evil' as the absolute knowledge of the Vedāntist or the absolute bhakti of the Vaiṣṇava. These latter may still be described as religious so far as they imply a surrender to the sacred but yoga as absolute will is explicitly a transcendence of the sacred. At the same time it is spiritual, unlike the absolute will in Nietzsche's cult of the superman, being essentially the will to nivṛtti and not to pravrtti, the will to mukti, to freedom as the power to stand as distinct from the power to create objective values indefinitely. Not that the mukti of Yoga is incompatible with a participation in the life of God for all time in His work of liberation of souls, but anyway such participation would not be to Yoga the self's own life as individual, the self being as in Sāṁkhya eternally individual and without any activity. The freedom of negative willing indeed implies the freedom of forward willing but, as has been pointed out, such forward willing is conceived in Yoga to be actualised and annulled at the same time.

135. The practical procedure for the attainment of samādhi includes many steps, some of which are only preparatory to absolute willing (bahiraṅga or external means) and others that are constitutive of it (antaraṅga or internal parts); and the lower forms of samādhi are themselves preparatory in rereference to the highest. Some of these are consecutive steps of which each higher is to be attempted only after the lower step has been efficiently practised; and some are only alternative steps. As to the consecutive steps, it is not necessary that one should

begin with the lowest; one may be competent to function on a higher level.[a] In fact, one should begin on the highest level and then gradually discover by trial the level that suits him i.e., on which he can function efficiently.[b]

136. The spiritual procedure of yoga consists in the last resort in abhyāsa and vairāgya, positive exercise of freedom and negative annulment of unfreedom. Two grades of vairāgya—para and apara—have been mentioned, of which the latter is desirelessness understood as the active conquest of desire and the former is the free withdrawal of the self from the mind itself. Both are forms of negative or retractive mental activity conditioned by the knowledge of the evil (doṣa-darśana) in the objective attitude of the mind and both may be regarded as the prasāda or realisation of the knowledge. The knowledge itself implies a residual objective attitude, the evil of which is manifest only in para-vairāgya which is accordingly a withdrawal from knowledge itself and may be described as such realisation (prasāda) of knowledge as amounts to the transcendence of it. Abhyāsa or practice is the free willing to stand,[c] the self-conscious effort of the mind to persist unchangingly as an isolated buddhi-vṛtti or as vṛtti-less buddhi, such willing being confirmed by constant repetition in the right spirit.[d] The right spirit is but vairāgya, the motive to the positive effort and not merely to its repetition, so that abhyāsa and vairāgya appear to be different aspects of the same activity, the difference lapsing altogether in the passage to asamprajñāta, where the positive activity is negative and the negative activity positive, freedom in the act and freedom in the end being coincident. The positive activity in all yoga is a prayatna or willing of which śraddhā, vīrya, smṛti, samādhi and prajñā are specific aspects.[e] 'Śraddhā' means here the active wish or aspiration for yoga. vīryā' the will to dhāraṇā, 'smṛti the effort of dhyāna, 'samādhi' the effortless activity to be and 'prajñā' the knowledge that shines out in samādhi: knowledge which

[a] YB. III. 6.
[b] YV. III. 6.
[c] YS. I. 13.
[d] YS. I. 14.
[e] YS. I. 20.

being practised in vairāgya for its object leads to the freedom of asamprajñāta.

137. All these are stages of abhyāsa which is here direct willing and not willing through means, prescribed in the first pāda of Yoga-sūtra for the uttama-adhikārin, the fittest aspirant who starts with śraddhā in the above sense and is already in a sense on the ekāgra level. This direct willing leads him on even to asamprajñāta, though here an alternative to willing—viz., Īśvara-praṇidhāna which implies surrender of the willing attitude—is prescribed which also is attained directly without means. The aspirant who can directly attain yoga and is on the way to it may, however, experience vikṣepa and certain auxiliary practices are prescribed for its avoidance which are not really means but serve only to strengthen and chasten the aspiration (and are accordingly called 'parikarma'). These include cultivation of a serene moral attitude towards other persons, breath-control, experimental production of certain magical experiences ('pravṛtti' as they are called) through the control of attention and so forth. The moral attitude mentioned is interesting. The aspirant is enjoined to cultivate maitrī, karuṇā, muditā and upekṣā for the happy, unhappy, the virtuous and the vicious person respectively.[a] He should avoid envy for the happy man, have good wishes for him, feel his happiness as though it were his own, these being implied in maitrī or friendliness through which he gets freed from rāga or the lure of pleasure. Karuṇā or compassion implies avoidance of indifference (tāṭasthyam) towards others' suffering, of the conceit of being superior to them (darpa) and of the wish to inflict suffering on the enemy (dveṣa): the feeling of others' suffering as one's own frees one from dveṣa or fear of pain. Muditā or joy (of approval) at others' puṇya (merit or virtue achieved) excludes asūyā or the carping tendency and leads one towards puṇya and the avoidance of the pain of a bad conscience (paścāt-tāpa). For the sinner one should have upekṣā or forgiveness (indifference or audāsīnya in the sense of seeking to forget his sin) and not amarṣa—anger or hatred. Unlike the first three, upekṣā is only negative and has no positive counterpart unless it be

[a] YS.I.33.

karuṇā, which, however, is for the relief of the suffering due to sin rather than for the conversion of the sinner (though it may not exclude what is called in Gītā 'loka-samgraha' or the compassionate teaching of others). That upekṣā is only negative comes out in Yoga-bhāṣya.[a] where it is pointed out that while the other three can be intensified by thought (bhāvanā) leading to realisation (samādhi) and spiritual strength (bala), upekṣā does not admit of realising thought and hence does not lead to positive strength.

138. No *means* to the attainment of yoga are apparently prescribed in the first section of the Yoga-sūtras which describes only the actual procedure of the uttamādhikārin, the aspirant who is already posted in the ekāgra level. The discipline for the madhyamādhikārin, the next best aspirant who has already the spiritual impulse and cannot yet spiritually will, is stated[b] as comprising tapas (asceticism), svādhyāya (study of sacred śāstra or meditation—japa— of sacred mantras) and Īśvara-praṇidhāna (contemplation of God), these making up what is called kriyā-yoga (inner religious activity which is external relatively to super-religious spiritual activity viz., the free willing of freedom). These attenuate the spiritual evil (kleśa) in our nature that prevents rise to samādhi.[c] They are prescribed for one already in the religious stage with aspiration for freedom or mokṣa. There are, again, others who have not yet risen to this stage, for whom a discipline of our relatively outward nature—moral and even physical—is necessary. The discipline for all who are on the vikṣipta level—for the vyutthita-citta (with a waking or discursive consciousness as distinct from the ecstatic sleep of samādhi)—is summed up in the eight stages—yama, niyama, āsana, prāṇāyāma, pratyāhāra, dhāraṇā, dhyāna and samādhi, samādhi being the end to which the others are consecutive means (and which is itself means to higher samādhi to one already on the ekāgra level).

139. Are these eight members of the yoga-procedure (yogāṅga) consecutive stages, each leading on to the next? In connection with Yoga-sūtra III.6, Vyāsa states in re-

[a] III.23.

[b] YS.II.1.

[c] YS.II.2.

ference to saṁyama comprising dhāraṇā, dhyāna and samādhi that one has to rise here consecutively from the lowest grade upwards unless one is already competent to function in a higher grade. Vijñāna-bhikṣu extends this rule to these eight stages in interpretation of the word 'yathākramam' in the Bhāṣya.[a] The rule, however, is taken by others to hold good about the last six stages, the first two—yama and niyama—being understood as only removing the obstacles to the attainment of samādhi.[b] Of the six stages the first three are taken to be preparatory steps (bahiraṅga) and the last three constitutive steps (antaraṅga), samprajñāta-samādhi itself being antaraṅga to asamprajñāta.

140. Yama and niyama constitute the ethical and religious setting of the specific yoga-activity. Five yamas are prescribed—ahiṁsā, satya, asteya, brahmacarya and aparigraha—all ethical in the sense of being negative or prohibitive in form and in reference to outward action. The niyamas are also five—śauca, santosa, tapas, svādhyāya and Īśvara-praṇidhāna, these being religious as implying the cultivation of certain positive inner virtues. The yamas as negative (or forms of nivṛtti), are prescribed for all irrespective of caste (jāti), place (deśa), time (kāla) and convention (samaya—restrictive condition, reservation in respect of purpose etc.), or in other words, they are universal and categorical rules of action. The niyamas as positive (or forms of pravṛtti) have reference to activity at a particular time and are not, therefore, universal (sārvabhauma) rules of action. Nor are they categorically prescribed i.e., for their own sake, for virtue is positive willing though in the inner spirit and as such demands to be retracted (nivṛtti). Not that it is implied that yama is more obligatory than niyama. Morality as abstinence, though from outward action, is continuous with vairāgya (or upekṣā for evil) and is directly willed for its own sake; while religious practice, though more inward than morality, is willed only as a means (kriyā-yoga) to the free activity of yoga (to abhyāsa, morality as an embodiment of vairāgya being co-ordinate with abhyāsa). Hence appa-

[a] YV. II. 23.
[b] BV° II. 29.

rently there is one morality but many religions. Morality is universal as the negative externality of spirituality, religious practice is its positive particularity and internality, while super-religious yoga is its transcendent individual reality.

141. The five yamas are forms of the will to nivṛtti or abstinence from violence, lying, stealing, sexual indulgence and acquisition of property—these forms of evil willing being understood not merely literally but as both generalised and inwardised. Hiṁsā or violence is taken to be the basal form of evil willing, the other four involving it or leading to it in spirit, if not in actual fact; and even the niyamas are taken to be intimately related to ahiṁsā which is thus taken to be central to all morality and religion.[a] Ahiṁsā and in fact, all the yamas are primarily the avoidance or arrest of hiṁsā etc. in thought i.e., as vitarka through the contemplation of their pratipakṣa, of their evil consequences. Hiṁsā etc. may be committed, abetted or approved; they may proceed from lobha (greed), krodha (anger) or moha (illusion that they are right or good, perverted conscience—dharmo me bhaviṣyati iti)[b] and may be directed towards an infinite variety of objects.

142. Of the five niyamas, the last three—tapas, svādhyāya and Iśvara-praṇidhāna—are specific religious practices (what are called kriyā-yoga in YS. II.1); and the first two—śauca and santoṣa—are religious attitudes in the sense of being not merely negative like the yamas and of forming the spiritual setting for the last three. Śauca is cleanliness, not natural but spiritual, cleanliness of the body as well as of the mind. The spiritual side of bodily cleanliness implies feeling of the association with the body itself (of oneself or of others) as unclean (aṅga-jugupsā)[c] which explains the inwardness of ceremonial or symbolic purification of the body (saṁskāra) by holy water etc. Mental cleanliness would imply freeing oneself from moral dirt (citta-mala) through the attitudes of maitrī, karuṇā etc. Santoṣa is contentment with what one has[d] or—as sometimes explained— with what is barely necessary for life. Tapas is asceticism (without prejudice to

[a] YB. II. 30.
[b] YB. II. 34.
[c] YS. II. 40.
[d] YB. 32.

mental serenity)[a] for the attenuation of the specific spiritual evils (karma-kleśa-vāsanā), consisting in deliberately bearing —accustoming oneself to—a pair of contrary experiences (dvandva) like heat and cold. It includes all self-chastening and expiatory religious practices and, according to Bhikṣu, even joyous religious practices like worship etc. Svādhyāya includes sacred meditation and study. Īśvara-praṇidhāna or meditation on God—understood here as an emotional activity rather than an impersonal or pure cognitive activity (as in YS. I.23) is the crown and consummation of niyama or religious discipline. Perfection in this meditative practice is said to lead directly to samādhi[b] which, as Yoga-vārtika exlpains, does not imply that the other items of the yoga-procedure are useless. It implies that it is only in the attitude of surrender to God that the later steps of yoga have to be performed for the sure attainment of samādhi.

143. The next three steps of yoga—viz., āsana, prāṇāyāma and pratyāhāra—constitute the process of direct energising of the body as an organ of the spirit in anticipation of the purely spiritual or bodiless willing that consists in dhāraṇā, dhyāna and samādhi. The moral and religious disciplines represented by yama and niyama are subjectivistic in attitude implying a flight from the merely natural bodily and mental life. The passage of subjectivism to concrete spirituality is effected by the conquest of the conscious body and not by flight from it, by spiritualising the body or attuning it with the infinite. The association with the body is due not to subjective error which implies ahaṁkāra but to transcendental error which originates ahaṁkāra itself, and which though attenuated by the subjective discipline of yama and niyama can only be conquered by the direct idealisation of the body. The willing implied in morality and religion is still bodily willing: normally there is no willing except in the body, the so-called religious willing being but a wishing or aspiration that tips bodily willing. Freedom from the body may come through grace in response to religious aspiration, but in the yoga-form of spirituality, this freedom has to be achieved by the will. Hence the necessity of reversing the direc-

[a] YB. II. 1.
[b] YS. II. 45.

tion of bodily willing: the natural movement of bodily willing which is pravṛtti towards finitising bhoga has to be turned into nivrtti-movement in the body towards the infinitude of the spirit (buddhi). Outgoing or assertive bodily willing has to be replaced by ingoing or retractive bodily willing in the form of the achievement of a tranquil posture, equable vital flow and the reversal of sense-activity.

144. The attitude of surrender to God makes directly for an effortless serene or sacred poise of the body called āsana. The poise is the consciously achieved expression of effortless strength, involving free relaxation of the will (prayatna-śaithilya) on the one hand and free identification on the other with the poise of our planet[a] or with the infinity of ākāśa.[b] The merely bodily posture may be induced by positive natural willing, the unconscious willing that holds the body together (vidhāraka-prayatna), but the spiritual poise of the body that āsana means is induced by the will not to exercise this prayatna which is in fact antagonistic to it[c] implying such strength as consists in the non-exertion of strength and in spiritual rapport with the infinite (devatā). Āsana spontaneously leads to prāṇāyāma which may be taken as control (negative—gati-viccheda, gatyabhāva etc.) of the life-function. Like vidhāraka-prayatna, prāṇa or vital activity is also an unconscious natural willing, and prāṇāyāma is the will not to exert i.e., to hold or arrest this willing. This vital willing is called vāyu and is taken in Sāṁkhya-kārikā as the function common to the karaṇas—buddhi, ahaṁkāra and indriya. Its manifest form is breathing—life felt or sensed as though it moved outwards and inwards and stood within the body; and prāṇāyāma means free breath-control. Here also, as in the case of āsana, the control though exercised in the body is spiritual willing, willing in tune with the universe, willing in the realisation of bodily life as the cosmic rhythm. This con-

[a] ananta-samāpatti or realised thought of being one with Ananta, the god holding the earth steady.

[b] 'ānantya-samāpatti'—an alternative reading, meaning ākāśādigatānantye cetasaḥ..... avyavadhānena tādātmyam— Bhoja-vṛtti II.48.

[c] cp. TV. II. 47.

[d] YS. II. 48.

trol of life spontaneously makes for control over the mind (dhāraṇā-yogyatā),[a] which in the first instance is manifest as pratyāhāra which means the retraction of the senses into the mind. The retraction is explained as the free act, objects being unpresented to the senses, absorbing the senses into the mental vṛtti that is concentrated on so that they appear to take the same form as the mind.[b] It is the mind that takes the form of the sensible, but in pratyāhāra the senses appear to take the form of the vṛtti: the free image of the object contemplated becomes sense-percept. Pratyāhāra is not mere indriya-jaya understood as the withdrawal of the senses from the objects presented to them, from evil objects or from all objects. The withdrawal, according to some, implies non-apprehension of the presented object and, according to others, the free apprehension of them.[c] Such withdrawal would in fact come under yama but pratyāhāra is a specific spiritual activity in the body like āsana and prāṇāyāma, not merely negative control of the senses but positive conquest and absorption of them by buddhi which supersedes the necessity of moral control.

145. Pratyāhāra is the consummation of spiritual willing in the body. The next three stages—the antaraṅgas or constitutive members of yoga—viz., dhāraṇā, dhyāna and samādhi imply bodi-less willing or willing in the pure spirit. These three apparently correspond to āsana, prāṇāyāma and pratyāhāra, the forms of spiritual willing in the body: willing is willing of a static attitude, of an outgoing action or of a retractive action, whether of the body or of the mind. Dhāraṇā is the fixation of the mind on a real space-position.[d] As a merely psychic process, it is interesting as a form of actual doing and not an imagined doing, the actual placing of an imagined object or image in the space-position attended to. The imagined object is the proposed content of dhyāna which in dhāraṇā is voluntarily visualised as *there*, referred to an actual position in the real world (including one's body). Ordinarily in imagining an object, if we visualise it at all with a background, the background or the spatial context is taken to be as unreal as

[a] YS. II. 43
[b] YS. II. 54
[c] YB. II. 55
[d] YS. III. 1.

the object itself. Here in dhāraṇā, however, the spatial context is real and the willing to visualise the imagined object in a position in it is just as real as the willing to see or looking for an actual object there. A presentation actually emerges in both cases as the result of and in response to the willing, the production of a desired effect being willing, whether the effect be a physical fact or a 'mere' appearance. Dhāranā is not mere imagining nor willing (attending) to know but willing to imagine in a known context, to visualise it there—it is added—for a certain desired duration. It is actually placing the imagined object there, the mind being fixed on it by its vṛtti.[a] The mind or the senses are taken in Sāmkhya[b] to be or to have their vṛtti where they function i.e., in the place where their object is referred to, not within the brain, their kriyā being not motion *in* space but the apprehending act which has space within it as its content. Dhāraṇā is, however, not a mere psychic process: like āsana, it is a spiritual process in tune with the infinite, implying a slackening of the natural effort of attention and an identification with the sacred—devatā or self or Īśvara, the visualising attitude here being a mode of negative *willing*, for otherwise real deśa or space-position would not be presented. Again, the deśa is not any arbitrary position but a position in the body or relatively to it that is prescribed as significant of the sacred content (devatā etc.) to be realised in samādhi, the significance being accepted in faith. Dhāraṇā is only a help to samādhi, to be practised in the earlier stages of yoga and may be dispensed with later.

146. Dhyāna is the continuous contemplation of the object on which the mind is thus fixed. The contemplation consists in the thinking or imagining of the object over and over again till the operation loses its intermittent character and is felt as a single process of willing and imagining, of the effort of the mind and the self-revelation of the object. Still there is a consciousness of subjective effort in fulfilment and supersession of which comes effortless samādhi where the conscious subjectivity lapses and the object alone shines out, the mind being expressed as the standing shine of the object. This samādhi is like

[a] YB. III. 1

[b] SS. V. 106

dhāraṇā and dhyāna only a member of the yoga-procedure and is distinguished from samprajñāta-samādhi or aikāgrya in which as the result of the continued practice of the three antaraṅga-yogas in successive levels of the mind, there emerges prajñāloka or the light of intuition in which all the implicit viśeṣa or particularity of the object concentrated on becomes self-evident. The antaraṅga triad—called saṁyama—is again preparatory or bahiraṅga to nirvīja or asamprajñāta-samādhi.

147. The eight-fold procedure of yoga is the spiritual discipline of willing in three stages—the subjectivistic-spiritual (or ethico-religious) stage comprising yama and niyama, the bodily-spiritual stage including āsana, prāṇāyāma and pratyāhāra, and the concrete pure spiritual stage divisible into dhāraṇā, dhyāna and samādhi. Each stage is bahiraṅga to the next stage as antaraṅga, this holding good also of the sub-stages within each stage. The whole procedure is bahiraṅga to asamprajñāta-yoga which thus is implicitly operative as the form of negative willing in all the stages and is more and more explicit and inwardised as one proceeds in the series.

148. Yoga is concentration on a variety of objects and in many grades. Each form of yoga is believed to yield a special siddhi or vibhūti—super-normal knowledge or magical control over objects. The general possibility of magical efficiency through spiritual willing has already been discussed. That a particular form of efficiency is acquired through a form of yoga is necessarily, to one who has not experienced it, a matter of faith. Yet as in the case of specific bhoga of a karma in a later birth, in some cases at least one can detect an imaginative affinity between the inward form of a particular spiritual willing and the specific vibhūti said to be acquired by it. Since yoga is a spiritual activity and not mere psychic gymnastics, the efficacy of it cannot be entirely unanticipable in imagination: the spiritual is the self-revealing. Incidentally it is pointed out that some preliminary experience of this magical efficiency of yoga is necessary for an aspirant in order to have a motive for the practice of yoga proper. In connexion with YS.1.35, Vyāsa says that faith alone in the super-natural helped by inference etc., is not sufficient to induce spiritual willing: there must be personal ex-

perience of at least some element of the super-natural content (including mukti) the realisation of which is prescribed. Without some experience of yoga-magic, spiritual activity is apt to be a matter of idealistic sentiment only.

149. The attitude prescribed for the yogin towards the magic siddhis or vibhūtis of yoga is of spiritual interest. Yoga-sūtra III.51 states about the yogin at a certain stage that the devatā of the level of buddhi conquered by him invites him to enjoy the paradise earned by him when he is expected to pass on unconcerned without desire and without conceit (saṅga-smaya). The magical powers come to be acquired but are not meant to be used for the gratification of desire. Nor should the sense of power induce the self-complacent feeling of being superior to the gods or an arrogant ascetic disdain for the paradise offered by them, which in fact is the name for a quality of spiritual satisfaction. If the yogin passes on, it is because he is genuinely afraid of slipping down and feels the urge to use the freedom already acquired to win final freedom.

CHAPTER X

THE NOTION OF ĪŚVARA

150. There is reference to Īśvara-praṇidhāna or the contemplation of God both in the first pāda and the second pāda of the Yoga-sūtras. YS. I.23 takes this praṇidhāna as an alternative procedure for the attainment of asamprajñāta. Sūtras II.1. 32,45 understand it as coming under kriyā-yoga or niyama and leading to the attainment of samādhi (II.45) which apparently is samprajñāta and only through it to the attainment of asamprajñāta. Praṇidhāna in II.1 is explained by Vyāsa as the dedication of one's willing and of the merit thereof to God, this being an emotional meditation enjoined as a karma-śesa, as an accessory to specific religious practice; while in I.23 it appears to mean pure intellectual meditation—though it is still called bhakti-viśeṣa, a special quality of bhakti. It is so called because it is still a surrender to God, surrender not merely of particular acts of willing but of the entire attitude of willing, of the willing behind knowledge itself for the sake of asamprajñāta. In other forms of bhakti there is surrender only of ahaṁkāra, not of buddhi as here. God is understood everywhere as the implicate or postulate of bhakti; but while bhakti as a kriyā-yoga implies meditation on an accepted God, God taken to be caught in buddhi, bhakti for asamprajñāta—as the surrender of buddhi itself—is meditation on a God that is manifest only through the meditative surrender or, to put it paradoxically, that is known not by knowing, by the renunciation of the conceit of knowledge. All the Sāṁkhya tattvas are known in buddhi, Īśvara as a new tattva being not included in them, because God as the object of religious bhakti would be either a feeling-construct and no tattva at all or only a self among selves with no qualitatively new character. Yoga admits God as a tattva, as a self qualitatively and not merely numerically distinct from the other tattvas. God only appears to be such in religious bhakti, and to super-religious bhakti, God is a tattva unknowable in buddhi.

151. Vijñāna-bhikṣu in his Sāṁkhya-bhāṣya makes the ingenious suggestion that the Sāṁkhya denial of Īśvara is only vyāvahārika intended in the interest of viveka to induce vairāgya for god-like power (aiśvarya); and as a matter of fact, Īśvara understood as the eternal God —not as janyeśvara, the existence of which is admitted—is taken to be only unproved[a] and not as non-existent. Any way the contemplation of God is not necessary to the distinctive spiritual discipline of Sāṁkhya and is even repugnant to it. To Yoga, the contemplation is necessary as a niyama in the lower stages of spirituality and has at least the status of an alternative sādhana for the highest stage—viz., asamprajñāta. To it but not to Sāṁkhya, God is a postulate of the activity of spiritual realisation. The exact meaning of 'postulate' here has to be determined in reference to the Kantian view of God as a moral postulate.

152. What is called the moral argument for the existence of God resolves into the position that since there is a higher and higher, there must be the highest. The question is whether it represents only an emotional or moral certitude or a logical inference. To Kant it is but a moral certitude about a content that is necessarily thought but not known. The content is not indeed an imaginative ideal like beauty or teleology, not a mere heuristic concept of rational imagination but is logically connected with the moral *ought* which, however, is only practically and not theoretically known. Not that it is therefore practically known; nor is there any moral obligation to entertain belief in it, the belief being there but apparently without any practical bearing on spiritual activity. To others, like the Mīmāṁsaka, there is an obligation to entertain the belief: the contemplation of Īśvara or of Brahman is prescribed as auxiliary to the performance of religious duty like worship or sacrifice, although the content is not regarded as a knowable truth or an absolute reality. To the Vedāntist, Brahman—not Īśvara—is the absolute truth and the knowledge of it is eternal, being contingent only in its manifestation to the individual mind and is no end the attainment of which is practically prescribed; nor is Brahman a mere symbol for a contemplation that is prescribed for its own

[a] SS. I. 92-5

sake. Between the Mīmāṁsā and the Vedānta positions, an intermediate position is conceivable viz.. that Īśvara is an absolute reality, the certitude about which and the contemplation of which emerge as one integral spiritual fact: Īśvara is not known first and then contemplated, nor does contemplation come first and then generate belief in Īśvara. Yoga apparently represents this position; and the Vedāntic position on Īśvara as distinct from Brahman is conceivably similar with the difference that Īśvara is here the eternal truth or Brahman itself with the sole vikalpa of being contemplated, or—what is the same thing—of revealing itself as absolute contemplation. To Vedānta there is knowledge of the eternal truth without the mediation of buddhi-vṛtti but not to Yoga to which the certitude about God that involves no buddhi-vṛtti is no knowledge of truth but a conviction about reality as in Kant.

153. Some proof of God is indeed attempted in Yoga-bhāṣya on the lines of the moral argument. God is mainly conceived as omniscient, as the infinite of knowledge, knowledge being the basis of spirituality, of power and goodness. Now this infinite of knowledge is inferrible on the ground that knowledge necessarily admits of increase i.e., knowledge of a content necessarily implies knowledge of a greater content that includes it, just as a magnitude is perceived necessarily as part of a greater magnitude. Whatever necessarily implies a greater implies a greatest or an infinite. This infinite of knowledge is the omniscient or sarvajña. The inference is, however, that there *must* be a sarvajña: that this sarvajña is God has to be accepted in faith. The infinite is an individual and assertorial certitude about the inferred (or necessary) existence of an individual that is unperceivable can only be yielded by the testimony of śāstra—or what is its nearest equivalent—by the testimony of our spiritual consciousness.

154. What is important in the present connection is that assertorial certitude about the infinite spirit is not yielded by inference or by any logical pramāṇa; and the implication is that the infinite spirit is not known in a buddhi-vṛtti. Faith is before and beyond knowledge though it may be quickened by it: it is through faith that spiritual knowledge (prajñā) reaches assertorial certitude. Where the knowledge is of a metaphysical content that is intuitable, the intuition is reached through yoga

started in faith. Apparently Īśvara in Yoga is unintuitable and there is no mention of the intuition of Īśvara in any form of samādhi. If He could be known at all, He would be known in some samādhi higher than samprajñāta but in asamprajñāta there is no knowledge at all. So about Īśvara, even if we know that He must exist, we can never know that he does exist. Like para-vairāgya, the śraddhā leading to the Īśvara-praṇidhāna that induces asamprajñāta is the samprasāda of viveka reached in samprajñāta, knowledge being realised negatively by the will to be free from it (para-vairāgya) and positively by the wish for such freedom (śraddhā). The motive to the will to yoga is vairāgya and the aspiration for yoga is śraddha or faith. The saṁvega or inner intensity of the will to yoga is or is determined by the depth of vairāgya. Asamprajñāta is said to be attained either directly by tīvra-saṁvega willing or indirectly by Īśvara-praṇidhāna, the former being determined by vairāgya and the latter by śraddhā. Viveka may be taken as realised by negative vairāgya into the positive will to yoga and by positive śraddhā into negative surrender of willing which is Īśvara-praṇidhāna, where Īśvara (who is nowhere mentioned as known in viveka) can only be the mystery of asbolute freedom bound up with the will-surrendering faith.

155. Faith or śraddhā has apparently two aspects—āstikya-buddhi or belief that there is a higher being than one-self and samprasāda or aspiration for a higher state of oneself. The concrete conception of the higher in either sense may be presented by śāstra but śāstra is recognised as śāstra because it is felt to interpret the faith in a higher that is already there. The concept of the higher is intrinsically bound up with the attitude of faith. The faith that emerges after viveka or self-knowledge reached in samprajñāta is faith in the existence of a higher self than the self-knowing self and in the attainability of a higher state of the self than self-knowledge, faith in Īśvara and aspiration for asamprajñāta. The aspiration is not merely subjective, for there is no place for subjectivism after samprajñāta but a self-fulfilling activity. Nor is Īśvara merely objective in the sense of being other than

the self but is higher in the sense of being capable of working in and annulling the self-consciousness (a buddhi-vṛtti) of the self and inducing in it the state of samprajñāta. The aspiration for asamprajñāta then fulfils itself through the inward working (antaryāmitva) of Īśvara, which in this connection is his grace. The aspiration thus matures into praṇidhāna or bhakti in Īśvara, which is at once a self-surrendering activity and the feeling of its fulfilment in His grace. Through this feeling of grace, self-knowledge as in viveka becomes the realisation of the self as like God. Thus God is primarily conceived through self-knowledge as higher than the self and absorbing its self-knowledge and then the realised feeling of God's grace transfigures the self with the reflection of divinity.

156. The conception of Īśvara that emerges in the faith after viveka which leads to praṇidhāna or bhakti requires to be elaborated. God is taken as a puruṣa-viśeṣa or a self qualitatively different from other selves. Other selves—as isolated from buddhi—are absolute self-repetitions: they differ only in the mode of buddhi that is their upādhi. The divine self may also be said to have a perfect buddhi (prakṛṣṭa-sattva) as its upādhi, but the difference is not only that the upādhi is perfect buddhi but also that God freely assumes the upādhi. Other selves are associated through beginningless avidyā with buddhi that is shot with this avidyā and although they can free themselves from it, they start as unfree while God is eternally free, free both to associate with and to dissociate from buddhi. Freedom means both mukti and free activity—positive and negative. God is free both in being and in activity and His free activity whether in the assumption or renunciation of buddhi—waking or sleep—does not prejudice His eternal freedom of being. In one sense, indeed, a jīvātman is eternally free, for he is only illusorily identified with buddhi as he finds out in viveka. But the illusion itself is a fact to him according to yoga and not illusory as to Vedānta, for even the jīvanmukta who recognises the illusion as such is conceived in Yoga not as passively watching the illusion that still binds him to his buddhi disappear of itself, i.e., turning out to be itself illusory but as actively seeking to free himself from it, from at least the potentiality of a body (sañcita-kar-

ma) by the creation of nirmāṇa-kāyas, such activity implying awareness of the illusion as a fact. There is apparently to Yoga no conscious realisation in life of freedom from buddhi. Yoga-bhāṣya II.27 points out that there is conscious realisation at best of freedom from the urge of the will, from the felt demand of something to be effected by buddhi but not from buddhi itself, freedom from buddhi—citta-vimukti as it is called—being an unconscious, unwilled process. The consciousness of the self in fact as eternally free is but a faith that is said to be realised through Īśvara-praṇidhāna.[a]

157. God is eternally free both in His being and in his will. The jīva's freedom of will does not belong to him as the self, being an intrinsic function of buddhi with which his self is illusorily and helplessly identified. But God's freedom in his will to assume or renounce buddhi as his upādhi belongs to him as a self: his identification with buddhi is free and does not involve an illusion. That is why his excellence (utkarṣa) and absolute reason (śāstra or logos) are said to justify each other, being in eternal mutual implication in his nature (prakṛṣṭa-sattva): his knowledge (revelation, śāstra) and his will (freedom, utkarṣa) are the same. But then it implies that his freedom to assume buddhi, to know or to reveal śāstra is his intrinsic attribute as a self. This involves a conception of the self as inactive (niṣkriya). Īśvara's freedom to assume a buddhi-body is an actual willing and hence the self generally may have to be conceived as having the capacity (yogyatā) for action which is actualised in the Divine self and is never actualised, except illusorily, in the other selves. In the case of God, there is real willing though as being absolutely free it is as much actual as unactual, his freedom of action being indistinguishable from his freedom of being or mukti. The freedom of being of other selves, even when actualised in their 'abiding in their essential nature' (svārūpāvasthāna), is not a willing to abide but only the capacity for such willing, so that there is no incompatibility with the Vaiṣṇava conception of their participation in the Divine work of the liberation of souls, though such participation would be to Yoga a mystery which is

[a] YB. I.29.

beyond philosophy. Hence, too, there is no knowledge of Īśvara in buddhi and if all knowledge of content is taken to be mediated by buddhi, there is no knowledge of Īśvara but only a faith in his reality conditioning praṇidhāna or upāsanā or bhakti. There is even no knowledge of the self as eternal and absolute (nitya-pūrṇa) but only a contemplative certitude bound up with the contemplation of God,[a] for such self-knowledge as we have is a buddhi-pratyaya.[b]

158. The buddhi with which God is said to freely identify himself is perfect or pure buddhi (prakṛṣṭa or śuddha-sattva), buddhi that is free from kleśa (transcendental error), karma (merit and demerit), vipāka (its maturation into bhoga) and āśaya (dispositions generated by bhoga). His mind represents the eternal limit (kāṣṭhā) of aiśvarya—the infinite of knowledge and will, knowledge of all that is real and resistless power having neither an equal nor a greater (sāmyātiśaya-vinirmuktam). Will (and wish) is but efficient or self-realising knowledge and what proves the existence of infinite knowledge proves the existence of the infinite mind. The existence of infinite knowledge is proved by the necessarily felt finitude of our actual knowledge though as what is inferred is only the necessity of existence, assertorial certitude about the existence of infinite knowledge can only be yielded by śāstra. The mutual dependence of the truth of śāstra and the reality of the infinite mind has already been referred to, the implication of which apparently is that the faith in the infinite mind or in the validity of śāstra is immediate. The fact of śraddhā (after viveka) is justification at once of the reality of perfect buddhi and of the truth of śāstra.

159. This justification—called 'nimitta' in Yoga-bhāṣya I.24 (interpreted as 'pramāṇa)—is cause rather than the logical ground of our belief in truth and reality, or more accurately is neither cause nor ground but something prior to both. Subjective reason or pramāṇa itself derives its prāmāṇya or validity from śraddhā or faith and that is why the inferred infinite requires to derive assertorial certitude from śāstra, requires to be given by objective reason, demands to be presented

[a] YB. I. 29.
[b] YS. II. 20.

to subjective reason independently of it. The faith in objective reason justifies subjective reason or logic in the sense of giving it assertorial certitude; and the faith in objective reason is itself justified by the infinite mind that is the content of objective reason, justified in the sense that truth is truth as emanating from or breathed forth by absolute reality. Reality emanates truth which reveals reality. That truth or objective reason or śāstra reveals reality or the infinite free self or Īśvara is because otherwise it would not be truth. Reality, too, would not be reality were it to emanate untruth, though it need not emanate either truth or untruth. The last clause implies that reality is the mystery of absolute freedom: there cannot be an unveracious God, but God may be silent as he is said to be in pralaya when he freely abstains from revealing himself. His self-revelation or assumption of buddhi-body or breathing out of śāstra as well as his self-concealment is absolutely free.

160. The infinite mind with which God is said to freely identify himself is conceived to be essentially the knowing mind. Knowledge is, however, regarded not only as receptive but as actively communicative or revelatory. God as with this mind is both sarvajña or omniscient and the eternal teacher, timeless teacher of all past teachers.[a] He is said to teach not for his own good but to save others, compassion or grace being the motive of his absolute free activity of revelation.[b] The work of this grace is conceived in different stages: he breathes forth śāstra, he quickens the reason of others from within (as antaryāmin) and he helps in their attainment of asamprajñāta. God's relation to other selves is that of the saviour to the saved, the saving work consisting in enabling others to work out their freedom, either by communicating to them knowledge in the shape of śāstra or by inducing in them inner intuitions or by directly devitalising the evil tendencies in their minds—the antarāyas or obstacles to yoga—that stand in the way of their realisation of freedom. The last is the specific work of grace responsive to Īśvara-praṇidhāna that facilitates the passage to asamprajñāta. The viveka in either presses towards absolute freedom in vairagya from viveka itself or

[a] YS.I.26.
[b] YB.I.25.

finds absolute freedom coming to him as the correlate of his bhakti.

161. For this bhakti or praṇidhāna, Īśvara is already revealed in sound as the mystic syllable 'Om' which may be regarded as at once his eternal expression and his perennial grace. The significance of language is eternal (sthita) and the restriction of particular words to particular meanings is beginningless convention which may be taken as God's will to particluarise the significance,[a] the will being free but not arbitrary, freely revealing or bodying forth the truth. The eternal significance of 'Om' which may be taken to symbolise language in general or the concept in general or truth is the absolute reality or Īśvara and the expression of reality in 'Om' would then symbolise Īśvara's permanent will to reveal or grace. Īśvara is eternally revealed in a symbol for contemplation and the contemplation is consummated not in knowledge or intuition but in a spontaneous liberation from the conceit of knowledge which is just the freedom of asamprajñāta. It is God who makes worship (praṇidhāna) possible and it is God who frees the worshipper from his own thinking mind--which is freeing him from worship itself and enabling him to work out his liberation. While then in lower stages God speaks to and vitalises man's reason, in the highest stage He frees him from his reason and from his feeling of dependence on Him which is conditioned by reason. There is no suggestion in Yoga of God raising man either into identity or into perpetual communion with Himself, though apparently Yoga would not oppose either suggestion. The precondition of such identity or communion is freedom—achieved or vouchsafed—from religious dependence and philosophy to Yoga apparently goes no further than this freedom.

162. There is no direct reference in Yoga to God's power to create or retract the universe. As in Sāṁkhya, so in Yoga, sṛṣṭi and pralaya are the functions of prakṛti or the object which is regarded as svatantra or free, uninfluenced by anything foreign to it whether in its downward path of causal pariṇāma or in its upward or anti-causal retraction of causa-

[a] YB. I. 27.

lity. Yet the movement of prakṛti is for the bhoga or mukti of embodied souls and may be regarded as in its essence the function of avidyā or aviveka that is illusorily referred to the self. Avidyā, however, is really the function of the object and its causal and anti-causal movement is nothing but this avidyā-function. Now if Īśvara operates in reference to the object, he operates primarily in the buddhi of other selves, buddhi with which they are unfreely and he is freely identified. He, in fact, operates as a nimitta primarily for the actualisation or retraction of their buddhi and through it for the creation or dissolution of the world of experience, nimitta being understood as a negative condition, the removal of pratibandha to the causal and anti-causal operation of nature. To operate as a nimitta is still his free willing: even in mahāpralaya or His sleep. He is said to freely will not to will.[a]

[a] YV. I. 24.

THE JAINA THEORY OF ANEKĀNTA

ANALYSIS

(1) Jaina Realism not only asserts a plurality of determinate truths but takes each truth to be an indetermination of alternative truths. (2) Sometimes an ultimate plurality of truths has been taken as one truth in the sense that there is one cognition of the plurality. The objectivistic equivalent of this unity of cognition is the bare togetherness of the facts known. (3) This category of 'togetherness' is the fundamental category of realism but it is only a name for quite different aspects of truth which do not make a unity in any sense. (4-5) Taking the distinction between 'subjective' knowing and 'objective' knowing what precisely is the counterpart of the knowledge of this distinction? Now, since togetherness or bare distinction is the form of objectivity, the counterpart in question must be 'distinction from distinction'. (6) This distinction from distinction has been taken as a kind of identity and the problem arises as to the relation between this identity and distinction in the objective. The Hegelian subordinates distinction to identity; Nyāya assigns priority to distinction. But the Jaina theory admits identity as indeterminate non-distinction and takes the two relations to be co-ordinate.

(7-8) The Hegelian subordinates distinction to identity in the sense that the dialectical movement ends in an absolute identity and not in an absolute distinction. But then this identity comprises all differences and is thus in the relation of identity with the differences. Identity would thus be at once a relation and a term. (9-10) To the Hegelian, identity as relation is nothing but mutual implication. But then the Identity of the Absolute synthesis with the retained being of the distinction within it is not identity as mutual implication. Apparently then the Hegelian has to admit two utterly different kinds of identity which cannot be reduced to further identity. This, however, is a contradiction. (11-14) There is a similar contradiction in the Nyāya view. We have synthetic identity of positives in this system in the form of samavāya. But this relation is a distinct existent only by self-identity. As a fact, it is only unrelated and cannot be even said to be definitely different from its terms. Relation, then, as an unrelated term is not even determinate and it is a contradiction to speak of it as self-related or unrelated and yet as determinate. (15-17) In the case of identity-in-difference then, the subordination of either relation to the other seems to lead to a contradiction. The relations of identity and difference may, however, be taken to be co-ordinate. But this would be no solution, for, on analysis it would be found that on this view, the identity of a determinate thing disappears and gives place to a dualism of the abstraction—thinghood and particularity.

(18) The only way of escape lies in taking the determinate thing to be 'simply given' i.e., to be existing as a distinct apart from distinguishing. This may be justified by the circumstance that the distinction between the subjective and the objective is itself a known object. But then distinction from the objective, taken as itself objective, implies that knowing is known as distinct from the known i.e., as *unknown*. This brings up the conception of the objective indefinite or the 'definite indefinite'. (19-22) What now is the relation indicated by the phrase 'definite indefinite'? According to the realistic postulate the 'definite indefinite' is a fact with two elements incompatible in thought. The factual equivalent of this incompatibility would be no-relation. Here then we have togetherness of unrelated or undifferenced elements. In the case of the given definite, likewise, we have the definite definite or differenced togetherness. We have thus two modes of togetherness—differenced and undifferenced—which the Jaina calls kramārpana and sahārpaṇa respectively.

(23-24) The different basal categories of objectivity corresponding to different forms of realism answer to the different aspects of the act of knowing. These categories are three in number, viz., distinction, distinction from distinction as other than distinction and the indetermination of the two. Ordinary realism is based on the first category. There are forms of realism that admit some kind of identity as distinct from distinction; and finally Jaina realism admits both in the form of indetermination. (25-30) The development of the Jaina conception of indetermination into seven alternative modes of truth analysed and assessed.

THE JAINA THEORY OF ANEKĀNTA

1. The Jaina theory of anekānta or the manifoldness of truth is a form of realism which not only asserts a plurality of determinate truths but also takes each truth to be an indetermination of alternative truths. It is interesting as suggesting a criticism of present-day realism and indicating a direction in which its logic might be developed. It is proposed in the present paper to discuss the conception of a plurality of determinate truths to which ordinary realism appears to be committed and to show the necessity of an indeterministic extension such as is presented by the Jaina theory.

2. The truth that we actually know is a plurality of truths and philosophy, rightly or wrongly, sets itself the problem of finding the *one* truth which either denies or in some sense comprises the plurality. Whatever differences there have been as to the actual conception of the truth, the rejection of the faith that there is *one* truth has generally been taken to argue a scepticism about the many truths that we claim to know. Sometimes, however, an ultimate plurality of truths has itself been taken as the *one* truth and the apparent contradiction has been sought to be avoided by taking it to mean only that there is one *cognition* of the plurality. Elsewhere the cognition of a fact is a further fact but here the addition of cognition as a fact to plurality as a fact yields us nothing but the plurality. The realistic or objectivistic equivalent of the unity of a cognitive act is the bare togetherness of the facts known; and the togetherness of cognition as a fact with the fact cognised is the exemplar of this relation.

3. The difficulty is about the objectivity of this bare togetherness. When two objects other than knowing are known together, they are ordinarily taken to be in some kind of whole, specific relation or unity. This cannot be said of object and its cognition as together. Objects also may, however, be barely together: the relation of a whole to its elements, of a relation to its terms or of a unity to its factors is nothing more specific than togetherness. This then is the fundamental category of realism; and whole, relation or unity would be understood as particular cases of it. We propose to show on the lines of the Jaina theory that this category is itself manifold, being only a name for

fundamentally different aspects of truth which cannot be subsumed under a universal and do not make a unity in any sense. Togetherness, as ordinarily understood by the realist, means distinction of determinate positive truths. The J a i n a category might be formulated as distinction from distinction which, as will be shown, has a definite range of alternative values, only one of which answers to the distinction or togetherness of the modern realist.

4. Prima facie there is a difference between the relation of a composite fact with its components and the relation of the components themselves. We may overlook for the present the different forms of the composite—whole, relation or unity—which imply varying relations to the components and provisionally admit composite truth as a single entity Now there is no difference between the togetherness of any one component with the rest and that of any other with the rest: the components in their various combinations are together in exactly the same sense. Taking, however, the composite on the one hand with the components on the other, we find that the two sides can be only thought alternately: while one side is thought by itself, the other can be thought only in reference to it; if the components are taken to be given, the composite can be understood as only *their* plurality; and if the composite is given as one, the components are known as only *its* analysis. Each side can be given by itself as objective and so it is not a cause of mere correlative *thoughts*. Neither side need be thought in reference to the other; but while one is thought as distinct by itself, the other has to be thought as only together with or distinct from it. We have in fact a correlation here between 'distinct in itself' and 'distinct from the other', between given position and what is sometimes called the negation of negation.

5. Is the necessity of thinking something *as other than its other* merely subjective? It would appear to be objective in the same sense and on the same grounds as the togetherness or bare distinction of positives admitted by the realist. Realism objectifies the subjective because it is *known* and is not simply transcendental. The question may be asked, is the distinction of subject and object, of knowing and the known, both taken to be facts—'enjoyed' and 'contemplated' respectively, to use Professor Alexander's phrase—a fact of the former or of the latter category

subjective or objective? Now just as knowing is known, the absolute difference of the two forms of knowing—enjoying and contemplating is also known; and if the unity of the knowing act be taken to correspond to objective togetherness, this absolute difference must also be taken to have its objective counterpart. Togetherness or bare distinction is the form of objectivity in general. The counterpart then of the difference of 'subjective' knowing or 'enjoying' from objective knowing or 'contemplating' would be distinction from objectivity i.e., from distinction. Thus both distinction and distinction from distinction should be taken by the realist as objective. These two, however, are not ordinarily distinguished: both are called by the same name—togetherness.

6. If however, as shown, these two forms of togetherness are fundamentally different, what is their further relation? Now distinction from distinction has sometimes been taken as a determinate relation, as identity or some unique relation, like 'characterising' or adjectivity, which also for our present purpose we may call a peculiar form of identity. The problem is accordingly about the relation of identity and distinction in the objective. We may consider two forms of identity as presented by the Hegelian and the Nyāya systems respectively. The Nyāya is avowedly a realistic system and the Hegelian theory may also in some sense be taken to be realistic. Realism proper, as we conceive it, has no place for the relation of identity in the objective except in a factitious sense, although it should—what it ordinarily does not—admit distinction from distinction as a specific category. The above two theories, however, admit both identity and distinction though they do not stress them in the same way. The Hegelian subordinates distinction to identity while the Nyāya assigns priority to distinction. The Jaina theory admits identity only in the sense of indeterminate non-distinction; and it takes the two relations to be co-ordinate without subordinating any one to the other.

7. In what sense does the Hegelian subordinate distinction to identity? No doubt he emphasises distinction to distinguish his concrete identity from abstract or formal identity but he does not admit—what a realist would admit—that an object can be distinct in itself and need not be in a comprising identity. The dialectic movement ends in an absolute identity, not in an absolute distinction. The thesis and antithesis at any stage are said to be re-

duced to 'ideality' in the synthesis, to be not only contained but also transformed by it. The identity progresses in concreteness in the sense that it dissolves in itself a deeper and deeper difference; but the absolute in the last resort is taken as the identity of the deepest differences, not as incommensurable bifurcations of an identity.

8. What, however, is this relation of *subordination* of distinction to identity? Distinction is in some sense negated by the identity; it is said to be dissolved or reduced to 'ideality' in the identity. Not that it is negated in the sense an illusory percept is said to be negated by a true percept: difference or the rich variety of the universe is not an illusion. If then difference still retains some kind of being, what is the name of the relation between this being and the being of the identity? Should it be called identity again, as apparently the Hegelian would call it? Identity then would occupy two positions: the synthesis or the composite, as we may call it, is the identity *of* the different factors and is also identical *with* them, being thus at once a relation and a term.

9. The Hegelian ordinarily understands identity as mutual implication or correlation. If A and B imply one another, each being wholly intelligible by the other, they are said to be identical. In this sense a synthesis would be taken as the identity of its factors. Is the identity of the synthesis *with* the retained being of the distinction within it also to be understood in the sense of mutual implication? The two implications that make up mutual implication must be envisaged as substantially different truths and must not be a purposeless repetition of each other in different verbal order only. If a synthesis and its factors be mutually implicatory, the synthesis implying the factors must mean some thing concretely different from the factors implying the synthesis. It cannot mean simply that the factors are *presupposed* by the unity; for that means substantially the same thing as that the factors presuppose the unity. The two sides are but the verbal explications of the same fact viz., the thought of identity-in-difference or synthesis. Synthesis implying the factors should mean then that the unity must break out *actually* into difference. In the last resort it will amount to saying that the Absolute should be *experienced*, not merely *thought*, as necessarily reproducing itself in actuality. But is the actual universe *experienced* as necessary? It is only thought to be necessary; and accordingly the implication

by the Absolute of actual differences—the necessity of its self-reproduction—is not distinct as a substantial truth from the mere *presupposition* of the Absolute by the universe.

10. The identity then of a synthesis with the retained being of the distinction within it is not an identity in the sense of mutual implication. If the relation be still called identity, it must be taken as simply intuited, as all identity is taken to be in the Nyāya. Apparently then the Hegelian, while subordinating distinction to identity, has to admit two utterly different kinds of identity, corresponding to the difference of thought and intuition, which cannot be reduced to further identity. This, however, is a contradiction.

11. A similar contradiction may be brought out in the Nyāya view. Here however, we start with the priority of distinction to identity and we have to end, as will appear presently, by admitting an identity that is not distinct from anything at all. Confining ourselves to positives, we have synthetic identity of positives in this system in the form of Samavāya or the relation of inherence. Without going into the subtle technicalities of the Nyāya in this connection, we may indicate that Samavāya is understood by it as the relation of attribute to its substratum and of a whole to its part. It is a relation of distinct objects and is regarded as what is presupposed by every other relation of existents. It is not a mere formal relation of identity: the distinction of the terms of this relation is taken to be real and to be in no sense superseded by it. Hence it is not *called* identity in this theory but it is pointed out that one term of the relation (attribute or whole) exists inseparably from the other (substratum or part), the inseparability being eternal although no term may be infinite or permanent. This eternal inseparability may accordingly be regarded as a form of concrete identity.

12. Now this identity is taken as knowable by perception, unlike the implicational identity of Hegel which is supposed to be known only by necessary thought. As a percept it is a distinct among distincts, not as in the Hegelian theory comprehensive of the distincts. Ultimately there are objects like the simple atoms distinct in themselves and not inhering in anything beyond them. Other objects like attributes and wholes exist as distinct but inseparable from their substrata. Finally, the relation samavāya or this concrete identity is also a distinct object. Thus

priority is assigned, as has been pointed out, in this system to distinction.

13. The relation of Samavāya implies three grades of distincts—objects that must be in some substratum, the substrata. and the relation itself. The question may be asked if relation is a distinct being in the sense in which the objects of the other two grades are distinct. These objects are distinct as the terms of the relation : objects which do not inhere in anything are still determinate as having attributes and wholes inhering in them. Not that the knowledge of a substance presupposes the knowledge of what inheres in it : it is known as distinct prior to the analysis. But in point of being, every object except relation must either have something inhering in it or itself inhere in something else or be in both these situations. Relation is not itself related to anything beyond, for then there would be a regressus ad infinitum. It is a distinct existent only by self-identity or sva-samavāya.

14. Self-identity, however, is not a relation of distincts at all. Granting—what is not admitted by all—that Samavāya is known by perception, this self-identity or Sva-samavāya is not a perceptible fact but is only an artificial thought-content. 'Self-related' means unrelated in the objective. Samavāya is certainly known along with its terms but as a fact it is only unrelated and cannot be even said to be definitely different from its terms. Can it then be determinate in itself? It may indeed be conceded that the determinateness of a related term does not in point of being depend on its relations : the relation of a term *presupposes* an intrinsic determination in the term. But that need not mean that the term is itself unrelated and has relation only added to it. In point of being the relation of Samavāya is eternal and so the related term is never unrelated, though as a term it is distinguishable from the relation. Relation then as an unrelated term is not even determinate and it is a contradiction to speak of it as self-related or unrelated and yet as determinate.

15. In the two conceptions of identity-in-difference above considered, the subordination of either relation to the other appears to lead to a contradiction. Shall we then take the relations to be merely co-ordinate? We may take one type of such a view as presented by W. E. Johnson (Logic, Vol. I. Chapter vii).

In the last two views, a term A can be both identical with and other than B. The present view denies it and keeps to the common-sense principle that distincts cannot be also non-distinct. Yet identity as a relation is admitted: a term X, viewed in connexion with the distincts A and B, would be said to be identical as against the distinction of A and B. Identity of X here practically means its self-identity: it is not merely the thing X but a relation in reference to the distinction. Identity of X thus implies a distinction outside X, viz., between A and B, not any distinction or plurality within itself.

16. The so-called mutual implication of the identity and distinction of two terms M and N means, according to this view, their identity *in one respect a* and their distinction in another *b*: the two relations are presented together, each being known independently. It amounts to saying that M and N are in the two relations the *same* two terms only in a factitious sense. They are two pairs of terms—M*a*, N*a* and M*b*, N*b*—presented together; and the identity of M*a*, N*a*, means that they are only different symbols of P.

17. But what does 'symbol of P' mean, it may be asked. Can we simply say that M*a*, N*a*, are P as in connexion with i.e., as distinct from and together with M*b*, N*b*, respectively? Apparently P *has* to be thought in two positions. The difference of symbols is not accidentally together with the identity P: it cannot be got rid of and cannot in the last resort be taken to be merely outside the identity, like the difference of M*b*, N*b*. In other words, a new relation—other than the mere co-ordinateness of distincts has to be admitted between P and its ultimate symbols or thought-positions. So far as the identity of P can be distinguished from this relation, it is only P-*ness* and not P; and the relation itself is but the particularity of P. The identity of a determinate thing then disappears and gives place to a dualism of the abstractions—thinghood and the particularity.

18. Ordinary realism starts with the determinate thing and would resist this analysis as artificial. But the alternative would appear to be to take the determinate thing as simply given, as implying no identity and to reject self-identity as only a meaningless phrase. What precisely is meant by 'simply given'? It can only mean 'independent of all particularising or symbolising thought'. It is to assume that the distinct exists apart from

distinguishing. If this is justified simply by the circumstance that the distinction between the subjective and the objective is itself a known object, we come back to the old difficulty about distinction within the objective and distinction from the objective. Distinction from the objective, taken as itself objective, implies that knowing is known as distinct from the known i.e., *as unknown*. If this is not a contradiction, knowing can only be understood as the *indefinite* that is known (i.e., is definite or objective) *as* the indefinite. The realistic equivalent of the relation of object and subject then is the relation of the definite and indefinite.

19. The objective indefinite has been admitted by some logicians with a realistic tendency, e.g., by Hobhouse in his Theory of Knowledge. The content of simple apprehension which to him is the standard fact is at once definite and indefinite. What is apprehended is a definite with an indefinite background. The indefinite as apprehended is so far definite but it is definite *as* indefinite, not as superseding the indefinite. Yet to Hobhouse there is knowledge only so far as the content is defined by abstraction. The knowledge of the indefinite as such is not regarded as necessitating any modification of the forms of definite knowledge. The difference of the definite and the indefinite is not understood as other than the difference between two definites. There is the other obscure relation approximating to adjectivity or identity indicated by the phrase 'definite indefinite'. But this relation, if not denied, is not considered by him at all. The Jaina recognises both these relations explicitly and obtains from their contrast certain other forms of truth, simpler and more complex.

20. The obscure relation in the content 'definite indefinite' requires elucidation. If the indefinite is definite *as such*, is this definiteness an objective character? To the realist, thought only discovers but does not constitute the object. Bare position corresponding to the simple positing act of thinking must then be objective. The indefinite is thought as *indefinite* and by the same logic the indefiniteness is also objective. The 'definite indefinite' is thus a fact but the two elements of it are incompatible in thought. The factual equivalent of this incompatibilty would be disconnexion or *no-relation*. The two elements cannot be said to be related objectively even in the way of distinction. Yet

as the elements have to be thought together, their togetherness is to be admitted as objective in the same abstract sense. Here then we have *togetherness of unrelated or undifferenced elements*. We cannot deny a plurality nor can we affirm a definite distinction: the relation is a magical alternation. This would be the J a i n a equivalent of the relation of identity. We may call it non-difference, distinction from distinction or indeterminate distinction.

21. If the given indefinite is definite *as* indefinite, the given definite is definite *as* definite. The given definite thus turns out to be a manifold, in contrast with the given indefinite. If the adjective 'definite' in 'definite indefinite' be objective, it is also objective in 'definite definite' and distinguishable from the substantive 'definite'. We use the terms adjective and substantive only in a provisional way. The adjectival definite is objective thought-position and the substantive definite as contrasted with it is objective given-ness or existence in general. As they are both distinct, their relation is definite distinction or differenced togetherness. Thus we have two modes of togetherness—differenced and undifferenced. The J a i n a calls them k r a m ā r p a ṇ a and s a h ā r p a ṇ a respectively—consecutive presentation and co-presentation, as they might be translated. To him the indeterminism or manifoldness of truth (a n e k ā n t a) presents itself primarily in these two forms of difference and non-difference.

22. The two definites in the phrase 'definite definite' mean thought-position and given-ness. They answer precisely to the elements of the determinate existent—viz., particularity and thinghood—which we obtained from the co-ordinateness of identity and distinction. In order to avoid the apparently artificial analysis, the realist takes the determinate existent as merely given. It is indeed given but so is the indefinite also given and the contrast of the two brings out the circumstance that the determinate existent is manifold—the very analysis that was sought to be avoided. The determinate existent then implies the distinct elements and is at the same time distinct from them.

23. Such is the logical predicament that is presented everywhere in the J a i n a theory. It may be generalised as a principle: the distinction from distinction is other than mere distinction and yet asserts the distinction. It is just the realistic equivalent of the simple statement that the subject is distinct from

the object and *knows* this distinction, or as it may be put more explicitly, that the knowing of knowing is the knowing of knowing *as referring to the object*. As we have already suggested, the different basal categories of objectivity with which the different forms of realism are bound up answer to the different aspects of the act of knowing. If knowing is a unity, the known is a plurality, the objective category being distinction or togetherness, If knowing is itself a duality of 'contemplating' and 'enjoying', the known or the contemplated is a duality of distinction and distinction from distinction. If finally knowledge is *of* the object, *refers to* the known, the known must present an equivalent of this *of-relation* or *reference*.

24. What is this *of-relation*? It is the relation of knowing and its content, the knowing or assertive function which is sometimes identified with the function of meaning. It is a relation, not of two contents, but of content and no-content; of being and no-being — something that is neither the one nor the other and is intelligible only by the concept of *freedom that can neither be said to be nor not to be*. This freedom, stripped of its subjective associations, is but the category of indetermination. Distinction and identity in fact—or as we call them, differenced togetherness and undifferenced togetherness (of particularity and thinghood)—are themselves related in the way of indetermination or alternation: particularity and thinghood are in *each* relation without being in the other relation *at the same time*. Identity is distinct from distinction and yet implies it, i.e., is in alternation with it. There are thus three basal categories—viz., distinction, distinction from distinction as other than distinction, and the indetermination of the two. Ordinary realism is based on the first category; there are forms of realism that admit some kind of definite identity as distinct from distinction; and finally, Jaina realism admits both in the form of indetermination, the identity being interpreted as indefinite.

25. The Jaina develops this category of indetermination into seven alternative modes of truth. The indetermination is ultimately of the definite and indefinite. Now this yields two relations—definite distinction between them and indefinite distinction. But indefinite distinction between them is to our knowledge nothing other than the indefinite as a term of it: we do not know more of the indefinite than that it is indefinite. The

most complex mode of truth then that we know is the definite distinction between the definite and the indefinite, or as we put it more explicitly, between the definite-definite and the definite-indefinite. Every other aspect of truth, as we shall see presently, is implied by it as distinct from and alternative with it.

26. Now the definiteness of the given indefinite, as has been shown already, though objective, sits lightly on the indefinite and is a detachable adjective. The conception of detachable definiteness being thus obtained, the given definite turns out to be a manifold, to be a togetherness or distinction of two definites—the detachable definite, on the one hand, or particular position which has no reference to existence or non-existence, and given-ness or existence in general, on the other, which as contrasted with the particular i.e., as characterless may be called its negation. No other negation is admitted by the Jaina to be objective: what is called absolute negation—one form of which is the contradictory—the negation of what it is not possible to affirm at all is to be rejected as not objective, as no truth at all. The definite-definite or the determinate existent may then be said both to be and not to be: particularity or pure position is its being and existence in general is its negation. There is no contradiction if we bear in mind that the being of pure position is not given existence but only what must be thought, what is objective in this sense. The same logic is sometimes expressed by saying that a determinate existent A *is* in one respect and *is not* in another respect. This does not simply mean that A is A and is not B: it means that existent A, as existence universal, is distinct from its particularity.

27. The determinate existent is, in the sense explained, being and negation as distinguishably together, together by what the Jaina calls kramārpaṇa. The given indefinite—the 'unspeakable' or a-vaktavya as it has been called—as distinct from the definite existent, presents something other than this 'consecutive togetherness': it implies sahārpana or co-presentation which amounts to non-distinction or indeterminate distinction of being and negation in the above sense. It is objective as given: it cannot be said to be *not* a particular position nor to be *non*-existent. At the same time it is not the definite distinction of position and existence; it represents a category by itself. The common-sense principle implied in its recognition is

that what is given cannot be rejected simply because it is not expressible by a single positive concept. A truth has to be admitted if it cannot be got rid of even if it is not understood.

28. So far then we have obtained four modes of truth—being, negation, their distinction and their non-distinction—all implied by the distinction between the definite given and the indefinite given. Now this distinction is itself a mode of truth: and as the definite given is taken to be being and negation or particularity and existence together, the indefinite may be considered as together with or distinct from each of these elements taken singly. It may be taken *to be* a particular i.e.. to be together with position, and it may be taken to be many undistinguishable negations, to be the universal—existence—as itself a confusion of the negations of many particulars, as not-A, not-B, not-C.... indefinitely together. Thus we have altogether seven modes of truth—bhaṅgas as they have been called—viz.. particular position or being, its negation or the universal—existence, position and negation as distinguishably together or the determinate existent, these as indistinguishably together or the indefinite, this indefinite as itself a being or particular position, as many negations together, and finally as distinct from the determinate existent. If there be an eighth mode, it would be non-distinction of the definite and indefinite, which however is but the indefinite, nothing more specific than the fourth mode.

29. The value of these modes of truth for logic cannot be fully discussed within the limits of this paper. We may conclude by pointing out that these modes of truth are not merely *many* truths but *alternative* truths. The last mode may be regarded as implying the other modes but is not therefore in any sense a comprising unity. What is implied by a mode is a different mode. The implying relation in objective terms is but indetermination. The implying mode and the implied mode are at once distinct and indefinitely non-distinct. Truth as an indetermination or alternation of truths is but manifold possibility. Each mode of truth as alternative with the others is a *possible* though it has to be taken as objective.

30. There is the conception of indeterministic will to which there are many possibles, any of which can be really chosen by it. Here we have already the notion of manifold possibility as objective to the will. But the logic of this notion has not been

sufficiently investigated, though the relations of objective possibles cannot be adequately expressed by the categories of ordinary logic. The J a i n a theory elaborates a logic of indetermination not in reference to the will—but in reference to the knowing, though it is a pragmatist theory in some sense. As a realist, the J a i n a holds that truth is not constituted by willing, though he admits that the knowledge of truth has a necessary reference to willing. His theory of indeterministic truth is not a form of scepticism. It represents, not doubt, but toleration of many modes of truth. The faith in one truth or even in a plurality of truths, each simply given as determinate, would be rejected by it as a species of intolerance. What is presented and cannot be got rid of has to be accepted as truth even though it is not definitely thinkable or is thinkable in *alternative* definite modes.

THE CONCEPT OF RASA

ANALYSIS

Artistic enjoyment (1-19).—(1-2) 'R a s a' in Indian Aesthetics signifies the essence of feeling and is to be taken either as an eternal feeling or as an eternal value that is felt. It is not, however, 'essence' in any intellectual sense and is to be understood purely in terms of feeling. It is the feeling par excellence and stands on a new level compared to other feelings. (3-6) In a direct feeling like enjoying an object, the contrast between the subject and the object becomes blurred; the object appears to have an enjoyable expression and the subject feels weighed down or attracted into the object. In sympathetic joy, on the other hand, where the direct object is another's joy, the sympathising subject does not lose the sense of distinction between his feeling and the feeling that is sympathised with. In the original feeling, again, the expression—joyous or otherwise—is presented as adjectival to the object of the feeling: in sympathy the expression is presented as detached from the object and as floating on it and the freedom of the sympathetic feeling is reflected in the object of the original feeling as this detachment of expression. It is because of these features that sympathy may be taken to belong to a higher level than the feeling sympathised with.

(7-9) Beauty, again, is not presented as a quality of the object. It is presented as an eternal or self-subsisting value very much like the expression of the original object in 'sympathy with sympathy'. (10-11) Aesthetic enjoyment thus stands on a level higher than ordinary sympathy and is on a par with duplicated sympathy. In some cases the artistic sentiment may be literally taken as sympathy with sympathy. My aesthetic enjoyment may be the feeling for an *actual* person feeling for an actual third person. In other cases, one or both of these persons may be imaginary. (12) Every feeling that is depicted in art is contemplated in aesthetic enjoyment as sympathised with by the Heart-Universal and the person who contemplates the feeling merges his private heart in this ubiquity. (13-14) We have thus three levels of feeling—contemplative, sympathetic and primary. This scheme of three levels can be kept up in the case of the enjoyment of natural beauty quite as much as in that of the enjoyment of a work of art. The beauty of an object implies three features distinguishing it from the object—expression, detachment and eternity. These three characters can be understood in the object as the projections of primary feeling, sympathetic feeling and contemplative feeling. (15) Artistic enjoyment is free. It is conceived not merely as free from the entanglement of fact but as the realisation of an eternal value, as the identification with the aesthetic essence without loss of freedom. (16-19) The nature of this realisation elucidated.

The beautiful and the ugly (20-29).—(20-21) The feeling for the ugly as an objective expression is quite as much aesthetic as the feeling for the beautiful. And in both cases the objective aesthetic quality cannot be discovered except through the aesthetic feeling. (22-23) Identity with the object is felt in all the grades of feeling. But distinction from this object is not felt or not felt uniformly in all the levels. In primary feeling, the distinction is not felt explicitly. In sympathy, it is felt explicitly while the feeling of identity is implicit. In the stage of contemplative feeling, both the feelings of identity and difference are explicit. (24) The feeling of identity is one of enjoyment and the feeling of difference is one of pain. The two feelings cannot simply stand side by side: one is subordinated to the other. The feeling of beauty emerges when pain is subordinated to the enjoyment, but where the enjoyment is subordinated to pain there emerges the feeling of ugliness. (25-26). The enjoyment of the tragic analysed. (27-29) The contemplative-aesthetic enjoyment of the ugly analysed and identified with the **bībhatsa-rasa** of Indian aesthetics.

THE CONCEPT OF RASA

I

ARTISTIC ENJOYMENT

1. Indian aesthetics presents the characteristic concept of r a s a for which it is difficult to find an English equivalent. Literally 'r a s a' means two things among others—it means essence and it means what is tasted or felt. The aesthetic conception of r a s a combines the two senses and signifies the essence of a feeling, which is indifferently taken either as an eternal feeling or as the object of it, an eternal value that is felt. 'Essence', however, is an intellectual concept and the phrase 'essence of feeling' requires explanation. 'Essence' here is not taken in the sense of a logical universal. There is no suggestion in the Indian theory of art, as in certain other theories, that the same universal that is known as the essence of things is apprehended in feeling in a confused way as r a s a. The logical universal has sometimes been identified with the ideal for life and the aesthetic essence has been conceived as the ideal that is felt or the feeling of the ideal. R a s a in the Indian conception is not identified with the Idea or universal truth, or with the ideal to be realised or as realised. It is understood purely through feeling and in terms of feeling; and if it is to be called essence or ideal, it can only be by way of metaphor. There is danger, however, of making too much of the metaphors both in the general theory of art and in the actual criticism of particular works of art. (Aesthetics—to start with at any rate—should not assume any speculative or religious postulates). What appears valuable to artistic feeling need not so appear—at least to the same degree—to the intellect or to the will, and feeling here should have the final say.

2. 'R a s a' means either aesthetic enjoyment or that which is aesthetically enjoyed. The significance of the concept is best interpreted by the orientation of aesthetic enjoyment in reference to other feelings. As will be explained presently, the artistic sentiment is not merely a feeling among feelings but the feeling par excellence, standing as it does on a new grade or level altogether as compared with other feelings. The place of a feeling is sometimes assigned in reference to the truth or known content with which

it is bound up or to the order of its emergence in mental evolution. It, however, does not help us far to find the significance or distinctive value of the feeling. This is best understood by the determination of the level or mental plane to which the feeling belongs.

3. We may begin by distinguishing between the direct feeling of an object and sympathy with such feeling. We speak of enjoying an object. What is the implication of the transitive use of the verb 'to enjoy'? It does not mean—at least to the enjoyer--that the object is only a means to the enjoyment: he feels no distinction between his enjoyment and the object. In this sense the clear-cut contrast of subject and object becomes obscured for feeling. The subject of the enjoyment unconsciously affects and is affected by the object. The object does not appear to him as a mere fact but as having a value, an enjoyable look or expression. The subject, too, does not feel his detachment from the object: he feels attracted into or weighed down by the object.

4. Consider next a feeling of which the direct object is another feeling, say, in a separate mind. This feeling of a feeling is to be distinguished from the mere understanding of it as a fact, which may leave one cold. Neither should it be confused with merely having a like feeling on the occasion of another's feeling. To sympathise with a person is to feel *him* feeling: only in this sense is his feeling the direct object of my feeling. We refer specially to sympathy, as it is the most familiar form of the feeling of feeling.

5. In sympathising with a child enjoying his toy, I am not interested like the child in the toy itself but in his enjoyment. Sympathy with joy is also joy but it is freer than the primary joy. I do not unconsciously project the joyous look or expression on the toy. I do not *see* it there like the child: I at best feel like *imagining it*. Nor do I like him feel fascinated by the toy, feel attracted into or glued down as it were to the toy. Not that I am altogether free in my sympathy, for I am still affected by the child's joy as a fact though not by the object of it, attracted by the particular feeling of the individual child as a compelling subjective fact. Even here, however, I do not lose the sense the child between my feeling and the child's feeling in the sense the child loses it between his feeling and the object of it.

6. By reason of this freedom then, feeling of feeling--of which we take sympathy as the type—may be taken as constituting a

higher level than the feeling of an object. We have next to consider if artistic enjoyment does not belong to a higher level still. That it has at least something of the freedom of sympathy can hardly be disputed. But it may be said that we seem to directly enjoy the beauty of an object and the beauty appears to be just as much *seen there* in the object as the terrible look of an object to one who feels terror. Where, it may be asked, is the distinction between such enjoyment and an ordinary object-feeling like terror? How does the former stand on a higher level—the level at least of sympathy? How sympathy with a feeling affects the object of the feeling requires first to be considered. Every feeling affects its object by lending a look or value to it. Sympathy does not indeed affect the object of the feeling sympathised with. To a person afraid of an object, the object has a terrible look but not one who sympathises with his fear. But the sympathiser, although he does not *see* the expression there, tends consciously to project something similar, to imagine seeing it there. The look or aspect that is consciously imagined differs from that which appears to be seen. The latter is presented as one with the given fact, as adjectival to it; whereas the former is presented as detached from the fact—as floating on it or as shining beyond it. The freedom of the sympathetic feeling, in fact, is reflected in the object as this detachment of expression from given fact, as expression 'in the air' without a substratum.

7. Now the beauty of an object, though not consciously projected on it by artistic feeling, does not appear to such feeling, as a quality or adjective of the object in the way the terrible aspect of an object does to one in fear. It is presented as a floating or transcendent expression like that which is consciously projected by sympathy on the object of the feeling sympathised with. The circumstance that beauty is not consciously projected but appears to be seen does indeed make a difference, to be explained presently. But that beauty is not presented as an adjective or quality of the object distinguishes it from the reflex of an object-feeling. That is why aesthetic enjoyment is taken to belong to a higher level than object-feeling. The question remains if it belongs to a level higher than sympathy.

8. We have pointed out that sympathy though unaffected by the object of feeling sympathised with, is still affected by and limited to the particular feeling and the individual subject to it.

In sympathy, the detachment is felt from objective fact but not from subjective fact, though the distinction from the subject sympathised with is not observed. But there may be such a feeling as sympathy with sympathy. One may sympathise, for example, with a mother feeling for her child suffering. Just as my sympathy with a person's feeling of an object is unaffected by the object, so my sympathy with a person's sympathy for a third person's feeling is unaffected by the feeling. It is thus on the level of this duplicated sympathy that a feeling can be emotionally contemplated in a detached way, felt as dissociated from its character as a given subjective fact, realised as self-subsisting value. To simple sympathy with a feeling, the object of the feeling has already a detached expression which, however, lacks reality by reason of the detachment. To this duplicated sympathy, the expression of the object is not only detached but self-subsisting, having a felt independent reality of which the given object is only a kind of symbol. Since it is altogether detached from the particularity of fact, it is a kind of eternal reality, a real eternal value.

9. Beauty, we hold, is just such an eternal value and aesthetic enjoyment accordingly belongs to the level of duplicated sympathy—sympathy with sympathy. That the beauty of an object appears to be seen rather than imagined shows that to feeling it has a reality not inferior to that of the object as a given fact. That it is not seen as a quality or adjective of the object and is yet not presented as another object side by side with it implies that it is reality to which the *object* is somehow adjectival or subordinate. As, however, there would be no sense in saying that the object is a quality of the beauty, the adjectivity of the object here has to be recognised as a peculiar relation—the relation of the symbol to the symbolised, an analogue in the sphere of feeling of the logical relation between a word and its meaning.

10. Aesthetic enjoyment thus stands on a level higher than ordinary sympathy which again constitutes a level higher than primary object-feeling. The artistic sentiment may in some cases be literally taken as sympathy with sympathy. I may, for example, enjoy contemplating an old man affectionately watching his grandchild playing with a toy. Contrast here the child's joy in the toy with the grand-father's sympathetic joy and this again with my contemplative joy. Although the old man is not immersed like

the child in the enjoyment of the toy, his feeling is not yet of the artistic character: it is still a personal selective interest in the particular child and his feeling.. My contemplative joy has no such personal complexion. I am interested in the child's feeling reflected in the grand-father's heart as an eternal emotion or value. I enjoy the essence of the emotion, get immersed in it even like the child in the toy, without, however, being affected by it and thus losing my freedom. I no longer feel the distinction between my feeling and the child's feeling, as the old man does between his feeling and the child's feeling. My personality is, as it were, dissolved and yet I am not caught in the object like the child. I freely become impersonal.

11. In the above example, my aesthetic enjoyment is feeling for another actual person feeling for a third actual person. But one or both of these persons sympathised with may be imaginary. Consider a case where the second person is imaginary. I may aesthetically contemplate a poor waif in the street. The waif is beautiful to me not as a dirty child but as it may be somebody's darling. I contemplate what the child would be to its mother, had she been living. The mother is here an imaginary person. A case in which the third person is imaginary would be where I contemplate a mother treasuring up the toys of her child who is no more. She sees the same value in the toys as though the child were living and playing with them. The child is here the imaginary person but the mother's emotion is still actual or personal and it is to me alone who contemplate the emotion a beautiful theme of art. Again both the persons are imaginary when, for example, I comtemplate a character in a drama. The character is here the imaginary third person or primary subject; but who, it may be asked, is the sympathising second person?

12. There is a difference between imagining an object as actual and imagining it as imaginary. In the former, the object is imagined as presented to an actual feeling of the person imagining as, for example, a savoury dish imagined by a hungry person. In the latter, the feeling bodying forth the image is itself imaginary: the object is imagined as what would be imagined by another person having the actual feeling. Now the character in the drama is not imagined by me as an actual person: I imagine some one imagining the character as an actual person and I sympathise with this imaginary 'some one' as the second person.

The imaginary second person is not one particular person but *some one* or *any one* person. He has the value of a concept of a person in general: only here we have in the concept an efflux of feeling and not of the intellect. This person is felt—not thought—by me who am aesthetically contemplating. The felt-person-in-general may be semi-mythologically called the Heart Universal. Every feeling that is depicted in art is contemplated as reflected in or sympathised with by this Heart Universal and the person who contemplates the feeling merges his personal or private heart in this ubiquity. Artistic enjoyment is not a feeling of the enjoyer on his own account; it involves a dropping of self-consciousness, while the feeling that is enjoyed—the feeling of the third person—is freed from its reference to an individual subject and eternalised in the Heart Universal.

13. Can we keep up the scheme of three persons or three grades of feeling—contemplative, sympathetic and primary—in the case of the enjoyment of the beauty of a natural object? Here also we may take the second and the third persons as imaginary and implicitly intervening between the contemplator and the object. Only here the third person is evanescent—some person rather than a particular imaginary person like the character in the drama spoken of. When I appreciate the beauty of a natural object. I imagine in the first place a particular primary feeling—say, joy or sorrow or fear—according as the object has a joyous or melancholy or fearful expression. This feeling is imagined as the feeling of 'some one', of an indefinite third person. The indefiniteness here, like the conceptual character of the second person referred to, is felt and not thought. It implies that the third person is indifferent to me: I am interested less in him than in his feeling. This feeling is next idealised by being contemplated as felt by or reflected in the second person—the Heart Universal. Lastly, I, the first person, feel this idealised feeling as my direct object.

14. Is this an artificial analysis? We have indicated that the beauty of an object does not appear as a mere fact—a quality of the object like its colour but as an expression or value. The expression, however, unlike the reflex of a primary feeling, is not seen as one with the object or adjectival to it but as floating on it or as irradiating beyond it. At the same time it is not presented like the reflex of a sympathetic feeling as an expression 'in the

air': it is to aesthetic feeling a real eternal value. The beauty of an object, thus, implies three characters distinguishing it from mere fact—expression, detachment from the object and eternity. These three can only be understood in the object as the respective projections of primary feeling, sympathetic feeling, and contemplative feeling. The feelings have to be understood as the feelings of three persons who may, however, all be in one person, viz., the aesthetic enjoyer in three different emotional levels at the same time. Since the last grade of feeling comprehends the other two, we have taken aesthetic enjoyment as not merely a feeling among feelings but as the feeling *par excellence*.

15. The conception of r a s a or aesthetic essence may thus be interpreted entirely in terms of feeling, without any reference to the intellectual Idea or the spiritual ideal. We have indicated the place and significance of aesthetic joy by determining the level or grade of feeling to which it belongs. A further elaboration is necessary to bring out the distinctive flavour of the Indian concept. Artistic enjoyment is conceived not merely as *free* from the entanglement of fact but as the *realisation* of an eternal value, as an identification with the aesthetic essence without loss of freedom. What is the precise sense in which this realisation or identification is understood? To answer the queston, we have to consider first certain features of primary feeling and sympathy.

16. We have pointed out that in a primary feeling—say, sensuous enjoyment of an object, the distinction of feeling and the object is obscured: the object gets an expression and the feeling loses its subjective detachment. Yet the confused unity of the object-immersed feeling has two alternative directions, the objective and the subjective. In the objective direction the self-feeling lapses: the object alone is perceived as with the expression adjectival to it. But the subject need not be in the perceiving or objective attitude; it may retain the feeling-attitude, while the object perceived gets indefinite and melts away, much as to a drowsy person the fixed world appears to swim and shimmer away into nought. This would be the subjective direction. Instead of the subject forgetting itself in the object, we have the object here getting dissolved in the subjective feeling. To understand it, we have to remember how in respect of an object in one's clasp, there is a difference between trying to enjoy it and actually enjoying it. When one is only trying to enjoy, the

feeling has indeed begun; but there is a constant sense of not being able to enjoy, of the object refusing to be enjoyed, to melt into the feeling. This tantalizing experience constitutes the unreal character that attaches to the incipient feeling. To successfully enjoy, to have the object dissolved in one's feeling, is to get rid of the felt unreality. The feeling here becomes subjectively real: it stands by consuming the object.

17. Two forms of sympathy may be distinguished corresponding to these two directions of object-feeling. Although in sympathy, the distinction between the sympathiser and the person sympathised with is never lost, the two subjects do not simply stand side by side. The sympathiser either feels through the other person's heart or feels the other person within his own heart. In the former case I feel *out* towards the other person, feel my detachment from him to be an evil, seek to forget myself, to feel as though I were the other person feeling and to become the other person in this sense. In the latter case, I feel my sympathy with him to be unreal so long as the other person is foreign and his feeling a mere fact which I cannot feel as mine. In the former I resent my detachment, in the latter his foreignness. In both I strive to feel freedom; in the former by expanding, by projecting myself outwards and in the latter by assimilating or drawing in, feeling his feeling as mine. We may accordingly call these the projective and the assimilative types of sympathy.

18. Similarly the identification with the object in the aesthetic enjoyment has two alternative directions—the projective or creative direction and the assimilative or abstractive direction. What is enjoyed in the object is its beauty which we have taken as an eternal self-subsisting value to which the object is related as a symbol. The symbolising function in the aesthetic sphere is of two kinds. The object that is the symbol may retain its definite character of fact and express a value as its transcendent significate, or its fact-character may get evanescent while the value symbolised gets defined out as a subtile spirit-form, as a dream floating in the ether of the heart and nowhere in space and time. Either way the enjoyer identifies himself with the eternal value. But whereas in the former he enters into the object freely, overcomes its opacity and sees himself as the soul of it, the heart of its reality; in the latter, he dissociates himself from the object as mere fact which accordingly tends to dissolve, to have its hard

outlines softened away, and feels rather than sees the soul of it freeing itself and merging in his enjoyment. In the former, the feeling becomes objective but does not get entangled in the given fact: it transfigures the fact into a value. In the latter, the detachment of the subject does not imply a feeling of unreality: the value or soul of the object is drawn out as it were and reposefully enjoyed. In the former, there is freedom in spite of enjoying contact: and in the latter, enjoyment or reality in spite of detaching freedom.

19. Indian art is prevailingly abstractive or contemplative in character and not dynamically creative: and in the Indian theory of art, the aesthetic essence is conceived as a subjective absolute or r a s a rather than as an objective absolute or beauty.

II

THE BEAUTIFUL AND THE UGLY

20. In the previous part, I did not distinguish between the feeling for the beautiful and the feeling for the ugly. I was concerned there mainly with the general level or grade to which both these feelings belong. In the present part, I have endeavoured to bring out the specific nature of the feeling for the ugly and the varying aesthetic values of ugliness as an objective expression.

21. As in the previous part, so here I rule out the question as to what there is in the object that makes it appear beautiful or ugly. Formal characters like symmetry or unity in variety, such as are ordinarily spoken of as constituting beauty, are not only inadequate for a definition but appear to presuppose the aesthetic feeling from which they derive their specific meaning. For one thing, an important element of beauty is subjective association: the objective formal element is not all. Besides, what does symmetry or unity in variety mean? Any geometrical symmetry is not beautiful: what particular symmetrical form is beautiful depends on the intuition of the artist and thus presupposes the artistic feeling. Similarly as to unity in variety: it all depends on what the artist *feels* to be the satisfying unity. The formal characters in their generality, apart from the particularising feel-

ing of the artist, mean almost nothing. Certain forms in certain contexts may indeed appear beautiful in many cases, though not in all cases. This, however, is a matter of technique which is but a summary of particular artistic experiences. A general theoretic discussion of the objective characters of beauty and ugliness appears to me, therefore, to be unprofitable. Not that I deny that there is something in the object that determines the aesthetic feeling. I believe, in fact, that the aesthetic attitude does not create but only discovers beauty or ugliness, and that while an object that appears indifferent to others has an aesthetic value to one already in the attitude, there are objects which perforce induce the attitude in many souls, if not in all. At the same time I hold that the objective aesthetic quality cannot be discovered except through the aesthetic feeling, that it is only by this feeling and not by any merely intellectual investigation that we can analyse beauty or ugliness in the object, and that the analysis can only be of a piecemeal character in the form of particular intuitions and can never be exhausted by any objective formula. So, as in the previous part, I confine myself here to an analysis of the mental attitude.

22. All feeling implies an identification of subject and object. Contrast the thought of an object with the feeling of it. The former implies a detachment from the object, the latter an intimacy with it. To thought, the intimacy appears to be a confusion, while to feeling the detachment means inanity or unreality of the subject. The subject feels itself real when it is filled with the object, when it feels the object united or identified with itself. What to thought is but a confusion is to feeling a real identity.

23. Identity with the object is felt in all feeling. Is distinction from the object also felt? Not in the grade of primary feeling. In some sense, indeed, all feeling of pain is a feeling of distinction between subject and object, but in the grade of primary feeling, the distinction is not explicitly felt as such. In the grade of sympathetic feeling, the distinction from the object of the feeling sympathized with is explicitly felt while the identity continues to be felt with the primary feeling. The two attitudes, however, do not enter into any relation in this stage: the feeling of identity here is only implicit and is completely merged in the explicit feeling of difference. In the contemplative feeling, both

the feelings of identity and difference are explicit. The subject freely merges into the object and the object tends to get dissolved in the subject. That is the identity. The object gets idealised into a standing expression, into a sort of objective mind and the subject feels real in joy by consuming the object. At the same time the feeling of identity is a process. There survive aspects of the object which stand out un-idealised as full fact and there is a persistent sense of not being able to enjoy along with the joy that has begun. The feeling (as un-idealised fact) of the inability to enjoy is the feeling of distinction between subject and object. It is still a feeling on the aesthetic plane because it would not arise but for the idealisation or enjoyment, the identity that is already felt.

24. If the feeling of identity be called enjoyment, the feeling of difference may be taken as a pain, both the feelings being on the artistic or contemplative level. Now enjoyment and pain cannot simply stand together side by side: one is subordinated to the other, subordination being a unique relation in the sphere of feeling. When the pain is subordinate to the enjoyment, we have the feeling of beauty. Where the enjoyment is subordinate to pain, there emerges the feeling of ugliness and its congeners.

25. To explain. Take the artistic contemplation of sorrow. A well-told tale of sorrow moves one to tears, who yet gets exquisite enjoyment out of it. The pain is here subordinate to the enjoyment. The pain is still explicitly felt and felt in fact more exclusively, though not, it may be, more intensely than by the primary subject of the sorrow. Sorrow to the primary subject has its distraction and has, more often than not, an admixture of other and sometimes quite incompatible feelings such as the subject may be ashamed to confess. But the contemplative subject is absorbed in the sorrow in its purity, stripped of all its accidents. That does not mean that he contemplates the mere feeling of sorrow and has no interest in its objective setting: that would be only logical abstraction. He contemplates the setting also—such circumstances as bring out the feeling and are suffused with the feeling-value, though there is a difference still between the centre of interest and the setting like that between a flame and its halo or irradiated light. But the primary subject of sorrow has not only the sorrow and its aesthetically relevant setting presented to him but also other feelings and objective cir-

cumstances along with them which have no affinity of tone with the sorrow. These are what I call 'accidents'. The aesthetic enjoyer contemplates the painful feeling of sorrow stripped of such accidents. To aesthetically realise or contemplate a person's sorrow is to *feel* the *sorrow*, not to think it, though it is to feel it as a pure eternal value such as the person himself is not privileged to feel. I say 'privileged', because though the sorrow is a more exquisite or penetrating (though not more intense) pain to the contemplator than to the primary subject, the former does not in the feeling lose his freedom like the latter, but feels himself more real as a spirit through the pain than if he did not experience it. So even where the pain is not itself artistically enjoyed, it is no mere evil to be avoided: its purity and depth are in themselves a spiritual value.

26. But the artistic contemplation of sorrow is an enjoyment. The sorrow is felt as an exquisite pain but it is still the object of the enjoyment and in this sense subordinate to it. As a felt object it is one with the enjoyment, turned into it, transfigured. As an object of contemplative feeling, it is still distinct, the sorrow continuing to be felt in its purity within the enjoyment. This relation of 'within' or subordination has only to be accepted as a matter of experience; it can only be explicated, not disputed. So any kind of primary feeling in its purity may be the object of enjoyment and subordinated to it; when the primary feeling is itself an enjoyment, it is completely merged in the contemplative feeling, merging being the limit of subordination.

27. But while any feeling may be subordinated to aesthetic joy, it *need* not be. That depends, so far as the subject is concerned, on the depth of his artistic realisation. Potentially, I believe the artistic spirit can swallow and assimilate every kind of feeling, subordinate the most refractory of feelings to itself, transmute all painful feelings into enjoyment. As a matter of fact, however, it cannot or does not in many cases transmute the presented feeling : it lacks either the energy or the transparency of the soul requisite for it, this being entirely a matter of inborn gift or previous discipline. Artistic feeling represents a new depth of the spirit: contemplative level is deeper than the level of primary feeling or sympathy. But there are varying depths within the contemplative level and a primary feeling which stands out untransmuted in one grade of aesthetic feeling

may be transmuted into joy in a deeper grade. Where a primary feeling presented to the aesthetic attitude is not assimilated, the joy of the attitude is present but gets subordinated to the presented feeling. The presented feeling is here a pain, a feeling that emerges in the joyous aesthetic attitude as distinct from it. So in the artistic contemplation of sorrow just considered, the sorrow is presented as distinct, as a pain to start with. But the pain is there the object of the joy while in the present case the joy is the object of the pain. The joy of the aesthetic attitude is here itself a torture which lends a new value to pain. But for the joy, in fact, the pain would not take the form of disgust. That is the sense in which I understand the subordination of enjoyment to pain. When the aesthetic feeling, unable to assimilate a presented primary feeling, gets thus subordinated to it, it turns into the feeling of ugliness. The implications of this account of ugliness have to be brought out. The primary feeling is here present to the aesthetic feeling. That means it is raised to the contemplative grade, stripped of accidents, isolated in its purity. A fact viewed in the scientific or practical attitude is neither beautiful nor ugly. It is only when it is aesthetically contemplated that it appears beautiful or ugly. When so contemplated, the fact as such retires into the back-ground and its expression or value as due to a primary feeling comes into prominence, this being viewed through the double medium of sympathy, as indicated in the previous part. The primary feeling as presented to the aesthetic attitude is thus itself turned into a contemplative feeling.

28. Next this contemplative feeling enters into a relation with the aesthetic feeling to which it is presented. The aesthetic attitude is in itself a joy, not merely an expectation of joy: it is joyous expectancy waiting to turn by its alchemy any new experience into joy. But the alchemy may not be potent enough. The new experience may be refractory and then the joyous expectancy is turned into bitterness or disgust so that the refractory experience gets an extra painful value, viz., the repulsive or disgusting value. The experience itself as a contemplative presentation is not repulsive: it is so only because of there being baffled expectation of joy.

29. When repulsion is thus felt on the contemplative level, there are many alternative ways in which the spirit saves itself.

The contemplative attitude may be withdrawn altogether and there may be a simple relapse to the normal practical attitude. Or it may happen that the spirit keeps on the contemplative level and the artistically refractory experience is side-tracked into contemplative channels other than the artistic. Received first in the artistic attitude as an un-welcome kill-joy, the experience may be presently draped off for philosophic or religious contemplation. The aesthetic expectancy is retracted but the spirit may be overborne by the hideousness of the world. The ordinary spirit is not artistic enough to stand ugliness for any length of time, to maintain the joy of the aesthetic attitude while either shaking off the repulsive experience or transmuting it into joy with the patience and faith of a courageous love. Yet there are spirits where joy is too deep to be killed by a repulsive experience and whose artistry is potent enough to evolve a beauty rich and strange out of presented ugliness. The aesthetic attitude survives the feeling of ugliness in two ways. It may, in the first place, turn into the feeling of the ludicrous which is just the joy of detaching oneself from or shaking off the repulsive experience. The feeling of ugliness is itself a contemplative feeling but the artistic spirit may retire to a deeper level and rejoicingly contemplate the ugly in an attitude of superior detachment. It rejoices either in having eluded its touch and in being able to watch it from a secure distance or in the sense of power to blow it away and turn it into thought—I mean the explosive power of laughter, these being the two directions of the feeling of the ludicrous. The other aesthetic attitude in which ugliness can be negotiated is what I have characterised as the patient faith of courageous love. The faith that the ugly can be transmuted into beauty is familiar enough in the artistic sphere. It is in fact what makes aesthetic education possible . No one will condemn more than the artist the conceit—which is unfortunately common to-day—that refuses to admit the need of educating the taste and the possibilities of realising what immediately appears ugly as beautiful through such education. It is this faith then that sustains what we may call aesthetic effort—the effort to deepen the feeling of ugliness into an enjoyment, to perceive the immediately ugly in its infinite setting and thus to realise it as beautiful. During the effort, the ugly remains ugly but becomes tremulous with the shimmer of expectant delight; the faith becomes objective as the suggestion of a beauty that is not yet manifest. And then as the aesthetic faith turns into vision and attainment, there emerges a Beauty Triumphant in which ugliness is itself realised in its quintessence as an object of enjoyment. This enjoyed quintessence of ugliness is just what Indian aesthetic daringly recognises as a rasa viz., the bībhatsa-rasa. Such recognition does credit to the virility of Indian art and to the Indian theory of art.

THE SUBJECT AS FREEDOM

VOL. II

ANALYSIS

CHAPTER I

The Notion Of Subjectivity (sec. 1—24)

(1) The 'object' is what is meant by the 'subject', and the subject is other than the object. The subject cannot, therefore, be a meant entity, yet it cannot be denied that there is some awareness of the subject. This awareness must then be something other than meaning-awareness. (2-3) (i) A word is said to *mean* an entity or produce a meaning-awareness when the speaker of the word and its hearer could use that word to understand the self-same entity. The word 'I' cannot be so used. It cannot then be said to *mean* anything. Yet it is undoubtedly understood by the hearer. This understanding is thus produced through the word but not through the meaning of the word. (ii) Again, the communicating act of the speaker is never a part of what is meant by a word. But when a person uses the word 'I', it is not his self only but the self as speaking or expressing itself that is understood. His self-consciousness is not merely expressed but is also *incarnated* in the word. (4) The term 'I', as *used* has a uniquely singular reference, but as *understood* it is general. It is thus unlike a term meaning an objective content which has the same reference to the hearer as to the speaker. What is meant by 'this' is not what is conveyed by 'I', though the latter may be indicated by 'this'. (5-8) The object is meant by 'this' and the subject is indicated by the three personal pronouns. There are six possible equations of 'this' with the three personal pronouns. But of these six possibles, three (viz., 'this is I' 'this is you' and 'he is this') are not believed, and the three that are believed (viz., 'I am this', 'you are this', and 'this is he') represent a felt but not a known content. None of the six equations is thus logically intelligible. (9) The object is known as distinct from the subject while the subject is known in itself. The subject is not known as related to the object : it is at best dissociated from the object with which it was identified. (10) The subject understood as the unique speaker of 'I' and the object that is meant as distinct from the subject are the two things that are known. But the object is not known with the same assurance as the subject. The unreality of an object or that

which is meant is perfectly intelligible : it is meaningless, however, to speak of the unreality of the subject. But the subject as a known fact is always a spoken fact unlike the object which may be known without being named.

(11) There is properly no metaphysic of the subject. The awareness of the subject is midway between mystic intuition and the consciousness of a meaning. The exposition of it is, accordingly, midway between mysticism and metaphysic. As, however, the subject is communicable by speech, it cannot be taken as falling outside philosophical enquiry. (12) The attitude of metaphysics is objective. It seeks to know reality as distinct from the knowing of it. Knowing is not known as a distinct fact, being only distinct through the self-conscious act of distinguishing it. To realise that the distinctness of knowing is entirely through the distinguishing of it is to realise knowing as a self-evidencing fact. (13) There is nevertheless the belief in the facthood of knowing as a 'function' i.e., as a positive something which can be literally expressed only in the negative way as what the known object is not. The awareness of this unmeant something involves, however, a higher certitude than the belief in the meant object. The knowing 'function' *is* only as the free reference of the subject to the object. (14) This felt reference is the positive freedom of the subject having different felt modes—like knowing, feeling or being—which can be symbolised by objective meanings. (15) In speaking of its function, the subject believes in it neither as meant nor as unmeant but as being constructed as fact by being spoken. The speaking creation of a system of subjective functions constitutes a study other than metaphysics and Epistemology.

(16) This new study may be called Spiritual or Transcendental Psychology which elaborates the believed facthood of the subjective functions into a system of symbolisms. The symbolism is the form of the non-theoretic or spiritually practical mode of escaping the objective knowing attitude and of cultivating a subjective attitude. Spiritual psychology symbolises the subjective attitude by the objective attitude from which it seeks to be freed. (17) The distinguishing of 'knownness' as an abstraction from the known object is *psychological* introspection and the consciousness of the subjective functions of 'knowing' etc., as other than this abstraction may be called *spiritual* introspection. These functions represent the modes of freedom from the corresponding psychological abstractions, and the philosophical study of these functions may be called Spiritual psychology. (18-19) The metaphysical problem—what it is in the object that determines its

known appearance—is only a problem in meaning and is outside the scope of spiritual psychology. The business of such a Psychology is two-fold : (a) to interpret Empirical psychological in terms of the felt and believed freedom of the subject from objectivity; (b) to elaborate modes of freedom that have no reference to object at all and thus to assign a place to spiritual mysticism. (20) Kant's Critical philosophy may be taken as a disguised form of Spiritual psychology as thus conceived. But the Kantian epistemology does not abandon the objective procedure of metaphysics and the sciences, and it thus misleads so far as it presents the function as an objective meaning and does not recognise that it is believed without being meant. (21) The persisting objective attitude of Kant explains his disbelief in the possibility of a spiritual discipline of the theoretic reason through which self-knowledge may be attained.

(22) According to Kant, the self can only be thought and not known. The view presented here is that the subject is known though neither thought nor intuited. The subject is known by itself and believed as relating to the object, the modes of relating being the modes of freedom from objectivity. (23) Spiritual progress means the realisation of the subject as free. According to some, this realisation involves a specific activity of the subject. There is a demand for some kind of activity of the subject towards itself. There is the demand that the subjective function of knowing which is only believed and not known as fact has to be known as the self-evidencing reality of the subject itself. This would be the supreme method of cognitive inwardising. (24) The possibility of such a method has to be exhibited in spiritual psychology. The steps involved in the method should correspond to a gradation of subjective functions or modes of freedom from the object. The stages of freedom are in the following order : (a) Bodily subjectivity; (b) Presentational subjectivity; (c) Non-presentational or Spiritual subjectivity. Each of these stages would comprise substages. The elaboration of these stages of freedom in Spiritual psychology would suggest the possibility of a consecutive method of realising the subject as absolute freedom.

CHAPTER II
Psychic Fact (sec. 25-56)

(25) Psychological introspection is the process of abstraction from the object of its modes of relatedness to the subject. This relatedness viewed as a character of the object is the so-called psychic

fact. 'Knownness' as one such psychic fact is a floating adjective like beauty and is an abstraction of the second degree. (26-30) Psychic fact is a character of the object and is bound up with object-cognition. (a) What does not involve *knowledge* of object is no psychic fact. (b) Again, what introspection does not reveal is no psychic fact. The consciousness of the imaginary is not revealed in introspection : it is not, therefore, a psychic fact. The feeling of an object that is believed to be illusory cannot also be asserted to be a psychic fact. (31-32) A mode of consciousness like the above is only a *fringe* of some psychic fact. The fringe may epistemologically be primary or secondary in respect of the psychic fact but it never stands by itself.

(33) A psychic fact involves not merely the *belief* in an objective fact but also the *knowledge* of it. Knowledge as distinct from mere belief involves the awareness of the distinction of the object believed from the belief. This distinction is just what is called 'presentation' of the object in which while the object is *given* distinct from the presentation, the presentation is only abstracted from the object. (34-37) Perceptual knowledge and perceptual illusion represent two extreme cases of this relation between presentation and object; and intermediate between perceptual knowledge and perceptual illusion are the other forms of knowledge involving a conscious distinction of the known object from its presentation. The distinctness of the object from the presentation does not, however, mean the distinctness of the presentation from its object.

(38) There are different grades of non-perceptual knowledge implying different modes of presentation, e.g., the knowledge of the body from within. the immediate apprehension of absence. memory. constructive imagination and inference. (39) Perception as the actual standard of knowledge not only lends the cognitive character to the other modes of apprehension but also prevents them from reaching their ideal completion. The objects of the non-perceptual modes of knowledge are adjectival characters of the perceptually knowable object. They are, however, necessarily symbolised as substantive by objective metaphors.

(40-41) In perceptual knowledge, though the presentation is not known as distinct from the object, yet it is believed or symbolised as what should be distinct. The psychic fact or the presentation is thus not accomplished as fact but only to be accomplished as such. As such the presentation may be said to be known as unknown and as to be known as object. (42) The complete accomplishment of psychic facthood is conceivable as implying presentation that is wholly turned into known object. It would mean the conscious objectivity of what in presentation is more than the sense-given object or the *metaphysical.* (43) The Kantian objection that the appearance of objectivity of the metaphysical element is only illusory cannot be accepted. The appearance is incomplete but not illusory and the demand to know it is quite legitimate. (44-45) To take the metaphysical as merely illusory is to assume the object to be alone knowable and to be incapable of being *known* freely. It is to deny the facthood of the constructive function by which the perceivable object comes to be for the subject. (46) The distinction of the object that is non-perceptually known from its knownness is just its character of being unknown. The known object is thus a problem to all knowledge other than the perceptual one. Non-perceptual knowledge is knowledge of the object as phenomenal with belief in a reality constituting it.

(47-49) To know the phenomenon is not *not* to know the reality but to know it as unknown. The knowledge of the unknown as such is the pre-condition as much of moral or aesthetic realisation as of cognitive realisation. (50) The knowledge of the unknown is what starts the actual problem of realisation whether in the cognitive or in the non-cognitive direction. The non-cognitive mode does not demand the belief that it is the only mode and that the cognitive mode implies a fanatical conceit or a theosophic illusion. Any denial of the cognitive mode would argue the impossibility of the non-cognitive modes as well. (51-52) To Kant, the metaphysical reality is only thought and is not really knowable. We agree that the introspective awareness of the metaphysical in the presentation is not knowledge of knowing but is only imagination of knowing the metaphysical. There is no question of turning this imagined knowing into actual knowing by sense-perception. It can be actualised, if at all, by the concreting activity of imagination itself. In this cognitive realisation, the metaphysical would have to be known as that of which the object is a free efflux and the empirical would have to be known not by being given but by the self-shining, substantively existent cognition of it.

(53-54) Psychic fact ordinarily appears as more concrete than objective fact only in promise and not in actuality. It does not, however, appear as co-ordinate with objective fact : it is what should be more real but is actually less real. The psychic is more concrete than the object in the sense that it can freely put forth the lesser reality. Nature is to the Psyche a magic or playful appearance. (55-56) The ordinary view of the psychic as co-ordinate with the object, the Hegelian view of it as comprehending the object as a real element and the theory of an experience-unity of subject and object have to be definitely rejected. The duality of psychic fact and objective fact is not again secured any better by making a distinction between the 'enjoying' and the 'contemplative' modes of knowing. The duality is not *known* but is only a symbolism for the felt dissociation of the psychic fact from the object.

CHAPTER III

Bodily Subjectivity (sec. 57-66)

THE BODY AS PERCEIVED AND FELT

(57) Perceptual knowledge is not directly the object of introspection and is not a psychic fact. There is, however, an awareness of the 'subject' even in this sub-psychic stage. The body as observed and felt is here the subject in relation to the environment. (58) Though the body represents a stage of being of the subject, yet one's own body, even as a perceived object, has a unique singularity. The objectivity of other perceived objects is constituted by their space-position relatively to the percipient's body. It is not, however, so in the case of the percipient's own body which is in this sense dissociated from the external world. (59) One's own body is uniquely different from other perceived objects and has no place in the objective world that he conceives to be presentable to him as a solipsistic observer. Even if the subject is taken as nothing but one's own perceived body, it involves knowledge of something that cannot be understood in terms of the perceptible object in the merely objectivistic attitude. It implies the mystic awareness of dissociation from the object in which subjectivity consists.

(60-62) One's own body is not only perceived from outside : one is sensuously aware of it also from within in the 'feeling of the body'. This body-awareness is indeed sensuous, but it can hardly be called 'sense-perception'. The felt body cannot be distinguished from the perceived body though the latter is distinguished from the former. (63) The relation between the felt body and the perceived body is similar to the relation of presentation and its object in non-perceptual knowledge. There is, however, the difference that introspection into such knowledge is possible because the presentation is felt to be dissociated from the object, while there is no introspection into body-feeling, as we are not aware of it as dissociated from the perceived body. Body-feeling may, accordingly, be regarded as not psychic fact but the potentiality of it. (64-65) The relations of body-feeling to (i) psychic fact, (ii) introspection of psychic fact, (iii) perceived body and to (iv) perceived object may here be considered. (i) The felt body is only half-distinguished from psychic fact and the latter is only potentially dissociated from the felt body. (ii) In introspection into psychic fact, this potential dissociation becomes imperfectly actual and the felt body begins to get resolved into a bodiless psychic feeling. (iii) The felt body is potentially dissociated from the perceived body because the latter is only half-distinguished from the former. (iv) The felt body is imperfectly dissociated from the perceived object and the latter is fully distinguished from the former.

(66) The feeling of detachment from the object is the feeling of freedom and the first hint of this freedom is reached in the feeling of the body. This first given feeling is what all freedom of higher grade involves. Subjectivity apart from spiritual discipline is rooted in body-feeling. The realisation of freedom from the felt body is the pre-condition of all distinctive spiritual activity.

CHAPTER IV

Bodily Subjectivity (Contd.) (sec. 67-79)

KNOWLEDGE OF ABSENCE AS A PRESENT FACT

(67-68) Like the feeling of the body, the perception of absence as a present fact is a fringe of object-perception. In both, again, there is a feeling of detachment. The feeling of the body is a detachment from the perceived object other than the perceived body. The direct knowledge of the present absence of an object is a detachment both from the perceived object and the perceived body but not from the felt body. (69) The sense-conditioned cognition of absence is not ordinary perception and is yet undissociated from it. The cognition is a fringe either of the perception of the locus or of the perception of the body and is in either case undissociated from the feeling of the body.

(70) Two cases of a direct cognition of absence in a locus may be distinguished : (a) one of the *absence* of an object and (b) the other of an object as being absent. Neither cognition need imply the other, yet each may develop into the other cognition. The two are, therefore, distinct; and each as primary may involve the other as secondary. (71) In (a), the perceived locus of absence is imagined

in the very perception of it as without the absence, and the absence is thus only a floating adjective that is felt to be dissociated from the locus. There is a suggestion of the absence being outside the space where the locus stands and of its being *nowhere* though it is believed to be objective fact. The suggestion is not actual imagination of positionless objective fact but only the feeling of detachment from objective space. This sort of perception of absence may be called aesthetic or imaginative perception. (72) In (b), the knowledge of the fact of a particular object as absent is present with the conscious imagination of the object as found being distinct from it as absent. It thus implies the feeling of the present fact being outside objective space altogether. Such knowledge may also be called imaginative perception. (73-74) The primary cognition of absence may be followed by the secondary cognition of the absent; and the primary cognition of the absent may be followed by the secondly cognition of absence. The secondary cognition in each case is not imaginative perception and has to be recognised as a new mode of knowledge called conscious non-perception.

(77) The relation of these two modes of cognition, viz., imaginative perception and conscious non-perception, with the apprehension of the body is remarkable. The primary is related to the perception of the body as the secondary is related to the feeling of the body. (78) The relation of the perceived body in imaginative perception and of the felt body in conscious non-preception to the known absence is like the relation of the perceived body to the felt body. (79) Conscious non-perception is a transitional stage between body-feeling and imagination with which psychic fact begins. It is free from space but not from the present. It is the distinguishing of the present from the detached presentation and is the immediate pre-condition of the felt detachment of the presentation from the present. Starting with object-perception as the actual standard of knowledge, the first clear hint of the subjective fact would be realised in the knowledge of absence through conscious non-perception.

CHAPTER V

Psychic Subjectivity (sec. 80-93)

THE IMAGE

(80-81) It cannot be denied that the image appears presented as a substantive something from which the object is distinct. It cannot also be denied that the image is a fact in a sense in which the object is not. The nature of facthood appears to change with different grades of fact. (82) (a) The facthood of the perceived object is constituted by position relatively to the percipient's body. (b) The lack of this relative perceived position is what constitutes the facthood of one's perceived body. (83) (c) Interiority or felt space constitutes the facthood of the *felt body.* (84) (d) Perceived *absence* as a fact is on a level with the felt body though its position is on the level of the perceived body. (85) (e) Absence that is known by conscious non-perception is not known as with position, though it cannot be said to be known as without position.

(86) The image has to be compared to absence. While absence as in (e) is not known with position, the image is known to be without position. Again, absence is known as *now,* while the image is not known as *now.* The image has thus no space-position and it cannot be asserted to have a time-position. (87) In the perception of the object, in the perception of one's own body and in imaginative perception of absence, the image involved is not felt to be dissociated from the percept. In the knowledge of absence through conscious non-perception, the image of the absent object is felt to be dissociated from the felt body but not from the present absence. But in imagination as a free psychic fact even the present absence is distinguished from the image. (88-89) The image proper is not known to be in time and is not felt dissociated from the present absence though it is potentially dissociated. The potential dissociation of the image from the *now* is realised in thought. (90) The image appears as a ghostly object. Its awareness is bound up with the perceiving attitude and is not introspective. (91) The distinguishing the object from the presentation is a phase of object-knowledge. The presentation as thus distinguished from is an indefinite quasi-object, and except in its lowest phase an image is felt also as not in time. In the thought of an objective fact, however, the meaning which is the presentation is not only not referred to time, its existence in time is meaningless.

(92) When the image is introspectively attended to, it changes its character and appears as imagining, as being formed though not as unformed, as functional without ceasing to be substantive. (93) The forming or the incomplete character of the image is not like the incomplete character of a perceived object. The incompleteness of a percept is in reference to a fuller percept : the image, however, is incomplete in itself. The image under introspection is a standing

process where the forming is not chronologically prior to the form and yet appears distinct from the form which is its interpretation. The consciousness of the finished form that interprets the forming is called the *idea* which as dissociated from the image would be the next psychic stage.

CHAPTER VI

Psychic Subjectivity (Contd.) (sec. 94-100)

THOUGHT

(94-95) The idea of an object that cannot be defined or concreted into image is thought proper that is definite in itself and is fixed in the mind by the images it may call up. It is other than pictorial thought which lies between the definite form and the definite intelligible and its object is definitely presented as unpicturable meaning. (96) The image implies a belief in its possible objectivity but thought involves a complete detachment from objectivity, though it is still about the object. (97) Non-pictorial thought which is definite independently of the image may be sought to be metaphorically or symbolically indicated by the image. Thought in its higher grade is detained in the mind by the word and not by its figurative representation. (98) Thought as distinct from the forming image under introspection is a completed product. It is oomplete as dissociated altogether from time and is in this sense eternal. Still it is about the object and as such should be called a presentation. (99-100) Thought is attained meaning and that it is a presentation comes out if it is contrasted to possible meaning which is exemplified in our consciousness of *trying* to think. This trying to think is beyond thought or meaning and is beyond all presentation.

CHAPTER VII

Spiritual Subjectivity (sec. 101-111)

FEELING

(101) The introspective awareness of meaning as distinct from the image is awareness of the explicitly unobjective. Feeling is also explicitly unobjective. It is not, however, merely negative but positive as *subjective* fact without any reference to objective fact. The consciousness of the merely unknown as distinct from what is known as

object that is also unknown is feeling. It is purely subjective in the sense that there is no conscious reference to object even in the way of dissociation from it. Feeling, again, involves belief in the unmeant as a distinct content. (102) In the awareness of thought, the content of thought appears distinct from thought, but in the awareness of feeling, the unthought content of feeling appears as only distinct in itself and not as distinct from feeling. Again, while thought or other psychic fact is believed to exist outside introspection, feeling is never outside introspection as a merely conscious fact.

(103) Introspection into feeling is an awareness of the feeling as apparently distinct from the awareness. But while introspection into psychic fact is a *distinguishing* of the fact which appeared undistinguished from itself, that into feeling is an *identifying* of the feeling which appeared to be outside introspection. Feeling is bound up with thought and imagination and is the awareness of their detachment as presentation from their objects. In introspection into feeling, the distinction of feeling from its presentative content is appreciated as definitely not known but only felt and symbolised. With this awareness of meaning as the symbol of feeling, the objective reference lapses altogether. Feeling as detached from meaning is awareness of the meaning as its symbolism and may be taken as implicitly introspective. (104) If feeling represents the complete dissociation from objectivity, willing means the free identification with objectivity. Willing starts as the free or playful expression of feeling. The freedom from thought is as much a progress as a regress, as much a willing as a feeling. With the cancellation of the objective attitude, there is the consciousness of being free, of being unrestricted by the object, whether for withdrawal from it in feeling or for conquest over it in willing. (105) Knowing means freedom both from blindness and from error. The freedom implied in knowledge means the outgoing of the positive attitude of not knowing, of conscious entertainment of the unknown—which is feeling—and of *conscious* projection of objectivity—which is willing.

(106-107) Feeling is the positive consciousness of detachment from meaning. It is the awareness of a content as *unmeant*. But as it is non-denial of a possible meaning, it is not without the persisting will to objectification. When a feeling has purged itself of this will, we have the awareness not merely of the unmeant but of the unmeanable. This is exemplified from the analysis of the experience of the illusory. The content there is the 'indescribable.' (108) Two stages of feeling can thus be distinguished: the lower stage where there is freedom from actual thought and the higher stage where there is freedom from possible thought. The lower grade is the feeling of self-being and the higher grade is one of self-negation. (109-110) The feeling of not having a feeling is itself a feeling. It can only be characterised as the *feeling* of a feeling. It is not introspection but the stage prior to it. It is the self-negation of feeling and is already the attitude of knowledge of what is neither felt nor unfelt, or of the unmeanable. (111) We are aware of the unmeanable in two stages, as the meant unmeanable and as the mere function of meaning. The knowledge implied in the former is of a contradiction while that implied in the latter is not *of* anything, being merely knowing. The feeling of feeling is the former kind of awareness, while the latter is just introspection which is the pure knowing *function* and is a complete detachment from felt being.

CHAPTER VIII

Spiritual Subjectivity (Contd.) (sec. 112-119)

INTROSPECTION

(112) The introspective awareness of a psychic fact is the awareness of its *distinction from object* and, therefore, of its distinction in itself also as existing apart from introspection. The introspective awareness of a feeling proper, on the other hand, is the knowledge of its *distinction in itself* only and is the recognition of the distinction as being entirely through introspection. (113) Introspection into feeling is just the function of meaning the feeling. It is a subjectivity that is detached both from being and negation, and it is positive as *freedom*. It is the positive of which the negation is not even tried to be meant. It is something which can only be sought to be impugned by the imaginary problem of conceiving its negation and is, therefore, never actually impugned. (114-115) The object and every subjective fact that is introspectively believed is capable of being doubted, but introspection as a function of believing or meaning which is not itself meant even as the unmeanable is not actually doubtable. It is just the first person 'I' and is not a believing in the 'I'. It is simply the function of speaking.

(116) Introspection into feeling implies the possible detachment from the being of feeling. This possible detachment from all distinct being is introspective awareness and is the conscious identity without being of the self. (117) The self is taken by Kant as the thinking function and also as an accomplished meaning. But here the

self has been identified with the function of introspection and has been taken to be detached from thinking and feeling. The self is a believing which is a self-knowing. (118) The self is the first person 'I'. The 'I' is neither meanable nor unmeanable. The word 'I' has a meaning-function but not a meaning. It is the expression of introspection or the I-function. (119) The meaning function of the word 'I' is to the speaker his actual introspection, but the understanding of the word by the hearer is indicative of a form of consciousness subtler than introspection. It is the awareness of a possible introspection.

CHAPTER IX

SPIRITUAL SUBJECTIVITY (Contd.) (SEC. 120-126)

BEYOND INTROSPECTION

(120) The word 'I' has no meaning either to the speaker or to the hearer and yet it stands like any other word for the same thing to both. This 'standing for' is not only not meaning but not also mere symbolising. The word 'I' may be said at once to symbolise and to be symbolised by my introspective self. It is this characteristic of a word other than its meaning-value or merely symbolising value that indicates a grade of self-consciousness higher than our actual introspection. (121) Actual introspection is unrealised knowledge because it is actually only self-evidencing to another and not self-evident to itself. One's own self should be self-evident and should be intuited by oneself even as it is intuited by another. The self should be at once self-evidencing and self-evident, but so far we have only the self as self-evidencing and evident to another. (122) The other self is to the self-evidencing self a possible introspector whose intuition of the latter is a possible intuition to the latter. The awareness of these possibles in oneself indicates the necessity of a spiritual discipline of realisation of the self already implied by introspection.

(123) Introspection into a possible mental state involves understanding of a word meaning the mental state. To mean a mental state is not, however, to think it but to remember it, to want it or to dreamily wish it. All these may be regarded as a stage of introspection prior to the introspection into an actual mental state and are capable of being themselves introspected into.

(124-125) Introspection into the awareness of a possible subjective state is possible or imaginary introspection and is half-dissociated from the actually introspective self. Complete dissociation from this actual awareness is reached when the content of it is a subjective state that is illusory. There are actual illusions about the subjective just as there are illusions about the objective.

(126) Ordinarily, introspection is the awareness of a subjective fact as owing its facthood to itself and is in tnis sense the appropriator of it. But there are experiences where one gets the hint of an introspection that is not appropriative. This kind of introspection would be self-intuition. The possibility of a silent self-enjoying 'I' is intelligible only because we are aware of certain subjective modes previously appropriated as utterly unappropriable and as appearing only as though they are distinct. The absolute intuitable self is only understood if the non-being of distinction is understood. The non-being of distinction is finally understood in the awareness of subjective illusion which is the explicit awareness *creating* a distinction that is no fact at all.

CHAPTER X

The Subject as Freedom (sec. 127-135)

(127) It is in introspection that we are aware of the demand for the consummation of the freedom that is felt in every grade of subjectivity in respect of the object presented to it. The introspective subject is free from possible objectivity and is thus freedom itself. But it knows itself not as itself but as a distinct subject that is only possibly identical with itself. It is thus aware of a demand to know this subject as *actually* itself. This demand is for the intuition of the subject as absolute freedom. (128) The subject is understood as freedom that is real. The idea of realising the subject arises only because we are actually indentified with the body while we are introspectively aware of ourselves as not objective and yet as definitely positive. We do not *know* ourselves as undissociated from the object, yet we are aware of a possible dissociation or freedom. (129) Actual freedom from the object is *known* in some measure in bodily subjectivity. In higher stages there is only a *feeling* of it. The higher the stage of subjectivity, the less is the freedom felt to be achieved though the more assured is the faith in its achievability. In the introspective stage, the feeling of achieved freedom lapses altogether but the faith in its attainability is completely assured. (130-135) The three broad stages of subjectivity and the several substages under each stage recapitulated.

CHAPTER I

THE NOTION OF SUBJECTIVITY

1. Object is what is meant, including the object of sense-perception and all contents that have necessary reference to it. Object as the meant is distinguished from the subject or the subjective of which there is some awareness other than the meaning-awareness. The subjective cannot be a *meaningless* word : to be distinguished from, it must be a significant speakable and yet if it be a meant content, it would be but object. It can thus neither be asserted nor denied to be a meant content and what cannot be denied need not be assertable. Apparently, the significant speakable is wider than the meanable : a content to be communicated and understood need not be meant.

2. A meaning that is conveyed by a word must be intelligible to the hearer as what he would himself convey by the word. What the speaker means by a word must be capable of being meant by the hearer if he were to use it. The word *this* as used by a speaker means primarily what he perceives; and although the hearer may use it of some other object, he can use it of the same object. A general term is always understood by the speaker and the hearer to mean the same thing but such identity of the general meaning is possible only because it applies to the same individual thing, the same perceived *this* to both. The word *this* may accordingly be taken as the symbol of the object or what is meant.

3. The word *I* as used by a speaker is not understood by the hearer to convey what he would himself convey by the use of it. If he used the word, he would intend himself and not the speaker. Actually, however, when he understands the word *I* as used by the speaker, he understands it to stand for the speaker. He may accordingly be said to understand the thing intended by the speaker through the word but not through the *meaning* of the word. The thing is not meant by the word for the further reason that the communicating act of the speaker which is never a part of the meaning of a word is itself conveyed by the word *I*. When the object-consciousness of the speaker is communicated, the object and not the speaking of the object is what is understood to be meant. But when his self-consciousness is communicated, it is not his self only but the self as speaking, communicating or expressing itself that is understood. His self-

consciousness may in this sense be said to be not merely expressed but *incarnated* in the word *I*. What is here intended by the speaker is not only what the hearer can never intend by the word if he were to use it : it is also the thing-subject—*as expressing itself* and not as merely expressed. What then is meant and is expressible as *this* is not what is conveyed by the word *I*.

4. Object as symbolised by the word *this* may be an individual object or a generality. The word *I* as intending the subject is not definitely either singular or general. It is indeed *used* to indicate not only one thing at a time but a thing which cannot be indicated by more than one speaker ; but then different speakers can be *understood* to use it—each of a distinct thing viz., himself—by the same hearer and understood to use as he would use it. As used, the term has a uniquely singular reference ; but as understood, it is general in the sense the term *unique* is general. It is thus unlike a term meaning an objective content, which has the same reference—singular or general—to the speaker as to the hearer. What is meant by *this* is distinct from what is intended by *I*, though the latter may be intended or indicated by *this*. The object is not the subject but the subject may be spoken of though not meant as object. The subject may be incarnated in the spoken word *I* which is objective. As incarnated in the object, the subject is the object which yet is distinct from it. In terms of *I* and *this,* we may say that the statement 'this is I' is false while the statement 'I am this' cannot be denied.

5. If *this* stands for a perceivable object including my body, there is no occasion to make the statement 'this is I' or 'I am this'. But *this* may stand for myself who *spoke* the word *I* ; and in answer to the conceivable question 'who is this speaker', I may say 'this is I'. The answer would imply not a judgment but a correction ; it would mean 'this speaker is not *this* or object to myself, *this* as distinct from me is here false, the fact being I'. So one may say 'that snake is but a rope' where what is meant is that the snake is illusory, the rope being the fact. But the statement 'I am this speaker' or 'I said *I*' would not be false in such a context : it would be a mode of expressing what is called personal identity. Nevertheless it is not a judgment : my consciousness of personal identity is not a recognitive judgment as it is ordinarily taken to be. In my answer 'I am this speaker', the predicate does not appear to me, as it appears to the questioner, as what the subject may not be. The pastness of the subject, moreover, as implied in the predicate—this speaker being I who *spoke*—is not consciously relative to the presentness of the subject.

In saying 'I spoke', I make no assertion at all about myself being *now*, the pastness of 'spoke' being consciously distinguished only from the present *objective* situation. The belief in my pastness can never be formulated *by me* as the judgment 'I who am now am I who was then'. It is only another person who can assert my personal identity in a recognitive judgment. I cannot deny the judgment and may take it as a symbolic expression of my felt belief. My personal identity, however, is to me only a felt content which though not false is not *asserted* by me. The equation of *I* and *this* is then logically unintelligible, being the rejection of *this* in the form 'this is I' and only a felt content in the form 'I am this'.

6. The object can be pointed out without the use of a word but it is expressible by the single word *this*. The subject cannot be indicated except by a word and the word for it is not *I* only but any personal pronoun (or any word the use of which is ultimately explained by a personal pronoun). The subject is what is intended by the words *I, you* or *he* and though it is always what can call itself *I*, the use of *you* or *he* is as directly intelligible as the use of *I* and need not be explained by it. There is, however, a characteristic difference between the first person and the other persons. If *this* means the object, there is no occasion to consciously identify it with *I*, though I may be implicitly identified with my body. But I am somehow conscious of an identity between another person and his body, conscious of them as distinct and yet one. The relation accordingly of *you* and *he* to *this* and *I* requires closer examination.

7. *You* and *he* are to me subjects individualised in the objective body, the body being, however, as much distinguished from them as from myself. Like their bodies they also can be spoken of as individual, but while the individuality of *he* is evidently derived from his body which is *this* to me, the individuality of *you* appears to be prior to that of your body. You are individual to me primarily through my act of addressing and only secondarily through what appears to my imagination as your identification with or appropriation of your body. *He* is individual to me only through his body being imagined as identified with or appropriated by him. *This* body is presented to me first through which I apprehend *this* subject or *he*. It may be—though it is not necessary—that before I can address you, I have to apprehend you as *this* subject or *he* ; but *this* subject appears to me as *you,* only as I address. To say 'this is you', is to mean, in fact, that this person is not *this* person, the third person or *he* : it is to imply a correction as in the statement 'this is I'. The

statement 'this is he', however, implies a belief though like 'I am this', it represents a felt content and not the content of a judgment. My identification of a body presented to me first with the subject *he* is not the knowledge of this object being identical with him, since the object is as much distinct from him as from me though I cannot assert his distinction ftom his body. I apprehend the third person as distinct from me, only as I take him to be individualised in his body. Conceived apart from his body, he would be known neither as distinct from me nor therefore as identical with me but only as one who can call himself *I*; and there would be as little occasion to say of him that he is his body as to say of me that I am my body. The statement 'he is this' is thus excluded but the statement 'you are this' would, like 'this is he', represent a belief that is not knowledge, a felt content that is only symbolised as a judgment. The apprehension of *you,* however, logically precedes while that of *he* follows the apprehension of *this* or the body appropriated. There is no occasion to say, as has been explained, either 'this is I' or 'I am this', where *this* stands for my body : and where *this* means a temporal determination of myself, the former represents a correction and the latter a felt and believed content.

8. Thus of the six possible equations of *this* with *I, you* or *he,* three are excluded and the three that are believed viz., 'I am this' (in the sense of myself as then), 'you are this' (your body) and 'this (his body) is he' represent a felt or imagined content that is not known. The object as meant by *this* is known as distinct from the subject as intended by a personal pronoun ; and the subject may also be said to be known in itself, being what is either illusorily or imaginatively spoken of as *this* but is not known to be related to *this* either in the way of identity or distinction. The correction implied in the statement 'this is I' indicates the nature of the subject such as it is aware of before it calls itself *I* and incarnates itself in the spoken word. *This* here means myself who spoke and was in the past and the correction is to the effect that the this-ness or pastness is not really mine and only illusorily appears so, that not *this I* but the unspecified *I* should be taken as the subject. There is no denial, however, of the subject being objectifiable as *this* or *then* but the objectification is an incarnation in which the projected objectivity is not known as a determination belonging to the subject, the subject being felt to be dissociated from it. The subject as *you* or *he,* so far as known, is not known as *this* or the appropriated body. You, as addressed and conceived to be logically prior to your body, are not known by me like

your body as distinct from me, being only felt to be the subject that I am distinct from. So, too, if *his* body is known to be distinct from him and from me, *he*, if conceived at all apart from his body, is known not as distinct from or identical with me but as only distinct. *You* and *he* are to my knowledge as much unique as what is intended by the word *I*, being, in fact, understood simply as one who can call himself *I*. The three persons are not known to be distinct from or identical with one another.

9. The object is known as distinct from the subject but the subject is only known in itself and felt to be free or dissociated from the object. I feel dissociated from the object as I feel dissociated from the subject *you* or *he* that appears to me somehow 'identified' with the object. I am aware of alienating you by the fact of addressing and of him being alienated from me as his body is alienated. I actively dissimilate' you and, therefore, also the body that you appropriate and feel unable to 'assimilate' him and, therefore, his body with which he is found identified. The object in either case is a body somehow one with a subject which I would not or cannot identify with myself. With regard to my own body, I only do *not* feel actually dissociated from it and am not *consciously* identified with it. I am indeed individualised in my body but I am not introspectively aware of it. I am aware of myself as *this* not in the sense of my body but only in the sense of myself in a temporal position, myself as having been, for example, in the past and having spoken of myself as *I*. *This* is here only thought and not known as distinct from myself and I am conscious not only of being dissociated from it but also of its distinction from myself being illusory. Thus everywhere the subject is known in itself and not as related to the object, being at best felt to be dissociated from the object with which it was identified.

10. The subject, understood as the unique speaker—actual or possible—of the word *I*, and the object that is meant as distinct from the subject are the two things that are known. The reality of what is meant can always be doubted and so the object is not known with the same assurance as the subject that cannot be said to be meant. There may be such a thing as an illusory object ; and in the statement 'this is I', as already explained, *this* is understood as an objectivity that is annulled. The idea of a possible annulment of objectivity being there, an object that is given as distinct from the subject can be conceived to be not distinct, though the distinction may not be actually cancelled. The denial of reality is intelligible only about what is meant, the negation of the meant being also either actually or problematically meant.

The unreality, however, of the subject as intended but not meant by *I* is meaningless. It is not only inconceivable like the opposite of an axiom ; it is not even tried to be conceived, a content being taken to be inconceivable only after it has been tried to be conceived. The word *I* expresses a unique and unanalysable content from which all that is meant is distinct and which yet is understood and unquestioningly believed. The belief cannot be called a grammatical superstition, though the fact believed is inexpressible except in language by a grammatical pronoun. The subject appears as a known fact, only as it is spoken of through a personal pronoun or conceived to be so speakable. One's private awareness of *I* before its expression in speech is indeed knowledge but the *I* here does not appear as a known fact distinct from the knower. To be aware of the subject as a known fact is to be aware of it as a spoken fact. It is not so about the object of which one may be aware as known even if unnamed. The subject as spoken fact is, however, a meant fact.

11. The metaphysical controversy about the reality of the subject is only about the subject viewed in some sense as object. The thinnest sense in which it is objectified is 'being taken as meant'. Ordinarily the validity of this degree of objectification of the subject is not questioned, nor therefore the possibility of a dispute about its reality. If, however, the subject is taken, as explained, to be what is expressed by the word *I* as expressing itself, it is not meant or at best meant as unmeant and is accordingly above metaphysical dispute. There is properly no metaphysic of the subject, if by metaphysic is understood an enquiry into the reality conceived as meanable. Even the unknowable thing-in-itself of Spencer and Kant is not taken to be unmeanable. It is at worst taken to be a problem in meaning. The knowable is meant and the negation of the knowable is, if not meant, tried to be meant, being not a gratuitous combination of words but a believed content that is problematically formulated. The subject which is also believed is formulated as *I* which is, however, understood as unmeanable though not as a mere word like *abracadabra*. The understanding here is not a mystic intuition though it may point to its possibility, nor the intuition of a meaning that can be a term of a judgment, nor yet the thought of a meaning that is not known because not intuited or that is known without being intuited. It is somewhere midway between a mystic intuition and the consciousness of a meaning, being the believing awareness of a speakable content, the negation of which is unmeaning and which, therefore, is not a meaning. What is claimed to be mystically intuited is speakable only in metaphor which

presents a contradiction in meaning and what is affirmed or denied in metaphysic is a meanable. The subject as I is neither contradictory nor meanable and the exposition of it accordingly is intermediate between mysticism and metaphysic. As, however, the subject is communicable by speech without metaphor, it cannot be taken as falling outside philosophical enquiry.

12. The attitude of metaphysics like that of the sciences including psychology is objective. It seeks to know reality as distinct from the knowing of it, as objective, at least, in the sense of being meant. Knowing as a fact from which the known is distinct is not properly the subject either of psychology or of metaphysics. Psychological introspection is at best awareness of the *knownness* of the object, the knownness being meant as an accident of the object, as an abstraction from the known object, as the difference between the object as known and the object that is only believed, or as the object *coming* to be known. If there be a metaphysic of the psychological fact of knownness, its problem would be to determine what it is in the object that makes it known and not what the subject should be in order that it may know. Knowing from which all that is known or objective is distinct is dealt with in epistemology which distinguishes it as a function from the object but does not, therefore, take it to be a known fact. Knowing is not given as distinct to introspection nor inferred as distinct, being only distinct through the self-conscious act of distinguishing it. Knowing cannot be known as a fact unless the distinguishing of knowing be the knowing itself, unless, in fact, the distinctness of the knowing from the distinguishing of it appears illusory, even as *this* appears illusory in the apparent judgment 'this is I'. To realise that the distinctness of knowing is entirely through the distinguishing of it is to realise knowing as a self-evidencing fact, as not distinct from the object known but as unrelated or illusorily related to it, as not the knowing *of* object but as the solitary fact of the subject itself. Knowing is not thus known in epistemology which, however, does not disbelieve in its facthood. Were it known as a meanable fact, there would be room for the metaphysical inference of the subject as the ground of it. As it is, knowing is only symbolised as an activity ; and the inference of the subject as the agent is rightly characterised as involving a grammatical superstition. There is no room for metaphysics after epistemology has worked itself out of the objective attitude of metaphysics and the sciences by distinguishing knowing from the object known.

13. At the same time the belief in the facthood of knowing is

there, as epistemology is not an enquiry into the significance of the mere phrase 'knowing *of* object'. The belief is in the facthood of the knowing function, function being a metaphor for a positive something which is literally expressed only in the negative way as what the known object is not and being thus not even an accomplished meaning. The awareness of this unmeant something involves, however, a higher certitude than the belief in the meant object. Epistemology claims this certitude though it cannot justify it and has to recognise it to be other than the certitude of knowledge. Thus it appears that while the subject can be said to be known by itself and the meant object to be known as distinct from the subject, a subjective function like knowing is only believed though it may be with greater assurance than the object. The knowing of an object is not given as distinct from the object and *is* only in being distinguished from it, as relating and not as related to it, as not distinct from the distinguishing but not therefore as identical with it, as the free reference of the subject to the object. The subject is, as explained before, free from the object in the sense of being known by itself and not as related to it either in the way of identity or distinction. The knowing function represents a positive mode of this freedom, the freedom of the subject to relate to object without getting related to it, which is believed to be more certain than the object but is not known. We are aware of knowing a content when it is formulated and believed to be independent of our formulating, speaking or distinguishing act. It is so believed when it is felt either to be a given distinct—as in the case of the object known—or to be 'incarnated' in the formulation, in the sense explained, of being expressed as expressing or self-revealing —as in the case of the subject. Subjective function or the positive freedom of the subject to refer to the object is felt to be neither and is accordingly said to be only believed. The belief is bound up with the knowledge of the self-evidencing subject and as belief in a content which is like the subject itself not presented as meant, it is incapable of being doubted and is more certain than the knowledge of a meant object.

14. The three believed contents—the subject, the positive freedom of the subject and the meant object—are all speakable and it is from the speakable that we have to start in philosophy. The subject is taken to be known, as one who says *I* is immediately understood by the hearer through the word but not as meant by the word. The speaker is understood as revealing himself to another of whom he is positively aware as distinct but not as independent of his distingui-

shing. The positive awareness may be called feeling of alienating the subject *you*. What is known is the body of the other subject as an object distinct from the speaker. The speaking subject may thus be said to have a feeling of relating itself to the object, of addressing itself to it as though it were *you*. This felt relating is the positive freedom of the subject having different felt modes like knowing, feeling or being which though not objectively meanable can be symbolised by objective meanings. Such symbolic elaboration of the felt or believed spiritual functions would be a procedure of philosophy intermediate between the recognition of the subject purely through the intention of the word *I* and the inferential inquiry into the reality behind the meant object which is called metaphysics.)

15. There is properly no metaphysic of the subject and the apparent problems about the existence of the subject and its relation to the object are really illegitimate. The question if the subject is real is unmeaning, for the subject as I is not a meaning. The reality of the subject is known in the direct understanding of the word *I* as used by a speaker, which is neither the understanding of its meaning nor a mystic intuition of an unspeakable content. There can be also no relation of subject to object if the subject is not objectively meant, the subject being only aware of its function of *relating* or referring to object. The subject may believe itself and the object without speaking of them but it believes its relating function only as it speaks of it. If it speaks of the object, it believes in it as meant and if it speaks of itself as I, it believes in it as unmeant. But in speaking of its function it believes in it neither as meant nor as unmeant but as being constructed as fact by being spoken. A believed content that is spoken appears objective but while the appearance is denied of the spoken subject and asserted of the spoken object, it is only not denied of the spoken function. The speaking creation of a system of subjective functions or the symbolising elaboration of the positive freedom of the subject constitutes a special study which as not asserting meanable and justifiable truth cannot be called metaphysic and as yet inviting to believe and exhibiting the interval between the self-evidencing I and objectively knowable truth has to be taken as coming within philosophy.

16. There is no theoretic passage from what is meanable or objectively knowable to the subjectively knowable I ; metaphysics cannot pass out of the region of meanings. Epistemology indeed deals with the subjective function behind the accomplished meaning but it does not assert it as fact. It *assumes* the facthood of the function—knowing *of*

object—and only paraphrases the intention of the preposition *of* in reference to the different modes of knownness of the object such as are presented in psychology. The facthood of the knowing function and of subjective function in general is believed though not known and is elaborated into a system of symbolisms in a new philosophical study which may be called Spiritual or Transcendental psychology. The symbolism is fact in the sense of being the form of the non-theoretic or spiritually practical mode of escaping the objective knowing attitude of which the meaning attitude represents the subtlest stage. No meanable truth is self-evidencing, its negation being at least a problem in meaning and yet the self-evidencing I is the type of truth. The implication is that meanable truth which cannot be denied to be truth has to be realised as self-evidencing, not by being objectively thought again but by the spiritual cultivation of a subjective attitude. As the positive freedom of relating—which is an objective attitude—is to the objectively meant relation, so is the negative freedom in the cultivation of the subjective attitude to the positive freedom of the objective attitude. Spiritual psychology symbolises the subjective attitude by the objective attitude from which it seeks to be freed. The modes of subjectivity are the modes of freeing oneself from the modes of objectivity.

17. Hence comes the justification of the name Spiritual *psychology*. Psychology, as has been pointed out, deals not properly with knowing but with knownness as a character or aspect of the object. It deals, as we may say generally, not with subjective function but with the object regarded explicitly as distinct from it, as known, felt or willed. If there be a metaphysic of psychology, its problem would be what there is in the object to make it known, felt or willed. We are aware of an object that was only believed as coming to be known though its existence is not asserted or denied before the knowing. The metaphysical problem about the objective knownness, feltness etc., is intelligible though it may not be capable of objective solution. The distinguishing of knownness etc., as an abstraction from the object, as the objectivity of the object is what is called psychological introspection. The distinguishing of the subjective function of knowing etc., as other than this abstraction of objectivity may also be called introspection and, it may be, with greater right. If psychological introspection be an abstracting from the object, this introspection is a creative symbolising, the functions being subjective facts and not mere abstractions, though they are only believed and not known. The symbolising of the subjective function

is by a mode of objectivity like knownness, dissociation from which is precisely indicated by the word function. Thus the functions represent the modes of freedom from the corresponding psychological abstractions. The consciousness of freedom is as direct as that of such abstraction and its content can only be indicated as some sort of negation of the abstraction. If the consciousness of the abstraction be called psychological introspection, the consciousness of freedom may be called spiritual introspection and the philosophical study that is based on it may be designated Spiritual psychology.

18. The metaphysical problem—what it is in the object that determines its known or felt appearance—assumes that an appearance of object that is not unreal is caused by object, which implies further that object has an assured reality independent of the subject. It has, however, been indicated that the reality of object is not incapable of being doubted like the reality of the subject ; and even if object be as real as the subjective process that refers to it, it is not necessary that its relatedness to the subject should be caused at all. The emergence of such relatedness of an object is an event in time, only so far as it is not other than the emergence of the object or of an objective situation comprising it. The knownness or feltness of an object is an abstraction, the problem of the causation of which is illegitimate. Change in the object, as distinguished from the object, is also an abstraction but it is still understood as objective fact though unseparated from the object. Knownness etc., or the objectivity of the object is an abstraction that has no objective meaning at all by itself and about which, therefore, the demand for causal explanation is meaningless. The explanation of the emergence of the object *as related* to the subject is an ordinary objective or scientific problem and no separate explanation can be demanded for the emergence of the abstraction of relatedness. The metaphysical problem is thus apparently only a problem in meaning—how relatedness to the subject can be spoken of as a character of the object.

19. Spiritual psychology, however, has a place because its business is not to explain or to solve a problem. Its business is in the first place to interpret empirical psychology in terms of the positively felt and believed freedom of the subject from objectivity ; and next to elaborate modes of freedom that have no reference to object at all, to conceive the possible illusoriness of all objects and thus to assign an intelligible place to what is ordinarily scouted as spiritual mysticism. In the objective attitude, the knownness or feltness of the object appears positive and knowing or feeling appears as its problematic

negation. In the subjective attitude, the case is reversed : freedom is positively believed and the relatedness of the object to the subject—its objectivity—appears as constructed, as not belonging to the object in the sense change belongs to it and is thus understood as the self-negation or alienated shadow of the subject. In the objective attitude again, *this* or object appears to exist beyond its *this-ness* or relatedness to the subject, while in the subjective attitude not only is the transcendent *this* rejected as meaningless, *this-ness*—meaning the so-called psychological entities, knownness or feltness—appears also not to be *given* as distinct to introspection but to exist only as distinguished or constructed, this distinguishing or constructing being felt as less certain than the self-evident subject behind it. The object or *this* beyond objectivity, *this-ness* or relatedness to subject is sought to be known not only in the metaphysic of psychology, but in all metaphysic. From the standpoint of spiritual psychology, this transcendent object is simply meaningless and metaphysic is the quest of a chimera . All so-called metaphysical problems are to it symbolisms for modes of freedom, the forms of spiritual discipline by which the objective attitude has to be renounced and the positive subjective functioning has to be reversed in direction towards the realisation of the subject behind it.

20. Kant's critical philosophy may be taken as a disguised form of spiritual psychology as thus conceived. The elaboration of the three modes of belief—theoretic, practical and aesthetic—is transcendental psychology, the spiritual equivalent offered by him for dogmatic metaphysics. The start is from epistemology which assumes the reality of the subject and subjective function though it does not explicitly confess in the case of the knowing function that it is only assumed or believed to be real and presents instead a make-believe of inference in the so-called transcendental deductions. The other functions are, however, definitely asserted to be only believed : the reality of the willing function, for example, is taken to be apprehended in the willing consciousness only. The confession is not made about the knowing function because epistemology is to Kant not so much a branch of transcendental psychology as a prolegomena to it, concerned not with the presentation of subjective fact but with the meaning of the preposition *of* in 'knowledge of object', the facthood of which is implicitly taken for granted. Its interest is still in the object, in the knownness or objectivity of the object which it seeks to understand theoretically as knowing . It does not abandon the objective procedure of metaphysics and the sciences, even though it sets itself to correct the conceit of independent objectivity. The objective procedure may be

necessary to show up the seamy character of objectivity and may also imply the truthful admission that we do not get rid of our actual belief in the independent object by the mere thinking criticism of it. But it misleads so far as it presents the function as an objective meaning and does not recognise that it is believed without being meant. Epistemology might be mistaken as only a philological study, unless it is consciously viewed as rooted in the faith in the facthood of the knowing function and unless the so-called deduction that it presents is definitely known to be not inferential and not literally meant but to be the mere symbolisation by logical form of what is immediately believed as spiritual fact.

21. The persisting objective attitude of Kant in his first critique explains not only his admission of the thing-in-itself and his denial of self-knowledge but also his disbelief in the possibility of a spiritual discipline of the theoretic reason through which self-knowledge may be attainable. From the subjective standpoint, object beyond knownness, *this* beyond *this-ness* is, as explained, meaningless. It may be that, wedded as we are to our body, we cannot get rid of the objective attitude and the tendency to look beyond the constructed object to the purely given. But not to be able to deny need not imply admission and though the Kantian disclaimer of idealism as accomplished knowledge is intelligible, his admission of the unknowable reality appears to be an unwarrantable surrender to realism. After the resolution of the objectivity of the object into the knowing function, the independence of the object becomes inconceivable though it continues to be believed. Such a belief cannot be asserted though it cannot also be rejected. Realism should, therefore, be held as suspect though idealism is only a faith and not knowledge. But the faith has to be cherished and there should be a subjective discipline to get rid of the persisting realistic belief. Kant does not admit such a discipline at least for the theoretic reason.

22. Self-knowledge is denied by Kant : the self cannot be known but only thought through the objective categories—unity, substantiality etc., there being no intuition of it. The view presented so far is that the subject is known though neither thought (meant) nor intuited. It is known as what the speaker of *I* is understood to intend by it. The understanding is a direct believing in something that is not meant but revealed as revealing itself, a question about the reality of which does not arise and is unmeaning. The subject is thus known by itself, as not meant but speakable and not as either related or relating to the object. It is, however, believed as relating to object and sym-

bolised as such by the objective relations. The modes of relating are at the same time the modes of freeing from objectivity, the forms of the spiritual discipline by which, it may be conceived, the outgoing reference to the object is turned backwards and the immediate knowledge of the *I* as content is realised in an ecstatic intuition.

23. Spiritual progress means the realisation of the subject as free. The realisation may or may not involve a specific activity of the subject. There are those to whom it is only a resultant experience. One lives an objectively good or full life and finds his self correspondingly realised. Others, however, recognise a specific discipline or consecutive method of activity for such realisation. The consciousness of perfection, freedom or salvation as the end is to them a demand for some kind of activity of the subject towards itself. This cult of the subject, as it might be called, takes various forms but they all involve a feeling of dissociation of the subject from the object, an awareness of the subject as what the object is not. The specific activity demanded is primarily in the inwardising direction and secondarily, if at all, in the direction of creating objective or social values. One demand among others—all being absolute demands—is that the subjective function being essentially the knowing of the object as distinct from it, this knowing which is only believed and not known as fact *has* to be known as fact, as the self-evidencing reality of the subject itself. This would be the cult of the subject *par excellence,* a spiritual discipline of the theoretic reason, a method of cognitive inwardising, the possibility of which, as indeed of any method of realisation, is not ordinarily recognised.

24. The possibility of such a method has to be exhibited in Spiritual psychology. A method implies a series of consecutive steps for the realisation of an end. The steps in this case should correspond to a gradation of subjective functions, of modes of freedom from the object. Identified as we are with our body, our freedom from the perceived object is actually realised only in our bodily consciousness, though even this, as will appear later, is only imperfectly realised. Bodily consciousness may as well be called conscious body, there being no dissociation at this stage of the subject from the body, though the extra-organic object is known to be distinct from it. The next stage of freedom is suggested by the distinction of the perceived object including the body from the ghostly object in the form of the image, idea and meaning which may be all designated 'presentation'. Consciousness as undissociated from such presentation, but dissociated from the perceived and felt body may be called presentational or

psychic subjectivity. The dissociation of the subject or consciousness from this presentation conceived as a kind of object would be the next stage of freedom which may be called non-presentational or spiritual subjectivity. The three broad stages of subjectivity would then be the bodily, the psychical and the spiritual and each would comprise substages. Wedded as we are to our body, actual freedom is felt only in bodily subjectivity and freedom in the higher stages as suggested by psychology is believed not as what is actual but as what has to be achieved or realised. The grades of subjectivity imply grades of objectivity, the terms being conceived in a relative sense. To spiritual subjectivity, the psychical is objective and so to psychic subjectivity, the bodily and to bodily subjectivity, the extra-organic is objective. The objective at any stage is known as distinct from the subjective next to it, which, however, is not known as distinct from the objective but only felt and believed to be free or dissociated from it. The elaboration of these stages of freedom in spiritual psychology would suggest the possibility of a consecutive method of realising the subject as absolute freedom, of retracting the felt positive freedom towards the object into pure intuition of the self.

CHAPTER II

PSYCHIC FACT

25. The facts of empirical psychology have to be interpreted from the subjective standpoint in spiritual psychology. What is called psychological introspection is apparently a process of abstraction from the object of its modes of relatedness to the subject. This relatedness, viewed as a character of the object, is the so-called psychic fact. There is a difference, however, between this objective character and other objective characters. A character of a thing is an abstraction distinguished from it but not imaginable as separated from it. As distinct *in* the thing, it is a fact; but as spoken of by itself, it need not mean a fact. An abstraction like colour, for example, means a fact while an abstraction like intensity does not mean a fact though the intensity of colour as in the colour is a fact. These two kinds of abstraction may be designated respectively as of the first degree and of the second degree. Knownness or any other mode of relatedness of object to subject, as taken by itself, is an abstraction of the second degree : it does not mean a fact though the object as thus related is a fact. There is a difference, again, between this relatedness and intensity as abstractions. In the knowing of a bright colour, colour is not known as distinct from brightness, being only spoken of as distinct while in the knowing of the knownness of an object, the object—at least as non-perceptually known—is known as distinct from its knownness or presentation. Knownness or relatedness is a floating adjective of the object like its beauty or like the absence of an object as a character of the object in which it is absent. The so-called psychic fact, as abstracted from the object by psychological introspection, may thus be taken as a floating abstraction of the second degree. It is interpreted from the subjective standpoint in spiritual psychology as a subjective function that is a fact.

26. To psychological introspection with its objective attitude, psychic fact is a character of the object, existing like the object even apart from introspection. It is, however, only quasi-objective : unlike the object which when not perceived is known to exist in some other mode of cognition, psychic fact that is believed during introspection to exist is believed on the testimony of the same introspection to exist also apart from it. The perception of an object is immersed in the object and as such is not, as will appear later, knowable in *direct* in-

trospection. As the object is only indirectly known to be distinct from the perception of it, perception cannot be taken as a given psychic fact for purposes of psychology. Feeling, again, is a psychic fact only as the feltness of a known object and as bound up with its knownness ; and if there is feeling not bound up with object-cognition, it cannot appear to introspection to exist apart from it and as such cannot be called psychic fact. To start with at any rate then, the term *psychic* has to be restricted to modes of subjectivity that lie between sense-perception on the one hand and such objectless feeling on the other.

27. Psychic fact is either the knownness of object or the feltness etc., of known object, being fact from which object is distinguishable. What does not involve the knowledge of object is no psychic fact. Is mere imagination then—imagination of the *imaginary* which is no known object—to be regarded as psychic fact? What is imagined need not be imaginary and even what is taken as imaginary is not wholly imaginary. The imagination of a golden mountain involves not only the awareness of what never is but also the belief in the possibility of a mountain being made of gold, in the compatibility of the objective facts, *golden* and *mountain*. This compatibility is not imaginary, is not merely an imagined relation of two images but is an objective fact expressed in an abstract and periphrastic way. The imagination of golden mountain is a psychic fact so far as it implies an unrejected belief in such objective fact.

28. But is the awareness of the content as what never is, to be taken as psychic fact? The belief in the absence of what is at some time somewhere is still knowledge of objective fact. Even the awareness of what never is, where there was wrong belief in it or a real question about it, implies an unrejected belief in some objective fact. But golden mountain is imaginary in the sense that it not only never is but that it does not even suggest a real question about its existence. The awareness of such an imaginary content implies the rejection of all belief in objective fact. Introspection is belief in the psychic fact of believing in an objective fact. Is there a belief in the absence of objective belief or, in other words, introspection into the consciousness of the imaginary? There may only be disbelief or no-belief in believing and so there seems to be no introspection into *mere* imaging, the awareness of it being other than, though on a level with, introspection. What introspection does not reveal is no psychic fact and hence the consciousness of the imaginary is no psychic fact.

29. Is there such a thing as objectless feeling, feeling that does not involve knowledge of an objective fact? The feeling that we introspectively believe as being a fact outside introspection is the feeling of an object as known, from which indeed the knowledge is distinguished but which is not itself distinguished from the knowledge. Objectless feeling, if such there be, would be like introspection itself only a non-psychic fringe of some psychic fact. The general possibility of such feeling will be exhibited later but it may be asked at this stage if the feeling of an object that is believed to be illusory should be taken as psychic fact. The past belief in the snake, for example, which is now known to be only a rope, was bound up with a feeling of fear. Is the fear now believed as a past psychic fact? Obviously, we do not believe it now as the fear of *that* snake. But it may be said that although *that* snake is not believed, the characteristic feeling of bodily reaction in the past is believed, which is just the past fear of the snake. A feeling, however, is essentially individual and its individuality is constituted by the belief in the individuality of its object. The reduction of what was taken to be the fear of snake to the feeling of bodily reaction would be the disbelief in *that* feeling. Belief in the past fear of some object, indeed, remains over with the belief in the past bodily condition. But it remains over only in the sense of not being rejected and not of being asserted, and it remains over not by itself but as only the non-psychic fringe of the memory of the past bodily condition.

30. When we speak of the feeling of an object, we are not introspectively aware of the feeling as distinct from and accompanying the belief in the object. We do not distinguish the feeling at all from the belief though we may be aware of the belief without the feeling. The feeling, in fact, refers to the object as directly as the belief and along with it. It is artificial to understand it to refer to the object in the first instance related to the belief in the object and, therefore, to take the fear of the snake now believed to be illusory as fear related to the past belief in snake as distinct from the snake. We cannot say that the fear of the snake was just as real as the past belief in the snake. The false belief, now that it is corrected, is known to have been a fact, for the correction can be expressed in the form 'what *was believed* to be snake was not snake but rope.' It cannot be said, however, about the fear that it was fear of the rope or of *that* snake or of that idea of snake or that it was fear of nothing at all. The rope was the cause but not the object of the past feeling; so, too, was the idea of the snake while *that* snake cannot be called

its object because it is now disbelieved. Nor can we take the object to have been snake-in-general, for fear of such a generality is, at best, a disposition to feel and not an actual feeling. We believe, indeed, in the past feeling of a characteristic bodily reaction but a bodily feeling is not the consciousness of the body as its object, there being as little conscious distinction between bodily feeling and felt body as between perception and perceived object, while the past feeling in this case was distinctly consciousness of something as object. We cannot say that the fear was of nothing at all, since we do not remember the feeling as unformulated. After the belief in the snake has been corrected, it is impossible to describe as past *fact* what was called fear of the snake when it was believed. It may be arbitrary to deny that the fear was a fact but it cannot be asserted to have been fact because its object is now indescribable. The feeling then of an object now believed to be illusory cannot, at least, be asserted to have been a psychic fact.

31. A psychic fact involves belief in an objective fact and introspection into it is a belief in such belief. The awareness of the imaginary as such, being a disbelief in objective belief, has been shown to be other than but on a level with introspection. Are these modes of subjectivity to be taken as psychic facts? A psychic fact may involve belief in another psychic fact but it is primarily a belief in some objective fact. One may remember, for example, an objective event and also be aware of the subjective fact of its having been previously known. Such awareness is not memory unless the past knowing of the event was itself known in the past and should be taken accordingly as nothing but introspection. It is no psychic fact by itself but is only the transitive fringe of the substantive fact of objective memory. Introspection is always awareness of a psychic fact that is past though the psychic fact need not be known as past as in this case and may persist at the time of introspection. In any case introspection into it is bound up with another psychic fact like memory as in this case, which is primarily a belief in the object and need not have this fringe. Like introspection which is belief in believing, disbelief in believing also—the consciousness of the imaginary, which is not introspection but may be taken as co-ordinate with it—is a non-psychic fringe of a substantive psychic fact. The correction of an objective illusion appears to present a difficulty, since in it we are aware not of the past object but of the past belief in object, the awareness being also introspection. It implies, however, a present disbelief in the object which as implying in every case an unrejected belief in something objective is psychic fact and

the introspective belief in the past fact of belief is the non-psychic fringe of this psychic fact.

32. So then we conclude that a form of consciousness which does not involve belief in an objective fact is no psychic fact but is only the fringe of some psychic fact that involves such belief and need not have the fringe. The fringe may epistemologically be primary or secondary in respect of the psychic fact but never stands by itself. Introspection, for example, is primary in respect of the psychic fact of which it is a fringe while the awareness of an illusory object is secondary in respect of the belief that remains over after the correction. Again, the individual feeling that cannot be denied as bound up with the past belief in the object that is now taken to be illusory is primary in respect of the remembered body-feeling and may be taken as secondary in respect of the present remembering of the bodily feeling.

33. A psychic fact is or involves not merely the belief in an objective fact but the knowledge of it. We are aware of a belief as having been belief in an object as now formulated if the object is now either known or disbelieved. It is in introspection into knowledge or in the consciousness of the unreal object as such that we realise that we believed before we knew or disbelieved and that there was then no awareness of a distinction of the object believed from the belief. Knowledge as distinct from mere belief involves awareness of the distinction, this being testified by introspection into knowledge even about such knowledge as precedes introspection. The distinction that is presented to introspection is believed to exist also apart from introspection. The distinction of the object from the belief in it is something more than the object itself, though it cannot be said to be not objective. It is just what is called presentation of the object, which is taken as a psychic fact only as it is in introspection abstracted from the object. Presentation and object are so related that while the latter is given distinct from the former, the former is not given distinct from the latter, being only abstracted or tried to be distinguished in introspection.

34. Two extreme cases have to be considered in understanding this relation of presentation and object. In perceptual knowledge, the object does not appear distinct from its presentation; and in perceptual illusion, there is apparently the presentation only, with no object distinct from it. We do not, indeed, introspectively distinguish perceptual knowledge from its object but still such knowledge is not mere belief inasmuch as in it the object is given as distinct in itself though not from its presentation and has not to be distinguished, as in the case of mere belief, in a later act of knowledge. The object explicitly ap-

pears distinct from its presentation in non-perceptual knowledge, such distinction being the condition of possible introspection into it. There is accordingly no introspection into perceptual knowledge, though other knowledge, when introspected into, may be distinguished from perceptual knowledge. Still the perceived object being consciously distinct in itself may *be* distinct from its presentation, though it is not consciously so appreciated. Knowledge involves only the conscious or evident distinctness of the believed object, whether or not there is the consciousness of the presentation as that from which it is distinct.

35. Perceptual illusion presents another kind of difficulty. The perceived object being disbelieved is not removed altogether from consciousness. The appearance may be still presented though such presentation would not embody belief in an object. Like mere imagination, mere perceptual presentation is no psychic fact at all to which object may be related in the way of distinction: the awareness of it is only the fringe of perception as a fact. In the correction of an illusion as expressed in 'not snake but rope', the rope is utterly unrelated to the mere presentation: the word *not* in it means rejection only and no distinction, the rejection being the fringe of the present perception of rope. The awareness of the mere presentation is not belief in it, though unlike mere imagination the presentation is not explicitly disbelieved. The mere presentation as this equivocal something that is neither believed nor disbelieved is very different from the presentation from which the object is said to be distinct in knowledge and which is definitely believed in introspection and taken to embody belief in an object. It should, in fact, be designated by some word other than presentation.

36. Intermediate between perceptual knowledge and perceptual illusion are the other forms of knowledge involving a conscious distinction of the known object from its presentation. It is in the awareness of the illusory that the presentation definitely emerges from the preceived object into which it was merged. But this emergence or freedom is also the death of the presentation in the sense that it no longer embodies belief. The presentation is a fact to introspection so long as the object presented is believed and distinguished from it. Introspection into non-perceptual knowledge is thus a belief in presentation. As introspection is the belief that its content is a fact even apart from introspection, the presentation is a fact, the facthood of which consists in its being a belief in a distinct objective fact. As there is no direct introspection into perceptual knowledge, there is no consciousness here, but not therefore a denial, of a presentation from

which the object is distinct. Introspection into non-perceptual knowledge is such consciousness of presentation of object from which object is distinct.

37. The distinctness of the object from its presentation does not mean the distinctness of the presentation from its object. The introspective belief in the presentation is belief in the object as well and so presentation is not not-objective, not illusory nor purely subjective. As the object, however, is distinguished from it in non-perceptual knowledge, it is the perceivable object and something more that is believed in, something that is not known but is wanted to be known. The knowledge of the distinction of the object as imagined to be perceived from the presentation is the belief embodied in presentation in something that cannot be imagined to be perceived but appears still as adjectival to the perceivable object. This believed something is, if known, known as unknown and as only wanted to be known.

38. There are different grades of non-perceptual knowledge implying different modes of presentation or belief in object. By 'perception' is meant here external perception of object. What is the knowledge of the body from within, body as internally felt and not externally observed ? The observed object including the observed body is distinguished from the internally felt body which thus is no part of the observable world and yet is believed not as other than the observed body but as its character of internality. Again, there is the immediate apprehension of the absence of an object which cannot be said to be known by external perception, at least, in the ordinary sense and yet is known as a present objective fact. There is memory which is belief in the perceivable object as past, pastness being an unperceivable character of the object. Imagination so far as it involves belief is non-perceptual apprehension of the object as forming or becoming formed to be a perceptible object. Inference, again, is belief in the perceivable object as involving the unperceivable character of necessity. None of these non-perceptual forms of apprehension is mere belief; the object cannot be said to be not known in them and yet each is a belief in something that cannot be known by external perception and, being still about the object and indefinite, is wanted to be somehow known or realised. Perceptual knowledge is the actual standard of knowledge. The other modes of apprehension imply it, are not taken in introspection to be mere belief and involve further a belief in something not yet known but which may be known in some ideal mode of realisation or intuition.

39. Perception as the actual standard of knowledge not only lends the cognitive character to the other modes of apprehension but also prevents them from reaching their ideal completion. The internality of the felt body, absence or pastness, forming or necessity as facts are wanted to be known as the object is actually known in perception. Yet these are facts of such a kind that if they were so known, the perception of the object could not remain unaffected in its cognitive character. So far as these modes of apprehension are knowledge, they are knowledge of these facts as adjectival characters of the perceptually knowable object. These facts however, as shown about the general character of knownness, are floating adjectives from which the object to which they are ascribed are distinct though as abstractions of the second degree, they have to be referred adjectivally to the object as substantive. They are, however, necessarily symbolised as substantive by objective metaphors, being not merely thought but sought to be believed as though they were substantive objects. If they could be known as such, the actual perceived object would be, at best, a particular manifestation of a more essential object. They are, however, not known as substantive and there is only the metaphysical *aspiration* to extend and deepen the conception of the object. They are not known because as a matter of fact, though not necessarily, we are wedded to the body and to the perceptual object that is organic to it. The identification with the object is so deep-rooted that, though not necessary, it is not annulled by any logic and may be regarded for all ordinary purposes as a 'permanent illusion'.

40. The believed object as perceived or imagined to be perceived is distinct from presentation but the presentation is not distinct from its object. In perceptual knowledge, if the object is not consciously distinct from its presentation, its distinction is yet knowable through some ordinary non-perceptual mode of knowledge. But if the presentation is not known as distinct from the object, it does not come to be known as such by any logic or in any ordinary form of knowledge. It is believed and symbolised as what should be distinct: the distinction here, not being a character of the object, cannot exist unconsciously. It can exist only in being achieved or realised subjectively. The psychic fact, being essentially presentation as embodying belief, is on the one hand not imaginary or non-factual and on the other not accomplished as fact but only to be accomplished. It is at once known and unknown, its facthood being what has begun to be achieved and is yet to be completed. Introspection is belief in the psychic, not as utterly unknown but as only not isolated or freed from objective fact. The complete

knowledge and facthood of the psychic has to be achieved by such isolation but the demand itself is roused by such knowledge as has already begun.

41. Psychic fact involves knowledge of object and such knowledge exists outside introspection as presentation from which object is distinct but which is not distinct from the object. Presentation is the object and more than the object, embodying, as it does, belief in something that can never be perceived by sense, from which the perceived object is distinct but which yet appears as a character of the object. As such, this presentation may be said to be known as unknown and as to be known and has to be symbolised as object, including, as it does, the object as its manifestation or appearance in some sense. Psychic fact accordingly is that of which the facthood is at once accomplished and to be accomplished, unlike the facthood of objective fact which is only accomplished and the reality like that claimed for the moral *ought* which is only to be accomplished.

42. The complete accomplishment of psychic facthood is conceivable as implying presentation that is wholly turned into known object, which would mean, not the lapse of the conscious distinction of object from presentation such as characterises sense-perception, but the conscious or evident objectivity of what in presentation is more than the sense-given object and suggests a metaphysical reality—what in ordinary psychic fact is only not denied as objective and may be conceived to be subjective. The image of a believed object, for example, is more than the perceivable object in the sense that it appears *being* formed and not given as formed. The forming is presented as a process of the object itself and yet somehow prior to its existence as formed. There is no ground to take it as merely subjective, for it appears to be seen in the non-introspective attitude though the object as formed is distinct from it. As a becoming of the object prior to its accomplished being, it implies a metaphysical fact that is not known as intelligibly related to the object, appearing as it does as an un-objective character of the object which is a contradiction. It is in this sense known as unknown in the object and felt as dissociated from it. If imagination were to be realised, this contradiction would disappear, the becoming would be evident as a substantive fact and the object would be seen as its contingent manifestation. The image would then be dissociated in knowledge and not in mere feeling from the object and would be said to have achieved a free existence. Similar suggestions of metaphysical reality and the possibility of realising it would be presented by psychic states higher than the imagination.

43. To such a view a Kantian may be supposed to object that the metaphysical reality thus adumbrated in the presentation is only subjective though it appears real in the object by illusion, by a permanent illusion which we can critically correct without being able to remove. The critical correction may only be sought to be strengthened in a non-cognitive way—the moral or aesthetic way—with the entertainment of the metaphysical reality in faith. Our contention would be that the appearance of its objectivity is incomplete but not illusory; that the illusion is to take it as known but not as knowable; that if it were unknowable, it could not be entertained in faith even for non-cognitive realisation and that the demand to know it is legitimate if not necessary. The thought of the metaphysical entity is a conscious problem but the problem is soluble in a mode of knowledge in which the object would appear as its free efflux, as what it can be but need not be. The metaphysical would appear in such knowledge as an evident real, as the existent fact of knowledge itself, with the object as its free possibility and as negated in its actuality.

44. That metaphysical reality is subjective is admitted in the sense that it is not an *object* behind the perceivable object. The objective attitude of metaphysics should terminate with the recognition of something that is known as unknown in the object, of the contradiction in the presented unobjective character of the object. But this unknown something that is known as such and formulated is not *merely* subjective in the sense of being illusory or in the sense of being the content of a faith that can never be turned into knowledge. To take it as merely subjective is to assume the object to be alone knowable and to be incapable of being *known* as put forth subjectively or freely. It is to deny the facthood of the constructive function by which the perceivable object comes to be for the subject. The epistemological functions are indeed believed and not known but they are not believed as merely subjective. They are, no doubt, symbolised by objective metaphors but the symbolism is necessary and has to be entertained in faith. The demand to entertain the objective symbolism in faith is inconsistent with the *denial* of the knowability or objectivity of the functions. To be aware of a description as metaphorical but necessarily so is to take it to be unknown in the sense of being unrealised, of being imagined to be known but not yet known. It implies the possibility of knowing not indeed by any logical procedure but by a specific self-realising activity of the imagination itself. It argues a gratuitous diffidence to take such activity to be a mystic chimera. The imagination of knowing or the symbolising faith would

not be faith at all if the possibility of such subjective achievement of the feeling of knowledge were to be denied.

45. A faith that is spiritually demanded to be entertained cannot be taken to be incapable of being turned into knowledge. The moral postulates of Kant, for example, are such faiths. There is indeed no *moral* demand to entertain them, for they proceed from the demand for moral willing and there is no obligation on the part of the will to contemplate their objects. But when they have proceeded, are they mere speculative luxuries ? Is the formulation of their objects with an *as though* spiritually indifferent or does it suggest a hope and a discipline to realise the hope of there being a grade of subjective realisation higher than the moral ? Such a grade may be admitted as 'religion within the limits of pure reason' but the conceit of possible metaphysical knowledge, it may be said, need not, therefore, be reinstated. The conceit would be to Kant a moral impurity and critical honesty as essential to moral purity is essential to moral religion. But the conceit that implies intellectual dishonesty is the belief that metaphysical reality is known, not that it is knowable. To take the spirit as finally known when its reality is to be achieved would be to take away the will to achieve. But if the spirit is believed to be unknowable, is not the will to achieve equally taken away ? The will to realise the self, whether in knowledge or otherwise—for there may be different modes of realisation, implies at any stage the knowledge of the self as not known and the belief that it is something more than as it is known. It cannot imply a belief in the self that is not knowledge at all, far less a belief in the self as unknowable.

46. The distinction of the object that is non-perceptually known from its knownness, presentation or idea is just its character of being unknown which is believed and sought to be isolated by introspection. The known object is thus a problem to all knowledge other than perception. Perception is at once full knowledge, and restricted knowledge, full in so far as no lack of knowledge is felt in it and restricted because nothing beyond the object is necessarily suggested by it. In imaginative knowledge, as in higher forms of non-perceptual knowledge, there is a felt lack of intimacy with the object known while something is known in the object—its becoming before being, for example,— which is unknown in the sense of not being as evident as the perceived object and of being incapable of being perceived. It is believed as constituting the reality of the perceivable object, the object being its appearance which is not unreal and in this sense a phenomenon of the reality. Non-perceptual knowledge is thus

knowledge of the object as phenomenal with belief in a reality constituting it.

47. There is no explicit belief in metaphysical reality except as thus implied in the knowledge of the phenomenal. To know the phenomenon is not *not* to know the reality but to know it as unknown and, it may be, as wanted to be known. Belief that is not knowledge at all is either unaccompanied by an idea of the object as distinct from the belief or is false belief. It is not possible, therefore, to say about the postulates of moral or aesthetic consciousness that they have only to be believed and cannot be known. They are, in fact, known as unknown, known as objects that are not to be rejected as permanent illusions but to be contemplated as symbols of the reality to be known. What in the case of the understanding is known as phenomenon is in the case of the reason known as symbol, neither of which can be taken in our ordinary consciousness to be illusory though they would be realised as illusory if the reality that is known as unknown were to be completely known.

48. It would indeed be wrong to say that what is known as unknown is necessarily wanted to be known, that there is a necessity for the idea of a believed object to get transformed into knowledge. The knowledge of the unknown as such is the precondition as much of moral or aesthetic realisation as of cognitive realisation. It would be equally wrong on the other side to say that for non-cognitive realisation it is necessary to give up faith in the knowability of the unknown. Belief in the unknowability of reality is not only not demanded ; it is impossible and although in a sense the unknowable real can be conceived, the confusion of this mere conceiving with belief will exclude the possibility of all spiritual realisation. We know or believe the reality to be unknown but we cannot believe it to be unknowable. We can doubt the knowledge of the phenomenon or symbol such as is implied in the knowledge of the unknown reality ; but either such doubt does not amount to disbelief or if it does, the belief in the unknown reality also disappears, for that stands so long as the knowledge is not doubted. While the belief in the reality persists, the doubt is only an imaginary doubt, only the conceiving of a disbelief—no psychic fact at all but only a fringe of it—a conceiving of the totally unknown that is yet real. The concept of the totally unknown reality is the imaginary concept of the unknowable.

49. The factors of actual knowledge can never be proved to be necessary to all knowledge. A content that is claimed to be known may be shown afterwards to have been only believed or to be known

as unknown but cannot be shown to be unknowable in the sense of being totally unknown and yet demanded to be believed. So long as it can be spoken of and believed, it is not to be regarded as totally unknown on the ground of some factor of actual knowledge being wanting. If the thing-in-itself or an Idea of Reason is spoken of and believed, it is already known as unknown ; and because of the two factors of actual object-knowledge—thought and intuition—either is wanting in this case, one has no right to doubt such knowledge as is there already or—what amounts to the same thing—to doubt the knowability of the unknown. To know something to be unknown implies, in fact, a demand to find a condition of its being known and if the conditions of other admitted knowledge be not there, it is a call to revise our epistemology and not to reject the knowledge of the unknown that sets the problem.

50. The knowledge of the unknown is what starts the actual problem of realisation whether in the cognitive or in the non-cognitive direction. The demand for either mode of realisation is absolute, though there is a spiritual choice—which is not merely the free choice of a will—between them. The non-cognitive mode does not entertain the demand that the unknown that is known as such should be known as known, that the belief in the reality has to be turned into the knowledge of it as evident. Not that it therefore demands that there should be a belief in its unknowability : it would, in fact, be impossible with such a belief. What is demanded for any mode of spiritual realisation is that there should be the knowledge of a reality as beyond the known and that it should not be known as unknowable. The non-cognitive mode of realisation does not demand the belief that it is the only mode and that the cognitive mode implies, as Kant would have it, a fanatical conceit or theosophic illusion. The impossibility of the cognitive mode would argue the impossibility of the non-cognitive modes as well.

51. Thus we meet the Kantian difficulty. Psychic fact, we said, involves presentation from which the perceivable object is distinct and which accordingly is object and more than object. It is *more* in the sense of being a metaphysical reality constitutive of the object which is its phenomenon, a reality that is known as unknown and as knowable, though the complete knowledge of it need not be demanded. Psychic fact as embodying belief in such reality is at once real and realising, realising as being already real, this being the objective counterpart of knowing the object as unknown. To Kant, metaphysical reality—what in presentation appears to be known as

unknown in the object—is only thought and believed and appears to be known by an inevitable or permanent illusion. We agree that the introspective awareness of the presentation as distinct from the object is not knowledge of knowing but only imagination of knowing the metaphysical. The imagination, however, is not an illusion but only incomplete or unrealised knowledge and hence the imagined knowing appears as the knowing of the unknown as such in the object. There is no question of turning this imagined knowing into actual knowing by sense-intuition : it can be actualised, if at all, by the concreting activity of imagination itself. Metaphysical reality is only symbolised in objective terms : it is not literally objective though the symbolising may be a step towards knowledge of it as a subjective reality and need not be in the service of willing or feeling only. The subject may be sought to be realised morally or emotionally and the conceit of knowing the reality may be dropped but there is no necessity to drop it. Cognitive realisation of the metaphysical reality as subjective has to be admitted, at least, as an alternative spiritual possibility.

52. In this cognitive realisation, the knowledge of the unknown as such implies the demand to know the metaphysical reality not as an object hidden behind the perceivable object but as that of which the object is a free efflux and to know empirical fact as real not by being given but by the self-shining substantively existent cognition of it. What appear as characters of the object—characters like forming, pastness or necessity revealed by imagination, memory or inference—would in such realisation cease to be adjectival and appear substantive. Psychic fact would not only appear isolated from its object in the stage of introspective realisation proper to it but would cease to be distinguished from introspection as its object, shining out as a mode of introspection itself, as a self-evidencing functional fact. The phenomenal object—the object as imagined to be perceived—would appear to be a possibility that is not actual by its own right, being negated or turned into illusion in this sense though not in the sense that when put forth, it is not real at all.

53. Psychic fact appears to our ordinary unrealised introspection as more concrete than objective fact only in promise and not in actuality. It does not, however, appear as co-ordinate with objective fact: it is what should be more real but is actually less real. To be more real is not to be a whole of which objective fact is an element, for the unobjective element of psychic fact that is known in introspection as the unknown character of the object is what constitutes the reality of the object. Psychic fact contains within it objective fact

as a possibility but it would be wrong to say that the realisation of the psychic *must* mean the actualisation of this possibility. Actualisation of a possible is, indeed, a necessity to knowing, provided we choose to know or to adopt the cognitive mode of realisation. Object is a possibility within the psychic only in the sense that it *can* be actualised, not that it will or need be actualised. It is not comprehended in the psychic in the Hegelian sense.

54. The Indian conception of a specific activity of realisation on the part of the individual spirit is alien to modern philosophy generally and specially to Hegelian philosophy. The individual spirit is supposed in the latter to be individual so far as he is subject and does not know his subjectivity objectively. He knows it objectively only as he finds it through non-cognitive spiritual activity. He asserts it non-cognitively but does not in such assertion will *towards* it as what is to be developed, does not know it and stand outside it in spiritual willing though in the consciousness of the resulting fulfilment, he knows the subjectivity to have been developed. To the absolute spirit, however, his will to realise his subjectivity is knowledge of his subjectivity *in* the willing and not *after* the willing : realisation in the Indian sense is thus admitted in the absolute spirit alone. So far as it is admitted, it is understood as cognitive, non-cognitive activity being only a stage or constituent function in it. So the object, so far as it is known as unknown in the psychic state, would be taken by the Hegelian to be known by the individual as eternally known by the Absolute, as what not only can but will be unfolded by the psychic, being eternally unfolded in the Absolute. It is this necessity that is denied here as against the Hegelian : object as an ideality within the psychic is what can be unfolded but need not be. The psychic is more concrete than the object in the sense that it can freely put forth the lesser reality; and even as it does put forth, it does not lend to it its whole reality but keeps itself still as more concrete than the manifested object. Nature is still to the Psyche a magic or playful appearance.

55. The parting from the Hegelian view is suggested at a comparatively late stage. But the view of the psychic as co-ordinate with the object and still more the view of it as comprehending the object as a real element have to be rejected at the very start. There is a tendency in certain recent developments of psychology to reject the ghostly psychic fact as co-ordinate with objective fact either in favour of an experience-unity of subject and object or in favour of the biological unity of the organism and its environment. We are not con-

cerned with the latter for the present. The experience-unity of subject and object is supposed to be known in introspection. It is the psychic fact as implying the object as a real element, the presentation which is not not-object and from which the object is differentiated out by 'inter-subjective intercourse'. Now the question is if this experience-unity is rightly claimed to be known by introspection, known so unambiguously that it can be proposed to be substituted for the current duality of subject and object. All that can be admitted is that we do not distinguish the presentation from the object as we distinguish the object from the presentation : we only cannot deny that the presentation is object though the object is other than presentation. The distinguishing of the object from its presentation is definite knowledge but the non-denial of the identity of presentation with its object does not amount to the knowledge of it. The presentation, in fact, cannot be known except as what the object is distinct *from*. By itself it is believed in introspection and it embodies belief in the object. Psychic fact as bound up with presentation cannot be asserted to *include* the object on the ground that presentation is not known as not-object or implies belief in the object.

56. The ordinary view of the ghostly psychic fact as co-ordinate with objective fact ignores the experienced non-distinction of presentation from its object while the view of experience-unity unwarrantably asserts it as identity. Is the duality of psychic fact and objective fact secured any better by the recognition of the distinction between the 'enjoying' and the 'contemplative' modes of knowing ? For one thing, it is doubtful if the enjoying knowledge of the psychic fact should be called knowledge at all. Even if it be taken as knowledge of it as objectively unknown, the difficulty is to relate the content of it with the content of contemplative knowledge. The distinction of objective fact from presentation or psychic fact may be taken to be itself an objective fact that is contemplatively known. But the distinction of psychic fact from the object, to be known, would have to be enjoyingly known. All that, however, can be said to be enjoyingly known is the psychic fact as distinct in itself. Its distinction from the object is only symbolically thought by an illegitimate extension of the reversible character of the relation of distinction within contemplative knowledge. It is not known but is only a symbolism for the felt dissociation or freedom of the psychic fact from the object.

CHAPTER III

BODILY SUBJECTIVITY

THE BODY AS PERCEIVED AND FELT

57. Psychic fact has been taken to be fact of which we are introspectively aware as capable of existing apart from introspection. Introspection is the distinguishing of the presentation from its object, the object being given as distinct from the presentation. In perceptual knowledge, the object is not given as distinct from its presentation and hence perceptual knowledge is not at least directly the object of introspection and is not a psychic fact in this sense. We are, however, aware of the subject even in the sub-psychic perceptual stage. The body as externally and internally perceived, as observed and felt may be regarded as the subject in relation to the environment and psychology has to start with this bodily subjectivity.

58. The materialistic view that the subject is but the body is true in so far as the body represents a stage of being of the subject. But it ignores the unique singularity of one's own body even as a perceived object. No merely objectivistic account can do justice to this singularity. The objectivity of other perceived objects is constituted by their position relative to the percipient's body which itself, therefore, cannot be taken to be so constituted. To the percipient, his body is an object situated in space relatively to some other percipient's body as imagined, being not perceived by himself in a space-position though not known, therefore, as non-spatial. The percipient as in his body or as his body is, in this sense, dissociated from the external world, being what his perceived world is distinct from: At the same time he cannot help imagining himself as included in the world though it may be as a privileged object.

59. One's own body is only half-perceived, the rest being eked out by imagination. The unseen face of a solid object that is perceived is imagined by the percipient by imagining his own body being placed in a different position. To imagine the unseen half of one's own body, however, the observer does not imagine his own body thus placed differently. He imagines *another* observing body, not his own, as thus placed. In this respect also his own perceived body is uniquely different from other perceived objects and has no place in the objective world that he conceives to be presentable to him as a

solipsistic observer. The world as a construction out of the views or perspectives of many observers cannot be simply identified with the world constructed out of the views of the same observer in different positions. The former is not, indeed, known as other than the latter ; but it is a world organic to a subject that feels dissociated from his body, a world therefore that has no perceivable position and involves a space that he as percipient cannot take to be objective to him. Thus even if the subject is taken as nothing but one's own perceived body, it involves the knowledge of something unknown as such in the object, something that cannot be understood in terms of the perceptible object in the merely objectivistic attitude. It still implies the mystic awareness of dissociation from the object in which subjectivity consists. What is intended by the word *I* cannot be characterised even in the lowest stage of subjectivity as simply *this* object.

60. One's own body is not only perceived from outside : one is immediately or sensuously aware of it also from within in what is called 'feeling of the body'. This feeling is not, like the feeling of an object, a psychic fact from which the object known is distinguished. The bodily feeling is but the felt body which is not known to be other than the perceived body. Yet the perceived body is distinct from it so far as it is an 'interior' that is never perceived and cannot be imagined to be perceived from outside. Introspection, indeed, is sometimes taken as nothing but sense-perception of the interior of the body. But the interior cannot be understood here as the interior that one may imagine oneself seeing. To say that it is the same spatial interior, only appearing indefinite, is to ignore the qualitative difference that is felt between the indefiniteness of a perceived position and the indefiniteness of a felt position, the position, for example, of a pain in the perceived body. Our knowledge of objective space may have been developed from the felt spread of the body or the felt location in it but we are always aware of such felt space as only *partially* defined into perceived space and, therefore, cannot assert the former to be nothing more than the latter. Perceived space, however it may be extended and complicated by the geometric imagination, can at best symbolise the uniquely felt space that sets the problem of objective interpretation and is always in advance of the interpretation. It is even as the uniquely singular *I* is symbolised by the objectively singular *this,* being never adequately interpreted by it.

61. Objective space that is indefinitely perceived is the same as the objective space that is definitely perceived and the definition does not involve any fresh objectification. But felt space is indefi-

nite in the sense that it is more than the objective space it is defined into, *more* in the sense already explained in which the presentation of an object is more than the object. The felt interior of the body may thus be regarded as the prototype of the observable interior, not merely the latter as presented indefinitely but what can only be symbolised by the latter in its full definiteness. Definite objective space is related to felt space as the objective exterior is related to the objective interior, the latter relation being, in fact, the reflection of the former relation.

62. The awareness of the body from within is, indeed, sensuous but it can hardly be called sense-perception. It is only not denied to be perception, though the perceived body as an object among objects is distinguished from the body as felt from within. The body is felt as extending from a vague interior to the outer surface that may be both felt and perceived. But the perception of the body stops at the surface and if it is extended by the imagination of the interior, the interior is still imagined as an external surface. The perceived and imagined body is always an exterior which may also be felt but the felt interior can never be imagined as perceived. Thus the felt body cannot be distinguished from the perceived body though the latter is distinguished from the former.

63. The relation between the felt body and the perceived body is similar to the relation of presentation and its object in non-perceptual knowledge. There is, however, the difference that introspection into such knowledge is possible because the presentation is felt to be dissociated though not known to be distinct from its object while there is no introspection into body-feeling, as we are not aware of it as dissociated from the perceived body. Body-feeling and felt body are only verbally distinct ; and the awareness of the felt body is not the awareness of anything but the perceived body though the perceived body is distinguished from the felt body. As in the case of the perception of objects, there is no conscious duality of presentation and object in body-feeling and as in the case of non-perceptual knowledge, the perceptible object—here the body—is distinguished from something which however here is the felt body and not presentation and is not suspected like presentation as the possibility of anything other than the perceived body. Body-feeling may accordingly be regarded as not psychic fact but the potentiality of it. The problem of dissociating it from the objective body does not yet arise, as it arises in the case of psychic fact. But the possibility of dissociation is there, in the actualisation of which body-feeling may be conceived to be transformed into psychic fact.

Actually in body-feeling, we are not interested in withdrawing from the environment : it is only an interest derived from higher stages of subjectivity that suggests such withdrawal.

64. We may consider body-feeling in relation to psychic fact and introspection into psychic fact on the one hand and to the perceived body and perceived object on the other. The perceived body is only potentially dissociated from the perceived object inasmuch as it is not merely like presentation not denied to be object but is positively known as object. There is no explicit awareness of dissociation from the object but since position relative to the body, which is a constitutive character of the object, may not be analysed out in perception, the object is only half-distinguished from the body, the body being, therefore, only implicitly or potentially dissociated from it. The object, however, is fully distinguished from the felt body: the perceived object presents exterior surface only, its so-called interior being, as perceived or imagined to be perceived, still an exterior. Corresponding to this full distinction from the felt interior, there is the actual but imperfect dissociation or freedom of the felt body from the perceived environment. The felt body, however, does not appear even imperfectly dissociated from the perceived body. It is only potentially dissociated because the perceived body is half-distinguished from the felt body in the sense one who observes his body as exterior to him may not feel it.

65. Again, the perceived body is fully distinguished from psychic fact—from the imagination of the body, for example—which however is imperfectly but consciously dissociated from it. There may be consciousness of the body as *mine* and at the same time as not other than myself, unlike the consciousness of the object which if felt as *mine* is felt as not *me*. The felt body is, however, only half-distinguished from psychic fact, since it is the feeling of the body on the one hand and is not actually dissociated from the perceived body on the other. Psychic fact accordingly is only potentially or implicitly and not actually or explicitly dissociated from the felt body. In introspection into psychic fact, this potential dissociation of the psychic fact from the felt body becomes imperfectly actual : there is no awareness of the psychic fact as not involving bodily feeling at all though bodily feeling as the felt body itself is other than the psychic fact. The felt body begins to get resolved into a bodiless psychic feeling in introspection and may be conceived to be fully resolved when introspection gets realised as assured knowledge. Meantime our ordinary introspection involves awareness of the felt body as

not other than the perceived body from which, however, psychic fact is felt to be completely detached. It is in this sense only that introspection may be taken as the sense-perception of the bodily interior. Strictly speaking, it is the awareness of a psychic fact felt as fully detached from the perceived body or the bodily exterior and half-detached from the felt bodily interior which also is half-detached from the bodily exterior.

66. The facthood of the subjective is constituted by this feeling of detachment or freedom. The first hint of this freedom is reached in the feeling of the body. In the perception of the object, there need not be the knowledge of the object being distinct from the body. Developed perception may involve such knowledge but still the body is taken as perceived object. When the perceived body is distinguished from the felt body, the exterior from the interior, we have an explicit feeling of distinction, detachment or freedom from the perceived object. Apart from the specific activity of realisation which subjectivity suggests, the first given feeling of freedom in body-feeling is what all freedom of higher grade involves and derives its meaning from. Subjectivity apart from spiritual discipline is rooted in body-feeling and is only imagined to be dissociable from it. Psychic fact is then fact because of the knowledge of object or the presentation that it involves, because of the consequent felt detachment of it from the perceived body and of its non-detachment from the felt body. In introspection, indeed, there is the initial detachment of psychic fact from the felt body but introspection itself is fact only as a fringe of some psychic fact which is undetached from the felt body. This initial detachment here is only imagined, for the felt body is not yet turned into a psychic feeling, introspection being only the faith that the detachment can be realised. The realisation of this freedom from the felt body is the pre-condition of all distinctively spiritual activity.

CHAPTER IV

BODILY SUBJECTIVITY (Contd.)

KNOWLEDGE OF ABSENCE AS A PRESENT FACT

67. The perception of objective fact does not imply a distinguishing of the object from the presentation of it. That there is a presentation here from which the object is distinct is not directly known by introspection. Perception as a psychic fact is known only in introspection into non-perceptual knowledge. In memory, for example, there is the distinguishing of the past object from the presentation (image) of it and in introspection into memory, there is the further distinguishing of the past perceptual presentation of the object from the present image of it, the object being thus known as having been unconsciously distinct from the past presentation. The perceived object may, however, be directly distinguished from the felt body which, as has been pointed out, is like the perceived object undistinguished from presentation but yet involves a feeling of detachment from all object other than perceived body. The feeling of the body may accordingly be taken to be an implicate of developed perception, of the perception of the object as distinct from the felt body and to be only a fringe of perceptual knowledge. The knowledge of absence as a present fact that now comes up for discussion is similarly a fringe of object-perception of a higher grade, involving like all perception no distinction of the fact from the presentation of it. The absence of object that is immediately known as a present fact is just midway between the body felt to be present and the presentation that is felt to be detached from present fact in non-perceptual knowledge.

68. Objective fact may be said to be present as external, as internal and as absent. The felt body is objective fact in its internal aspect. An object may be also directly known to be *now* absent, to be 'present as absent' in this sense—a paradoxical phrase to be justified presently. All these three aspects may be said to be known in connexion with sense and involve no distinguishing from presentation. A present object as external may be distinguished from other present objects as external, from a present object as internal or from the present absence of itself. The feeling of the body is already a detachment from the external object though not from the body as

external. The direct knowledge of the present absence of an object is a detachment not only from the object but also from the perceived body though not from the body as internally felt. The absence of an object, so far as it is located, is located like its presence in reference to the body but the reference is in opposite directions. The object as present is there away from my body. In the case of absence, the object being missed or unreached by my body is what my body is away from : the absence is where my body is not. Thus the body as external is distinguished from the object as absent and not the latter from the former. Corresponding to this distinction, there is the felt detachment from the body of the present absence of the object or of the object as now missed, the consciousness of the absence or the absent being thus removed from the space round the body.

69. The sense-conditioned knowledge of an object being now absent is not to be confused with the memory, expectation or imagination of the object. None of these need involve knowledge of its *present* absence. An object may be remembered, expected or imagined though it is now present : non-perceptual knowledge of it may co-exist with perceptual knowledge. There are cases, again, in which there is no distinct image of the absent object at all and where yet we may be aware of the perceived locus of the absence as empty or devoid of an indefinite something. A consciously imagined object as now absent or the absence of an object not consciously imagined that characterises a perceived locus as empty is known in connexion with sense and known, if not in perception, in a cognitive mode undissociated from perception. The cognition is a fringe either of the perception of the locus or of the perception of the body and is in either case undissociated from the feeling of the body.

70. The cognition of an object as now absent may but need not involve the cognition of its absence as characterising a locus and the latter also may but need not involve the former. The two cognitions are, therefore, distinct and each as primary may involve the latter as secondary. A field, for example, was observed in the past with a tree standing on it, which might not have been particularly noticed at the time. The observer comes to the place when the tree has been removed and finds a new bare look about the place. He may not know that it is absence of the tree that makes the difference but he notices the difference, bareness or absence. To take another example, a person is looking for a book in a room but does not find it. He knows the book to be absent without being conscious of any empty look about the room and without, in fact, consciously referring the

absence to the room at all. The former example would be a case of cognition of the *absence* of an object (tree) and the latter of cognition of an object (book) being *absent*. Neither cognition here need imply the other and both are direct sense-conditioned cognitions of objective fact. Yet each may develop into the other cognition : what is absent may come to be realised as tree in the first example and the absence of the book may come to be realised in explicit reference to the room in the second.

71. Should the primary and secondary cognitions in each case be called perception ? In the first case, the absence of the tree is known as a character of the locus, the perceived field where the tree stood. The tree may not be definitely remembered but if remembered it is recognised to be the specification of the absence that continues to be known, the place not ceasing to wear the bare look because of the definite memory. As the place is perceived, absence as a character of the place may also be claimed to be perceived. There is, however, a distinction between the sense in which absence is a character and that in which a quality like colour is a character of the place. The place in being perceived with the bareness or absence is, if not perceived, at least imagined as what need not have the character, being presented as with a new look or, in other words, as distinct from what it might be. But to perceive the place with a colour is not necessarily to imagine that it might be without it. The perceived locus of absence being imagined in the very perception of it as without the absence, the absence is only a floating adjective that unlike colour is felt to be dissociated from the locus. There is a suggestion of the absence being outside the space where the locus stands—the space round the body, of its being *nowhere* like an image, though it is believed to be objective and not psychic fact. The suggestion is not actual imagination of positionless objective fact but only the attempted symbolising of the feeling of detachment from objective space. The absence cannot be said to be not known as objective but it is implicitly felt to be dissociated from objective space. The perception of it as a character of the object in the feeling that it is not a character and with the conscious distinguishing of the object from it may be called aesthetic or imaginative perception to distinguish it from ordinary perception.

72. In the second example, what is known in the first instance is not the absence of the book but the book as absent. The book is not found and the room where it is not found is not perceived, at least immediately, to have any empty look owing to the absence.

The book as absent is immediately known as a present objective circumstance that is neither remembered nor merely imagined. The missing of the imagined book is a characteristic experience, implying a feeling of the body not reaching it, which is interpreted as the objective fact of the book being absent. The knowledge of this fact of the book as absent is with the conscious imagination of the book as found being distinct from it and implies the feeling of the present fact being outside objective space altogether. Such knowledge also may, therefore, be called aesthetic or imaginative perception. The difference from the previous case is that what is imaginatively distinguished within the perception is not the perceived locus of the absence from the absence but the imagined object-as-present from the perceived object-as-absent. In neither case is the positive object distinguished from a presentation as in non-perceptual knowledge. It is distinguished in both cases from the objective fact of absence or the absent and not from a psychic fact. This objective fact that is distinguished from may thus be said to be perceived.

73. The primary cognitions of absence and the absent which are both perception may be followed by secondary cognitions. The perception of the absence of the tree in the first example may develop into the cognition of the tree as absent and the perception of the book as absent in the second example into the cognition of the absence of the book imagined explicitly as the book *in the room*. The interest may shift in the former case from the bare look of the locus to what was in it but is no longer existing and in the latter case from the book that is missed to the locus which might have been but is not with the object. Are these secondary cognitions also perception ?

74. When after the perception of the absence of the tree as a character of the place, the tree as remembered is known to be now absent, there is no missing of a looked-for object like the missing of the book in the second example. If an object is looked for and not found, the object as it might be now, with presentness as its adjective, is perceived to be absent. Again, when absence is known as a character or adjective of a present locus, it is taken to be perceived. But when as in this case *that* object tree is known to be *now* absent, the presentness is not adjective either to the object or to the locus but is only an adverbial mode of the adjective *absent*. What is consciously referred to as *now* is neither the object nor the locus but the absence only. *That* object is not now perceivable and the perception of this place is irrelevant to the knowledge of the tree as absent.

Such knowledge is not perception : there is no perception that is not or does not consciously imply apprehension of a concrete as present.

75. The secondary cognition of *that* tree as now absent is not perception, though it is immediate and sense-conditioned cognition of the present. What is known to be *now* absent is known in the consciousness of not perceiving it, with the belief that it would have been perceived had it been present. Not that it is, therefore, *inferred* to be absent : the consciousness of not perceiving what, it is inferred, would have been perceived is itself no inference and is at once the objective knowledge of the present fact of absence. Present absence by itself is then immediately known in connexion with sense and inference by what may be called conscious non-perception. This has to be recognised as a new mode of knowledge and is comparable with the pure perception of object, conceived as that to which the object is not given but before which it floats up like an image and is none-the-less believed. Conscious non-perception is, indeed, in connexion with sense but what is perceived by sense is irrelevant to its content.

76. The secondary cognition in the second example is also a case of conscious non-perception. To make it more readily intelligible, we may vary the illustration and consider the absence of a beloved person instead of a book that is looked for in a room. When such a person is missed or imaginatively perceived as now absent, there may not be any relevant reference to the locus viz., the room. But one may come to imagine the room as with the person and then realise his absence in reference to this imagined content. To imagine an object in a perceived locus is a special form of imagination in which the present locus is viewed as characterising and not as characterised by the imagined content. The belief in the absence of the object as thus characterised by the locus, the absence here of the imagined room as sentimentally associated with the beloved person, is immediate knowledge but not perception. The absence is not taken to be fact *in* the present locus ; and as the presentness of the absence is not the presentness of any concrete thing, it cannot be said to be perceived. The secondary cognition is conscious non-perception, the room that is perceived by sense being turned into the imagined character of location of the imagined person.

77. The primary cognition of absence and the absent is imaginative perception and the secondary cognition of them is conscious non-perception. The relation of these modes of cognition with the apprehension of the body has now to be brought out. The primary cognition is related to the perception of the body as the

secondary cognition is related to the feeling of the body. The absence of the tree in the first example is where its locus is. The tree as absent, however, is not essentially referred to the locus, being felt in fact as outside the space round my body, as detached from reference to the perceived body. The positionlessness is felt and believed as a mode of my body-feeling which is dissociated from the object. The *now* or presentness of the absence is the *now* or the presentness of the body-feeling. But while the *now* of the body-feeling is not distinguished from the *then* as remembered or the *might be* as imagined, being only an implicit *now,* the *now* of the absent tree in this case is so distinguished. The *absent-now* is felt dissociated from the perceived body as the felt body is not. Thus the felt body is imperfectly distinct from the *absent-now* which, therefore, only appears to be a mode of the felt body, being undetached from it but really represents a stage higher and just falling short of the detached image. There is a similar relation of the primary and secondary cognitions in the second example to the perceived body and the felt body.

78. In the imaginative perception of absence and the absent, there is no explitly felt dissociation from the position of the perceived body, which however is imperfectly distinguished from the imagined position of absence or of the absent. In conscious non-perception, there is the explicitly felt dissociation from the perceived body but not from the felt body, though the felt body has begun to be distinguished from the fact of absence or the absent. The relation of the perceived body in the former case and of the felt body in the latter to the known absence is like the relation of the perceived body to the felt body. The perceived body is half-distinguished from the felt body which, however, is not felt to be dissociated from the perceived body. Absence imaginatively perceived is thus on a level with the felt body, both being felt undissociated from the perceived body which however is half-distinguished from them. Absence known by conscious non-perception is on a higher level, being felt half-dissociated from the perceived body which, however, is fully distinguished from it and undissociated from the felt body which is half-distinguished from it.

79. Conscious non-perception then is a transitional stage between body-feeling and imagination with which psychic fact begins. It is the consciousness of presentness without space-position, the same as the presentness of the felt body but distinguished from such absence of the perceived object as is realised in imagination, memory or expectation as the *might be,* the past or the future. It is free from

space but not from the present and accordingly does not imply a presentation of the object as dissociated from the object. Psychic fact begins with the distinguishing of what the present is not. Conscious non-perception is the distinguishing of the present from the detached presentation and not reversely and may be taken as the immediate pre-condition of the felt detachment of the presentation from the present. Were one to start with object-perception as the actual standard of knowledge, the first clear hint of the subjective fact would be realised in the knowledge of absence through conscious non-perception.

CHAPTER V

Psychic Subjectivity

THE IMAGE

80. Psychology does not begin till the perceived object is distinguished from the half-perceived body. The body may not be felt as dissociated from the objective world but it is still realised as a uniquely central object round which the world is disposed. To those who would not go farther in psychology, introspection is only observation of the indefinite body-interior and psychic fact is only a bodily attitude, the beginning of the behaviour of an organism to the environment. Some, however, would go one step farther and admit the image as a unique fact, appearing as a quasi-object from which object including the body is distinguished. Psychology to them cannot ignore the image, even if it be only ancillary to bodily behaviour. The image may be functional in character as a reference to the object, the reference being ultimately a behaving mode ; but that it appears presented as a substantive something from which the object is distinct and exists in a sense in which the object does not exist cannot be denied.

81. The meaning of facthood appears to change as we pass from the perceived object as fact to the image as fact. This is realised if we interpose between them the three entities so far discussed—the perceived body, the felt body and absence of object as known in conscious non-perception. Each later term in the series appears to be fact in a sense different from the term before it—the perceived body from the perceived object, the felt body from the perceived body and so on. Facthood as an abstraction has an unformed symbolic meaning : its actual meaning depends on the nature of the content that is taken as fact. Fact in general means only what is believed or asserted but what fact means as a predicate applied to a content apart from the subjective function of assertion is indeterminate. Its meaning depends on the form of knownness of the content, the knownness that is its constitutive character and is abstracted by the so-called psychological introspection. The object is object to us so far as it is given and not self-evident like I, so far as it is presented and believed as more than it is known, so far, in fact, as it is known

to be unknown. Knownness as an abstraction emerges only with this positive awareness of the unknown and has meaning only in reference to it. If the abstraction by itself has a meaning, it stands for an indeterminate which is not given nor yet is self-evidencing like the knowing I, being at best what is to be known. The concept of fact in general or knownness by itself is thus a problem in meaning and not an accomplished meaning. Meantime facthood is but a name for many grades or modes of fact which have no *actual* relation of similarity or point of similarity. We have accordingly to begin by accepting the different grades of fact as implying different meanings of facthood.

82. A perceived object is necessarily a spatial object having a position relatively not only to other perceived objects but also to the percipient's body. The perceived parts of his body are to him like outside objects situated relatively to some part of his body that he does not perceive nor even imagine himself perceiving but imagines only as perceivable (by another) and yet as continuous with the part that he perceives. His perceivable body as a whole is not perceived by him as situated relatively to the object. The perceived positional relation of one object to another is reversible but that of the object to the percipient's body as a whole is not reversible. Position relatively to the percipient's body is a character that constitutes the facthood of the perceived object, but his body as a perceivable fact is not constituted to his perception by position relative to the object though it is imagined by him as situated relatively to another spectator in a perceived objective position. This lack of perceived position is what distinguishes the facthood of one's perceivable body from the facthood of the objects perceived by him.

83. The imagined position of the perceived body is in objective space, space that is all exterior to the actual or imaginary percipient. Interior and exterior within objective space are understood relatively to two spectators : what the same actual spectator perceives is only the exterior. What he apprehends as interior is the felt space : his felt position consists in withdrawal from objective space, though it is not known as other than the imagined position of the perceivable body. The body is still felt to have a position which objective position is not but which is not, therefore, known as other than objective position. The interiority of the felt body is what distinguishes its existence from that of the perceived body.

84. The absence of an object is immediately known as a present objective fact. Has its facthood any reference to space-position?

In what we have called the aesthetic or imaginative perception of absence, the absence is taken to be where the thing absent is imagined to be. Now in imagining an object in a perceived position, the position is turned into an imagined character of the object. The position of the absence of the object is thus imagined though not imaginary. The position of the perceived body is also imagined and of both it may be said that they are not unperceived because imagined, being, in fact, perceived through the imagination. The difference is that the body is half-perceived by sense while the absence is perceived wholly through imagination. Absence has a factual position only as the felt body is undetached from the perceiving body. The position of absence as distinguished from the absence itself, is like the perceivable body half-perceived through the imagination : the locus is perceived by sense and it is also imagined as turned into a character of the imagined object. Perceived absence then is on a level with the felt body but its position is on the level of the perceived body. Such absence is undetached from its position as the felt body is undetached from the perceived body.

85. Absence that is known by conscious non-perception is not referred to objective space. It is not known as with a position though it would be going too far to say that it is known as positionless. It is felt even as the body is felt, the belief in it being a bodily feeling of not feeling the object. Yet as the felt body is not detached from the perceived body and appears spatial as the mystic interior, absence in conscious non-perception is referred to this interior. It is as though the absent object was in the felt body. Yet the felt body is half-distinguished from it, just as the perceived body is half-distinguished from the felt body. Absence is here not known as with position while the felt body is known as with an unknown position from which objective space-position is distinct. There is the further distinction that the presentness of the absence is asserted explicitly while bodily feeling is only the implicit feeling of presentness. It is the explicit presentness that makes it possible for absence to be known as objective and yet without position.

86. The image is known to be without position while absence in conscious non-perception is only not known with position. So, too, absence is known as present or *now*, while the image is not known as *now*. The image has no space-position and it cannot be asserted to have a time-position, which, however, is not denied. To imagine an object is not necessarily to know it as now absent. We may imagine it while we perceive it e.g., when the object is our body and

we may perceive it wholly through imagination as in what has been called aesthetic perception. But we imagine the object also when we know it to be absent. In such a case we imperfectly distinguish the object as *now* absent from the image of the object, which however is undissociated from the absent object and as such is not denied to be *now* but is not, therefore, asserted to be *now*.

87. The ordinary perception of object is said to involve imagination but the image here is only inferred and cannot appear to introspection. In a perception like that of one's own body, there is the direct consciousness of something in it as not sensed, from which the sensed portion of the body is distinguished but which itself is not distinguished from it. In what has been called aesthetic or imaginative perception, not only is the sense-perceived locus of its object distinguished from it : the object as imaginatively perceived is distinguished from itself as merely imagined though not conversely. In none of these cases is the image felt to be dissociated from the percept. In the knowledge of absence through conscious non-perception, the image of the absent object is felt to be dissociated from the felt body but not from the present absence. What is known to be wholly distinct from the image at this stage is the object as present and not as absent. The knowledge of present absence is still a mode of bodily subjectivity; but in imagination as a free psychic fact, even the present absence is distinguished from the image; and so the image, though not explicitly dissociated from the presentness, is not known as with this character which is the last vestige of perceptible facthood. The image here appears with objective form but does not appear with objective position.

88. The relation of the image and of psychic fact generally to objective time has been the subject of controversy. There is the current banality that psychic facts are only in time while objective facts are in both space and time. We have pointed out on the one hand that absence that is known in conscious non-perception is not known to be in space though it is objective and that the image proper on the other is not known to be in time. We cannot assert nor can we deny that such objective absence is in space and that the image is in time. The image is assertable as not in space, neither in perceptible space nor in felt space. It has, indeed, spatiality as a character or form ; and it is even possible to imagine an object on a perceived locus, where, however, the image is not in space but has space-position as an aesthetic expression. Thus there is a felt dissociation of the image from objective space and even from the felt

5

interior of the body. Since the absence known in conscious non-perception is not consciously dissociated from the felt body, it is only half-distinguished from the image, being not deniable as in space while the image is so deniable ; and thus the image is not felt dissociated from the present absence though it is potentially dissociated.

89. This potential dissociation of the image from the *now* is realised in 'thought'. In the examples of non-perception so far given it has been assumed that the object that is absent is imaged. But there may be cases where the absent object is only thought, as for example, when we say 'no man is present here' : man in general is here thought and not imaged. The vague image of an individual man may float up but the absence that is known is the absence not of this man in particular but of all men. The image here as symbolising the thought may be said to be consciously dissociated from the presentness of the absence. Thus though the image need not be denied as *now*, it may be denied. We cannot assert that the image of the object now absent is *now* and we can in higher stages e.g., in the stage of image with thought definitely deny it.

90. The lowest stage of psychic fact is represented by the image without thought, emerging in the conscious non-perception of the absent as such. Just as the perception of the object half-consciously implies the perception of the body, this the feeling of the body and this again the conscious non-perception of the absent, so this last implies the image of the absent from which the absent as such is imperfectly distinguished. Attention here is primarily directed to the objective absence but in distinguishing it we attend indirectly to the image of the object that is absent. As thus indirectly attended to, the image is not distinguished and appears without thought. There is no awareness yet of its being not objective : it appears as a ghostly object that does not consciously imply belief, much as the half-perceived body appears when an object is perceived to be *there*. The awareness of the image is still bound up with the perceiving attitude and is not introspective. The image is still consciously as though it were an object. It is like the illusion of the object persisting after correction, though it is only without belief and does not imply as in the case of illusion a conscious disbelief. It is only potentially psychical, being an object for possible introspection.

91. The distinguishing of the presentation of an object from the object is introspection which does not amount to the knowledge of the presentation as a given distinct. The distinguishing of the object

from its presentation is, however, a phase of object-knowledge. The presentation as thus distinguished from is an indefinite quasi-object. It is felt dissociated from the object as having no position in objective space and except in its lowest phase as image is felt also as not in time. In the case of the image, there is only no consciousness of its being an event in time : it is not felt to be not in time. Conscious non-perception of an object implies, indeed, the conscious image of the object but what is believed to be present fact is the *object* as absent, as distinct from the image which is neither believed nor disbelieved to exist at the moment. In the thought of an objective fact, however, the meaning which is the presentation is not only not referred to time : its existence in time is meaningless.

92. In conscious non-perception of an object, its image is not directly attended to and there is no introspective distinguishing of it from the object as absent. When it is introspectively attended to, it changes its character ; the image appears as imaging, as being formed though not as unformed, as functional without ceasing to be substantive. A presentation like meaning also appears functional under introspection but loses its substantive character. The completed meaning is turned into the meaning act and loses its ghostly objectivity. All psychic fact conceived in introspection to be outside introspection is the quasi-objective fact of presentation which, however—with the exception of the image—appears as a mere function or act under introspection. The ghostly psychic fact cannot accordingly be taken to be a mere illusion ; it is what introspection testifies to as existing consciously outside itself and the lowest form of it viz., the image is apprehended even in the objective attitude apart from the testimony of introspection. The view of psychic life as the self's transaction with quasi-objective presentation is suggested by the image. A presentation like meaning that wholly melts into function under introspection does not stand before the self as object for its attention.

93. The image appears under introspection as functional and substantive at the same time, as a form being formed. This forming or incomplete character of the image requires fuller consideration than it has received. There is a qualitative difference between the incompleteness of an image and the incompleteness of a perceived object, much like the difference between felt space and perceived space. The incompleteness of a percept is in reference to a fuller percept ; taken by itself, a percept is finished and definite and an indefinite and unfinished sense-appearance is not yet a percept. The sense-given cannot be incomplete in itself without being indefinite and without fall-

ing short of a percept. The image, however, is incomplete not merely in comparison with a percept but in itself ; it could not, in fact, be complete without being a percept. There cannot be a finished form that is not believed as the form of a perceived object. The imagined form is always being formed without, however, being indefinite like the sense-given content which is being formed into a percept. It is definite because the consciousness of the forming is at once the consciousness of the form to be completed. The forming and the form appear to be seen together, as they are actually seen together in what has been called aesthetic or imaginative perception. The image under introspection is, in fact, a standing process where the forming is not chronologically prior to the form and yet appears distinct from the form which is its interpretation. Under introspection accordingly the image appears as not in time while the image before introspection, as in the stage of conscious non-perception, is only not known to be in time. The consciousness of the finished form that interprets the forming is sometimes called *idea*. But the idea at this stage is not a separate presentation but only a fringe of the image. It is not dissociated from the image as forming, which, however, is distinguished from it. The idea as dissociated from the image would be the next psychic stage.

CHAPTER VI

Psychic Subjectivity

THOUGHT

94. The image under introspection appears as a forming form in which the finished form is evident in the forming process as its interpreting idea. The idea as dissociated from the image is idea of the object as not imaged and sought to be imaged. The object here appears indefinite and the imagining or forming that is started by the conscious want of the image is the process of defining it. This process which may be called the materialising of the dissociated idea is intrinsically incomplete and is ever to be completed. The undissociated idea of the previous stage is the complete form that as much appears to be seen as the incomplete forming. The dissociated idea thus implies the imaging process and the conscious want of the image. The want is here only partial but there may be idea of something in the object that cannot be defined or concreted into image at all. Such idea is thought proper that is definite in itself and is not defined in meaning but at best fixed or detained in the mind by the images it may still call up. The images here have a consciously metaphorical or symbolising value for the idea.

95. Image or thought here is considered as presentation that embodies or at least does not exclude belief in the object. The mere image or the mere meaning, the object of which is disbelieved from the start is, as indicated before, no psychic fact at all. Now what in the object is believed specifically through imagination—viz., the form, though not posited in the space that is organic to the body, is still represented as spatial, appearing as though it were felt like the body. What is believed specifically through thought, however, does not thus appear to be intimately felt and is yet as defiinite as the imagined form. The dissociated idea lies midway between the definite form and the definite intelligible, being non-spatial in form but indefinite and only partially definable by an incomplete forming. It may be called pictorial thought to distinguish it from thought proper, the object of which is definitely presented as unpicturable meaning. Picturable metaphors and symbols may be used to fix the identity of such meaning and for purposes of easy communication but they do not help to define or elaborate it.

96. The image lacks space-position but still appears spatial in form and temporal as forming or becoming and as such implies a belief in its possible objectivity. Thought as the awareness of the unimaginability of its specific content is the awareness of its objectivity being impossible and thus involves a complete detachment from objectivity. Thought is still about the object but it is of something about the object that is definitely unobjective. In lower stages and even in the stage of body-feeling, something unobjective in the object is also presented but it is not known explicitly to be unobjective, not completely denied as objective. It is completely denied in thought and if it is still said to be something in the object, it is understood to be what *appeared* as objective, what the object was not distinguished from in the lower stages. The thinkable universal or relation, for example, was presented as objective in the lower stages and the object was never sufficiently distinguished from that presentation. Even in the stage of pictorial thought or the dissociated idea, the universal appeared as a quasi-spatial whole and relation as a quasi-temporal transition. In non-pictorial thought, this conceit of their quasi-objectivity is dropped, though the object continues to be referred to as what exists and is known without name and without relation. The universal and relation in the object are recognised, if not as thinking, as not distinguished from thinking, the object given as distinct being reduced to unrelated singulars or unique contents such as may be conceived to be 'purely perceived'. As thus referring to the object, meaning is still objective though explicitly through thinking, being a presentation and not a free subjectivity.

97. Non-pictorial thought which is definite independently of the image may be sought to be metaphorically or symbolically indicated by the image. Metaphor differs from symbol : the object that is thought is imagined as though it were the same as the metaphor but not as though it were the same as the symbol. Both are recognised to be other than the object thought; but while the metaphor is consciously employed as similar to the object, the symbol which is also remotely similar to the object in relational constitution is not employed *as* similar. The word is a symbol and not a metaphor for the object meant; the metaphor is only half-distinguished from the meaning while the symbol is fully distinguished. Thought in its higher grade is detained in the mind by the word and not by its figurative representation.

98. Thought as distinct from the forming image under introspection is a completed product and the thinking that does not

amount to a complete thought is a misnomer and should only be called a trying to think. This complete thought is about an object and the object thought is quite definite, whatever indefiniteness or incompleteness there may be in the symbolic imaging of it. Thought is complete as dissociated altogether from time, not merely from time-position from which the image (at least under introspection) is also dissociated but also from the forming or ideal timing that characterises the image. It is complete in the sense of being eternal; and spatial or temporal objectivity is distinguished from it. Still thought is about the object and as such should be called 'presentation'. Its content is such as is *necessarily* characterised as what the object is distinct from. Thought is thus a psychic fact, having a facthood apart from introspection. Despite its eternity, it would be incorrect to speak of it as a pure subjective activity. Much of the mysticism in Kantio-Hegelian philosophy has sprung from the confusion of thought with pure subjective activity, of reason with the spirit. Compared with the awareness of *I*, thought is objective and objective in its very dissociation from objectivity. It has still to be characterised in reference to the object as what the object is not.

99. That thought is a presentation comes out in the form of consciousness which we have called *trying* to think. Thought outside introspection is the accomplished meaning. The meaning stands in higher thought, at any rate, through the word. The word is quite distinct from the meaning but as *being used,* it is only half-distinguished from the meaning while the meaning is not dissociated at all from it within thought. The identity of the meaning with the word cannot be denied though it would be going too far to assert it. The identity is disturbed in the consciousness of missing the meaning of a word-combination of which the constituents have a meaning. The problem as to what a combination of significant words means, if it means anything, is an intelligible problem and so attained meaning is distinguished from possible meaning. Attained meaning has accordingly a kind of being outside subjective activity and is a presentation in this sense.

100. What, however, is this possible meaning, the missing of an actual meaning, the trying to think? The logical form of word-combination or syntactical connexion is a generality that has no actual meaning apart from the constituent words but cannot be denied to have a meaning when the word-combination has a meaning from which the meanings of the constituent words can be distinguished. The form of connexion here is not itself distinguished as an actual

meaning, being only distinguished from. As itself distinguished, it is possible meaning ; and in the problem of finding the meaning of a word-combination, the possible meaning is what symbolises the lack of actual meaning. Within thought, the image or the word furnishes the symbolism but here the form of thought itself constitutes the symbol for the felt problem. The feeling of the problem with the unrejected active faith in its solubility is the trying to think which is beyond thought or meaning, beyond all presentation.

CHAPTER VII

SPIRITUAL SUBJECTIVITY

FEELING

101. Thought is still presented as meaning, as the unobjective something about the object, being characterisable only in reference to the object as what the object is not. The introspective awareness of meaning as distinct from the image is awareness of the explicitly unobjective. Feeling is also explicitly unobjective but it is not merely negative but positive as *subjective* fact without any reference to objective fact. The thought of object may accompany a feeling but it is recognised as only a symbolism for the feeling, as what no longer intends the object, being not consciousness of *object* as unknown but an avowedly over-definite representation of the merely unknown. The consciousness of the merely unknown as distinct from what is known as object that is also unknown is feeling. The consciousness may be called knowledge, such knowledge as has been sometimes supposed to constitute dreamless sleep. It is purely subjective in the sense that there is no conscious reference to object even in the way of dissociation from it though not yet in the sense that the meanability or thinkability of its specific content is denied. Feeling is as much undissociated from its content 'absence of knowledge' as conscious non-perception is undissociated from the objective absence that is its content. In the *trying* to think, as in feeling, thought is distinguished from the conscious absence of thought which itself is not distinguished from thought. While however in the trying, there is no belief in the unmeant as a distinct content, feeling, involves such belief, much as perception involves belief in an object as distinct but not as distinct from perception.

102. To introspection, the content of thought appears distinct from thought though it does not appear to be *given* as distinct. Feeling, so far as we are aware of thought as only symbolising it, may be said to have a content, an unthought or unmeant content which, however, appears to introspection as only distinct in itself and not as distinct *from* feeling. While again in the case of thought or other phychic fact, introspection seeks to distinguish it from its content, it seeks to distinguish the unmeant content of feeling from the feeling

and not *reversely*, though the seeking to distinguish does not amount to the knowledge of distinction in any case. Because psychic fact is distinguished in introspection from its object, it is believed to exist also outside introspection. But as the feeling is not thus distinguished from its content, it cannot be believed to exist outside introspection as a merely conscious fact. Feeling is never outside introspection, just as perception is never within introspection.

103. Introspection into feeling, however, is an awareness of the feeling as apparently distinct from the awareness. Introspection into psychic fact is a distinguishing of the fact which appeared undistinguished from itself, consciousness being implicitly self-consciousness in this sense. Introspection into feeling, however, is an *identifying* of the feeling which appeared to be outside introspection as a psychic fact illusorily bound up with a presentation and implies the annulment of this illusion. Feeling is bound up with thought and imagination, being the awareness of their detachment as presentation from their objects, corresponding to the known distinction of the objects from their presentation. In introspection into psychic fact, the felt detachment is symbolised as a thinkable distinction of the psychic fact from its object, though its merely symbolic character is not appreciated as such. In introspection into feeling, the distinction of feeling from its presentative content is appreciated as definitely not known but only felt and symbolised. The content as presented is recognised to be not *its* content. To distinguish a feeling from the meant content is to view the content as a mere symbolism. When thought views the image as its symbol, the symbol still stands as presentation though it is not meant. But when along with feeling, there is the awareness of meaning as its symbol, the symbol is not only not felt: its object-reference lapses altogether. The meaning loses its actuality and turns into the form of a possible meaning. Possible meaning is no presentation, as the awareness '*as though* feeling meant something' is no belief in it as fact. There may be a faith that some meaning of feeling will emerge but the faith is not a belief in what is, at least, partly meant actually. It may imply a trying to think which is not so much a doing as a wishing, being but the free self-expressive play of the feeling. When a presentation is reduced to mere play, there is a make-believe and no belief. Not that the faith must be there but the belief in the object must lapse. Feeling as detached from meaning is awareness of the meaning as its symbolism and may in this sense be taken as implicitly introspective, being never a merely conscious fact outside introspection. Explicit introspection into feeling means only out-

growing the necessity of thus symbolising feeling by meaning and recognising that feeling does not mean anything but itself.

104. The place of willing may be indicated here as co-ordinate with feeling. If feeling represents the complete dissociation from objectivity, willing means the free identification with objectivity. Throughout we have been tracing the movement of dissociation, beginning with the dissociation of the perceived body from the object. To knowledge, the object is *there* and the body *here* is its presupposition ; and as knowledge deepens, there is a regress to prior presuppositions, the felt body etc., up to feeling or what we have called the knowledge of the merely unknown. Each presupposition persists undistinguished in a lower stage and hence feeling may be said to inform even the perceived object, though this is known only when feeling has been dissociated from thought. It is at this stage also that the identification in the lower stages is known to have been free in the sense of not being necessitated by the object. The playful self-expression of feeling in a meaning or thought as its symbol is the first conscious identification with a lower stage, self-objectification without the lapse of dissociation, the initial act of objective willing as distinct from spiritual willing. Willing starts as the aesthetic expression of feeling. The freedom from thought is as much a progress as a regress, as much a willing as a feeling. Regress and progress are two distinct movements in the lower stages, distinct because the object as known is there the starting point. With the cancellation of the objective attitude, there is the consciousness of being free, of being unrestricted by the object whether for withdrawal from it in feeling or for conquest over it in willing.

105. Knowing means freedom both from blindness and from error, escape from the confusion of the object with the subject and from the identification of the subject with the object. As we have shown at many points, the distinguishing of the object from its presentation implies a half-detachment of the presentation from the object when a consciousness emerges of something in the object that is unknown, the presentation being however not denied to be object. The consciousness of the unknown is at the stage we have reached understood as feeling inwardness ; and the consciousness of the presentation as a ghostly object, as what cannot be denied as object but cannot, therefore, be asserted as such is now interpreted as the objectifying or self-externalising function of the will. The so-called knowledge of the object thus appears to be a single function of inwardising and objectifying, of regress and progress, of feeling and

willing. The freedom or detachment implied in knowing means the outgrowing of the positive attitude of not knowing, of conscious entertainment of the unknown—which is feeling—and of *conscious* projection of objectivity—which is willing. Thus to the knowing attitude, feeling and willing appear as what are jointly outgrown and as what also symbolise the inwardness and reality of knowledge.

106. The positive consciousness of detachment from meaning which is the last residuum of the object is feeling. Feeling is the knowledge of the purely unknown as such, the unknown that is not even meant. It is only symbolised as knowledge *of* the unknown, though the unknown being unmeant, the preposition *of* has no meaning and is recognised as a mere exigency of language. There is no distinguishing of the knowledge from its content : the knowledge stands by itself and is the awareness of its content as no content, as unmeant. The next stage would be the awareness of the content as unmeanable. In feeling there is still the demand for a symbolical meaning to be denied, a will to expression, the awareness of the absence of actual meaning and the non-denial of a possible meaning. That will to expression is a trying to think and there may come after the trial the consciousness of a failure to think and the consequent abandonment of the trial. Such consciousness of failure may be regarded as feeling that has purged itself from the persisting will to objectification, as the awareness not merely of the unknown but of the contradictory or unmeanable, of what is not imaginary but is given as false. It is feeling in the sense that it *comes* : if trying to think is still an activity, the consciousness of inability to think is what is borne in upon us.

107. The consciousness of given falsity or objective illusion has to be distinguished from the consciousness of the imaginary. In the example of the illusory snake corrected into the perceived rope, the snake appears after correction to have been not merely a sport of the imagination like golden mountain but to have been believed as real: At the same time while the disbelief in golden mountain implies no uncertainty as to its being merely imagined, the present disbelief in the snake implies an uncertainty as to its having been perceived. What we are conscious of now is that it is *as though* it was perceived. So we say about a dreamed object—'it is as though it was seen'. The snake, we say now, was believed and not merely imagined but not known. What is now remembered as having been believed and appears as though it was known was not, therefore, merely imagined. Belief in an object ideated, as a psychic fact existing outside introspection, is presentation. The present awareness of an object as though

it was known might be called appearance of presentation. The appearance of presentation is a disbelieved possibility of object. It cannot, however, be taken as imaginary, for an imaginary thing does not appear presented (with belief) at all. The awareness of an imagined thing may not be a belief in the thing but is belief in the presentation. The awareness of an imaginary thing is disbelief in the thing and is no belief in the presentation. The awareness of a thing as illusory is not only disbelief in the thing but implies, at least, a positive doubt about its presentation. Disbelief in the imaginary thing may still be called knowledge, knowledge of the negation of all objective facthood. But disbelief in the illusory thing is not even knowledge of such negation, being the consciousness of an indetermination which is neither factual nor imaginary, neither presented with belief nor not presented at all. What being first presented with belief comes to be disbelieved cannot be asserted to be presented without belief : that it is presented cannot only be denied. Disbelief in the illusory object is not *knowledge* of its falsity but the awareness of what cannot be asserted or denied to be true. When this 'indescribable' content is altogether rejected, there is knowledge not of falsity but of the self.

108. The indescribable is unmeanable and so there may be a consciousness of the unmeanable and not merely of the unmeant in feeling. This consciousness cannot be said to be not feeling, though there is no longer the belief in the possibility of symbolising it by a meaning. Introspection into the first stage of the feeling process means, as has been shown, not a distinguishing of the feeling from thought—for feeling does not exist except in being thus distinguished—but an identification of it, the positive assertion of the feeling being itself only, of freedom from thought constituting the very being of feeling. Such freedom is a positive being because there is no rejection yet of *possible* thought or meaning. The awareness of the unmeanable then, as implying such rejection, is freedom from the being of feeling, though as the lapse of the trying to think *comes* as a result of such trying, it cannot be said to be not felt. Roughly then two stages of feeling can be distinguished—freedom from actual thought and freedom from possible thought, from the faith in a possible meaning, from the will to think. It is the persisting will to think that constitutes the being of feeling in the lower stage. Freedom from the will to think is thus feeling that has no being, possible feeling that yet is possible not to a will or trying but to feeling itself, being the feeling of self-negation as distinct from the lower feeling which is feeling of self-being.

109. The feeling of not having a feeling is not an uncommon experience. The awareness of wanting a feeling—whether sense-enjoyment, aesthetic satisfaction or spiritual serenity—is itself a feeling. All desire involves a present feeling of not having a feeling, an awareness of the 'inferiority' of the anticipatory pleasure to the actual feeling that is to come. It is not simply one feeling *due* to the want of another feeling but the feeling of the want of its own being or actuality. Nor is it yet the disinterested awareness of the want, a detachment from it such as introspection would imply. It can only be characterised as the *feeling* of a feeling, with which are bound up interesting spiritual attitudes like sentimentalism on the one hand which confuses the felt want with the actual feeling that is wanted and the experience of the want on the other as a pain that miraculously ends in a fulfilment.

110. This feeling of a feeling is not introspection but the stage prior to it, even as the trying to think is prior to feeling. It is the negative of which introspection is the positive equivalent—the self-negation of feeling or feeling detached from its being. Such detachment or self-negation is already the attitude of knowledge, knowledge of what is neither felt nor unfelt, of a negation that cannot be denied, of the indeterminate unmeanable or indescribable. Such knowledge may be regarded as introspection that yet has a being and is not denied to be the object of introspection. Introspection proper is not the object of further introspection.

111. The nature of this pre-introspective knowledge may be intelligible through the analysis of a puzzle about the unmeanable. *Unmeanable* is itself a significant word and so the unmeanable, it may be said, is meant. The puzzle suggests a two-fold function of the significant word. Speaking as to the speaker has to be distinguished from speaking as to the hearer ; and to the speaker himself, the word being spoken has a function different from the word as already spoken. What the speaker means as unmeanable after having tried to mean may be to the hearer what he does not even try to mean. Again, while in speaking of the unmeanable, as in any act of speaking, the speaker only means without contemplating the meaning as accomplished, the word as spoken appears either to his or to the hearer's contemplation to have an accomplished meaning. If the speaker does not contemplate it, the hearer (or he himself later) may contemplate it ; and if the speaker contemplates, the hearer may not. There is thus a difference between the meaning being coined out or being understood and the meaning as accomplished and contemplated. We are

aware of the unmeanable in two stages, as the meant unmeanable and as the mere function of meaning or speaking. The knowledge implied in the former is of a contradiction while that implied in the latter is not *of* anything, being merely knowing. The feeling of feeling is the former kind of awareness while the latter is just introspection. Self-negation in feeling of feeling is still a felt being, existent knowledge rather than the function of knowing. Introspection is complete dissociation from felt being and is the pure knowing function.

CHAPTER VIII

Spiritual Subjectivity (Contd.)

INTROSPECTION

112. Introspection into a subjective fact means a distinguishing of it. There is no direct introspective awareness of perceptual knowledge. In non-perceptual knowledge, object is already distinguished from presentation and the introspective awareness of such knowledge is the awareness of its distinction in itself with a feeling of its dissociation from the object. This feeling is symbolised as a thinkable distinction from the object by a reversal of the known distinction of the object from the presentation. Introspective distinguishing is only the knowledge of a subjective fact as distinct in itself, though in the case of subjective fact lower than feeling, it appears through such symbolised feeling of dissociation as the knowledge of the fact as distinct *from the object.* Feeling is nothing but this conscious dissociation, as is realised when presentation in the attenuated form of meaning is known to be distinct from feeling. Introspection into feeling from which meaning is known to be distinct—feeling which is nothing but the conscious dissociation from the object—is the awareness of feeling being distinct in itself only and does not involve the further symbolism of being distinct *from* anything. Thus while the introspective awareness of a psychic fact is the awareness of its distinction from object and, therefore, of its distinction in itself also as existing apart from introspection as presentation, the introspective awareness of a feeling proper is the knowledge of its distinction in itself only and is the recognition of the distinction as being entirely through introspection. Such recognition may be called an identification.

113. Introspection into feeling is the recognition of the distinct being of the feeling as entirely through the introspection. It is just the function of meaning the feeling, of distinguishing, referring to or speaking of the feeling. Meaning as a function as distinct from the meant is intelligible only after the self-negation of feeling, feeling of wanting a feeling, the detachment of feeling from its being or the awareness of the meant unmeanable. To mean not merely the conscious absence but the conscious impossibility of meaning is the pure function of subjectivity, the function of introspection that is not objec-

tive even in the form of the meant unmeanable. If the feeling of feeling is already a detachment from subjective being, it is as a contradiction, as a be-ënt want of feeling. Introspection is a subjectivity that is detached both from being and from negation, being positive as *freedom.* It is not simply like the meant unmeanable or the 'indescribable' what is neither be-ënt nor non-be-ënt, a negation that cannot be asserted or denied. It is the positive of which the negation is not even tried to be meant. The negation of the function of meaning is a gratuitous problem in meaning which there is no call to solve. Unlike the illusory object which is first presented and then reduced to the unmeanable, this negation is an imaginary problem in meaning which can, indeed, always be asked in logical sport but suggests no actual uncertainty about the introspective function. The imaginary problem is never ousted but never amounts to an uncertainty about any actual belief. Introspection is an actual believing which can only be sought to be impugned by the imaginary problem of conceiving its negation and is, therefore, never actually impugned. The content believed in introspection is, as will appear presently, capable of being impugned but not the believing itself. We speak only of introspective believing because a belief the object of which turns out false is no longer a belief in the object but is still a fact to introspective memory as the past believing in an unmeanable, as a contentless believing that is not other than the introspection.

114. The old argument against absolute scepticism that it is doubting on the strength of believing is untenable if it is intended to exclude doubt about the *object* of belief. The object of belief is always impugnable though the grounds of the doubt must be actual or believed to constitute a relevant doubt. The argument, however, is valid if it intends to say that believing cannot be doubted. It will be presently apparent that not object only but every subjective fact that is introspectively believed, even though it be meant as unmeanable, is capable of being doubted. Believing then would not be fact at all, being not even meant as unmeanable. Nor is it, therefore, an illusion, for an illusion about the subjective has a place, as will be shown, beyond the introspection that we are now considering.

115. Introspection is the function of believing or meaning which is not itself meant even as the unmeanable and is, therefore, not actually doubtable. It is just the first person I, the speaker who is not an object to introspection but is simply the function of speaking. Introspection is not believing *in* the I : it is the I, the believing that is not fact at all but is not, therefore, illusory. As not believing even in the

meant unmeanable, it is not believing in anything distinguished from it and so may be loosely expressed as believing in itself. The conscious inadequacy of the expression is itself evidence of the believing being not believing *in* anything.

116. Introspection as a conscious dissociation even from feeling that is distinct only through it is an annulment of the distinction—what we have called identification. Introspection into a psychic fact bound up with presentation reveals that its subjective facthood is nothing but the facthood of feeling. Such introspection appears to be a believing in a distinct because the distinctness of psychic fact is not immediately annulled by introspection, being reduced in the first instance to the distinctness of feeling. The direct unidentifiability of the psychic fact is what constitutes its apparently independent being ; and it is thus that the psychic fact is pronounced by introspection itself as having a ghostly existence outside introspection. That it is directly unidentifiable is due to the fact that it is never a complete detachment from the felt body and that accordingly psychic fact never appears to it as having only the facthood of feeling. But there is the conscious semi-detachment of feeling from the meanable psychic fact pointing to the possibility of complete detachment ; and there is the identifying introspection into feeling implying possible detachment from the being of feeling. This possible detachment from all distinct being is introspective awareness. Introspection is essentially the annulment of all distinct being, being self-identification or the conscious identity without being of the self.

117. . The self is taken by Kant as the thinking function. The thinking function is thinking of a thought or accomplished meaning and Kant does not deny that the self as an Idea of the Reason is an accomplished meaning. There is, however, the awareness not only of trying to think without any accomplished meaning but also of the impossibility of meaning. We can mean the unmeanable and thus the speaking or meaning function is more fundamental than thinking. In calling introspection the self, we not only bespeak the detachment of the self from thinking and feeling but also take it to be a believing or self-identifying, the negation of which is not even a meant unmeanable and which, therefore, cannot be denied to be a self-knowing. The introspective self is self-knowing, not as having the self as the object of knowledge but as denying the distinct being of feeling, as identifying it without denying its being and as having itself no deniable being.

118. The self is the first person I. The *I* is not unmeanable nor is it meant—meant even as unmeanable. It is not unmeanable in the sense that it presents no problem in meaning at all and can be said to be neither meanable nor unmeanable. Meaning is the thinnest presentation of the object, as existing apart from introspection. *I* has no meaning in this sense : it has not even the meaning of being unmeant or unmeanable, which feeling in its two stages may be supposed to have. The word *I* is used by the speaker not for what is distinct but for what is only being distinguished by him ; and it is not understood by the hearer to *mean* a distinct content. No two persons would use the word *I* of the same thing ; but the speaker and the hearer must be agreed about a meaning. Yet if a person understand me when I call myself *I*, though he does not use the word himself about me, it is—it may be contended—because of the meaning of the word. But in that case it would be a kind of general term meaning any speaker, in which sense, however, it is not used, not being applied to more than one thing at a time. The term, in fact, is not singular in the sense that different people use it of the same thing and not general in the sense that it is *understood* by any of the different things at a time. If a person using the word *I* is understood as referring to himself by another, it is not because the latter means the speaker by the word and would use the word to refer to the speaker. Thus it may be said that a speaker calling himself *I* is understood through the word but not through the meaning of the word. The word here has a meaning function but not a meaning : it is the expression of introspection or what may be called the *I*-function.

119. Like the word *unmeanable,* the word *I* illustrates a use of language other than for purposes of thinking, the former being still the expression of an inability to think while the latter has not even this negative reference to thought. The meaning function of the word *I* is to the speaker his actual introspection but the understanding of the word by the hearer is indicative of a form of consciousness subtler than introspection. It is the awareness of how the speaker would introspect, awareness of a possible introspection.

CHAPTER IX

SPIRITUAL SUBJECTIVITY (Contd.)

BEYOND INTROSPECTION

120. The realisation of what a speaker means by the word *I* is the hearer's awareness of a possible introspection. Such awareness is as much knowledge as actual introspection. The speaker calls himself *I* and may be understood by the hearer as *you.* As thus understood, the introspective self is individual, not an individual being—for introspection is not a subjective *being* like feeling—but the function of addressing to another self. The speaker does not understand himself through the meaning of the word *I*: his introspection is through the word and not through its meaning and is less a self-knowing than a self-revealing, revealing to a possible understander of the word *I*. Yet as the addressing attitude is only implicit, it is to him accidental and posterior to his self-knowing. To the understanding self however, although he understands the speaker's self-knowing because he is himself self-knowing, his understanding of the other I is primary while his own self-knowing is accidental and secondary. The speaker knows himself in implicitly revealing to the hearer and the hearer knows the speaker in implicitly knowing himself. Neither self-knowing nor other-knowing is through thinking or the meaning of the word and both might be called 'intuition' in this negative sense. There are thus two cases—self-intuition with other-intuition implicit in it and other-intuition with self-intuition implicit in it. Both are actual knowledge implying the use other than the thinking use of a word like *I*, which is like a pointing gesture at once self-evidencing and self-evident. My self-consciousness is not the understanding of the meaning of the word *I* : the word only reveals it to another. His understanding of the word as referring to me is not the understanding of it in the sense he would use it himself. The word has no meaning either to him or to me and yet it stands like any other word for the same thing to both. This *standing for* is not only not meaning but not also mere symbolising. It is on the one hand revealing and on the other an accomplished revelation, at once self-evidencing and self-evident. The word may be said at once to symbolise and to be symbolised by my introspective self. The hearer takes it to symbolise myself but I, the speaker, symbolise it by myself or in a sense explained before, incarnate my-

self in it. The reference of the word *I* varies with the user of it: its meaning function is through his self-consciousness, is symbolised by his meaning function which is what he is primarily aware of, the symbol being better known than what is symbolised by it. Because the word *I* is at once the symbol and the symbolised, it cannot be said to have simply the symbolising function. It is this characteristic value of a word other than the meaning value or merely symbolising value that indicates a grade of self-consciousness higher than our actual introspection.

121. Actual introspection is implicitly social, being a speaking or addressing or self-evidencing to another possible introspection or self to which its conscious solitariness or self-identity is evident. The evidencing and the evidentness are actual to different selves, speaker or hearer. The evidentness as to the hearer is, however, only a possible evidentness to the speaker. Actual introspection is unrealised knowledge because it is actually only self-evidencing to another and not self-evident to itself. One's own self should be self-evident, should be intuited by oneself even as it is intuited by another. The introspection that is actually reached by the annulment of the alien character of feeling as subjective being is, as already shown, only a speaking, self-evidencing or self-revealing, a function in the Kantian sense though not thinking function, a kind of transcendental willing which is not known by the introspector but should be known as it is already known by another self. The self should be at once self-evidencing and self-evident but so far we have only the self as self-evidencing and evident to another.

122. The other self is to the self-evidencing self a possible introspector whose intuition of the latter again is a possible intuition to the latter. It is because the actual introspector is thus aware of the possible introspector that he can conceive a possible introspection of his own beyond his actual introspection ; and it is only as he is thus aware of a possibly intuited subjectivity that he can understand the possibility of a subjective illusion. The awareness of these possibles in oneself—possible knowledge and possible illusion of subjectivity—indicates the necessity of a spiritual discipline of realisation, realisation of the knowledge of the self already implied by introspection.

123. Introspection into a possible or non-existent mental state is or involves understanding of a word meaning the mental state. To mean a mental state is not to think it : it is either to feel the want of it or to give it a distinction which it has not, which is like creating it. Where the mental state is not present, to mean it is to remember it,

to want it or to dreamily wish it. All these are forms of awareness of a possible mental state and may be regarded as a stage of introspection prior to the introspection into an actual mental state. If it is introspection, it cannot be said to be completely dissociated yet from subjective being and as such it is capable of being itself introspected into. There can be, for example, introspection into the conscious want of a feeling.

124. The want of a feeling is an actual feeling and introspection into it, as into any feeling, means its identification with the introspection. It does not, however, mean identification with itself of the feeling that is wanted. The introspector is not aware of such a feeling as his feeling : the possible feeling is an unappropriated feeling. The introspective awareness of an unappropriated subjective state is like the awareness of another self having it. To the introspector it is the awareness of what he himself *might* appropriate. There may be actual knowledge, as immediate as introspection and standing on a level with it, of another self and his subjective state. But as the introspector only imagines and does not know his own being, his awareness of his possible subjective state is not actual knowledge. Introspection into the awareness of a possible subjective state is thus possible or imaginary introspection. Such introspection is half-dissociated from the actually introspective self, half-dissociated in the sense that we only cannot deny it to be *our* introspection. It is, indeed, completely dissociated from the possible subjective state but not from the actual awareness of it. Complete dissociation from this actual awareness is reached when the content of it is a subjective state that is illusory and not merely absent or possible.

125. There are illusions about the subjective just as there are illusions about the objective. A subjective state appears illusory to later introspection into the subjective state that supersedes it through, it may be, the effervescence of interest or other subtle subjective cause. But a simple form of subjective illusion may be presented in connexion with an objective illusion. When the objective presentation with which a psychic fact is bound up turns out to be illusory, there is at least a partial reduction of the psychic fact to illusion. In the example of the correction of the presentation of snake into the presentation of *this* rope, the fear as of *that* snake—that individual fear—is, as pointed out before, also felt to be, if not illusory, at least incapable of being asserted as a past fact. We cannot say that we feared *that* snake if we now know that the snake never was. Some feeling bound up with the bodily reaction was, indeed, felt but *that* feeling of fear or fear

of *that* snake was never felt. The specific character of the feeling bound up with the past belief in the snake cannot be said to have existed. Introspection now not only does not identify *that* feeling with itself : it rejects it as what it cannot possibly appropriate. There is a doubt, if not a denial, of possible appropriation of it by any individual self, of its being knowable by any introspection and yet it is introspection itself that denies the possibility.

126. Introspection is the awareness of a subjective fact as owing its facthood to itself and is in this sense the identification or appropriation of it. Such subjective fact may be itself the awareness of the absence or possibility of another subjective fact and introspection into it is the awareness of this other fact as not actually appropriated but as possibly appropriated by another introspection. The subjective fact introspected into may be again the awareness of the impossibility of a subjective mode previously taken to be fact. Introspection here would be the awareness of this mode as beyond all possible introspective appropriation. One gets here the hint of an introspection that is not appropriative, of the appropriative function being accidental to the introspective self, of the distinctness or exclusiveness of *I* being an eliminable feature, of an intuitable self-identity that has not any subjective fact distinct from it to identify. Introspection that is not appropriation would be self-intuition, the *I* that is evident to itself and not merely to another, that does not like the individual *I* create a distinct subjective mode by distinguishing to resume it by identifying and proclaim this resumption again by speaking in the first person to another possible person. The possibility of such a silent self-enjoying *I* is intelligible only because we are aware of certain subjective modes previously appropriated as not only now unappropriated but as utterly unappropriable and as accordingly appearing only *as though* they were distinct. The absolute intuitable self is only understood if the non-being of distinction is understood. Objective illusion is still a meant unmeanable, meant and therefore distinguished. But subjective illusion is not even meant as unmeanable. Introspection too is an unmeant meaning function; it is not known as distinct nor is it primarily so much a distinguishing as an identifying so far as it is knowledge. It is, however, still a distinguishing in the act of self-revealing and therefore also a distinguishing from itself as possible. The awareness of subjective illusion goes beyond introspection, being the explicit awareness of illusorily distinguising, of *creating* a distinction that is no fact at all. The non-being of distinction is finally understood here and hence too the conception of the absolute self.

CHAPTER X

The Subject As Freedom

127. The subject is understood as what intends by the word *I*. The subject that intends is other than the subject that understands, being self-evident as self-evidencing to another and not to itself. The intuited subject is not only revealed but revealing: it is directly known as self-expressing in the spoken word *I* without being meant by it. It does not, however, intuit itself, as the intuiting subject also does not reveal itself. There is no introspective awareness of being revealed or incarnated in the word *I*, of one's freedom to self-expression as itself an evident fact. There is at best an imaginative demand for such awareness, for the realisation of the felt identification with the word (or the object) as presupposing dissociation from it, for the transformation of the felt freedom into the intuition of freedom. It is in introspection that we are aware of this demand for the consummation of the freedom that is felt in every grade of subjectivity in respect of the object presented to it. The object appears alien to the subject up to the stage of thought. The feeling subject is free from the thought or meant content in so far as the latter is reduced to a symbolism. But it is still subject having being, subject that can still be object to introspection, being free but not freedom itself. The introspective subject is, indeed, free from this being or possible objectivity and is thus freedom itself but it is still a distinct individual though only unconsciously. It knows itself not as *itself* but as a distinct subject that is only possibly identical with itself. It is thus aware of a demand to know this subject as actually itself, to annul its possible distinction from itself and, therefore, also its actual distinctness through the word *I*. The demand is for the intuition of the subject as absolute freedom.

128. The introspective self is aware of itself as the psychic self and the bodily self. At all stages it knows itself as to be known. It knows the bodily self indeed as known not only as object but also as definitely separated from other objects. But it does not know it like other objects as having a space-position and is aware of the demand to realise its positionless objectivity. The psychic self is also known as identified with objectivity as pure form or pure meaning but it is only felt as dissociated from the perceived body; and in introspection we are aware of the demand to realise this felt dissociation in knowledge.

The introspective self is unaware of being objective to itself though it understands another self calling itself *I* and thus knows it as having objective distinctness, the distinctness of the word *I*. As, however, itself revealing through the word to another self, it is aware of itself as a possibly understood distinct entity. It knows itself not as known like the psychic or bodily self but as only to be known. As to be known, it is understood as what is only symbolised as distinct like the word *I* and what would lose its distinctness in being actually known. The subject is understood as freedom that is real and is characterisable by no objective category, not even by the category of distinctness. As we do not in introspection cease to be the bodily self which alone is actually evident to us, the subject that is absolutely unobjective or is freedom itself is to us only a possibility to be realised. The idea of realising the subject arises only because we are actually identified with the body while we are introspectively aware of ourselves as not objective and yet as definitely positive. Introspective awareness of oneself is awareness of the subject as not only not objective in the sense of being thought or meant but also as what cannot be said to have the being of feeling nor to be contradictory like the feeling of the want of a feeling nor even to be distinct like the subject to which it reveals itself. At the same time it is not awareness of a mere negation or of an indefinite. This definite positive cannot be said to be not known, though as actually undissociated from the object we cannot assert it to be known. We are only aware of not being dissociated, being dissociated to the extent implied by such awareness. Such implied dissociation is possible freedom that is to be realised as evident.

129. The consciousness of not being actually dissociated is present even in the stage of bodily subjectivity where alone actual dissociation is known in some measure and not merely felt as in higher stages. It is known, as has been pointed out, as the perceived separation in space of the body from the outside object, though there is a feeling still of one's body not being perceived in a space-position, all position being relative to it. In higher stages, there is no knowledge of freedom from the object but only a feeling of it, the feeling so far as it falls short of knowledge being the implicit awareness of not being actually free from the object. The higher the stage of subjectivity, the less is the freedom felt to be achieved though the more assured is the faith in its achievability. In the introspective stage, the feeling of achieved freedom lapses altogether, since it is here that the possibility of freedom is first definitely known. The faith in its achievability, however, is completely

assured in this stage and takes the form of a conscious spiritual demand for the intuition of freedom as evident.

130. Three broad stages of subjectivity have been exhibited—the bodily, the psychical and the spiritual. In the bodily stage, three substages have been discussed—the body as externally perceived. the body as internally perceived or felt, and the absence of object known as a present fact. As externally perceived, the bodily subject is the centre of the perceived world but is not itself perceived as in it. As felt, it is definitely known to be not in this world though it is not known as not the externally perceived body. The subject that imaginatively perceives the absence of an object is also like the felt body not consciously dissociated from the perceived body but the subject that knows absence through conscious non-perception is consciously dissociated from it. He feels himself unlike the felt body as definitely without reference to space-position and as only the time-position—present or *now*, as distinct from the image of the absent object, which also is without this reference but is not consciously felt as *now*.

131. The image of the object whose absence is known in conscious non-perception marks the transition to the psychic stage. It appears as the object that is absent and is not yet felt to be dissociated from it. The psychic stage begins when attention is shifted from the objective fact of absence to the image. As attended to, the image appears as imaging or the forming of a form, the process and the product being presented at once. The consciousness of the form as evident in the forming process and as a product that does not yet come in time *after* it is the idea as undissociated from the image. A later stage is the idea as dissociated from the image, or pictorial thought which wants to be imaged and is definite so far as it is imaged. Non-pictorial thought comes next, thought that is definite in itself and has properly no image though an image may serve as its metaphor or symbol. These grades of image and thought are the grades of presentation which is explicitly felt to be dissociated from the object. Such dissociated presentation is known in introspection to have no space-position and is at least not known to have time-position. The image still appears, however, as though it had spatial form and to be forming as though it were a temporal process. Some trace of this quasi-temporal process may persist in thought but thought as a non-pictorial meaning is felt to be free from it and to be eternally complete. Still such meaning appears as though it were object, being introspectively believed like other psychical facts to exist outside introspection. Its presentational character is explicitly indicated by the consciousness of

the absence of accomplished meaning in what we have called *trying* to think which may be taken as pointing to the positive freedom from objective meaning such as characterises the non-presentational or spiritual stage of subjectivity.

132. The positive freedom from objectivity appears in the first instance as feeling. Feeling still seems to mean something but the meaning here so far as it is formulated is avowedly a symbolism for it only. To introspection indeed, feeling appears to be object but not as what may exist outside introspection. Its alien character is to introspection only apparent, being distinct only through introspection and not capable of existing outside introspection except as illusorily bound up with a presentation. The feeling subject has a being to introspection so that it is free and is not freedom itself. The next stage is the feeling of wanting a feeling, which is, in fact, a felt contradiction or self-negation that still appears distinct from the introspection into it. The introspecting subject, however, is not introspected into and is self-revealing through the word *I*. It is aware of being revealed or evident not to itself but to the subject addressed and therefore of being *possibly* revealed to itself also. As thus only possibly evident to itself, it is unappropriated by itself while as introspecting, it is aware of addressing a subject and of being dissociated from it by the very fact of addressing. It thus feels being distinct but does not know itself as distinct. It is aware of the subject as possibly free from distinctness, as its very self but not as exclusively its own.

133. I am introspectively conscious of my body as subject but not as not mine or the appropriated. I am conscious of a psychic fact as not mine, as subject that is not, however, not *me* as the known. As, however, I speak of *I* in introspection, I intend what before I spoke was not *me* but not what was not a distinct *I*. There is no introspection into introspection but just as perception is known indirectly in introspection into some other subjective state like memory, so introspection is known indirectly in introspection into feeling. Feeling appears to introspection as subject that has no reference to object, as I but still as I distinct from I, as the be-ent I illusorily distinct from the introspective I. Introspection into the feeling I then is awareness of the introspecting I as not distinguished but as only distinguished *from*, as that from which being and non-being are both distinguished, as that which cannot be denied to be distinct in itself but of which such distinction is not known.

134. The apprehension of I as not even distinct in itself is indicated by the consciousness of subjective illusion, of a mode of sub-

jectivity that is not only unappropriated but unappropriable. There is occasion to correct the conceit not only of *my* body and of *me* as a presentation, not only of I as felt being but also of I as an actual distinct introspector. The introspecting self that I am indirectly aware of in introspection into feeling appears to be an actual self. In introspection into the feeling of wanting a feeling it turns out to be only a possible self that is still distinct as an introspector. But there may be the consciousness of a feeling being illusorily wanted: I may, for example, recognise not only that I am not religious but also that even my hankering after religion is not real but only a sentimental make-believe. Such recognition would be the awareness not only of an unappropriated but of an unappropriable religious aspiration, of the self that only appears as I aspiring and *is not it,* is not an actual introspector and not even a possible introspector.

135. I am never positively conscious of my present individuality, being conscious of it only as what is or can be outgrown, only as I feel freeing myself from it and am free to the extent implied by such feeling. I do not know myself as free but I conceive that I can be free successively as body from the perceived object, as presentation from the body, as feeling from presentation and as introspective function from feeling. I am not introspectively aware of my actual introspective individuality but I am aware in my introspection into feeling that the self from which the feeling is distinguished may not actually introspect and may not even possibly introspect, that individual as it is as introspecting—individual or distinct freedom without being, it may be free even from this distinctness, may be freedom itself that is de-individualised but not therefore indefinite—absolute freedom that is to be evident.

THE CONCEPT OF PHILOSOPHY

ANALYSIS

I. Orientation to Kant (1-5)

According to Kant, the self is not knowable but is thinkable; but according to the view presented here, the self is not thinkable, though not therefore utterly unknowable. Kant's 'Idea of Reason' is not 'thought' in the literal sense: it is only the verbal form of thought as a symbol of an unthinkable reality. The self is knowable without thinking and has to be so known. It may be a moral postulate but it is formulated for the contemplation of it as a truth to be known. This contemplation is the process of reaching the truth without thinking. What applies to the self applies mutatis mutandis to other metaphysical entities. Philosophy is then not only not actual knowledge: it is not even literal thought.

II. Grades of Theoretic Consciousness (6-18)

(6) Philosophy presents beliefs that are speakable. To speak is to formulate a belief and it is the understanding of what can be spoken that constitutes the theoretic consciousness. (7) Such understanding may not be knowledge, but it involves belief in something as known or to be known. (8) All forms of theoretic consciousness as involving the understanding of a speakable are sometimes called 'thought'. Four grades of thought may be distinguished: (a) *empirical thought* which involves reference to an object perceived or imagined to be perceived; (b) *pure objective thought* which has reference to an object but not necessarily to a perceived object; (c) *spiritual thought* which has no reference to any object and is subjective; (d) *transcendental thought* which is neither objective nor subjective. The content of (a) is 'fact', of (b) the 'self-subsistent', of (c) 'reality' and of (d) 'truth'. Science deals with (a), the other three being the subject-matter of philosophy. (9) The grades of thought are really grades of speaking. Speakability is a contingent character of the content of scientific thought, but it is a necessary character of philosophic thought. (10) (b), (c) or (d) is not assertable as fact. Belief in it may indeed be expressed in the form of a judgment, but the form would be only symbolic. In a real judgment about a 'fact', the predicate amplifies or explicates the meaning of a subject that is already believed. But in the apparent judgment concerning the other three contents, the subject

is believed as a self-evident elaboration of the predicate that is already believed to be self-evident.

(11-15) Philosophy is such self-evident elaboration of the self-evident which is spoken but not spoken of. There are three forms of this self-evident according as it is spoken in the objective, the subjective and the transcendental attitudes. The objective self-evident is spoken as the apparent judgment "the relation of A and B is", where 'is' means an objective content that is self-subsistent and where the objective attitude is still retained. The subjective self-evident is spoken as "I am", where 'am' means something that is subjectively 'enjoyed'. Here the objective attitude is explicitly dropped and the content is only spoken *as though* it were objectively contemplated. In 'I am' the predicate is a symbol of a literally spoken subject. The transcendental self-evident is spoken as "the absolute self is". But unlike the above two cases of the self-evident it is not even literally spoken. Still it is not meaningless and it symbolises 'truth' i.e., what is believed and is not literally speakable.

(16-17) The self-subsistent entity meant by 'object is' demands to be known in absorbed contemplation or intuited as simply 'object'. The real 'I' demands to be known without the objective intuitive attitude i.e., in pure enjoyment. In these two cases there is no demand to know the content without the speaking attitude. Transcendental consciousness starts by regarding all speaking as only symbolising and is accordingly conceived as completed when this symbolising speech is dispensed with. (18) We have three grades of philosophy corresponding to the three attitudes, viz., philosophy of the object, philosophy of the subject and philosophy of truth.

III. Science and Metaphysics (19-24)

(19) Both science and the first grade of philosophy deal with the object. But object as discussed in philosophy is believed to be self-subsistent. (20) Science has no interest to formulate the concept of the self-subsistent object and it apparently believes that the object must be knowable or usable. To it the object is just what is known and though it may be unknown, there is no question of its being unknowable. (21) The implicit belief in the necessary knowability and usability of the object is, at least, questioned in philosophy. It is this spiritual attitude of science towards the object that suggests the need for a speculative theory of the object. The concept of the self-subsistent object is the first corrective that philosophy offers of the predatory outlook of the scientific intellect. (22) The problem of piecing together

the results of the sciences is wrongly taken to be a philosophical one: wrongly, because the expected synthesis can be accomplished only by the employment of the distinctive technique and methods of science. A world-view of this kind can at best be an aesthetic view. (23) The so-called philosophy of evolution as the significant story of cosmic evolution is neither science nor philosophy but only a piece of imaginative literature. (24) The so-called philosophy of science as the formulation of the postulates or the structural concepts of science ignores the impassable gulf between fact and the self-subsistent.

IV. Philosophy of the Object (25-31)

(25) That object is called 'fact' in which the reference to the subject or the speaking function is not necessary. This fact is dealt with in science. The object that has necessary reference to the subject is called the self-subsistent and is dealt with in philosophy. (26) 'Objectivity' which is common to these two objects is itself no fact, being only the self-subsistent form that is elaborated in Logic. Logic is thus no science but only a branch of the philosophy of the object. The pure object of which Logic is the form is the metaphysical object. Logic and metaphysics are thus the two branches of the philosophy of the object. (27) The concept of the object is first reached by contrast with the subject as the self-evident content of spiritual consciousness. Thus object is understood as self-subsistent before fact is understood as object. Logic in this sense presupposes metaphysics. (28) Metaphysics involves the objective attitude and is philosophy of the object. There is no metaphysic of the subject. The rationale of any division of metaphysical contents, e.g., into matter, life and mind is to be found in the introspected distinction within spiritual experience. (29) The characteristic abstractions of metaphysics are symbolic meanings which derive their whole value from spiritual experiences that they symbolise. Metaphysical beliefs are not reached by inference and metaphysical reasoning is only the systematic exposition of symbolic concepts. (30) The spoken fact and the spoken self-subsistent agree in having certain unavoidable speech-created forms. Logic presents a system of these unavoidable forms. And since Logic presupposes metaphysics which presents alternative theories, there may be alternative systems of Logic. Apparently, every metaphysical system has its distinctive Logic. (31) The contrast between Logic and Metaphysics suggests the distinction between the self-subsistent and the real.

V. Philosophy of the Spirit (32-37)

(32) The suggested distinction between self-subsistence and reality is verified in the 'enjoying' consciousness of a content (viz., I) as symbolised by a 'contemplated' meaning (viz., 'am' in 'I am'). This 'enjoying' understanding is what should be meant by 'introspection'. Its content is not understood as fact nor even as the self-subsistent object. It is understood as what object is not, as the speaking subjectivity. (33) Introspection, in the proper sense of the term, is to speak in the first person—actually or ideally—with the consciousness of the 'I' as what the object is not. When such speaking involves the consciousness of *being* what is spoken, it may be called spiritual introspection. (34) In spiritual introspection, the subject 'I' is never enjoyed by itself. It is always enjoyed first (a) as unaccountably embodied, next (b) as having personal relation to other selves and lastly (c) as having identity with the over-personal self. The study of all contents enjoyed in explicit reference to the subject 'I' may be called the philosophy of the spirit. (35) In (a) the object is conceived not as self-subsistent but only as a shadow or symbol of the 'I'. In (b) 'I' and the other person are each not the other and each contradictorily the symbol of the other. In (c) there is the consciousness of the over-personal reality as symbolised by 'I': this conscious symbolising is consciously being nought and is the soul of religious experience. (36) Religious experience is consciousness of being and, as simple, it admits of no variation within itself. There is, however, an infinite plurality of unique religious experiences and the Hegelian notion of a single and exclusive gradation of religions is unacceptable. (37) The theoretic form of a religious system is a philosophy of religion. Every system of religious philosophy has its distinctive theory of the spirit, Metaphysic and Logic. All philosophy is systematic symbolism and symbolism necessarily admits of alternatives.

VI. Philosophy of Truth (38-41)

(38) There is a theoretic consciousness of 'I am nought'. But the denial of the 'I' is possible because we already believe that the absolute is. Reality as apprehended in religion is expressed literally in so far as it is expressed as a self. The positive character of the Absolute, however, is expressible only by the negation of the 'I' and, as such, is not literally expressible at all. If then it is said that the Absolute *is*, the 'is' means not reality but truth. (39) Truth is believed as independent of speaking, as self-revealing. As a positive to which even

the 'I' is nought in itself, it is nothing to be distinguished from and is, in this sense, absolute. It is, however, symbolically spoken, and as such it has to be believed as distinct. If, then, truth as absolute is distinguished, it can only be distinct from itself. There is, however, no necessity in this self-distinction. The absolute may be truth, or it may be freedom or it may be value. There is no sense in speaking of the absolute as the unity of truth, freedom and value. It is each of them. (40) This triple Absolute is the prototype of the three subjective functions—knowing, willing and feeling--which are elaborated not in the introspective but in the transcendental consciousness. (41) The theory of truth is the theory of the other two absolutes also, but it recognises the possibility of elaborating a primary theory of each of them in reference to the other absolutes.

THE CONCEPT OF PHILOSOPHY

1. An explication of the concept of philosophy appears to me more important than the discussion of any specific problem of philosophy. The possibility of philosophy as a body of knowledge distinct from science is nowadays called in question. I may indicate my general position by stating wherein I differ from the Kantian view of the subject.

I. Orientation to Kant

2. With regard to the knowability of the self as a metaphysical entity, Kant holds that the self is a necessity of thought and is the object of moral faith, but is not in itself knowable. My position is, on the one hand, that the self is unthinkable and on the other that while actually it is not known and is only an object of faith, though not necessarily only of moral faith, we have to admit the possibility of knowing it without *thinking*, there being a demand, alternative with other spiritual demands, to realise such knowledge. This is practically reopening the entire epistemological question of the meaning of thought and knowledge.

3. In taking the self to be unthinkable, I understand Kant's Idea of the Reason to be not only not knowledge, but to be not even thought in the literal sense. The so-called extension of thought beyond experience and the possibility of experience means to me only the use of the verbal form of thought as a symbol of an unthinkable reality, such symbolising use not being thinking. I go further and hold that a form of thought as understood by itself in logic and apart from its symbolising use is not literally thought. Some present-day positivists who deny not only metaphysical knowing, but also metaphysical thinking, would not go so far as to deny logic itself to be a body of thought. They rely, in fact, on logic which they take to be pure thinking, in order to deny metaphysical thinking. I take logic to be a philosophical and not a scientific subject: the logical forms are shadows of metaphysical symbolisms and are as such themselves to be understood as symbolisms.

4. On the negative side then I go much further than Kant. On the positive side, however, I would tone down his agnosticism. That the self is believed in and is yet actually unknown is itself to me ground for holding that it is knowable without thinking and has to be so known. The self or freedom is taken to be a moral postulate, but why

is a moral postulate formulated at all? Neither morality nor metaphysical theory gains anything by the formulation in theoretic form. A moral postulate is not simply an Idea of the Reason, nor is it a construct of the aesthetic imagination. It appears to me to be formulated for the contemplation of it not as a moral good or as an enjoyable value but as a truth to be known. Such contemplation cannot be a spiritual luxury or make-believe, but must have behind it the faith that it is just the process of reaching the truth without thinking. It is not indeed a duty to contemplate, but the contemplation being already there, it demands fulfilment in knowledge. The contemplation of the self as truth may start from consciousness other than the moral, nor need moral consciousness develop into it. A distinctively spiritual activity comes spontaneously and has no necessary origin. The contemplation of the self as truth demands fulfilment in knowledge only by one in whom this activity has already started. It is an absolute demand co-ordinate with the other absolute demands.

5. What applies to the self applies with necessary alterations to other metaphysical entities. Metaphysics, or more generally, philosophy including logic and epistemology, is not only not actual knowledge, but is not even literal thought; and yet its contents are contemplated as true in the faith that it is only by such contemplation that the Absolute can be known.

II. Grades of Theoretic Consciousness

6. Whether philosophy is knowledge or embodies literal thinking may be open to dispute. But in any case it presents beliefs that are speakable or systematically communicable and is like science an expression of the theoretic consciousness. Theoretic consciousness at its minimum is the understanding of a speakable. What is spoken must be in the first instance believed. What is disbelieved must be, to start with, a believed content. The meaning of a sportive combination of words like the "hare's horn" or "square circle" is only not believed and cannot even be said to be disbelieved. Nor is such combination said to be spoken except as an example of what is not spoken. To speak is to formulate a belief. Even imperative or exclamatory speech expresses some kind of belief of the speaker, though the belief is not primarily intended to be communicated. A lie which is not believed by the speaker is not felt by him to be informatively spoken, being felt to be spoken only as incorporated in the implied prefix of all speech, viz., the imperative "believe me." It is believed content that is spoken

and it is the understanding of what can be spoken that constitutes the theoretic consciousness.

7. Such understanding may not be knowledge, but it involves belief in something as known or to be known. The belief may not be explicitly an awareness of the actual or possible knownness, but it can always be made explicit as such. The belief in knowledge may be implied in the explicit awareness of unknownness. The agnostic or the anti-rationalist or the absolute sceptic is primarily conscious of unknownness, but to be conscious of unknownness is to be conscious of knownness also. They may not be said to *know* the unknown as such but they *believe* it and impliedly believe also in something as known, even though it may be speakable only as unspeakable. They are said to present a philosophy so far as they express the theoretic consciousness which implies belief in something as known.

8. All forms of theoretic consciousness as involving the understanding of a speakable are sometimes called 'thought'. Of these, as will appear presently, only one form is literal thought, the others being symbolistic thought which should not be called 'thought' at all. Four forms or grades of thought may be distinguished. They may be roughly called empirical thought, pure objective thought, spiritual thought and transcendental thought. Empirical thought is the theoretic consciousness of a content involving reference to an object that is perceived or imagined to be perceived, such reference being part of the meaning of the content. There are contents that are objective but have no necessary reference to sense-perception and the consciousness of such contents may be called pure objective or contemplative thought. The content of spiritual thought is no object, nothing that is contemplated in the objective attitude, being subjective in the sense of being appreciated in a subjective or 'enjoying' attitude. Transcendental thought is the consciousness of a content that is neither objective nor subjective, the further characterisation of which will come later. The contents of the four grades of thought may be provisionally called fact, self-subsistence, reality and truth. Science deals with fact, the content of empirical thought. Philosophy deals with the last three, the contents of pure thought in the objective, subjective and transcendental attitudes.

9. All contents of the theoretic consciousness are speakable. The so-called grades of thought are really grades of speaking. Fact in science is spoken of as information and understood without reference to the spoken form. It is what need not be spoken to be believed. Speakability is a contingent character of the content of empirical thought, but it is a necessary character of the content of pure philo-

sophic thought. In philosophy, the content that is spoken is not intelligible except as spoken. Pure thought is not thought of a content distinguishable from it and is accordingly sometimes regarded as a fiction, philosophy being rejected as a disease of speech. Philosophical contents are, indeed, believed to be self-evident and the self-evident means what is independent of the spoken belief of an individual mind. This independence of speaking is, however, a part of their meaning. It is not part of the meaning of a scientific content which is understood without reference at all to be linguistic expression of it.

10. Now a believed content that has necessary reference to the speaking of it is not spoken of as information. Self-subsistence or enjoyed reality or truth is not assertable as fact. Belief in it may be expressed in the form of a judgment, but the form would be only artificial or symbolic. Fact is always expressible as a judgment of the form "A is thus related to B", this being the only judgment-form that is literally intelligible. A judgment of the form "X is", if it expresses belief in a fact of science, is only a periphrasis for a judgment of the above rational form. In "X is", if X stands for "A is related to B", the assertion means either only that A is related to B or that A that is thus related is related to something else. Fact is always a fact related to facts. If anywhere "X is" means something other than the relational assertion, it means that X is self-subsistent, real or true, which is only an apparent judgment. The subject is here understood as presupposing the predicate. The predicate does not, as in a judgment proper, amplify or explicate the meaning of a subject that is already believed. The subject is here believed as a self-evident elaboration of the predicate that is already believed to be self-evident.

11. Philosophy is such self-evident elaboration of the self-evident and is not a body of judgments. The self-evident is spoken, but is not spoken *of*. Of what is only spoken and contains a necessary reference to the speaking of it there are three forms according as it is spoken in the objective, the subjective or the transcendental attitude. The difference between the first two forms is the difference between the imports of the apparent judgments "The object (-in general) is" and "I am". In a judgment proper "A *is* thus related to B", if the word *is* by itself means anything, if in other words the assertion means any content more than "A related to B". the content as isolated would be objectivity. It may be expressed as an apparent judgment "the relation of A and B is". In a judgment proper, the word 'is' expresses only the objective attitude of the subject, but in this apparent judgment, 'is' means an objective content which is self-subsistent but not

fact. To express or formulate this content is still to retain the objective attitude. The attitude is explicitly dropped in saying "I am". The content here also is spoken and not spoken *of,* but it is explicitly understood as not objective and as only apparently objective or symbolised by objectivity. What the word 'am' means is not contemplated in the objective attitude but is subjectively enjoyed and only spoken *as though* it were objectively contemplated. If fact is spoken of and the self-subsistent object is only spoken—both being spoken as *meant,* reality is spoken not as meant but as only *symbolised.*

12. All the three are literally speakable. To say that the object is not the subject and that the latter is symbolised by the former is still to speak literally. The word that is used as symbol is not indeed literally understood, but what is symbolised by it (and that it is symbolised) is literally spoken. The subjective is a positive entity through which the objective is understood. The concept of the object is not reached through a generalisation of the objective facts of science. Were it not for the direct consciousness and speakability of the subject *I,* the concept of the object would never be precipitated. The first person *I* is the primary instance of a content that necessarily refers to the speaking of it. It is, in fact, the spoken that is understood as the same as the speaking function. In "I am" then, the predicate is a symbol of a literally spoken subject. What is taken as self-subsistent or real is literally spoken and understood. What, however, is taken as true is not literally understood.

13. How then is truth as beyond reality spoken? To answer the question, the connection between the notions of fact, self-subsistence and reality has to be further elucidated. The denial of each of these is possible. The judgment "A is thus related to B" may be denied in the form "that A is so related is not fact". "That A is so related" is no judgment, but what is nowadays called a 'proposition'. The enunciation and denial of it are possible because we have already a belief in the self-subsistent. If the proposition is understood as not fact, it is because we cannot deny its self-subsistence[1]. So we may deny the self-subsistent in the form "object is not", meaning "What is other than the subjective is not a definite or self-identical content for contemplation"—a recognised philosophical view that is not *prima facie* meaningless. The denial is possible because we already believe in the

[1] The term 'self-subsistence' instead of 'subsistence' is used because we *mean* only in reference to a belief. The believed subsistent is the self-subsistent as meant. A meaning that is not a believed content of one grade is a believed content of a higher grade.

subjective as enjoyed reality. We may also deny reality in the form "I (as individual subject) am not". This, too, is *prima facie* intelligible and it represents a new grade of negation, for the individual subject is understood to be real as subject and not as object though it may be individual through some sort of identification with the object. Even as individual, the *I* is enjoyingly believed and the denial of such a content is possible because we have already the notion of truth beyond reality.

14. Taking a sentence of the form "X is", it is a judgment proper if 'X', 'is' and their combination (or the judgment-form) are each literally understood. Where X stands for the self-subsistent, both X and 'is' are literally understood but the combination is not, since X is intelligible only through 'is'. Where X stands for the (individual) self as enjoyed, it is literally understood, but the word 'is' is only an objective symbolism for enjoyed reality and the combination, therefore, is also symbolic. Where X stands for the negation of the (individual) self, it is not literally understood, because no positive is understood as equivalent to it. The self is unintelligible except as the subject *I* or as what the subject *I* is not. There is no consciousness of an absolute or transcendental self without reference to the subject *I*. If such a self is understood, it is only as the implication of the enjoyed *I* and never by itself. It is indeed positively believed, but there is no positive formulation of it independent of the notion of *I*. Thus here X is only symbolically understood and consequently the word 'is' and the judgment-form also are symbolically understood. "Object is" is no judgment, being tautologous as a judgment and "I am" is no judgment because 'am' is only symbolism, but both are literally spoken because the subject is literally understood as positive. But the sentence "the absolute self is" is not only no judgment but is not even literally spoken. Still, it is not meaningless and symbolises what is positively believed, viz., truth. What is believed and is not literally speakable (and is as such undeniable) is truth.

15. So there are the four grades of speakables. There is the primary distinction between what is only symbolically speakable and what is literally speakable. The literally speakable comprises what is spoken of as information and what is only spoken and not spoken *of*. Of these, what is only spoken is spoken either as symbolised or as meant. Truth is only symbolically spoken, reality is literally spoken as symbolised and the self-subsistent is literally spoken as meant. None of these are spoken *of* as information, while fact is spoken of as information. These correspond to what were roughly called empirical,

contemplative, enjoying and transcendental thought. It is only what is spoken of as information or fact that is or can be meant literally. In contemplative, enjoying and transcendental thought, the content is not spoken *of* but is only spoken. If it is put in the judgment-form "X is", the form is only symbolical. In the first two, X being literally understood, the content though not literally thought is still said to be literally spoken. In contemplative thought, the judgment-form is only symbolical; even in enjoying thought, the word 'is' is also used symbolically. In transcendental thought, X also being symbolical, "X is" is not only not literally thought but not also literally spoken.

16. A content that can be literally spoken of is the content of a judgment. The content of a judgment is information or fact that is intelligible without reference to the speaking of it. A content that is necessarily understood in reference to the speaking of it is in some respect, at least, symbolically understood and is not information, fact or content of judgment. Beliefs in science alone are formulable as judgments and literally thinkable. If a content is literally thinkable in a judgment, the belief in it as known is actual knowledge. If it is only symbolically thinkable, it is not said to be known but to be only believed as known.

17. Theoretic consciousness was said to be belief in a speakable content involving belief in a content as known. When the content is spoken symbolically, it may not be believed as known, but is at least understood as pointing to what is believed to be known. In science, the content is spoken literally, and is just the content that is believed to be known and is as such actually known. In philosophy, the content is spoken as at least partially symbolised. The self-subsistent content meant by "object is" where the judgment-form is symbolical and not actually known and demands to be known in absorbed contemplation (or intuited) as simply 'object'. The real *I* similarly demands to be known not only without the judgment-form, but also without the objective intuitive attitude, i.e., in pure enjoyment. Yet in all these cases something is literally spoken and there is no demand to know the content without the speaking attitude. The speaking function is the final form of individual subjectivity and even the pure form of spiritual thought implies it. Transcendental consciousness starts by regarding all speaking as only symbolising and is accordingly conceived as completed when this symbolising speech also is dispensed with. What transcendental consciousness amounts to and whether it remains consciousness at all when it frees itself from speech or individual subjectivity we do not know, for absolute or impersonal consciousness is

only conceivable in a negative way. All that can be said is that truth which consciousness starts by symbolising continues to be believed and becomes more and more self-evident as the symbolising accomplishes its purpose.

18. Theoretic consciousness is embodied in science and philosophy Science alone speaks in genuine judgments, the content of which is fact intelligible without reference to speaking and is alone actually known and literally thought. Philosophy deals with contents that are not literally thinkable and are not actually known but are believed as demanding to be known without being thought. Such contents are understood as self-subsistent object, real subject and transcendental truth. We have accordingly three grades of philosophy which may be roughly called philosophy of the object, philosophy of the subject and philosophy of truth.

III. Science and Metaphysics

19. The philosophy of the object requires to be further distinguished from science. Both deal with the object understood as what is believed to be known in the objective attitude as distinct from the subjective, enjoying or spiritual attitude. The object in science, however, is understood as fact and not as self-subsistent. By 'fact' is meant what is perceivable or has necessary reference to the perceivable, is speakable in the form of a literal judgment and is believed without reference to the speaking of it. The self-subsistent is an object that has no necessary reference to the perceivable, is not literally expressible in a judgment and is believed only as it is spoken. A speakable is understood in necessary reference either to sense-perception or to the speaking of it. What is believed and understood in necessary reference to the speaking of it is, however, believed as self-evident or independent of the belief of any individual mind. As understood in the objective attitude, the self-evident is the self-subsistent. Fact in science is not believed as self-subsistent, as what would be even if no one believed it.

20. The self-subsistent object is a concept of philosophy, and it is not only not a concept of science but may be even denied by science. Science has no interest to formulate the concept of the self-subsistent object; and it apparently believes that the object *must* be knowable or usable. The self-subsistence of the object implies that the object *may be* in its very nature inaccessible to the mind. To contemplate the object as what would be if there were no subject to know it is to believe that it may be unknowable, that in any case it is not known as

of right. Science would not only take this suggestion to be gratuitous but would positively deny it. The notion that truth freely reveals itself and is in itself a mystery or even that it is its very nature to reveal itself would be scouted by science as obscurantist or anthropomorphic. To science, there is nothing in the object to make it known; it is just what is known and though it may be unknown, there is no question of its being unknowable.

21. The implicit belief of science then is that the object is knowable and usable *as of right*. This belief is at least questioned in philosophy to which it is an expression of solipsistic self-sufficiency on the part of the subject. In normal practical life, nature is not consciously exploited as a tool but is negotiated in the primitive spirit of sociableness. It is the arrogant exploiting attitude of science towards the object that provokes a self-healing reaction of the spirit in the form of philosophy or some cognate discipline. The spiritual demand is that nature should be contemplated and not merely used or manipulated. Science even as theory is evolved in a practical interest. What is more significant is that its very intellectual method is practical, being the use of actual or ideal *contrivances*. It is the wrong spiritual attitude of science towards the object rather than the so-called contradictions and problems left unsolved in scientific theory—as imagined by the philosopher but never felt by the scientist—that suggests the need for a speculative theory of the object. The concept of the self-subsistent object is the first corrective that philosophy offers of the predatory outlook of the scientific intellect. Realism is a philosophical faith among faiths: the creed of science. if formulated, would be a pragmatist form of solipsistic idealism.

22. The relation between science and the philosophy of the object may be brought out by a reference to certain problems which have been wrongly taken to be philosophical. There is the problem of piecing together the results of the sciences into a world-view. The synthesis wanted is sometimes imagined to be the generalisation of the primary laws of the sciences into more comprehensive laws. To suppose. however, that it can be accomplished by philosophy without the employment of the distinctive technique and methods of science would be nothing short of a presumptuous folly. If a law as distinct from a loose descriptive concept could be thus established, philosophy might well take in hand the entire work of science. All that can be achieved in this direction is an imaginative description of the world, which would be not only actual knowledge but not even a hypothesis that is intended to be turned into knowledge. Nor could it claim the

a priori certitude of a theory of logic or of metaphysics. Philosophical contents, if not known, are at least theoretically believed, but a world-view of this kind cannot even be claimed to be believed. It can be only an aesthetic view, having at best a suggestive value for science and an illustrative value for philosophy.

23. As an example of such speculation, I may refer to what is called evolutionary philosophy as distinct from the scientific account of evolution. Metaphysics may discuss the general concept of evolution which is but the concept of life and its materialistic, spiritualistic or other interpretations. For this, however, it does not require to piece together the results of science, all the data needed—matter, life and mind—being presented in the knowledge of oneself as in the body. The details and specific generalisations of science are utilised in the so-called philosophy of evolution not as evidence but as only illustrative material intended for visualising the metaphysical theory on the subject. The scientific account of evolution is knowledge or hypothesis, the metaphysic of life in relation to matter and mind is believed, if not known, but the so-called philosophy of evolution, so far as it is different from either, is only an organised presentation of the known or supposed facts of evolution *as though* they constituted the history of a single cosmic life. Cosmic life is not known as a fact, but may still be believed as self-subsisting. The single significant history of this life, however, as rounding off the jagged groupings of facts in science and bridging over the gaps left by it, is only imagined, and is understood to be neither self-evident nor verifiable. The significant story of cosmic evolution then is neither science nor philosophy but only a species of imaginative literature.

24. There is another problem, viz., the formulation of the postulates or structural concepts of science, which used to be regarded as a philosophical problem. Pure physics, for example, was taken by Kant as a branch of knowable metaphysic established by deduction from the *a priori* principles of synthetic knowledge. There is a similar confusion of thought at the present day in the romantic philosophy that has sprung up round the physico-mathematical theory of relativity, although here the confusion is of science with philosophy and not of philosophy with science as in the other case. In both, the impassable gulf between fact and the self-subsistent is ignored. The so-called axioms of science are but postulates, the formulation of which is the work of science itself. The postulates are hypothesis of a kind which are intended not for the anticipation of facts, but for the organisation of them into a system. They admit of rival hypotheses and may be

rejected though not as contradicted by fact, but only as clumsier and less expeditious to work with than the rival hypotheses. Again, there is no passage from a postulate of science to a concept of the object in itself. Whether the real world is four-dimensional or is intrinsically indeterminate in its behaviour can never be determined from the basic conceptual devices that happen to organise the facts of science at the present day. The postulates of science neither lead to nor are deducible from any metaphysical conception of the object.

IV. Philosophy of the Object

25. What then has philosophy to say about the object? The objective attitude is understood only in contrast with the subjective or enjoying attitude. What is believed in the objective attitude, viz., the object, need not, however, be understood in reference to the subject. Where the reference to the subject is no part of the meaning of the object, the object is called fact and is dealt with in science. Philosophy deals with the object that is intelligible only in reference to the subject. By 'subject' is meant the individual subject or *I* which is understood in the theoretic consciousness as the speaking function that is symbolised by itself as spoken. The object that has necessary reference to the speaking of it is the self-subsistent object for philosophy.

26. Philosophy formulates and elaborates the concept of the self-subsistent object. What is common to such object and scientific fact is objectivity which is itself no fact, being only the circumstance of being understood in the objective attitude. This is just the form of the object, the self-subsistent form that is elaborated in Logic. It is indeed the form of spoken fact. but as it is the form of the self-subsistent object also, it cannot be said to have necessary reference to fact or the perceivable. Logic as the study of this form is thus no science, but a branch of the philosophy of the object. The form is itself a pure object and is also the form of pure object. The pure object of which Logic is the form or shadow is the metaphysical object. The two branches of the philosophy of the object then are Logic and Metaphysics.

27. Logical form or objectivity is not a concept reached by a comparison of the objects or facts of science. The concept of the object is reached in the first instance by contrast with the subject as the self-evident content of the spiritual consciousness. It is in the theoretic consciousness of the spiritual grade that one is first explicitly conscious of the object as such. In the consciousness of "I am", one appreciates the objective attitude of judgment as distinct from the enjoying attitude and understands it to be assumed only as a necessary make-believe.

The consciousness of the asserted being (*am*) or object as such here emerges as the consciousness of a necessary symbol of the subject *I*. That object is symbol of subject implies that object is not subject. The consciousness of negation as such, in fact, emerges only in this symbolising consciousness. One may be conscious of the object without being explicitly conscious of the subject, but object has no meaning except as the negation and the symbol of the subject. The symbolism here is necessary, and hence when the reference to the subject is only implicit, the object appears as the immediacy of the subject, as implicitly real. Thus object is understood as self-subsistent before fact is understood as object. Hence objectivity or the form of the object is intelligible in reference to the object that is taken to be implicitly real or what is called metaphysical object. Logic in this sense presupposes Metaphysics.

28. Metaphysics is philosophy of the object and involves theoretic consciousness in the objective attitude. There is properly speaking no metaphysic of the subject. What passes as such is either the metaphysic of the mind understood as a particular type of object or is no metaphysic but a self-symbolising form of spiritual activity. Metaphysics elaborates the concept of the object in reference to the subject. The rationale of any distinction of metaphysical contents is to be found in an introspectively appreciable distinction within spiritual experience. Even the crude division of the object into matter, life and mind is not intelligible as an inductive classification of fact. That these are *all that is* can at least never be known by induction. The notion of the objective universe is that of an infinite singular and not of a universal; and an *exhaustive* division of such a singular into items that are *all positive* can only be reached if the singular self-evidently unfolds itself in them, if, in other words, each item means every other item or means the entire system. Such a system is self-evident only as the symbol of an introspective or enjoyed content, as the symbolic analysis of the simple or unitary consciousness of oneself living in the body. The analysis is symbolic because the so-called constituents of the content—matter, life and mind—are intelligible not by themselves but only in reference to this consciousness. Their difference is such as is immediately felt and every apparently factual characterisation of them is understood in reference to this feeling.

29. No metaphysical concept is intelligible without reference to the subject or spirit which itself goes beyond metaphysics. The characteristic abstractions of metaphysics which are supposed on the one hand to be of an 'extra high grade' and on the other to be only diseases of speech are really symbolic meanings which derive their whole value

for belief from the spiritual experiences that they symbolise. There are no judgments, accordingly, in metaphysics and, paradoxical as it may sound, the metaphysical beliefs are not reached by inference. The elaborate parade of deductive proof in metaphysics is only a make-believe, unless proof is taken, as it is sometimes taken, as the exposition of an unperceived tautology. Metaphysical reasoning is only the *systematic exposition of symbolic concepts,* concepts that are implicitly taken as symbols of contents that are enjoyingly believed.

30. Fact and the self-subsistent are both literally spoken and in both the believed content is figured by being spoken. Fact is understood as independent of this figuration while the self-subsistent is presented as constituted by it. What is common to these spoken contents is this speech-created form. There are accidental forms of speech, but there are also certain structural forms that are unavoidable in the communication of belief and which are believed to belong to the understood content and not to the speech only. When a fact is spoken, there is a peculiar dualism in the understood content of the meant and the believed, the latter being meant as beyond meaning or as perceivable. When a self-subsistent is spoken, the dualism lapses, the meant and the believed being coincident. The unavoidable forms of speech are constitutive of the meaning. Logic presents a system of speech-created forms of meaning. There may be alternative systems, for logic presupposes metaphysics which presents alternative theories. The fundamental disputes in logic are unavowed metaphysical disputes. Apart from the question of accidental inconsistency within a logical system, whether one logical system is better than another is settled not by logic but by metaphysic. Metaphysical dispute, however, is not settled by logic, for apparently every metaphysical system has its distinctive logic.

31. The suspicion that the subject is not believed in the same sense as the metaphysical object does not arise within metaphysics. Metaphysics is unaware of the distinction between the self-subsistent and the real. There seems to be nothing wrong, for instance, in the characterisation of matter or mind as real. The distinction is suggested by a contrast of logic with metaphysics. The forms of meaning as discussed in logic are a kind of entity that must be said to be believed in, but it would be absurd to say that they are real. They are believed in as not real and yet not nothing, or in other words, as self-subsistent. If logical form or objectivity is self-subsistent, has the object of metaphysics any higher status? The distinction of abstract and concrete has meaning only within fact and hence the object cannot mean anything more than objectivity. The metaphysical object is defined, in contrast

with fact, as objectivity or self-subsistent meaning. Metaphysic defines itself in logic.

V. Philosophy of the Spirit

32. The suggested distinction of self-subsistence and reality is explicitly verified in the spiritual or enjoying consciousness of objectivity as a symbol of the real subject. As already pointed out, in 'I am', *am* meaning self-subsistent being as understood in the objective attitude is the symbol of *I* as understood in the subjective attitude. Enjoying understanding of a content, in fact, is the consciousness of it as symbolised by an objectively contemplated meaning. Without such a symbolism, the subject would be enjoyed but not enjoyingly understood. It is not only understood like the self-subsistent in necessary reference to the speaking of it: it is understood further as symbolised by its spoken form. This enjoying understanding is what we mean or should mean by introspection. Introspection proper is a form of the theoretic consciousness that implies an abjuration of the objective attitude. Its content is not understood as objective fact nor even as self-subsistent object. The content is not the 'interior' of the body which is fact nor is the 'mental' which as unintelligible without reference to the speaking of it is a self-subsistent object. The content is *I* or implies *I*, and although it is spoken as though it were an object, it is understood as what object is not, as the speaking subjectivity.

33. To introspect is actually or ideally to speak in the first person. To speak in the first person may not be to explicitly conscious of the I as what the object is not. When it involves such consciousness, it amounts to introspection. Again, introspective speaking may or may not involve the explicit consciousness of *being* what is spoken. When it involves such consciousness, it may be called spiritual introspection. The consciousness of being what is spoken (*I*) is itself a new achievement of the subject, its realisation or deepening of being. All introspection involves such achievement: introspection cannot be like the knowledge of objective fact, which leaves the fact unaffected in being. But there is a form of introspection which *apparently* leaves the content thus unaffected, where really there is an alteration of subjective being which is enjoyed only in the non-theoretic way This may be taken to be an implicit form of spiritual introspection. Sometimes there is a conscious suspension of theoretic consciousness about such alteration, a deliberate exclusion of it from introspection.

In such a case, introspection tends to degenerate into objective consciousness of the mind as distinct from the *I*—what is ordinarily called psychological introspection.

34. The subject *I* is never accepted by itself in spiritual introspection. Something else is always enjoyed along with the subject and enjoyed in reference to it. This may be of three grades. There is in the first place the explicit consciousness of the subject as *unaccountably* embodied, this being the same as the consciousness of the subject as what the object including the mind is not. Next there is the consciousness of personal relation to other selves. Lastly there is the consciousness of the over-personal self. The over-personal self is enjoyingly understood not only in reference to the subject *I* but as implying the specific experience of communion, the felt form of identity with the *I*. Such enjoying identity is what is called concrete identity or identity-in-difference, a relation that is unintelligible in the objective attitude. Identity in the philosophy of the object is conceived as abstract identity of the form 'A is A' and there is no place for *relation* of identity in the sphere of fact. The consciousness of the over-personal self as thus one with the *I* is the religious form of the spiritual consciousness. The study of all contents enjoyed in explicit reference to the subject *I* may be called the philosophy of the spirit.

35. Spiritual consciousness is not mere consciousness of reality but is reality itself. Except in the specifically religious form of it, however, it involves some consciousness of reality as distinct from what may be called empty objectivity. In the enjoying consciousness of the self as embodied or symbolised by the object, the object is conceived not as self-subsistent, but only as a shadow or symbol of the *I*, the consciousness of the shadow as such being said to be empty. In the consciousness of personal relations—the moral consciousness, for example—*I* and the other person are each not the other, each the symbol of the other, there being an alternation of symbolisms. The other person is to me 'another *I*' which taken literally is a contradiction through which alone, however, he is understood. Or I (first person) am aware of being 'this person' (third person) to him, which too is symbolising by a contradiction. Each alternative is real in being but contradictory or empty in meaning or theory. The experience of religious communion or worship is the consciousness of the over-personal reality as symbolised by *I*. The conscious symbolising by *I* is a non-theoretic experience of self-abnegation: it is consciously *being* nought and not consciousness *of I* as nought. What emerges to theoretic religious consciousness is the over-personal reality alone. In this sense

the religious consciousness is said to outgrow all empty subjectivity and to be the enjoyed fulness of being.

36. Religious experience as consciousness of being is simple and admits of no variation within itself. There is, however, an infinite plurality of unique religious experiences. Their relation is determined by themselves and not by any external reflection. Each experience by its self-deepening gets opposed to or synthesised with other experiences. One experience may enjoy another as a stage outgrown or as in absolute conflict with it, where a third experience may emerge as adjusting them to one another. There is no possibility of systematising them by secular reason and so far as they systematise themselves, they present themselves in many alternative systems. Each experience, in fact, is a revelation and we believe in a system only so far as it is actually revealed. Extensive internally coherent systems with indefinite boundaries are actually revealed, though there is no *a priori* necessity of a system and still less of a system admitting of no alternative systems. The Hegelian notion of a single and exclusive gradation of religions would appear from this standpoint to be intrinsically irreligious.

37. The theoretic form of a religious system is a philosophy of religion, there being as many forms of this philosophy as there are religious systems. This form expresses itself in the lower grades of philosophy—in the theory of the sub-religious spirit, in the metaphysic of the object and even in logic. Every system of religious philosophy has its distinctive theory of the spirit, metaphysics and logic. The fundamental differences within logical theory are, as has been suggested, implicitly metaphysical, those in metaphysic are implicitly spiritual and those in the theory of the secular spirit are implicitly religious. Religions may indefinitely multiply and indefinitely get synthesised. So is there indefinite scope for differences and syntheses in philosophical theory in general. There is no question of philosophy progressing towards a single unanimously acceptable solution. All philosophy is systematic symbolism and symbolism necessarily admits of alternatives.

VI. Philosophy of Truth

38. In religion, there can be no theoretic denial of the subject *I*. In worship, indeed, the subject abnegates itself but the abnegation is there an affair of enjoyed being and not of theory. There is, however, a theoretic consciousness of 'I am nought', of the possibility at any rate of the subject or the individual self being unreal. The denial of the *I* is possible because we already believe that the absolute is. The absolute is not the same as the over-personal reality that is enjoyed in

religion. It means what the subject *I* is not, but the reality of religious experience while it is enjoyed and symbolised by *I* does not mean such theoretic negation of *I*. What is called the absolute is a positively believed entity that is only negatively understood. It is an entity that cannot be understood as it is believed, and is speakable only by way of symbolism. Reality as apprehended in religion is, indeed, symbolised by *I*, but so far as it is expressed as a self, it is expresssed literally. The positive character of the absolute, however, is expressible only by the negation of *I* (or more accurately by 'what-I am not') and as such is not literally expressible at all. If then we say that the absolute *is*, we mean by 'is' not reality but truth. Reality is enjoyed but truth is not. The consciousness of truth as what is believed in but not understood either in the objective or in the subjective attitude, as not literally speakable at all but speakable only in the purely symbolistic way, is extra-religious or transcendental consciousness.

39. What is believed in and understood as literally unspeakable may be said to be self-revealing. Reality is still literally speakable and may be taken to depend on the speaking for its revelation, though the speaking (which means the *I*) is not there empty subjectivity. Truth is believed or revealed *as* independent of it, as *self*-revealing, what is true being spoken as what the speaking *I* is not. At the same time, to be even symbolically spoken, it has to be believed as a distinct. As a positive to which even the *I* is but a symbol and, therefore, nought in itself, it has nothing to be distinguished from and is absolute. If, then, truth as absolute is distinguished, it can only be distinguished from itself. The self-distinction of the absolute cannot mean self-identity as it appears in the religious consciousness in which the identity-in-difference is conceived to be necessary. There is no necessity in this self-distinction. The absolute may be truth or it may be what truth is not or it may be their mere distinction without any unity in the background, which means their indeterminate togetherness which cannot be denied to be either of them. What truth is not and is yet positive is the absolute freedom beyond being (the absolute freedom of the will) and what is indeterminately either truth or freedom is absolute value. There is no sense in speaking of the absolute as the unity of truth, freedom and value. It is *each* of them, these being only *spoken* separately but not *meant* either as separate or as one. The theoretic consciousness of truth, then, is the consciousness of truth as distinct from itself as freedom and from this identity-less self-distinction or value. The absolute as transcending the enjoyed reality of religion is positive being

(truth) or positive non-being (freedom) or their positive indetermination (value). The absolute is conceived rigorously as truth in (Advatia) Vedānta. What is loosely called nihilist Buddhism apparently understands the absolute as freedom. The Hegelian absolute may be taken to represent the indetermination, miscalled *identity* of truth and freedom which is value. All these views belong to what may be called the transcendental grade of philosophy.

40. This triple absolute is apparently the prototype of the three subjective functions—knowing, willing and feeling. These functions are primarily the self-distinction of the transcendental consciousness. The distinction of the functions does not emerge in the spiritual consciousness. Spiritual consciousness is simple and integral in its very nature. The consciousness of *I* is not only not the consciousness of a complex unity of these functions, it is not even the consciousness of a unity revealing itself in each of them. It not only does not analyse itself: it supplies no motive for such analysis. The tripartite elaboration of consciousness is not introspective but transcendental. The absolutes reveal themselves and the *I* appears trinal only as their shadow or symbolism. As the absolutes are not related into a unity, neither can their subjective shadows be said to be related. The simple *I* has no enjoyed elements or aspects to be related. Nor are the so-called functions intelligible as pure acts or interests *of the I*. They cannot be defined in subjective terms nor can they be taken as unique subjective experiences, being not presented as distinct to introspection at all. Their whole meaning is derived from the self-revealed absolutes.

41. The theory of truth is the theory of the other two absolutes also. At the same time it recognises the possibility of elaborating a primary theory of each of them in reference to the other absolutes. We have shadows of these primary theories in the lower grades of philosophy. The theory of truth, for example, as conceived in its explicit transcendental form has its shadow in the theory of knowledge which belongs to the philosophy of the spirit and in the theory of objective categories which is somewhere intermediate between metaphysics and logic in the philosophy of the object.

THE CONCEPT OF THE ABSOLUTE AND ITS ALTERNATIVE FORMS

ANALYSIS

(1) Philosophy starts in reflection which is the awareness of a content *as to* a mode of consciousness. The nature of this relation of 'as to' has got to be analysed. (2) There can be no consciousness of a relation prior to reflection. Yet the relation between content and consciousness has to be understood in terms of the relation between two contents of consciousness. (3) It is sometimes held, on the contrary, that the relation between two contents of consciousness has to be understood in terms of the relation between consciousness and content, which is claimed to be one of identity-in-difference. That the relation under reference is actually what it is said to be has got to be examined. (4) To reflection, the relation of content and consciousness appears to be one of asserted implication. Now if A is asserted to imply B, a factual relation is always meant and this relation is one which obtains between a term which must be definite and independent of the relation and the implied term B. Unless such a definite independent term is found, the implication has to be taken as an indefinite formulation of a factual relation. In the case under reference, the independent term is not a definite nameable thing, and thus in the reflective stage, we have only an indefinite relation between content and consciousness. (5-8) This indefinite relation appears to reflection as at once distinction and non-distinction. But this non-distinction cannot be positively asserted as an identity. Neither can it be denied to be so. The relation, then, of content and consciousness appears to reflection as an indefinite distinction only and not as an indefinite identity. The demand is for this distinction to be defined and for a supra-reflective consciousness where this distinction can be visualised.

(9) The absolute has to be understood not as the identity but only as a completely definite distinction of content and consciousness. (10) Now, as consciousness is of three kinds—knowing, feeling and willing—the implicatory distinction is also threefold. The mode of resolution of these implicatory distinctions into corresponding non-implicatory distinctions will accordingly vary in these three spheres. Thus the absolute has to be formulated not as a unitary something but as an un-unifiable triplicity. (11) The variations of the implicatory distinction in these three spheres may be represented by three modes of distinction that are recognised to hold between known contents. The content may be spoken of (a) as unconstituted by consciousness, or

(b) as constituted by consciousness, or, again (c) as along with consciousness constituting some kind of unity. (12-16) The content of knowing, i.e., the object known is independent of and thus unconstituted by knowing. The content of willing, i.e., an act, an end or an empirical embodiment of the end is not independent of willing and is, in this sense, constituted by the willing. Reflective knowing, as also reflective willing, is the consciousness of the content as distinct from the consciousness. Reflective feeling, on the other hand, is the consciousness of the content as in unity with the feeling.

(17-19) The content of knowing is necessarily understood in reflection as what is perfectly distinct from knowing. The content implies such a reference to knowing and apparently means nothing without it. To say that the reference is necessary is not, however, to say that the content is a fact necessarily related to knowing. But the content is not also apprehended as only accidentally related to knowing. Reflection tells us nothing either way, and both the idealistic and realistic positions appear to be over-statements. (20) The realistic position that the known content may exist unknown cannot either be denied or asserted. The possibility, however, of such a content is understood in reference to what is taken as self-evidently known. The self-evident is that which reveals itself and which might not have been to the knower at all. (21) The realistic view of the independence of the known content can only be admitted in the sense of the content being in some respect self-evident.

(22) The self-evident is not 'necessary' in the sense of being that whose opposite is unintelligible. It is rather that in regard to which the problem of thinking the opposite is not entertained at all. To be conscious of a content as self-evident is to be conscious not of its negation being unmeanable but of the problem of meaning the negation not even arising. (23) The self-evident is that of which we cannot be conscious except as true. It cannot as a rule, be the content of a judgment in the true sense of the term. (24) That a conclusion follows from a premise or premises is the only content that can be claimed to be self-evidently known, but it is not, properly speaking, a judgment. (25-26) A disguised form of this inferential 'following' is found in 'to know A is to know B'. This content cannot, however, be said to be no judgment and yet we are not conscious here of the problem of meaning its negation. It is the primordial and the only self-evident judgment. (27) The copula of this judgment is not known like other copulas. It is understood as *spoken* but not as *spoken of*. The word 'is' in the judgment is known, no doubt, but is not under-

stood as known *content*. (28-29) It may, accordingly, be (loosely) called a known no-content. It is explicitly known as what known content is not. (30) This then is the element in all that is reflectively known that is known as what need not be known. It is the element that is free from the implicational relation of the content to the knowing of it. This is the absolute for knowing that demands to be freed from its immanence in the implicatory distinction of content and knowing.

(31) The implicative distinction is demanded to be resolved in willing also. The content of willing is something that is foreign to and is thus a limitation to itself. But in the reflective stage this limitation is not realised as a self-limitation or the free limitation of the will to realise itself. But reflection demands that the limitation should be realised as self-limitation in this sense. (32-34) The relation between two contents willed suggests the relation between the willed content and willing. Now, two contents are said to be willed at once when one of them is a means to the other. This relation of means and end has to be understood as the relation between the willed content and willing. It is difficult, however, to understand how one can be said to act in a particular way to act freely. Reflection indicates that it is to be understood by contrasting 'I will this act' with 'I will this act that I ought to will'. The contrast yields the implication that willing as represented by the former is itself a being that is to be superseded by willing as represented by the latter, and that we will an act in order to get rid of the being of the act. But reflection cannot understand this willing or freedom at its limit.

(35-39) In reflective feeling, there is the definite consciousness of an indefinite distinction of the content felt and the feeling of it. Reflection demands that this idefinite distinction be resolved into a definite self-subsistent unity, that is to say, a unity where the constituents are distinguishable from it. We try to understand this relation on the analogy of the relation between two contents which are felt together, as for example, in the feeling of a beautiful object. We do not completely succeed. The constituents (i.e., the felt content and the feeling) appear to be imperfectly distinct, and the unity here means an imperfect distinction of the constituents and not the self-subsistent unity that is demanded to be realised in reflection. Value as such unity is not thus realised as self-subsistent like the beautiful object. The felt content and the feeling-consciousness are not together distinguished from the value that is their unity. (40) Recapitulation of sections 22-40.

(41) In the case of knowing, a known content has to be under-

stood as what need not be the content of any knowing, that is to say, as utterly unrelated to knowing. In the case of willing, the reality of willing has to be understood as the negation of being or of an emergent distinct. In the case of feeling, the being of value has to be understood as a being from which known being is distinct: it is to entertain an indifference of being and non-being. All the three—unrelatedness, negation of the emergent and the indifference of being and non-being—imply unmeaning modes of negation to reflection. In all these cases, what demands to be understood cannot actually be understood, because such understanding would involve a species of negation that is unmeaning to reflection. To admit the absolute in any form is to admit a negation that is unintelligible to the logic of the understanding.

(42) The absolute may be defined from the standpoint of reflection as what is free from the implicational dualism of content and consciousness. There are three ways in which this freedom can be understood: (a) the content may be freed from its reference to consciousness and we have *truth*—the absolute for knowing; (b) consciousness may be freed from its content and we have *freedom* of the will—the absolute for willing; (c) the implicational relation of content and consciousness may be freed from their distinction as a unity and we have *value*—the absolute for feeling. (43) The absolute has thus to be formulated in a triple way. It is meaningless, however, to cognitively assert that there are three absolutes or one absolute, for the absolute is not *known* content and it is only about a known content that the question 'one or many' has any meaning. (44-45) Freedom may alternatively be called reality and, as it is not known, it is meaningless to call it truth. Truth is the self-evident and is known, though it is not a known content. What is known, however, may be either the self-evident in its purity or some relation of *given* contents with the form of self-evidence. The self-evident in its purity is truth and not reality: but a relation of given contents is not only said to be true but cannot also be said to be not real. The real then is not true, but the true may be real. (46) Similarly, truth is not value, but value is not un-true. The predicates 'valuable' and 'worthless' do not apply to truth. (47) The predicates 'real' and 'unreal' do not apply to value. But reality or freedom cannot be said not to be a value. (48) Thus it is meaningless to speak of truth as a value, of value as real and of reality as true: while value may be truth, reality value and truth reality. The absolute may be regarded in this sense as an alternation of truth, value and reality.

THE CONCEPT OF THE ABSOLUTE AND ITS ALTERNATIVE FORMS

1. Philosophy starts in reflective consciousness. Reflection is the awareness of a content *as to* a mode of consciousness. The phrase 'as to' means some relation and it is in reference to this relation that the concept of the absolute has to be understood. What is this relation?

2. We ordinarily understand a relation as between the contents of consciousness and we have here apparently to conceive some such relation as subsisting between content and consciousness. Of the two relations—between content and content, and between content and consciousness—the latter has to be understood in terms of the former. Not that we know relation in objective consciousness before we come to be reflectively conscious of a relation between content and consciousness. To be aware of a relation *as such* between two terms, of their relation as distinct from their whole having the form of being, is to be aware at the same time of the possibility of the terms being not related in that relation. Now unlike a term known to be existent, a relation known to subsist between two terms cannot be *imagined* to be absent. The possible absence of a known relation, in fact, can never be apprehended in merely objective consciousness. Hence we can know a relation *as such* of two contents only in reflection which is specifically the consciousness of a relation between content and consciousness. Yet although there can be no consciousness of a relation prior to reflection, the relation of contents may be said to be prior to the relation of content and consciousness in the sense that the former is intelligible by itself while the latter is intelligible only in terms of the former.

3. There are those who hold that because we are only reflectively conscious of relation, the relation between content and consciousness should be read into the relation of content and content and not vice versa. The relation of content and consciousness is to them a transparent identity-in-difference and all relation of contents is to be understood as the same relation in an implicit form. The difficulty is that the relation of content and consciousness is not explicitly or self-evidently appreciated as an identity-in-difference by reflection itself, being, in fact, claimed to be so appreciated only in a higher consciousness called absolute or speculative consciousness. The possibility, however, of this supra-reflective consciousness may be disputed and it is

necessary in the first instance to show if and how reflection itself points to it.

4. Prima facie to reflection, the relation of content and consciousness appears as an implicative distinction. We are reflectively aware of the content as distinct from and in necessary reference to consciousness and the reference is not merely verbal but is implicitly an assertion. In the case of an asserted implication between two terms, the fact asserted is a relation (or unity), the terms of which are not the terms asserted to be in implication. If A is asserted to imply B, a factual relation is meant but A is not understood as a term of the relation. A here stands for a fact which need not have the relation but is thought as having it, the fact being not altered by being so thought. This fact should be capable of being expressed by a term that does not refer to the relation and the relation should be taken as between this term and the implied term B. For every implying term, it is necessary to find such a non-implying term, if possible; and until and unless it is found, the implication has to be taken as an *indefinite* formulation of a factual relation (or unity). To reflective consciousness there is implication between the content and the consciousness of it and the implication points to a factual relation (or unity) of which one of them at least is not really a term. One of them at least stands for an unnamed something which need not be related to the other. Some factual relation then appears to be only *indefinitely* formulated as the implication of content and consciousness in the reflective stage.

5. Now if it can be shown within reflection that this indefinite relation cannot be denied to be a distinction and cannot be denied also to be an identity, a stage of consciousness in which distinction and identity of the same terms are positively known together may be taken to be demanded by reflection which cannot understand them together. That the content is somehow distinct from consciousness is obvious to reflection but identity is not so obvious. What immediately appears is an indefinite distinction between content and consciousness: the terms are undoubtedly distinct but they are not wholly distinguishable. Have we the right to interpret this vague indistinguishability as an identity?

6. The indefinite relation of content and consciousness appears to reflection at once as distinction and as not distinction but this non-distinction cannot be positively asserted as an identity. Things may come to be distinguished that were undistinguished but what are once distinguished cannot be later taken to be non-distinct without at least one of the terms being taken to be illusory. Hence to distinguish terms

imperfectly is to be able to assert their distinction but neither to assert nor to deny their identity.

7. But it may be contended that distinction and identity stand on the same footing in respect of undeniability : like distinction identity also once apprehended cannot be denied. That we distinguish what were undistinguished does not mean that we knew their *relation* of identity which is now denied. We reply that it is possible to deny the relation of identity even when it is explicitly apprehended. There is something peculiar about the relation of identity, as expressed in the dilemma: if its terms are not distinct, they are not related at all, and if they are distinct they are not identical. We cannot get rid of the dilemma and admit identity as a relation unless we hold that while the distinction of its terms is cognitively undenied, it is positively entertained only in non-cognitive consciousness. The fact A in the context M is said to be identical with A in the context N and A has the differential characters x and y in the contexts, which are presented and yet as neither factual nor non-factual. If the characters be facts, A cannot be identical in the two contexts and if they be no facts at all, there is no distinction of terms and, therefore, no relation. They have accordingly to be taken as not cognised characters but aesthetically apprehended expressions which do not preclude the cognised identity of A and yet are themselves cognitively undenied. To assert a relation is not to *assert* a distinction between its terms but only not to deny it. We may be affectively or conatively aware of a distinction where we do not intellectually disbelieve the distinction but do not also assert it. Identity then such as is knowable is a relation of terms, the distinction of which is undenied but unknown. Now what is unknown and yet speakable as felt *may* come to be known. If the differential characters *x* and *y* come to be known, the identity of A would be denied. Identity cannot accordingly be taken to be undeniable like distinction.

8. The indefinite relation then of content and consciousness should not be interpreted as indefinite identity. There is no demand, therefore, in reflection for a stage of conscious in which content and consciousness may be explicitly seen to be identical in difference. The only necessary demand in knowledge is that what appears as indefinite in an assignable respect should be definable in that respect. If further the indefiniteness is such as *necessarily* appears to a stage of consciousness, that stage is taken to demand a higher stage where the indefinite gets defined. To reflection, the relation of content and consciousness appears necessarily as an indefinite distinction only and not as an indefinite identity. The demand is for this distinction to be

defined and for a supra-reflective consciousness where this distinction can be visualised.

9. The concept of the absolute in any form is taken to belong to a supra-reflective consciousness. The possibility and nature of this consciousness have to be understood in reflection as a necessary problem. The conception of an explicit identity-in-difference of content and consciousness is not demanded in reflection. Reflection demands only a non-implicational distinction of them to define the necessarily implicational or indefinite distinction that is presented to it. The absolute accordingly has to be problematically understood within reflection as meaning not an identity but only a completely definite distinction of content and consciousness. It may be that the supra-reflective consciousness in which the reflective implication of content and consciousness is turned into a non-implicatory distinction is itself consciousness of identity in a symbolic or metaphorical sense. But in any case identity as *a logical relation* has to be definitely denied between content and consciousness before this mystic identity can be appreciated.

10. We are concerned for the present with the conception of the absolute such as is intelligible as a problem to reflection. We have to trace in detail how the indefinite distinction of content and consciousness can be defined, how their apparent identity can be denied, how, in fact, the implicatory distinction can be resolved into a non-implicatory distinction. We shall find presently that the implicatory distinction of content and consciousness varies according as the consciousness is knowing, feeling or willing. The implication is resolvable in different ways in these three spheres and the absolute is understood in the reflective stage in terms of the mode of resolution in each case. Knowing, feeling and willing will then each have its own formulation of the absolute—viz., truth, value and reality (or freedom) respectively, as will be justified later. In the reflective stage these absolutes or formulations of the absolute will be found to be un-unifiable and to be in a sort of alternation. Whether a mystical identity of the absolutes can be reached in the supra–reflective consciousness does not concern us. Our problem is to show how reflection demands a specific absolute in each case.

11. What is specifically apprehended in non-cognitive consciousness cannot be literally formulated in terms of knowledge. Philosophy which cognitively deals with the contents of all consciousness should claim to know *not* the non-cognitive contents themselves but only *that* they are non-cognitive, that we believe in contents which we do not know. It can, therefore, speak of these believed contents

only by a sort of intellectual symbolism *as though* they were known. To reflection, the implicative distinction of content and consciousness varies according as the consciousness is knowing, feeling or willing. The variations may be represented by three modes of distinction that we recognise as between known contents. If A is distinct from B, B may be simply an other, or it may be constitutive of A, or A and B may be both constitutive of C. So the content that is distinguished in reflection from consciousness may be spoken of as unconstituted by consciousness or as constituted by consciousness or as along with consciousness constituting some kind of unity. The first mode of distinction is the relation of content and consciousness in knowing and the last two will be found to appropriately symbolise the relation in willing and feeling respectively.

12. The content of a knowing act is unconstituted by the act The *particular* act of knowing discovers and does not construct the object known, even if the object be admitted to be constructed by *some* knowing. Knowledge would appear to mean that the object known is in some sense independent of it though it may be a question whether what we ordinarily claim to know is properly said to be known and to be independent of the knowing. Where the object is coloured by the particularity of the act of knowing, it may be said to be only empirically known but it is still taken to be known so far as it is believed to be independent of it.

13. The content of willing may be said to be an act, an end, or the empirical embodiment of the end—the organisation of certain objective facts (including the means) by the end. None of these is a fact that can be said to be known in the willing, believed as independent of the willing in the sense the content of knowing is independent of knowing. Each is constituted by willing in the sense that apart from willing it is nothing at all. It cannot be said that it is a future fact that is *known* in the willing. Willing is, indeed, some form of consciousness of the future but the future here, unlike the future that is said to be known, is not a fact but a contingency, not what *will* be but what *would* be *if* it were willed, not as already determined but what is being determined by the willing and as therefore apart from the willing nothing at all. Yet the content of willing is distinct from willing, distinct as what is constituted is distinct from what constitutes it.

14. Reflective knowing is consciousness of the known object as distinct from the knowing. Reflective willing is consciousness of the act willed as being distinguished by the willing from itself. Neither is consciousness primarily of the distinction itself or the distinguishing.

Reflective feeling is primarily consciousness of the distinction (or the distinguishing) of content and consciousness. To be conscious of a content *as* felt is to be conscious of the content in unity with the feeling or of feeling unified with the content. The unity of two contents means—whatever else it means—an imperfect distinction between them ; and we have to understand the unity of content and consciousness on this analogy. The unity of which reflective feeling is conscious is the imperfect distinction between content and consciousness, taken itself as a content. To be conscious of a content as known or willed is not even to be implicitly conscious of a unity of content and consciousness. The known content appears to reflection as perfectly distinct from knowing and a unity of perfect distincts cannot be reflectively conceived to be knowable. The content of willing as constituted by the willing alone cannot be understood to constitute along with the willing any unity other than the content itself. It is only in reflective feeling that we are conscious of something, viz., value that is as much content as consciousness, that is not indeed *both* of them at once but what each of them is and is not alternately. The felt content is imperfectly distinguished from feeling but not constituted by it in the sense that apart from it, it is nothing at all. We do not, indeed, know but cannot deny that the value of an object is really in it.

15. Reflective consciousness is definite consciousness of something. The content of feeling of which we are reflectively conscious is not a definite content. What is perfectly distinct from another or constituted by another in the sense of being nothing without it is definite in itself. What, however, is imperfectly distinct from another and unconstituted by it is not definite in itself. Now an indefinite can only be referred to in connexion with a definite content. What we are definitely conscious of in reflective feeling is the imperfect distinction itself of content and consciousness, this indefinite *as such* being, in fact, their unity. The indefinite content of feeling can only be referred to as a factor of this unity.

16. The content of knowing then is perfectly distinct from knowing and is unconstituted by it. The content of willing is imperfectly distinct from willing though distinct in itself and is constituted by it. Content and consciousness make a unity in the case of feeling but not in the case of knowing and willing. There are thus three modes of distinction of content and consciousness of which we are reflectively conscious. Each of these is an implicative or indefinite distinction in some sense and the indefiniteness will be found to consist in the fact that a relation that is intelligible as between content and content is

only half intelligible when taken to be the relation between content and consciousness.

17. To begin with knowing. If the content of knowing be perfectly distinct from knowing, how can the distinction be implicative or indefinite at all? It is implicative in the sense that the content of knowing is *necessarily* understood in reflection as what is perfectly distinct from knowing. The content *implies* such a reference to knowing and apparently means nothing without it. When one content is asserted to imply another, a relation is asserted of which, as we said, the implying content is not really a *relatum* but some other content which need not have the relation and which as thought with the relation is the implying content. This irrelative content may not be actually formulated but we conceive it to be formulable. It is difficult to conceive, however, what the known content apart from the knowledge-relation can possibly mean, since it is before the mind only as known.

18. The consciousness of a content as known is not, indeed, the consciousness of it as a fact necessarily related to knowing but it is not also the positive consciousness of it as only accidentally related to knowing. Reflection, in fact, on knowing tells us nothing about whether the content known is or is not necessarily known. The known content *means* indeed what is perfectly distinct from knowing but this verbal reference to knowing need not mean a *necessary factual* relation. The perfect distinction, too, does not mean that the content stands for something that would be even if it were not known by any one. Both the idealistic and the realistic positions here appear to be over-statements. In one sense, however, the realistic position may be said to have an advantage, for although reflection does not testify that what is known need not be known, it does not deny it while the idealistic view that the content is constituted by the knowing of it appears to be plainly opposed to reflective testimony.

19. It may be, however, that if and when the realistic conception of the known content as what need not be known is realised, the idealistic notion of its being constituted by knowing will be found to have a meaning. Criticism of knowledge may show that all that is actually taken to be known in the reflective stage is in some respect constituted by the particular act of knowing and, therefore, is in that respect not properly known though its known character cannot be denied altogether. Meantime we may reject the ordinary idealistic argument that to be aware of knowing an object is to be aware of recognising it, aware therefore of the object as necessarily known. There is actually no consciousness of recognising the object in the

literal sense of remembering the past knowing of it. All that is actually meant is that to be aware of knowing an object is to be aware of knowing *truth,* knowing something—in other words—to be eternal or timeless. The object may be temporal but that it is in time is not itself a temporal fact. To know is to have a timeless truth revealed but this does not mean that it is timelessly *known* and so known *again* in the present act of knowing. There is apparently no ground to assume either a previous knowing or of a timeless, impersonal or universal knowing along with the present knowing to justify the use of the word 'recognition'.

20. The realistic position that the known content may exist unknown is not denied but cannot also be asserted in the reflective consciousness. It may be said, however, that it cannot be denied or asserted because only the proposition is meaningless. Can reflection understand it as a possibility? The possibility, we reply, is understood in reference to what we take to be *self-evidently* known. Certain known contents appear at least to be self-evident, not simply evident. So long as the evident is not contrasted with the self-evident, we say about it 'it is' and not 'it is *to me*'. When it is contrasted however, we say 'it is *to me*' (though not 'to me only'), while of the self-evident we say simply 'it is'. To say 'it is *to me*' is to suggest that it may not be; and to say—in denial of this possibility—that 'it is' is to imply that it might not have been to the knower at all, that it is eternally true, that it is truth literally revealing itself. If anything then is known to be self-evident, it is known as what need not be known.

21. That the known content may exist—or more accurately—may be true without being known is then intelligible as a problem to reflection. It is, therefore, deniable, and it is not denied (though not asserted) because some content claimed to be self-evident appears to be implied in all knowledge. What is taken to be known is thus implicitly believed to be self-evident and only in this sense to be what need not be known. The realistic view of the independence of the known content, of its knownness being accidental, can only be admitted in the sense of the content being in some respect self-evident or self-revealing. The realist's definition of knowledge has to be accepted; but the question against him would be if what is claimed to be known is really known, is independent of the particular act of knowing or knowing generally. It is not the question if what is taken to be true is true. Value, for example, may be claimed to be known but it may be legitimately asked if it is known at all, if it is not merely believed in a non-cognitive way. So one may ask if what is taken by

Kant to be only empirically known as involving construction of experiences is, as the realist will claim, really known, known as independent of the constructivity of the knowing act. The Kantian view may or may not be accepted but the question is certainly legitimate if what is claimed to be known is known in the realist's sense of the term. The realist apparently would not admit the necessity of testing whether what is supposed in the first instance to be known is really known.

22. The known content should be what need not be known but where is the content that is known as such? The self-evident, we take it, is what is known to be independent of knowing in the sense of being eternally true without requiring to be known; but is anything admitted to be self-evident in the reflective consciousness? No known content is absolutely indubitable and in any case there is no agreement as to what content is indubitable. But some content or other appears self-evident in the sense of there being an explicit consciousness of doubt about it being unintelligible. The unintelligibility of doubt about a content should be distinguished from what is called the inconceivability of the opposite. Inconceivability of the opposite is understood only by trying to conceive it and to try to conceive it is to entertain a problem in thinking or meaning, if not of knowing. But there are cases where the problem of thinking the opposite of the content known is not entertained and one is conscious of its not arising at all. To be conscious of a content as self-evident is to be conscious not of its negation being unmeanable but of the problem of meaning the negation not even arising. We are conscious of the self-evident in this sense though the negation of what appears as such may later come to be conceived through a new self-evident cognition or revelation.

23. What we reflectively speak of as true or false is a judgment. The self-evident is that of which we cannot be conscious except as true. Is there then any self-evident judgment? To form a judgment is apparently always to be conscious of the *problem* of meaning its negation. This applies even to what is taken as a necessary judgment. Its negation is found to be inconceivable only after it has been tried to be conceived, and it is so found because it is but the elaboration of a systemic concept which, is really a *postulate* that is neither true nor false and may admit of rival postulates. It is a direction of imagination in which what tends to be imagined is eo ipso believed. The belief is here not properly cognitive but is what may be roughly called a feeling of cognition. It is the consciousness that something *must be* without the consciousness that it is: it is as though one

dimly felt what must be. The so-called necessary judgment is an analysis of the content of such felt cognition and is not properly knowledge.

24. What however is inferred, i.e., believed as what *must be* because something *is,* is believed also as what *is* and as such cannot be said to be merely felt as known. It is only the necessary that is not consciously inferred that should be so characterised. That a conclusion follows from a premise or premises is the only content that can be claimed in reflective consciousness as self-evidently ksown and not merely necessarily known i.e., felt to be known. Properly speaking, indeed, that a conclusion follows from a premise is not a judgment though expressed as such. The 'following' is not a relation of contents that is itself a content co-ordinate with them. Still as it is not an arbitrary subjective relating of contents, we cannot say it is not a *believed* relation though it is not content of consciousness.

25. A disguised form of this inferential 'following' we have in a judgment like 'A implies B' which may be paraphrased 'to know A is to know B'. What does the word 'is' here stand for? The two knowings stand for subjective acts but the connecting word 'is' does not mean another act co-ordinate with them. Nor does it mean a relation of the contents A and B that is a third content. It appears to be a relation not of the contents but of the cognitions in respect of their content, being itself however no subjective act of cognition. It cannot be said not to be known though it is not content of the knowing of which A and B are contents. Whether it is the content of the reflective consciousness is not known in the reflection itself and so *for the reflective consciousness* it means neither the consciousness nor the content of consciousness.

26. The self-evident is to reflection a relation that *is* without being the content of a knowing that is known. 'To know A is to know B' cannot be said to be no judgment and yet here we are not conscious of the problem of meaning its negation. It may well be that the assertion is a mistake but when it is made, it is made on the basis of an immediate unquestioning belief which is yet on the reflective level. The problem of meaning the negation of a perceived content does not arise during the perception because perception is not on the reflective level. But it, is only reflectively that we say 'to know A is to know B' and yet the knowledge here is immediate so that if later it turns out to be false, it is taken to be an illusion and not merely a thinking error. Since the knowledge is reflectively immediate, there is not only no conscious problem of meaning its

negation, there is the consciousness of such a problem not arising. It is only about what is known as the *content* of knowing that such a problem arises. So it is about judgment generally (which is on the reflective level) except what we take to be the primordial judgment viz., 'to know A is to know B'. It is primordial judgment because it is the basis of necessary judgments that are the bases of all other judgments. A necessary judgment is still known mediately through the baffled attempt to conceive the opposite. This also is based on a judgment like 'to know the inconceivability of the negation of a judgment is to know the judgment to be axiomatic'. A judgment of the form 'to know A is to know B' is self-evident judgment which is implied in all other judgments. That the terms of a judgment *have* a relation i.e., appear to be related to the relation only means that to know the terms is to know the relation—which is just a judgment of this form.

27. That the copula of this primordial self-evident judgment is not known as a content requires further explanation. The judgment is, indeed, knowledge and knowledge of the contents A and B as known, but so far as it is knowledge of the relation implied by the word 'is', it is not knowledge of it as a content that is known. In the case of a judgment like 'A is B', we understand the copula as a relation that is at least partially a content on a level with A and B. But in the judgment 'to know A is to know B' the 'is' is not on a level with the cognitions of A and B, far less with A and B. It is not known as known like the cognitions and their contents in the reflective consciousness. How then do we say that it is known? Because the sentence 'to know A is to know B' is significant and what it signifies cannot be disbelieved. The import of the sentence or of the word 'is' in it is, in fact, understood only when already spoken and not in the speaking of it. When even understood as already spoken, it is not retrospectively taken as the content of that speaking and *distinct from it*. It is understood, in fact, as *spoken* but not *as spoken of*. The word 'is' in the judgment is not understood as known *content*.

28. What is understood (without disbelief) only as already spoken and not in the speaking of it is understood as known but not as known content. By 'known content' is meant what is *knowable* as distinct from the knowing of it. It may not sometimes be so known in the knowing of it but it may be known later. The import of the word 'is' in the judgment 'to know A is to know B' is not so knowable at all and may accordingly be (loosely) called a known no content. It may be suggested that the import of the word 'is' here,

therefore, is the knowing act itself (or I) that is known by first appearing as content and then getting denied. It does not, however, appear at all as content to be negated : it is only symbolically spoken of later as content in the full consciousness that it is only verbally distinguished from the problematic knowing of it. Meantime the knowing of A and B that appears to reflection is definitely distinguished from it. What then the judgment 'to know A is to know B' signifies is known but does not appear as content to be accepted or rejected. It appears neither as known knowing nor as the content of such knowing.

29. This judgment is the only self-evident entity of which reflection is aware and the copula in it is not only not known as content but is explicitly known as what known content—including the apparent reflective content 'known knowing'—is not. The known position from which all content is distinguished—as represented by the copula here—is implied in all reflective knowledge, in all judgment like 'A is B' where the 'is' means this over and above a relation that is a content.

30. To sum up. In reflection on a content as known, the content implies knowing and is indefinitely distinct from it in the sense that it *means* this reference to knowing (though it means perfect distinction from knowing), that it does not mean independence of this reference and is not known as what is accidentally known. Reflection demands that it should be so known. The content is known to be only accidentally known i.e., to be only accidentally a content, when it is self-evident. The only self-evident of which we are reflectively aware is a judgment of the form 'to know A is to know B' or what the word 'is' in it stands for, this being meant in all judgments or knowledge on the reflective level. This then is the element in all that is reflectively known that is known as what need not be known, the element that is free from the implicational relation of the content to the knowing of it, the element that reflection demands to be isolated but cannot itself isolate. This is the absolute for knowing that demands to be freed from its immanence in the implicational distinction of content and knowing.

31. So far about knowing. We may now rapidly indicate how the implicative relation of content and consciousness is demanded to be resolved in the case of willing and feeling. What implication of content and consciousness does reflective willing present ? The willed content, as has been pointed out, is constituted by willing in the sense that apart from willing it is nothing at all. Yet the constituted content as definite in itself appears as a limitation to the constitutive willing :

willing appears to be necessarily the willing of what is foreign to itself. In the reflective stage the willed content is appreciated as real through the willing but yet as its limitation, not as its self-limitation. It is not apparent at this stage that the will limits itself to realise itself, freely commits itself to a being to annul it and become freer. Reflection demands that the limit that is necessarily constituted by willing should be realised as self-limitation in this sense. That is how the implication of content and consciousness is problematically understood to be resolvable in the sphere of willing.

32. To elaborate the problem. The relation of two contents willed at once may be taken to suggest the relation between willed content and willing. Two contents e.g., two acts are said to be willed at once when one of them is a means to the other. Two unrelated acts cannot be said to be willed at once and two acts that are jointly means to a third act cannot be *distinctly* willed in the willing of the third act. A conscious will-relation of two contents must be a relation of prior and posterior, the prior being that through which the other is possible. In the relation of means and end as *willed,* the end is the prior through the willing of which it is possible to will a content *as means*. Now this relation of means and end has to be understood as the relation of willed content to willing. A willed act has to be taken as a means to the willing of it though it is through the willing that the willed act is possible. It is difficult to understand, however, how the willing of an act is the end of the act willed, how in other words willing is realised by the putting forth of the act, how one can be said to act in a particular way in order to act freely.

33. That we objectively act to be subjectively free, that the good will and nothing but the good will is the value for which we will an act—the view, in fact, of Kant—may be called the idealistic view in this connexion. The realistic view here then would be that we act for an objective end and not for the subjective end of being free; and an extreme form of the view may be conceived that we objectively act in order that we may objectively act for evermore. In the case of knowing, we pointed out, the realistic view is prima facie more acceptable than the idealistic view. In the case of willing apparently, the idealistic view is acceptable in the first instance. The realistic view amounts to saying that there is no willed act that is good in itself and the view that we objectively act in order that we may objectively act is just its logical consequence and its reductio ad absurdum. The idealistic view is consonant with the nature of reflective willing—viz., that the prior is the end, but in the reflective stage it appears to

amount to the barren statement that it is good to will what it is good to will. The demand is to find a vital meaning for the statement, to understand how willing is a willing of itself.

34. Reflection indicates how it is to be understood. There is the difference between 'I will this act' and 'I will this act that I ought to will', when the former is not contrasted with the latter, the will-consciousness is expressible as an imperative 'let this act be done'. When, however, it is contrasted, it is expressed as mere information 'I am doing it' while the latter is properly expressed as an imperative 'let this be done' which implies 'I may not do it'. In contrast with it, the former appears as a statement of fact though by itself it appears as an imperative. The implication is that willing as represented by the former is itself a being that is to be superseded by willing as represented by the latter, that what is taken as free is implicitly not free, that therefore we will an act in order to get rid of the being of the act, get rid of the self-complacent will to continue in this being—what may be called the will to indolence. Reflection indicates the way but cannot understand willing or freedom at its limit.

35. In reflective feeling there is the definite consciousness of an indefinite distinction of the content felt and the feeling of it. The content felt is not definite in itself like the known or willed content and is understood in reference to this indefinite distinction definitely appearing to reflection *as though* it were a unity. We say 'as though', because the unity does not appear as a definite self-subsistent unity from which its constituents are distinguishable. The implication of content and consciousness would be resolved in the sphere of feeling, if a unity of this kind could be apprehended. In the feeling of two contents together, we can reflectively apprehend a self-subsistent unity. Reflection accordingly demands such a unity of felt content and feeling but cannot itself understand it.

36. To explain. In the apprehension of an object having spatial parts as beautiful, both the whole and the parts are felt but differently. The whole as a known content is distinct in itself and even if it be conceivably distinguished *from* the parts, the parts *as in the whole* cannot be distinguished from the whole and, therefore, can only be imperfectly distinguished from one another. The parts are, however, distinguished in the feeling way from the whole, being, in fact, felt as not felt in the way the whole is felt. The whole is felt to be beautiful but the parts are felt to be indifferent, felt to be 'only known', such feeling of their mere knownness being necessary for the appreciation of the beauty of the whole. To feel two contents at once then is to

feel their unity and to feel them otherwise than the unity. We try to understand the relation of the felt content and the feeling of it on this analogy. They appear imperfectly distinct and unity means to reflection an imperfect distinction of the constituents. But the unity does not appear to reflection self-subsistent in the sense of the constituents being distinguishable from it. Such a self-subsistent unity is, however, demanded.

37. As in the case of knowing and willing, so here one may imagine an alternation of realistic and idealistic or objectivistic and subjectivistic views. The unity of felt content and feeling may be understood as content that is indefinitely other than consciousness or as consciousness that is indefinitely other than the content. Value may be regarded as a kind of object though not as completely distinct from the consciousness of it as the known object or it may be taken to be an impersonalised feeling as somehow expressed in the object and thus objectified symbolically but not as a known character. Neither view appears to have any advantage over the other. Does reflection, however, indicate how consciously the alternation may be stopped and the unity come to be definite in itself ?

38. Taking value, the unity of felt content and feeling, realistically as objective, we are reflectively aware of the value as referred to the known object that is distinguishable from it. We feel the object as known to be not the value, to be neutral, felt otherwise than the value. This is *feeling* the distinction of the object from the value of it and it is thus that the value tends to appear distinct in itself by having the object distinguished from it. So also if we take the value as an impersonalised feeling rather than as an objective character, in understanding it as expressed in the object we may feel the knowing of the object as somehow *inside* the impersonal feeling, involved in it without being confused with it, much as the image in a mirror shows the mirror to be unaffected by it. Thus we may be said to be aware of the felt object as well as of the individual feeling as distinct from their unity.

39. So far the relation of felt content and feeling appears to be similar to the relation of two contents of the same feeling. In both there seems to be a unity from which its constituents are felt to be distinct. There is, however, discrepancy in an important respect. In appreciating a beautiful object where we feel the object as a whole as well as the parts, the parts that appear neutral are *together* felt to be distinct from the whole that appears beautiful. The beautiful object as beautiful thus appears in feeling as a whole isolated not only from

other objects but also from its own knowable parts and thus shines as a self-subsistent something in the air. We cannot understand such a thing about the unity of content and consciousness called value. The felt content and the feeling consciousness are only *alternately* distinguished from the value that is their unity. The demand is for them *together* to be feelingly distinguished from value so that it may shine in isolation as a self-subsistent unity. To put it more correctly, the demand is for the concept of a value that is independent of valuation, of its reference to a known object. Reflection understands the problem but does not see the solution.

40. In all these cases then, reflection tries to understand the relation of the content of a mode of consciousness to the consciousness on the analogy of the relation of the contents of the same consciousness and finds that the analogy can be definitely extended only halfway, although it can indicate the way in which the indefinite aspect that remains over could conceivably be defined. In the case of knowing, how the known content could be without being known is not reflectively understood although the consciousness of the self-evident as distinct from the evident is consciousness of such a *possibility*. In the case of willing, it is reflectively indefinite how willing is the end of the act willed but the consciousness of the *ought* is consciousness of the possibility of getting rid of the being of the act willed. In the case of feeling, value should be understood but cannot be reflectively understood as the definite self-subsistent unity of felt content and feeling, but there is the consciousness of its possibility in the reflective appreciation of a beautiful object as what 'never was on sea or earth', isolated from its knowable relations not only to other objects but also to its own parts.

41. In all these cases, again, it will be noticed that what demands to be understood cannot actually be understood because such understanding would involve a species of negation that to reflection is unmeaning. In the case of knowing a known content has to be understood as what need not be content of any knowing. In the case of willing, the reality of willing has to be understood as the negation of being, of the being even of the content that is willed. In the case of feeling, the being of value has to be understood by the known as such being distinguished from it. To reflection, for the known content to be without being known is for it to be intrinsically unrelated to knowing in the way of distinction or identity. To be conscious of A and B, not to be able to deny either and yet to say they are utterly unrelated is apparently to state a contradiction. So to understand the willed

act to be distinct from willing and yet to be nothing apart from it, or—to put it differently—for the act not to *be* and yet to be real as willing is to conceive the negation of an emergent distinct or the emergent distinction of a negation. To take the felt value also as a being from which known being is distinct is to be definitely conscious of an indefinite, to entertain without disbelief an *appearance* or an indifference of being and non-being. All the three—unrelatedness, negation of the emergent or the emergence of negation, and the indifference of being and non-being—imply unmeaning modes of negation to reflection ; and yet the specifiable indefiniteness in the content of reflection demands to be defined precisely through such modes of negation. To admit the absolute in any form is to admit a negation that is unintelligible to the logic of the understanding.

42. The absolute may be generally defined from the standpoint of reflection as what is free from the implicational dualism of content and consciousness. There are three ways in which this freedom can be understood. The content may be freed from its reference to consciousness i.e., from its contenthood. Or consciousness may be freed from its reference to content, in which case it ceases to be conscious of anything beyond itself. Or the implicational relation itself may be freed from its terms as a definite self-subsistent unity. The known that is free from its contenthood is known as the content that need not be content, is the self-evident *is,* just what we call *truth*—the absolute for knowing. Consciousness that is free from its content (in the sense that it solely constitutes its content, makes the content a content, creates its distinction from itself) is *freedom* of the will—the absolute for willing. The implicational relation of content and consciousness that is freed from their distinction as a unity is *value* in itself—the absolute for feeling.

43. Truth, freedom and value then are absolutes for knowing, willing and feeling. It is impossible to avoid this triple formulation of the absolute though the notion that there are three absolutes would be just as illegitimate as the notion of there being only one absolute. The absolute is not a *known content,* about which alone the question 'one or many' has meaning. Truth is self-evident and is as such known but is no content; of value as the self-subsistent unity of content and consciousness, we cannot say either that it is not known or that it is like truth self-evident and, therefore, is no content; and there is no question even of knowing freedom, the belief in freedom being, as Kant pointed out, no intuition but willing itself. It is meaningless therefore to cognitively assert that there are three absolutes or one

absolute. The absolute has, however, to be formulated in this triple way. Each is absolute but what are here understood as *three* are only their verbal symbols, they themselves being understood together but not *as together*.

44. For freedom, an alternative name would be reality. The real is understood either as will or what is given to will. Will means free will or freedom which though not theoretically known is not disbelieved, the belief in willing being willing itself. The expression of willing is always an imperative 'let this be done', which means no known being and, if anything, means 'let this known situation here be negated, *used* as means, melted into the future'. Willing in this sense is the negation of being and is yet real, its reality consisting in the supersession of being. This comes out more explicitly in the consciousness of the imperative as the moral *ought*. *Ought* is real as the explicit rejection of the *is* or the actual that is known, explicit annulment of the known being of the presupposed 'natural willing'. Known being may be real but reality is understood in its purity as the conative rejection of known being; or more accurately, since everything has to be understood here in conative terms, as the freedom to withdraw or abstain from 'natural willing'. Natural willing, called 'natural' in reference to the *ought,* is in itself an imperative : the person who wills says to himself 'let this be done' and not 'I am doing it'. So any willing and specially the willing to abstain from willing is unknowable freedom or reality. What is given to the will is also said to be real because either it is consumed by the will as a means to itself as end or if it cannot be so consumed, it has to be taken as an opposed will. Freedom or reality may accordingly be taken as synonymous.

45. Freedom or reality then is not known or, in other words, it is meaningless to call it truth. The true is the self-evident, that of which we are conscious as known but not as known content. Freedom or willing is not known at all or if we are aware of knowing it, we are aware of its knownness as illusory. We are only aware in one grade of willing that a presupposed willing of another grade—natural willing, as we have called it—had an illusory being or appeared to be known. What is known, however, may be either the self-evident in its purity or some relation of *given* contents—meaning contents given *to the will*—with the form of self-evidence. Every judgment, as has been pointed out, involves a self-evident judgment of the form 'to know A is to know B'. The self-evident in its purity is eternal truth and not reality : but a relation of given contents is not only said to be true but cannot also be said to be not real.

46. The real then is not true but the true may be real. So speaking of truth and value, we may say that truth is not value but value is not untrue. Just as the predicates true and false do not apply at all to freedom or reality, so the predicates valuable or worthless do not apply to truth. Truth is not felt or if it is felt, it is felt as unfelt i.e., as no value. But the predicate false applies to value in so far as the falsity of a felt value is denied though its truth cannot therefore be asserted. A value like beauty is evident but not self-evident; it appears as a content to an appreciative consciousness and appears without being disbelieved as an illusion but not as what need not have reference to the consciousness. The self-evident is the true and the evident is true if it implies self-evidence and till the self-evidence becomes explicit, it cannot be said to be false.

47. Again in respect of reality and value it may be said that while the predicates real and unreal do not apply to value, reality or freedom cannot be said not to be a value. Value is a felt being and is neither given to willing nor is itself willed into existence though it may appear as the fulfilment of willing. It is in this respect similar to truth which may shine out in fulfilment of willing in the form of attention but is not brought into existence through its causality. Reality or freedom may, however, be felt and an act that is claimed to be willed is at least not morally indifferent if it is felt to have been genuinely willed. An act, in fact, that is felt to be morally indifferent is eo ipso felt to have been not free, not willing at all, the sole proof of freedom being in the retrospective moral valuation. To say that an act is free is to take it as not valueless though it may be going too far to assert that freedom is a value. Value is a felt *being* while freedom or willing is felt as the real *negation* of a known being and can at best be the felt being of a negation (of known being).

48. Thus it appears to be meaningless to speak of truth as a value, of value as real or of reality as true while we can significantly speak of value as not false, of reality as not valueless and of truth as not unreal, although we cannot positively assert value to be truth, reality to be value and truth to be reality. Each of them is absolute and they cannot be spoken of as one or many. In one direction their identity and difference are alike meaningless and in another direction their identity is intelligible though not assertable. Truth is unrelated to value, value to reality and reality to truth while value may be truth, reality value and truth reality. The absolute may be regarded in this sense as an *alternation* of truth, value and reality.

KNOWLEDGE AND TRUTH

ANALYSIS

(1-2) The doctrine of truth and error stands on a different level of self-consciousness from that occupied by Logic or Epistemology. The level is indicated by the contrast between falsity which is the content of rejection and negation which is the content of disbelief. Disbelief is a kind of knowledge and negation is said to be *known* in the sense that truth may be asserted of it. But rejection is not knowledge and falsity cannot be said to be known, though it is something of which we have some kind of awareness. The consciously unknown or the unknowable, the false, the abstractly possible, the impossible or the unnameable and what is only willed or felt—these are only 'half-thoughts' and not accomplished meanings. These should be the subject-matter of a new philosophical discipline and not of Logic or Epistemology which is concerned with complete thoughts or accomplished meanings. The doctrine of truth and error would really belong to this new discipline. (3) Epistemology as the study of the knowing function is based on a kind of introspection which is neither logical mediation nor mere internal perception. It is a self-evident transition in self-consciousness, and is exemplified by Kant's transcendental method. (4) Since the time of Kant there have been rival epistemologies each with its assurance of finality. It is only a doctrine of truth and error that can possibly adjudicate between them. This doctrine must, therefore, be based on a still deeper assurance of finality. And the possible falsehood of a theory based on epistemological introspection suggests that the concept of falsity belongs neither to Logic nor to Epistemology as they are commonly understood. (5-7) Kant gives a hint of a transcendental Psychology behind the general theory of knowledge. The systematic doctrine of truth and error would be the same as or a part of transcendental Psychology and it must itself be a body of knowledge.

(8) Knowledge and truth have to be defined in terms of each other. Knowledge is what alone is true and truth is what alone is known. It is only metaphorically that we speak of the truth of a feeling or willing. (9) An object may be known without being known explicitly to be true. But knowing is never known except as implied in the assertion of the truth about its content. This, however, may be disputed and a perception may be held to be known in memory without any question arising as to the truth of the memory.

(10) There are reasons, however, to hold that the past perception is not known by any method by which an object is known. (11) There is occasion to know a past cognition only if its content is challenged or confirmed. (12) Neither is there any perception of knowing at the time of knowing. In perception, a content is never distinguished from it, so that it is not possible to know whether they are synchronous or not. The question, therefore, about the temporal relation of cognition and its perception does not arise at all.

(13) Cognition is not thus known by psychological introspection conceived either as perception or as memory. It is known by epistemological introspection such as is involved in the explicit awareness of truth. (14-15) Though there is this kind of introspective knowledge of knowing, there is no such knowledge of feeling or willing. There may, however, be a belief in the latter along with and implied in the knowledge of knowing. (16-18) Three consequences follow from the above : (a) there is no such thing as false knowledge; (b) there is no knowledge of objects as merely distinct but not otherwise related to one another : that is to say, the known content must be explicitly coherent and not merely co-existent with other known contents; (c) interpretations of knowing in terms of non-cognitive modes are unacceptable.

(19-22) The view that truth is predicated of the subsistent 'proposition' and that it is a relation between knowledge and its object cannot be accepted. The so-called 'proposition' or the merely meant is an illegitimate abstraction and no predicate may be asserted of it. It is, again, a misleading use of the term 'relation' to speak of the knowledge of an object as in relation or as the relation to the object. The reference of knowing to its object is no relation at all. For, there cannot be any relation without mutual distinction. And in the present case, though knowing is known as distinct from its object, the object is not known as distinct from knowing. The so-called distinction of the object from knowing is only unrelatedness. (23) Though this one-sided distinction is not, properly speaking, a relation, yet it has to be necessarily symbolised as a relation. (24) To knowledge, the object is only evident and not related to it though symbolised as such. To willing and feeling, however, this symbolism is real and unrelatedness is a believed quasi-relation.

(25) It has been said before that knowing is known only when confirmed by other cognitions and as so confirmed. But this entails the paradox that the confirming relation constitutes knowing and yet falls beyond it. (26) Confirmation is not a character either of the

cognition or of its object. It is not felt as a character of the complete cognition that is confirmed. The object, again, is unrelated to the object of the confirming cognition. (27) The confirmation of which we are aware in the awareness of a cognition implies a conscious distinction of it from the confirming cognition but not the distinction of the latter from the former. Though it is not a known relation, it has to be symbolised as a relation. And what is symbolised is a metapsychical or spiritual process. (28) There is symbolising in another direction. Confirmation in the epistemic sphere is a spiritual overtone of cognition as a psychic fact. It is itself a metaphor for a mode of cognitive realisation.

KNOWLEDGE AND TRUTH

I. Place of the Doctrine of Truth and Error

1. The present-day doctrine of truth and error may be regarded as a part of Logic or Epistemology but it is to be recognised as standing on a level of self-consciousness different from that on which these subjects, as ordinarily conceived, appear to stand. The level is indicated by the contrast between the concept of falsity and the concept of negation. There arc two grades of negation from both of which falsity has to be distinguished. When we disbelieve a content, we may only exclude it from a particular context while believing it to exist in another context. Such exclusion may be regarded as negation of the first grade. In the second grade, there is exclusion from a context without inclusion in another, disbelief without a positive complementary belief. It is what is sometimes called pure negation, the content negated being only known to be non-existent. Negation in both the grades is said to be known in the sense that truth may be asserted of it. Disbelief here amounts to a kind of knowledge which, however, is not the case when we reject a content as false. (The false is not simply the non-existent but the non-existent *as appearing existent,* to reject which is not logically to deny). We cannot say that we know the falsity, for then falsity would be regarded as a truth. We should only say that we are aware of the falsity : we only disbelieve the content without knowing its non-existence. The non-existence of the possible, as in the second grade of negation, is a tautology but the non-existence of the false is meaningless.

2. Objective Logic recognises only the first grade of negation. It takes note of existents only, disbelieving them only in the sense of believing them as outside or distinct from the context in question and knows nothing of pure non-existence, far less of falsity. Pure non-existence is admissible as a known content only in epistemology and in such logic as is undistinguished from it. The believed and the disbelieved are taken here as two classes of known content and what is common to them is the *possible* which is a *quasi*-objective or 'subsistent' content from the epistemic stand-point. But epistemology confines or should confine itself to the known, the possible being known in the disbelief in its existence as a complete meaning. It should have nothing to do with what is only a problem in meaning

as distinct from an accomplished meaning, with the consciously unknown or the unknowable, and with the false. We have no knowledge of the absence of knownness ; we speak of it and are aware of it variously in respect of the abstractly possible, of the impossible or the unnameable, or of what is only willed or felt but such awareness is not knowledge. Half-thoughts like these should find place in a new philosophical subject though they are as a matter of fact admitted in epistemology or logic. The doctrine of truth and error would really belong to this subject.

3. Epistemology is founded on a species of introspection different from what is called psychological introspection. The latter, if it knows knowing at all, knows it as indistinguishable in quality from mere believing. A qualitative distinction between knowing and believing is, however, known, being just what is called the logical character which is apprehended by a new quality of introspection. It is a confusion to speak of the function of knowing or the logical character being known by a logical procedure again. Kantian criticism is sometimes distinguished as logical from the criticism of Locke which is taken to be psychological. But the particular logical method by which Kant obtained his transcendental constants has never been identified or named in logic. There is, indeed, a quasi-logical transition from the logical forms to the apriori functions but it is not transition from one objective content to another as one would expect in logic. The transcendental method is a self-evident transition, a process in self-consciousness and not in consciousness and, as such, should be taken as a kind of introspection which is neither logical mediation nor mere internal perception. To be necessarily implied or presupposed by the logical content is no logical relation at all nor is it a name for the mere psychological mode of knowing the content.

4. Epistemological introspection knows only this presupposition, the functional character that distinguishes the known content from the merely believed content. It claims a special quality of certitude, deeper than that claimed by mere objective or logical cognition, cognition through what Kant would call the uncritical employment of reason. Kant, in fact, hoped that critical reflection, as he understood it, would establish a final science of knowledge above the reach of philosophical controversy. The hope has not been realised and rival epistemologies have been put forward since his time, each claiming the same degree of certainty as that set up by him. The conflict of these assured theories of knowledge has brought to the fore

the importance of a doctrine of truth and error competent to adjudicate between them and, therefore, based on a still deeper assurance of finality. The possible falsity of a theory based on epistemological introspection suggests the unique character of the general concept of falsity which, as we have indicated, belongs neither to logic nor to epistemology, as these subjects are ordinarily conceived.

5. The assurance of critical reflection does not in itself constitute the subjective criterion for distinguishing truth from error and cannot be the level of self-consciousness from which one can sit in judgment on an epistemology. A criticism of epistemology is demanded to-day, of the very subject that emerged as the criticism of the logical or dogmatic procedure of reason. The doctrine of truth and error, if it could be systematised according to a principle, would furnish such a criticism of criticism. The two degrees of criticism are not distinguished and there is so far no principle on which we may decide between rival epistemologies. In the Kantian critiques, there is the hint of a transcendental Psychology behind the general theory of knowledge, with an occasional recognition of the necessity of distinguishing between them. Kant speaks, for example, of error being due to the 'subjective use' of reason as distinct from its intrinsically logical function and of certain principles being real to reason as employed in an extra-theoretic 'interest'. His theory of knowledge is properly concerned with the general logical function which is common to true knowing and error. His references to reason as a subjective faculty capable of perverse or extralogical use are accordingly to be looked upon as mere obiter dicta within his epistemology and as really belonging to transcendental Psychology which was always assumed but never sufficiently distinguished by him.

6. The systematic doctrine of truth and error would be the same as or a part of this transcendental Psychology. To empirical psychology, the logical function going astray and yielding a false *content* conveys no meaning at all. Logic can recognise error only as a blind fact and epistemology should regard it as a miracle : the question of explaining its possibility does not arise at all in these subjects. Yet a theory of truth and error is ordinarily claimed to be established by a conscious or self-conscious logical method and there is no recognition so far of any mystery of cognitive level about it. One tendency, however, is noticeable in theories thus established—viz., to slur over the absolute distinction that is recognised in commonsense between truth and error. The suggestion is put forward in different forms that error

is a partial truth, truth within a limited context; and it is sometimes proposed in a manner to drop the conception of truth itself, a content being taken to be true only in the sense that it is known or 'asserted'. Such flagrant opposition to commonsense requires to be justified by something more than the consideration that it is conceivable and logically irrefutable. It is necessary to show on the one hand that a doctrine of this kind is itself knowledge and not a mere hypothesis and on the other that a theory admitting the absolute distinction of truth and error cannot be maintained.

7. Here we have the hint of a principle or criterion for deciding between rival theories of knowledge. *An epistemology must itself be a body of knowledge;* there is no room for a hypothesis or a mere conceivability in this region where finality is claimed for every assertion. With regard, for example, to a voluntarist theory of knowledge, the preliminary question must be asked in what sense, if at all, willing is *known,* if psychological introspection yields *knowledge* of it, and whether some spiritual consciousness of the practical kind amounts to the knowledge of the impossibility of pure knowing. There is the connected negative demand that *theoretic* reasons have to be adduced for the rejection of a theory that keeps within the commonsense distinction of truth and error. Such a theory, in fact, has a prior claim to consideration, even if these theories can interpret knowing all the way without stumbling. The interpretation of the cognitive by the non-cognitive—by willing or feeling or any superior spiritual process—is prima facie suspect and can be accepted only if a purely cognitive interpretation is shown to be impossible.

II. Mutual Implication of Knowledge and Truth

8. Two propositions may be stated about knowledge—that knowing is known only as implied in the explicit awareness of truth and that truth is asserted only of a content that is known. Knowledge and truth have to be defined in terms of each other, the former as what alone is true and the latter as what alone is known. It is only metaphorically that we speak of the truth of a feeling or willing; and values in the non-cognitive sphere are what we only believe but do not know We may examine in this connexion two positions that appear to be fundamentally opposed to our view, viz., that knowing is known by psychological introspection and that truth is a relation, not to a known, but to a suggested possible content, an idea or mere meaning.

(i) KNOWING IS NOT KNOWN BY PSYCHOLOGICAL INTROSPECTION

9. We may know an object without knowing it explicitly to be true but do we ever know the psychic fact of knowing except as implied in the assertion of truth about its content ? It may be contended that knowing is known by memory or internal perception, like any other psychic fact. The past perception of an object, for example, may be taken to be remembered in the remembering of the object without any conscious reference to the truth of it. When we remember an objective event, we do not at once reproduce every detail of it and need not know that it was perceived. But just as omitted objective details are gradually reinstated, so also, it may be said, does the subjective fact of perception come to be known in the course of the mere fulfilment of the memory without any question arising as to the truth of the memory. Is such a contention tenable ?

10. There is in the first place the obvious difficulty that the past perception was not perceived in the past and so cannot be said to be now remembered, unless we admit either that all perception is implicitly perception of perception or that we can remember without having perceived. Nor can the past perception be said to be now internally or introspectionally perceived, for the object of perception is ordinarily understood to be synchronous with the perception. There cannot be also any question of inferring the past perception from the remembered object of it, for that presupposes, what we never had previously, knowledge of other objects and their cognition as together. To know the cognition of object is not to know the cognition and the object to be together.

11. The past perception is, indeed, known but it is not known by memory, perception or inference,—by any method, in fact, by which an object is known. There is occasion to know the past psychic fact if the object or content of it is challenged or confirmed. If any grounds now present themselves for doubting the reality of the past objective event, the doubt is laid by the assurance that we actually perceived it. Or, again, if any facts or inferences now yield an explicit confirmation of the reality of the event, the sense of confirmation implies the awareness of the past perception of the event. We cannot imagine any other occasion for such awareness. Not that we can say why the awareness of the past cognition emerges. We know only that this awareness is at the same time awareness of the confirmation or the rejected doubt that is involved in the explicit assertion of the objective content as true. Properly speaking, the knowledge of cognition does not emerge

in time as the cognition itself emerges and so does not demand explanation. We start with this knowledge which is the same as the knowledge of the truth of the objective content. The time-position of the content determines, not the time position but only a differential quality of its cognition,—a quality, however, which does not appear to affect the knowledge of the cognition at all.

12. There is apparently then no memory of a cognition in the mere interest in fact, as distinct from interest in the truth of the fact. Is there an introspective perception of knowing at the time of the knowing? The question is really illegitimate; for, as just shown, there is no possibility of knowing the synchronousness of a content and the perception of it. A content and its perception are never known independently to be taken as together or successive : the content is never distinguished from its perception, though the perception distinguishes, manifests or reveals the content. If this holds good when the content is objective, it holds good with greater reason when the content is cognition itself. The cognition as we have said has no time-position but only a quality due to the position of its objective content; and the knowledge of the cognition has not even this quality, so that there is no question at all of the cognition and the knowledge of it being temporarily related. We conclude then that neither a past nor a present cognition can be said to be known as such for the purposes of psychology.

13. Cognition is, indeed, known but not by the so-called psychological introspection, conceived either as perception or memory. It is known by what we have called epistemological introspection such as is involved in the explicit awareness of truth. All that psychology claims to know about cognition, it gets either through this unconfessed epistemological reflection or through a blend of imagination and verbal interpretation which yields only the appearance of knowledge. This blend is what passes by the name of psychological introspection which can never know a psychic process as a fact as distinct from fancy or mere meaning. Belief in psychic reality emerges only as the implication of belief in a spiritual value like truth or beauty or obligatoriness.

14. The object of cognition is distinguished by the cognition though it is not known as distinct from it. In the awareness of the cognition, the cognition is distinguished from its object which then as not appearing distinct from it becomes indefinite. In the awareness of a feeling or willing, however, the psychic fact is not distinguished from the object, the object being only distinguished from it. The psychic fact and its object are in neither case presented as mutually dis-

tinct : the cognitive fact is only distinguished and the non-cognitive fact is only distinguished from. This is apparent from the nature of the value in apprehension of which the awareness of the psychic fact is implied. Truth does not appear as a *character* of the object while beauty or sacredness appears as such. Hence in the awareness of truth, the object is indefinite and its cognition definite while the consciousness of beauty etc., implies the reverse—viz., the object as definite and the corresponding psychic fact as indefinite. The awareness of the fact of cognition accordingly itself amounts to a cognition, while that of the non-cognitive psychic fact is nothing more than a belief. There is no introspective belief in the reality of the mental except as the implication of belief in value, and there is introspective knowledge, as distinct from belief, of knowing only, not of feeling or willing.

15. There may, however, be a belief in willing or feeling along with and implied in the knowledge of knowing. In the knowledge of knowing, the object of the knowing is cognitively indefinite but that does not prevent it from being definitely real to a non-cognitive interest. Such indefiniteness of the object does not prejudice the completeness of the cognition of it, though the feeling or willing that it implies points to a new conception about cognition—viz., the necessity of subjectively realising it. The non-cognitive value of the object known—e.g., its beauty or scaredness—demands to be realised as the truth-value (if that can be called value at all) of the cognition, though the truth which has already presented itself does not suffer because it is not yet realised. Again, just as there is the demand to realise other values as truth, so there may be demand in the non-cognitive interest to realise truth as other value, realise it, as we say, in life. Thus something can be done through feeling or willing to secure the subjective maturation of knowing, as these too may be matured by a discipline of knowing.

16. We have so far tried to establish that psychological introspection is not knowledge of psychic fact, that psychic facthood emerges only as the implication of belief in value, and that knowing alone among psychic facts, as implied in the belief in truth, can be said to be known. Certain consequences follow. There is, in the first place, no such thing as false knowledge. If knowing could be known as an indifferent psychic fact, both truth and falsity would be predicable of it. But if knowing is known only as the implicate of the awareness of truth, to know an object is to know it as in some sense implicitly true. Truth cannot be taken simply as additional confirmation of what already is known indifferently, though the explicit knowledge of truth itself testifies to a prior knowing of the object without this conscious asser-

tion of truth. Not that the truth of this mere object-knowledge can be said to be now *recognised*: the loose use of the term 'recognition' is responsible for a good deal of epistemological superstition. Knowledge is implicit knowledge of truth only in the sense that the explicit knowledge of truth is the knowledge of a knowing that was not known. It does not mean that truth as a character or content of the knowing was somehow hidden in it. We can only say that the knowing, when it was not known, could not be false, as then it would be no knowing at all. An object to be known need not be known explicitly to be true; but if it now appears to be not true, it is never said to have been known but taken at best to have been believed.

17. Another consequence of the view that knowing is only know in the knowledge of truth is that there is no knowledge of objects as merely distinct but not otherwise related to one another. To be known, an object must not only be distinct but consciously confirmed by the contents of other cognitions. The known content must be explicitly coherent and not merely co-existent with other known contents. The coherence emerges not only within the content of a particular cognition but also between it and the contents of cognitions that fall beyond it. The content as a whole of a given cognition, without losing completeness or self-sufficiency, is felt to be confirmed by the contents of other cognitions that retain their distinction from it and do not get fused. The coherent plurality within the content may be taken as representing a fusion of cognitions, although the coherence does not appear as conscious confirmation but not, therefore, also as a mere relation of co-existent elements in a whole.

18. A third consequence of our view about the knowing of knowing is that interpretations of knowing in terms of feeling or willing are excluded as not themselves amounting to knowledge. If the awareness of willing, for example, is not knowledge but at best a belief, a voluntarist interpretation of knowledge has to be regarded, not as a scientific or factual theory, but as a prescription to imagine or believe the fact of knowing in a particular way for some practical end or purpose. It is a contradiction, in fact, to claim a voluntarist epistemology to be true, though it may be practically useful or even obligatory as an imperative to the imagination. If cognition is only a means to activity, the knowledge that it is so cannot again be a means to further activity without leading to an infinite regress. The awareness that a belief works and is, therefore, cognition does not itself appear again as an *efficient* belief.

(ii) TRUTH IS NOT RELATION TO A MERE MEANING

19. We have examined the proposition that knowing is only known as the implication of the awareness of truth. There is next the converse proposition that truth is asserted only of knowing. The affirmation of truth in respect of a feeling or willing is, as we have said, only a rhetorical expression of its non-cognitive value. Within knowing, however, truth is sometimes taken to be asserted, not of the known content, but of the merely suggested content, of what has been proposed to be called 'proposition' as distinct from judgment. We have said that the awareness of the truth of a content is knowledge of the content as *known,* not merely suggested. The content is known as known for the first time in such awareness; and to say that it is true is to say that it is known as known. In the view just suggested, however, the assertion of the truth of a content means only the assertion that it is known, not that it is known to be or to have been known. The subject of the assertion 'it is known' is taken to stand only for a meant or 'subsistent' content as distinct from a known or existent content. The predicate *known*—or what is its equivalent, *true*—is understood to be external to it, to be however, not *in relation* to it, but the relation itself, being thus at once term and relation, constituting what is described as a 'flavour' of the content.

20. Our objection to such a view is two-fold. On the one hand the merely meant or subsistent content—the *possible,* as it may be called—is an illegitimate abstraction of which no predicate may be asserted, and on the other, the knowledge or assertion of a content cannot be understood as a relation, far less as *in* relation to it. The first objection comes out definitely if we consider an existential judgment of the negative from 'A is not'. As we have already indicated, the disbelief in A here may be knowledge but need not imply belief in A as having being in some context. Properly speaking, therefore, such knowledge cannot be called a judgment at all. A is here known as the possible only through the apparent predicate *non-existence,* it being a mere tautology to say that the possible is not actual. The possible has no positive being except as implied by verbal fixation. 'A is not existent' is only an illegitimate extension of the form of a negative judgment like 'A is not B' which implies the existence of A. It should accordingly be recognised as a mere trickery of language: there is no belief in A here, the disbelief being the whole of the knowledge.

21. Our second objection is that it is a misleading use of the word 'relation' to speak of the knowledge or assertion of an object

as in relation or as the relation to the object. The realist, we hold, is right when he takes knowledge as external to or distinct from the object: knownness cannot be understood as an attribute or character of the object. When we are aware of the knowledge of an object, we distinguish the knowledge from the object though the distinguishing does not amount to the knowledge of a factual distinction. It appears to be wholly wrong, however, to speak of the object as distinct from the knowing of it. We are not aware of the distinction from knowing as an objective fact. Nor is the knowing of the object the *distinguishing* of the object *from itself*. The object known is simply distinguished: it is not related at all to its knowing in the way of identity or distinction. If the act of knowing or distinguishing be knowledge of the distinction of the object from itself, that *itself* would be a term known as distinct from itself and so on indefinitely. We have, therefore, to recognise that the reference of knowing to its object is no distinction or relation at all, that though we are aware of the knowing of the object as distinct from the object, the so-called distinction of the object from knowing is only unrelatedness of which we are aware but not cognitively.

22. To explain the concept of unrelatedness. When two contents are known together, they need not be known *as* together. They may not only be known as unrelated in space, time or nature: they may not even be known as barely distinct from one another. To know *two* contents, it is only necessary to know that one is distinct from the other but not that the other is distinct from it. When two contents A and B are thus known, A being distinct from B, B is known, not as distinct from nor therefore identical with A, but as unrelated to A. In fact, even when we know them as mutually distinct, the two distinctions are not known as making up one distinction. They alternate and the alternation appears, not as distinction between A and B, but as their unity or whole in space, time or nature. They are then not only known together but also *as* together, though the distinction of A from B and that of B from A do not cease to be themselves distinct. Hence it follows that to know one content as distinct from another is *in no case* to know the other as distinct from it but only to know it as *unrelated*, though the two distinctions may sometimes be known together. It is thus intelligible how while knowing is known as distinct from its object, the object is known, not as distinct from, but as unrelated to the knowing.

23. When, therefore, in the view under discussion it is held that knowledge *is* the relation to the object, what is really meant is that

knowledge is distinct from its object but not reversely. Our contention is that such onesided distinction is not relation at all. There is no relation without *mutual* distinction which implies some form of objective togetherness. Knowing and its object are not objectively together and, therefore, even the known distinction of knowing from its object, which we admit, is not relation. Yet such onesided distinction has to be necessarily symbolised as a relation. We have to speak of two things—knowing and object, though we know they are not objectively two, not known as two. The awareness of the distinction as onesided is the awareness of the evidentness, manifestation or prakāśa of the object, which is no relation but is only symbolised by it. The evidentness of the known content is a category utterly distinct from relation, to recognise which is to appreciate the differential character of knowing.

24. We have said that the object is known, not as distinct from or identical with its knowing, but as unrelated to it. Properly, however, we should say that it is known simply as evident and that it is *not* known as related to knowing. There is no knowledge of the circumstance of unrelatedness but only an extra-cognitive awareness of it. As already pointed out, it is only in the awareness of willing or feeling, as distinct from that of knowing, that the object referred to is distinguished from the psychic fact. This distinguishing is not the knowledge of distinction or relation but only a direction or phase of willing or feeling. The object is not known as related to knowing but is willed as an end to be realised or felt as a value that is being realised. There is, therefore, no conflict between the deliverances of cognitive and non-cognitive consciousness; what we are *not* aware of cognitively we are aware of *non*-cognitively. The distinction between these deliverances is sometimes overlooked; and we have realistic and idealistic theories of knowledge asserting the object to be distinct from or identical with the knowing of it. The former take the willed distinction and the latter the felt identity-in-difference as though it were the known distinction of the object from or the known identity of the object with the knowing of it. To knowledge, the object is only evident and not related to it though symbolised as such. To willing or feeling this symbolism is real and unrelatedness is a believed quasi-relation which is by confusion taken to be a known relation.

III. Nature of Logical Confirmation

25. Truth, we have said, is asserted of the known content. The assertion amounts to saying that the content is known as known.

Knownness or truth is external to it in the sense that knowing is distinguished from its object. Knownness is no character of the object, being but the fact of knowing, the knowing that reveals the object as evident, as distinct but not distinct from itself. This knowing is also known, known only when confirmed by other cognitions and as so confirmed. The confirmation is not known as a relation within the content of the knowing, for then there would be no break between the content of one knowing and that of another. We have as a matter of fact many cognitions and a cognition does not, consciously at any rate, refer to the entire universe. The elimination of the distinction between cognitions or—what is the same thing—the conscious presentation of truth as single may be a spiritual ideal but we have no right to assume it in the characterisation of an actual cognition. Since a cognition, however, is not known except when confirmed, there emerges the paradox of the confirming relation constituting it and yet falling beyond it. A cognition, as we have seen, must be complete but it is never known except as confirmed by other cognitions.

26. Not that confirmation is known as a character of the cognition, or of its object. The object is unrelated to the object of the confirming cognition and the so-called systemic relation is only an imaginary objectification of the subjective circumstance of confirmation. Nor is the subjective circumstance felt as a character of the complete cognition that is confirmed. There are cases, indeed, where the confirming cognitions get telescoped into the confirmed cognition; but there the latter gives place to a new cognition of which the content is a synthesis of the contents of previous cognitions and presents the confirming relation as some immediate relation of coherence like that between the substantive and the adjective. The cognition, however, that is said to be confirmed by others without prejudice to its completeness does not get modified in the confirmation; it only gets to be known through it. There may be a strengthening of belief but that is only a psychological circumstance. Logically then, confirmation is not a known character either of the cognition or of the object of it.

27. The confirmation of which we are aware in the awareness of a cognition implies a conscious distinction of it from the confirming cognitions but not the distinction of the latter from the former. It is accordingly no known relation of the cognitions, though as the one-sided distinction is there, it has to be symbolised as a relation. What is symbolised here is a metapsychic or spiritual process which though not itself a cognition is not indifferent to cognition. The given cognition is known only in the assertion of truth in respect of it, truth that

is manifested in conscious confirmation symbolised as a relation. It is this pseudo-relation that has been elaborated into the objective symbolism of a system of relations, the system that is said to constitute the known object and which may be regarded as a shadow of truth, an imaginary projection of the knowing of knowing or self-consciousness. It is important to recognise that system is but a symbolism.

28. There is symbolising in another direction. Confirmation in the subjective or epistemic sphere is no psychic character or relation but a non-cognitive or spiritual overtone of cognition as a psychic fact. It is itself a metaphor or symbolism : the strengthening or maturation of knowledge is but a figure of speech for a mode of cognitive realisation. The process may be otherwise symbolised as the shining out of thought, with the attenuation of error, as a mirror that catches the reflection of truth. Truth cannot be characterised; it has only to be symbolised by the evident content of a cognition, appearing within its magic interior. The interior or reference of a cognition is the conscious gap or discontinuity between the cognition and its object, the sphere of what may be called problematic thought—comprising incomplete but completing meanings, the consciously unknown, the contradictory, and this circumstances of confirmation—all centering round the evident content that is known. Truth is known as this evident content but not reversely : the particular known content is not known as the truth but is only demanded to be so known, by the process of confirmation and the consequent or independent process of the dissipation of error inherent in it.

FACT AND THOUGHT OF FACT

ANALYSIS

(1-2) 'Fact' means that which is believed. It may be the existent, or the non-existence of a possible existent, or, again, that which is neither existent nor non-existent e.g., the moral 'ought' or freedom. (3) The possible existent or that about which there can be an *actual* question of existence is a fact that is said to be 'thought'. That which does not imply the question of existence cannot properly be said to be 'thought'. (4-5) This may be disputed and the 'subsistent' may be cited as an instance of a thought-content which does not necessarily involve the question of existence. The contention, however, is inadmissible. The 'subsistent' is, no doubt, a meaning or thought-content, but there appears to be no escape from the view that the subsistent also *means* the possible existent. A content abstracted from its possible existence is not a thought-content but only a significant speakable. (6) A speakable content that is not thinkable may or may not be a fact. The false or the unreal is a significant unthinkable that is not a fact, for the assertion of falsity implies *pure* disbelief. (7) The purely disbelieved content has no reference to existence. There is no actual question about its existence : we may have at best a possible question. (8-10) The 'false' is sometimes distinguished from the 'unreal', the former being taken to be asserted of a proposition and the latter of a thing. The distinction is not tenable in the case of the 'illusory'. The illusory snake e.g., can be spoken of indifferently as false or unreal. The term 'unreal', however, is apparently wider than the term 'false'. An unreal content is properly said to be false if it was believed and hence could be the subject of an actual question.

(11) Belief in some fact is implied in all negative assertion. To say that a content is non-existent implies belief in some actual existent; to say that it is false implies belief in some possible existent; to take it as imaginary or contradictory requires no belief in a possible existent but only, in fact, about which there is no actual question of existence. (12) Though falsity implies belief in a possible existent, the thing believed in is only *some* possible existent which is not anything determinate. As an indeterminate entity, it is the unthinkable. (13-14) A speakable content is either fact or no-fact. Fact is either thinkable or unthinkable. The unthinkable fact is either assertable or unassertable. Just as the thinkable fact is the possible existent as determinate, the un-

thinkable assertable is the possible existent as indeterminate. The indeterminate possible existent is believed to be other than the believing, i.e., to be something that is objective. What is believed without being objective, viz., concrete subjectivity would be the unthinkable, unassertable fact. (15) The indeterminate fact that is said to be possibly existent is the objective or the assertable in general. It is possible to ask if objectivity is fact or no-fact. The question would be an actual one representing a spiritual uncertainty. (16) A subjective or spiritual fact is, like bare objectivity, a fact beyond the question of existence. But while there cannot be any actual question about the latter, about the former there cannot be even a possible question. The suggestion that objectivity is unreal is not meaningless. It is not worthless either, for there is a spiritual feeling of the symbolistic character of the object and of the vanity of the object-interest as independent of the spiritual interest. (17) A question about the facthood of the spiritual is meaningless. (18) No question arises about the facthood of the spiritual itself unless it is artificially objectified by language or otherwise. To realise that it is an unmeanable content would be to reject the question itself as illusory and not to obtain an answer to the question. (19) Doubt about an object implies the belief in *some* object or in bare objectivity. The apparent doubt about a subjective fact implies certainty about the fact itself and uncertainty about its symbolic characterisation by an objective category. (20) The bare object or objectivity cannot be disbelieved but there may be a spiritual doubt about its being other than the spiritual, for the object may be conceived as only the self-symbolising function of the spirit. The suggestion has value for the spiritual consciousness but it is not assertable in the secular consciousness.

FACT AND THOUGHT OF FACT

1. Fact means what is believed : what a person believes is a fact to him. The characterisation of fact as what stands in a constant system of relations or as what is given and not constructed by the mind or as what conditions and constitutes successful willing is no definition, as it itself assumes some fact. Fact does not admit of an impersonal definition.

2. Fact need not be the existent. The non-existence of that about which there can be an actual question of existence is also a fact that one believes and asks others to believe. A content about which there is no such question is, if believed, a fact and, if not believed, is no fact. There may be believed contents like the moral 'ought' or freedom which are facts that are neither existent nor non-existent. What is taken as false or unreal is no fact and one cannot speak of its non-existence also as fact, there being, as will appear presently, no question of its existence.

3. The existence or non-existence of a content about which there can be an actual question of existence is a fact that is 'thought'. Other facts are not properly said to be thought and the consciousness of a content as false or unreal is not a thinking consciousness. That about which the question of existence is asked is the possible existent. What is thought is either the possible existent or the existence or the non-existence of the possible existent. Nothing is properly said to be thought which does not imply the question of existence.

4. This restriction of the use of the word 'thought' requires justification. In the question 'does A exist or not', A does not mean an existent; it is a thought-content that is sometimes said to be subsistent. Must such a thought-content be understood as a possible existent? Is anything souhgt to be known about it except whether it exists or not? One may, it may be said, seek to analyse it to find out if it is compatible with another thought-content. Are such problems answered by thinking without reference to existence and non-existence? The answer in any case, it may be contended, is self-evident, however it is reached. But it is not self-evident like an axiom, being no judgment if a judgment is understood to imply a reference to the fact of existence or non-existence. Is the explication of a meaning or its compatibility or otherwise with another meaning a thought-content at all? Is the awareness specially of contradiction properly called thinking?

A contradictory thought is no thought, being only a loose expression for a combination of words meaning contents in contradiction with one another : the contradiction itself is no meaning. A synthesis of two meanings may, indeed, be a meaning but the so-called relation of compatibility is no meaning. It is only a symbolic expression for the problematic synthesising process which, if called thinking at all, is thinking without any thought-content of which we are actually conscious. So, too, when a given meaning is known to be equivalent to the synthesis of two meanings, the equivalence is a symbolic expression for an equating process which is at best a thinking without an actual thought-content.

5. What then is sought to be known about a thought-content or objective meaning without reference to its existence or non-existence is not itself an objective meaning. If anything is objectively known about the subsistent as other than a possible existent, it is its distinctness. If the reference of the distinct subsistent to existence be not necessary, how is the relation understood at all? In 'A has or has not existence', is the relation of *having* itself a subsistent or existent? If it is subsistent, how does it again get related to existence and if it is existent, how does A which means only a distinct get related to it? It will not do to say that the reference of the subsistent to existence is no objective content at all, for then the judgment 'A exists or does not exist' would have no objective meaning. There appears to be no escape from the view that the subsistent *means* the possible existent. A content abstracted from its possible existence is not even subsistent.. Not that a content as thus abstracted is an unmeaning phrase : it is only not subsistent, not a meaning or thought-content, though it is still a significant speakable. Even a contradiction which is no thought is a significant speakable.

6. A speakable content that is not thinkable as having no reference to existence may or may not be fact. The false or unreal is a significant unthinkable that is no fact. It is unthinkable as implying the absence or withdrawal of the question of existence and is thus distinct from non-existence, to assert which of a content is still to entertain the question of its existence. What is said to be false is a speakable content that is sometimes wrongly taken to be a proposition understood as the thought-content that is asserted or denied in a judgment. A negative judgment is the denial of a proposition or of a possible existent but the awareness of a content as false is not a negative judgment. To take something to be false is to reject or negate it without being aware of the negation as a thought-content. The

negative judgment also implies rejection or disbelief but the disbelief there is always a qualified belief. If the judgment 'A is not B' be a denial of the proposition 'A being B', it is also an affirmation of the proposition 'A being not B'. Even in the limiting case of the negative judgment—the negative existential judgment 'A is not', the disbelief in the existence of A is a positive belief in the non-existence of A, non-existence being understood as a factual determination of the possible existent A. But the assertion of falsity implies *pure* disbelief that is not equivalent to any belief. The content that is disbelieved here is not even understood as a possible existent and is accordingly no thought-content. If it is still called a proposition, we have to distinguish it as a merely speakable proposition from the thinkable proposition that is affirmed or denied in a judgment.

7. But has not the purely disbelieved content, it will be asked, a reference to existence? If the golden mountain or the hare's horn is disbelieved, do we not take these to be thinkable and as possibly existent? The question is if the person who disbelieves such a content takes it to be a possible existent during the disbelief. In forming a negative judgment like 'A is not', one entertains the question of A's existence, the content of the undecided question being just the proposition. But in stating the hare's horn as an example of the false or unreal, we do not have an undecided question of its existence in our mind. We do not actually ask if it exists : we can only imagine ourselves asking it. If then a purely disbelieved content admits of a question about its existence, the question is not actual to the disbeliever, being only a *possible* question. The content of an actual question being the possible existent, the content of a possible question would be the possibility of a possible, an entity that we need not regard as unmeaning but which is not the same as the thought-content called proposition that is asserted or denied in a judgment. If the content that we take to be false or unreal has a reference to existence at all, it is this possible or imaginary reference. Such reference we may deny only to a contradiction like square circle; a question is not even imagined about the contradictory. Not that it is absolutely unimaginable, for the contradictory is not meaningless like the word 'abracadabra'. We can ask about two thoughts if they are compatible and hence a possible question of existence about the possibly compatible—the doubly possible question, as we may call it—is not altogether excluded. If the content of a possible and a doubly possible question were to be called proposition, it would be only a speakable that is not thinkable, a significant entity that is yet no meaning.

8. What is rejected as false then is a speakable but not thinkable proposition. Must it be even a speakable proposition? The terms 'false' and 'unreal' are sometimes distinguished, the former being taken to be asserted of a proposition and the latter of a thing about which there is only a possible question of existence. Is the distinction tenable in the case of the perceptually false or the illusory? A perceptual judgment like 'this stick exists'—expressed, it may be, in the interjectional form 'this stick'—may be said to be the affirmation of the proposition 'this stick existing' or 'the existence of this stick'. A proposition of this kind is, indeed, a useless paraphrase of the word 'this' but it is not meaningless. When a stick is mistaken for a snake and the mistake corrected, the correction is properly expressed not as 'this is not a snake' but as 'this snake is not a snake'. It is not the thinking denial of a proposition, for the proposition 'this snake being snake' cannot be denied. It is no judgment but is only the symbolisation in the form of a judgment of the peculiar experience of perceptual annulment, of the visible reduction of the percept to unreality. Correction is the correction of a falsity and so it is the thing snake as apparently perceived and no proposition that is taken to be false. The snake can be here spoken of indifferently as false or unreal.

9. What is false then need not be a proposition. Where it is a proposition, it is speakable but not thinkable and is equivalent to a content about which there is no actual but only a possible question of existence. Such a content is said to be unreal and so, the false—whether perceptual or non-perceptual—may also be called unreal. The term 'unreal', however, is apparently wider than the term 'false'. A content that is said to be unreal may or may not have been previously believed and the question of its existence may or may not have been raised. All that is necessary is that it should be disbelieved and that there should not be an actual question of its existence during the disbelief. If the question was previously raised about it, it is now wholly dropped, and if it was previously believed, the belief is now wholly or partially withdrawn. About the unreal in the form of the contradictory, no question of existence could have arisen and it could not have been believed. What is called 'imaginary' may or may not have been believed and made the subject of a question but in any case the belief and the question are now wholly withdrawn. An unreal content is properly said to be false if it was believed and hence could be the subject of an actual question, the question being now wholly and the belief only partially withdrawn. What does the partial withdrawal of belief mean?

10. The possible existent is fact that is indeterminately known as either a determinate existent or a determinate non-existence. We speak of the falsity of what was previously believed to be a possible existent. Existence or non-existence is itself a determination of fact but each again has its particular determination : we speak of the previously believed existence or non-existence *of A* as false. The falsity would imply disbelief in *this* existence or non-existence but not in *some* possible existence as a determination of fact. When A is taken to be false, the non-existence of A may also be false but *some* possible existent must be believed. One may, for example, dream of the room in which he actually is and on waking take the dream to be false without believing in the non-existence of the room. So, too, the falsity of the belief in the non-existence of A need not imply belief in the existence of A, though in neither case is the belief in the possible existence of *something* rejected. This is the sense in which belief is to be understood as *partially* withdrawn in an assertion of falsity.

11. Belief in some fact is implied in all negative assertion—the assertion of non-existence of falsity or of other forms of unreality. To say that a content is non-existent is to continue to believe in some actual existent. To say that it is false is still to believe in some fact as possibly existent. To take it to be imaginary or contradictory requires no belief in a possible existent but only in fact, about which there is no actual question of existence. The assertion of falsity presupposes the belief that reality or fact can be existent fact or the fact of non-existence. The belief is not denied or rejected in the assertion of a content as contradictory or imaginary but it is irrelevant to such assertion of unreality.

12. The notion of the possible existent may appear to present a confusion. A fact is taken to be 'thought' if there is an actual question of existence about it or, in other words, if it is a possible existent. The consciousness of falsity, however, has been said to imply a belief, that is not questioned, in some possible existent. Falsity is not a thought-content and the possible existent that is presupposed by falsity is also presumably not a thought-content and yet thought-content is defined as the possibly existent. There is no confusion if we remember that what falsity presupposes is *some* possible existent, only an indeterminate assertable, an unquestioned and, therefore, unthinkable fact; and that thinkable fact as a determination of this indeterminate is the subject of a question of existence. The determinate assertable is thinkable fact, the indeterminate assertable is unthinkable fact and there may be unthinkable fact that is not assertable at all.

13. A speakable content then is either fact or no-fact. The false, the imaginary and the contradictory are forms of unreality or no-fact. Fact is either thinkable or unthinkable and unthinkable fact may or may not be assertable. Thinkable fact is the possible existent as determinate and the unthinkable assertable is the possible existent as indeterminate. Is there any unthinkable fact that is not assertable and if so, is it co-ordinate with the unthinkable fact that is assertable?

14. The false or the unreal as such is an unassertable content that is not fact. It is unassertable in the sense that it is purely disbelieved. The believed content may be distinguished from the believing but the disbelieved content is not distinguishable from the disbelieving. As thus indistinguishable, the disbelieved content is not asserted and so if there be a believed content that is not other than the believing of it, it would be said to be unassertable fact. A fact that is not yet known to be existent fact or the fact of non-existence but is known as not other than these alternatives—the indeterminate possible existent—is believed to be other than the believing, to be presented or objective in this sense. Unassertable fact then would be what is believed without being presented or objective. Not that it would be only the believing : it would be believed as not distinct from the believing, believed to be the subjective that is not merely consciousness of fact but is itself the fact of which it is conscious. Concrete subjectivity, as we may call it—the spiritual in our ordinary parlance—is thus the fact that is not only unthinkable but unassertable.

15. Unthinkable fact—whether assertable or unassertable—is fact about which there is no actual question of existence. About the assertable unthinkable there may be a *possible* question, just as there may be possible question about the false or imaginary. The indeterminate fact that is said to be possibly existent is the objective or the assertable *in general* about which there is no question of existence because the question presupposes it. But it is possible to ask about it—what idealism actually asks—if objectivity or distinction from the subjective or spiritual is fact or no-fact, real or unreal. It would be an actual question not of existence but of facthood or reality, representing a spiritual as distinct from logical doubt. Spiritually actual, it can be admitted in logic only as a *possible* question of existence. The idealist's doubt about the object is properly not about its existence, not whether it is an existent among existents. Since the object *means* the possible existent, the existent *or* non-existence, the doubt is whether the existent is existent and non-existence non-existence. It is

an unintelligible question which is none-the-less real, being, in fact, a spiritual uncertainty symbolised by the logical form of a question.

16. The possibility of existence and non-existence or bare objectivity is a fact beyond the question of existence. Subjective or spiritual fact is also beyond the question but the difference is that a question about the former is not meaningless, while it is meaningless about the latter. No question is actually entertained about the former, while about the latter there cannot be even a possible question. The possible question entertainable about bare objectivity is, as already said, whether the existent is existent and non-existence non-existence. It is the question whether existence and non-existence are not both unreal. If the possible means *either* existent or non-existent, what is neither existent nor non-existent would be the impossible. It may be a contradiction to speak of a content as both existent and non-existent but to say that it is neither is only to imply that it is not thinkingly known, that it is impossible to thought but not that it must be unreal. The impossible may be fact, though this 'may be' is a motiveless possibility to logic, a possibility that cannot be thought but cannot also be rejected by thought. Hence it is not meaningless to suggest that objectivity—meaning both existence and non-existence—is unreal, though in the absence of a positive spiritual feeling or experience of such unreality, the suggestion would be worthless. It is not worthless because there is a spiritual feeling of the symbolistic character of the object or of its unsubstantiality in itself or of both, of the vanity of the object-interest as independent of the spiritual interest—the heart of religion and the perennial spring of all idealism.

17. Thus the facthood of objectivity though unquestioned in logic is questionable from the spiritual standpoint, the question being not meaningless but motiveless for logic, no actual intellectual question. A question about the facthood of the spiritual, however, is meaningless. We may contrast three forms of certainty—the necessity of an axiom, the unquestioned character of the object in general and the self-evidence of the spiritual. All the three are logically undeniable. The axiom, however, admits of an actual question; there is only a possible question about the object in general; while a question is altogether meaningless in respect of the spiritual. An axiom is at once a law and an intuitable form of a particular organisation of thinkable facts. The law is necessarily true for the organisation but it does not exclude the possibility of an alternative organisation of the facts under a different axiom. Objectivity again, as presupposed by the logical question, is not itself questioned in logic; but while

logic does not entertain, it does not exclude a doubt other than the intellectual, which is symbolised by a logical question. That doubting cannot be doubted is true not of the logical but of the spiritual doubt. Spiritual uncertainty is itself a certainty and if objectivity is spiritually felt to be suspect, it is as much unreal as real. The object is never felt to be more than suspect, to be altogether unreal, though one may feel the want and the desirability of such feeling.

18. No question arises about the facthood of the spiritual itself unless it is artificially objectified by language or otherwise. The question about the reality of the self arises when the self is represented—it may be, through a word like 'I'—as a meant thing among things. To realise that it is an unmeanable or unthinkable content would be to reject the question itself as illusory and not to obtain an answer to the question. So if an alleged spiritual value of a thinkable object is pronounced unreal, it means either that it is not a spiritual value or that the value is not embodied or incarnated in the object but not that the spiritual value that it is alleged to be is itself illusory. So a doubt about the facthood of what is called a subjective state is an uncertainty about the naming of the subjective fact or about its being a fact in the mind of the doubter as appropriated by him or even about its being subjective at all, but not about there being the subjective state.

19. Doubt about an object need not imply the belief that the object exists at any time but only implies the belief that there is *some* object, belief in bare objectivity which is not questioned within logic, though a question about it is not meaningless. What appears as a doubt about a subjective fact implies certainty about the fact and uncertainty only about its symbolic characterisation by an objective category. Uncertainty about the spiritual is a spiritual certainty about its persisting objective aspect being merely symbolic or superinduced and is, in fact, the beginning of the correction or elimination of the aspect. The spirit is born in the uncertainty about the facthood of objectivity and it realises itself on the one hand by freeing itself from or correcting away the objectivity that sticks to it and on the other by consciously symbolising or contemplating itself as object to consolidate its freedom.

20. While the bare object is an unquestioned fact, it is not coordinate with self-evidencing spiritual fact. Objectivity cannot be disbelieved but there may be spiritual doubt about its being other than the spiritual. As the spirit realises itself by symbolising itself as object, the object may be only the self-symbolising function of the

spirit. The suggestion has value for the spiritual consciousness but is not assertable in the secular or logical consciousness, being only not denied in it. So long as the dualism of the spiritual and the secular consciousness remains, we have to regard the object as an unquestioned fact and the subject as an unquestionable fact without being able to assert their unity or duality.

CORRECTION OF ERROR AS A LOGICAL PROCESS

ANALYSIS

(1-3) The correction of an error, e.g., of taking a rope for a snake cannot be adequately expressed by the single sentence 'this that I believed as this snake is not snake'. It has to be expressed in the two sentences '*this* was taken as *this* snake' and 'what *this* was taken to be was no fact'. There is no unitary 'logical form' to express correction. It is an epistemic function without any unitary logical content. (4) There is an extreme view that the corrected consciousness was no belief and no consciousness of any unity like 'this snake'. The position cannot be accepted. (5-6) There may, again, be the suggestion that the corrective consciousness is no disbelief of the form 'this was not snake' and no awareness of 'this snake' as having been false when it was believed. But this appears to be an extreme statement that is not warranted by introspection. The testimony of introspection is not, however, clear as to whether the disbelief is in the form 'this *was* not snake' or 'this *is* not snake'.

(7-11) It may be contended further that the content 'this snake' as false to my present belief does not contradict 'this snake' as true to my previous belief and that the former may even be said to be a 'transformation' of the latter. But this alleged transformation or ideal inclusion is inclusion only in a constructive sense and, even as such, cannot be demonstrated. Secondly, it is hardly intelligible at the stage of disbelief to describe the content of the previous belief as a 'this'. Thirdly, the previous belief stood only on the conscious level, while the present disbelief stands on the self-conscious level. But the conception of falsity—and, therefore, of truth as well—does not emerge on the level of the merely objective consciousness. It is thus meaningless to speak of '*this* snake'—as to the previous belief—as true or false. The suggestion, therefore, that a belief that is false in conscious reference to another belief may be still true in itself has to be rejected as futile.

(12) Falsity has no reference to the time-position of a cognition at all. What is taken as false cannot be specified in purely objective terms, and the expressions considered in sec. 1-2 are all a mixture of subjective and objective terms. (13-14) What is false is a meaning to self-consciousness and is *this fact* to the corresponding consciousness. As meaning, it cannot be spoken of as *this,* though it cannot be indicated except in reference to *this* fact. A false content is a mean-

ing with a necessary reference to the thisness of fact. There may be the realistic view, however, that 'meaning' or 'content' is but the fact that is meant and what is false is not content of a belief but the belief itself. The belief is false not in respect of *its* content—for it has no content—but in respect of the content that is now thought to describe the particularising character of the belief. (15) Now this thought-content is not a true description of the belief but is only a constructive or symbolic description. The meaning of 'correction', accordingly, changes in this view : it is not a disbelieving in a previously believed *content,* but only disbelieving that the previous belief had a content at all. (16-17) The realistic view thus admits a contentless belief and is perilously near to the idealistic view that the object is nothing but belief with its subjectivity heterised. In the former, however, the contentless belief was only a believing and no presentation; in the latter, it is a presentation. The idealistic view is to be preferred to the realistic view.

(18) Taking the disbelief implied in correction to be adequately expressed in the form 'this snake is not', the *'this'* in it would not mean a perceived substrate of the snake-character. *This,* here, is not even a believed substrate but only an imagined specification of the imagined snake. (19) *This* in 'this snake' stands for no fact at all. The disbelief is absolute and is not capable of being expressed as a negative judgment. (20) It cannot, again, be said that what *this* was believed to be was not presented, nor that it was presented as *this.* I cannot now describe in objective terms what I then believed, nor can I say that there was only the subjective fact of contentless belief. I believed in a content that was neither fact nor absolute nought.

CORRECTION OF ERROR AS A LOGICAL PROCESS

1. I am said to correct and error of mine when I disbelieve in what I am aware I believed. The correction of the error of taking a rope for a snake may be expressed as two processes. I am now aware that I believed this object before me to the *this snake* and I now believe that this was not a snake. Is the singleness of the corrective process expressed adequately by the complex sentence, 'this that I believed as this snake is not snake'? The clause 'that I believed, etc.' only gives subsidiary information though the corrective function is directed primarily towards what is meant by the clause, towards what *this* was taken to be and not towards *this*. Again, what is now taken to be no snake is a content that *was* believed to be fact and is not now believed. It is not believed as a past fact, nor can it here be said to be merely suggested to me as a possible fact about which there may be a genuine question whether it exists. The subject of a negative judgment is what is believed or suggested as a fact in the judgment. The complex statement above is no negative judgment and does not adequately express correction.

2. The predicate of the complex sentence '(this...) *is not snake*' is also open to objection. The disbelief implied in correction is primarily disbelief not in a certain naming of a previously believed content (that it is *snake*) but in its facthood. I now know that what *this* was taken to be was no fact. Correction has to be expressed in the two sentences, '*this* was taken as *this snake*' and 'what *this* was taken to be was no fact'; and these cannot be combined in one sentence.

3. Not only is correction not expressible as a negative judgment : there is no unitary logical form to express it. By 'logical form' is here meant a form in which there is reference only to the content of a believing or thinking and not to the believing or thinking itself. Correction cannot be formulated in language without reference to the subjective fact of a past believing. It is an epistemological function that has no unitary logical content corresponding to it.

4. Correction has been so far described in terms of two subjective processes—a previous belief and a present disbelief referring to it. Are the processes rightly designated 'belief' and 'disbelief'? Was the previous consciousness a belief, the content of which could be called 'this snake'? There is the extreme view that it was no belief, no consciousness at all of the unity 'this snake'. There was belief

in *this* and belief in snake and these beliefs that were together were simply not distinguished. Or it may be allowed that the facts *this* and snake were the contents of a single belief but they were not distinguished. Or this view may go with the admission of some consciousness of the unity 'this snake' other than belief—suggestion or thought or speaking consciousness. There is no error according to these views and, therefore, also no correction. What is called error is only not distinguishing, the privation of the knowledge of distinction; and correction is nothing but the knowledge of the distinction that was previously unappreciated. Such a position can hardly be refuted except by an appeal to the testimony of consciousness. The appeal is not indeed decisive, for the testimony is indefinite. We are not clear at the time of correction whether the previous consciousness was of a definite unity but in any case we can say that it was not consciousness of an indefinite content, consciousness of this and snake as utterly unrelated. What was not appreciated as indefinite may yet have been indefinite but there is at least a presumption in favour of its having been a definite unity.

5. Admitting then that there was a belief in the unity 'this snake', we ask if there is now a disbelief in it. That there is no longer a belief in 'this snake' is not disputed but it may not mean that there is now a disbelief in the form 'this is not a snake' or 'this snake is not a fact.' Even if such a disbelief be admitted, it may not mean disbelief in *this* having been a snake when it was believed as such. These may appear to be unreal objections but they gain plausibility when developed. The present consciousness, it may be said, is primarily a belief in *this* being a rope. It refers indeed to the previous belief in 'this snake' but the reference is only a belief in a positive distinction between *this* and snake which ousts the previous belief psychologically but does not amount to a disbelief in it. I may now say 'this is not snake' but the word 'not' here only means a distinction and does not imply a rejection. Negation in the objective content means nothing but distinction and even if there be a subjective feeling of rejecting or disbelieving as distinct from distinguishing, it has no content other than distinction. Even if 'this is not snake' means the non-existence of snake here and not simply its distinction from *this,* non-existence being as much an objective fact as distinction, it is the content of a belief and not of the alleged process of rejection or disbelief. Again, admitting that the disbelief has for its content the *falsity* of the previous belief, this falsity, it may be said, is only an additional character, the knowledge of which means the psychological cessation of the

previous belief but does not affect its truth. There is no contradiction in speaking of the content 'this snake' as both true and false, true in itself when the belief was there and false now in relation to the content now believed, viz., 'this being rope'.

6. The suggestion throughout is that there is no disbelief in the form 'this was not snake', no awareness of the content 'this snake' as having been false when it was believed. That there is now only belief and no disbelief appears, however, to be an extreme statement that is not warranted by introspection. I am aware of having a disbelief, and also a belief not only in 'this rope' but also in the non-existence of snake here though hardly in the distinction of *this* from snake. The testimony of introspection is not, however, clear as to whether the disbelief is in the form 'this *was* not snake.' If it be suggested that the disbelief is only in the form 'this *is* not snake', the suggestion does not appear to be definitely opposed to my introspection. Not that the snake has now only ceased to exist and that it was when believed. Introspection apparently does not say anything about my present belief being in a snake having existed when it was believed.

7. But, it may be said, the truth or falsity of a believed content does not mean its existence or non-existence in time. Disbelief in its existence now may be regarded as *belief* in its falsity as an additional character. The content 'this snake as false now' does not contradict the content 'this snake as true then' and may even be said to contain it ideally, to affirm it as not negated but positively transformed. The notion of ideal retention or transformation is difficult to understand in the case specially of perceptual error. But then perception as knowledge would be taken in this view to be an implicit judgment. How is the content of the judgment 'this is snake' contained in that of the judgment 'this is rope'? A judgment cannot be taken by itself : it has to be taken as implicitly cohering in the inferential way with other judgments. A judgment is to be understood as an epistemological condensation of a system of judgments and perception that is knowledge is a further integration of such a judgment into psychological immediacy. The percepts 'this snake' and 'this rope' are each an integration of a system of believed contents and one may be said to contain the other in the sense that the system integrated in the one is inclusive of the system integrated in the other. The relation of inclusion between the percepts is not indeed perceived and hence it may be called an ideal inclusion which appears to perception as the magic relation of transformation.

8. The strictly logical assertion in this view is that the content 'this snake' as false to my present belief does not contradict 'this snake' as true to my previous belief. The rest of the view is couched in imaginative language and whether it can be fully presented in literal logical terms is disputable. The metaphors mainly employed are the *implicit* working of one cognition in another and the content of one cognition being present in *ideality* or transformed in the content of another. Implicit working of inference in judgment and of judgment in perception means in strict logic that the included cognition is cognition of a content other than the content of the inclusive cognition, which yet is no new fact. When again the content A is said to be reduced to ideality or transformed in another content X, nothing more is meant than that the cognition of X is the cognition of A in relation to B and that the cognition of this relation is implicitly contained in the cognition of A in the sense explained that it is cognition of no fact other than A. Whatever else appears to be meant by these notions is purely subjective and is only figuratively represented in objective language.

9. When then the belief in 'this rope' is said to contain the belief in 'this snake' as transformed, what is literally meant is that the belief now is in the content 'this snake' in relation to new contents, the relation being no new fact. The perceived *this* taken with certain relations to outside facts makes a system which is constructively the same fact as 'this snake'. (Again, *this* taken with the relations to these and other outside facts makes a fuller system which is the same fact as 'this rope'.) The facts and relations contained in each system, however, can never be fully specified and it would, therefore, appear to be impossible to show that one system is included in the other. Even if this objection is waived, it is hardly justifiable to deny that the percepts integrating the systems are incompatible on the ground that one system includes the other. The percepts 'this rope' and 'this snake' are wholly incompatible characterisations of the given *this,* one of which can be said to ideally include, define or transform the other only in a remotely constructive sense.

10. The belief in 'this rope' is a disbelief in 'the snake' now, but does it mean that 'this snake' *was* false when it was believed? It all depends on what is meant by the content of a belief or disbelief. Is believing a content the same as believing a fact ? If a content is believed, it is believed as fact. If later it is disbelieved, taken to be false, it is no longer believed as fact. The disbelief is a conscious reference to the previous belief, to the previous apprehension of the

content as fact. Can the content be *now* spoken of as 'this snake'? I can say now that what I believed and could have then spoken of as 'this snake' is false but can I say 'this snake' is false? Can what is known as false be spoken of as *this?* Does not *this* at once mean *this fact* in time? If a content does not mean a fact in time, can we apply the word 'this' to it?

11. The content of the consciousness 'this fact' can be called 'this meaning', if introspection into the consciousness of a fact as *this* is admitted to be itself the consciousness of the fact as a meaning. If what is now disbelieved be said to be 'this snake', 'this snake' is a meaning and not a fact to the disbelief, though the same expression stands for a fact to the previous belief. The present disbelief refers to the previous belief and is on a self-conscious level relatively to it which stood only on the conscious level. What then is false to self-consciousness need not be false to consciousness. Properly speaking, however, the concept of falsity does not emerge on the level of merely objective consciousness. We can speak of the content of consciousness as fact or no-fact, existent or non-existent but not as true or false. It is meaningless to speak of '*this* snake'—as to the previous belief—as true or false. The suggestion running through the views just examined that a belief that is false in relation and conscious reference to another belief may be still true in itself has, therefore, to be rejected as futile.

12. What was taken as 'this snake' cannot be said to have been false. What is now taken as false cannot also be expressed as 'this snake'. Falsity, in fact, has no reference to the time-position of a cognition at all. What is taken as false cannot be specified in objective terms. If the disbelief is expressed in the form 'this that was believed and could be spoken of as *this* snake was not a snake', the subject is a mixture of subjective and objective terms. If the disbelief be formulated—preferably for reasons explained—in two sentences 'what this was believed to be is no fact' and 'this was believed (or more accurately, could be spoken of with belief) as *this* snake', both the sentences are a mixture of subjective and objective terms. The difficulty, it would appear, is not merely verbal.

13. What is false is a meaning to 'self-consciousness' and is at the same time *this fact* to the corresponding consciousness. As meaning, it cannot be spoken of as *this,* though it cannot be indicated except by a reference to *this* fact. A false content is a meaning with a necessary or constitutive reference to the *this*-ness of fact. It may, however, be held that meaning or content is but the fact that is meant.

The content of a belief that is not fact but mere meaning is a chimera. Meaning as distinct from fact meant is but the subjective function of thinking. It may be symbolically or figuratively spoken of as though it were objective but it is not objective at all. What is false then is not the content of a belief but the belief itself. There was the belief formulated by the phrase 'this snake' which, however, was not belief *in the content* 'this snake'. It was belief in *this* and belief in snake but not belief in the unity 'this snake'. Yet it cannot be said that the two beliefs were simply not distinguished—a view already examined. They were positively combined into a single belief which had, however, no content. It was not belief *in* 'this snake' and can only be figuratively spoken of as such. Correction indeed is disbelief but the content of the disbelief is the negation 'this is not snake' which, however, is not the whole content of the corrective consciousness. What is false or is corrected is not the judgment 'this is snake' : it is the previous belief which was not a judgment or inference but a perception. But as there was no fact corresponding to the phrase 'this snake', the perception was only a perceiving and not the cognition of a content or fact which are the same.

14. Can belief as a mere subjective fact be said to be false? It can be said to be false only in respect of its reference, of what it says, unless the falsity of a belief means nothing but its ineffectiveness in a will-context. Falsity may be ascertained partially by a reference to the will-context but it does not *mean* ineffectiveness. Apparently then this view has to admit a content that is spoken of, thought or suggested without belief. What is false is belief in respect of this thought-content. There was a belief combining the beliefs in *this* and snake, which had no content, no fact corresponding to it. But the belief is now interpreted by a word-conditioned thought of which 'this snake' or 'this being snake' is the content. This thought is formulated at the time of disbelief and is taken to be the description of the belief. The belief then is false not in respect of *its* content—for it has no content —but in respect of the content that is now thought to describe the particularising character of the belief.

15. But is this thought-content a true description of the belief or is it only a constructive or symbolic description? It is the latter, though as no belief is claimed for it, there is no question of truth or error. The meaning of correction accordingly changes in this view : it is not disbelieving in a previously believed *content* but only disbelieving that the previous belief had a content at all. This is expressed by the negative judgment 'this is not snake' which, however, does

not presuppose the suggestion that the belief had 'this snake' for its content. The negative judgment is ordinarily taken to presuppose an affirmative judgment or a question which suggests a possible fact. Here, however, the judgment 'this is not snake' would be taken to presuppose a belief that has no content and is only characterised by the thought 'this being snake' at the time of the judgment. The belief is false in respect of what is now constructively taken to be its content.

16. The admission in this realistic view of a contentless belief would bring it perilously near an idealistic view according to which object is nothing but belief with its subjectivity alienated or heterised. There was, according to both, no belief *in* 'this snake' but only belief *of this form,* belief as factitiously characterisable by the present thought of 'this snake.' In the realistic view, however, the contentless belief was only a believing and no presentation; while in the particular idealistic view, it is a presentation. A further difference is that the belief that is corrected is in the realistic view contentless so far as 'this snake' is not a unitary believed content, though it is still belief *in* the contents *this* and snake; while in the idealistic view, the belief *of the form* 'this snake' is not only not belief in the unity but not also in *snake.*

17. The idealistic view here appears to have an advantage over the realistic view, for it is difficult to understand a unitary belief which is only partly determined or characterised by its content. Now that we have the thought of the unity 'this snake' or 'this being snake' which is disbelieved, the thought that symbolises the subjective unity of the belief, can we say that the predicate or determinant *snake* in it means the fact snake as remembered to be elsewhere? Is it believed at all within this thought? As the thought of 'this snake' now rises with disbelief, it implies an empty contingency like 'if this could be snake, as it cannot be'. The emergence of the idea of snake may be through memory but does the idea continue to be believed memory-content within such a contingent thought? Apparently it continues only as *meaning* and for the belief now characterised by the thought of 'this snake', 'snake' is as little a believed content as the unity 'this snake', being only the *mode* of the belief—the believing or the presentation.

18. To the idealistic view, the previous belief is no belief *in* snake but is still belief in *this* as a presentation, though not as objective fact. 'This snake' was a presentation and since *this* as believed now is objective fact (or heterised presentation), the word *this* appears to be a specification both of the objectified and of the unobjectified presentation. Taking the disbelief implied in correction to be

adequately expressed in the form 'this snake is not' rather than in the form 'this is not snake', would *this* in it mean a perceived content, the perceived substrate of the snake-character? If neither 'this snake' nor 'snake' be a believed content for the previous belief, can *this* be regarded as a substrate at all? When I imagine a lion on a perceived object like the wall before me, the whole content 'lion on the wall' being imaginary, the term 'wall' in the whole means not the locus as perceived but the imagined character of location of the imagined lion. So here *this* is not a believed substrate but only an imagined specification of the imagined snake. The previous belief in the mode 'this snake' has thus no content at all or has for its content something that is no fact at all but absolute nought.

19. The illusion 'this snake' is then a presentation in which there is no belief in *this* or snake or their unity as fact. The word 'this' is here not only not the specification of an objective fact but not also of the presentation as a subjective fact. *This* in 'this snake' which is disbelieved stands for no fact at all. The disbelief is absolute and is not capable of being expressed as a negative judgment. If it is at all expressed as a negative statement, its form would be 'this snake is not' which would not be a negative existential judgment like 'ghosts do not exist' in so far as the subject 'this snake' is not even the suggestion of a possible fact. It is not even the psychic fact of presentation, being only the appearance of presentation, if such a phrase could be allowed. At the time of disbelief, we feel it is only *as though* 'this snake' was presented.

20. All this follows from the meaning of *this* in the disbelieved unity 'this snake': every part of an imaginary content is imaginary. The objection to this view is that 'this snake' was believed and was not merely imagined like the lion on the wall. I disbelieve it now not in the form 'this snake is not' but in form 'what I believed this to be is not', where the word *this* stands for a fact that is now believed. But then I believed *this* to be 'this snake' in which phrase or thought the word 'this' means what is like *snake* no fact. Yet the two *this*'s mean the same perceived content. I cannot say then that what *this* was believed to be was not presented nor that it was presented as *this*. Now that I disbelieve, I cannot assert that I perceived *this* snake nor can I deny that I perceived something as *this*, as an individual fact before me. I cannot now describe in objective terms what I then believed, nor can I say that there was only the subjective fact of contentless belief. I believed in a content which was not fact nor absolute nought.

THE FALSE AND THE SUBJECTIVE

ANALYSIS

(1-2) The consciousness of the false and the consciousness of the subjective imply one another. A. *The consciousness of the false is the consciousness of the subjective.* The consciousness of the false is the consciousness of a content that is not speakable except as the content of a belief. (3) The false is what is corrected and disbelieved. 'Disbelief' is a positive mode of consciousness and is not merely the privation of belief. (4-6) The content said to be disbelieved cannot be expressed except as what was believed. The content of belief is formulated loosely as 'this is A', artificially as 'this being A' and naturally as 'this as A'. The content of the corresponding disbelief cannot, however, be expressed in this form. It can only be described problematically as '*What* was believed'. (7) Disbelief of correction has thus to be taken as a form of reflective consciousness. It is not, however, a cognitive belief in the prior belief: it is only a consciousness of it in necessary reference to itself. (8) It is not cognitive belief, for a cognitive consciousness is the conciousness of something which is speakable without reference to the consciousness.

(9-16) B. *The consciousness of the subjective is the consciousness of the false.* That is to say, (i) the consciousness of a belief implies disbelief in its content; (ii) all consciousness of the subjective implies consciousness of a belief. (i) The consciousness of belief is the consciousness of having the belief *as past* for present rejection or re-affirmation. The consciousness of a past belief is either belief or disbelief in its content and never a mere non-committal consciousness of the content as merely subsistent. The consciousness of the subjective is not a substantive conscious state like the consciousness of the object. To be conscious of a belief, in the way of rejection or re-affirmation, is in all cases to be conscious of a dissociation of the content of the belief from fact. This dissociation even in the case of re-affirmation implies that re-affirmation is really the rejection of disbelief. In all cases then in which we are explicitly conscious of a past belief, we have a disbelief in the content of that belief. To be conscious of the subjective fact of belief is thus to be conscious of its content as false.

(17) (ii) All consciousness of the subjective is consciousness of a belief. There is no consciousness of a subjectivity that is not consciousness of a content referred to fact. What we are reflectively

aware of is the consciousness of a content as what is or may be believed. (18-20) Introspection is only distinguishing a mode of consciousness from its content. It cannot literally be said to be the consciousness of a subjective content, for that would lead to a vicious regress. Introspection is itself a subjectivity and we speak of it with belief without having any consciousness of it. Much of what we call 'introspection' appears to be only a naming of a subjectivity. (21) We have no consciousness of a subjectivity that is not the consciousness of a content referred to fact. Thus to be conscious of the subjective is to be conscious of a belief.

THE FALSE AND THE SUBJECTIVE

1. The thesis elaborated in the present paper is that the consciousness of the false and the consciousness of the subjective imply one another. It may be analysed into two propositions (A) that the consciousness of the false is consciousness of the subjective and (B) that the consciousness of the subjective is consciousness of the false. The first denies that the false is but the objective fact of non-existence and the second denies that the subjective can be known without belief or disbelief in its content—which is apparently the theory behind what is called psychological introspection. The further implications of the thesis would be that the object is through the self-alienation of the subject and that the subject is not known except by a denial of the object. These implications are not discussed in this paper.

A. Consciousness of the False is Consciousness of the Subjective

2. The proposition may be thus developed:

The consciousness of the false is consciousness of a content that is not speakable except as the content of a belief which, again, is not speakable except as that the content of which is false.

3. The false is what is corrected or disbelieved. Properly, 'disbelief' should mean correction or rejection of what was believed, though the word is sometimes used loosely to mean rejection of what is suggested or the mere absence of belief in the imaginary or the contradictory. To be conscious of a content as imaginary or contradictory is to have no belief in it. Disbelief is a positive mode of consciousness and is not merely the privation of belief. The so-called disbelief in a suggestion is really a belief. A content is suggested as what either is or is not and never, as will appear, without all reference to fact; and the rejection of it means that the negative alternative is accepted or believed. We take disbelief then in the sense of correction which we hold is incapable of being regarded as equivalent to a *belief* in negation.

4. Correction of error means disbelief not merely in what was believed but in what we are explicitly conscious of having believed. The content said to be disbelieved cannot, in fact, be expressed except as what was believed. What is it that we are said to disbelieve? If we start with the belief 'this is A'— all belief in the last resort is in a

this or given reality—and then correct it, what is it that we take to be false? What we disbelieve may be taken to be what we believed. In the belief or judgment 'this is A', how should the content believed be formulated? Is the correct formulation of it 'this *is* A' or 'this *being* A' or 'this *as* A'? If we accept the first two formulations, there is no difficulty in accepting them also as the formulations of what we disbelieve. If, however, the believed content be taken to be 'this as A', what we disbelieve cannot be said to be also 'this as A', for the word 'this', when used as the principal word in a verbal combination, can mean only what is believed and never what is disbelieved.

5. We contend that the first two formulations of the content of belief are inadmissible. The judgment-form 'this is A' in which the principal word is the copula stands neither for the fact believed nor for the believing act but for an undifferentiated or confused unity of the two. There is nothing in believed fact or in the believing act—each taken singly—answering to the distinction between 'this A' and 'this is A', i.e., to the copula, the meaning of which nevertheless has to be understood in reference to the fact and the act. The content of belief cannot, therefore, be formulated as 'this *is* A'. Nor should it be expressed as 'this *being* A'—what is nowadays called *proposition* as distinct from judgment. In 'this being A', the principal word is *being* which means here a relation, in a wide sense of the term, between *this* and A. What is believed, however, is not the relation but the concrete fact this as related to A. It is briefly expressed as 'this as A'[a] in which the principal word is *this* standing for the substantive fact. It is this fact as characterised by A and not the characterising relation that is properly said to be believed.

6. The content of belief is formulated loosely as 'this is A' and artificially as 'this being A', the natural expression of it being 'this as A'. The content of the corresponding disbelief—meaning *what* is disbelieved—cannot be expressed in this form. It cannot, in fact, be expressed in any form except problematically as '*what* was believed', the *what* being unspecifiable at the time of the disbelief in purely objective terms. We cannot then even say that what *was* believed is 'this as A', for the word 'this' would mean content of a *present* belief.

7. Disbelief or correction then as necessarily involving the consciousness of something subjective, viz., the previous belief has to be taken as a form of reflective consciousness. To be conscious of the

[a] In more complex cases the content may have to be expressed as 'this A as related to B'.

false as such is to be conscious of the subjective. Not that the consciousness of the false is a belief in the prior belief as a definite subjective fact. Disbelief, indeed, is a conscious reference to the prior belief but the prior belief can be spoken of at the time of disbelief *only in reference to the disbelief*. Although the previous belief is not disbelieved, it is not *now* specifiable by its content, for the content is specifiable only by reference to it. The belief can be specified only as that the content of which is false or is now disbelieved. The content cannot be spoken of without reference to the belief and the belief cannot now be characterised without reference to the present disbelief. Disbelief is not a cognitive belief in the prior belief but a consciousness of it in necessary reference to itself.

8. It is difficult to define cognitive consciousness but it may be characterised as the consciousness of something which is speakable without reference to the consciousness. Will-consciousness, for example, is distinguishable from it by the circumstance that it implies a belief in something that cannot be formulated without reference to the willing. To will an action is to be conscious of the action not as merely going to happen but as going to happen *through the willing*. What we believe here may be called the content of the willing but the content, if literally expressible at all, is expressible *not* in the form 'this action is coming' but in the form 'this action is coming through the causality of my willing'. Now the belief of which we are necessarily conscious in disbelief is such that the content of it cannot be spoken of without reference to the belief and is accordingly to be regarded as a non-cognitive belief. The disbelief also, the content of which is the content of the belief which is speakable only in reference to the disbelief, is a form of non-cognitive consciousness.

B. Consciousness of the Subjective is Consciousness of the False

9. The proposition may be split up into two propositions: (i) that the consciousness of a belief implies disbelief in its content and (ii) that all consciousness of the subjective implies consciousness of a belief. Both would appear paradoxical, if not obviously false.

10. (i) The first proposition may be thus elaborated: The consciousness of a belief is consciousness of *having* the belief *as* past for present rejection or re-affirmation, the re-affirmation implying rejection.

11. The statement may be hazarded that the consciousness of a

past belief is either belief or disbelief in its content and never a non-committal consciousness of the content as merely subsistent. We may be conscious of the content of a past belief without being conscious of the belief itself. Such consciousness need not be actual belief or disbelief: it may be only an idea or suggestion.[a] If however we are conscious of the belief as a subjective fact, our consciousness of its content is always a judgment that it is or is not a fact.

12. Strictly speaking, the consciousness of a past belief, as of any subjective fact, is not memory but whether it is called memory or not, it differs from the memory of an objective fact in an important respect. To be conscious of a subjective state is to *be* in a subjective state referring to the content of the primary state, of which the consciousness of the primary state is a transitive fringe or function. The consciousness of the subjective is not like the consciousness of an object, a substantive conscious state subsisting by itself.

13. To be conscious of a subjective fact like belief is to have a present dealing with the content of the belief in the way of rejection or re-affirmation. Either way, it implies *having* the belief. How can we be said to have the belief when it is rejected? When we disbelieve the content of a belief, we understand the content, as already explained, not by itself but *as* what we believed. We are thus conscious of the belief as past but as the belief is now understood *only* as rejected, we may say that to reject it is to *have* it now in the mind *as past*. 'As past' means 'as rejected': the consciousness of the pastness of the belief is but the consciousness of the belief being rejected.

14. To reject a belief is to have the belief as rejected. It is to be aware of a dissociation of the content of the belief from fact. Again, to re-affirm a belief is not only to continue believing in its content but to be conscious that the content might not be fact. It also implies the dissociation of the content from facthood. To be conscious of a belief then is in all cases to be conscious of such a dissociation. When the belief of which we are conscious is the belief of another mind expressed through speech, we are conscious of the content of the belief being dissociated from our own belief in the very act of understanding the speech. To understand a person's assertion may be primarily to believe the content asserted but it is also *from the very start* to be aware that the content might not be fact.[b] When however we are conscious of our own belief, we are conscious

[a] The consciousness of a content without all reference to fact is not even an idea which has a problematic reference to fact.

[b] The content, however, is not here dissociated from the asserting act.

of the dissociation of the content from fact *only through positive disbelief*.

15. We are explicitly conscious of a subjective fact like belief when we distinguish its content from it and we distinguish it only as we disbelieve it. The dissociation of the content of a belief from its facthood in the re-affirmation of the belief implies that re-affirmation is really the rejection of disbelief. To know a belief to be true is to reject a disbelief in its content that is already emergent. Just as the rejection of a belief implies having the belief as past, so the rejection of a disbelief means having the disbelief as past. To be conscious of a past belief as true is also to have consciousness of its being false. In all cases then in which we are explicitly conscious of a past belief, we have a disbelief in the content of it.

16. It may be said that to be conscious that the content of a belief might not be fact, it is not necessary that it should be disbelieved. It may be simply doubted or there may be only a question in the mind, a desire for information as to whether the content is existent or non-existent. But a question of this kind does not imply consciousness of the *belief*: it implies only the consciousness of its content as possibly existent or possibly non-existent and does not accordingly involve a dissociation of the content from *fact*. Existence and non-existence both come under believed content or fact. Doubt indeed—as distinct from such question—involves a dissociation of the content from fact, being the consciousness of the content as either fact or no fact (where 'no fact' means 'not even the fact of non-existence'). It is the consciousness of an alternation not of two beliefs but of belief and disbelief, of a belief as past and the disbelief in its content, both being present in the mind. Doubt cannot indeed be said to be *both* belief and disbelief but it cannot be *denied* to be either. Where then the content of a belief is doubted, it cannot be said to be not disbelieved.

We may accordingly hold that we are conscious of a belief as past only when we have a disbelief in its content. To be conscious of the subjective fact of belief is to be conscious of its content as false.

17. (ii) We now come to the other proposition that all consciousness of the subjective is consciousness of a belief. It may be thus paraphrased:

There is no consciousness of a subjectivity that is not consciousness of a content referred to fact.

What is not the consciousness of a content is not the content of introspection, though it may be subjective fact. Again, there may be the consciousness of a content without any reference to fact and this also cannot be said to be the content of introspection. What we are reflectively conscious of is the consciousness of an actual or possible fact, of a content as what is or may be believed. The consciousness of a content as what may be believed is still an actual consciousness of belief.

18. Some explanations are necessary. Introspection should be taken as at once *meaning* the distinguishing of a mode of consciousness from its content. To be conscious of a mode of consciousness is to be conscious also of the content of the mode; and to be conscious of the mode and the content together is to distinguish them. Not that it can be said to be the consciousness of their distinction *as a content;* the distinction cannot be regarded as an actual content that is either objective or subjective. The distinguishing here is not the consciousness of distinction and the consciousness of the subjective is but the distinguishing of the subjective from its content. Introspection accordingly cannot be literally said to be the consciousness of the subjective content, though the form of expression is unavoidable. If it were the consciousness of a content, there would be introspective consciousness of introspection and therefore introspective consciousness of this consciousness and so on ad infinitum.

19. The subjective is not definable as the content of introspection. Introspection is itself a subjectivity and we speak of it with belief, though we have no consciousness *of* it. A subjectivity, then, of which we are not conscious may not be denied and may be significantly spoken of. One example of it is the so-called consciousness of a content without a believing or disbelieving reference to fact. To be conscious of a content without reference to fact is to be conscious of it *as* without reference, as with the referring consciousness suspended. The so-called consciousness of the bare content is the suspending act which is the consciousness of the referring consciousness and not of the content only. If to introspect be to distinguish consciousness from its content, a content without reference to fact being incapable of being distinguished from, there can be no introspection into the consciousness of such a content. The consciousness of a content without intentional reference is a non-relational *acquaintance* with the content.

20. To the definition of introspection as the distinguishing of a subjectivity from its content, it may be objected that it would exclude introspection into perception and into all consciousness on the perceptual level. The very character of perceptual consciousness is that it is not immediately distinguishable from the object perceived and yet we

seem to be obviously aware of such consciousness as when we say 'I see the table.' Nor does this awareness of perceiving the table imply any disbelief in the table, as would be demanded by our theory. Such awareness of perception, however, is not introspection but only a significant speaking of it. Just as there is no introspection into introspection though we may speak of introspection, so the fact that we speak of seeing the table does not imply that we are introspectively conscious of the seeing. We have no direct enjoying consciousness of the seeing operation—as distinct from the organic-muscular experience of using our eyes—being performed by us. Much of what we call introspection appears to be only a speaking or naming of a subjectivity. All introspection may imply a naming of the subjective but all naming of it is not introspection.

21. We have no consciousness then of a subjectivity that is not consciousness of a content with intentional reference. Intentional reference is a believing or disbelieving reference and disbelieving reference involves a believing reference. Thus if we are conscious of the subjective, we are conscious of a belief.

22. The consciousness of a belief has been shown to involve disbelief in its content. As to be conscious of any subjective fact is to be conscious of a belief, all reflective consciousness may be said to involve disbelief in the content of the corresponding unreflective consciousness. Thus the consciousness of the false is the consciousness of the subjective and vice versa. We are necessarily aware of the false and the subjective together.

SOME ASPECTS OF NEGATION

ANALYSIS*

(1-5) The problem is to formulate the logic of the view that truth is manifold. There are many radically different types of logic based on incommensurable views of negation. What *is not,* viz., the illusion may be regarded (1) as having some kind of abstract being or (2) as contradiction itself. Illusion may be (i) a being only to be denied, (ii) a being as positive as fact but different from it and positively related to it, (iii) identical with fact, relation being but identity, or (iv) no being at all but negation transcending all being.

(6-10) These four views indicate four distinct attitudes towards truth, four stages of attention. The positive direction of attention is alone emphasised in the first three views. Pragmatism which recognises the fourth view in one form does not yet suggest a definite discipline of attention in the negative direction. This negative attention is very like introspection, being the consciousness of the absence of object and as such implying cognition of the object as well. The faculty is explicitly recognised in the fourth view of negation which accordingly brings out the need of an intensive discipline of it.

(11-15) The analysis of the meaning of '*not* illusory', of negation of negation shows the concrete shapes which the above four views assume. In (i), 'not illusory' means 'not merely subjective', and all relation being illusory or merely subjective, there arises the notion of the self-identical reals. Self-identity or self-conservation as a function, and what is opposed to it, viz., the thinking function of the subjective ideas are only grades of illusion, each of which is indifferently one or manifold. In (ii), 'not illusory' is what is different from the positively subjective and coordinate with it, viz., the objective. Each side of the difference is a relation of terms, subjective relation is distinct from objective relation, and while there is one object-system, there are many idea-systems connected with many substrata. In (iii), the truth that is 'not illusory' is the necessary identity of the subjective and objective, of the known and the unknown. In (iv), this necessary identity is not positive at all. To say that the limiting unknown is *necessary* is not to know the unknown. Nor will it do to make any positive use of it as a transcendent negation, to take it, e.g., either as positively conditioning the known or as negative matter in relation to (Platonic) Ideas. 'Not illusory' in this view can only mean the unknown of which we are aware through the absence of positive knowledge. The principle is uncertainty itself, the uncertain alternation between the unknown and this awareness of the unknown.

(16-18) The feeling of this alternation is a religion in three forms: (i) an absolute dissatisfaction with the definite dualism of truth and untruth, (ii) an absolute condemnation of the attitude in which any religion is taken to be false, and (iii) a faith that all religions are not only true but identical. These are bound up with the views (i) that the negation of negation is negation, (ii) that the negation of absolute negation is the absolute truth of all affirmations, and (iii) that absolute negation and absolute affirmation are mutual negation in indentity. Such is the absolute, as distinct from the subjectivistic, interpretation of the view that truth is manifold.

SOME ASPECTS OF NEGATION

1. The aim of this paper is to bring out the fact that there are certain ultimate modes of logical thought embodying types of negation which are really incommensurable and that all philosophical dispute resolves itself in the final analysis into a conflict between such types. Every system of philosophical thought or religion has its own logic and is bound up with one or other of the fundamental views of negation. Each furnishes its distinctive criticism and orientation of the others: it is impossible to refer them all to a single court of trial and probably the only demand should be that a philosophy or religion and its distinctive logic justify each other. Not that, however, subjectivism or scepticism is the necessary consequence: all the types may be true and truth itself may be manifold. It is necessary to formulate, if possible, the logic of this view of the manifoldness of truth.

2. Negation is intelligible as illusion. When an object is known to be illusory, what kind of being or non-being do we attribute to it? We answer the question too easily when we say that it has a subjective being but no objective being. The antithesis between subjective and objective has only been reached very gradually in the history of thought and there is every reason to regard it as contingent. There is a too facile falling back upon psychology as a secure anchorage, although it should be an open question whether psychical fact is fact at all.

3. To say 'this object is not existent' is to imply either that *this* is no object but something else is, or that this object is no object. In the former case, 'this' is something which can be spoken of without being object; it has a being which is not objective being, and so negation means only a *difference* between this peculiar being and objective being. This peculiar being need not at once be spoken of as subjective being: that would be to identify without sufficient proof yet a mental state with the content of it i.e., with what it refers to. Such an abstract being would be the starting point of a view which interprets negation as mere difference: concrete being would be only a determination of it—determination in a sense which will appear presently. In the latter case where the illusory object is regarded as an object which is no object, negation does not mean mere difference: contradiction itself which is no abstract being is the starting point. We begin then by distinguishing these two starting points—abstract

being and contradiction and these we expect to indicate a deep line of cleavage throughout philosophy.

4. The different shades of views in the first type of thought require to be developed in order to be brought into definite relation to the second type.

(i) Negation emerges only when an illusion has been corrected, when, for example, we say 'A is real, *not* X'. Has X here anything to do to determine or define A? It may be held that A is here by its own right and that it owes nothing to X which is simply to be rejected or outgrown. 'A' which is wholly given is not X: it gains or loses nothing by rejecting X. There is no relation between A and X to define A: truth is never determined by relation, truth *is not* relation, i.e., all relation is illusory. Negation is always difference in this type of thought; all relation implies difference, and the primal relation is the difference between fact and illusion. Hence the relation between two facts A and B is itself no fact: each of them is a fact by its own right and each rejects the other as illusion. Positive relation between A and B is only this mutual rejection *by* two given beings: what *are* only rejected are not related at all, are neither identical nor different, and so the region of negation is the region of the indefinite.

(ii) If, however, A and B are negations of each other and yet facts, it may be said that an illusion X, by the correction of which A is posited, is only the name of *another fact;* only, this is not X, this is A. Something else is X, X is not nothing, and the illusion is only in the inherence of X in *this.* The illusion is not in the 'that' or in the 'what' of the given content but in their particular relation: a judgment alone can be false, not any term of the judgment, nor the bare relation apart from the terms. The false judgment however has a definite form, as definite as the corresponding true judgment; and the relation between these judgments is expressed in the definite negative judgment. 'This is X' is the false judgment corresponding to 'this is A', the true judgment; and their relation is 'this is not X'. In fact the primal judgment is simply the opposition between two terms like 'this A' and 'this X' expressed as 'this A is not this X', through which there emerge the affirmative judgments 'this is A' and 'this is X' and the concepts of truth and falsity as applied to them. The simple negation appears as a difference between two terms but is really an opposition between two judgments and in fact the judgments are judgments because of this simple negation. All relation is at bottom this simple negation or difference, the opposition of truth and falsity is the opposition of a true and false relation, and so relation is not necessarily an illusion as in the previous view. Truth, however, in this view is the *relation* of two beings as set against some other relation: not the abstract beings but these as related constitute the true starting point. This relation is never without the terms, nor the terms without the relation; and yet neither side is *constituted* by the other. This relation which keeps up the difference of the terms and is itself different from them is *inherence.* So we have as facts not only particular given beings but also particular relations of these beings, illusions being included in such particular relations. In this view then, illusions are particular and definite relations: the relations of terms, which are facts are not constituted by these illusions and so terms too are not constituted by their relation.

(iii) It may be asked however, if terms and their relation are inseprable, if in the primal negative judgment, 'this A is not thisX', the illusion is inseparable from the fact, and if both the illusion and the fact are particular and definite, by what criterion are illusion and fact distinguished at all? In the view just considered, each negation is at once the distinction; but then as there is no *universal* negation, so there can be no universal fact-character also. This means that fact and illusion are not distinguishable by any general character at all. A particular fact is *not* the corresponding illusion and it is *not* also another fact: there is nothing to distinguish these two negations. So the conclusion should be that a particular fact and the corresponding illusion are *identical* and that the positive relation of inherence, therefore, is reducible to this identity of position and negation.

Particularity in the first two views as above considered is ultimately *given.* In the present view however, the particularity of a position is constituted by that of its negation and vice versa. Each position is different from an infinity of other positions and is thus constituted by an infinity of differences, by infinite negation. Each negation too would thus be the negation of infinite position i.e., a negation identical with infinite position. There would thus emerge the conception of the identity-in-difference of the finite and the infinite, and of infinite negation and infinite position. Every term, however, is not only constituted by its negation of other terms but it is also, as explained in the previous view, through such negation turned into a judgment, relation, or negation opposed to i.e., negating other judgments, relations or negations. A whirl of negation then alone remains but it is still regarded as the positive.

(iv) There is nothing however to distinguish such a positive from negation. Here then we definitely leave behind abstract being which was our first starting point and start with contradiction itself or transcendent negation as our first principle. We may next take being as only *posited* by this negation. The uniqueness of particularity is then not removed and need not also be removed. It is not taken indeed as ultimately *given*: it is held as *free* determination by this negation but yet as inexplicable or unpredictable. From the vortex of negation *any* particular may spring and so particulars have only to be accepted as they come and related into a world, positive for all particular purposes but with an absolute inexplicability as the ground of it all. We have accordingly equal right to take particular being as *superseded* by this inexplicability or retracted into this whirl of negation.

5. Being then is progressively reduced to negation in these four views. In view (i), the particular simple beings are ultimately given and are not in any way determined by negation or the indefinite. In view (ii), both the beings and their negations are given as particular and so all relations are also given as facts. In view (iii), particularity is not given but posited or constituted by definite absolute negation. This however does not abolish their dualism: their identity and their difference remain as inexplicabilities, though not as given beings. In view (iv) finally, being is abolished and absolute negation alone remains, not only as inexplicably definite but also as inexplicably self-related or self-negating i.e., as a free function or activity.

6. The true value of these views of negation appears in the concrete types of philosophy and religion in which they take shape. They indicate certain distinctive temperaments or attitudes towards truth, certain familiar modes of handling a given content. One's first impulse is to attend to what is confusedly given, to break up its continuity, to single out its elements, to analyse. It is the attitude of positive attention to the elements and although it means the withdrawal of the mind from the given confused content, this negative direction of attention is not itself attended to. The given confused aspect also is not attended to, it is simply forgotten or left behind. The next stage is that in which the given aspect is remembered along with the elements analysed out, is distinguished from them and is recognised to contain them. The elements are separated and also related. The given complex and the relation of the elements alternate in the mind, though the alternation itself is not attended to. In the next stage again, the given complex is taken as identical with the related elements and so the elements themselves are felt to be identical. When thus however alternation is stopped and difference superseded by positive attention

to this identity, the identity has lost the placid being of the given: it is felt to be an inexplicability, a dream, a being that is negation through and through—a perfect revel of negation. Positive attention denies itself utterly and the denial itself is known, not by positive attention to it but by attention directed to the positive object alone. Positive attention is recognised as a withdrawal from its own withdrawing activity; in other words, negative attention is known by negative attention to it.

7. In all accounts of attention, the positive direction is alone emphasised: it alone is taken to be under control and capable of being cultured. To try to know or to do something is to positively attend: and even to try to forget it or avoid is to attend to something else. And yet in all knowing and in all doing, one has a consciousness of the problem before the effort to solve it, a very peculiar kind of consciousness rousing and regulating the effort, containing in fact both the solution and the effort already within it. It is the 'aching void' of James, of which all determinate knowledge and action are the materialisation. This materialisation is ordinarily left to chance and it is never suggested that negative attention which is the very heart of all mental process can be controlled or cultured by any intensive discipline.

8. The modern pragmatist resolution of truth into will means a recognition in one form of this fourth type of negation. The will that constructs all truth and therefore denies the right of all absolute truth is nothing but this creative negation. Not that pragmatism has suggested any system of discipline for this truth-constructing will: it has not yet told us *how* to construct any particular truth. In this respect it is on a par with absolutism which pronounces reason to be creative of truth but cannot present any method of obtaining a particular truth other than the method of experience. So too the neo-Hegelian formula of self-realisation furnishes no ethical discipline other than that presented by positive morality. When Hegel and others sought to *deduce* physics or history, they recognised the legitimacy of this demand for a method other than experience for obtaining particular truths, though they did not satisfy the demand. This method cannot be other than a discipline of negative attention, the process of accentuating the 'aching void', the deliberate endeavour to see what we *want* to see i.e., to know the want itself or the particular ignorance.

9. We know the absence of an obejct, say of a book on the table by a faculty which is neither perception nor inference. It is not perception, for the absence gives no sensation; and it cannot be inference, for inference must be based on perception. The faculty

however being there, it may be helped out by the perception or inference. It is nearest to psychological introspection, though it knows objective non-existence and not subjective existence merely. The non-existence of a book on the table is an objective fact known by negative attention, defined by relation to the facts obtained by positive attention. Through this negative attention then, we also know a particular negation or absence of knowledge, know the want of a solution and therefore the solution itself. Negative introspective attention accordingly is the faculty that requires to be controlled.

10. The first type of negation which we have considered implies no recognition of the necessity for this control. It leaves the discovery of truth entirely to chance. It suggests nothing but the anxiety to escape the given. It is a mode of self-will in the intellectual region: let only attention assert itself and some truth will come. Still the escape here is nothing but negative attention which however does not know itself. The will is unregenerate here, uncontrolled, capricious: it wants to possess or to rest in the positive, wants anyhow to discharge itself only. In the second type, there is already some sort of recognition of negative attention. There is the positive eagerness still to catch the truth but there is no satisfaction or rest in what is caught and hence there is the positive anxiety to return to the given. The consciousness of the possession of a truth is accompanied by a haunting sense of the truth left behind and so each truth is alternately possessed and left behind. Nothing is rejected, everything is only distinguished, and all judgments are taken to be true but different. This haunting sense of the truth left behind, this positive attention to difference is negative attention itself turned inside out. The unregenerate assertive tendency is still regnant but it is the *negation* that is asserted as a positive difference. The difference is however not taken as constitutive of the position, as it is taken in the third view. This would be the next stage then where positive attention and negative attention are employed as one process, where what is known and what is unknown are viewed as in one necessary system of truth which however is still only positive. This truth in which the will finds rest—for it is still anxious for rest—is not dull being but a free play, a moving identity. So the dream of the construction of truth arises here: truth appears at least as a play of reason, as a music which the mind follows and feels it can reproduce but cannot reproduce. The will cannot construct a particular truth, for it has not faith enough in its omnipotence, though there is an irresistible feeling of omniscience i.e., of truth being absolutely transparent. Hence arise on the one hand the absurdities of

Natur-philosophie and the indolent acquiescence on the other in all given reality as rational. The newness or uniqueness of intuition remains over after all dialectic which proves at best that intuition must be unique. The experience of quality is still utterly unpredictable and religion mocks all attempts to trace its evolution. Faith lours ahead as a dark cloud that refuses to be transparent to reason. The free and undoubting play of reason, the facile dream of the transparency of truth gives place to the absolute abruptness of quality and the deathlike seriousness of faith. Negative attention refuses to be positive: it denies its assertive tendency utterly. All truth is retracted into this self-denying negative attention and what remains over is but the demand for its intensive discipline.

11. We began with a discussion of illusion as a clue to the ascertainment of the several types of negation. To bring out their nature in more concrete terms, it is necessary to consider the illusion of an illusion. It involves a double correction or negation. Something is believed to be real, it is next taken to be illusory, and then again on closer observation it may be pronounced to be *not* illusory. The question is what 'not illusory' means. In the first view, illusion which is the name of the utterly indefinite gets some kind of definition in this connexion. Negation being negated becomes definite though not positive, being set against a positive. This definite negation or 'definite indefinite' is the subjective, the *merely* subjective, which the corresponding positive is *not*. The subjective not only does not constitute the positive, it does not determine it in any way. It means a double triumph for the positive alone: it is not merely by its own right, it asserts this right explicitly. So to say 'this object is not illusory' is to say that this object is not *merely* subjective but is self-identical. There emerges then against the notion of the subjective the notion of the self-existent simple which explicitly rejects all relation and all complexity and is the self-conserving real or monad. So then a double series comes out, the series of the reals as rejecting the subjective series, real atomism *versus* psychical atomism. The self-conserving function of the real is only the function of rejection, for which the real is neither the better nor the worse and so it is nothing real by itself. Yet here it gets a pseudo-objective character: it is the activity or energy of the real. On the other side the subjective is rejected i.e., the definiteness of the idea is proved to be nothing and this predicament of being rejected, like the function of rejecting, gets a pseudo-definiteness as the conscious activity of the idea. This conscious activity of the idea would be called 'thought', being more unreal than the idea and yet on that very ac-

count nearer the positive as the cognition of truth. In this negative or illusory region lies the concept of identity-in-difference. The reals are distinct as rejecting all relation and each idea is distinct as being rejected by a distinct real. But the energies of the reals, which are essentially illusory, have not the distinctness of the reals and hence would arise the notion of one energy or self-activity turning up many different energies. This objective self-activity again would be taken as negating a corresponding subjective self-activity, viz., a self-conscious self determining all cognitions of truth. Such then would be the illusory emanations of negation, the implications of the illusion of illusion in the first view.

12. In the second view, negation being negated becomes not only definite but also positive. Only, this positive would be of a different order from the positive of which it is the negation. This positive being of illusion is our ordinary subjective idea which is not to be disparaged as the merely subjective i.e., as nothing at all. Here too this idea does not constitute the object: each of them is self-identical by being distinguished from the other. We have nothing but particular negations in this view and the relations among these neagtions are of a different order from the relations among the positions. Not-A and not-B are like A and B distinct but not-A rejects A in a way different from that in which A rejects not-A. The idea is conscious of not being object but the object distinguishes itself from the idea by not being conscious. Hence arises the circumstance that an object is definitely related to other *objects* only. In the subjective region, two ideas are not the same though they know, i.e., consciously distinguish themselves from, the same object and so the definite objective relations need not be reflected in correspondingly definite relations of ideas. The ideas may have orders of their own which do not reflect the objective order at all: hence the distinction between true and false cognition. False cognitions would be relations of ideas without the definiteness of the relations of things. Hence while we have the notion of a single system of objects, we cannot speak of the system of ideas as single, which as distinct from the single object-system must be regarded as *many* systems, many minds each definitely related to other minds but indefinitely within itself and to the object-system. Yet the indefinite as such has no place in this view: definite cognitions and indefinite cognitions are alike definite as ideas, definitely connected with the selves as unconscious substrata.

13. In the third view, the illusion of an illusion is not only definite and positive subjective being but as the original illusion which

was pronounced subjective is turned objective, the given is taken to be the identity of the subjective and objective. The distinctness of a particular given position and the corresponding negation vanishes altogether: what is now taken as objective may appear to be subjective and this subjective again may turn out to be objective and so on indefinitely. It may be said that the objective at which we stop at any stage is only *possibly* subjective and has not yet been actually corrected. But every stage is believed to be contingent because there is no ground to believe that it is final. One may be uncertain whether it will turn out to be illusory but uncertainty or indefiniteness has no place either in this view or in the previous view. The uncertainty itself is here a definite negation of knowledge: the stopping at any object is a definite illusion or definite subjective being which is identical with the corresponding reality of absolute knowledge. Limit itself is posited by reason. All truth is hypothesis and all hypothesis is true: the particular truth which is not yet turned into hypothesis is only a hypothesis in relation to the absolute truth. Thus there emerges the identity-in-difference of the given truth and its explanation. The given by itself is abstract thing-in-itself and the explanation by itself is abstract reason. Each is the negation of the other and their synthesis is the concrete positive, the absolute Idea.

14. In the fourth view, this synthesis of mutual negation is not positive at all. The manner in which the present actual stage of knowledge is resolved into a contingency in the previous view may not be accepted as satisfactory. The difference between the problematic and the assertory statements—that the present object *may* be illusory and that it *is* illusory—may be felt to be an absolute difference; and to cover the defect by saying that all particularity *must be* resolvable into universality may sound very much like a bravado. That uncertainty whether or not what is now believed to be real will turn out to be illusory either appears not to affect the belief at all or if it does, it points to a feeling of certitude about the unknowable which is stronger than all knowledge. To say that the feeling is itself the highest knowledge, that this uncertainty is what is *reasonably* to be expected will not remove the uncertainty itself. The uncertainty in fact deepens: it is uncertain whether we should begin philosophy with the *assurance* that uncertainty is necessary or with the *uncertainty* itself.

15. This deeper uncertainty about the starting point of philosophy should, for all we know, be itself the starting point; but meanwhile there may be attempts at compromise. The assurance of reason may be accepted along with the inexpressible negation of it. The posi-

tive may be taken along with the negative but as transcending it. On the one hand, Ideas of Platonic type may be believed to transcend a negative matter and yet to work with it, or on the other the unknowable or unknowables may be regarded as transcending all knowables and yet as positively conditioning them. In either case a positive use is made of negation: it is either the matter that is formed or the real cause, never a bare nothing. There are those who object to all such positive use of negation, although they do not bring out the real implication of their objection viz., that a negative use is to be made of negation. In the fourth view of negation then, what is 'not illusory' is the unknown of which we are aware by the absence of positive knowledge. Here the principle is uncertainty itself, the uncertain alternation between the unknown and this awareness of the unknown.

16. It is this alternation which takes the form of the uncertainty whether philosophy is to start with the faith that all our finality or positiveness, all unique quality, all our present truth in fact is explicable or necessarily to be expected in respect of us as merely finite beings—with this very halting and withal very assured form of omniscience, or with these inexplicabilities themselves. Neither the given nor the explanation, no positive in fact is the beginning or the process or the goal of philosophy. The identity of the given and the explanation, or of the objective and subjective is the last thinkable positive which alternates with negation. This identity (or reason) is a process and as such is itself a negation opposed to a transcendent negation. This latter negation may be indifferently called subjective will (or interest) constructing all truth, or vital impulse moulding a matter known only as its negation, or absolute will determining at once reason and Ideas. It is not the merely subjective of view (i), nor the subjective co-ordinate with the objective of view (ii), nor the absolute reason of view (iii). The negative use of this transcendent negation is religion which is the negation of philosophy and therefore also the true philosophy.

17. Here also in the final stage, the first three views of negation may alternate. The first type would be the religion of nirvāṇa, consisting in an absolute dissatisfaction with the definite dualism of truth and untruth. The negation of negation is itself negation, the dualism of true and false is itself false. The second type would be the religion of absolute toleration, which is a dissatisfaction with all negation, an absolute condemnation of the attitude in which any religion is declared to be false. The negation of any religion is absolute negation and the negation of this absolute negation gives the absolute

truth of all particular affirmations, all particular religions. The third type would present the faith in all religious being not only true but identical. The absolute negation and the particular absolute affirmations are mutual negations in identity. This identity and this mutual negation are then the terminal points of all philosophy. Either side is beyond the dualism of definite truth and untruth.

18. Such is the logic of the manifoldness of truth. The pragmatist interpretation of this manifoldness makes philosophy subjectivistic and logic temperamental. We have endeavoured here to give an absolute, instead of a subjectivistic, interpretation.

PLACE OF THE INDEFINITE IN LOGIC

ANALYSIS*

(i) Logic which ordinarily deals with the definite refers to the indefinite (i) as only subjective, (ii) as an epistemological element of the definite, or (iii) as the dialective function of negation constructive of the definite. Should not logic find place for the absolute indefinite, in view especially of the metaphysic of the irrational?

(2-5) Logic as dealing with the form of all thought-content should consider primarily if there is any form which is not matter i.e., which is prior to all determinate doctrine and controversy, scientific and metaphysical. Epistemology, as it is, presupposes determinate principles supposed to be above criticism and hence it lapses into metaphysics. Logic should criticise the basis of this science and start with an absolutely abstract first principle which can be neither a self-evident axiom nor a contingent law, viz., with the bare dualism of the definite and the indefinite, to deny which is to admit it. All dualisms except this admit of a third something beyond. If stated as a law at all, the principle would be 'the definite is not and is the indefinite', i.e., the line between the definite and the indefinite is itself indefinable.

(5-7) It is different from the dialectic principle of the identity of being and non-being which lays more stress on identity than on difference. Against dialectic, it urges that there is an alternative—unreason—beyond the identity of being and non-being which is reason; against conceptualist logic, that there is the indeterminate beyond determinate affirmation and negation; and against empirical logic, that the positive object of experience is a determination carved out of the indeterminate. It not only thus extends but modifies the logic of the definite: it brings out the indefinite given character of determinate experience, of relation (including contradiction), and of systemic or necessary unity quite as much as it emphasises their character as determinate negations of the indefinite.

(8-10) Logic starts neither with pure being and non-being nor with determinate being and non-being but with '*this* determinate', where determinateness or 'this-ness' is being or negation or their identity and the 'this' a transcendental indefinite. This indefinite is determined into the relation in a judgment—identity and difference; and so of affirmation and negation, neither is prior to the other. The necessity in reasoning, again, is in reference to this indefinite, whether taken as a given system of position as in empirical logic, as a given system of analytic relations as in conceptualist logic, or as a given self-creating system of functions as in dialectic.

(11-16) Dialectic only shows that a given category *was* necessary: it does not create it and yet *somehow* such prophecy after the event is synthetic knowledge. As, however, the inferential expectation of material truth is only probable, the ideal form of inference has to be distinguished from the material process. To conceptualist logic, this form of analytic necessity is *given* and is *somehow* applied to the matter of experience. To empirical logic, the material process—from particulars to particulars—which is really indefinite is *somehow* definite. Kant shows that the forms of conceptualist logic are not merely given but are synthetic necessities, they being necessarily applicable to experience which, however, in its particularity is unanticipable. So Spencer shows against empirical logic that inference is not only a psychological transition but implies a consciousness of necessity or justification and that the given definite experience is but the unknowable breaking forth into the relation of difference. Both bring out the transcendental indefinite but both take it uncritically to be *real*. But the indefinite is really a third category, beyond reality and negation, and thus not a transcendental implicate only but a content of positive logic. It may be called unknowable negation or reality and so metaphysically we may deny the knowable world, not only in absolute intuition but in logical thought and admit at the same time determinate noumena or phenomena or both as real specifications of the indefinite. We may make a metaphysical use of the indefinite in either way; and in reference to this indefinite, the distinction between necessity and fact, negation and position itself becomes indefinite.

(17) Two applications : (i) *all and some*. In 'all A', the denotation determined by the definite connotation is definite as denying the indeterminate differences of the particulars which are still implied; and 'some A' means not only this indefinite but also a definite, suggesting that the connotation of A is indefinitely modified by a determinative x. So sub-alternation may or may not be opposition.

(18-26) (ii) *Negative conditional propositions*. In logic of the definite, conditionals are admitted only as intending a definite element *explicitly against* a mass of indefinite implication; and negation (i.e., indefinite negation) of this definite element is supposed only to yield abortive propositions. Yet such negation may be practically useful and so the negative hypothetical should be a definite form in logic. The indefinite disjunctive 'A is either B or not-B', where not-B stands for a definite or an indefinite positive or for nothing at all, is really *negative* in relation to the definite 'A is either B or C' and is in fact the very form of ultimate alternation between knowledge and ignorance, between the definite and the indefinite.

PLACE OF THE INDEFINITE IN LOGIC

1. The purpose of this paper is to examine what modifications of logical doctrine would be necessitated by the admission of the indefinite in logic, side by side with definite position and definite negation. In logic which ordinarily deals with the definite content of thought only, the indefinite is considered in at least three ways. It may be regarded explicitly as extralogical, as only something subjective or psychological which it is the purpose of the science to outgrow or supersede. Sometimes it is treated as provisionally definite; both the uncertain and certain relation of the knowing faculty to the object is taken to yield definite forms of positive logic, the indefinite in fact being admitted as only an epistemological element of the definite content of logic.[a] In dialectic, it is taken as definite function of truth itself, as the *function* of negation which is neither a mere epistemological element nor a static truth by itself but still a constructive factor of definite truth only. Our inquiry is whether and how logic should find place for the absolute indefinite as distinct from the indefinite that is only constitutive of the definite and our prima facie justification for the inquiry is that there is such a thing as a metaphysic of absolute doubt—at least a philosophy of the irrational—and that logic as the prolegomena to all science and metaphysics should not commit itself to the particular metaphysical faith in the finality of a definite system of truth. The indefinite has found in fact a place in metaphysics in many forms. To mention only a few at random, there is the 'negative' matter of Plato, the māyā of the Vedāntists, and the śūnyam or 'void' of the Buddhists. There is the notion of objective chance in Aristotle and of the inexplicable change of direction of the atoms of Lucretius. There is the conception of the indeterminate will, specially in the extreme form of unmotived or irrational activity, as presented by a Duns Scotus, a Schopenhauer, or a Bergson and there is finally the Unknowable whether of Kant or of Spencer. These notions are at present homeless in logic; there is no category to express them and disputes arise in connexion with them in metaphysic which properly should have arisen in logic itself.

2. It is necessary to begin by clearly defining the scope of logic as conceived here. Whatever may have been the origin of the science, in its present state it can hardly be treated except mainly as a positive

[a] See ref. to Venn § 19.

science distinct alike from psychology and the objective sciences and concerned with the most abstract principles, not only of all science, but of all philosophy. It deals with the object or content of all knowledge claimed as such and in this sense is an objective science, though the object here means all thinkables, subjective, objective, and absolute. It considers only the form of the object, not the matter and so its primary problem should be whether there is any form which is not matter, which is not determinate, which is undeniably presupposed in all determinate concrete thought, accepted or disputed, which in fact—paradoxical as it may sound—is not affected even by the uncertainty of this problem. It is not the primary purpose of logic to develop this form, if it can be discovered, into the ground-principles or categories of the several concrete departments of thought. That would be committing oneself to a particular system of metaphysic; and logic, as prior to all metaphysic, can only indicate these by way of bringing out all that it does not deal with. For purposes of logic, in other words, it should be assumed that all intuitions that are claimed as such and all sciences and philosophies *may* be true; it must be universal in the sense not only of presenting the form common to all that is claimed as knowledge but also as presenting the form of all doubt and dispute.

3. This view of logic is forced upon as by the circumstance that it has to take account not only of the positive sciences but also of metaphysics. Metaphysics in re-opening the fundamental questions assumed to be settled in the sciences presents many alternative solutions of which it is not for logic to accept or reject any on the ground of commonsense, for the whole purpose of the science is to replace the rough and ready rule of the thumb. A similar problem gave rise to epistemology as a prolegomena to all branches of knowledge claimed as such but there is this difference from logic as we conceive it here that it itself represents a body of knowledge that is determinate or uncriticised, resting as it does either on the authority of introspection or on that of traditional logic for the solution of the critical problem without a prior criticism of these authorities themselves. This prior criticism, if undertaken, would yield us logic proper, with its absolutely abstract or fundamental character. If epistemology has not been able so far to maintain its role of a prolegomena and has come to be a mere chapter in some metaphysical system, dialectical or other, it is because it has not stripped itself, to start with, of all determinate presuppositions, because in fact it has not been fundamental enough. That the transcendental logic of Kant, for example,

led to the positive dialectic logic of Hegel only shows that the antithesis between the transcendental and positive is not absolute in the sphere of the determinate. In both, the abstractions with which logic is taken to be conversant are taken to be constructive functions: they are viewed as at once analytic and synthetic. In Kant, the analytic moment indeed remains transcendental in view of a consciousness of a limit to reason, of an indefinite thing-in-itself; but this consciousness of the indefinite is not taken seriously to affect the epistemology itself. The definite unity of the self and its synthetic specification into a definite system of categories are obviously suggested by the presuppositions of a particular system of metaphysic, viz., the developmental, and the indefinite itself is taken to be *real* without criticism. Logic in our present conception, however, in endeavouring to supply the abstract form of epistemological knowledge itself would stand on a height of abstraction where the distinction of the transcendental and the positive is obliterated. The synthetic developmental principle has no necessary place in it any more than the principle of determinate identity, for it has no right to build on a determinate metaphysical presupposition: the principle of logic should be absolutely abstract.

4. Can we have such a science at all? If we demand a criticism of epistemology, should we not demand a criticism of the criticism and so on ad infinitum? Epistemology starts with a principle that it believes to be self-evident or necessary. If however, a real doubt is cast on the principle, if the basis of intuition or axiom in general is challenged as it has been challenged, logic as such has no right to enter into the dispute and to take sides; and so on in criticising epistemology, it cannot stand on any so-called necessary or self-evident principle. To start with a determinate contingent principle would be equally absurd and so it can only stand on an indeterminate principle which can indifferently be called necessary or contingent. This principle can be no other than the bare dualism of the definite and indefinite, in which neither has even the specific implication of reality or unreality. A further criticism of this dualism is unintelligible, for the negation of the principle is nothing other than the principle itself.

5. To explicate this principle. The most abstract and comprehensive dualism that can be conceived is that between the definite and the indefinite. It is possible to show in the case of any other dualism that can be proposed that there is a *third* something beyond it. Even in the case of being and non-being, one can cite an indefinite

that is neither, call it the unknowable or freedom or whatever else. It is not necessary to present the dualism of definite and indefinite in the form of a judgment as a law of thought, for the law-form is only a form among forms: the judgment is not the necessary logical unit in such logic as is conceived here. But if a law-form is demanded for this principle—the word 'principle' is sufficiently general in philosophical usage, it may be presented in the paradoxical form—the indefinite is not and is indefinite at once. It is similar to the dialectical principle of the identity of being and not-being but there is the difference that in the latter, more stress is laid in the last resort on the identity than on the difference between the opposed terms: the synthesis of position and negation is uncritically taken to be only positive, and the final synthesis viz., the absolute is taken as a positive system of truth. In the principle we have presented, equal stress is laid on the identity and difference of the opposed terms; what it amounts to is that the line between the definite and the indefinite is itself indefinite that the minimum of difference from the indefinite that constitutes the abstract definite is a vanishing quantity.

6. The difference from the dialectical principle can be stated in another way. The ground principle of logic has been formulated in at least three ways—in the form of system or reason, in the form of relation or judgment, and in the form of an irrelative term, intuition or experience. The identity of being and non-being points to the conception of system as the ruling conception of dialectic. In conceptualist or intuitionist logic, the fundamental principle is best conceived as a relation between positive terms i.e., as an ordinary judgment like 'this being is not another being'. In empirical logic, an experience is the test of its own truth and so the basal principle may be formulated as 'this determinate being (Mill) or this determinate becoming (Bain) which is not non-being.' In the principle proposed for the logic of the indefinite, no preference is implied for any of these three forms. It is best put as a mere dualism or opposition, definite *and* indefinite, the 'and' expressing apparently the very form of illogicality or the despair of knowledge. It really however expresses the inadequacy of the three forms aforesaid. As against the form of reason, the dialectical principle, it indicates an alternative —unreason—beyond reason: position and negation are not necessarily the moments of the positive absolute. As against the form of judgment, the conceptualist principle as we may call it, it suggests that beyond determinate affirmation and negation, there is the indeterminate (though it may be practically useful) form of doubt or

ignorance. As against the form of the irrelative determinate term—we call it the experimental principle provisionally—it points out that the positive object of experience is always a determination carved out of the indeterminate. It suggests, in fact, that the indefinite has to be recognised as standing outside the term, the judgment, and the inference, that one should go beyond ordinary logic which simply turns its back on the outlying indefinite and looks to the definite as the sole content of thought.

7. Such recognition of the indefinite implies not only an extension of logical doctrine: it involves also a material modification of the logic of the definite. With regard to the term, for example, the determinate object of experience, our principle shows that the boundaries that demarcate it from the surrounding indefinite are themselves indefinite or indefinable, that the particularity of 'this determinate' is something unique which can neither be taken as a separate definite category nor as a necessary determination of the universal and accordingly the 'this' may be indifferently taken as either being (Mill) or as transition (Bain).[a] With regard to the judgment-form, it is pointed out that definite relation, affirmative and negative, is itself indefinite, that if relation is given fact, the 'givenness' is an indeterminate which can be regarded either as an abrupt positive or as a negation of the indefinite and that the negation of the indefinite is indifferently affirmative or negative i.e., the distinction between affirmative and negative is indefinable or in other words, contradiction is just as conceivable as otherwise.[b] With regard to the form of reasoning, our principle would indicate that system or necessary relation is as much a given fact as a negation of negation and that this negation

[a] Within empiricism in fact is reproduced the opposition between the conceptualistic and dialectic views of the *principium individuationis.* To conceptualist logic, individuality as such is properly a unique category of thought, a simple ultimate thought, and there is sometimes a tendency to abolish it altogether. To dialectic, it is a construction through thought as a function. (i) In the empiricism of Mill, corresponding to the simple *thought* of 'this', appears 'this' individual experience, this given simple being. (ii) In Bain however, experience is taken to be a transition; properly no term is given but only a passage, a differentiation between terms. Individuality is only an arbitrary point in this transitional process; it is a conflux of relations or generalities. Existence is admitted as a separate category, distinct from co-existence, sequence, and resemblance by Mill but not by Bain. These conflicting views only show that the unit-term or the individual is at once definite and indefinite, the latter aspect being systematically ignored in ordinary logic.

[b] Here within conceptualism is reproduced the opposition between empirical and dialectical views of *relation.* To empiricism, relation is a given experience; the elementary relations of likeness and difference are taken as ultimate feelings. To dialectic, it is the *function* of negation, the negation of immediacy, the self-distinction of the given. The conceptualist view splits up into at least two types: (i) relation is an ultimate given thought and here the ultimate difference between empiricism and intuitionism is a vanishing one. All relation in fact is positive;

of negation may be taken as equivalent to position or negation indifferently.[a]

8. With the Hegelians then, we admit the identity of being and non-being or necessity but hold that this necessity is itself a contingent fact. So the contradiction between being and non-being is to us as much an object of thought as their non-contradiction; a contradictory judgment is neither inadmissible nor is merely a moment in the necessity of dialectical identity. So, too, the determinate *this* has not simply being and negation in its constitution but also the indefinite or the Unknowable.

9. The indeterminate being or non-being with which Hegel starts is not the same as our indefinite. In the term, 'this determinate', 'this' is something unique to which neither the terms, 'being' or non-being can be applied, though 'thisness' or determinate being may be taken as an identity of being and non-being. As constitutive of 'thisness' then, the indeterminate being or non-being of Hegel is still definite in our sense: 'this' as transcending 'thisness' is unanalysable, indefinable, or indefinite. 'This determinate' may thus be analysed into the three principles—the indefinite, being, and non-being. In reference to the criticism of the Hegelian position that logic should start with determinate being rather than with pure being, we hold that the indefinite, being, and non-being can all be taken as the starting point indifferently, these being all implied in 'this determinate'.

10. With reference to the judgment, our contention is that it is equally true to say that the terms are or are not constituted by their relation, that in it a given matter of fact, a 'this' which is neither definite being not definite non-being is determined into a relation of

negation itself is but positive difference. (ii) Positive relation and negative relation are co-ordinate: absence or void is a category side by side with existence. The given positive stands over against its definite negation: the primary difference is not difference between two positives but between position and negation, this negation being thus a sort of being or position. Thus the distinction between affirmation and negation becomes indefinable. Negation is not being and yet a sort of being. These conflicting views show again that what is taken to be definite relation in ordinary logic is really indefinite.

[a] The opposition between empiricism and conceptualism has to be traced as affecting the integrity of the dialectic view of *system* or necessary relation. To empiricism, system is no given being: the past does not *exist* in the present and yet the present is what it is *because* of the past. The ground of present knowledge is always non-existent. To conceptualism, the relation of ground and consequent is an eternally existent thought. The dialectic movement presents both these tendencies without reconciling them. As the ground of itself (natura naturans), it is a transition, negation of negation, freedom—no existent being. As the consequence of itself (natura naturata), it is the *existent* absolute, the *truth* that is thought through and through. This alternation of the dynamic and static aspects in dialectic points to the fact that system or reason is indefinite in its very constitution.

terms, that the relation is at once identity and difference in reference to this indefinite, and that apart from this indefinite, it is just as true to say that there is as that there is not necessary mutual implication between identity and difference, that the affirmative relation is and that it is not prior to the negative.* As to reasoning, the necessity implied in the 'therefore' is taken by Hegel as the self-creating dialectic of truth itself, as the position created by the negation of negation. In empirical logic, it is taken to be the position contingently reached through other positions, as a particular reached through particulars; and in conceptualist logic, it is the mere explication of a position by negation, as a rendering of a universal premise analytically definite by an individualising minor premise. We, however, hold that the new something reached in the conclusion is really a definition of the indefinite matter to which reasoning has reference and that the necessity is but a contingent fact in this reference.

11. Hegelian Logic does not admit the indefinite but holds instead that dialectic necessity is creative. Its strength lies however only in *seeing* that a real category of given experience *was* necessary, not really in yielding any new category or creating it. Hence where it has sought to create, critics have only seen a dismal failure or found that it was a sort of prophesying after the event. This inability to create is, in fact, the implicit admission of the indefinite. What the critics do not bring out however is that this retrospective prophecy, this *seeing* that a stage which has emerged *was* necessary is a true seeing: they have yet to explain why the dialectic exposition which is not at least explicitly analytic *fits* the category deduced, how an apparent continuity between an old and a new category is at all established by the mere process of negation of negation. It is a form of the old question how what is anticipated by inference comes to be verified by experience and to call it a mere accident or to understand

* The judgment 'A is B' has been understood in at least three ways: (i) A does not exist when A B exists. (ii) A exists when A B exists, (iii) A exists *because* A B does not exist but is a function—the empirical, conceptualist, and dialectic views respectively in typical form. Taking ii, A is in the limit the unique 'this', transcending the determination A B. As indeterminate, it is as much definite being as negation and thus (i) is justified along with (ii). So in (iii), A B, the function or negation, *is* i.e. constitutes A, the existent. Thus A or 'this' is negation, being, and their identity in i, ii, iii respectively: it is in (i) the not-given (not-now-given), in (ii) the given and in (iii) the existent through not being given. A B then is (i) not A, (ii) is not A and yet in A, and (iii) is A by being not A; in other words, the negative relation is *after* the affirmative, *co-ordinate with* the affirmative and *before* the affirmative in the three views.—All these variations of view point to the circumstance that relation is at once definite and indefinite: the admission of the indefinite justifies and falsifies all these views.

a preestablished harmony is simply to give up the problem of explanation.

12. At the same time it is true that such anticipations of inference are not sometimes verified, that only probable truths are reached actually by inference and hence the justification for taking the inferential form as only an ideal and for distinguishing it from the material process of inference itself. This amounts on the one hand to the admission of the analytic necessity within this ideal form as itself *given* and as *somehow* applicable to the indefinite matter of experience and on the other to the view that the synthetic material process is a definite necessity inexplicably emerging out of the indefinite. In conceptualist logic, the definite analytic necessity within the syllogism is understood as the given or intuited ideal and error or uncertainty is taken as only the accident of application. In empirical logic where the ideal is nothing and the material process is all, it only amounts to saying that *somehow* as a matter of fact we pass from particulars to other particulars which are sometimes verified.

13. As against conceptualist logic, Kant holds that the forms of positive logic are not merely given but are synthetic apriori necessities at bottom, that their applicability to experience is not accidental but necessary, that however although matter in general is necessarily demanded by form, *what* specifically the matter will be is unknowable. The Kantian view thus brings out the latent implication of the indefinite in the intuited character and applicability of the forms admitted in conceptualist logic. As against empirical logic, Spencer points out that unless logic is to lapse into psychology, the ideal form has to be taken as necessarily presupposed in the material process, that inference is inference only as implying the consciousness of justification or necessary ground, that this necessary ground or axiom is not only the consolidation of contingent experiences but has the implication of the inconceivability of the opposite and that experience taken as the *given* definite in empirical logic is really the indefinite breaking forth into the relation of difference.

14. Both Kant and Spencer thus bring out the transcendent character of the indefinite but both uncritically take this indefinite to be the unknowable *reality*. Against this however we hold that the indefinite may as well be called the unknowable negation, that in fact it is a third category side by side with position and negation, that it is as much immanent in the definite as transcendent, and that therefore it is not simply the transcendental implicate of definite logic but the content of positive logic itself.

15. Our logic thus finds categories for widely different metaphysical notions of reality, for the notion of the knowable world as unreal in the last resort as well as for the notion of it as a real evolute in all different senses in which it has been taken. Logic as here conceived renders intelligible the denial of the unique positive reality of the given, not only in the sense in which Hegel understands it who admits the reality and takes it to be constructed by negation, but also in the absolute sense. The assertion of the ultimate falsity of the world—falsity not only to absolute intuition but to logical thought itself—is thus conceivable. In positive logic itself, not only is position to be conceived as negation of negation as it is conceived in dialectic: it is to be admitted also that negation of negation may be indefinite negation. At the same time we recognise that the indefinitè may be regarded as real and as embodied in the definite axioms and experiences that we start with as positively *given*. We admit the truth both of conceptualist and empirical logic or—what is the same thing —we can conceive the metaphysical view that determinate noumena or phenomena or both side by side constitute the knowable world. There is nothing finally to prevent us from conceiving that this immanent being is to the transcendent real indefinite a real mode, effect, or objectification, that the definite is a real specification of the indefinite. We thus frankly make a positive use, logical and metaphysical, of the indefinite, unlike Kant and Spencer who while deprecating such positive use of the indefinite view it implicitly as the *real*. Conflicting epistemological notions are also thus logically conceivable: both necessity and fact can be understood alike as an emanation and evolute of the indefinite, and each may be regarded as the other—i.e., necessity may be taken as an inexplicable fact, as the positive stress of the indefinite real and given fact may be viewed as implying negation of an indefinite negation.

16. The general implications of our principle—the indefinite and definite are and are not one—have been brought out as demarcating the logic of the indefinite from other types of logic. The bearing of it on some details taken at random may be discussed by way of further elucidation.

17. *Conception of 'all' and 'some'*. Logic as dealing with the most abstract content of thought, definite and indefinite, has no direct interest in developing the determinate categories of the several departments of knowledge. If it refers to quantity then, even in the vague form of 'all' and 'some', it is only by way of bringing out what it does not deal with. The primary question is whether it starts

with the determinate or the indeterminate and our answer is that the starting point is 'this determinate', where 'this' is the unique indefinite. The difference of the definite and indefinite being itself indefinable, the difference of the determinates from one another is also indeterminate in the last resort. From the side of the definite as fixed by language, we deny this indeterminate difference which we are conscious of, by using the word 'all': the connotation is primarily meant as definite, in view however of the indeterminate differences of the particulars constituting the denotation. The word 'some' on the contrary primarily means this indeterminate difference in view of the definite connotation. The secondary accompaniment in each case is affected by the primary intention. We have said that the definite and the indefinite are not only different but identical and so the indefinite denotation of 'all A'—indefinite as fixed by connotation and not by enumeration—is itself a definite function or form in logic: and the definite connotation of 'some A'—viz., the connotation of A—is itself rendred indefinite, 'some A' being equivalent to 'all A *x*' where *x* is an indefinite determination of A. In so far then as we say that the definite is *not* the indefinite, subalternation may be regarded as an opposition and not so in so far as we admit their identity: the truth of 'all' both denies and admits the truth of 'some'.[a] This only means that quantity-difference which is the object or content of thought and not merely psychological is itself indefinite and that these contradictory views about 'all' and 'some' may be both true. Logic should consider this fact of alternation only: it should not be its business to develop the quantitative doctrine itself into some sort of logical algebra or geometry. Nor is it its business to settle the psychological or metaphysical question of the concept, although in thus defining its own business, it would indirectly indicate the germs of the concrete solutions of the question that have been presented.

[a] There are the two ordinary views: (i) 'some' means *not* 'all'; (ii) some does not deny 'all'—i.e. (i) some is a definite negation of 'all'. (ii) 'some' is indefinite. In both views, 'some' is taken as both definite and indefinite in a sense e.g. in (i) though it means 'not all', it is indefinite which individuals and how many are meant.—Still it is held that this indefiniteness is only subjective: to logic, it means the definite 'not all', definite because 'not all A' means 'all Ax' —i.e. the connotation of A as qualified by an unknown but real adjective *x*. In (ii), though 'some' is indefinite as not denying 'all', it means definitely at least one individual having the connotation of the class: the indefinite is thus provisionally treated as definite in logic. The second view does not assume what the first does that 'some A' is necessarily equivalent to *another* universal, viz., A*x*; and the first does not assume what the second does that any individual A is definitely known to have the predicate B in the judgment 'some A is B'. The first would assert 'some A is B' on the two definite grounds (1) that at least one individual A has been found to be *not* B and (2) that therefore the real connection of B is not with A but with A*x*. The second would assert it on the ground (1) that at least one A *is* B and (2) that other A's are either B or not B.

18. *Negative conditional propositions.* Can conditional propositions be negative? (1) There are the opposite views about the hypothetical proposition—(a) As distinct from the categorical, its sole function is to express the logical or objective dependence of one relation on another. Non-dependence is no objective relation at all and requires no logical form to express it. The consciousness of it is purely privative: that I cannot connect a consequent with an antecedent is a mere subjective incapacity. There is therefore no negative hypothetical. (b) It may be contended however that in any case the negative categorical is allowed in this view (we need not discuss the extreme view according to which no negative relation is admitted in logic) i.e., the negative relation is admitted as objective, though with the implied assumption that it is equivalent to a definite affirmative which may not be known yet. As a logical form then, the negative categorical is admissible where subjectively there is the ignorance of its affirmative equivalent. Now there should be a difference between the dependence of an affirmative consequent and that of a negative consequent on a given antecedent. The quality of the dependence itself varies with the quality of the consequent and hence a negative hypothetical should be admitted if a negative categorical is admitted. To be negative the hypothetical need not express non-dependence but only dependence of a negation.

19. The dispute here really turns on whether the quality of the dependence is affected by the quality of the consequent. Where we do not know yet what affirmation is equivalent to the negative consequent, should we say that the hypothetical proposition itself is negative? Should we express the state of knowledge there by a hypothetical form at all? We take the example—'if the keys cannot be found in this room after so much search, they are not here'. I do not know *where* the keys are then and still it may be useful to

The first emphasises the defect of connotation (A should be determined into A*x*), i.e. the indefiniteness of the connotation which is taken to be definite in 'all A' and the second emphasises the indefiniteness of the denotation in 'some A' which is already indefinite in 'all A', though the point is provisionally ignored there. 'All A' in fact is both definite and indefinite, definite in connotation and indefinite in denotation. 'Some A', as *in*definite in connotation (A—A*x*) is a negation of 'all A'; but 'some A', as indefinite in denotation, is no negation of 'all A', the indefinite being indefinitely related to the indefinite.—The recognition of the indefinite as a logical and not merely a subjective, element brings out the truth of both the views of 'some' and 'all'. The logic of the indefinite thus not only makes conflicting logical doctrines intelligible: it points out the essential indeterminateness of the concept, and the really extralogical character of quantity—showing that logic is here uselessly racked with disputes about what as outside its scope must be disputed and indicating that the doctrine of quantity is capable of being developed, not only from the side of the determinate but also from that of the indeterminate.

express the circumstance in the negative hypothetical form: I need not waste time searching for it in this room for the reason stated. But it is urged in the first view that what is expressed in this proposition is only something subjective: there is no objective connexion between the antecedent and the consequent, the absence of the keys here being not conditioned by the fruitless search. But this only means that the keys have not been removed from the room in consequence of the fruitless search. The absence of the keys need not however mean this positive removal and may yet be a useful truth that is inferred from i.e., is conditioned by the fruitless search as its reason or ground. It is not the content of mere ignorance. Mere ignorance, it may be said, need not be expressed in logic: what is called the privative judgment in logic is *useless*. The proposition about the keys is useful and yet is not the expression of an objective dependence of a positive fact. Should this intermediate state of consciousness between mere ignorance and positive objective knowledge be expressed in logic? Venn has pointed out the fallacy of over-objectification in logic: to him, logic deals with the *passage* from the subjective to the objective. We hold that logic as dealing with object in the abstract sense of content of thought can never *over*-objectify and that the real truth of Venn's view is that logic deals with the passage from the indefinite to the definite in the object. The useful knowledge about the keys which is not yet positive objective knowledge has a content or object distinct alike from the absolutely indefinite and useless content of ignorance and from the definite object of the positive knowledge of the whereabouts of the keys: it is at once indefinite and definite and as such should have a logical expression. The logic of the indefinite would therefore admit the negative hypothetical and point out that its logical status is indefinite—somewhere intermediate between the forms of positive knowledge and absolute ignorance, and a stage removed in point of definiteness from the negative categorical judgment. The negative categorical is already the explicit objective embodiment of partial ignorance: it assigns a provisional being to negation in relation to a position. In an affirmative hypothetical also, the *contingent* being of the relation in the consequent is such an explicit objective embodiment of partial ignorance: the assertory being of the categorical relation is modified by a negation into a possibility. The negative hypothetical then is an objective embodiment of a double ignorance or negation but is still in view of a position and therefore useful.

20. It may be noted in passing that the issues here are similar to those which arise in the Vedāntic discussion of the illusion of illu-

sion.[*] An illusion being positively *given* has an 'indescribable being' according to Vedānta, even when it is corrected. Has the illusion of illusion such a being also? A compromise between plain yes and no is given by some Vedāntists viz., that the illusion of illusion is *given* in a way different from i.e., more indefinitely than illusion itself. A similar difficulty may be pressed against Bradley's view of the negative judgment. It presupposes, he says, not a full-formed affirmative judgment but only a question. What is the nature of the question? He himself takes it to be *only psychological,* an ideal suggestion, a floating idea. Bosanquet however would take it as a logical content, a rudimentary disjunction. Sigwart would call it a rudimentary positive judgment—i.e., a merely *given* relation. They all admit that a full affiirmative judgment need not be presupposed by the negative and yet *what* precisely do they contend about? It is really somewhere intermediate between the *content* of thought and the mere psychological *fact* of thought. This transitional something between the definitely psychological and the definitely logical can only be taken cognisance of in such logic as has been conceived in this paper.

21. (2) As to the disjunctive proposition, the ordinary view is that it cannot be negative in the disjunctive form. The definite element in 'A is either B or C' is that A is in B and C taken together and sometimes the definite side is pushed further to imply the mutual exclusion of B and C. There is indefiniteness then at least as to *which* of the two, B and C, is predicated of A: the disjunctive is so far an explicit embodiment of partial ignorance. It would be held then that 'A is either not B or not C' is not the logical denial of 'A is either B or C', for if the ignorance-element in both is considered, there is no denial, an indefinite being only *indefinitely* related to an indefinite, and if the knowledge-element in both is considered, B plus C is either the same as or a part of not-B plus not-C. In reference to the knowledge-element however, we intend to point out as in the case of subalternation that if the connotative side as distinct from the denotative side of B and C is considered, there is an intelligible sense in which B plus C may be taken as the negative of not-B plus not-C.

22. Those who hold that 'A is either B or C' do not deny that A may be both really point to this connotative side: the precise relation between the denotations of B and C may remain indefinite according to them when the disjunctive is asserted. From this stand-

[*] Something is believed to be real it is next taken to be illusory, and then again on closer observation it may be pronounced *not* illusory. What does 'not illusory' mean?

point then 'either not B or not C' would be doubly indeterminate. In 'A is either B or C', it is only affirmed that the connotations of B and C are compatible with that of A. This compatibility is a definite logical content but the mutual relation of B and C understood connotatively is indefinite; the mutual relation of not-B and not-C then would be doubly indefinite. The problem is to find out the value of this double indefiniteness.

23. We may distinguish our position here from at least four positions that may be conceivably advanced. (1) It may be held that the negation of the indefinite 'either B or C' in the form 'either not-B or not-C' has nothing definite in it and is absolutely useless. (2) There is just the opposite view that 'either not-B or not-C' is the same as 'either B or C', B and C being already exclusive. (3) Or it may be held that the mutual exclusion of B and C is indefinite in 'either B or C', and that 'either not-B or not-C' makes this definite, that it amounts to a more definite affirmation and is therefore no *negation* at all; it is *extra* affirmation, an *added* truth *side by side* with the definite truth of 'either B or C' . Or (4) it may be urged that this extra affirmation is a *development* of 'either B or C' rather than an accretion, that it is undoubtedly a negation but amounting to an affirmation. 'Either not-B or not-C' is taken as (1) no logical form at all or (2) as identical with 'either B or C' or (3) as different from it but not a denial of it or (4) as a denial of it that amounts to a definite affirmation which is at once same and different. Our position however is that 'either not-B or not-C' is the form of the *indefinite denial* of 'either B or C'. It is denial of the definite element in it—viz., the compatibility of B and of C with A: that the compatibility itself is partial or indefinite, is *not* definite is pointed out by 'A is either not B or not C'. As the denial of what is believed to be a definite element in 'A is either B or C', it is itself *believed* in and is not dumb ignorance: it has a useful content which yet is not positive, not the same as the given affirmative nor something co-ordinate with it, nor a negation amounting to a definite positive.

24. That 'A is either not B or not C' is the negation of 'A is either B or C' may be shown in another way. The ordinary form given of its negation is 'A is neither B nor C'. This however states more than the mere negation which should be simply 'A *may* be neither'. If not-B and not-C are understood as the negation of the connotative side of B and C, 'A is either not-B or not-C' is equivalent to 'A is either B or C or neither', which means precisely that A may be neither.

25. In speaking of a logical form being useful, we have assumed only for the sake of the argument that the merely privative judgment, the expression of mere ignorance is useless. It is necessary now to point out that the word 'useful' is itself a question-begging term: it dogmatically assumes that the knowing self ought to move towards more and more determinate truth. This assumption itself may be questioned and the logical impulse may be taken to be satisfied in the correction of the given error of determinateness, not in the attainment of new determinations, in getting rid of the limitation of the definite and not in securing increase of definiteness, in the direction of the indefinite and not in that of the definite,—freedom or the absolute state being reached either way. In this 'undefining' process, as we may call it, it is not even necessary that empirical truth should be held fast provisionally. All doubt, including what is taken to be the most irresponsible form of it—viz., absolute scepticism, would be *useful* in this connexion, though there might be grades of usefulness here also. Logic, conceived to deal with the bare dualism of the definite and indefinite can make room for either kind of usefulness or truth.

26. This may be presented in terms of the disjunctive proposition. The proposition 'A is either B or C or neither' may be taken as equivalent to 'A is either B or not-B', the bare form of the Excluded Middle. Now this form may be taken (1) as absolutely useless, a joke, the mere form of ignorance; (2) as the limiting form of disjunction, and therefore a particular case of disjunction, giving us the form of truth i.e., of the universe as constructed by thought out of the unique given; (3) as the form of the determinate— determinate position and negation as co-ordinate—present in all particular disjunctions; or (4) as the abstract form of truth *developed* in all concrete disjunctions, in all grades of determinate knowledge. Not-B in these views is (1) nothing logical at all, (2) logical only in relation to the unique but definite 'givenness' of B, (3) a positive logical content side by side with B and (4) the logical implication of B, as B is of not-B. In conformity to what we have said above, we hold that not-B is something logical, though not definite: it is the logical useful indefinite. 'A is either B or not-B' is a logical negative of 'A is either B or C'; utterly indeterminate in contrast with it but determinate as expressing the fundamental logical principle of the disjunction of the definite and indefinite, the form of the knowable-unknowable, the form of mystery rather than of absolute truth, the limiting mystery of all philosophy.

THE DEFINITION OF RELATION AS A CATEGORY OF EXISTENCE

ANALYSIS

(1) An attempt is made here to establish a definition of 'relation' in objective terms on the assumption that 'relation' of objects is not a mere mode of knowing them but is as definite and objective as the terms themselves. (2) Two terms A and B may be presented together to thought (a) either as mere distincts or (b) one may be thought as distinct from the other. (b) again has two varieties: the distinction may be thought (i) either in both 'directions' or (ii) only in one direction. (3) On the alternative *a, distinction* is not thought at all and the thought of the 'and' cannot be said to be definite like that of A and B. On the alternative *b (i),* we get either the reinstatement of *a* and so of the indefiniteness of *and* or the indefiniteness of A and B which, however, would be contrary to the starting assumptions. (4) The alternatives *a* & *b* (*i*) thus getting eliminated, it is only *b* (*ii*) that remains over to be examined. In 'A distinct from B', there is no confusion between the thinking of B and the distinguishing of A. The distinction of A is together—not with the thinking of B but—only with B. Thus 'A distinct from B' represents a distinct act of thinking. (5) Is it also definite as a content? Now, B here may be said to be *given* as distinct or the intrinsically distinct and A is only distinct *from* or the extrinsically distinct content. The togetherness of the extrinsically distinct and the intrinsically distinct is more definite than the togetherness of two mere distincts, for the concepts 'extrinsic' and 'intrinsic' distinction serve to fix the relative positions of A and B.

(6-7) Relation has sometimes been taken to be definite but holding between terms one of which is indefinite. But the indefinite is what we are barely acquainted with and cannot be described and used as a term. (8) Mere *togetherness* of two distincts has sometimes been taken to be a relation. But this 'togetherness'—A *and* B—is not distinctly thought. (9) There is, again, the infinite regress if 'A and B' is taken as a single definite thought. This regress can be avoided on the theory of 'pure togetherness'. (10) But 'pure togetherness' as what is common to the definite whole and the definite disjunction of A and B amounts to 'either both or not both A and B' which is nothing but an indefinite alternation and is no definite relation at all. (11) Not 'pure togetherness' but togetherness in a unity may be taken to be the relation of A and B. This unity may be (i) a disjunction or (ii) a whole. (12-13) (i) Now, disjunction of A and B, even if it be taken to be a definite unity, is a standing cycle A B A. But this cycle is hardly a relation being just an indetermination of term and relation. (14-15) (ii) Neither can the relation of A and B be taken to be a static whole of the two. That would be only to invite an indefinite regress. (16) The notion that elements are related by the fact of their being in a whole may be replaced by the theory that relation is always between element and whole. The whole may be a substance (or unity of attributes) or it may be a unity of such substances. The two relations are incommensurable and appear to be only nominally described as the *same* relation of element and whole. (19) The difference may be expressed by saying that though attribute is spoken of as *in* a substance and part as *in* a whole, in the former what is *in* is dependent and in the latter it is independent. (20) We have thus to avoid the concept of 'whole' in trying to characterise 'relation' in general.

(21-23) 'Relation' is to be understood in terms of 'dependent' and 'independent' which are intelligible as characters of terms without reference to relation. A term is said to be a 'dependent' when it is not only intrinsically distinct but *necessarily* so. It is said to be an 'independent' when it is thinkable as object apart from a given dependent. When then a dependent is thought as an object along with and distinct from an independent, the former is said to be objectively related to the latter. (24) This definition avoids the petitio of using the concept of relation. The use of the term 'along with' is harmless, for it is understood as not objective but only as a character of subjectivity. The definition amounts to saying that if we think in a certain way, we think of *objective* relation. (25) It is to be noted that relation like distinction is irreversible. Mutual relation is not objective relation: mutual contact is only an attribute. (26-29) Elaboration of the distinction between attribute and relation. (30) Objective relation implies a reference to thinking on the one hand and to the objective *fundamentum* on the other. The reference to thinking must not be more than the bare thinking together of objects. The objective *fundamentum*, again, must not be the mere distinctness of each object.

THE DEFINITION OF 'RELATION' AS A CATEGORY OF EXISTENCE

1. The paper starts with the postulate that objects exist as distinct from the knowing of them and that knowing itself exists as an object for a further act of knowing. It assumes that objects including knowing may both be related and unrelated and that relation of objects is not a mere mode of knowing them but is as objective as the terms. The question has arisen whether such relation is definitely intelligible and can be defined in objective terms that do not presuppose the concept of relation so as to be distinguished from other categories of existence. It is the purpose of the present paper to establish such a definition by a criticism of certain conceptions of relation that claim to keep within the above assumptions.

2. Relation involves at least two distinct terms. Assuming that the terms stand for contents that are definite and objective, our first question is if two such distinct terms can be said to be the object of a single thought unconfused with other thoughts. Now two terms A and B may be presented together to thought as mere distincts, or one may be thought as distinct *from* the other. Again, the distinction of A and B may be thought in both directions at once—A distinct from B, and B distinct from A; or it may be thought only in one direction. In what sense, if at all, is the content 'two terms as distinct' said to be definitely thought?

3. If A and B are mere distincts and *distinction* is not thought at all, the thought of the 'and' cannot be said to be definite like that of A and B. Each of the two terms can by the hypothesis be separately thought, but 'A and B' is not thought separately from the thought of each (4, foot-note). 'And' here means no whole, distinction, or relation but simply 'togetherness', the claim of which to the status of relation will be refuted presently (8-10). Neither is *mutual* distinction of A and B capable of being definitely thought. We can conceive 'A distinct from B' and 'B distinct from A' to be different thoughts, but are these two directions together present to a single distinguishable thought? If they are, as together, fused into the mere distinction *between* A and B, such distinction is nothing more than A and B as distincts together (13). If they are not so fused, we have the indefiniteness of the mere 'and' or togetherness of the two distinctions. If finally, mutual distinction alone is taken to be definitely thought,

each direction of distinguishing being an indefinite abstraction mixed up with the other, the terms A, B would be themselves indefinite, contrary to our original assumptions. The consequences of dropping the assumption will be considered later (12).

4. Is then the content 'two terms as distinct' definitely thought only as a single direction of distinction, say as 'A distinct from B'? Whatever B may be distinguished from, the distinguishing of A from it is a single act of thinking. The distinguishing of B from something else, if presupposed, is presupposed as a separate act. But since B is thought in the distinguishing of A, is not there confusion, it may be asked, between the thinking of B and the distinguishing of A? That depends on the value of B when *not* thought as distinct from something else. B then is still a distinct, and presupposes the distinguishing of it as an act that is finished and no longer there. There are, in fact, two modes of thinking a content. The content may be thought to be distinct from the thinking of it *as continuing* or from the thinker of it *as ended.* In the latter case, it is still together with another thinking, the content of which is distinct from it. In the present instance, B—a distinct presupposing a past act of distinguishing —is together with the thinking of A, A being distinct from it. The distinguishing of A is together—*not* with the *thinking* of B—but only with B, is in fact the thinking of B as an *implication.* But what is B as an implication as distinct from B thought on its own account? A content *as other than itself* is not indeed definite as content but can yet be said to be definitely *thought.* B as implied in the distinguishing of A is here definitely thought as other than itself—viz., as the B that was distinguished in a previous act.[a]

5. We conclude then that 'A distinct from B' represents a single distinct act of thought. Is it also definite as a content? The distinguishing of B from something else in a previous act has bequeathed only the *term* B to the present act of distinguishing A: B in the present act is distinct only from the indefinite and is as such nothing but the distinct B. But the present act has to do with two distinct terms, A and B, B being its implication and A the direct content. B here may be said to be *given* as distinct and A is only distinct *from* it. They may be designated intrinsically distinct and extrinsically distinct contents respectively for this particular act of thought. Now the

[a] The distinguishing of B and the distinguishing of A are here two separate thoughts in spite of B being the implication of the latter. This cannot be said of the thought of 'A and B' and the thought A (or of B) in 3, for A there is not the mere implication of the former but is thought on its own account while the former is there.

togetherness of the extrinsically distinct and the intrinsically distinct is at least more definite than the togetherness of two mere distincts. Anything that is spoken of is by the very fact a definite; even the indefinite is definite in this sense. Mere 'A and B' is also so far definite, but the extra definition through the concepts of intrinsic and extrinsic distinction consists in the fixing of what we may call the relative positions of A and B. Not that complete definition of the content is yet attained, for we can still speak of 'A distinct from B' *and* B, where the 'and' points to the uncertainty whether the distinction is objective or merely a distinguishing. The extent of definiteness attained may be brought out by a criticism of certain current views of relation.

6. Relation has sometimes been taken to be definite without both the terms being definite. One term may be indefinite, the other term being definite either only as distinguished from it or as with an intrinsic or given distinction. In the former case, the definite term is said to be the same as or to be constituted by the relation. In the latter case, the relation is additional to it, being like a line or an interval extending away from it. Either way, it is taken to be definite as a function.

7. But should the indefinite be regarded as a *term* of a definite relation? Something may indeed be definitely thought *as* indefinite, but there 'indefinite' is only a term in a factitious sense. It is in fact a problem: a whole may be presented to thought through language where the elements and even the abstract form of the whole are definite, but the form *as applied* to the elements is not yet capable of being thought and is only sought to be thought. If the particular combination of definite thoughts at all yields a definite content which is not known, that content is the indefinite formulated in advance as a term. In any other sense, the indefinite is what we are barely acquainted with and cannot be described, far less used as a term. The factitiously or problematically definite term 'indefinite'—in a proposition like 'this is indefinite'—cannot be said to be either denied or affirmed as a character or *predicate* of *this;* and there is no question of its being used as the *subject* of an assertion. We can indeed have a negative assertion like 'this is not indefinite'; but it only amounts to the thought of the definite term 'this', the negation or distinction being here no relation but only the subjective act of distinguishing viewed as finished.

8. We may conclude then, what we assumed at the beginning, that relation must be between two definite terms. Is the mere

togetherness of two distincts a relation, as it has been taken by a school of writers at the present day? We have already seen that mere togetherness—A *and* B—is not even distinctly thought. Can it be then a definite content? But it may be said that a content may be definite, even if it has to be fixed by more than one definite thought.[a] So without raising the psychological issue of the thinking here being single or manifold, we may consider the strictly logical aspect of the content 'A and B'.

9. If the content 'A and B' be distinct from A and from B, it is yet together with them. If it be called C. then C is C and A and B, for 'and' is here the symbol of togetherness. But C and A and B may be taken as D—distinct from and together with each of the terms and so on indefinitely. Can this indefinite process be avoided? Togetherness of A and B, it may be answered, is just what is common to 'A and B' as a definite whole and 'A or B' as a definite disjunction; in both cases we have A, B as purely together. In both, however, C together with A and with B is but C, *not* a further content D; and thus the indefinite process is avoided.

10. But is there anything common to the whole and the disjunction of A and B? Is pure togetherness in fact a legitimate abstraction? Whole and disjunction agree in the circumstance of involving two terms but this circumstance can as little be regarded as a common object of thought as table can be said to be common to the maker of it and the price of it. If there be anything common, it would be either of them *minus* its speciality. The speciality of the definite whole of A and B—what it is as distinct from their disjunction—is that it is *both* A and B. So the speciality of the definite disjunction of A and B is *not both* A and B. Pure togetherness of A and B then would mean abstraction from *both* and *not both* at once, which would leave nothing behind. We can only abstract from one at a time and then togetherness amounts to 'either both or not both', which as a disjunction without a standing universe is but an indetermination or indefinite alternation of one and many and is therefore no definite relation.

11. Shall we then reject pure togetherness and take togetherness in a unity—as whole or disjunction—to be the relation of A and B? The mutual distinction of two terms of which neither is intrinsically distinct is regarded in an influential school of thought as the primordial

[a] When a content is made definite by two thoughts, there is a single thought of the two thoughts as finished, the contents of which make a single implication for it (4). This implication of the single thought is here a construction (27) by the thought. If togetherness be such a construction (say, an abstraction from the thoughts of whole and disjunction—9), it must be still shown to be definite as a construction.

relation through which the terms become definite, the relation itself getting defined again through the terms. The view takes two forms according as the relation is admitted to be definite prior to the definition of the terms or is regarded as definite only after the definition. In the former, mutual distinction is definite as disjunction of alternating and therefore indefinite terms. In the latter, such disjunction is rejected as merely subjective, relation being definite only as the whole of the terms as elements.

12. To begin with disjunction. Disjunction of A and B, it may be said, is a definite unity, being the standing cycle ABA which means that A is definite as distinct from B which again is definite as distinct from A. Is this cycle a relation? If ABA is definite when A as well as B is indefinite, then, as a relation, it is indistinguishable from a term; and each term too, so far as it is defined by the relation, is indistinguishable from the relation. In other words, the cycle is but an indetermination of term and relation. If A and B as defined are thought along with the defining cycle, the alternation ceases and the cycle becomes indistinguishable from a static whole. But why should A and B, as alternating, be taken to be indefinite? Could we not take disjunction as the alternation of definites? Why should alternation cease when the terms are definite and taken along with the cyclical unity?

13. The reply is that the *alternation* of definites cannot be taken along with their unity. Each of the two thoughts—of alternation and of unity—presupposes the other as a finished act and, therefore, the content of it as only an implication. As we said in 3, the implication is definitely thought as other than itself, though 'other than itself' is but an indefinite content. It is, at best, the problematic 'definite indefinite' of 7. The alternation of definites, so far as it is a definite content, means either nothing more than the togetherness of mere distincts, or if it means more, it means the precipitation of the abstract content—extrinsic distinction—as an attribute of each of the distincts. That each distinct has a distinction may be regarded as a relation, but it does not mean a relation *of* the distincts. The extrinsic distinction of the one may be correlative with that of the other; but, as will appear later (27), this does not oblige us to admit that the terms are related.

14. Is then the relation of A and B a static whole of the two? Here, by the hypothesis, A, B, and their whole C are all definite. Wherein is C different from A, B that it should be called 'relation', while the other two are called 'terms'? It is no use saying that A, B may be separately definite, but not C; for C also, with A, B yet

unanalysed, may be definite. We are besides concerned here with A, B as definite *in* C and not with the previous history of the situation. In the given situation, A and B are by hypothesis mutually distinct, but are C and A (or B) mutually distinct? To understand the mutual distinction of A and B, we have recourse to their whole C, and if C and A (or B) are also distinct from one another, should we have a further whole and so on *ad infinitum?*

15. There appear to be two alternative ways of avoiding the difficulty. Either C is only a distinct and is not distinct *from* A or *from* B, *or* C and A (or B) make a whole which is C itself. The first alternative amounts to saying that the togetherness of C with A or B is no distinct thought at all and that C is but a third term and is no relation between A and B. The second alternative admits that C and each element are mutually distinct but holds that C is not only a term of the distinction, but also the whole comprising itself and what is distinct from it. The contradiction in the last phrase is sought to be avoided by saying that it only verbally analyses the meaning of 'whole' which as perfectly simple cannot be really analysed. But the verbal analysis does not appear to be arbitrary. A whole may be thought with its elements unanalysed and indefinite, or with its elements definitely emergent. The difference of the latter from the former is not merely subjective. Analysis or emergent difference of elements is a character of the latter content and is not simply analysing or distinguishing thought. The whole *of* distinct elements is, in fact, no mere third term like the whole with elements unanalysed. As a relation it must mean a cyclical triplicity of relations. If C is but the equivalent of the mutual distinction of A and B, the equivalent of the distinction between C and A should be taken as B and *not* as C and that between C and B as A. But is this triplicity of relations a definite content? As before, we argue that either the relations are each indefinite, their whole being alone immediately definite or the relations are all definite, the *and* joining them standing for indefinite togetherness.

16. But why not drop, it may be suggested, the notion that elements are related by the fact of their being in a whole? In the first alternative above, the whole is an unrelated term and has no extrinsic distinction from the elements. In the second alternative the whole is both intrinsically and extrinsically distinct. Why may not there be a third alternative viz., that the whole has only extrinsic distinction? When A and B are each intrinsically distinct, their whole C is not intrinsically distinct but only distinct *from* them. Relation

then would still involve the whole and the only relation, it would be said, is between an element and a whole, though the whole is not the relation between the elements. The indefinite triplicity of relations then would define itself out as two relations between C and A and between C and B, A and B, being *unrelated*. Where A and B are related, one being an element of the other, C would not be the whole of A and B only but of a third element as well, say, X. If A be an element of B, C—if distinct from B—would be the whole of B and X. In the sense in which we use the word 'whole'—viz., as the static equivalent of the mutual distinction of the elements, the whole of A, B, X is not also the whole of A, B. So where C and A, C and B, and A and B are all mutually distinct, they do not make up a cyclical system; for if C and A make B, and C and B make A, as understood in 15, A and B do not make C but only some unanalysed element of B.

17. In this third alternative then, where relation is understood as between element and whole, *not* between elements in a whole, the whole as the equivalent of mutual distinction is but a term and a further mutual distinction between this and the elements is a meaningless supererogation. But the relation of element and whole appears to cover at least two incommensurable relations. The whole may be a unity of attributes, a substance or it may be a unity of such unities or substances—e.g., a spatial whole of parts. Whether the substance is simply the whole of its attributes or an underlying something, it is still a unity of the attributes in some sense. Now, the addition of a new attribute to a substance does not disturb its identity while the addition of a new part or extra bit to a spatial whole makes a new whole. So the two relations—that of an attribute to a substance and that of a part to a whole appear to be only nominally described as the *same* relation—viz., of element and whole.

18. This difference may be sought to be whittled away by saying that extensity is but a character of every quality and that substance is only a synthesis of the extensities of many qualities. But that substance is not disturbed in its identity by the addition of a new quality should imply that the extensity-synthesis here differs from that in the addition of a new part to a whole. The difference would be some qualitative equivalent of the difference between spatial superposition and side-by-side arrangement. The term 'extensity-synthesis' implies in the two cases no *common* logical content that is distinguishable; it means either the one or the other. The difference,

therefore, between the two forms of the relation would still stand out as absolute.

19. We may express this difference by saying that though we speak of attribute in a substance and part *in* a whole, in the former what is *in* is dependent and in the latter independent. An attribute is never thought except in a substance but what is conceived as a part in a given whole need not be so conceived elsewhere. A space, it may said, is always part of a larger space but the spatial thing need not be part of a bigger spatial thing. In this sense, then, attribute is always dependent whereas part may be independent. But why should the substance be taken to be independent? It is independent in the sense that without the particular attribute given as dependent, it would still mean something. But how if the particular attribute be what is called an essential attribute? Without an essential attribute, substance would not indeed *be* anything actual, but would still *mean* either the underlying unity, the hidden something, or if that be not admitted, the persistent extensity-measure of the given substance from which the abstraction is made. The spatial whole however, unlike substance, is dependent on a part, since without that part it would not mean the same whole.

20. It appears then that to characterise relation in general, we have to avoid the concept of 'whole' altogether. It was shown in 5 that relation of A to B, whatever else it means, implies that A is distinct *from* B *given* as distinct but not vice-versa; or, in other words, for the single thought of A, B, they have fixed relative positions as extrinsically and intrinsically distinct respectively. The view that the sole relation is that of an element to a whole has to be rejected, because the relative position of the terms varies in the two cases of the whole—viz., as substance and as spatial whole. Incidentally the criticism of the view has suggested that in both the cases the relation is properly of a dependent to an independent. Dependent and independent, however, while satisfying the condition of fixed relative position appear to go further, and there is the prima facie doubt if they make up the content of a single thought.

21. Do the extrinsically distinct and the intrinsically distinct together make up a unitary objective content? We said in 5 that the fixing of the relative position of A and B does not secure complete definition of the content. We have still *two* positions; we can still speak of 'A distinct from B' and B. Relative position here is the content of a single thought but is not yet more than an abstraction to characterise the particular thought. It is not objectively unitary in the

sense in which A or B has been assumed to be at the outset. The distinction of A from B need not be objective, because A and B are each separately objective. When we say 'whiteness is distinct from the Soul', we mean that the *thought* of whiteness only is distinct from the thought of the soul, though each of the terms, taken separately, is objective. The question therefore arises: under what circumstances if at all, the relative position of A and B may be regarded as objective relation. In other words, is the content of the thought of relative position distinguishable from the particular thought?

22. That depends on whether the position or extrinsic distinction of A can be thought apart from the position or intrinsic distinction of B, or what is the same thing—apart from the thought of the abstraction, *relative* position. Can A be known to have *necessary* extrinsic distinction, i.e., to be *always* together with and distinct from something else which may not be B? Now whether there are any terms that are thinkable as only intrinsically distinct or absolute; never extrinsically distinct, may be disputed. But there are at least some terms, viz., those which stand for attributes and wholes that must have an extrinsic distinction. When A is always thought as together with some other term (not necessarily B) which is however thinkable apart from A (though, it may be, still together with a third term), A is said to have necessary extrinsic distinction without specific reference to B. Now if such a term A is thought together with B in any particular case where B need not be thought together with A, their relative position is said to be distinguished from the particular thought of it, or in other words, said to be objective.

23. We are now in a position to understand relation of a dependent to an independent as a definite and objectively unitary content. Dependent and independent are intelligible as characters of terms without reference to relation. A term is said to be a dependent when it is not only extrinsically distinct but *necessarily* so. It is said to be independent when it is thinkable as object apart from a given dependent.[a] This reference to a given dependent is no dependence, but only the thought of the absence of dependence. When then a dependent is thought as an object along with and distinct from an independent, the former is said to be objectively related to the latter.

24. In thus defining relation, we have avoided the petitio of

[a] When A as object is thought as distinct from B as object, if B is also distinguished from A, it only means another co-existing thought of the *thought* of B as distinct from the *thought* of A (21). B *as object* is then thinkable however *apart* from A i.e., not as distinct from or together with A but as by itself or as the content of a past or finished act of thinking of, say 'B distinct from X'.

using the concept of relation. The terms we have used in the definition are distinct objects together, one of them always distinct as together with some other which is either distinct by itself or as together with something else. *Distinct* is here the character of a term, and the only relational word used—viz., 'together' is understood here as thinking together, as not objective but only as a character of subjectivity. We begin in fact with a confusion of subjectivity and objectivity, of thinking with the object of it. Our definition is only an attempt to distinguish the object from the thinking and practically amounts to saying that if we think in a certain way, we think of *objective* relation. The reference to this thinking together is indeed necessary to the thought of the objective but it does not on that account prejudice the independence of objectivity. The thinking together of two contents we take to be a unique experience which we somehow symbolically describe by an objective term. Whatever account may be given of this symbolism, it does not affect objective logic.

25. We note also—as about distinction, so about relation—that objectively it is irreversible. If A is related to B, B cannot be said to be related to A: mutual relation is not objective relation. When, for example, A and B are said to be in mutual contact, contact is no relation but an attribute that is related to both of them. Why it is ordinarily called 'relation' will be explained below (26-27). But why offer violence to ordinary usage, it may be asked. The reply is that the categories of attribute and relation have to be distinguished. An attribute, whatever else it means, is understood as that which has necessary extrinsic distinction. Relation, we have seen, is the togetherness of an object with necessary extrinsic distinction with another object that in reference to it is intrinsically distinct. Relation cannot be said to have a further necessary extrinsic distinction, for then relation would be a term and there would be a demand for a further relation between relation and its terms and so on ad infinitum. If what can be regarded, like contact, as having a necessary extrinsic distinction be called a relation, there would be nothing to differentiate the category of attribute.

26. That an attribute like contact is plausibly called relation is due to the circumstance that two relations having such an attribute as a common term sometimes yield an inference involving the other two terms. It happens in fact that certain characters of an object can be inferred from the characters of an object in contact with it. But this inferribility need not mean an objective relation between the two objects. In some cases, indeed, inference is possible through an objective relation, as for example, when an attribute or spatial whole is given,

we infer a substance or spatial parts. There are other cases where if we infer a predicate about B from a predicate of A, it is because the predicates are the same attribute or substance, there being no reason to suppose that it does not persist. An attribute of a part may ordinarily be inferred to be an attribute of a whole constituted by it; and given a concomitance of attributes we can under certain circumstances infer a single substance underlying them. In such a case the given objects are not related; they are either each related to a third object or have a third object related to each of them. There is a more complex case—covering most of our really productive inferences—where what is inferred about B is either directly or remotely correlative with, but not the same as, the given circumstance about A from which it is inferred. This case demands special investigation.

27. If the given circumstance be X and the inferred circumstance, Y, X is either directly correlative with Y or there are intermediate circumstances M. . . .P such that X and M,. . . .P and Y are correlative terms. Correlatives need not always be in a pair: sometimes more than two terms may be directly correlative with one another. The principle, however, is that inference is possible through groups of correlative terms. Does the admission of correlative terms imply the admission of correlation as an objective relation? How else, it may be asked, could we have objective correlations? Object is indeed distinct from the thought of it but such thought also is an object to the further thought of it. The cause of an object other than thought may be other than thought, or it may be in some cases a thought regarded as an object. In the latter case, the object is said to be a construction of thought, meaning by it nothing mystical but only the objective *effect* of thought which is itself an object to some other thought. Now correlative terms stand for such an objective effect, for the joint effects of the same causal thought. The effects are objective though they have no objective relation to one another. Though each is objective, two correlatives are not together as objective: the *thoughts* of two correlatives can alone be said to be together. The cause of an object need not be a part or element of it and there is no objection to starting with effects as data of inference, whatever their causal history might be. We can then start with correlative objects as our data without admitting any objective relation between them. That they have the same thought as their cause does not mean that they are objectively related.

28. The inferibility of Y from X then does not necessarily mean that X is related to Y. The contact of A and B is no relation because contact is capable of being regarded as an attribute. It is

ordinarily called a relation, becauce A and B in contact have correlative positions X and Y which are indeed objective but are only unrelated effects of the same mental cause. To speak of a relation between A and B when they have a common circumstance or correlative circumstances is to confuse a mere subjective attempt to relate or infer with a unitary objective relation. A and B are here objectively unrelated, there being relation only between each of them and the common circumstance or the correlative circumstances.

29. Although such a complex situation is no single object, there may be a single thought of it, and this thought may have a special working value. It sometimes happens that the form of the thought enables us to infer a new truth with other given terms. Taking for example the symbolism A X—Y B, where there is a relation between A and *X* and also between B and *Y*, X and Y being correlative terms, we find that by arranging given terms A, X, Y in that form, B which is not given can be imagined and is sometimes verified as a fact. In such a case Y may on subsequent verification be found to have the same relation to B, as Y has to B. Sometimes, especially in complex cases, this subsequent verification is not forthcoming: the symbolism anticipates B without bringing to light its objective relation. The symbolism stands for a mode of imagining and thus a subjective activity discovers, by a leap as it were, a new truth the objective relation of which to the data may yet be unknown. There is ground indeed for regarding this mode of imagining as more than mere subjective play, if it happens to uniformly hit a new truth. It cannot be by a mere accident that the symbolism happens to be so systematically useful. But the mystery is not removed by taking the symbolism to be a single objective relation. The commonsense description which we find verified in simple cases of inference—viz., unrelated terms related each to each with correlative terms, the complex being nothing objective but only a unitary act of thinking—should not be rejected in complex cases merely because the constituent details of the situation cannot be completely exhibited. Still less is there excuse for rejecting it in favour of the conception of relation as a living *objective function,* which as altering the fundamental meaning of objectivity cannot at least claim to be justified on ordinary objective grounds. To exclude this conception from objective logic is not to deny the subjective mystery of the inferring imagination.

30. Objective relation, as we have defined it, implies a reference to thinking on the one hand and to an objective *fundamentum* on the other. The reference to thinking must not be to more than the

bare thinking together of objects. Many apparent relations alleged to be objective will accordingly have to be ruled out as involving a reference to a more complex subjectivity. Again, the objective *fundamentum* must not be the mere distinctness of each object, for then we would only have unrelated objects. Nor are objects necessarily related when they have a common circumstance or correlative circumstances. Nor are correlative terms themselves objectively related, for though they have an objective ground, there is a ncessary reference to a single thought as the cause of them, a reference thereore to much more than the terms, but in the *objective* not like that of correlatives in a complex *thought*. The objectivity is secured only where thc complementariness is in a single direction, or in other words, where the thought of relation has an unshiftable starting point in a term having necessary extrinsic distinction. The thought of such complementary objects is alone the thought of objective relation. There are other more complex unitary thoughts of an objective manifold which are useful for inferring objective truth, but it is only in a figurative sense that they are called 'thoughts' of 'objective relation'.

OBJECTIVE INTERPRETATION OF PERCEPT AND IMAGE

ANALYSIS

(1) Percept is a spatial object as perceived and the image is the spatial object as cognised but as unperceived. An attempt is made here to translate the subjective terms 'perceived' and 'un-perceived' into objective terms. (2) A spatial object is sometimes perceived with its outside indefinite and so un-perceived, e.g., an emerging flame. (3-4) An object is perceived as existent when it is perceived as defining an outside. Two cases: (a) where the object emerges in time but not in space, e.g., a scar coming to be perceived on a man's face; (b) where the object is perceived to cease in space, e.g., a fire perceived to go out. (5) In (a) the object is not perceived to *happen*. It is known only to *exist*. It is known to emerge in time only and not in space. Its outside or spatial negative is perceived as definite, though not as emergent either in time or in space. It is perceived only as constituting the existence of the object. (6) In (b) the fire is noticed to exist in being seen to go out. The spatial negative of the fire (to wit, the field) is perceived to emerge in time only. This emergence of the field is the perceived existence of the fire in space. (7) The spatial negative of a perceived object is the *whole* of space in which the object is distinguished. The limit of the bounded space is not set by the *object* occupying it but by the *sensed matter* that fills space and is not itself spatial. Space that is outside the limit has nothing spatial outside it and is as such the whole of space. (8) The perception of the object as existent or emergent in time only is the consciousness of the percept which is not anything other than the perceived object. Percept is a *mental* object not in the sense of being a datum for introspection but in the sense that it is an external object as perceived *explicitly* to be existent. (9) Two kinds of percept—the non-cessant and the non-emergent. (10) To know perceived space as non-emergent is to know it as having been and to know it as non-cessant is to know it as continuing to be. There is thus knowledge of persistence either in the form of *having been* or in the form of *continuing to be.* (11-12) This knowledge of persistence is not, however, perceptual.

(13) To know a perceived object as persistent is to be aware of an image which, like the percept, has two varieties—the non-emergent and the non cessant. (14) The image is nothing other than the perceived object as persistent. (15) The objective equivalent of the *unperceived* character of the object is its non-existence in time.

OBJECTIVE INTERPRETATION OF PERCEPT AND IMAGE

1. To be conscious of a spatial object as perceived is to be conscious of a percept and to be conscious of it as unperceived is to be conscious of an image. 'Perceived' and 'unperceived' are subjective terms and the problem is to translate them, if possible, into objective terms.

2. To perceive is to perceive a spatial object with a spatial outside or the spatial outside of a spatial object. It is to be conscious of a definite shape and of an outside that may or may not be defined. When we perceive an object emerging in space e.g., a flame emerging as a match is struck, the outside of the object as emerging does not appear with a definite boundary. As it is only a definite shape that can be said to be perceived, the outside of the flame is not perceived but is only the content of an indefinite sensational awareness. The emerging flame is perceived with an outside that is not perceived.

3. When an object and its outside are perceived together, the former defines the latter but not vice versa. The object is definite in itself while the outside is definite through it. The definite object is perceived as existent, its definite outside being its perceived existence. But the outside may not itself be perceived as existent, though it is perceived as definite. An object emerging in space like the flame is also perceived as only definite and not as existent. But the flame is perceived as definite in itself while the perceived outside is definite through the object of which it is outside.

4. An object is perceived as existent when it is perceived as defining an outside. There are apparently two cases where an object is perceived as defining its outside. The first is the case where the object emerges in time but not in space and the second is where the object is perceived to cease in space. A scar comes to be perceived on a man's face as he draws near. The scar here begins to appear at a certain moment but does not then begin to exist. It does not like the flame appear or emerge in space but emerges in time only. There is explicit perception of the scar as *there,* as existent: to come to be perceived without being perceived to happen is to be perceived *as* existent. Again a fire is perceived to go out, the going out or cessation being, unlike the emergence of the scar, a perceived happening in space. The fire need not have been explicitly perceived as

existent before its cessation is perceived. Its existence, however, is perceived as involved in the perception of its cessation. The fire may be for the first time perceived to exist in being perceived to cease. To see it ceasing is not to cease to see it but to notice its existence.

5. In the first case, the scar is seen to exist in the face but not to emerge *in* it. To emerge in space is to happen and the scar is not perceived to happen. Its outside or what may be called its spatial negative is perceived as definite but not as emergent in space or in time. To know that the scar *emerges* in time only and *not in space* is to know that it *exists* in space. But its spatial negative as being not known to emerge at all is not known as either existent or non-existent. It is perceived only as constituting the existence of the scar. Existence to perception is spatial existence and the spatial negative of the perceived object here is its perceived existence.

6. In the second case, the fire is noticed to exist in being seen to go out. To see the fire ceasing is to see it as existent against its outside or spatial negative perceived *not* as not emerging at all like the outside of the scar, but as emerging in time only like the scar itself. To see the fire going out is to see the field in which it exists getting defined without happening, such definition being emergence in time only. The emergence of the field in time only is the perceived existence of the fire in space or—what is the same thing—the emergent non-existence of the fire in time. The scar, as emerging against a field that emerges neither in space nor in time, is perceived as existing both in space and in time. The fire as ceasing is perceived, against a field that emerges only in time, as existing in space only.

7. The spatial negative of a perceived object is the *whole* of space in which the object is distinguished. The object indeed occupies some space but the outside or the negative of this space has not this space outside it. The limit of the bounded space is not set by the object occupying it, for then there would be a clrcle, since to occupy space is to have *so much* space constitutive of it. The limit is set by the sensed matter that fills space and is not itself spatial. Space that is outside the limit has then nothing spatial outside it and is as such the whole space that might be filled. The existence of an object to perception is space defined as outside the object but not having the object as its outside. Space is defined as outside the object when either the object emerges in time only or ceases in space.

8. The object is perceived to exist when it emerges in time only or when its spatial negative emerges in time only. The perception

of the object as thus existent is the consciousness of the percept. The percept is not other than the perceived object, not a ghostly or diaphanous object—as it is sometimes conceived to be—apprehended in psychological introspection. There is no introspective awarenesss of the percept, although it has to be taken as a 'mental' object. The mental object is nothing but the external object as perceived explicitly to be existent. The object is said to be *perceived* as existent when existence is seen in the object without being reflectively known as seen. Its emergence in time only or its cessation in space is its existence unreflectively seen as an objective predicament of the object. The external object in this objective predicament is the percept.

9. Such is the objective interpretation of the percept. Corresponding to the two kinds of perceived existence viz., that of the scar in both space and time and that of the fire in space only, there are two kinds of percepts. The scar is perceived as beginning to appear but not as disappearing while the fire is perceived as disappearing but not as beginning to appear. The percept scar is non-cessant while the percept fire is non-emergent. The scar must indeed disappear to the observer as the scarred face recedes from him but the beginning of the disappearance is never perceived. The fire again begins to be perceived in the perception of its cessation but this beginning is not itself perceived. Unlike the scar, the fire is perceived to exist only and not to emerge at all.

10. The spatial negative of an object perceived as existent in space is perceived as not existent in space. As pointed out, the outside of a perceived object has not the object outside it; and it is the outside of an object that constitutes its perceived existence. The outside of an object then is perceived along with the perception of the object but not as with the object as its outside i.e., not as existent *in* space. It is perceived as space itself and this perceived space differs according as the object, perceived as existent i.e., as in space, emerges in time only or ceases in space or, in other words, according as the percept is non-cessant or non-emergent. Space as the outside of the scar is known as non-emergent against the scar as emergent in time only and space as the outside of the fire is known as non-cessant against the fire perceived as cessant i.e., existent in space only. To know perceived space as non-emergent is to know it as *having been* and to know it as non-cessant is to know it as *continuing to be*. In the perception of space then as the outside of an object perceived

as existent, there is the knowledge of persistence either in the form of *having been* or in the form of *continuing to be.*

11. The perceived outside of an object is presented as a definite extending away into the indefinite. What is known to persist is the definite—e.g., the face on which the scar emerges or the glowing ember that may be taken as perceived to survive the fire. When the scar is perceived as existent, the face is known as having existed and when the fire is perceived as existent, the ember is known as continuing to exist. The face and the ember are both known to persist but while the former is known as non-emergent, the latter is known as non-cessant. Both are perceived as the definite outside of a perceived object but is the knowledge of their persistence in the two forms to be called perception?

12. The outside of an object is known as what the object is not, not as what is not the object. The face and the ember are known as what the scar and the fire are spatially and temporally demarcated from. The perceived content that is known as persistent is as much a percept as the perceived content that is known as existent. The distinction of the scar from the face .or of the fire from the ember is perceived, for there is a single perception of an object as in its field or outside. The distinction of the face from the scar or of the ember from the fire is really the distinction of the *percept* of the outside from the *percept* of the object of which it is outside. The distinction of the former percept viz., percept of the persistent from the latter percept viz., that of the existent is however no percept, being known as definite but neither as existent nor as persistent. A persistent is known as persistent when what is known as existent is distinguished from it or—what is the same thing—when the percept of the persistent is distinguished from the percept of the existent. There is thus no *perception* of a content *as* persistent.

13. To know a perceived object as persistent and not as existent is to be incipiently aware of an image. The persistent is not non-existent, but to be known as persistent is not to be known as existent. A perceived content may be known as persistent or existent but while to know it as existent is to be aware of a percept, to know it as persistent is to be aware of an image. Just as corresponding to the perceived object as emerging in time only and ceasing in space, there are the non-cessant and non-emergent percepts, so corresponding to the knowledge of the perceived object persisting as what *has existed* and as what *continues to exist,* we have respectively non-emergent and non-cessant images.

14. The image here is still, like the percept, nothing other than a perceived object. The percept is the perceived object as existent and the image is the same as persistent. The persistent perceived object is the outside of the existent perceived object, which however *as* persistent is not perceived though immediately known. As thus immediately known as persistent, it is the incipient image. The awareness of such image is the knowledge of an object as what the existent is not though not yet as what is not existent. The knowledge of an object as non-existent is the awareness of an image proper, where the object is no longer a perceived object.

15. For the interpretation of the image proper, the objective equivalent of the *unperceived* character of the object has to be found. The scar, we said, disappears as the face recedes from the observer though the disappearing is not perceived. The face still perceived is immediately known to be different without the belief in its identity being disturbed. The difference is known to be the scar itself as non-existent in time only, which is known as much in the unreflective objective attitude as the scar emerging in time only. Again, varying the example of fire, we may imagine seeing black charred wood instead of the glowing ember directly as the fire goes out. Here, too, there is the undisturbed belief in the identity of the charred wood with the ember in the fire but a *discontinuity* is immediately known without being perceived of the wood from the fire such as is not known when the glowing ember is seen to *survive* the fire. It is known in the objective attitude as an emergence not, like that of the surviving ember, in time only but also in space. The emergence of the charred appearance is known as the non-existence of the fire not only in space but also in time, the fire being here not what is ceasing but what has ceased. Thus the objective equivalent of the unperceived character of the scar and the fire is their non-existence in time as contrasted with the persistence of the face in the case of the former and with that of the ember (that glowed in the fire) in the form of charred wood in the case of the latter.

REALITY OF THE FUTURE

ANALYSIS

(1) The object of this paper is to discuss whether the reality of the future expected on a known ground can be said to be an object of 'knowledge'. (2) That which is believed on a known ground and is not directly known may comprise two cases: (a) 'if A, then B'; (b) 'since this A, therefore B will be'. (3-4) (a) may be admitted to be *known,* (b) is claimed to be a case of inferential knowledge, but what we really may claim to know is that B *can* be. That B *will* be is only a matter of non-cognitive expectation. (5) The future as real is thus a real contingency or an indeterminate potentiality. (6) But objective indetermination has no accomplished being and we cannot claim to *know* it. (7-8) Belief in the future is expectation either as initial willing or as faith. The future is real but as what might not be and what is being brought into existence or being revealed.

(9) The ordinary view that the past, the present and the future are facts of the same status seems to be an oversimplification. The time-positions differ in factual status and are not *mutually* distinct. The past is distinguished by itself, the present is distinguished only from the past and the future is distinguished only from the present. (10-11) The past may be remembered without being known to be remembered and as such it is known as *that* existent and thus as fact. The belief in the *that* is direct and does not involve a consciousness of its present non-existence. The past is in this sense distinguished by itself. The present may not be distinguished at all and may only be felt and not known. When it is at all distinguished as *this,* it is only known as beginning to be. It may not, again, be so known. But in either case the past is an accomplished fact. The present is only half-known and is known simply as *not* the past. (12) The present is known only as beginning and not as ending. It is not distinguished from the future, though what is now believed to be the future is distinguished from the present. This distinguishing is not, however, knowledge. The future is a fact to faith which the present only symbolises. (13) The future then, if distinguished at all, is distinguished from the present and taken either as being actualised or as being looked for. (14) The process of actualisation is an imaginary movement from the present towards the future: the other process is an imaginary defining out of the future towards the

present. Neither process reaches its end. The apparent knowledge in the former case takes the form of inference and in the latter case the form of justification of inference. (15) The consciously willed future is not really inferred. What is really inferred from the present is the potential future. The interpretation of this potentiality as a fact is not inference but ungrounded expectation. (16) The future that is real to faith can be justified by the present only in the sense that faith is extra-logically confirmed by an inference from the present. It is not logically justified as is a conclusion by its premise in retrospective explication. (17-22) The future is real to us in two ways—to will and to faith. Elaboration of this distinction.

REALITY OF THE FUTURE

1. The future, if expected without a ground, cannot be said to be known as real. If expected on a known ground, it is believed to be real. Is this belief knowledge?

2. What is believed on a known ground may be also directly knowable or it may be intrinsically unintuitable. The latter comprises two cases—(*a*) a conditional relation—'if A, then B'; and (*b*) 'since this A, therefore B will be'.

3. The conditional relation may be admitted to be known, though the point is open to dispute. From the joint perception of A and B in the past, we may claim to infer 'if A, then B' where the dependence is independent of the time-position of A and is timeless in this sense.

4. On the ground of this timeless relation and of the perception of A as present, we are said to *infer* that B will be. Really, however, we infer at least that B *can* be and only expect non-cognitively that B *will* be. We infer that B will be, *if* there is nothing to counteract it and we never *know* that there is nothing. That there will be no counteraction is but a faith. What we may claim to know or infer is that B can be, that there is a tendency for B to be.

5. The future then, so far as it is real to us now, is not what actually will be but only can be. It may not be actual at all and yet it is believed to be real. It is the real contingent, real in the sense in which a possibility which is willed or, if not willed, can be willed is real. The future or the anāgata as real is taken by Patañjali to be avyapadeśya just in this sense. With this we may connect the present day notions of reality in the making and of the intrinsic unpredictability of the future. The mechanical conception of the real being determinate and of the future being what must be, the present being what it is has considerably lost its hold on the modern mind. The principle of objective indetermination or real contingency is now-a-days presented with assurance in many forms.

6. Our question is if this principle can be said to be *known*. What is known is the complete or accomplished being, the parinișțhita or bhutartha. The unaccomplished in the sense of what is real without being actual cannot be said to be known. It may be that in God's consciousness, the real future is accomplished or determinate: it is the old conception of God knowing our free action beforehand.

It may be also that we can rise by yoga to some kind of transcendental intuition of the future as future. As it is however, the future as real is only an indeterminate potentiality to us: we cannot claim to know it.

7. We may now state our position briefly. Belief in the future is not knowledge but expectation. Expectation is either initial willing or faith. Will and faith are antithetical attitudes, their dualism being ever sought to be overcome but never actually overcome.

8. The future is not eternally existent or necessary. It is real but as what might not be. The contingency itself is real, being believed and not merely imagined. The future is what is inexplicably being determinate as being and as meaning: it is either being brought into existence or being signified or revealed. Here, too, is a dualism that is only being overcome.

9. The past, the present and the future are ordinarily taken to be all facts of the same status, disposed in an imaginary time-line and mutually distinct like facts in different space-positions. It is an illusory simplification of a complex situation. The time-positions differ in factual status and are not *mutually* distinct. The past is distinguished by itself, the present if distinguished is distinguished only from the past and the future is distinguished only from the present.

10. To explain. The past fact may be now remembered without being known to be remembered and hence may be said to be believed as a distinct fact without being distinguished from the present. When the past is known to be remembered, it is not distinguished by itself but *from* the present. As so distinguished, however, it is the non-existent which is no fact at all, its non-existence being a fact that is present. Fact or what is believed is either an existent or the non-existence of an existent: the non-existent is only imagined and is not fact. The past that is merely remembered without self-consciousness is known as *that* existent and thus as fact. The belief in the *that* is direct and does not involve a consciousness of its present non-existence. The past is in this sense distinguished by itself. The present, however, if believed without reference to the past is not distinguished at all, is felt but not known. *That* or the past, though psychologically prior is logically posterior to *this* or the present. *That* means *not-this* but *this* does not *mean* though it is *not-that*. The present may not be distinguished at all but only felt. But if after the past is known, there be any occasion to distinguish the present as *this*, it is known only negatively as *not* the past, as *beginning* to be.

11. There are cases in which no break appears between the

past and the present, and the present is not known as beginning. But the past here is just as complete or accomplished a fact as the past from which the present is marked off, the only difference being that in the latter case, the present non-existence of the past is *also* known. The past is the type of the existent: the existent is the accomplished. The present is only half-known, known simply as *not* the past but not as existing by itself, as beginning but not as ending. Where the past does not consciously cease, it is not incomplete as fact like the present. It is at once complete and continuing, unlike the present existent which is only continuing. There is no incompatibility between *complete* and continuing. The past is not distinguished *from* the present, the latter being only distinct from the former. Hence the past does not lose its pastness or accomplished character, if it is also present. The past can be present though the present cannot be past.

12. The present is known only as beginning, not as ending. So the present as fact is not distinguished from the future. What is now believed as future is however distinguished from the present. Is such distinguishing knowledge? If the present is not known to end, the break between it and the future cannot mean a *known* distinction. The future cannot begin as the present begins. If it is believed at all to begin, it can begin either in the present without being present or actual or begin absolutely without any adjacent past. In either case, its distinction from the present amounts only to unrelatedness. If the future now begins without actually being, it means that its existence is being brought about, that it is now willed. Known relation implies an existent continuity but the will-continuity of the present and the future is nothing that exists now. If, again, the future is believed to begin absolutely, there is no continuity at all—known or willed—with the present. There is awareness of the present, not as the *past* of this future, but as its *symbol,* the signifying function of which is no factual relation. The future is here a fact to faith which the present only symbolises, which is helped somehow to get defined as a meaning by the present.

13. The future then if distinguished at all and not merely implicitly expected is distinguished from the present and taken either as being brought about or as being looked for—the content of will or faith. As explicit, either content takes the appearance—but only the appearance—of the known fact. The future as beginning to become without actually existing is symbolised as a potential existent actualising itself; and the future as absolutely beginning which is only

timelessly set against the believed *contingency* of its non-emergence tends to be pictured as having this contingency temporally *before* it, as heading backwards in time towards its actual present non-existence, as *presupposing* the present. The symbolisation in either case means an imaginary transformation of the discontinuity between the present and the future into a continuous process.

14. The process of actualisation is an imaginary movement from the present towards the future but never reaching the future. The other process is an imaginary defining out of the future towards the present, a magic development of the future as a meaning and may be called the process of idealisation. Neither process reaches its end because the farther it goes, the more does the interval become indefinite: we become only less and less aware of the gap and do not see it getting filled up. The apparent knowledge in the former case tends to take the form of inference and in the latter case the form of justification of inference, of the explication of presupposition.

15. The consciously willed future appears to be inferred from the present but is not really inferred because what is inferred is necessary i.e., is not temporally related to the data at all. What is inferred from the present is at best that something *tends* to be, can happen, will happen if there be no counter-acting circumstance. The interpretation of this potential future as factually future is not inference but only ungrounded expectation.

16. Again, the future that is real to faith may appear to be justified by the present, as a fact already known is retrospectively justified—or explained—by the explication of its reason. Such retrospective explication is already a strange process within logic. But there is difference between the justification of a known conclusion by its premise *within* an inference and the justification of a fact that is expected *by* an inference. The future as a fact to faith is justified by the present only in the sense that the faith is non-inferentially or extra-logically confirmed or strengthened by an inference from the present. This subjective (not merely psychological) confirmation of faith by an inference outside it is ordinarily confused with the inverse justification of a conclusion by its premise within an inference.

17. The future is real to us in two ways—to will and to faith. Reality to the will-consciousness is a current conception, some going so far as to say—what we may deny—that even the past and the present are real as somehow ideally willed. The future alone, we hold, requires this pragmatic interpretation. But the future may be real not to any ideal willing but to faith which is utterly distinct from

it. A voluntarist will ordinarily reduce faith to ideal willing. What I believe will *come,* I either actually will, or imagine I can will, or imagine as willed by some other will I imagine myself energising. If faith be an ideal willing, it would be this imaginary willing of another's willing. Whether this reduction is correct or not, reduction in the opposite direction is also equally conceivable. My consciousness of willing may be sought with equal justice to be resolved into the faith that my will is *coming.* If I can imagine another's willing as being brought about by my willing, I can also look for my willing to come with absolute spontaneity. As a matter of fact, neither of these reductions is really accomplished or believed: we only *aspire* to believe either way.

18. We may start from actual willing—say, willing to move a limb—and trace the steps by which we extend it ideally and aspire even to incorporate faith in willing. We may start also from implicit faith in the free rationality of persons and trace how the faith is extended downwards, how faith in the behaviour of the object is justified by this faith and how my own willing comes to be imagined in faith as the last link of this object-behaviour.

19. When I will to move a limb, I implicitly expect this movement will be brought about. The movement need not even emerge in a conscious anticipative idea. Where I will to bring about an extra-organic change through my limb-movement and cannot at once bring it about, I have an anticipative idea of the object, though I may not be conscious of the movement that is a means. Where again an objective change is willed through another objective change brought about by my movement, I have a conscious idea of the objective means which however is undistinguished from my initial willing. I have a sort of feeling of 'double touch' with the objective end. This is the sense in which I go on ideally extending my will. Mechanical causality is thus imagined as an extension of my bodily willing.

20. A difficulty emerges when the objective means appears unpredictable in its behaviour, cannot be believed as simply transferring its motion to the object in which the end-change is to be brought about. The feeling of this discontinuity affects the belief in the future which thus appears only probable. Still the will asserts itself in imagining a continuity: we believe there must be continuity though we do not visualise it. There are cases however where this general belief in necessary continuity is pulled up—e.g., where the means is a living thing or a person, where the unpredictability of its

behaviour is felt to be due not to my subjective uncertainty but to its objective uncertainty. We need not ask why this belief in objective indetermination comes, but it is a fact that we sometimes cannot *believe* even generally that there *must be* some continuity of motion between the means and the end. Here we only *imagine* with a definite abandonment of the will-claim to bring about the end of right.

21. .This is just where the attitude of faith should come in, so far as I still believe that the end will come though the behaviour of the means is intrinsically unpredictable. Not that the will-attitude always gives place to the faith: it may persist as a satanic or āsurika will-aspiration. I may choose to exploit the living or free object as a means, though I feel I have no right to use it as means. I do not identify my will with it as I do with a dead objective means. I seek not only to take advantage of its behaviour so far as it is mechanised: I employ it much as I make an evil spirit by incantations do my bidding. It is like hypnotising the means: I command, for example, a person to act and make his own will lapse. It is through such a hypnotising will that one feels making history—the culmination of the āsurika ambition.

22. Thus we may trace the ideal extension of willing including the stage in which faith itself which ought to mean surrender of will is incorporated in aspiration with willing. We do not trace here the other process of the ideal extension of faith and its aspirational incorporation of willing.

THE CONCEPT OF VALUE

ANALYSIS

(1) We speak of the value either of a known object or of a willed content. (2) A known object is valuated in the form of a judgment—'The object has this value', (3-4) Here the object is known and the value is felt. The judgment apparently means that there is a single consciousness of the object and the value. The knowing and the feeling do not, however, make up one consciousness. They are the objects of a single reflective consciousness. In spite of the judgment-form, this consciousness is not reflective knowing. It is primarily reflective feeling. Value cannot be said to be reflectively known though the object to which it is referred may be said to be reflectively felt. (5) Valuation implies a feeling-consciousness both of the felt content as such and of the known content as such. The known content does not cease to be known by being reflectively felt and the felt content, though not known, is endowed with a kind of objectivity by reflection. Both being objective, they can be spoken of as though they were related in a judgment. (6) The felt content is objectivised in reflective feeling in a peculiar manner. The content of a reflective feeling as the feeling of the impersonal feeling of the same content is definitely objectivised through the mediation of the impersonal feeling. (7) Though the felt content is thus objectivised, it is not turned into a known object. Though value is referred to a known object, it is not known as a *character* of the object. (8) To speak of the relation of the known content and its value would be really to *speak* the reflective feeling and not to *speak of* it. When we speak of a value in an object then, we only indirectly express as information what we should only speak exclamatorily.

(9) That the known object is in a manner 'subjectivised' is not so obvious as that the felt content is objectivised. We may feel that something is *only known* in the sense that we feel it as unfelt or neutral. In valuation, we are feelingly aware of the known object as unfelt even when the object is being felt. (10-11) It is possible for the *same* content to appear *at once as felt and unfelt,* in the valuating reflective feeling. The known object is not felt as one with the value, though the value is felt as one with the object. The known or unfelt character is not the felt value though the latter has the former involved in it. Value is thus referred to the object which is understood as not really *having* it and may in this sense be called a *floating* or *free*

adjective of the object. (12-13) Strictly speaking, however, value cannot be taken as an adjective of the object like red, green etc. In 'red flower', though the substantive is one with the adjective, the adjective is not one with the substantive. In an object that is felt to have value, the value is not felt as other than the object, but the latter is felt as other than the value. (14) Value, however, appears to be necessarily referred to the object and to be subordinated to the object. But this notion of subordination can be got rid of and it can be shown that value is independent of valuation. (15) Value is not appreciated as such until the object to which it is referred is felt as known. When the known object is so felt, it is felt to be subordinate to the value. (16) It is not enough to understand that value is felt to be objective but not known as such. We have to appreciate that value is absolute and that the speakability of value as information is a necessary illusion. (17-19) There are cases of feeling a possible feeling and feeling the want of a feeling. They indicate the possibility of the feeling of an actual feeling. Valuation as reflective feeling is of an imperfectly distinct content, viz., the possibly felt and the felt unfelt. We have also a feeling of feeling in which there is not even this imperfect distinguishing. The value of an object gets freed as a substantive from the object of which it appears as an adjective and acquires the status of an absolute only in this feeling beyond reflective feeling. (20) The expression of this absolute feeling is not only no information, it is not even a speakable valuation. The term 'value' should properly be confined to this absolute; value is nothing if not absolute.

(21) The valuation of a willed content is not, like the valuation of a known content, a pure feeling but is a feeling with willing somehow involved in it. Moral valuation is to *feel* the sacredness of the 'ought'. It is properly expressed as an exclamation of the 'practical feeling' of respect for the 'ought'. (22) Aesthetic valuation is the type of valuation. (23) To be valuated, what is valued should be a finished content. Willing, then, as simply the process as distinct from willing as completed is no content of consciousness and the rightness of willing as a process is no value at all. (24) The moral valuation of an object as clean or sacred occurs when the purity or holiness of an *impersonal* will is felt to be embodied in the object. (25) A willed act is the content of willing only and is distinct from the willing through the willing itself. It has an embodiment which is no content at all apart from the willing. (26-27) The judgment on an embodied willing is aesthetic relatively to the judgment on ideal

willing which determines it, though the value depends on or involves the moral value of the ideal willing. (28) Valuation ranges from the pure aesthetic valuation of an object to the moral valuation of an act. All valuation is expressed in an informatory sentence, though as feeling it should be primarily expressed as an exclamation. (29) Valuation—whether aesthetic or moral—is no judgment. Aesthetic valuation is not judgment because the subject here is subordinate to the predicate. Moral valuation is not judgment because it is not even literal information. (30-33) Analysis of the form of the moral judgment that is furthest removed from the aesthetic judgment. (34) Valuation in its different forms may be conceived to be a process, intermediate between knowing and willing.

THE CONCEPT OF VALUE

1. We speak of the value either of a known content or of a willed content. Value is itself a felt content and so the value of a felt content is but a higher grade of the value of a known or willed content.

I. VALUE OF A KNOWN OBJECT

2. A known object is valuated in the form of a judgment—'The object has this value.' The difficulty about the judgment is that the object is known and the value is felt and there can apparently be no relation between the incommensurable contents. One may evade the difficulty by saying that value is only symbolically spoken of as content, the real judgment here being 'we thus feel the object.' But this form also is not easy to understand. What does 'feel' as a transitive verb mean in reference to the object? It cannot mean simply 'we thus feel *when* we know the object'; and even if it does, there is the further difficulty how one speaks of 'we' having the feeling in respect of the object. Probably it is one and the same circumstance that is expressed by 'feeling the object' and '*we* thus feeling about the object'; and to speak of value as a content is apparently to symbolise the same mystery. It is as well therefore that we accepted the judgment-form—'The object has this value' and tried to find out its implications.

3. How is any relation sopken of between the known object and the felt value? The relation may be only symbolical but it is not obviously unintelligible. What is at least meant literally is that there is a single consciousness of the two terms—the object and the value. We cannot say, however, that the knowing and the feeling make up one consciousness. We are aware of what is known as completely distinct from the knowing and of what is felt as only imperfectly distinct from the feeling. We cannot speak of the object as content of the single consciousness for then it would be at once known and felt, at once completely and incompletely distinct from the consciousness.

4. The knowing and the feeling cannot make up one consciousness but it may be that there is a single reflective consciousness of both. Is such consciousness the consciousness of the content of the

knowing and the feeling making some sort of unity? It depends on what is meant by reflective consciousness. There are apparently two kinds of reflection on a conscious process: it is either the distinguishing of the conscious process from the content or the distinguishing of the content from the process. The former is what is usually called psychological introspection in which attention is withdrawn from the content of the conscious process and fixed on the process itself which is thereby sterilised and turned into a ghostly temporal event. In the latter, it is the content of the conscious process that is attended to as in the unreflective stage, though it is defined by being distinguished from the conscious process which we thus do not distinguish but only distinguish from. The reflective consciousness of knowing and feeling that we postulate to understand the so-called value-judgment is reflection in the latter sense. It is consciousness not directly of the knowing of the object and the feeling of the value but of the object and the value as known and felt respectively. Reflection in this sense is consciousness of the conscious process not as an event but as a function implied in the content. It is not necessarily cognitive: reflection on the knowing or feeling or willing of a content may be but need not be the reflective knowing or reflective feeling or reflective willing of the content respectively. To understand the so-called value-judgment then, the object and the value should be taken as the contents of a reflective consciousness of knowing and feeling. Is this consciousness, reflective knowing or reflective feeling? The judgment-form would suggest that it is reflective knowing but we contend that the form is here only artificial, if not symbolic and that the so-called value-judgment is primarily reflective feeling. Value is here spoken of *as though* it were known but the object is not here spoken of *as though* it were felt. The known object in fact is actually felt in the reflective feeling. Its knownness is felt: there is a feeling of the object as in space and time being *merely known* in the sense of being *unfelt* or indifferent. In the reflective stage we may feel that something is only known but we do not know that something is only felt. To know is to know a definite content but to know that a content is only felt would be to be aware of it as indefinite. In other words, value cannot be said to be reflectively known though, like value, the object to which it is referred may be said to be reflectively felt.

5. The so-called value-judgment then is not reflective knowing but reflective feeling. The judgment-form or the form of knowing here is only an indirect if not symbolic expression of the reflective

feeling of valuation. Valuation implies a feeling-consciousness both of the felt content as such and of the known content as such. The known content does not cease to be known by being reflectively felt and the felt content, as will be shown presently, though not known, is endowed with a kind of objectivity by reflection. Both being objective in a sense to the same reflective feeling, they can be spoken of as though they were related in a judgment.

6. How is the felt content objectivised in reflective feeling? When I am conscious of my own past feeling or of another's feeling, the consciousness is a feeling and not a spectator's consciousness, though the feeling of which I am conscious is in some sense alien to me. The content of this alienated feeling is not however consciously distinguished from it in my reflective feeling of it. Now when I say that a person feels in a certain way towards an object, I say it on some evidence over and above the mere evidence of my feeling. But sometimes I am aware without any such evidence that one *must* or *should* feel in the way I feel. When I take something to be beautiful, for example, I feel implicitly that any one will find it so, as I believe when I take it to be of the colour red. I do not say that it is red to *me* but only that it *is* red; and so I say it *is* beautiful. If asked how I know it is beautiful to others, I would say it *must* or *should* be so and if it is falsified, as it well may be, I would doubt as I would doubt my senses. I am, in fact, here implicitly aware in my feeling towards the object that it is not my feeling only, that the object would be so felt by any one, or—what is the same thing—that the felt content is somehow *in* the object. To believe unquestioningly without evidence that *we* feel in a certain way in respect of an object and to believe that the felt content is in the object are one and the same belief, neither being prior to the other. Here then the feeling that I reflectively feel is not taken as any one's feeling in particular: it is unappropriated or impersonalised rather than universalised. The content of it also is consciously distinguished from it and taken to be on a level with the object to which it is referred. Thus the content of a reflective feeling as the feeling of the impersonal feeling of the same content is definitely objectivised through the mediation of the impersonal feeling.

7. The felt content is thus objectivised but it is not therefore turned into a known object. Value is objective and is somehow referred to a known object but it is not known as a *character* of the object. The word 'objective' here is wider than the word 'known.' Whatever can be spoken of as information may be said to be objective.

Now the objective may be either capable of being spoken of without reference to the consciousness of it or not so capable. It is only in the former case that it is said to be known. Value which is objective to reflective feeling is not speakable without reference to the feeling. It is unintelligible without reference to the impersonal feeling which is not speakable without reference to the reflective feeling. Value accordingly is not said to be a known content.

8. We can speak of the known content and this value together as both objective to the reflective feeling. To speak of their relation would be really to *speak* the reflective feeling and not to *speak of* it. In exclaiming, we speak our feeling and not speak of it; and when we command, we speak and do not speak of the command. What we thus speak may be, however, spoken of in a symbolical or periphrastic way. When we speak our feeling in the way of exclamation, we may also artificially speak of it or express it as information in the form 'this is my feeling about the object' or 'the object has this value'. When we speak of a value in an object then, we only indirectly express as information what we should speak exclamatorily in a form like 'how fine is this object'. Why do we thus express ourselves? It is to mark the objectivity of the feeling-content induced by the impersonalisation of the feeling, to indicate in fact that it is not arbitrarily that we thus valuate the object.

9. That the knownness of the object is felt in reflective feeling, that the known object is thus in a manner 'subjectivised' is not however so obvious as that the felt content is objectivised. As pointed out, we may feel that something is *only known* in the sense that we feel it as unfelt, neutral or indifferent. To the extent a known object appears flat and uninteresting is it felt as merely known. We speak of truth as beyond our likes and dislikes: the feeling of the truth of a content is the feeling of its being independent of our feeling (and of being no value at all). To be aware of a content being known is not necessarily to be aware of the content as unfelt but to be feelingly aware of the known as such is to be aware of it as unfelt. In valuation, we are feelingly aware of the known object as unfelt even when the object is being felt.

10. How is it possible, it may be asked, for the content to appear *at once as felt and unfelt,* as interesting and as neutral in the valuating reflective feeling? We may put it in some such formula: the known object is not felt as one with the value, though the value is felt as one with the object. In feeling at least if not in knowing, if a content A is one with a content B, B need not be one with A.

Something, for example, may be felt to be pleasurable and painful at once: one may enjoy a tragedy with a breaking heart and one may grieve over the loss of one's beloved in the enjoying reminiscence of the love. The pleasure and the pain are not really mixed here, the feeling being either pleasure or pain, *one* of them with the other somehow *within* its content and not side by side with it. The enjoyment of the tragedy is undistinguished from the pain that is felt, the pain itself being enjoyed; but the pain is distinguished from the enjoyment in the sense that it does not detract from the enjoyment. So in the other case, the pain through the pleasure and not vice versa. Likewise we say about the valuated object that its neutral or unfelt character is distinguished from its felt character or value which however is not distinguished from it. The known or unfelt character is not the felt value though the latter has the former involved in it. Value is thus referred to the object which is understood as not really *having* it and may in this sense be called a *floating or free* adjective of the object.

11. Unless the known object is appreciated as unfelt at the time we feel towards it, the felt content cannot be called value. The value of a known object is a content felt to be one with the object which is however felt as other than the content. The oneness of the content with the object or the objectivity of value is through its being felt as the content of an impersonalised feeling in respect of the object. The object is felt as other than the content through its being felt as unfelt. The reflective feeling of the value as felt and the object as known is the feeling of the objectivity of value and of the unfelt character of the object.

12. We have spoken of the value as a free adjective of the object. But is value an adjective at all? We say about a red flower that the flower is red flower but the red colour is not the flower, implying in this sense that the substantive is one with the adjective which however is distinct from it. Here however we have said that the value is not felt as other than the known object but the known object is felt as other than the value. So properly speaking, value is no adjective of the object.

13. We may elaborate the argument. A substantive need not be distinguished from its adjective to be known as a distinct. But an adjective to be known as a distinct must be distinguished from or in the substantive. When an adjective has been distinguished in a substantive, the substantive is not distinguished from the adjective at

least in the sense of being taken to be *without it.* But when value is distinguished in object, the object is distinguished from it in the sense that it is felt to be intrinsically without value, felt as unfelt or merely known. Value accordingly cannot be taken as an adjective of the object.

14. Apparently however we are still unable to deny that value is in some sense subordinate to the object, that while the object does not imply value, value has necessarily to be referred to the object. We have to get rid of this notion of subordination, of this necessary reference of value to the object. Value as such is not understood unless we clear our mind entirely of intellectualist prejudice. We speak of value indeed in connexion with the valuation of a known content, which though a feeling is necessarily symbolised as a judgment. But a critical examination of valuation shows not only that it is no judgment (amounting to knowledge) but also that value should be independent of valuation.

15. Value-judgment, we have seen, is primarily an exclamation somehow toned down into information. Exclamatory speech is like an impersonal proposition: the predicate is all and the subject seems to be nowhere. A person exclaims 'grand' and so he can say 'lightning' or 'rains'. There is a difference however, for when the exclamation 'grand' is completed into a sentence, we should say 'how grand is this scene' and not 'this scene is grand,' the predicate still retaining the principal position. This indicates the relation between object and its value: the known content is here subordinate to the felt content. 'How grand is this scene' means that grandeur—the value—is expressed or embodied in the scene. In the Platonic way we may say, the scene partakes of grandeur as the individual partakes of the Idea. Expression appears to be the least mystical description of the relation: value is expressed in the object as a feeling is expressed in the face. Both the terms here—object and value—are here substantive and both are interesting though we are interested in the object because of the feeling or value embodied in it and not in the latter because of the former. It may be, the object *as expressive* is as interesting as the value expressed but the object *as merely known* is in any case subordinate in the so-called value-judgment to the value expressed in it. Value, we said, is not appreciated as such till the object to which it is referred is felt as known or unfelt or neutral. When the known object is so felt, it is felt to be subordinate to the value, being so felt because of the value. The neutral character of the object is, as we pointed out, within the content of the feeling that is felt.

16. Value-judgment is an exclamation disguised as information. How do we realise it? It is not enough to understand that value is felt as objective but not known as such and that the known object that is said to have it is also felt in the valuation as unfelt. We said that we cannot primarily speak *of* value, that we really speak of the value and then artificially speak of it. We have to appreciate that value is *absolute* and not merely objective or in other words, that the speakability of value as information is in the last resort *a necessary illusion* like the speakablity of the unspeakable.

17. We spoke of feeling a possible (impersonal) feeling and feeling the want of a feeling. These are both on the reflective level but they indicate the possibility of a feeling on a higher level which would be the feeling of an *actual* feeling. The possibly (or impersonally) felt and the felt unfelt both appear as objective or as content to the reflective feeling of them. Valuation is a reflective feeling, feeling of this content which implies a distinguishing (though imperfect) between consciousness and content. Do we have a feeling of feeling in which there is not even this imperfect distinguishing?

18. A person says informatively 'It is a cool breeze'. He may exclaim 'How cool is the breeze'. He may go further and say 'How I enjoy the cool breeze'. The first statement expresses the felt character of the breeze and not the subjective feeling of it, the second statement expresses this feeling and the third expresses the further feeling of this feeling. To speak exclamatorily of the cool breeze is to express reflective feeling but to speak exclamatorily again of the reflective feeling is to express feeling of a higher grade. The value of an object gets freed as a substantive from the object of which it appears as an adjective and acquires the status of an absolute only in this feeling beyond reflective feeling.

19. To illustrate by a more complex example. 'Tat tasya kimapi dravyam yo hi yasya priyo janah', says the poet; 'What a treasure is one's beloved to oneself.' One may unreflectively discover a thousand excellences in a person or may reflectively speak of him as beloved but to speak of the value of the beloved to oneself implies a consciousness of the reflective content as such. This consciousness may be more intellectual than emotional, in which case it is what is called sentimentalism. Or it may be a genuine emotion, a mystic wonder at the *unspeakable* value of the loved character of the person, which is apparently what is voiced in the passage by the poet. The loved character of the known person is already a value. This wonder

then is consciousness of the value of the value, feeling of reflectively feeling the value.

20. Such is the feeling of an actual feeling to which the feeling of a possible (impersonal) feeling and the feeling of the unfelt (merely known) alike point. It is a stage of feeling beyond reflective feeling, an absolute or transcendental feeling, the expression of which is not only no information but not even a speakable valuation. It is a pure exclamation in which we do not speak *of* anything or rather in which we symbolically speak of the *unspeakable* as such. It is the expression of what is undeniable yet unintelligible, of the absolutely unique or new, or of the absolutely contingent—what is *believed* as might-not-have-been while it is there or as might-have-been while it is not, what is perpetually being lost or wanted when attained and being attained when it is lost or wanted. What is spoken but not spoken of in the pure exclamation may as much be called value of value as feeling of (actual) feeling, being in fact a form of the absolute. The term value should properly be confined to this absolute; value is nothing if not absolute. Loosely however we speak of absolute value and relative value, the former as the value of the latter.

II. VALUE OF A WILLED ACT

21. Valuation of a willed content is not like the valuation of a known content a pure feeling but feeling with willing somehow involved in it. Both the valuations are expressed as information but while the latter is properly expressed as an exclamation, the natural formulation of the former is an exclamation that is at the same time an imperative. To say that an act willed is good is a periphrasis for 'how good is this act' which again means 'how we *should* all act thus'. To say simply 'we should act thus' is no valuation or exclamation, being only an imperative. But to say '*how* we should act thus' is to wonder at this universal or impersonal obligatoriness, to *feel* the sacredness of the *ought*. Moral valuation is thus properly expressed as an exclamation of the 'practical feeling' of respect for the *ought*.

22. Aesthetic valuation is the type of valuation. Moral valuation is valuation as approximating to aesthetic valuation, there being intermediate valuations. There is the feeling, for example, of an object being clean or sacred, which may be called moral or spiritual valuation of the known object. Again, we feel admiration for a willed act as noble or magnificent, this being a sort of aesthetic valuation of the *look* of the act. Moral valuation proper would be the valuation

of the act—not as it looks but as the inner willing that is finished—as good or evil. This again may be distinguished from the consciousness of right or wrong willing in the willing itself, which is not the valuation of the willing as finished and therefore not valuation at all.

23. For valuation it is apparently necessary that what is valued should be a content having the form of being. It may be a known object that is definitely distinct from the consciousness of it or it may be indefinitely distinct from it in different degrees, the minimum distinction being that of the willing as completed from the willing as process. Willing as simply the process without the form of being is no content of consciousness and cannot be valued. The rightness of willing in process as distinct from the goodness of willing as completed is not felt and is like truth no value at all.

24. To begin with the valuation of an object as clean or sacred. Cleanness is a simpler value than sacredness. Dirt may be matter in the wrong place but the wrongness is what is felt as such in a specific feeling and does not admit of objective definition. So the clean is what appears as such to a specific organic feeling which has a close affinity with the feeling of moral goodness. Cleanliness is next to godliness and the feeling of having sinned is the feeling of being polluted. The clean suggests purity as the beautiful suggests joy. The sacred object has a further mystic significance: it is not merely clean in itself—what one dares not pollute—but what will clean the soul by its touch or presentation. Cleanness or sacredness of an object then is the purity or holiness of an *impersonal* will felt to be embodied in the object just in the sense in which the beauty of an object may be taken to be an impersonal joy embodied in it. This valuation then is an aesthetic feeling of a moral or religious value, of a will-value or a soul-value.

25. A willed act is the content of willing only and is distinct from the willing through the willing itself, having indeed an empirical embodiment which however apart from the willing is not even a known content. By 'embodiment' is here meant not an already distinct empirical 'body' into which the will somehow enters but what is made distinct by the willing alone. Taking for example the act at the lowest level—viz., the bodily act as willed, the embodiment of the willing is not some objective attitude of the physical body but some internal motor experience which cannot be described even as a given internal sensation. It is doubtful whether the motor experience—experience of moving a limb or even of having it moved—should be called muscular *sensation*. There is no consciousness of its being *given* to

willing i.e., of being other than willing when we are conscious of the willing. This applies even to the consciousness or having one's limb moved, for it is only imperfectly distinguished from the experience of moving and is only appreciated as a partial privation of the latter experience. This motor experience is apparently nothing but bodily willing that one is conscious of in reflective willing. Tactual and other sensations bound up with motor experience are adjectival to it in the content of reflective willing and cannot be regarded as independent facts that are only mixed up with it. A similar consideration will apply to willing at higher stages of consciousness. The embodiment then of a willing is no content at all apart from the willing.

26. There is a distinction between the embodied willing at any stage and the next higher willing that constitutes it. Each may be morally judged but the judgment on the embodied willing will be more of an aesthetic valuation than the judgment on the higher willing. Mere bodily act e.g., an acrobatic feat is almost like an object and is valuated almost wholly in the aesthetic way. Yet the fact that it is willed makes some difference. It is not merely the outward look of the act that is judged; the look as expressing the success of the willing is judged, its value being the efficiency of the psychic effort put forth. To say that the acrobatic feat is splendid is to say that the will is wonderfully efficient though the will is judged because of its triumphant expression in the body. So at a higher stage we speak of a splendid act of bravery, the psychic act being here judged more or less aesthetically, though its value consists in the measure of freedom of the willing behind it which however would not be judged as splendid but for its expression in the psychic act. Everywhere then the judgment on an embodied willing is aesthetic relatively to the judgment on the ideal willing that determines it though the value depends on or involves the moral value of the ideal willing.

27. When we speak of a splendid act of bravery, we judge the *look* of the act to have the aesthetic quality of splendour. What does *look* mean here? It is the empirical being of the free willing, meaning not only the bare being of the willing as a finished process but also an entire objective situation as conatively incorporated in it. The look of the act is judged aesthetically according to the moral value of the willing behind it. This willing too is judged as good or evil only as it is taken to have some kind of being. It has to be understood at least as *this* act in order to be valued even morally.

28. Valuation then ranges from the pure aesthetic valuation of an object to the moral valuation of an act considered simply as the

finished being of free willing without any further determination. All valuation is expressed in the form of an informatory sentence, though as feeling it should be primarily expressed as an exclamation. The informatory expression of aesthetic valuation, though not primary, cannot be said to be merely symbolical. Beauty has an objective though not known being, the objectivity being mediated through an impersonal feeling. Moral valuation is not only not judgment; its expression as information is symbolical and not literal. Moral value is indeed objective in the sense of being mediated through an impersonal willing; goodness, as will appear presently, consists in being eternally or impersonally willed. But it is not objective being but objective negation or freedom that is eternally willed. Negation is information when the subject of which a predicate is denied is not itself denied at least as a possible existent. But when it is so denied, there is nothing about which the information is given and the expression of it as information is only symbolic. Now to say that an act is free—and that is, as will be explained, what is meant by saying that it is morally good—is to deny the being, the bare temporal being or other empirical being of the act. In the sphere of knowing, the subject of an apparent judgment which is denied absolutely in the judgment is just the unreal in some form. In the sphere of willing, the act of which the being is taken to be nought by being felt to be free is understood to be *real* beyond all being or empiricality. The statement therefore that the act is free is no information and is only symbolically expressed as information.

29. Valuation, whether aesthetic or moral, is no judgment. Aesthetic valuation is not judgment because the subject here viz., the object valued, is subordinate to the predicate 'beauty' which appears at best as a floating character and is really no adjective but a substantive that is *expressed* in the substantive subject. Moral valuation is not judgment because it is not even literal information.

30. Moral valuation of the form that is furthest from aesthetic valuation is that in which the subject is an act of willing considered as a being in the sense simply of being finished or of having a bare position in time. The value of it viz., goodness, we have suggested, means only felt freedom. This requires explanation. It is clinched best on the negative side: to say that an act of willing is evil is to imply that it was not willing at all, that there was an illusion of willing. An illusion of a particular subjectivity means no denial of subjectivity itself but only of its particularity or specification. The specification or naming of a subjectivity is however vital to introspection: one is

said to be introspectively aware only of a subjectivity that is named or specified at least as different from named forms. Now we are said to have an illusion of willing when we somehow will but do not will the particular content that we claim to will. We may think we are running of our own accord when we are being mainly dragged along a slope or that we are speaking to a person for his good when we are really speaking to him in anger or that we are acting on principle when really some unavowed selfish motive is operative. What does such an illusion imply?

31. The consciousness of not having willed a content is always consciousness of having positively willed not to will it and not simply of having willed some other content. In the moral valuation of an act of choice, we consider not simply the content that we have not chosen but also the fact of having positively rejected or willed not to will it. So generally we cannot be conscious explicitly of the *subjective fact* of not having willed a content unless we are conscious of having rejected it. Unless we are so conscious, we should only say that *another* content was willed but not that there was *no willing* of this content. The fact of willing or no-willing is not known but is only conatively believed. So the correction of the illusion of an act of willing means awareness of having willed not to will it. But then it may be said we are not actually conscious in the valuation of an act as evil of having willed not to will the act. There is however an unspecified consciousness, in all retrospective consciousnes of an act as evil, of having willed not to will in the form of willing to remain what one is, the will to spiritual indolence. That is the general willing of omission that is bound up with all consciousness of willing—even of good willing: it is the consciousness of not having sufficiently exercised one's freedom. The consciousness of freedom in fact is belief in it as not completed, as having no *being*.

32. Moral self-approbation is not complacency but the consciousness of having exercised our freedom which could have been however further exercised. To exercise our freedom is always to work against the radical evil in us of the will merely to be or the will to indolence, against the downward current—what has been called pāpavahā nādi—which however is still will or freedom and not nature, the freedom to be not free, freedom to suicide. Moral self-condemnation is the feeling of not having exercised our freedom against this will to be, of not having shaken off the will to indolence, of having willed to drift or not to will, of having only had an illusion of willing otherwise. All consciousness then of *having* willed wrongly— as distinct

from that of the willing in operation—is consciousness of having had an illusion of willing. The consciousness of wrong willing in the willing itself is however not being aware of the willing as illusory. In fact it is to be more explicitly aware of it as willing, aware of *individual* freedom, than in the case of right willing. To the retrospective valuating feeling however, what was believed as a specific wrong willing was not that specific willing but only the radical will to indolence. What we are conscious of as right willing in the willing itself appears to the valuating feeling as a finished act that is good. It is the valuating feeling that on the one hand turns the process of willing into a finished act with bare position in time and distinguishes its freedom on the other as its constitutive reality. To say that an act is good is to say that it was free; that it was genuinely willed. Moral value is the *reality* of the act willed and does not even appear as its *character*. While the subject of the so-called moral judgment gets bare objectivity through it, the predicate viz., good is not objectified into a being at all, being only freedom that is felt as negation of the objectivity of the subject and yet as its constitutive reality. We have pointed out that it is not for the same reason that aesthetic valuation and moral valuation are denied to be judgments.

33. We have discussed the form of the moral judgment that is furthest removed from the aesthetic judgment. Still it is valuation so far as it is aesthetic, so far in fact as free willing is aesthetically represented as an act with the form of being. The aesthetic character is more prominent in the valuation of an empirically embodied willing as noble or magnificent and still more so in the valuation of an object as clean or sacred. In the aesthetic judgment proper, the joy that is embodied as beauty in the object completely loses its naked subjectivity. We have here in fact the least mystical and the most self-forgetful mode of embodiment of subjectivity. In the judgment of an object as sacred, the spiritual value retains a raw subjective character though mystically referred as a character to the object. In the judgment of empirically embodied act of willing as noble or splendid, not only the value but also the substrate of it has an element of subjectivity. In moral judgment proper, the substrate of value has only bare being as its objectivity and the value itself is felt as freedom or subjectivity and not objective *being* at all.

34. Valuation means aesthetic valuation which though not judgment may still be regarded as information and as such the least removed from logical judgment which is no valuation. On the other side, the consciousness of willing being right or wrong *in the willing*

itself is no valuation and the moral valuation of a finished willing as good may be taken to be just on this side of purely subjective willing. Valuation then in its different forms may be conceived to be a process intermediate between knowing and willing.

STUDIES IN KANT

CHAPTER I

Idea of Transcendental Philosophy

1. Kant's critical philosophy is a form of transcendental philosophy, and is avowedly only the first sketch or 'architectonic plan' of it. The 'transcendental' may be taken provisionally to mean what we are certain about as not objective. By 'object' is meant a content that is other than the consciousness of it. The transcendental then would be a content that is not distinct from the consciousness of it. One may be conscious of a content as simply distinct or as distinct from the consciousness of it or as not distinct from the consciousness of it. Instances of the last would be negation as the content of disbelief and the self as the content of self-consciousness, variously called consciousness, pure being, pure act or freedom. To Kant, the transcendental is the self as conscious act or freedom. He does not conceive it as quiescent consciousness or undifferenced being like the Vedāntist, and he vigorously denies intuition of the self. The self is to him an active consciousness or conscious act, whether as knowing or as willing. The primitive act is not unconscious, as it is conceived by Fichte, but conscious freedom in willing and conscious apperception in knowing. The thinking act in knowing is to him not only conscious in reflection but conscious also as constructive of the object. He does not also admit a primitive act in the Fchtean fashion as the common prius of knowing and willing. Knowing and willing are to him entirely different acts, and although each implies thinking, it implies it in different ways, and in any case thinking is not to him an act that is fact by itself prior to knowing and willing. Willing as free is the realising of thinking, practical assertion of reason; while knowing or the theoretic assertion of reason is thinking not as realising itself but as dealing with reality as given in intuition. Willing is real as realising, while knowing is only true and not real by itself, being real or existent only so far as its thinking form is realised in willing. Knowing is not willing but fits in with willing, being dependent on willing for its existence and not for its truth. Speculative thoughts which as lacking intuition do not amount to knowledge may indeed be turned into certainties in being realised in willing but certainty is not truth. ('Primacy of practical reason in its union with speculative reason') One of these thoughts, however, is the thought of the self itself, which is

turned in moral willing not merely into certainty or faith but into knowledge. The self then would appear to be at once reality and truth. Still it is neither as real nor as true that the self is taken as formative of the object known. It is formative only as the thinking form or the purely logical unity of the object. All the transcendental constants of knowledge are the possibility of object and this possibility is only the form of truth and not a truth that is known. This form of truth is indeed real as the thinking act involved in willing, but it is not therefore as real or realising or willing that it is said to determine the object that is known. Thus Kant's theory of knowledge is neither voluntarism nor intuitionism of the Vedāntic type. To the former, willing or realising which may be called the reality of the subject is constitutive of the object known, and to the latter, it is the self as truth that is so constitutive. To Kant, the subject as constitutive of the object known is only the form of truth and is conceived neither as an existent nor as a truth.

2. Transcendental or critical reflection may be supposed to arise through the necessity of adjusting two different kinds of certitude —practical and theoretic. We have in moral willing a certitude about the reality of the self, and we have in our theoretic consciousness a certitude about the existence of the object. The former is faith, the self as freedom being one of the postulates of moral consciousness. There is a difference, however, between freedom and the other two postulates, freedom being an *immediate* implicate of the consciousness of the moral law. The belief in freedom accordingly is called cognition[a] and not merely faith, cognition of the practical and not of the theoretical kind. Knowledge then to Kant need not be theoretical knowledge and need not imply intuition : it is only theoretical or objective knowledge that has intuition as a necessary factor. Both practical knowledge and theoretical knowledge imply thinking, the former being thinking *in* categories and the latter thinking *under* the categories[b]. In neither form is belief induced through thinking. In theoretic knowledge of the object belief comes through the intuition or the sense-givenness or blind pressure of the thing-in-itself, the matter that is brought *under* the categories. In practical knowledge of the self, there is the thinking of the self as cause, as *in* the category of causality, but the belief in the self is through the willing or the realising of the thought. Willing is free as *thinking* of itself as cause

[a] Critique of Practical Reason p. 200 (Tr. Abbott).
[b] Critique of Pure Reason (Tr. Maxmüller) p. 324, and Critique of Practical Reason (Abbott), p. 233.

and realising the thinking. Free willing is known as real in the willing itself, not in introspection; known therefore not as an object but only as not empty concept, as form to which 'object belongs', though *what* the object is is not *understood.* In theoretic knowledge of the object too, there is the thinking of the object as causally constituted and related, which is taken to be fact because the thought is found to apply to sense-experience. There is the common thought of causality and the practical cognition is of the self as not object. The cognition of the self as free in moral willing has reference to sensibility as what "affects but does not determine" the will and also as that on which a rational system is to be imposed. Free will is determined by reason in conscious rejection of sensibility; and to realise the rational idea or the idea of the good is to have faith in the sensible world being changed in response to it. To will or freely cause is in fact to think and expect a causal change in the world, and the expectation is at least partially fulfilled. Thus there is a fitting of free causality with objective causality, a meeting of practical cognition of the self and theoretic cognition of the object in the thought of causality. It is difficult however to understand how a change in the object is caused at once by another object and by the self, and thus arises the necessity of adjusting the two kinds of cognition. The adjustment is effected by the view—to be explained presently—of the known object as only phenomenal. To critical reflection that is roused by the meeting of practical cognition with theoretical, the object becomes suspect in its determination or form, though—as given—its reality in point of matter is undeniable. This brings in the problem of transcendental analysis of the object into matter and form, matter that is undeniably given and form that is indistinguishable from the self.

3. That critical reflection is roused through the practical consciousness may not be readily admitted. It is ordinarily assumed that the critique of knowledge is an independent enquiry and that it refers to willing only at the end when it takes the Ideas of the Reason to derive their reality from the moral consciousness. Many passages in the Practical critque however, and especially the elaborate discussions of the relation of freedom and necessity suggest that the relation between the theoretic and the practical reason is much more intimate. The entire conception of apriori thinking as a factor of knowledge appears to be connected with the moral apprehension of free causality. All the transcendental constants of knowledge are comprised in the category of causality. The last category—necessity—is

but causality on a reflective level, and necessity not only comprises all the other categories but is also an anticipation of the forms of sense—time and space. Now this causality in the known object is intelligible only in reference to free causality as practically cognised. That the object or knowledge of the object is constituted by the self-functions would not be an assertory proposition at all, unless the functions were believed to be real and not mere logical entities. If, as Kant says, the self is not theoretically known as real, the entire conclusion of the theoretic critique that the self constructs the known object would be but a metaphor of speech and no assertion meant for acceptance.

4. In fact, the very problem of the first critique—how knowledge and object of knowledge are possible—would be gratuitous and almost meaningless unless the object were already suspect in the light of a certitude higher than that about the object, and that certitude can only be a spiritual certitude which in Kant amounts to the certitude of the moral consciousness. The idea of the phenomenality of the object must have already been suggested from the practical side to start the enquiry—if certain contents that are claimed to be known as objects are really so known and if what is known as object is known as noumenal. The standard of reality can only be suggested by the apprehension of the self in the subjective or spiritual attitude. It might be supposed that the distinction of phenomenon and noumenon is suggested by our objective apprehension of appearance and illusion. But that only implies a distinction within the object between the mental and the external, the mere appearance of the external object being somehow conditioned by the mental object. The suspicion that the mental object is itself phenomenal would never emerge so long as one knows in the objective attitude. By far the most important pronouncement of Kant is that about the transcendental ideality of time or the mental world, implying a distinction between self and mind. It is doubtful whether this is really proved in the Transcendental Aesthetic alone without the assumption of or faith in a real self that is utterly unobjective.

5. That brings up the question: in what sense is the object taken to be phenomenal? Phenomenon has to be understood from the standpoints of all the three critiques, from the practical, theoretic and aesthetic points of view. In the first critique, the objective is taken as phenomenal because its forms, space and time, are taken to be not objects, not given in experience but apriori as supplied by the self They are taken to be, if not the self, at least indistinguishable from

the self. Causality including other relations constitutive of the object is understood as the thinking or apperceiving *act* of the self, but the forms of time and space are taken as the receptivity of the self and not its act. As constitutive of the object, the self is logical form. This form is real as the implicate of the act of freedom and is itself accordingly called the act of thinking, apperceiving or understanding. The knowing self being thus an act, what is its receptivity? If the act has to be understood to be real as free will, the facthood of the receptivity—of time and space—has to be understood also from the practical standpoint. Moral willing involves the certitude that free causality is being realised in the sensible world. The certitude has two forms—that free causality is being realised in internal sense as a temporal or mental series and in external sense as causality in the spatio-temporal world. The first certitude is that free choice will be expressed as sensible *life* i.e., a necessary chain of mental appearances[a] and the second is fulfilled in its objective as an objective rational *system* or nature[b]. The former is time and the latter space (-time) to practical consciousness. Thus we may understand time and space or the pure receptivities as the expectations involved in the act of freedom, as not acts of the self but as their fulfilment in knowable objectivity. Willing involves thinking of itself as 'successful' or objectively realised, realised as time and space, as mind and the world. If freedom could be known in intellectual intuition, as it is not known, it would be known to put forth time and space. As a matter of fact we only know freedom practically and know time and space practically as what *must be* and not as what *is*. Freedom is known in moral willing as *not* the object, not in time and space. To know the real self to be *not* in time and space and to know time and space to be not fact but only necessary is to know the object as less real than the self. Thus we practically know the object to be an emanation of the self as freedom.

6. From the practical standpoint then, the object is phenomenon in the sense of being an emanation of the self. The temporal world or the mind is not theoretically known as distinct from the self which however is practically known to transcend it. Thus the mind is known to be a phenomenon of the self. But the spatio-temporal world is theoretically known as distinct from the self as thinking and is not merely mental or mere idea of the self. How it can be an emanation of the self and yet not an idea is not theoretically understood and

[a] CPrR—pp. 192-3.
[b] Ibid.—p. 161.

hence it is taken to imply an unthinkable given element and to be indistinguishable from an unthinkable but believed—i.e., an unknowable reality or thing-in-itself. Yet it does not itself appear indefinite: it appears as definitely known. This definite appearance has to feeling or imagination an intrinsic value and is thus appreciated to be self-subsistent. The object thus appears as a contradiction—an emanation of the self and yet not mere idea, unthinkably real and yet having the definiteness of the idea; and the contradiction is resolved in aesthetic consciousness into a self-subsistent value. Though practically indistinguishable from the self as real and theoretically indistinguishable from an unknown reality, the object is not known as real nor therefore known as unreal, being aesthetically apprehended as a self-subsistent emanation from reality. Mind however,—the merely temporal object is not apprehended in aesthetic consciousness.

7. In transcendental reflection then the free self alone is known to be real and the object is known to be phenomenal. This may be regarded as the simple teaching of Kant's transcendental philosophy.

CHAPTER II

MIND AS PHENOMENON

8. Mental facts unlike external facts which are spatio-temporal are in time only. What is in time is change. A change in the external world is perceived or understood as a persisting spatial object in change. Mental fact has to be taken as a change but it cannot be objectively known to be in a persistent. The persistent can be either a spatial object or the self. The mind is not spatial and the self is not objectively known. A change in a spatial object is as real as the object, the reality of the object being primarily known through the matter of sensation being given to space. About mental fact as change then, which is not objectively known to be in a persistent, the question arises for the first time how it is fact, though that it is fact of some kind cannot be doubted. The question whether the spatial object is real or phenomenal does not arise in the first instance. It arises only after the mental fact is known to be phenomenal. Hence though in the order of exposition in the Transcendental Aesthetic, the phenomenality of space is presented before that of time, in the order of truth the former is dependent on the latter.

9. The question, in what sense the mental is to be regarded as fact is suggested by its contrast, as explained, with external fact. As a change for which no persistent is known and yet of which the facthood is undeniable, the mental appears as a problem. The solution that it is a phenomenal fact and that it is a phenomenon of the self could not have been reached on objective grounds. It is, as was suggested in the previous chapter, because we practically know the self as free causality with a negative and positive reference to a life of sense, know that the self is free only as refusing to be determined by the temporal and yet as having its causality realised in the temporal that the mental which is the purely temporal is understood as the phenomenon of the free or the noumenal self. The proof of the phenomenality of time in the Transcendental Aesthetic on the ground of time being an apriori notion must be taken as already assuming the reality of the free self, all apriori theoretic function being understood as emanating from free causality.

10. If the apriority of space and time proved the phenomenality of the external and mental object, why should the former

be taken as phenomenon of an unknowable reality and the latter as phenomenon of the self as real? Both the objects are presented: we do not know object except as affecting us, though we may conceive an infinite spirit knowing (and creating) object entirely by thinking. Now the mental object unlike the external object is not presented through sensation: it is the self that affects itself in its form of receptivity called time.[a] Why the self has the forms of receptivity is to our theoretic knowledge an ultimate fact and no necessity. The question how the self 'affects the mind' cannot be answered; we are only assured that it does. Apparently this is not theoretic assurance.

11. That we are affected in our external sense may be admitted to be theoretically known in our internal sense. But that we are affected in our internal sense cannot be said to be known in the internal sense again. We can only be apperceivingly aware or aware in the subjective attitude that we do not know the self as object, i.e., as mind by mere apperception. Such subjective awareness of our inner sensibility in the negative way is apparently involved in the practical cognition of ourselves as free cause.

12. There is a good deal of obscurity in Kant's conception of the internal sense, and the exposition of it presented here is to a certain extent tentative. The external sense is said to be affected by the object, the form of the sense being space and the matter the sensations. If the object affects, it is not as spatial but as given, i.e., as the unknown reality phenomenalised in space. The internal sense is also affected by its object, viz., a mental object, not by the object so far as it is temporal (for time is the form of the sense) but by the real self phenomenalised in time as mental. The mental object has a form and a matter, the form being time, the form of the internal sense or the internal sense itself, but what is the matter? 'The representations of the external senses'—the percepts as we may call them, rather than the perceived things—are the matter of the internal sense.[b] In the case of the external object, the matter (i.e., sensation) is only understood in reference to the form (i.e., space) as what fills space, although space is not understood in reference to the matter, being imaginable as empty. Sensation *means* what is involved in space, this involution of content being apprehended in the internal

[a] 'If the faculty of self-consciousness is to seek for i.e., to apprehend what lies in the mind, it must affect the mind and can thus only produce an intuition of itself'.—Critique of Pure Reason (Tr. Max. Müller)—p. 733.

[b] Critique of Pure Reason (Tr. Max Müller)—p. 732.

sense. In the case of the internal or mental object, the matter—spatial percept—is similarly understood only as the filling of time, as involved in time. How is this involution apprehended? Not by the internal sense but by apperception. The reference of the image to the percept may be taken as the type of involution here. This reference is not itself presented: there is awareness of it only in the subjective attitude, in the form of 'I refer'. This awareness or apperception is only self-feeling, not knowledge of the self.[a] The matter of the internal sense is thus the spatial percept as floated in time, as involved in time, as referred to in an image. The mental object is the image which is not so much in time as time itself, time figured as variously as the image varies. So the external object is not so much in space as a determination of space. The varying determinations of space or space-figures are through timing, through the imagination of possible motion in space. Similarly the varying time-figures—each image being a time-figure—are through the working of apperception or understanding in time, of the self or the mind,[b] this working being called the transcendental synthesis of the imagination or figurative synthesis.

13. The mental is thus understood by Kant to be time as figured by the self and as involving or engulfing percepts, to be image constructed by the self in time (as pure intuition) and referring to spatial percepts. We have spoken of the work of the self on the internal sense in connection with knowing. We may now generalise it and understand the work of the self on the internal sense as willing or feeling also after the analogy of the schematic imagination in knowledge. The internal sense as thus figured is the empirical mind. The images belong to the internal sense, while the feelings of pleasure and pain and the will do not belong to it except as bound up with the images and as thus representing the work of the self on time. The mind then will mean the images as figured—cognitively, conatively and affectively—by the self. A mental fact is thus an image as formed out of time by the self and as informed by the self. An image, we said, is not so much in time as time itself as figured, so that that mental facts are in a series is only a verbal proposition while that external facts are in time is a synthetic proposition. If mental facts being in time be taken as implied by the very concept of the mental,

[a] Prolegomena (Tr. Mahaffy & Bernard)—p. 97, ft.n.

[b] Critique of Pure Reason (Tr. Max Müller)—p. 758-9—where the internal sense is distinguished from the faculty of apperception, the mind from the self.

[c] Critique of Pure Reason (Tr. Max Müller)—p. 732.

Kant's view even of the (empirical) mind would be very different from the Humian view of the mind as a mere series of mental states. To Kant, mind would be time itself as a unity, as a permanent or duration, not mere succession, and so in sundry passages he speaks of mind and its modifications. Only this permanent mind cannot be pictured: it is on the one hand presented with the self-feeling and on the other symbolised by the spatial world (as gathered up in body—a point which Kant did not bring out), time being symbolised by space. The symbolism is necessary and adequate because the body felt as referring to (or in specific response to) the external world is the content of the mind as self-feeling.

14. The time-relation of mental facts (images) though not a succession within a spatial permanent and therefore not a causal succession is yet an objective fact and not a merely imagined content or image. The paradox requires to be explained. Empirical Psychology is taken by Kant as a descriptive but not an explanatory science. 'It' (Empirical Psychology) 'can never . . . be anything more than a historical and as such, as far as possible, systematic natural doctrine of the internal sense i.e., a natural description of the soul but not a science of the soul . . .'.[a] It cannot be a science because, as pointed out in this connection, 'mathematics is inapplicable to the phenomena of the internal sense'. These may no doubt be represented in time symbolised as a line, but the inapplicability of mathematics means really inapplicability of causality which is known only in the *spatio*-temporal world. The applicability of mathematics makes science proper only because such applicability means precision of causal explanation.

15. This is brought out in another way. The object of the internal sense, unlike that of the external sense, has no 'quantity as substance' 'consisting of parts outside one another'. Not that it has no intensive quantity or degree but its 'increase or decrease is possible, notwithstanding the principle of the permanence of substance'. The intensity of an external object increases or decreases, only when *substantial* units are added to it or taken away from it. But when a mental state decreases in intensity, we do not know of its losing any parts or substantial units so that a total annihilation of a conscious fact unlike that of a material fact is intelligible. This is practically saying that the law of conservation of matter or energy is inapplicable to the mind; and it amounts to the statement that the category of causality is inapplicable to mental phenomena.

[a] Metaphysical Foundations of Natural Science (Tr. Belfort Bax)—p. 141.

16. Succession, says Kant in connection with the second Analogy of experience, is objective only as causal. Now if, as shown, the succession of mental states is not causal, must it be taken as only subjective? Must we say only that we are aware of one mental state after we are aware of another and *not* that one mental state *is* after the other? No: the succession of mental states is to Kant as much a fact as the succession of external events, the same time being the form of the mental object and of the external or spatio-temporal object bound in causality. How is this possible? We may imagine—for I am not aware of any actual passage of Kant in support—that it is because each mental state is, as pointed out, necessarily and adequately symbolisable by an external situation (as gathered up into a felt bodily state), is non-distinct from it (though it is distinct from the mental state). The time-relation of two mental states is then the time-relation of the external situations with which they are bound up, and it is only thus that it is objective fact without being causal.

17. It may be asked: if there is no causal relation among mental facts, why does Kant hold in connection with freedom and necessity that the self as noumenal is free and as phenomenal i.e., as mental is causally determined? The answer is that causality within mental phenomena is not theoretically or objectively knowable, being only a practical expectation. Moral or free willing involves the belief that it is being realised in the empirical world—mental and spatial. The belief is only partially realised theoretically: we may see the effect in the objective without being able to see the *modus operandi,* to understand how the effect so far as it is seen is brought about, how e.g., an inclination is weakened and rendered impotent on the occasion of moral willing by the free act or by some mental antecedent, though neither alternative is excluded, and an adjustment of the two causalities is conceivable. The belief in the operation of causality within the mind is only practical, being bound up with the practical belief in or knowledge of free causality.

18. The external world as phenomenal is felt, heuristically imagined or reflectively judged to be self-subsistent. The mental world cannot be similarly imagined to be self-subsistent. It may be suggested that the self-feeling in the mind can be *symbolised* by the external world imagined to be teleological i.e., to be a self-subsistent mind (not self). The mental world would then only be symbolised, not judged, as self-subsistent phenomenon.

CHAPTER III

SENSE AND SENSATION

19. Kant speaks of 'sense' not only in connection with knowing but also in connection with willing and feeling. Inclination, for example, and pleasure and pain are taken as belonging to sense, though they are not like sensation matter of knowledge. Sense generally is thus understood in a spiritual or transcendental reference rather than in a psychological or physiological connection. 'Sense' is taken by Kant as a mode of the faculty of representation. It is defined as 'the faculty of receiving representations according to the manner in which we are affected by objects'. The primary dualism apparently is of the thinking act and the faculty of representation, sense being the latter with the further attribute of being 'affected'.

20. The self is, to Kant, essentially the conscious thinking act which has three incommensurable 'interests' or directions—theoretic practical and aesthetic. We have representation in each of these directions of thinking. Representation is received in knowing, put forth in willing and entertained in feeling. In none of these is representation a mere floating image, the self having certitude of some kind about its content. Representation is apparently nothing to Kant apart from the thinking act, though distinct from it; and the thinking act means to him a necessary act or an act with immanent certitude about its content. Pure thought, to him, has no content distinct from it: the so-called logical entity is either not purely logical or is no content of thinking but the thinking act itself. The first content of thinking is representation.

21. To confine to representation as the content of *cognitive* thinking. Here the representation is received or is given. As given it is intuition and the receiving of it is intuiting. There is no reflective consciousness of intuiting as distinct from the intuited and so somehow representation is at once the object and has the object given to it. Thinking, however, is reflectively distinguished from representation, though in knowing it is not distinguished from the representing. Thinking as undistinguished from representing is Kant's pure productive imagination. Representation as distinguished from thinking in reflective knowledge is the image, not floating image but image of the believed or existent object which is not other than the object.

It is at once imaging and image of the existent and comprises memory, apprehension (internal perception of external perception) and perception (external perception of external object). The faculty may be called reproductive imagination and its function is to Kant as much apriori as the productive function, being an anticipation of the given.

22. Representation in knowing is then imagination of the existent and the faculty may be taken as the mind itself as distinct from the self. Thinking as undistinguished from representing—pure productive imagination is as much the self as the mind. How in it the self retains the thinking activity and how the mind as image of the existent is distinct from the self and is given to it is what we do not know. To Kant, the self is somehow the mind and the mind is somehow not the self—a mystery that can be only exhibited in transcendental reflection but cannot be understood. It is probably the same mystery as the practical self being somehow at once free and not-free, free as good willing and unfree as the 'intelligible character' behind wrong willing, free as act and unfree as being.

23. The mind as the faculty of representation is sensibility when the representation emerges through the self being affected by the object. A 'pure' mind is conceivable in which the image of the existent emerges to the self without an affection of the self; but as a matter of fact an image of the existent arises in us human beings through affection or in other words, we have sense-intuition only. How are we conscious of the affection? We are conscious not merely of receiving i.e., not thinking but also of the thinking act being arrested, of a positive limitation of thinking or, more accurately, of productive imagining. We may conceive a clairvoyance of the object, a veridical image of the existent floating up before the mind as a spontaneous fulfilment and not as a limitation of our productive imagining. Actually, however, we receive such an image as a limitation i.e., through an affection. The veridical image comes in memory, apprehension and perception as a check to our free imagination.

24. Sensation is to transcendental reflection the conscious limit to free imagination. It is defined by Kant as 'the effect produced by an object upon the faculty of representation, so far as we are affected by it'. If the image of the existent emerges—as it always does as a matter of fact—through an affection of the self i.e., as a limitation of the free imagining act, it is a sensible or empirical representation. To be aware of a limitation of free imagining is to be aware of something positive and not of a mere privation, aware of

something other than the free act—viz., a given object—as positively limiting the act and as thus conditioning the emergence of the conscious representation of the object. This conditioning is understood as the causality of the object towards the mind. The representation—call it the percept here—is an event that emerges in the mind as the object is given. The percept is not other than the perceived object and cannot be said to be the effect of the object. It is in fact the mental object or event as reflecting the external object or as one with it. But the emergence of the event is not an event or representation. Not the event but the conscious emergence of it is the effect of the object and this emergence, as meaning a conscious arrest or limitation of the free imagining act, is sensation.

25. Sensation is not a representation but the emergence of it (as percept) on the one hand and the arrest of free imagining on the other. The causality of the object in respect of sensation is a conditioning, though it does not mean temporal succession. The causality of the phenomenal object in respect of the sensation which is not an object at all is not phenomenal or temporal causality. It is like the causality of the self in respect of a phenomenal event or the problematic conditioning of a phenomenal causal sequence by a noumenal ground. The emergence of a percept as mental event is not itself an event, nor is it a mere abstraction, being a state or affection of the self that is timelessly or transcendentally real, as real as the free imagining act of which it is limitation.

26. It may be asked how the object which to Kant is only a phenomenon constructed by the self can be said to cause the affection of the self called the sensation. The objection implies a misconception about the status of the phenomenal object. Representation received or given is intuition and it is empirical intuition as received or given through sensation. 'The undefined object of . . . an empirical intuition is called phenomenon'. Now, consciousness of sensation as an affection of the self is consciousness of a positive something that affects i.e., of a given that is transcendentally real. The phenomenal object is this given real as represented in the mind. The representation or percept or perceived object is not a mere idea other than this given real or thing-in-itself. The mental view of the thing-in-itself is the thing-in-itself as viewed. Not *falsely* viewed, for there is question of falsity only where the truth is knowable. The consciousness of the thing-in-itself is indeed a certitude involved in the certitude of the self being affected, but it is certitude only about the affecting positive *somewhat* and is not knowledge. It is certitude

involved in phenomenal knowledge and running beyond it. The certitude is not falsified in phenomenal knowledge, for it is reached only in the latter and never in isolation from it. We may say that the phenomenal object is the thing-in-itself as symbolised and given only in the symbolism. Thus to say that the phenomenal object causes the affection of the self is to say that the thing-in-itself causes it.

27. The sensation is not a mental event in time. Nor is it a quality of the spatial object. 'Colours' says Kant, 'are not qualities of a body, though inherent in its intuition . . . . but are modifications only of the sense of sight as . . . . affected by light'. In 'the table is red', the table as perceived is so much occupied space and this space is not red, even as the image of red is not red. The so-called quality of the phenomenal object is to transcendental reflection only the *filling or content* of the space *occupied* by the object.

28. Apparently to Kant, the relation of thing and quality has no application to objective existence. Thing is understood as a *simple* existent unity with a manifold of qualities and not as a *whole* of the qualities. How a simple can have a manifold in it is objectively unintelligible and is understood only in the case of the self as the subject of conscious states. Taking 'quality' in the proper sense as what the thing is and what yet is not the thing, we understand (though we do not know) the relation of thing and quality literally only in the case of the subject; and in the case of the object, we should take it merely *as though* it subsisted in it. The object or—what is the same thing—the space that is the object or is occupied by it has the apparent quality as its *content* or filling—as matter *within* it much in the sense in which the mirror has the image within it—and not as its real determination which quality proper should be.

29. The sensation then is neither mental object nor external object (as it would be, if it were quality) but what is mystically 'involved' in the external object or occupied space. Not that it is unreal like the image 'involved' in the mirror, but it is real not as object but as an affection of the subject and is known as such in the emergence of the percept as a mental event. The *content* of the external object, the *emergence* of the (percept as) mental object and the *affection* of the subject are one and the same real fact, viz., sensation, The content of the external object is (the degree of) its affecting causality; the consciousness of the affection of the self is the consciousness of the affecting causality of the object; and it is in the reflective consciousness of affection that the external object is known as the emergent mental object—the percept.

30. The external object is 'involved' in the percept as sensation is involved in the external object or occupied space. The external object is analysed into space as the form and sensation as the matter given by the thing-in-itself. The corresponding internal object—the percept—is similarly analysed into time as the form and the spatial matter which is paradoxically taken by Kant to be given by the self. The material for the internal sense to him is the external object which fills time as its content as sensation fills space as its content. The percept occupies time (i.e., emerges in time) as the perceived object occupies space; and the perceived object is the matter or content of the percept, internal sense or time as the sensation is of the perceived object.

31. How to understand however that the spatial object is matter given to internal sense *by the self,* as the sensation is matter given to external sense by the thing-in-itself? The affection of the self as internal sense is the spatial object and the cause of the affection is taken to be the self. It is only as the spatial object is reflectively known by the self that the mental object —percept —emerges in the mind. To reflectively know the object is to judge the object, to categorise it, or in other words to know it as externally and internally related. It is only of the explicitly related object that we have a conscious mental representation. The percept emerges to consciousness as mental (and not merely as the perceived object) only in the context of a judgment where one is aware of the relation in the object as undistinguished from the relating activity of the subject. The mental as mental emerges only as the matter of a judgment. The relation explicitly constituting the matter is known here to be given to the self (as internal sense) not from without but by the self as judging or relating. Precisely then in the sense in which the thing-in-itself is the excitant of the external sense is the self the excitant of the internal sense.

32. Sense to Kant is an apriori or transcendental receptivity, being the self itself (which is essentially active) as *somehow* passive. The forms of sense are just this apriori sense or receptivity. Sensations are the affections of the sense by the thing-in-itself. Sense as the transcendental ground or potentiality of sensations is called the apriori form of the sensations.

CHAPTER IV

Space, Time, and Causality

33. The analysis of known object into matter and form emerges in the transcendental consciousness only : matter and form are not empirical abstractions. The analysis is understood as self-evident : that the object has a given factor and an ungiven factor is taken by Kant as not requiring proof.[a] That the ungiven factor is Space, Time and Causality has indeed to be appreciated and exhibited step by step, but it is not really inferred or argued out. The formal arguments that are presented to bring out the apriority of space, time etc. are more directions for transcendental reflection than logical demonstration. This reflection may be described as a sort of experimentation with the knowing activity, a subjective exercise that can be specifically regulated. Objective reasoning is only a seeing of objective connections and does not involve an explicit introspective exercise. Transcendental knowledge—epistemology, to take a form of it—is not reached by logical reasoning without this conscious introspective deepening. In fact,-reasoning is here one among other indications of the kind of subjective exercise that is demanded. The knowledge that we get through such introspective exercise does not come after the exercise (as in the case of reasoning) but is an aspect of the exercise itself. So willing is in itself knowledge of the willing or the willed content. Like the knowledge of willing epistemological knowledge is self-evident without being intuitive.

34. The external world under transcendental reflection i.e., in such introspective exercise with the knowing of it along the line of logical reasoning gets stratified into sensed matter and the forms of Space, Time and Causality. It is stratification rather than analysis into co-ordinate factors. The sensed matter is apprehended as involved in space, the spatial matter as involved in time and this spatis-temporal matter as further involved in causality. Causality as known fact implies change, change as known fact implies the spatial object in change and spatial object as fact implies a given matter. The matter at every stage is known only as the filling of its form : whether apart from the form, it is anything is not known though it cannot be denied. The form however is understood everywhere as what can be empty, empty

[a] CPR—p. 16.

form being not fact but a possibility i.e., transcendentally *known*. We have an anoetic consciousness of matter apart from space (manifold of intuition[a]), of spatial object not in time and of non-causal succession of spatial objects. A spatial object may not be explicitly known to be in time, but we may have explicit consciousness of such object as *not* in time[b]—a sort of aesthetic consciousness which does not amount to knowledge. So a succession of spatial events may not be known as causal but there may be consciousness of their succession[c] as non-causal which is not knowledge of it as fact. The spaceless manifold of sense, the timeless spatial object and non-causal succession are not known as fact, though apparently they may be content of a non-theoretic consciousness. Empty form, however, is transcendentally *known* as a possibility. Empty space can be imagined as the possibility of sensed matter, empty time can be symbolised as the possibility of spatial object, and empty causality can be schematised as the possibility of an objective succession. The three empty forms are imagined in three stages. Empty space is picturable i.e., imaginable by itself. Empty time is only vicariously imagined or symbolised, being not picturable but representable (necessarily and completely) by the analogy of space; while empty causality is not only not picturable but not even symbolisable by any space-picture, being only sketched out or schematised by a half-formed time-figure or a direction of timing. None of these are known as facts but are not therefore chimeras; they are imagined and imagination here is knowledge of an objective possibility. This possibility is a kind of subsistent entity which to Kant is distinguished from mere chimera by being identified with a transcendentally evident subjective function. Empty space is the receptive function of the self called the external sense, empty time the receptive function called the internal sense, and empty causality the active function called thinking. All these functions are evident to transcendental or critical reflection.

35. The external object as being perceived is imagined, viewed

[a] The manifold is *known* as implied in perception, but whether it is psychologically given prior to perception is not denied by Kant.

[b] What is not known to be in time may yet be fact but *not* what is known not in time. A changeless spatial object is contemplated in an aesthetic intuition without being claimed to be fact. It can however be known as implied by time, in the knowledge of change.

[c] Whatever succession is believed to be objective fact is explicitly or implicitly believed to be causal. Even causal sequence is causal, the terms being members of a pervasive causal context. It is only what is taken as merely causal sequence between the terms taken by themselves that we are aware of as not objective fact. This will be discussed in the next chapter.

through the internal sense ['apprehended*], such viewing from within being transcendental relatively to the positive (or forward) perception. As thus viewed, the object shows itself as space which might be empty as involving or engulfing sensed matter. Space, in other words, detaches itself from the spatial object and becomes a distinguishable content of the apprehension, which may be called the possibility of spatial objects. This subsistent form of space — which may be now called an image or mental object — is next viewed from within i.e., sought to be thought as it is being imagined, and presently it shows itself as time detached from the mental object, time that can be empty but is filled with the matter of the mental object, viz., the spatial object. This detached time as the content of thought appears as a reference to space, only *as though* it were space, as space in the making, as the tracing out of space. Time as such symbolic space is again viewed from within, i.e., sought to be apperceived as it is being constructed and thus itself appears as in the making, as the sketching out or figuring of a possible image. Picturing, symbolising and schematising are the three consecutive grades of imaginative viewing of the external object, of viewing it from within or transcendental reflection on it through which its forms space, time and causality get successively detached from it and show themselves as the subsistent possibilities of the object. The grades of imaginative viewing are respectively the viewing of the object of the external sense from the level of the inner sense, of the object of internal senses from the level of thought and of the object of thought from the level of the apperception itself.

36. Form in the wide sense as comprising space, time and causality means qualitative unity or self-identity of the objective world, being just its known aspect or knownness. Space is this unity as presented, time as imagined to be presented and causality as thought to be presented. Space is pictured as object, time symbolised as object and causality schematised as object. Everywhere the form is taken as a single content, the world being understood as a unity and is contemplated as a detached subsistent. The detachment is transcendental and may be likened to aesthetic detachment. The object is in the first instance what is practically dealt with, intended for use. To the mind in the aesthetic, imaginative or contemplative attitude, the object floats up like an appearance and gets loosened from the practical context. Still the aesthetic attitude is objective; there is no suggestion of the appearance being *in point of truth* internal to the practical reality, being more essential

* CPR—p. 98-99.

than, or constitutive of this reality. In transcendental reflection, there is this suggestion: the form by being detached from the object contemplated appears constitutive of the object. The detached form is understood in the first instance as standing by itself as empty, and then it is appreciated as having formed or constituted the object, contained or engulfed the matter. The formative form next appears as self-limiting and self-constructing and as thus self-repeating.

37. To illustrate it in respect of space. The first grade of transcendental reflection is that in which space gets detached from the spatial object. The arguments for the apriority of space are really modes of this reflection on the spatial object, of viewing it from within, of imagining it as being perceived. The aim is not so much to *prove* the apriority of space as to some to *see* space as a detachable form, that form is apriori being taken to be self-evident. The five arguments point out the character of space as a detachable form paraphrased in different ways. The aspect of detachable space that first emerges is its conceivable emptiness, the ground relied on in the second argument. Emptiness is the negative aspect, and the corresponding positive aspect is what is brought out in the first argument, viz., space as having constituted the object, space as the mutual externality of objects (including one's body) to the internal sense, as a single all-comprehensive system of their positions, blown out in anticipation from the internal centre[a]. To be transcendentally aware of space as detached from objects is to be aware of its being their pervasive location and to organically feel oneself pervading them. To appreciate space as what can be empty i.e., a pure percept (intuition) is to appreciate it as a pure perceiving (form of intuition) or to feel oneself pervading out. Space as at once intuition and form of intuition (intuiting) appears as a living entity limiting or contracting itself into finite shapes, constructing or expanding itself also into finite sizes and thus perpetually reproducing itself. The argument about the oneness of space asks one to view space as having finite spaces emerging in itelf through self-limitation. Finite space is a shaped size. Shape rather than size should be taken to be meant by this argument as appearing through limitation, for there is no question yet of the spread of space out of which finite sizes are carved out, the limitation being thus a contraction of the one formless space rather than a division of one pervasive spread. In the argument about infinity, the size-aspect is pointed out as emerging

[a] An object is nothing without a perceivable position. To perceive an object in a position is to perceive—or (imaginatively) apprehend—its relativity to every other position including the position of the percipient's body. It is to apprehend the entire system of positions as constituting the object.

through expansion. 'Infinity' of space here means not a helplessly pervasive spread but "infinity in the progression of intuition", every finite size presenting this infinite progression or construction through an infinite number of expansive spurts.

38. Whether in the contraction or in the expansion, space is understood as reproducing itself, and thus each finite space-size may be said to be a repetition of every other, to be a type or paradigm of the whole of space. This character is brought out in the argument presented in the transcendental exposition of space. The typical or self-reproducing character of space which might be objectively viewed after Plato as the process of an Idea is understood in the subjective or transcendental way by Kant "as a form of the external sense in general", as an external intuition "having its seat in the subject only" "anterior to the objects themselves." The apodictic character of geometric propositions implies the assurance that the properties of any parts of space hold good of all space. Thus the arguments for the apriority of space amount to a *seeing* of space as a form in its varying aspects.

39. As time is necessarily and adequately symbolizable by space, the arguments for the apriority of time are exactly parallel to the arguments for space and indicate similar modes of transcendental viewing of time as a form. What difference there is between the forms of space and time is intelligible as the difference in the mode of imagining empty space and empty time. Empty space, we said, is picturable while empty time is only symbolizable. The former is represented as possibility of spatial objects and is subjectively evident as the external sense itself (form of intuition) or as one big image (intuition). The latter is representable by actual spatial object as simply persistent or "continuant" and is evident as internal sense, felt duration or what may be called self-feeling.

40. We have, for the sake of convenience, used the term 'form' to indicate not only space and time but also the categories as comprised under the one heading, causality. Kant uses the term of space and time only, of the former literally and of the latter analogically or symbolically, restricting the term to such unity or self-identity of the object as is presented. Causality is also a mode of unity but is not presented. Of space and time, it is said that they are not only forms of intuition but also intuitions. As forms of intuition, they are indeed transcendentally felt as subjective, but as subjective receptivity and not as subjective activity. "The form of .... intuition may lie *apriori* in our faculty of representation, without being anything but the man-

ner in which a subject is affected" (C.P.R. p. 744). The manner of being affected is not even an implicit act of the subject.[a] It would in fact be taken only as unconscious capacity (a bodily function—organic or internal and special or external sense) but for the fact that space and time are themselves conscious intuitions (images as we may call them directly or indirectly referring to experience). Causality is a 'connection' or 'synthesis' of presented objects (p. 744 above) that is not presented or intuited, though the objective *fact* as we believe it necessarily implies it. This necessary implication is not inferred but is evident to transcendental reflection (on time) as a conscious *act* of the subject and not as a sense or receptivity or the manner of being affected.

41. The forms of sense have sometimes been loosely characterised as subjective acts. They are indeed *apriori* conditions of objective knowledge and as such anticipations of experience. But the anticipation is subjectively a feeling rather than an act. From the practical standpoint they may be regarded as expectations of the fulfilment of moral willing and not as moral self-assertion. They would be evident as practical assertion or as put forth by the will if, as was pointed out previously, we had intellectual intuition. As we have no such intuition, we have to take them as passive expectations of sensuous intuition. We may connect it with the Kantian statement that space and time are only known as the forms of *human* intuition : if we have to know, some form of intuition is necessary but that it should be space or time i.e., in reference to *sense*-experience only is no necessity but an ultimate transcendental fact for us. Space and time are as a matter of fact constitutive of the object that we know, necessary only in this sense and not necessary in the sense in which category or apperception is necessary, i.e., as self-justifying like willing which is indubitably real to itself. Even apperceptive consciousness *of the object*— that we should know object at all—is not a certitude like that of willing. *As* we practically *expect* a knowing of the fulfilment of willing and as we therefore *happen* to know object, the categories are self-evidently necessary to knowledge of object.

42. Causality is an unpresented act and as such no 'form' in the Kantian sense, although we may take it as 'form' in the wide sense of form of unity of the object. As Kant says[b] 'the concept of connection includes, besides the concept of the manifold and the

[a] Kant admits implicit act, not in the sense of unconsciousness (for apperceptive act is to him self-evident) but only in the sense of faint consciousness connected with the effect only and not with the act itself (C. P. R. p. 86).

[b] CPR—p. 745.

synthesis of it, the concept of the unity of the manifold also'. Synthesis is the act of relating, relation as a transition from one intuitable object to another. But the external world that we know is not merely a related plurality but is a standing unity. It is in this sense that causality can be called a form.

43. As in the case of space and time, we may understand the form of causality as empty. Connection as empty is the form of unity, being variously called 'qualitative unity', 'synthetical unity of the manifold' and 'objective unity of self-consciousness'. Apperceptive unity by itself is but 'self-identity: 'the principle of the necessary unity of apperception', 'says Kant[a] 'is itself identical, and therefore an analytical proposition'. 'But', he continues, 'it shows, nevertheless, the necessity of a synthesis of the manifold which is given in intuition, without which synthesis it would be impossible to think the unbroken identity of self-consciousness'. As the possibility of such synthesis, the apperceptive unity is called objective as 'distinguished from the subjective unity of consciousness which is a form of the internal sense'. Transcendental reflection on the object of the understanding viz., causal succession dissociates its form of causality as the empty form of unity which as empty is but the subjective unity of consciousness or what we have called self-feeling (of the mind or internal sense). But the empty form is now recognised as the positive possibility of the objective *world* or the unity of experience. 'The same transcendental unity of apperception constitutes, in all possible phenomena which may come together in our experience, a connection of all these representations according to laws'.[b] [Cf. the relation of the second argument for space to the first argument—the general principle being that in the reflective detachment of a form (which is the representation of it as empty) there is the recognition of the positive constitution or constructive character of the form. The whole of the theoretic critique may be regarded as the recognition of the possibility of the object, i.e., of the construction of the object in and through the reflective dissociation of form from the object].

[a] Ibid.—p. 747.
[b] Ibid.—p. 89.

CHAPTER V

CAUSALITY

44. Kant enunciates the second Analogy of Experience in the Second Edition in the form : "all changes take place according to the law of connection between cause and effect". By "change" here he means objective change, change in the spatial world, as distinct from the mere succession of mental states which cannot, except symbolically, be said to be in causal connection. In fact, not merely the laws of succession among the objects of the internal sense, but apparently any specification in it e.g., the distinction of the succession of two mental objects A and B from that of A and C or of the order A-B from the order B-A would be taken by him to be known only through the knowledge of causal dependences in the spatial world. Space to Kant is, as has been pointed out, known before time is known; and connected with it is the fact that causal change—in the spatial world, for causality is (theoretically) known nowhere else—is known prior to mental change[a] Succession as imagined[b] presupposes succession as perceived, objective succession, or succession as fact—factual or given (perceived) succession being the same as causal succession. Given succession is irreversible succession, irreversibility being not the criterion but only the analytic description of causal succession. When one looks from one end of a house to another and back again, one is not aware of a *given* succession of two perceived objects; but only of the succession of their apprehensions. Every perceived succession in the spatial world is at the same time a succession of apprehensions of two objects but the perceived succession is not necessarily a fact *as between* those objects. What is called a causal sequence of A and B is indeed a given or causal sequence, but of X and Y (which may be undiscovered yet), not of A and B. A and B being somehow bound up with X and Y so that the causal sequence is represented subjectively as between the apprehensions of A and B.[c] There is no question here of reversibility, so that causality —as here between A and B—is not denied on the ground of rever-

[a] Critique of Pure Reason (Tr. Maxmüller)—pp. 161-62.

[b] Succession of images (internal presentations) is—apart from succession of spatial objects—imagined succession.

[c] AX—BY may, as succession of presentations be called indifferently succestion A-B, A-Y, X-B or X-Y; as of spatial objects it is only X-Y.

sibility. A given or perceived sequence then is always causal and irreversible though the precise terms of the sequence may not be the terms, the apprehensions of which we are aware of as successive in the internal sense. All perceived succession is irreversible succession of two (spatial) facts which may not be known and which can be ascertained by the criterion that the antecedent among them should contain the condition of the rule by which the consequent follows at all times and necessarily. Thus two characters are given of causal succession—irreversibility and inevitability, each a sufficient character —the former presenting the problem of finding the precise terms of the succession through the application of the latter as a criterion.

45. That every given or perceived succession is causal succession of *some* objective facts is not capable of objective proof. It, however, follows immediately from the transcendental reflection that if succession which should not be perceived (by the external sense) is yet perceived, it can only be through the imaginative production of the perception.[a] The internal sense is necessarily anticipative of the continuous extension onward of time, and since whatever is to be known would be represented in the internal sense as presentable to external sense, it would necessarily be known as a series of phenomena in space in which each succeeding necessarily depended on the preceding.

46. To explain. Time is not externally perceivable and yet we apparently perceive a change in the external or spatial world. Succession is believed as an intuited fact and is not taken as an imaginary content. It cannot be intuited by the external sense nor by the internal sense which can intuit only an external percept. So succession in the external object and the intuition of the succession in the mind must be apriori or timelessly constructed by the sense. Apriori construction of succession is timeless construction of time in space. Time is not given before this synthesis.

47. But it may be asked, why may not a change be perceived in the ordinary way? To apprehend a change as change, it is necessary not only to have the idea of different states together but to have the idea of their being in order of succession. The time-order cannot be said to be remembered unless it was perceived. Now it cannot be said to be perceived for the first time at the time of sensing, for then it would be perceiving without a sense-basis. Elsewhere e.g., in the visual perception of the orange where the colour is sensed and the touch aspect ideated, the latter is sup-

[a] CPR—p. 171.

posed to have been sensed along with the colour in the past. Here, however, the prior and the posterior moments of the change could not have been sensed together. If the succession is taken to be only perceived now, it is non-sensuously *intuited* by the mind. The mind then has to be credited with an original power to know the pastness of the external object without the help of sense. One has to choose between this view and the Kantian view of the mind's constructive anticipation of the posterior moments of a change at the time of sensing the prior moments—or—what is called "production of the perception" of change—which, we may suppose, is completed in the sensing of the posterior moments. The latter would be consonant with the view that the mind (internal sense) can apprehend only what is or appears given to sense perception (external sense). The anticipatory apprehension of the coming moment of the change is possible through the apprehension of the direction of the change or motion that is presented in space. This initial *direction* appears at least to be externally perceived. In the other theory there is no such apparent external content to guide us from the present to the past, and one has to admit a purely internal intuition of the pastness of the external object.

48. The production of the perception of change is anticipative, starting from the sense-perception of the external state on which the change supervenes. To apprehend the state in the internal sense is at once to expect and to perceive a state of depending on it, to necessarily produce the percept of it in advance. Now, since we can know the external world only by floating the representation of the external sense in the internal sense—that being the condition of apperception, the external world is known as intrinsically involved in change, as a continuous succession of spatial facts in which the consequent followed the antecedent necessarily, that is, according to a rule.

49. It is thus that Kant transcendentally deduces the possibility of the factual world being spatio-temporal. On our ordinary notions of space and time, of perception and imagination, spatio-temporal facts as well as the perception of time would be a mystery. The mystery has been sought to be made intelligible in other ways—e.g., by the conception of a single entity that is somehow both space and time, though called either space or time. But apparently such a conception is not feasible except as a mere problem, being unrepresentable as presented or intuited, since the distinction of space from time is the inalienable distinction of perception from imagination.[a]

[a] The very condition of perception is a distinction of space from time.

Yet, since as a matter of fact we *do believe* in the world being spatio-temporal—without which belief too, the merely temporal (or mental) cannot be believed, we have to overcome the ordinary notion of space and time as a duality of co-ordinate entities in a different way. Kant's solution is apparently that space is involved in time and yet distinct from it—or to put it otherwise, space is distinct from time but not vice versa. The solution he presents in the transcendental or epistemological way rather than as an objective metaphysical view. Space and time are no doubt to him transcendentally ideal but the identity is understood in contrast with the transcendental reality of the free self as practically apprehended. Within phenomenal objectivity, they are real and we can have *apriori* a metaphysical view of the relation of space and time, such metaphysic being never repudiated by Kant but only postponed after the critical enquiry. Now his metaphysical view as indicated by his epistemology of the perception of change may be imagined to be that space is within time but is not time; the external world is real within the mental but is not itself mental. The object is within the mind in the sense that while the object appears given to, and therefore distinct from the mind, one is aware of the mind not as distinct from the object but as constituting the object in so far (primarily) as it appears in change (and motion, and secondarily as a determinate shape-size). Change is an explicitly equivocal presentation: it is not spatial and yet it is in space. To distinguish space from time and yet to perceive time in space as change is to be transcendentally aware of this immanence as the immanence of the mind in the object.[a] So one is aware of the changing object as what has mind immanent in it and aware of it, yet as perceived by the mind and as such distinct from it, and reflected in a mental presentation.

50. Thus apparently the law of causality as presented in the Second Analogy of Experience is legitimated by the epistemology of the perception of change. The concept of objective change requires to be elucidated. Change is a transition from one mode of existence to another mode of existence of the same object. Further 'every transition . . . . from one mode of existence into another takes place in a certain time between two moments, the first of which determines the state from which the thing arises, the second that at which it arrives. Both . . . . . are the temporal limits of a change or of an intermediate state between two states and belong as such to the whole of the change. Every change, however, has a cause which proves its causality during the whole of the time in

[a] Cf. Alexander on time as the mind of space. Only take mind literally and all within phenomena.

which the change takes place. The cause, therefore, does not produce the change suddenly (in one moment) but during a certain time.... All change, therefore, is possible only through a continuous action of causality which so far as it is uniform is called a momentum. A change does not consist of such momenta but is produced by them as their effect'.[a]

51. Change then means change of state, and not merely difference of certain relations which we have even in a uniform movement which is no change.[b] It does not mean the state which arises (or an event) but the passage from one state to another of the same object. Between the states, there is always an intermediate state: 'neither time nor a phenomenon in time consists of parts which are the smallest possible; nevertheless, the state of a thing which is being changed passes through all these parts, as elements, to its new state'[c], this being the law of continuity in all change. The 'thing' or the spatial object in change emerges out of a state which is apparently at once the initial state of the object and the terminal state of another object. 'Arising or perishing absolutely, and not referring merely to a determination of the permanent, can never become a possible perception'.[d] But a spatial thing would not be said to arise out of a state that belonged to it only. 'Every substance .... must contain in itself the causality of certain determinations in another substance'[e],'....according to the principle of causality, actions are always the first ground of all change of phenomena and cannot exist therefore in a subject that itself changes'.[f] Now the action through which a change or a changing thing arises cannot belong to the same thing. This action or influence of one thing on another implies 'a relation of the subject of the causality to the effect.' The 'subject of the causality' is a substance other than that in which the effect is produced. The relation of the two substances must appear in a single mode of their coexistence in space, this being the state out of which the spatial object in change, which is the presented form of the substance influenced, arises.

52. The question may be asked about the status of these substances and of the causality of which the influencing substance is said to be 'the last subject'.[g] These substances cannot be metaphysical in the sense in which the free self is metaphysical, nor are they unknow-

[a] CPR—p. 170;
[b] Ibid. p. 169n;
[c] Ibid. p. 170;
[d] Ibid. p. 153-4;
[e] Ibid. p. 173;
[f] Ibid. p. 167.
[g] Ibid. p. 167;

able things in themselves. Kant calls them substances in phenomenon: they are not presentable in external or internal sense and yet are the contents of *perceptions,* perceptions that are produced by imagination only. They are metaphysical in the sense of not being given in sense, in the sense the fundamental principles of natural science are called by him metaphysical. These substances are embodied in spatial object in change, are indicated by them, but are not themselves spatial. As to the causality of which the acting substance is said to be the last subject, it is not the temporal action but what is embodied in it and is determinative of the change that follows it. It is what he calls "real powers, which can be given empirically, ... motive powers" which "certain successive phenomena (as movements) indicate".[a] These then are the causes: the previous spatial *event,* the last state of the influencing substance is not the cause. The effect too is not an event in the sense of a stage of change, but the whole change which may be called a unitary continuous series of events. The cause that is said to operate "during the whole of the time in which the effect takes place" is thus a motive power or force, a metaphysical entity in the sense explained. Thus Kant's conception of causality differs from Hume's not merely in the recognition of necessary connection, but also in the recognition of the metaphysical entities of substance and force as necessarily in phenomena. (So too, as was pointed out previously, he admits not only mental phenomena but a substantial empirical mind in which a pure self is embodied).

53. It is important to note here that why one substance should cause a change in another we do not know; and it is permissible here to suppose that the ground of the causality is something noumenal.[b] The connection of such "metaphysical entities in phenomena" with free causality is thus easily suggested as a problem.

54. Causality to Kant implies the category of substance though substance need not imply causality. Causality is understood in respect of a change of a substance, of change as implying a static permanent. But after the recognition of causality, there arises the concept of action which implies again the concept of the "subject" of the action, the "last subject of the causality" which must be permanent. As time necessarily refers to space which without reference to time is not known as fact, and cannot yet be denied, so causality presupposes substance which as a merely static permanent cannot be denied. Thus though, according to Kant, nothing is known as objective fact

[a] Ibid. p. 169;
[b] Ibid. p. 441.

unless it is causally related, the terms of this relation are not therefore taken to be constituted in their facthood by the relation: causality is a regulative and not a constitutive category. The effect must be outside the cause and dependent on it: causality means an order of time, a rule of succession. There would, however, be no rule or necessity represented in phenomenon if there was a *lapse* of time between the cause and effect. The effect must be co-existent with the causality of its cause, though the cause cannot produce its whole effect in one moment.[a] The dependence of effect on a co-existent in which the causality resides—or *action* which is the same thing in another way—is symbolically, necessarily though, represented spatially e.g. by a line of motion. This symbolizing is a constructing so that we may say that causal influence is the construction of a pure motion. The subject of the action and the subject of the change that follows are understood as two substances. The time-order of the action and change can be only known as an objective fact if the corresponding substances are embodied in co-existent spatial objects. But spatial co-existence is fact only if *each* object acts on the other i.e., if the subject of the change also acted on the subject of the action. In other words, causality as a fact entails reciprocity between two substances, i.e., phenomenally presented as a spatial co-existence of spatial objects. Time is an objective fact only as a change in space and space is a fact only as changes dependent on each other which would be a contradiction unless understood as substances acting on each other and having a change in each dependent on the others. Change is only of the unchanging and is accordingly only a sensible phenomenon of an intelligible reality. Here we have an analogue within the knowable object of the practical dualism of the self as free and determined, as noumenal and phenomenal.

55. The Second Analogy of Experience states only that change takes place according to the law of causality or in other words, that it does not happen by *chance*. It does not exclude the possibility of a causal transition (from an action to a change) being itself only a fact, being conditional on nothing else, or–as it may be put—being unintelligibly *fated*. This fate is excluded as a knowable object by the Third Postulate of Empirical Thought. There might be, one can argue, unconnected causal laws (or reciprocity system) in which the cause is not caused and at least the effect does not cause. The Third Postulate may be taken to assert that uncaused cause and uncausing effect cannot be known objects, that whatever is known as object is knowable

[a] Ibid. p. 166.

as at once the effect of something and the cause of something else. No object is known that is not in change and no change that is not caused. This may indeed be taken to be implied even in the Second Analogy, (though it is explicit only in its formulation in the first edition —"everything that happens presupposes something on which it follows as a rule"). But in any case an uncausing effect is not excluded by it. An effect or rather the last stage of a change, that terminates of itself may be still admitted, for its existence or its cessation after the last moment of the change would be no happening and, therefore, does not fall under the Analogy. But, as has been shown at the beginning, the perception of a change is *anticipatory*: given a perceived situation, one apriori expects some existence (in change) to emerge out of it.[a] Since the last stage of a change is a perceived situation, the anticipation of the perception of a change after it is necessary. Some such deduction of the impossibility of an uncaused effect (as an empirical object) may be supposed to be implied in the Third Postulate, though it is not explicitly stated.

[a] Ibid. pp. 184-185.

CHAPTER VI

JUDGMENTS OF FACT, VALUE, AND OUGHT-TO-BE

56. Kant discusses the judgment in all the three critiques. Theoretic judgment is judgment of fact, and there is no theoretic knowledge to Kant outside the judgment. But judgment to him need not be knowledge: the third Critique is of judgment considered as a faculty co-ordinate with knowing and willing and identified with feeling. This is judgment of value or, as he calls it, of purposiveness, purposiveness being value in its relational aspect. Moral judgments such as he deals with in the second Critique are judgments of something being 'good', the good being understood as presupposing the 'ought' or the moral imperative. A judgment is expressible as a sentence indicative and so prescriptions of 'ought to will' are not judgments. But 'good' means what ought to *be*: to say that an action is good is to state a judgment, to assert that it fulfils the moral law or the 'ought to will', is such as ought to exist as an object. Neither 'ought-to-will' nor 'ought-to-be' is a value: value is nothing if not at least partially actualised in an object, while 'ought' means what completely transcends the actual. In Kantian ethics at any rate, there is no moral value, for the 'good' means nothing apart from 'ought to will', no *self-subsistent* value which the will is to realise. *Value,* however, may be possessed by what is morally, good, beauty or teleology being explicitly taken by Kant in the third Critique as symbol of morality.[a] Fact as a concept would be to Kant positively opposed to value, and goodness too is not value, though it may be symbolised by value.

57. Judgment in all these cases refers to a phenomenal object and is the appreciation of a concept or an intelligible being somehow immanent in it. The appreciation amounts to theoretic or practical knowledge about the object in judgments of facts and of ought-to-be, which accordingly are called *determinative judgments*. It does not amount to knowledge but only to an imaginative or subjective satisfaction in judgments of value which are called by contrast reflective *judgments*. In all judgment, however, the content viz., the immanence of the intelligible in phenomenon is actual or accomplished to imagination, though it is assertorially believed only in reflective judgment, not in determinative judgment where it is only taken to be necessary. It

[a] CJ. p. 248, p. 370.

is (in any case) what is imagined with certitude and not merely what is sought to be or might be imagined.

58. The subject of a judgment is always a phenomenon and the predicate an intelligible. The phenomenon may be actual or possible, perceived or perceivable, but never what we are conscious of as imaginary or illusory or problematic (*might be* imagined). The possible phenomenon means here that which *is* imagined as what *can* be, not merely *might* be. The subject again is not nothing without the predicate, though it may be nothing *known*; and as having the predicate immanent in it, it is still phenomenon and not phenomenon-cum-noumenon. The subject must be presented in intuition, empirical or pure: there is no judgment about the purely intelligible. The immanence of the predicate in the subject also cannot be purely rational, the copula being apprehended in an apriori imaginative synthesis as phenomenon in the making, as the form*ing* of the subject phenomenon.

59. Phenomenon is at once the other of the intelligible and what is constituted by it, a term of the relation of immanence and the relation of immanence itself. In the first chapter, phenomenon was explained from the moral standpoint as less real than the (free) self, from the theoretic standpoint as somehow mixed up with the self, and from the imaginative (reflective) standpoint as yet self-subsistent. These three aspects of phenomenon are brought out in the three types of judgment—moral, theoretic and reflective—, and in the three types of imagination that they involve. It may be stated in advance that the moral judgment takes the subject as a *symbol* (typic) of the predicate (*ought,* 'final purpose', good), the theoretic judgment understands the predicate (concept) as *approximation* to (or schematically figured by) the subject, and the reflective judgment regards the subject as the *expression* (self-specification) of the predicate (reason, 'pur-posiveness').

60. To begin with the theoretic judgment. Every judgment is understood in the form 'S is P', where S is a perceived content, actual or possible, P a thought-content or concept, and the copula *is* the immanence of the concept in the percept. The subject is an object of the external sense or of the internal sense, and each may be actual or possible. An actual object of the external sense is a spatial (spatio-temporal) object, and a possible object is some pure determination of space as mere form (external object in general), the judgment being either physical or geometrical (phenomenal-mathematical). An actual object of the internal sense is a temporal presentation of a spatial object, actual or possible; and a possible object of the internal sense

is some pure determination of time as mere form, of presentation in general. A judgment about the former would be psychological or pure—mathematical (according as the subject is presentation of an actual or of a possible spatial object); and a judgment about the latter would be transcendental—what Kant called 'principle of the understanding' (comprising apparently two grades—the metaphysical principles of natural science making up what is called 'pure Physics' and the transcendental principles dealt with in the first Critique). The predicate is a concept which may be empirical (like 'dog'), pure-intuitional or mathematical (like 'triangle') or a category (form of concept or necessary connection). The different grades of the subject may be grouped conformably to the predicate into the three heads of individuals—empirical object, particular determinations of space–time and space-time; the corresponding judgments being called physical, mathematical and metaphysical judgments in a generalised sense.

61. The transcendental equivalent of the copula in these three classes of theoretic judgments is the schema, a generic form in the making as half-presented form of the spatial (spatio-temporal), vicariously or symbolically presented form of the (purely) temporal and unpresented (but intended to be presented) form of the intelligible. The schema is not a complete image but is what is intended to be completed in an image. It is not image at all in the case of the category, but in the case of the other concepts, there is some actual indefinite image which is sought to be further defined. The defining out of the image is in every case a conscious act and not merely an unconscious process in which one finds the image progressively defined. The schema being of a universal is a generic or typical image which is only in the making and unlike an individual image which is found complete so far as it goes and found, it may be, to be presented with increasing definiteness, is being defined by a conscious continuous act. The act is with a definite intention i.e., thought of the perceived object to be comprehended or apperceived. The manifold of sense as received primarily in space and secondarily in time is only arranged, not yet related, is only a given whole of elements which are not yet *necessarily* connected, connected in such a way that each is known to be a fact only as implying the whole, that the implication itself is believed to be as real as the given whole. When a given or perceived whole is thus known to be interconnected, it is said to be comprehended or apperceived. Implication is the universal form of objectivity which being unknown, the given whole is only undeniable but not assertable as objective fact. The categories are the different modes of logical implication, the primary

differentiations of the universal form of objectivity or of the apperceptive unity. These again comprise the modes of mathematical and physical implication which may be regarded as secondary universals. Schema in general then may be defined as implication in the conscious process of being imaged.

62. Judgment as a transcendental function implies the schematisation of the universal. The universal in Kant is understood in a very wide sense. There are universals of quantity, quality, relation and modality, each including category, mathematical concept and physical concept. The ultimate universal in the theoretic sphere is objectivity, implication or apperceptive unity. In both theoretic and non-theoretic judgment, the universal is the self as asserting itself in reference to the phenomenal object. In the theoretic sphere, the self in such reference is logical implication or the implication called truth; in the practical sphere, it is the good or the objective obverse of freedom; and in the imaginative sphere, it is self-subsistent value. In all spheres, the self in reference to the given phenomena is a thinkable which is in the process of being phenomenalised as an anticipatory image of the phenomenon. In the theoretic sphere, the self thus becoming flesh is called schema.

63. In theoretic judgment, the concept to apply to the percept seeks to imaginatively anticipate it. The question has been asked if this is not a gratuitously mystical account of the judgment. We start, it is said, with the fact of knowledge which is judgment, the concept and the percept being only unreal abstractions from it. To Kant, in the practical sphere at any rate, the free self and the inclinations with which the known objective world is bound up are no mere abstractions, the dualism being of two hard concretes. The latter is, no doubt, a phenomenal reality, less real than freedom, which, if holiness could be attained and intellectual intuition were possible, would be realised as an emanation from the one reality of the self. As a matter of fact, holiness is an absolute imperative and we have no positive conception of intellectual intuition, though the being of the former and the facthood of the latter, cannot be denied. In actual consciousness then, phenomenal reality has to be admitted as opposed to transcendental reality. Some sort of unification is taken to be attained in the reflective concept of value, but the unity is self-subsistent only as phenomenal object or nature, not as a beautiful soul; and even in nature, the union of mechanism and teleology is not actually imagined but only what may be imagined, being no content of reflective *judgment*. The dualism of spirit and nature then remains and in the theoretic sphere, it appears

as the dualism of the infinite (Idea of Reason) and the finite (content of judgment), and as its shadow within the judgment—the dualism of concept and percept. Had the sphere of object-knowledge (theoretic judgment) stood by itself, the view of concept and percept as mere abstractions would be plausible, and the two unknowns at the background—viz., the self as a pure logical entity and the thing-in-itself might have been dismissed as chimeras. As a matter of fact, we have actual belief in, though not knowledge, of the self and the thing-in-itself as concretes, in the setting of which belief the transcendental analysis (which is knowledge) of the judgment into concept and percept is understood. Hence it is that there is a problem as to how the concrete concept and percept meet in the judgment. The cognitive questions 'what is it? (the given)' before a judgment and 'Is this judgment true?' after a judgment point to the judgment as a union of factors that can be dissolved. If it can be dissolved, the uniting has to be recognised as a function.

64. The uniting function is constructive imagination, imagination that produces belief, produces the perception of the given spatial object as figured by it. The figure is not given in passive or receptive perception but it appears consciously as though it were given i.e., as the content of perceptual judgment. The spatial object as passively perceived is still distinguishable from this content which however appears one with it. In contrast with the passive percept, the figure appears in the internal sense as in the making and is from the point of view of thought or apperception the conscious making or figuring. This figuring that is at the same time an incomplete figure is called a schema. In the case of concepts lower than the category, the incomplete figure is partially or symbolically pictorial, but in the case of the category, the figure is purely temporal, just barely intended to be pictorial. In the former case, the judgment is not purely theoretical but partly *reflective* or aesthetic, there being a feeling of actual or realised immanence of the concept in the percept. In the case of the category and the purely theoretic judgment, this feeling is absent, the percept being accordingly completely distinguishable from the judgment. The schema proper is a process of the concept that barely touches the percept i.e., is represented in the internal sense as what is not but is to be or must be represented in the external sense.

65. Since the schema is intrinsically non-pictorial (at least partly) or in other words the percept is distinguishable from it, the theoretic judgment or object-knowledge is realised only in an *internal* percept in figured *apprehension*. The concept thus only approxi-

mates to the percept, its immanence in the external or spatial object being only intended, not accomplished. Such knowledge, therefore, as we actually have is always unsatisfying, is only necessary and not self-evident. The known phenomenon is only a mixture of concept and percept, of thought and the given and is not self-subsistent like the phenomenon of the reflective judgment or judgment of value. To the reflective judgment, the phenomenon is living nature, external percept inter-penetrated with the concept, a sort of spatialised mind. But just because the concept is here spatialised, there is no longer knowledge. The perceived phenomenon is no longer apprehended in inner sense and therefore no longer apperceived. Knowledge implies apperception of the apprehended or internally perceived phenomenon.

66. To elaborate the account of the reflective judgment or judgment of value. The phenomenon to it is self-subsistent, a spatialised mind that specificates itself. Its figuring by the concept appears as its own elaboration or expression. The union of the concept and the percept is not here a schema, a presentation in the making but the accomplished presentation of expression—what is called 'specification of nature'.[a] The concept here appears immanent in nature as *its* purposiveness, the specification being of the purpose. In the theoretic critique, the understanding is said to make nature: the object is no known fact unless it is figured through the schemata by the categories. But what is thus constructed by the understanding is the bare form of nature, the object so far as it can be apriori anticipated in the *principles*. The object must have *some* extensive or intensive quantity, *some* causal law etc., but we do not know the *particular* quantity or law apriori. We know this by experience i.e., nature gives it. There is no necessity that nature should give us specific forms and forms that are connectable into a system. As a matter of fact, however, nature does give us such. Each specific form or specific connection of forms is such as can be known by us, fits in with our general apriori anticipation or principles, appears purposively designed not for our desire but for our cognitive faculty. It is as though there was an objective mind speaking to our mind in a language intelligible to us. That we can know aposteriori, that the matter of knowledge which we could never anticipate happens to wear the apriori forms of our knowledge is a wonder that we can never theoretically explain—for that would be apriori knowing the given particular. We have only to accept it as a fact and feel the problem and reflectively interpret it as the purposiveness of nature. Such interpretation would be a judgment of

[a] CJ—p. 26.

impersonal value—an altogether new kind of judgment. A judgment of personal value or purposiveness for desire would be only a theoretic judgment.

67. The purposiveness of nature is purposiveness to our knowing, not to our desire, and is imagined as such in the expression or interpretation of an actual or given feeling of pleasure of a disinterested kind. The imagination is, as compelled by an actual feeling, necessary, and the principle of purposiveness (to knowing) is a transcendental principle of the faculty of judgment. Judgment has to be recognised as a faculty distinct from knowing, for this imaginative interpretation of a feeling of knowing as purposiveness is necessary without being inferential. It is necessary for reflection or understanding of the subjective faculty of knowing, of the union of the two factors of knowing—apriori and aposteriori—reached in transcendental reflection but not necessary for the understanding of the object known, for the union is not given as a perceivable character of the object but only a felt content. Judgment such as we have within cognition is not other than the faculty of understanding which is indifferently described as a faculty of conceiving (categories) and of judging (principles or rules), the two being distinguished at all in view of this extra-cognitive reflective judgment which has a specific transcendental principle. Within knowing, concept that is not for judgment is but subjective apperception and has no objective meaning. At the same time it may wait for application in a judgment and is in this sense prior to it. This reflective judgment however is prior to the concept of purposiveness; the immanence of the concept (of purpose) in the percept,—the judgment function–is given in feeling in the first instance, and the concept is then sought to be formulated through the reflective elaboration of the feeling. In judgment of fact, the concept seeks application but in judgment of value, the application seeks the concept.

68. The purposiveness of nature is felt and imagined in two ways—the aesthetic and the logical (teleological). In the former, the purpose is imagined in reference to the cognitive faculty in general while in the latter, it is imagined in reference to the cognition of something objective. What the specific purpose is we do not know in either case: but while in the teleological judgment, it is known as some *intrinsic* purpose of the object that is yet to seek, in the aesthetic judgment, it is not so known, the object being only imagined as fitting the apriori conditions of knowability. In the teleologic judgment, the purpose or the ideal is not merely imagined but thought as objective, being imagined as the completion of some thinkable and not merely

felt character of the object. In the judgment of an object as living i.e., with "an inner end" the end is explicitly thought as formative of the object[a], though it is not known in specific detail. In other words, while the aesthetic judgment starts with an empirical percept, the teleologic judgment starts with an empirical judgment, the starting cognition being reflectively sought to be specificated in either case. In both, the purposiveness is imagined as an interpretation of empirical knowability, of what is only felt to be knowable in the former and of what is both felt as knowable and partly thinkingly known in the latter.

69. The judgment of ought-to-be like the judgment of value is the expression of a felt immanence of the concept of the good in perceivable object, though the feeling is a practical feeling, not one of enjoyment. At the same time it is a determinative judgment amounting to practical knowledge. The predicate as in theoretic judgment is fully formulated and transcends the subject, determining only the apprehension or the internal perception of it. Its immanence in external nature is indeed felt: nature is felt as the body of the holy law, though a mystic and not a manifest body, not as informed by the law of freedom, but as its distant symbolism (typic). In the theoretic judgment, the transcendence of the concept is expressed by its indefinite approximation to the percept in the *schema*. In the practical judgment however, the transcendence is expressed as the approximation of the percept to the concept, of the felt perceivable nature to freedom, such approximation being understood as symbolism or 'typic'.

[a] Judgment of external end is not reflective but theoretic judgment.

CHAPTER VII

FREEDOM AND MORALITY

70. Kant starts with the appetitive faculty (which to him is life itself), being the faculty of desire and aversion, which he understands as 'the faculty of being by means of one's ideas the cause of the objects of those ideas'. Desire (or aversion) is an act (as distinct from a sensible state) of the appetitive faculty, an effort (*nisus*) to be and is a causality at least within the subject. It is conscious as idea of an object to be caused and may or may not be conscious in the actual causation, and even where it is so conscious, may or may not pass out to the object itself. In any case it is conscious as an anticipation of causality. Where it is conscious in the actual causation, it is called will or wish (both being sometimes called *will*), according as it passes out or not to the object. Free will is taken as a particular form of the will.[a]

71. Desire is connected by a subjective rule with pleasure either as its cause or effect, such connection by rule being called interest. Pleasure that is so connected is practical pleasure as distinct from contemplative pleasure. As the cause of desire, it is called appetite, the habitual form of which is inclination. Desire is said to be caused by pleasure or the interest of inclination when the causal idea is of pleasure to oneself.[b] But the causal idea may be of an object only irrespective of pleasure: one may desire an object for its own sake, in which case the desire is said to be caused by an interest of reason, which as habitual may be called interest of sense-free inclination. There is, however, pleasure here as the effect of desire which is apparently not the pleasure of gratification but pleasure felt in the idea of the object to be caused, the 'felicific aspect' of the object ideated.

72. Pleasure as the effect of desire in this sense appears in the process, where it is conscious, of the causality of the idea of the object desired in the form of pleasing or choosing to act.[c] The causal process

[a] Kant uses the term *will* in two senses—(i) elective will which may be free or unfree, (ii) free or rational will. Sometimes *will* means also wish: the most general sense would be *pleasing* to act (or forbear).

[b] Its connection with desire being by a subjective and not objective rule, pleasure causes only an *idea* of pleasure and hence there is no question of an actual feeling of pleasure taking form as desire for more pleasure.

[c] Pleasure as necessarily and subjectively connected with desire determined by the interest of reason as its effect cannot be the pleasure due to the objective

of the idea is conscious when the desire depends on concepts; when, in other words, one is conscious of the object as desired on a general ground, as a case of a subjective rule or *maxim* of action. To be conscious of desiring an object because of a maxim is necessarily to be conscious of pressing towards gratification, of pleasing or choosing to act. Desire or aversion as such, 'doing or forbearing as we please', is called *wish,* and it is called *elective will* when there is the further 'consciousness of the power of its action to produce its object', consciousness of its causality passing out to the object.

73. This pleasing or choosing need not be choosing between alternatives. It is not necessary for willing that one should be conscious of an alternative course of action, and even where one is so conscious, that the idea of it should be an effort or *nisus* towards materialisation, conflicting with the idea of the object chosen. The rejected alternative may be an idea that only *might be* acted on without actually soliciting the will. In good willing, for example, there is the consciousness of the wrong course rejected; but this consciousness is not a rueful contemplation of a good opportunity of gratification *being* missed.[a] Choice need not mean conflict: the bearing of this on Kant's rejection of indeterministic freedom will appear presently.

74. The elective will is not necessarily free. There is animal elective will which is determined by inclination. Man in individual elective will is conscious of being only affected by inclination, being not determined by it. Both are determined by the subject, choice[b] being an act of the subject, the subject as embodied in the empirical

fruition of the desire. The effect here comes before the objective fruition which may or may not come. Because an object is desired, the contemplation of it is a pleasure. Desire in such a case cannot directly pass into objective action: it must develop first into a consciousness of causing, a subjective activity. This conscious activity can be only a choosing i.e. adoption into a maxim. Such adoption cannot but be a pleasure. All fitting of an object into a general subjective rule is a pleasure, and since the fitting is here practical, the pleasure is a pleasing. To find an object pleasant as the result of desiring it is to please to adopt it into one's general will-attitude.

[a] Where there is such contemplation, the choice is determined not by pure reason but only by a 'sense-free inclination', is not properly free. Kant's morality is not *reluctant* choice but only choice not determined by feeling though accompanied by feeling in the form of a *pure pleasing* to act. In the case of willing that falls short of good willing, the choice is determined by feeling (as in wrong willing) or by reason incorporating feeling in it (as in being honest by policy); and the *pleasing* to act is not a pure pleasure of self-approbation, where the rejected temptation still retains its tempting character, the *pleasing* to reject cannot be pure pleasure and cannot have been motived by the law but at best by the habit of acting according to it.

[b] Even the animal chooses, though apparently the concept or maxim of the choice *can* be only an attitude of specific adaptation to a class of circumstances in the environment, the adoption of an object into this attitude being represented by a pleasing to act.

mind. The animal subject does not distinguish itself from the mind or inclination, i.e., is not self-conscious.[a] The human subject is self-conscious, aware of itself as only solicited by the inclination. The human will may be still determined by inclination, but the subject is then conscious of *letting* the inclination determine it. But even this act of letting on the part of the subject does not mean free willing. Human elective will is said to be free when the subject that determines it is not only self-conscious or aware of the inclination being distinct from it but does not also let the inclination determine the will, and is conscious of itself as *pure* reason determining it. 'Freedom of the elective will is just that independence of its determination on sensible impulses: this is the negative concept of it. The positive is the power of pure reason to be itself practical'.[b]

75. Even in free willing, the determining subject is embodied in a mental attitude, motive or maxim which as distinct from the transcendental or 'objective' law of reason (moral law) is said to be a *subjective* principle of action, which the subject makes a rule to himself (viz., 'how he chooses to act).[c] Free will is still elective will: moral willing though proceeding from pure reason is still a conscious rejection of inclination and has, therefore, a necessary reference to the life of sense. Kant conceives a rational will beyond free will. 'The rational will which is directed to nothing but the law cannot be called either free or unfree, because it is not directed to actions but immediately to the legislation for the maxims of actions (and is therefore practical reason itself). Consequently it is absolutely necessary and even incapable of restraint. It is therefore only the elective will that can be free'.[d] The rational will here means the super-moral holy will which is beyond freedom and to which the human will as free is a perpetual approximation, being presented to man only as the moral law. '. . . Holiness of will is practical Idea which must necessarily serve as a type to which finite rational beings can only approximate indefinitely and which the pure moral law which is itself on this account called holy constantly and rightly holds before their eyes'.[e]

76. This freedom is not indeterministic. 'Freedom of elective will however cannot be defined as the power of choosing to act for or against the law (*libertas indifferentiae*) as some have attempted to

[a] Apparently there is a lower stage of animal desire not amounting to will, where there is no choice but only an idea of the object, not only not self-consciously but not even consciously, causing its existence.

[b] Critique of Practical Reason (Tr. Abbott), pp. 268-9.

[c] Ibid. p. 282.

[d] Ibid. p. 282.

[e] Ibid. p. 121.

define it, although the elective will as a phenomenon gives many examples of this in experience'.[a] Choice in itself is only phenomenon, while freedom of choice is noumenal. Empirical causality is necessary connection between phenomena. Why there should be a causal law connecting two particular phenomena we do not theoretically know, and it is quite permissible to suppose that the law itself has its ground in a noumenal cause.[b] Such a supposition of noumenal causality which would in no way conflict with phenomenal causality but which cannot be verified elsewhere is turned into a certainty in our moral consciousness. Free causality may or may not be the only form of noumenal causality but it is the only form that is known. It is known to us only through the moral law: *ought* implies *can*. A person acting from the moral law as motive and not merely according to it is practically cognisant of being a free cause, noumenal i.e., independent of sensible elective will and yet inexplicably constraining it. The phenomenal will[c] theoretically known as cause of the outward action is here practically known to be itself caused by or grounded in noumenal freedom. This is known only in good willing or willing of the moral law. We are not aware of being free cause in wrong willing so that there is no neutral or indeterministic freedom known to be a cause choosing to obey or disobey the moral law. We are indeed theoretically cognisant of obedience or disobedience as alternatively possible phenomenal directions of the elective will. But we know obedience only as free noumenal causality which cannot accordingly be defined as the power to choose between alternatives.

77. Wrong willing requires further discussion. Wrong willing is choosing to act from a maxim of inclination and consciously against the moral law. Choice is an event in time, a phenomenal causation, and human choice may be between reason and unreason (sense or inclination) as possible motives. Where the choice is of reason or *ought* or the moral law as motive, the phenomenal causality itself is known to be noumenally determined or caused by the supra-mental free subject. Where the choice is of inclination in rejection of the law, it must also be noumenally determined by the subject but as not supramental or free. Inclination is a mental phenomenon, and the subject as choosing it is aware of being identified with or embodied in the mental, is consciously unfree. The subject is noumenal cause but it is not aware of becoming unfree by any *act* of freedom but only knows

[a] Ibid. p. 282.
[b] Critique of Pure Reason (Tr. Maxmüller), p. 441.
[c] Not as merely mental but as involving body.

itself to be unfree. It *lets* itself be embodied in the empirical motive in the sense that it is *aware* of not acting independently of it, such inaction being itself a known phenomenal fact. At the same time, since the subject is self-conscious, the inaction or unfreedom is known to belong to the noumenal self and constitutes a noumenal and not merely a phenomenal evil. Wrong willing though not a noumenal *act* is a noumenal fact embodied in a phenomenal fact. The self as the noumenal but consciously unfree determinant of the wrong choice is the *intelligible character*. It is to our practical knowing a being and not an act: the self is practically aware of itself as essentially moral act and yet somehow as a determinate being also, just as it is theoretically aware of itself as essentially apperceptive and accidentally (though inalienably) receptive at the same time. This duality within the self is to Kant an ultimate fact presupposed by transcendental philosophy.

78. Like freedom, this intelligible character is known only practically as the implication of the moral quality of willing (as good or evil). The noumenal or transcendental duality of the self as free act and the self as intelligible being or character is known in self-conscious good willing and evil willing. This intelligible character, though actually evil, may have potentiality for good, originating, it may be, from previous good or free willing. There may be accordingly a willing that is not good or free i.e., *from* the moral law but not also against the law; one may be honest, for example, not because honesty is commanded but because it is the best policy. Here one not only knows theoretically that his action conforms to the moral law but also practically i.e., in spirit conforms—though only conforms—to it, is practically aware of *not dropping respect* for the law though not acting out of respect for it. Kant would say in such a case that 'the empirical character is good but the intelligible character is bad'.[a] Strictly speaking, to him the intelligible character is perverse rather than morally bad. Moral badness to him would imply evil not only in the intelligible but also in the empirical character, evil passing from the noumenal self to the phenomenal choice or elective will. Although the transcendental evil is still *imputable*—being therefore called *innate guilt*[b]—it is still not an imputable *choice*. The man is evil, not his willing. Kant speaks of three degrees of transcendental evil or rather propensities to evil[c]—frailty (i.e., not following adopted maxims), impurity (not distinguishing between good and evil springs) and perversity; a man being properly called evil when

[a] Critique of Practical Reason (Tr. Abbott), p. 344.
[b] Ibid. p. 345.
[c] Ibid. p. 344.

frailty and impurity mature[a] into perversity, the perversity of *subordinating* reason to sense[b], the moral motive to inclination, of 'reversing the moral order in respect of the springs of elective will.[c] The case of a person acting from the maxim of honesty being the best policy is a case of transcendental perversity which has not vitiated the phenomenal choice or elective will. Here there is a subjective mixture of two motives—rational and sensible, although the will is objectively determined by one only—in this case, the sensible motive. The willing here is not wrong though not good also: good willing as well as wrong willing implies the passing over of the transcendental determinant—adoption of a motive or maxim in the spirit—into the empirical choice.

79. The intelligible character is practically known in the first instance in (transcendental reflection on) wrong willing where there is a consciousness of rational motive as antagonised by sensible motive. The adoption in spirit of the sensible motive in transgression of the moral law implies a determinant other than but co-ordinate with freedom and therefore transcendental. The intelligible character is next known as operative in the case considered of willing that is right but not good where there is transcendental evil which does not vitiate the empirical will. That the empirical character here is good shows that although the intelligible character is actually evil, it is still potentially good. This potential goodness may be taken to have matured into the actual goodness of the empirical character. In fact, even in the case of wrong willing, one has to admit a potential goodness in the intelligible character which however does not mature or matures only as acceptance of natural law. There may be however a diabolical willing in which though there is no *free* transgression, there is non-acceptance of natural law through the stress of inclination. Belief that my inclination has a claim superior to that of reason implies disbelief not only in moral but also in natural law, disbelief in all constraint to inclination. This is conscious acceptance of insanity or 'stupidity'. Here the potential goodness of the intelligible character does not mature at all. 'Man (even the worst) does not in any maxim, as it were, *rebelliously* abandon the moral law."[d] There is no *free* transgression, so far as we practically know, obedience to the moral law being alone practically known to be free. Why the self is sometimes free and sometimes unfree, and why the unfree condition or evil of the noumenal character sometimes passes over to the empirical character and some-

[a] Ibid. p. 344.
[b] Ibid. p. 343.
[c] Ibid. p. 336.
[d] Ibid. p. 343.

times not we do not know: the fact is however practically known, known only assertorially. At the same time the question *why* cannot be stifled and there is the faith (not practical cognition and much less theoretic cognition) that, 'what man is or ought to be in a moral sense he must make or must have made himself.[a] What is to our cognition an ultimate transcendental fact *demands* explanation by an antecedent free act: the evil or good in the noumenal character, as imputable, cannot be simlply given but must be somehow through one's free causality, though it need not be through an act in time. This freedom cannot be a freedom appearing in an empirical choice and as such cannot be known (the freedom that we know—good freedom—appears in choice). Nor do we know *how* evil antecedent to free or good choice leaves a trace (in the form of a potentiality for good) in the noumenal character:[b] we only know that it does. The freedom that does not appear in a choice is a matter of faith, the being or character of the self being to us not only an ultimate fact but also a mystery to our practical consciousness. This freedom is not only the ground of the intelligible character which is itself the ground of wrong willing and right willing that is not good: it is also the ultimate ground of good willing. Even in good willing, reason determines the choice in *conscious* supersession of inclination. That the inclination should at all emerge as an alternative motive to reason to be rejected shows that the intelligible character (from which the inclination rises) is a necessary condition of the causality of reason. Our free will is not holy will: holiness is in us not in will but in the moral law as the transcendent determinant of the will.[c] The freedom which is to our faith behind intelligible character and behind even good freedom of which this character is a condition is what Kant calls the radical evil in human nature, a mystery co-ordinate with holy will (being the same as the primal viparyaya as avidyā which to the Yoga is even behind viveka and which matures into the more concrete degrees of evil like asmitā etc.) It is the free principle of evil which like the holy will is a matter of faith, not of practical cognition. As such it is not co-ordinate with our good freedom and hence it is that within moral philosophy proper as founded on practical cognition, we have to deny a bad freedom and therefore also a neutral freedom.

[a] Ibid. p. 352.

[b] Compare the question how asaṁprajñāta-samādhi leaves a saṁskāra.

[c] We could conceive a divine will which would be holy but not a choosing phenomenal will—what can not be called free or unfree. It would be freedom creating its own being and not having it somehow given to it, an intelligible character that never gets phenomenalised. It would be like the Iśvara of Yoga philosophy, sadaiva mukta and with prakṛṣṭa-sattva.

80. We can have a metaphysic of morals only on the basis of practical cognition, not of faith. Practical cognition is consciousness of the reality of freedom and of moral law in one process of good willing. The master principle of Kant's transcendental philosophy is good will or free will which is necessarily self-cognisant, knowing itself as free in the knowledge of the moral law and as the condition of the moral law. *Ought* is *known* as real, not merely thought or felt—as the rational self *actually* constraining the sensible self, freedom being this actual act, not a *may* nor a theoretic *can* but a practically assertorial *can*. Freedom is the condition of the *ought* in the sense that *ought* is real only in being acted, not in being merely felt or thought[a] (before good willing or wrong willing): *ought* is only as it is causal, being not an eternal truth or value. There is to our *faith* freedom beyond *ought,* the freedom to sin, the radical evil in man, although it is not known. There is no faith however in *ought* beyond freedom. The faith in holiness is faith in holy *will,* no faith in *ought,* which is only the holy *law* as that is known by us (and not as a matter of faith) *as being acted.* Thus in the single cognition of good willing, freedom is known as the (transcendent) condition of the moral law.

81. *Ought* is known only as being knowingly (freely) acted and as therefore wearing the form of knowability or reason. The form of reason is universality and so *ought* is known as the law and is formulable as a prescription to act only on the form of universality. Reason is primarily practical or imperative, and theoretic reason may be taken to presuppose it not as constitutive of objective knownness, but as constitutive of the *fact of knowing.* Hence if we started with theoretic reason, how it becomes practical would be unintelligible. Practical reason then is the form of universality or imperative in general as causal (categorical imperative). The form as causal is real: it is not merely a thought-possibility.

82. It has been sometimes objected that Kant gives us only a formula of morality, the mere form and not the content of morality. As will be presently seen, in his three-fold formulation of the moral law, the last two give some kind of matter, though it is pure matter. In the *Groundwork* and the *Critique,* again, he is mainly concerned with the form:[b] he reserves the division of concrete duties for a future metaphysic of morals. The main reason why he deals with the form in the *Groundwork* and the *Critque* appears to be that to him the form of morality is not mere form but the essence, the real spiritual

[a] *Ought* felt or thought as real without being acted is not (practically) known and may be taken to be imaginary.

[b] CPrR p. 93.

attitude that matters, morality being to him noumenally real only as this attitude.

83. The attitude is differently formulated as that of one legislating for all or treating humanity as the end or regarding oneself as a member of a possible kingdom of ends, i.e., regarding every person to be a universal legislator. The formulae refer primarily to the attitude: it is not meant, for example, that one should before acting try to find out the *consequence* of his maxim of action being followed by all. The consequence cannot be and need not be fully known: one has only to assure oneself that there is no contradiction in the inner spirit, no making of an exception in one's favour, no treatment of other persons as less than a person and a universal legislator. The rationality of the attitude prescribed is practical rationality which is not merely the implementing of a principle known first theoretically (i.e., in the consequence) to be generalisable without contradiction. The form of practical rationality unlike that of the theoretical is concrete and real in itself independently of application, The imperative universal is the concrete Idea of humanity as the legislative self of every individual self. Practical reason is of itself concrete as a person: the concretion or matter is here not other than the form and is called pure matter. The universal in the moral sphere is the *real* rational self which is real not as found common to many individual selves but as the noumenal individuality of every individual self. The self knows itself as a real individual only by practically asserting itself as legislative towards itself as somehow embodied in empirical inclination; and to be in this legislative attitude is to recognise other such individual legislators and to be in conscious harmony (and not identity) with them. To be in the attitude is to be aware of oneself as not consciously ignoring other individuals as in wrong willing. Good willing is conscious repudiation of wrong willing i.e., of conscious exclusion of other individuals: it is the practical apprehension of harmony with other individuals. Inclination is the principle of exclusiveness which is not however, the principle of real individuality, being itself only known by a moral self as unaccountably its body, a moral self that already knows itself as individual in harmony with other individuals. So the practical universal—humanity–means many individual selves in harmony, a society of spirits ('kingdom of ends') which is in inner attitude asserted by every individual spirit. The self that is free is, indeed, universal, but the universal self is not, as undertood by some, the *singular* Absolute or divine self working in us but is *each* individual self as in harmony with other selves.

84. The moral formulae can all be reduced to the form; act *as if* the maxium of the action were to become by the will a universal law of nature. Nature is theoretically known as the sphere of universal (causal) law. The practical idea of a kingdom of ends is necessarily symbolised as nature—necessarily, because to will morally i.e., to will the kingdom of ends is to have faith that the kingdom is being realised in a life of sense and in sensible nature. The *as if* here is a make-belief so far as this realisation in nature is not known even practically, but it is practically real not only as an attitude, but also as a contemplative act. The imaginative contemplation is not indeed prescribed but free willing as self-conscious is in itself a theoretic thinking (that is not knowing) of the form or meaning of the willing. The contemplation is practical in the sense of the willing being self-expressing, using theoretic thought as the medium of its expression, its self-consciousness being not a theoretic self-knowing but a self-symbolising by the theoretic concept of law of nature.

85. The imperative is called a law by way of symbolism, being envisaged *as though* it were a judgment indicative. The moral judgment of an object e.g. an action being good is a literal judgment, but the object here symbolises the concept 'good' through the typic of system of nature. Moral good means sensible nature as realising the moral law, as what ought to *be* corresponding to the ought to *will*. If a particular action is judged to be good, it is so far as it is known to realise the *ought-to-be* or rational or purposive system of nature. Such a system is understood as an infinite time or perpetual life in which the good will may be perfected into holy will (immortality) and as a nature organic to the happiness of the virtuous (and the opposite)*. The good as the predicate of moral judgment—this system of nature—is here envisaged *as though* it were the prescribed 'kingdom of ends' realised. The particular object, judged to be good is so practically known but the good itself or the ethico-teleological system of nature is not known but is necessarily entertained in faith. Such a system involves the concepts of immortality and of God (as the cause of the synthetic connection of virtue with happiness embodied in nature). This faith means a further symbolism: to believe in the reality of the *ought* (ought-to-be corresponding to ought-to-will) is to believe *as though* immortality and God were facts. Thus there are three stages of practical symbolism or consciousness of *as though*: in the formulation of the moral law, in the concept of the good, and in the postulates of God and immortality.

* The 'good' is understood as my own perfection and the happiness of others.

ANALYSIS

CHAPTER I

Idea of Transcendental Philosophy (Sec. 1-7)

(1) The Critical philosophy is a form of Transcendental philosophy. The 'transcendental' may be taken to mean the non-objective or that which is not distinct from the consciousness of it. To Kant, the transcendental is the self as conscious act or freedom—whether in knowing or in willing. This self is, according to him, formative of the object known but it is formative only as the purely logical unity of the object. The Kantian theory is thus different both from Vedāntism and Voluntarism.

(2) There are two different kinds of certitude or knowledge, viz., the practical and the theoretic. The former which is about the reality of the self is found in moral willing and the latter which is about the existence of the object is found in theoretic consciousness. In theoretic knowledge of the object, belief comes through the factor of intuition; but in the practical knowledge of the self; intuition is not present and the belief is through the willing or the realising of the thought. To will or to freely cause is to think and effect a causal change in the world. There is thus a fitting of free causality with objective causality and a meeting of the two certitudes in the thought of causality. It is difficult, however, to understand this. The difficulty arouses critical or transcendental reflection which effects an adjustment by taking the known object as only phenomenal.

(3) The relation between the theoretic and the practical reason is much more intimate than what is ordinarily assumed. The conception of apriori thinking as a factor of knowledge appears to be connected with the moral apprehension of free causality. Causality in the known object is intelligible only in reference to free causality as practically cognised. (4) The very problem of the first Critique would be gratuitous unless the object were already suspect in the light of a certitude higher than that about the object. That certitude is, to Kant, the certitude of the moral consciousness. The standard of reality can only be suggested by the apprehension, in the subjective attitude, of the self as utterly unobjective. (5-7) When Kant describes the object as only a 'phenomenon', the word has to be understood from three points of view—the theoretic, the practical and the aesthetic or reflec-

tive—elaborated respectively in the three Critiques. From the theoretic standpoint, the objective is taken as phenomenal because its forms—space, time and causality—are taken to be not objects but indistinguishable from the self : from the practical standpoint, the object is known to be an emanation of self as freedom; from the aesthetic standpoint, the spatio-temporal object is just a self-subsistent value.

CHAPTER II

Mind as Phenomenon (Sec. 8-18)

(8) A mental fact is in time only and what is in time is change. A mental fact is thus to be taken as change. But this change is not like a change in a spatial object and is not objectively taken to be in a persistent. This contrast suggests the question as to how it is to be regarded as a *fact*. (9) As a change for which no persistent is known and of which the facthood is undeniable, the mental appears to be a problem. The solution of the problem lies in the theory that it is a phenomenal fact. That the mental as the purely temporal is known as a phenomenon of the free self is grounded in the fact that we *practically* know the self as free causality. (10) The external object is taken by Kant to be the phenomenon of an unknowable reality and the mental object of the self as real. As objective knowledge depends on the affection of our sensibility, the knowledge of the mental fact must depend on some affection of the mind. But the question as to how the self 'affects the mind' cannot be answered. We are assured, however, that it does and this cannot be theoretic assurance through inner sense. (11) That we are affected in our external sense is theoretically known in our internal sense. But that we are affected in our internal sense cannot be known in the internal sense again.

(12) The internal sense, like the external, has its form and its matter, time constituting the form and the 'representations of the external senses' the matter. This matter involves time and the involution is apprehended not by the internal sense but by apperception. The matter of the internal sense is thus the spatial percept as floated in time or as referred to in an image. The mental object is the image which is not so much in time as a figure of time. Just as the different space-figures are through the imagination of possible motion in space, so are the varying images or time-figures through the working of apperception in time of the self or the mind. (13) The 'mental' is thus understood by Kant to be image constructed by the self in time and

referring to spatial percepts. The internal sense as thus figured not merely in knowing but also in willing and feeling is the empirical mind. A mental fact is thus an image as formed out of time by the self and as informed by the self. Kant's view of the empirical mind as time itself as a permanent unity would thus be very different from the Humian view of the mind as a mere series of mental states.

(14-15) The time-relation of mental facts is not a succession within a spatial permanent and, therefore, not a causal succession. It is yet an objective fact and not a merely imagined content. For Kant, Empirical psychology is not a science of the soul only because mathematics is inapplicable to mental facts. The inapplicability of mathematics means really inapplicability of causality. (16) According to Kant, succession is objective only as causal. The sucession of mental states is not thus objective. But it is not, therefore, merely subjective. The paradox can be resolved only by imagining that, to Kant, the time-relation of two mental states is the time-relation of the external situations with which they are bound up. It is only thus that it is objective fact without being causal. (17) There is no causal relation among mental facts. Kant, however, held that the self as phenomenal is causally determined. This would be intelligible on the assumption that the belief in the operation of causality within the mind is only practical, being bound up with the practical belief in or the knowledge of free causality. (18) The external world as phenomenal is reflectively judged to be self-subsistent. But the mental world would only be symbolised and not judged to be so.

CHAPTER III

Sense and Sensation (Sec. 19-32)

(19) Kant defines 'sense' as 'the faculty of receiving representations' by being 'affected', and the primary dualism is of the thinking act and the faculty of representation. (20) The self is essentially the conscious thinking act having three directions—the theoretic, the practical and the aesthetic. We have representation in each of these three directions. Representation is received in knowing, put forth in willing and entertained in feeling. Representation is the first content of thinking. (21) In cognitive thinking, the representation is given. As distinguished from thinking in reflective knowledge, it is at once imaging and the image of the existent object. (22) Representation as the faculty of imagination is the mind as distinct from the

self. (23) The mind is the faculty of sensibility when the representation emerges through an affection of the self. We are conscious of this 'affection' not merely as receiving but also as a limitation to free imagination. (24) To be aware of a limitation of free imagining is to be aware of something other than the free act—viz., a given object—as limiting the act and conditioning the emergence of the conscious representation of the object. The emergence of the mental event, which is not an event or representation, is just the sensation. (25) Though it is not an event, it is not therefore a mere abstraction. It is a state or affection of the self that is timelessly real.

(26) There is no harm in saying that the affection of the self is caused by the phenomenal object, for to say that is really to say that it is caused by the thing-in-itself. (27) The sensation is neither a mental event in time nor a quality of the spatial object. The so-called sense-quality is only the content of the space occupied by the object. (28) To Kant, the relation of thing and quality has no application to objective existence. The object has the apparent quality as within it much as the mirror has the image within it and not as its real determination. (29) The sensation then is neither mental object nor external object but what is 'involved' in the external object. (30) The external object is 'involved' in the percept as sensation is involved in the external object. (31) The self is the excitant of the internal sense precisely in the sense in which the thing-in-itself is the excitant of the external sense. (32) Sense as the transcendental ground or potentiality of sensations is called the apriori form of the sensations.

CHAPTER IV

Space, Time and Causality (Sec. 33-43)

(33) The analysis of known object into matter and form emerges in transcendental reflection which is a form of introspective activity and which is quite other than the act of reasoning. The knowledge that we get through such introspective exercise is an aspect of the exercise itself and does not come after the exercise as in the case of reasoning. (34) Under such reflection, the external world gets stratified into sensed matter and the forms of Space, Time and Causality. The sensed matter is apprehended as involved in space, the spatial matter as involved in time and this spatio-temporal matter as further involved in causality. The matter at every stage is known only

as the filling of its form, but form is understood everywhere as what can be empty. Matter without form is not *known,* but it may be the content of a non-theoretic consciousness. Form without matter is, however, transcendentally *known* as a possibility. This possibility is a kind of subsistent entity which is distinguished from mere chimera by being identified with a transcendentally evident subjective function. (35) There are three consecutive grades of transcendental reflection or imaginative viewing of the external object: (a) Picturing—where the object as being perceived is imagined through the internal sense and shows itself as the space-form which might be empty; (b) Symbolising—where this subsistent form of space as being thought is viewed from within and shows itself as the time-form which can be empty. Here time appears as symbolic space or space in the making; (c) Schematising—where this detached time, as viewed from within, appears itself as the figuring of a possible image.

(36) In the non-reflective attitude, the object is what is practically dealt with; in the aesthetic attitude, the object floats up like an appearance; in the transcendental attitude, the form by being detached from the object appears constitutive of the object. The detached form is understood in the consecutive stages of transcendental reflection (i) as standing by itelf as empty, (ii) as having constituted the object and (iii) as self-limiting and self-constructing and thus self-repeating. (37-39) The three grades illustrated in respect of space and time. (40) Unlike the forms of space and time which are presented, the form of causality (comprising all the categories) is never intuited, though objective fact necessarily implies it. (41) The forms of sense are not subjective acts. Though they are anticipations of experience, the anticipation is subjectively a feeling rather than an act. (42) Causality is a form in the wide sense of form of unity of the object. (43) Transcendental reflection on the object of the understanding, viz., causal succession dissociates its form of causality as the empty form of unity. This empty form is recognised as the positive possibility of the objective world.

CHAPTER V

Causality (Sec. 44-55)

(44) Causal succession possesses two characters—irreversibility and inevitability. The former presents the problem of finding the precise terms of the succession through the application of the latter. (45)

Every perceived succession is causal succession of *some* objective facts, but this is not capable of objective proof. It follows only from the transcendental reflection that if succession which should not be perceived (by the external sense) is yet perceived, it can only be through the imaginative production of the perception. (46) Succession in the object is believed as an intuitable fact, but it cannot be intuited either by the outer or by the inner sense. It follows that the apparent intuition of succession is only an apriori or timeless construction of time. (47) The only alternative to this Kantian view would be to admit that succession is nonsensuously intuited by the mind. But the Kantian theory would be consonant with the view that the mind can apprehend only what is given to sense-perception.

(48) The production of the perception of change is anticipative and the external world is known as intrinsically involved in change. (49) On our ordinary notions of space and time, of perception and imagination, spatio-temporal facts and the perception of time would be a mystery. The mystery has been sought to be solved by the conception of a single entity—space-time. That conception is, however, inadmissible. But since the ordinary conception of space and time as a duality of co-ordinate entities cannot be maintained, the true solution appears to lie in the Kantian view that space is within time but is not time. Space is thus distinguished from time and time is yet perceived in space as change. In the transcendental consciousness, this immanence of time in space is nothing but the immanence of mind in the object. (50) Thus the law of causality is legitimated by the epistemology of the perception of change.

(51-53) Kant's conception of causality differs from Hume's not merely in the recognition of necessary connection but also in the recognition of the metaphysical entities of substance and force as necessarily in phenomena. (54) Causality presupposes substance. According to Kant, nothing is known as objective fact unless it is causally related; but the terms of the causal relation are not, therefore, taken to be constituted in their facthood by the relation. Again, causality as a fact entails reciprocity between two substances.

(55) Uncaused cause and uncausing effect cannot be known objects. Whatever is known as object is knowable as at once the effect of something and the cause of something else.

CHAPTER VI

Judgments of fact, value and Ought-to-be (Sec. 56-69)

(56) Kant recognises three types of judgments. A theoretic

judgment is a judgment of fact and embodies knowledge. A feeling-judgment is a judgment of value and embodies imaginative satisfaction. A moral judgment is a judgment of ought-to-be and like the theoretic judgment it embodies knowledge. (57) Judgment in all these cases refers to a phenomenal object and is the appreciation of a concept somehow immanent in it. (58) The subject of a judgment is always a phenomenon—whether actual or possible—but never the imaginary or the illusory or the problematic. The predicate is always an intelligible. The copula represents the immanence of the predicate in the subject and is apprehended in an imaginative synthesis as phenomenon in the making.

(59) The three types of judgment bring out the three aspects of phenomenon mentioned in Chapter I. (60) The different grades of the subject in the theoretic judgment may be grouped conformably to the predicate into the three heads of individuals—empirical objects, particular determinations of space and time and space-time. The corresponding judgments are called physical, mathematical and metaphysical. (61) The transcendental equivalents of the copula in the three classes of theoretic judgments are respectively the schema or the half-presented form of the spatial, the symbolically presented form of the purely temporal and the unpresented form of the intelligible. The nature of schema elucidated.

(62) Judgment as a transcendental function implies the schematism of the universal. In both theoretic and non-theoretic judgments, the universal is the self as asserting itself in reference to the phenomenal object. In the theoretic sphere, the self in such reference is truth; in the practical sphere, it is the good; and in the imaginative sphere it is the self-subsistent value. In all spheres, the self in reference to the given phenomena is a thinkable which is in the process of being phenomenalised as an anticipatory image of the phenomenal. (63) In theoretic judgment, the concept to apply to the percept seeks to imaginatively anticipate it. The objection that the concept and the percept are only unreal abstractions from the concrete fact of judgment cannot be accepted in the light of the transcendental analysis of the judgment into concept and percept. There is a problem as to how the concrete concept and percept meet in the judgment. The judgment is a union of factors that can be dissolved. If it can be dissolved, the uniting has to be recognised as a function. (64) This uniting function is constructive imagination or the imagination that produces the perception of the given spatial object as figured by it. The figure is not given in passive perception. In contrast

with the passive percept, the figure appears in the internal sense as in the making. (65) Since the percept is distinguishable from this schematic figure, object-knowledge is realised only in an internal percept in figured apprehension. The concept only approximates to the percept and its immanence in the spatial object is not accomplished. Such knowledge as we actually have is, therefore, only necessary and not self-evident.

(66) To the reflective judgment, the phenomenon is self-subsistent. Its figuring by the concept appears as its own expression. The union of the concept and the percept is not here a schema but the accomplished presentation of expression. The concept here appears immanent in nature as its purposiveness. (67) The purposiveness of nature is purposiveness to our knowing and is imagined as such in the interpretation of an actual feeling of pleasure of a disinterested kind. The reflective judgment is prior to the concept of purposivenesss. The immanence of the concept of purpose in the percept is given in feeling in the first instance, and the concept is then sought to be formulated through the reflective elaboration of the feeling. In judgment of fact the concept seeks application; but in judgment of value, the application seeks the concept. (68) The purposiveness of nature is felt and imagined in two ways—the aesthetic and the teleological. In both the purposiveness is imagined as an interpretation of empirical knowability—of what is only felt to be knowable in the former and of what is both felt as knowable and partly thinkingly known in the latter.

(69) The judgment of ought-to-be, like the judgment of value, is the expression of a felt immanence of the concept of the good in perceivable object, though the feeling is a practical feeling amounting to practical knowledge. The predicate is fully formulated and transcends the subject. The transcendence is, however, expressed as the approximation of the percept to the concept, of the felt perceivable nature to freedom and the approximation is understood as symbolism or 'typic'.

CHAPTER VII

Freedom and Morality (Sec. 70-85)

(70) Desire is conscious as an anticipation of causality. Where it is conscious in the actual causation, it is called will or wish. Free will is a particular form of the will. (71) Desire is connected by a subjective rule with pleasure either as its cause or as effect. As the

cause, it is called appetite or inclination. As the effect it is the 'felicific aspect' of the object ideated. (72) Desire or aversion as such i.e., doing or forbearing as we please, is called 'wish'. When there is the further consciousness of its causality passing out to the object, it is called 'elective will'. (73) This pleasing or choosing need not be choosing between alternatives and choice need not mean conflict.

(74) The elective will is not necessarily free. Human elective will is said to be free when the subject that determines it is conscious of itself as pure reason determining it. (75) Free will is still elective will. There is, however, a rational will beyond free will. This rational will is the supermoral holy will. (76) Freedom of elective will is not indeterministic. Choice in itself is only phenomenon, while freedom of choice is noumenal. The phenomenal will which is theoretically known as cause of the outward action is practically known to be itself caused by noumenal freedom. This is known only in good willing or willing of the moral law.

(77) Wrong willing is choosing to act from a maxim of inclination and consciously against the moral law. In both good willing and wrong willing, the phenomenal causality is known to be noumenally determined by the subject. But while in good willing the subject that noumenally determines the choice is the supra-mental free subject, in wrong willing the subject is consciously identified with the mental and is consciously unfree. In the latter case, the subject is not, however, aware of becoming unfree by any act of freedom. The self as the consciously unfree determinant of choice is the *intelligible* character.

(78-79) This intelligible character, like freedom, is known only practically as the implication of the moral quality of willing. There is to our faith a freedom behind this intelligible character, and behind even good freedom of which this character is a condition. This is what Kant calls the 'radical evil in human nature'. (80) Practical cognition is consciousness of the reality of freedom and moral law in the single process of good willing. (81) 'Ought' is known only as being fully acted and as weaving the form of reason. Practical reason is the form of universality or imperative in general as causal.

(82) The charge of 'formalism' is not wholly justified. In his three-fold formulation of the moral law, the last two give some kind of matter. The main reason, again, why he deals with the form appears to be that, to him, the form of morality is not mere form but the essence as well. (83-85) Kant's standpoint and his moral formulae analysed in detail.

APPENDIX

'TRANSCENDENTAL METHOD'

Kant's method of philosophic investigation is a method of transcendental reflection. Ordinarily in philosophy, we reason or argue as in science from data to conclusion. Kant also seems to reason, but a closer consideration shows that his procedure is very different from objective reasoning as in science. In objective reasoning, the conclusion is taken as what must be and not as what is, and the subjective operation of passing to it from the data is not understood as constituting the connection between data and conclusion. The content of the conclusion is only expected to be perceived, experienced or realised and is not felt to be realised in the reasoning itself; and that the conclusion follows from the data is taken to be an eternal fact no way depending on the work of the reasoner's mind. In the transcendental procedure of Kant, there is the exhibition of data and conclusion; but the conclusion is not merely expected to be realised but is felt to be realised and felt not after the reasoning but in the very consciousness of the reasoning. The reasoning is like willing, the fulfilment or success of which is felt in the willing itself which, in fact, is expectation and fulfilment in one, realisation of the end in the consciously expectant operation. Within knowledge, we have this kind of immediately successful operation below reasoning also in intuitive construction: the line is there before us as we draw it. So in the presentation of a motion, there miraculously emerges the presentation of the path of motion. Transcendental reasoning is similarly a realising of the conclusion in the very operation of reasoning. Everywhere it is a sort of seeing in the doing: the transcendental procedure is an experimental knowing, the experiment being consciously made with the self itself. Ordinarily we take knowing as what *comes* to us. There might be voluntary regulation before the knowing—e.g., knowing of the conclusion in a reasoning where one regulates one's thinking through a certain mode of arranging the data in one's mind. But the knowing comes after the arranging and does not shine in the arranging itself: even then it does not amount to a seeing or assertory certitude but only to the faith that it will be verified. In the apprehension, however, of the line emerging into being in the imaginative drawing of it, there is assertory certitude about the line in the conscious process of reaching it. So in all the apparent reasoning in the demonstration of the apriority of time, space etc. in the Critique, we have an assertory certitude about the conclusion in the conscious procedure. It is not a matter of proving so much as of inwardising the knowledge of time, space etc., of what may be called an introspective knowledge of the object, of realising of the objective fact as being bodied forth by the subject. We may see a line simply as there or we may apprehend it as being seen by being imaginatively traced. The apprehension may be helped by a distinguishing of the objectivity of the line from that of a perceived empirical fact, and the distinguishing may be expressed in the form of a reasoning—*because* the geometric entity has such distinctive characters, *therefore* it cannot be a merely seen fact as it appears to be. Really however the distinguishing is the whole cognition and the reasoning is but a scaffolding. The distinguishing here again is not a comparison, the mere consciousness of an objective point of distinction. It implies the emergence of a new grade of subjectivity, viz., imaginative seeing, the line being perceived by being given like the empirical object but by being imagined. The point of distinction between the line and the empirical object occupying it is not objective fact but a content corresponding to the introspective distinction between imagination and perception. The distinction between an objective fact as perceived and the same as imagined cannot be said to be objective nor merely subjective. The fact as imaginatively apprehended can only be described as internal to or constitutive of the fact as simply perceived, this internality being a transcendental (and not an objective) grade of the objective fact. Everywhere, reasoning in transcendental investigation is seeing the conclusion as the internality of the data through a methodical subjective deepening of the cognition of the data. The deepening is a doing, a specific experimentation with the subjective level of knowing. To adduce proof of the line being there through imaginative tracing is in fact a prescription to others to subject the perception to imagination or a recalling of one's own act of thus having constructed a line. So everywhere, transcendental proof is the indication of a subjective experiment with the knowing activity. To find the proof from oneself is to retrace the process by which one constructed or put forth the data. Transcendental reflection is the reverse of the process of transcendental construction. It is a form of aesthetic contemplation of the object through which the object is seen as being or having been expressed or bodied forth from within. It is like reflecting on a poem and to retrace the steps by which the original formless feeling in the poet's mind came to take its present articulated shape.

B. 'On The Sensum'

I used to believe with Kant-as I thought-that the sensum was a thinking abstraction from the physical object, which alone is properly known. But now I take it to be an 'aesthetic' abstraction which, unlike an aesthetic content like expression, I regard as known. I understand the sensum as of different stages the lowest of which (I consider at present) is the stage in which it is still reffered to a space position relatively to my body, like the physical object. Both the sensum and the object I take to be known, but in different senses. I understand knowledge in the ideal form to be consciousness of a content as completely distinct from the consciousness of it. Neither the object nor the sensum (in the lowest stage) is known in the ideal sense. Both are phenomenally known, known as somehow still mixed up with the subjectivity, localisation, for one thing, being still somehow at once subjective and objective. The mixture, however, does not mean a complete denial of knownness; both are known to the *extent* they are distinguished from the subjectivity. Relatively to the object, however, the sensum is better distinguished and therefore more properly said to be known. There is, however, another consideration, *viz.* about the sense of reality in respect of the known content, about the felt degree of the subjective actuality of the knowing. In this respect, the knowing of the object is more actual than the knowing of the sensum, though both are actual as distinct, for example, from imagining, which is only possible knowing. In other words, the sensum is a content of a higher grade than the object, though the knowledge of it is less 'subjectively' real. If the sensum could be subjectively realised (a mystical affair, it will be said, but not very different from what Descartes and others indicated by their demand for the clearness and distinctness of ideas), in the degree in which the object is naturally realised, it would be realised as what is only actually adumbrated as metaphysically more real that the object. Our metaphysic is only knowledge in promise, there being only this distinction about the status of the sensum as distinct from higher entities that its metaphysical reality is in some degree actually realised. The physical object is not known at all to be metaphysically real, while the sensum is, its reality being, however, half realised subjectively. The sensum (in the lowest stage) is still somehow phenomenal also, being referred to a space position, but relatively speaking, it is known as metaphysical. Now of the metaphysical and the physical, I say, if the one is known, the other is not known. So far, however, as the sensum is still phenomenal, it and the object are both said to be known phenomenally. I understand the phenomenal character of location to be an excrescence *to be* eliminated from the sensum. *To* reflect on the sensum is to be aware of its being an imperfect 'aesthetic' abstraction from the object.

Is the sensum related to the object? Taking it in its proper metaphysical aspect, it is known as what the object is distinct from, but not reversely. Distinction is the basis of relation rather that a relation; but waiving this point, I say that this one-sided distinction is the only relation that is known, being in fact the objective formulation of what I call aesthetic abstraction. So far as the sensum is still phenomenal, the space position is like its *expression* and it can be said to be coexistent with the object in this sense, the relation being other that the coexistence of the objects. The colour expanse (sensum) for example, coincides with the coloured surface of the object which is the object itself in one aspect, conincides and yet is apprehended as what the latter is not, and not *inversely*. If two objectives surfaces - opposed surfaces of the section of an object, for example - coincide, they are either only imagined to be distinct or are known to be *mutually* distinct. As phenomenon then, the sensum is related to the object in a peculiar sense, for all objective relation implies *mutual* distinction of the terms.

Knowledge is understood by Kant as an activity, though it is not the conative activity. Knowledge in its *ideal* form I take, with the Vedāntist and others, as a quiescent certitude and no activity at all, and *our actual* knowledge always has some activity in it, which implies that its object is partially undistinguished from the knowledge; and the higher the grade of knowledge, the less is the activity. (This of course is an unKantian view.) In the lowest grade, *viz.* knowledge of the physical object, I would take the activity in all grades of actual knowledge to be conative of different degrees of subtlety, and so I would, *by way of criticism,* take his phenomenal knowledge to be voluntaristic, though Kant would not admit it. But after all it is a minor point.

If and as the sensum is known in its true or metaphysical aspect, the object is understood as having no autonomous existence, but as an appearance projected by conative affective organic consciousness, by what I call the 'felt body' (or by the self as one with it). Is this projected or constructed object then known? Known, as I said, phenomenally, half distinguished from the consciousness of it and with a sense of its reality. Taken by itself, the consciousness of it cannot be said to be not knowledge, but taken in contrast with the knowing of the sensum, it is not knowing. To comparative reflection on the apprehension of the sensum and that of the object, both are not knowledge. In contrast with the knowledge of the sensum, what is called knowledge of the object may be called belief.

I shall explain what I mean by this 'organic projection' of the object or construction by the 'felt body'. My body, I both observe and internally apprehend ('feel' in this sense). My body, I both observe it as distinct from me, but do not 'feel' myself to be distinct from it. Again, I am not aware of the felt body as other than the seen body. I am aware only of the seen body as not the felt body. I am aware also of the felt body as distinct from (object to) myself, (though not reversely), this self being thus higher that relatively *subject* to bodily self or self not distinguished from body. This felt body is what I have *roughly* called organic sensum, thought it is not sensum proper, since organic consciousness or consciousness of the body from within is hardly sensation, being, as I take it, a conative-affective dealing with sensation rather than sensation. I call it sensum to indicate that it is distinct from or object to myself, though in reference to the seen body, it is subject or this conative-affective *consciousness* (on-distinct from the seen body). The 'felt body' is object in one reference, subject in another.

Now this felt body as subject, as dealing with the sensum (object of the special sensation), is projective or constructive of the physical object. The object is constructed as a reduplication of the body (the seen body felt as *mine*), in an extra-organic space (which is the felt organic space turned inside out) in reference to an actual or possible feeling of pressure (touch as 'mechanical sense' being in my opinion no presentative sense at all but a mode of organic feeling). Extra organic space, represented by the distance of the object from the body, is *constitutive* of object, or rather is an object in the making, only half-distinguishable form the body felt as mine, unlike the object in space. It is at once a projection and a projecting process. (Cf. Kant on space as at once an intution, and a form of intuition). 'The object there' is just what the percipient, identified with the body, is going out to feel (touch). The object is localised relatively to the body but it is indefinite to *which point* in the seen body. It is localised apparently relatively to the whole solid body, so far as it is also felt from within and hence the object is itself constructed as a solid, as a replica of the body. I take this projection to be the empirical interpretation of Kant's transcendental construction.

Sensa (the objects of the special sensations) are thus organised by the conative-affective organic consciousness into the physical object. The co-existence of different sense qualities in the object appears to me intelligible only on the analogy of the felt unity of the body. Since it is the only analogy, I take it to be more than analogy; the body felt as mine is constitutive or constructive of the many-qualitied solid hard object out there in space. The construction is unconscious and is in fact the psychological formulation in the forward direction of the aesthetic detachment of space as the constitutive and containing *from* of the object from the object. (What we know in reflection is the 'aesthetic' detachment of the form of the object from the object - corresponding to the cognitive distinction of the object from the form. This detachment is a *discovery* of the sensa, and reflection on the detachment is the relisation of the sensa as *having been* organised, constructed or projected out). The object apart from the form is the sensa of which we are aware in reflection as not constituted by, i.e. as distinct from the perceiving consciousness. The sensa appear to this reflection as received in this consicousness which, though subjective relatively to the sensa (and the object), is objective relatively to the reflection, is the felt body. The sensa may thus be said to be in the felt interior space of the felt body. This space has to be admitted as what the outward space is distinct from and to be conceived as engulfing the outward space, the boundary of the latter being the seen body felt as mine. (Unless we admit it, I do not know how to understand a pain to be in the finger). As a mater of fact, the sensa (in the lowest stage) are only imperfectly detached form the outward space though they are never quite *in* this space like the object. In the case of sound-sensum, the detachement is most definite - a sound is as much heard 'out there' as heard 'in the mind', in the felt interior of the felt body, sound unlocalised (in outward space) being still appreciated as objective (unlike an unlocalised pain).

I will state how I differ from Price. To start with, I say, here is the surface of a *physical* object. The fact of variation, etc. do not invalidate the belief in such object and are in fact intelligible only on the admission of such object. I next say that with the slackening of the practical stress and the emergence of theoretic-aesthetic consciousness, what was taken as surface is apprehended as a self-subsistent expanse. The practical stress still continues and the object is still believed and so also the surface of the *object*. The red expanse and the red surface may be said to coincide in the peculiar sense I have brought out above. The surface is distinct from the expanse which, however, cannot be said to be distinct from the surface. In any other sense, coincidence of the two appears to me unmeaning. I see no harm in calling expanse surface 'taken by itself' or detached from the object; for it is just in this detachment that the surface which is but a thinking abstraction and no 'entity' is realised or discovered as an aesthetic abstraction or 'entity' or a self-subsistent. The physical object is believed from the beginning as an occupant of space and the belief is never dropped (though I conceive it dropped when the sensum is subjectively, or as one would say, mystically realised In its isolation). When the sensa are explicitly known, the occupant cannot be said to have the sensa or family of sensa; for the only relation between it and sensum is one-sided distinction and at best one-side coincidence.

I do not *prove* a sensum at all. I certainly refer to variation and illusion *by* way of example. That an object has varying or illusory appearance is known already as the distinction of sensum and object. Nor do I begin with the sensum and then in practical interest interpret it as object. More often that not, one begins with the object and realises later its distinction from sensum.

Only I do not admit that we necessarily begin with the practical attitude; a child may begin in the aesthetic attitude.

To detach the sensum from the object is to know it to be an actual something. An abstraction (aesthetic or thinking) is understood only in reference to a concrete. The aesthetic abstraction in this case, moreover, is known to be real in the abstracting process itself.

As soon as the practical interest slackens, the sensum comes to be known as what the object is not. It does not begin to be but only begins to be known. So if we start with the aesthetic attitude and then become practical the sensum does not vanish but may cease to be attended to.

I believe that the object has only one colour. I have some definite knowledge of it, say, as red, though the exact shade of red may be indefinite to my knowledge. I take this to be real till it is contradicted, the mere possibility is nothing to me. (Nor do I deny that more about this red—viz. its distinction from other reds—may come to be known). When it is contradicted I take some other colour to be real. My theory does not require that what is once taken as real can never be falsified, or that I may not be ignorant of the real. Only, when an object successively appears to have different colours, one colour only is believed, really to belong to it, provided no objective change has taken place, and the others are not so believed. It is not that different colours are seen without any reference to an object and then the question arises which, or whether more than one, belong to it. The object is believed to have some colour at the start and the same object is seen later to have some other colour. The starting colour continues to be taken as real (and the other is taken as unreal), unless it comes to be ousted from belief by the other colour. No one can anticipate which will oust which; like a belief, the correction of a belief only comes, and each has to be accepted as it comes. There is no question of a privileged colour; whatever is believed to be real at any time is privileged.

The appearance of an object continuously varies owing to position of observer within a certain range. This range, I suppose, is what Price means by family. It is all privileged in the sense that any variation beyond the range would not be taken as appearance of an object. If you can speak of many continuous ranges, each with a nucleus. Begin, however - as I say everyone in common sense does - with the objects, each having appearances, you can still speak of range or family of appearances of an object, the object as *what* it is believed to be, this *what* being its real appearance or the nucleus. There is no question of the object having to be discovered in the autonomous appearances.

By primary qualities, I mean the space qualities. (The resisting character of the object I do not call a *quality* presented to sense-knowledge, being apprehended conative affectively and not cognitively, though as the background of object-cognition). Colour is, however, presented only as coloured space, so that the contrast is not between space and colour, but between the mere form - space and colour - space, secondary quality being in this sense but a determination of primary quality - whether space as unqualified (colourless, etc.) should be admitted as *quality* of object may be disputed. But admitting it, secondary quality (colour-space) is less detached from the perceived object than the primary quality (unqualified space) but more distinguished from the perceiving consciousness (or felt body). (A 'mere appearance' is the appearance of the perceived space. A hallucination is the appearance of the sensed field at the time. A dream is the appearance of the time before waking).

Can the bent look of the straight stick be called a *shape of* the stick detached from it? My answer is that what is perceived and believed in the first instance is bent *stick* and not bent *shape,* that next, the belief is corrected - inferentially and not perceptually - in the form 'not bent *object* but straight object and that the correction starts (and does not cause, the aesthetic detachment of the bent shape from the *bent* object (which still stands before perception, though discredited by inference), the detachement being a discovery of the 'bent' sensum (which is not corrected). Hence the sensum in every case is the detached shape of the object that *stands before perception.* Here the bent shape is detached from the bent stick and not from the straight stick, but as the straight stick is inferentially taken to be the fact, it is *spoken* of as the look or appearance of the straight stick.

The detachment of the look of the object from the object, of the bent look from the bent stick is occasioned or started by the correction of the object. It means at the same time consciousness of the *possibility* of detaching the look or *seem* of the object that is taken as real, e.g. the straight look from the straight stick. So in the case of the really red rose, its look or *seem* is not detached but detachable. (The correction of any object, e.g. bent stick, is enough to suggest the *detachability* of the look of any object from it.) Its red shape, it is believed, *can* be but *is* not actually appreciated as sensum. Now as in the case of the bent look, its actual detachment means a discovery and not the production of the sensum, what is only believed as detachable is also admitted as sensum, actual in being, but not yet subjectively realised. The red look of the of the rose is sensed, but there is no reflective appreciation of the sensed as such and the perceived as such being different. The real appearance is sensum, but not reflectively appreciated as sensum.

To meet the case of illusion and hallucination, I develop what I said earlier about the sensum being of different grades. I distinguish first between actually sensed sensum and sensable sensum. (The red look of the red rose is sensed sensum though not reflectively appreciated as such). When I see a fire from a distance where I do not sense its heat, I take the look to be sensed sensum and the heat to be sensable sensum. I still believe the heat to be there, but in some cases (e.g. when I see a firefly and take it at first to be hot), my belief is falsified. In both cases, I take the heat (as detachable from the object) to be an *imagined* sensum. There are cases where I only *think* a sensum without imagining it, e.g. where I believe a rose at distance to have a characteristic smell which I not only do not sense but do not also imagine, there being no *image* of smell. This also may or may not be falsified, but either way the smell is a *thought* sensum. Both the imagined and thought sensa are unsensed but sensable sensa.

This means incidentally that a sensum, even a sensed sensum, may be doubted. You cannot say about the bent look of the stick that it is undoubtedly there, that you have pure acquaintance-knowledge of it. What is undoubted here is that the *consciousness* of seeing is there, not the seeing nor the seen sensum. There may be confusion between seeing and imagining, and what is imagined may not be even really sensable. So there may be confusion between imagining and thinking, and what is thought may not be really imaginable.

I take an illusory appearance to be the 'appearance of a sensum', which would be meaningless if the consciousness of a sensum be undoubtable acquaintance knowledge. (I may admit *acquaintance* of sensum in a *relative sense*, in contrast with the knowledge of object). As contrasted with the sensum, the appearance is undoubted, but there may be a further appearance of appearance in contrast with which the appearance (of the sensum) is doubtable. Illusory appearance of sensum gives the idea of real appearance of sensum also. Now appearance of sensed sensum, whether illusory or real, is an imagined sensum and appearance of appearance is a thought sensum (a sensed sensum being itself *appearance of object*). Appearance at any stage is either illusory or real.

(I cannot understand the illusory appearance of a thought *sensum* as a sensum again of a higher grade. I admit that a thought sensum may be illusory but the consciousness of this illusoriness is not the consciousness of a higher *sensum*. It is consciousness of something that is not distinct from the consciousness-call it intuition or by any other name.)

The snake in the stock example is illusory *object*, and the illusory object *in contrast with* the real object is taken as a sensed sensum to start with. By 'illusory', I here mean the object that is apparently seen to vanish when the real object (rope) is perceived. This is distinct from the 'bent stick' which is not *seen* to be nought in inferential correction. The snake on correction is understood only as snake-shape (sensum), while the bent stick on correction is understood still as object - the snake-shape detached by the correction of the illusion into a sensum is presented in the correction as a *passing* of the object into sensum, as the vanishing of the object.

So far the question of the illusoriness of the sensum does not arise. But one may ask if this vanishing of the object, which is apparently sensed, is not merely imagined, or in the other words, if the snake-shape (as appearing in the correction) is a sensed sensum at all. It may well be an imagined sensum. In contrast with the detached shape of the standing (i.e. continuing to be perceived) 'bent stick', the snake-shape of the vanishing snake (*object*) is itself a vanishing *sensum*. Not that it is realised as an image but it is at least indefinite in its sensed character. The vanishing sensum (or what I may call sensed appearance of sensum) is midway between the yet undoubted sensed sensum (bent shape of the stick) and the unsensed, sensable or imagined sensum. One may go further and speak of an illusion about an imagined sensum and even about thought-sensum, i.e. about sensum in general.

On my general theory of presentations, we are aware of the presentation only as what the object is distinct from, but I make an exception in favour of the sensum so far that it is not only known as what the object is not but also known as *by itself* but *not as distinct from the object.* A content can be distinguished from another, distinguished in itself or only distinguished from. What is distinguished in itself *only* is the Self; an object is distinguished in all the three ways; but sensum is only *not* distinguished from the object. Taking an image in contrast with a sensum, it is not *known* as distinct in itself though imagined or thought to be distinct in itself, being known only as what the object or sensum is distinct from.

As I understand it, presentation (including the sensum) is to Reid 'the object as appearing to the mind.' I can admit it but I do not take the complex phrase to mean a complex entity. I wonder what Kant would have thought of the sensum. I think I was wrong in holding that to him it would be a thinking abstraction from the object. The object is to him just an object of the external sense. Such object is also to him object of the internal sense, *viz.* as a percept. The perceived object as received into the internal sense is taken by him to be 'apprehended' (C.P.R. tr. by K. Smith p. 144). I take this apprehended object to be *percept.* I would add that the percept is not other than the perceived thing which, however, is other that the percept. (That is how I would understand his statement that what belongs to external sense belongs also to internal sense). The sensum is to me just this percept or the perceived object 'as appearing to the mind'. The sensum thus may appear complex, as involving the object. It is, as mind is, said to involve the external world. This *involving,* however, is not containing, not like one object involving another. It is as the mirror has the image within it - (the question of the unreality of the image being neglected). So the percept or the sensum is simple, even thought it involves the perceived object. In fact, the sensum is the reality, the object *apart from it* being an abstraction, but as in it real and distinct from it (but no reversely). In that phrase 'object- as-perceived-through-a-medium-in-an environment' (Reid), is the environing space also taken to be perceived? Also the medium? If not, at least in the sense the object is perceived, is the sensum only a thought function of the object space and medium, or is it sensum only a thought function of the space and medium, or is it an immediate content of consciousness?

The (imperfect or lowest) sensum is still referred to a space position. Even then it is not *in* space in the sense an extended object *is in* space (where space is at once attribute and container of the object). The image is never referred to a space position. The image is the unactual sensum of a higher grade. The sensum can be, while the image cannot be, localised in reference to the body.

The image also means aesthetic detachment; but as detached it is not realised and known while the sensum is so realised.

The stick *looks* bent. It really, looks or falsely looks. In the former case, it is judgement and is equivalent to 'the stick if *known by me* to be bent'. In the latter case, it involves a correction which is no judgement. 'Known' is properly no predicate by itself; it is predicate in the case of true knowledge, because what it is known *to be* is predicate. In the case of false knowledge, because what it is known *to be* is predicate. In the case of false knowledge (as known in correction) it is not at least a cognitive judgement. It is, if judgement at all, what Kant calls a reflective judgement-a judgement of *as though.*

KRISHNA CHANDRA BHATTACHARYYA

We are indebted to Dr. J.N. Chubb of Bombay and Dr. J.N. Mohanty of Calcutta for these interesting comments of the late Prof. K.C. Bhattacharyya on the notion of sense-datum. These comments were originally contained in a letter which Professor Bhattacharyya worte, more that two decades ago to Dr. Chubb in response to certain questions which the letter had asked him concerning this subject. Dr. Chubb made a type-script of these comment and handed it over to Dr. Mohanty in order to get them published in some suitable journal. Dr. Mohanty got the same published in **The Journal of Indian Academy of Philosophy** (vol. XI, 1972 pp.1-10). We also extend our thanks to Professor A. Raghuramraju (University of Hyderabad) for having provided the article to us for this revised edition of the Studies in Philosophy.

-EDITOR